Creative Technologies for Multidisciplinary Applications

Andy M. Connor
Auckland University of Technology, New Zealand

Stefan Marks
Auckland University of Technology, New Zealand

A volume in the Advances in Media,
Entertainment, and the Arts (AMEA) Book Series

Published in the United States of America by
    Information Science Reference (an imprint of IGI Global)
    701 E. Chocolate Avenue
    Hershey PA, USA 17033
    Tel: 717-533-8845
    Fax: 717-533-8661
    E-mail: cust@igi-global.com
    Web site: http://www.igi-global.com

Library of Congress Cataloging-in-Publication Data

Library of Congress Cataloging-in-Publication Data

Names: Connor, Andy M., 1972- editor. | Marks, Stefan, 1973- editor.
Title: Creative technologies for multidisciplinary applications / Andy M.
  Connor and Stefan Marks, editors.
Description: Hershey, PA : Information Science Reference, 2016. | Includes
  bibliographical references and index.
Identifiers: LCCN 2015050769| ISBN 9781522500162 (hardcover) | ISBN
  9781522500179 (ebook)
Subjects: LCSH: Technology and the arts. | Creative ability in technology. |
  Technology--Social aspects.
Classification: LCC NX180.T4 C73 2016 | DDC 700.1/05--dc23 LC record available at http://lccn.loc.gov/2015050769

This book is published in the IGI Global book series Advances in Media, Entertainment, and the Arts (AMEA) (ISSN: Pending; eISSN: pending)

British Cataloguing in Publication Data
A Cataloguing in Publication record for this book is available from the British Library.

For electronic access to this publication, please contact: eresources@igi-global.com.

Advances in Media, Entertainment, and the Arts (AMEA) Book Series

Giuseppe Amoruso
Politecnico di Milano, Italy

ISSN: Pending
EISSN: pending

MISSION

Throughout time, technical and artistic cultures have integrated creative expression and innovation into industrial and craft processes. Art, entertainment and the media have provided means for societal self-expression and for economic and technical growth through creative processes.

The **Advances in Media, Entertainment, and the Arts (AMEA)** book series aims to explore current academic research in the field of artistic and design methodologies, applied arts, music, film, television, and news industries, as well as popular culture. Encompassing titles which focus on the latest research surrounding different design areas, services and strategies for communication and social innovation, cultural heritage, digital and print media, journalism, data visualization, gaming, design representation, television and film, as well as both the fine applied and performing arts, the AMEA book series is ideally suited for researchers, students, cultural theorists, and media professionals.

COVERAGE

- Visual Computing
- Blogging & Journalism
- Digital Media
- Traditional Arts
- Communication Design
- Digital Heritage
- Applied Arts
- Color Studies
- Computer aided design and 3D Modelling
- Fabrication and prototyping

IGI Global is currently accepting manuscripts for publication within this series. To submit a proposal for a volume in this series, please contact our Acquisition Editors at Acquisitions@igi-global.com or visit: http://www.igi-global.com/publish/.

Titles in this Series

For a list of additional titles in this series, please visit: www.igi-global.com

Political Influence of the Media in Developing Countries
Lynete Lusike Mukhongo (Moi University, Kenya) and Juliet Wambui Macharia (Moi University, Kenya)
Information Science Reference • copyright 2016 • 303pp • H/C (ISBN: 9781466696136) • US $200.00 (our price)

Impact of Communication and the Media on Ethnic Conflict
Steven Gibson (Northcentral University, USA) and Agnes Lucy Lando (Daystar University, Kenya)
Information Science Reference • copyright 2016 • 344pp • H/C (ISBN: 9781466697287) • US $185.00 (our price)

Handbook of Research on Media Literacy in the Digital Age
Melda N. Yildiz (Walden University, USA & Unite to Educate, USA) and Jared Keengwe (University of North Dakota, USA)
Information Science Reference • copyright 2016 • 532pp • H/C (ISBN: 9781466696679) • US $295.00 (our price)

Analyzing Art, Culture, and Design in the Digital Age
Gianluca Mura (Politecnico di Milano University, Italy)
Information Science Reference • copyright 2015 • 329pp • H/C (ISBN: 9781466686793) • US $185.00 (our price)

Handbook of Research on the Societal Impact of Digital Media
Barbara Guzzetti (Arizona State University, USA) and Mellinee Lesley (Texas Tech University, USA)
Information Science Reference • copyright 2016 • 789pp • H/C (ISBN: 9781466683105) • US $350.00 (our price)

Handbook of Research on Digital Media and Creative Technologies
Dew Harrison (University of Wolverhampton, UK)
Information Science Reference • copyright 2015 • 516pp • H/C (ISBN: 9781466682054) • US $310.00 (our price)

Handbook of Research on the Impact of Culture and Society on the Entertainment Industry
R. Gulay Ozturk (İstanbul Commerce University, Turkey)
Information Science Reference • copyright 2014 • 737pp • H/C (ISBN: 9781466661905) • US $345.00 (our price)

www.igi-global.com

701 E. Chocolate Ave., Hershey, PA 17033
Order online at www.igi-global.com or call 717-533-8845 x100
To place a standing order for titles released in this series, contact: cust@igi-global.com
Mon-Fri 8:00 am - 5:00 pm (est) or fax 24 hours a day 717-533-8661

Table of Contents

Detailed Table of Contents

This chapter provides a historical overview of the emergence of the creative technologies, tracing the usage of associated terms back to the close of the Second World War. An overall analysis of the reviewed literature suggests that the growth of the field was relatively slow prior to the year 2000; however since the turn of the millennium there has been an explosion of interest. The origin of creative technology is firmly places in the engineering disciplines with a focus on soundness of technology; however over time the field has expanded to include more artistic foci. This change in focus is discussed in light of how the creative technologies are viewed today and future directions of the field are discussed.

Chapter 2

In 2012, a Belgian company called Materialise hosted a fashion show featuring designs from a worldwide millinery competition. The featured pieces were paraded down a catwalk by professional models, and an overall winner chosen. What made this fashion show unusual was that the attendees were predominantly clinical and industrial engineers, and the host was a specialist engineering and software development company that emerged in 1990 from a research facility based at Leuven University. Engineers and product designers rather than fashion designers created the millinery and the works were all realized through additive manufacturing technology. This chapter provides an example of how fashion design has become a creative stimulus for the development of the technology. It illustrates how disruptive creativity has the potential to advance scientific research, with the two worlds of engineering and fashion coming together through a collaboration with industrial design. The chapter highlights the challenges and possible implications for preparing trans-disciplinary research teams.

Chapter 3

Jennifer Loy, Griffith University, Australia
Peter Tatham, Griffith University, Australia
Ry Healey, Griffith University, Australia
Cassie L. Tapper, Griffith University, Australia

This chapter provides an introduction to the discourse informing humanitarian design research practice and a context for evaluating problem solving strategies in this area of research. Advances in the development of creative technologies, and in particular 3D printing, are stimulating innovations in approach and practice. This chapter is based on a design research project that uses advances in digital technologies to address the logistical challenges facing Oxfam's Water, Sanitation and Hygiene (WASH) projects in East Africa, whilst simultaneously responding to current design theory in humanitarian design research. It takes into account people, process and technology in developing a response to the opportunities provided by creative technologies that offers a new approach to achieving an appropriate balance between paternalistic and participatory design research in this discipline. The field study informing the research took place in Nairobi in 2014/2015 and was principally supported by the Humanitarian Innovation Fund.

Chapter 4

Stefan Greuter, RMIT University, Australia
Sarah Kenderdine, University of New South Wales, Australia
Jeffrey Shaw, City University of Hong Kong, Hong Kong

The Mogao Grottoes located in Gansu Province of north-western China consist of 492 cells and cave sanctuaries carved into the cliffs above the Dachuan River in Mogao. A UNESCO World Heritage Site, they comprise the largest, most richly endowed, and oldest treasure house of Buddhist art in the world. However, for preservation and conservation reasons most of the caves are now closed to the public. This chapter discusses the range of technologies currently available for the virtual representation of Cave 220, just one of the many caves located at this site. In particular, the chapter focuses on the latest prototype, developed by the authors called Pure Land UNWIRED which uses a virtual reality platform specifically designed for a unique single user full-body immersive virtual reality experience. The discussion includes technical and evaluative analysis of this prototype.

Chapter 5

Wendy A. Powell, University of Portsmouth, UK
Natalie Corbett, University of Portsmouth, UK
Vaughan Powell, University of Portsmouth, UK

Virtual Humans are here to stay. From the voice in your satNav to Apple's "Siri", we are accustomed to engaging in some level of conversation with our technology, and it is rapidly becoming apparent that natural language interfaces have potential in a wide range of applications. Whilst audio-only communication has its place, most natural conversations take place face to face, and believable embodiment of virtual humans is the necessary next step for them to be fully integrated into our lives. Much progress has been made in the creation of relatable characters for film, but real-time facial animation presents a unique set of design challenges. This chapter examines the role of the virtual human, its history, and approaches to design and creation. It looks at ways in which they can be brought to life, interacting, assisting and learning. It concludes with a view into popular culture and perceptions of the future, where fact and fiction meet.

Chapter 6

The chapter focuses on convergence in creative computing between simulation and gaming. It examines the collapse of categorical differences between games, play and simulation, categories that were rarely used concurrently. The chapter uses a media archaeology – the study of historical conditions enabling emerging technology – to explore gamification, or the design practice of embedding game mechanics into everyday applications and activities. Gamification is employed as a prominent design tactic for motivating users to perform contextual tasks based on strategically deployed game dynamics. This analysis highlights convergence and creative technologies as a historical process.

Chapter 7

This chapter presents an overview of machinima, an important socio-cultural movement that originated in the 1990s gameplay movement known as demoscene. The chapter presents a review of literature and key issues related to its evolution. Modes of its production (perfect capture, screen capture, asset compositing, bespoke machinimation) are described, along with the range of different genres that have emerged, including fan vid, parody, documentary, music video, advertising, reportage, reenactment, activist, pre-visualization and artistic forms. Thereafter, the chapter identifies channels of distribution and growth trajectories for each. The chapter then presents four key phases of the emergence of machinima, identifying the key actors and roles of organizations within each phase. As a movement that continues to evolve, the discussion presented is by no means a final analysis, thus the aim of the chapter is to present a 'state of the art' overview of its emergence and development.

Chapter 8

Current discussions within videogames focus on the ways in which gameplay or narrative can be analysed by themselves, and rarely as a collaborative effort to explore a text. Although there have been a number of alternative approaches to this debate, none have succeeded in becoming prevalent within the field. This contrasts greatly with the study of graphic novels in relation to the application of multimodal analysis. In this field, discussion about the interplay between the mode of the image and the mode of the written text are more frequent. This textual analysis takes into account the two modes to focus on their collaborative effects in how the graphic novel can be understood. This chapter suggests that current videogame scholarship can benefit from pre-existing multimodal discussion that exists within graphic novels.

Chapter 9

A universal problem in the disciplines of communication, creativity, philosophy, biology, psychology, sociology, anthropology, archaeology, history, linguistics, information science, cultural studies, literature, media and other domains of knowledge in both the arts and sciences has been the definition of 'culture' (see Kroeber & Kluckhohn, 1952; Baldwin et al., 2006), including the specification of 'the unit of culture', and, mechanisms of culture. This chapter proposes a theory of the unit of culture, or, the 'meme' (Dawkins, 1976; Dennett, 1995; Blackmore, 1999), a unit which is also the narreme (Barthes, 1966), or 'unit of story', or 'unit of narrative'. The holon/parton theory of the unit of culture (Velikovsky, 2014) is a consilient (Wilson, 1998) synthesis of (Koestler, 1964, 1967, 1978) and Feynman (1975, 2005) and also the Evolutionary Systems Theory model of creativity (Csikszentmihalyi, 1988-2014; Simonton, 1984-2014). This theory of the unit of culture potentially has applications across all creative cultural domains and disciplines in the sciences, arts and communication media.

Chapter 10

The Selfie project was not only inspired by the long history of the self-portrait, but also intended to create a genealogy between the self-portraits of masters from the Modern art era and the selfie. The project, designed as a walkthrough experience, consisted of three major engagement areas. On entering the space, children were directed into a 'transformation' area – a typical theatrical wardrobe, where they could dress up in a variety of costumes, including hats and wigs. Once garbed, children were given smart phones and led to the area where they could take a selfie with a celebrity such as Gauguin, Cézanne, Monet, Van Gogh, Modigliani and Munch. Finally, they could manipulate the selfie using gesture-based technology and post it online. The attraction proved to be extremely popular and the children who participated were extremely satisfied with the experience.

Chapter 11

As computer artists, we might ask: can the computer serve as the artist or a proxy thereof? There seems no possible conclusive answer to this. Rather, we approach this question from a different angle: Why do humans make artifacts/praxis, which might be experienced by conspecifics as art (e.g. visual art, music, dance)? To investigate this subtle issue, computer technology provides an important tool for artist-engineers, namely allowing programmatic integration of audio analysis and visual graphic animation. We initially discuss the history and problems of the role of an intuitive model of cognition, in the pursuit of an automated means of the synthesis of intelligence, versus what has been learned about organic brains. This comparison, while somewhat critical of empiricism, is meant to zero in on the cognitive function of art for humans, as an evolutionary adaptation. We are thus lead to an alternative programming paradigm regarding art's very particular but crucial role for our species.

Chapter 12

The development of software to produce Visual Effects is based on a unique model. The majority of large companies across the film industry have taken a distinctive approach for three decades, which might explain their ongoing business success, despite the same tough conditions that other technology companies have to face in light of shrinking margins and several financial crises. This chapter examines the model and proposes an Artist-Driven Software Development Framework for visual effects studios. A brief insight into the recent history of successful applications of this model is discussed and suggestions on how to employ this framework and improve on it are given.

Chapter 13

This chapter proposes a computerized tool to promote inspiration in a specific, but very important, kind of scientific creativity, for significant scientific breakthroughs are often enabled by conceptual revolutions. The creative process is often divided into four phases: preparation, incubation, inspiration, and verification/elaboration. The proposed tool enhances the incubation phase of scientific creativity, with the goal of inspiring fruitful reconceptualization of a problem. It accomplishes this by exposing the scientist-user to continuous sequences of images designed to engage innate, unconscious cognitive structures. The sequence is not fixed, but may vary either randomly or under user direction. When this image flow seems relevant to the problem, users can record their position in it and their own ideas with a variety of low-interference recording techniques. Several simple image flows are described, along with the computational engine for generating them.

Smart homes have been predominantly pointed as one of the key constituents of intelligent environments. These are residential units substantially integrated with a communicating network of sensors and intelligent systems based on the application of new design initiatives and creative technologies. This study provides a holistic overview on the essence of smart homes besides demonstrating their current status, benefits and future directions. The study reveals that smart homes embrace significant potentials towards achieving comfort, security, independent lifestyle and enhanced quality of life. Findings urge the necessity to focus on further exploration of the social and environmental benefits derived from the application of creative technologies in smart homes. The study concludes that smart homes play a fundamental role in shaping the future cities. Finally, the study identifies a research gap indicating that there has been less consideration towards linking the fundamental potentials of smart homes to the overall performance and key indicators of smart cities.

This chapter suggests that in terms of preparing creative technologies graduates it is better to define what skill sets will be in the future rather than attempting to define either what creative technologies is now or what a current creative technologist should be capable of. The chapter is a collaborative attempt to explore the future definition of a creative technologist through a form of creative expression. The chapter utilizes a combination of self-reflective narrative and performative writing to develop position descriptions for jobs that may exist in the future, where each job is an extension of an author's life trajectory. A cluster analysis is undertaken to identify common themes that define the possible characteristics and attributes of future graduates that can be used to design the curricula for creative technologies programmes to meet the needs of the changing world.

Preface

In many regards the nature of a University environment has remain unchanged for hundreds of years, both in terms of the relationship between the three pillars of academic life and the way in which the University is structured around disciplines. Since the founding of the University of Bologna in 1088, there have of course been many changes in what these disciplines are. Though in reality it may be that the emergence of new disciplines is simply a process of creating a boundary around areas where existing disciplines overlap. In many these overlaps produce a short lived "interdiscipline" that quickly emerges as a discipline in its own right. Perhaps one reason why we feel the need to categorise and subdivide disciplines can be traced back to early Greek philosophers and their influence on Western thought. The argument that knowledge may be categorised according to disciplines can be traced back to Plato. Aristotle later developed the concept into a hierarchy of subject areas. However, at times it seems that we have lost one of the key elements of Plato's thinking, that knowledge itself maintains a unity which transcends any divisions created by the presence of disciplines.

It is therefore an exciting time to see the emergence and growth of Creative Technologies, perhaps not so much as a discipline but as a practice that crosses boundaries and draws together knowledge from disparate disciplines in the production of knowledge or artefacts that contribute to a wide agenda. In particular, this production of knowledge has no regard for the distinction between the sciences on the one hand and the arts and humanities on the other.

As teachers and researchers in this emerging field, our goal for creating this book was to explore the rich diversity that Creative Technologies embraces. It is a field that defies definition, which seems to adapt and change easily over time. In its brief heritage to date there have been few publications devoted to this field and this book represents a snapshot of consolidated knowledge as a record of what this field represents now, before change sweeps it onwards in a rapidly changing world.

As teachers, we strive to challenge our students to embrace diversity of disciplines and to draw knowledge together for the purpose of developing meaningful student projects. As researchers, we sit on the edges of many disciplines and are acutely aware of the potential that exists for interdisciplinary collaboration. This book therefore acts as an inspiration for both teachers and researchers to see the potential of Creative Technologies and become part of its future.

During the production of the book there has been no fixed definition of what Creative Technologies is, or what it could be. Chapters were invited leaving this open to interpretation from the contributors, and this has produced challenges in managing the diversity of the content. Indeed, it would seem that at this stage even amongst scholars in the field that there is some uncertainty about what Creative Technologies is, and what it is not. We have come to the conclusion that there is a power in not defining Creative Technologies as a discipline, but more as an approach of inquiry and action that can deliver outcomes that disciplinary approaches cannot.

Due to the diversity of the contents of this book, we have decided to not structure or group the content in any way. Each chapter stands alone as a work in its own right and we leave it to the reader to draw relationships that exist between chapters, and of course between chapters and their disciplinary heritage.

The first chapter emerged from the initial goal of wanting to define what Creative Technologies was and is authored by one of the editors, Andy Connor. Instead of defining the field, this chapter traces the usage of the terms "Creative Technology" and "Creative Technologies" in the academic literature to illustrate how the field has emerged. Such an undertaking is of course not exhaustive, but illustrates the elusive nature of the field and opens the door for further work focused on specific timescales of interest.

Chapter 2 has been contributed by Jennifer Loy and Samuel Canning. This chapter not only outlines an interesting application of additive manufacturing in fashion, but provides a wealth of insight into the clashes of culture that can occur when working across different disciplines. Such clashes are inevitable in any form of interdisciplinary work and the chapter therefore serves well as reference for those embarking on such projects for the first time.

Jennifer also contributed to Chapter 3 along with Peter Tatham, Ry Healy and Cassie Tapper. This chapter truly embraces the multidisciplinary goals of this book by outlining the outcomes of using additive manufacturing in humanitarian logistics projects in remote areas.

Our fourth chapter is contributed by an international team across three Universities in two countries. Stefan Greuter, Sarah Kenderdine and Jeffrey Shaw have come together to describe how virtual reality technologies can be used to provide access to at-risk heritage sites whilst limiting risk by reducing physical visitations.

Chapter 4 continues the virtual theme and outlines the rise of the virtual human. In this chapter Wendy Powell, Natalie Corbett and Vaughan Powell outline the past, present and future of virtual humans and the technologies involved in their production.

We see the first consideration of games in Chapter 6, where Nathan Hulsey provides an analysis of the convergence of simulation, games and gamification in the context of Creative Technologies.

In Chapter 7, Tracy Harwood continues on the game theme by describing the phenomenon of machinima, the making of original works using and reusing the content of 3D computer games engines. This is inherently a contemporary example of Creative Technologies in action, based on the artistic and aesthetic competencies of those making the work, but embedded within hacking and modding cultures typically associated with Creative Technologies.

The journey through the book continues in Chapter 8, where Daniel Dunne utilises graphic novels as a robust model for understanding the multimodality in videogames. This chapter provides a link from the digital environments in to wider cultural aspects of Creative Technologies.

This link is followed in Chapter 9 where JT Velikovsky attempts to define a formal structure for the unit of culture in media, entertainment science and the arts. Again, this chapter exemplifies some of the fundamental possibilities of work cutting across traditional disciplinary boundaries.

Chapter 10 describes a project organised by Alexei Dingli, Dylan Seychell and Vince Briffa that involves using technology as a means to help children explore and discover art using the modern day phenomenon of the "selfie" facilitated by mobile technology.

The theme of combining art and technology continues in Chapter 11 where Judson Wright describes a novel approach for using computers as a tool in art, in particular the use of computation as an approach to exploring musicality through the principles of intelligence and evolution. Both Chapter Ten and Eleven very much deal with crossing the disciplinary divide between the arts and science.

Chapter 12 is contributed by Jan Kruse and covers new perspectives on visual effects tools and pipe-line engineering as it encourages the studios that have not yet made it common practice, to embrace the idea of artist-driven software development. As with the previous chapter this deals with the integration of computational tools to support creativity and artistic practice.

The role of creativity in Creative Technologies is an area addressed by Bruce MacLennan in Chapter 13, with particular reference to enhancing scientific creativity. This chapter opens a discussion about the ongoing relationship between technology and creativity in various disciplines.

The topic of Chapter 14 is the consideration of the foundations of smart home technology that is contributed from an international team of authors. Smart homes embrace the concept of integrating intelligent technologies into residential spaces, and the ideas in this chapter may lead into a consideration of intelligent technologies integrate into the wider context of our increasingly interconnected world.

The book closes with Chapter 15 where authors from Auckland University of Technology ask questions about the future of Creative Technologies. This is not a question of the future of the field itself, but if the field continues on its trajectory then what capabilities will future graduates of Creative Technologies programmes need to have? This chapter brings together a varied group of teachers, researchers and students how project their own story into a possible future of Creative Technologies.

With our journey through the chapters of this book coming to a close, we as editors feel very much like Alice following the white rabbit but we are not yet sure where the tumble down the rabbit hole will take us. The book provides an overview of some of the work in this area, but much is left to be discovered and clarified. Whilst the book addresses some of the history and the current state of Creative Technologies, it leaves more questions unanswered about the future.

In a world that is rapidly changing, becoming more connected and smarter, what is the role and purpose of Creative Technologies? Some researchers feel that the purpose of Creative Technologies is self-actualisation and the promotion of creation by the general public. This is certainly borne out through the proliferation of Maker Spaces and the growth of user generated content in digital mediums. Yet others feel that Creative Technologies has a role to play in bringing together disciplines to solve otherwise so-called "wicked problems" involving technology. It is our belief that these two views are not mutually exclusive, that Creative Technologies can indeed be both of these and many more. We believe that Creative Technologies is an approach that defies traditional disciplinary norms and embraces creativity and technology (in its widest sense), it can embrace both the hacking and modding culture as well as the more formal approaches to creation. Creative Technologies is a practice of integration, limited only by our own imaginations. It has an exciting future and we are glad to be part of it.

Andy M. Connor
Auckland University of Technology, New Zealand

Stefan Marks
Auckland University of Technology, New Zealand
November 2015

Chapter 1
A Historical Review of Creative Technologies

Andy M. Connor
Auckland University of Technology, New Zealand

ABSTRACT

This chapter provides a historical overview of the emergence of the creative technologies, tracing the usage of associated terms back to the close of the Second World War. An overall analysis of the reviewed literature suggests that the growth of the field was relatively slow prior to the year 2000; however since the turn of the millennium there has been an explosion of interest. The origin of creative technology is firmly places in the engineering disciplines with a focus on soundness of technology; however over time the field has expanded to include more artistic foci. This change in focus is discussed in light of how the creative technologies are viewed today and future directions of the field are discussed.

INTRODUCTION

In a modern context, creative technologies is normally considered to be a broad interdisciplinary and transdisciplinary domain that typically combines knowledge from a variety of disciplines that include art, computer science, design, engineering and the humanities. In education, degrees of this ilk are typically presented as a modern degree intended to address needs for cross-disciplinary interaction and to develop lateral thinking skills across other more rigidly defined academic areas recognized as a valuable component in expanding technological horizons.

The lack of rigid definition of the field is a challenge in terms of understanding what is (and what is not) in scope of creative technologies. This chapter addresses this by undertaking a literature review that traces back the history of the field to the early uses of "creative technology" or "creative technologies". The goal of this chapter is therefore to provide a very high level overview of how this field has emerged and transformed over time. The chapter adopts a chronological reporting style in order to mirror how the field has evolved with common themes and relationships identified in the discussion.

DOI: 10.4018/978-1-5225-0016-2.ch001

BACKGROUND

It seems that the use of the phrase "creative technologies" is a recent trend, particularly in academia where the last few years have seen an explosion in number of undergraduate programs that utilize the phrase "creative technologies" in the program title or otherwise articulated in the curriculum. The trend is not limited to academia, with the emergence of the job title "creative technologist" becoming common around the globe. Whilst a casual glance may suggest that creative technologies is a recent trend, the field can trace its origins to the 1940s and potential drivers emerging from the Second World War that were focused on rapid technological development and economic stability.

Figure 1 shows the outcomes of a search conducted using Google Scholar using the search term ["Creative Technologies" OR "Creative Technology"], where patents and citations were excluded from the search results. The number of articles that contained either of the search terms was limited to year of publication to give an indication of how the use of the term in academic literature has changed over time. In this approach, typically 1-4 articles occurred per year between 1940 and 1979 and so for convenience these are reported in five year blocks.

In terms of the emergence and definition of the field, these early publications provide an interesting insight in terms of heritage and lineage. This early, pioneering work will be discussed later in this article.

Continuing with the analysis, the period from 1980 to 1989 shows an increase in the number of articles published, though throughout this period it remains roughly constant. However the late 1990s see the start of a year-on-year growth. Figure 2 shows this growth in publications.

Such simple analysis is by no means a perfect tool for evaluating the growth and impact of creative technologies. It is recognized that the Google Scholar database varies over time, so the results may not be repeatable. Similarly, due to limitations of scale, not every article has been fully documented to provide insight to the history and relevance of creative technologies and further studies should be conducted to provide more detail of the key milestones. Instead, the prominent trends have been extracted from the literature to provide an overview of the emergence and evolution of the field for which the publication data suggests that there is a growing interest.

Figure 1. Publications by year (1945 – 1979)

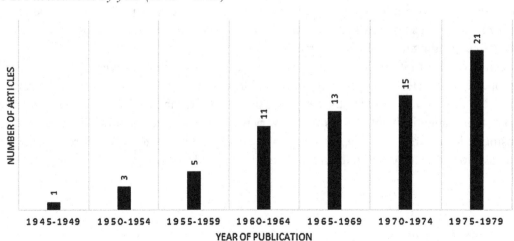

Figure 2. Publications by year (1980 – 2014)

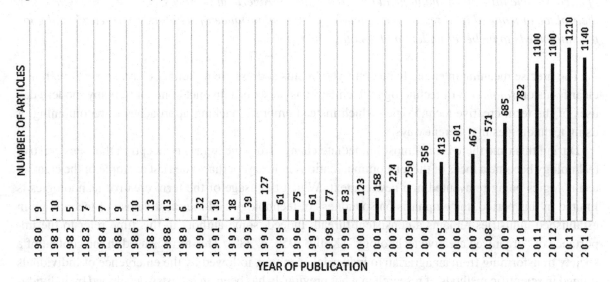

The approach utilized in this chapter is a simple literature review using a single database (Google Scholar) and two search terms ("creative technologies" and "creative technology"). From a broad range of materials gained there is a low chance of researcher bias from this methodology. Furthermore the search terms is open enough to lead to both the exploration of creative technologies, in the scope of technology that is creative, but also practitioners who creatively use technology. This has led to a varied range of results, however the potential for a more systematic and more in-depth study of literature based on a smaller range of dates is acknowledged and this potential will be discussed later in the chapter.

A HISTORICAL REVIEW

This section of the chapter undertakes a review of some of the key literature in the field of Creative Technology. The purpose of this section is to provide a detailed insight to the early literature in this field and explore how Creative Technology has evolved from its inception.

The Post War Inception (1945 - 1954)

The first traceable use of the phrase "creative technology" can be found in the academic literature, written just a few months before the formal end of the Second World War. In a timely address, the President of the American Dairy Science Association, Arthur Ragsdale made the following statement:

Whether we are engaged in research, teaching, extension, milk production, processing, manufacturing or merchandising dairy products, we have before us the greatest opportunity in history. One lesson of this war is that the possession of a sound and creative technology tends to assure military and economic security. It seems clear that in the years ahead the progressive nations of the world will pursue a policy of intensive scientific and technological research. Can our American Colleges and Universities maintain their place of leadership in research and teaching? The importance of scholarship, research and good teaching needs to be better understood. (Stoltz, 1945, p. 625)

The precise meaning intended to be conveyed by this address are no longer clear, however there is a clear focus on *soundness* of technology which perhaps presents a distinct contrast to many modern day uses of the term creative technologies which instead embrace hacking approaches to recombining or using technologies in different ways.

During this time there is an almost immediate change from the agrarian inception that sees creative technology become a focus of the telecommunications industry, perhaps the first example of the creative technologies being reinvented in a new context. Whilst the usage of the term creative technologies is limited in this period, the emphasis on soundness of technology and the creative use of technology in established industries remains a consistent thread. Indeed, some authors in this time refer to the importance of "organized creative technology" (Kelly, 1950, p. 288). This term is used in the context of a society transforming from an agrarian to industrial economy, followed by the emergence of individuals trained in scientific methods of research in what previously has been an industry developed by individuals with practical skills and knowledge. Kelly uses the term organized creative technology to refer to the integration of scientific based research in the engineering and manufacture of products before going on to outline the role of creative technology in Bell Telephone Laboratories. Kelly describes this as a process of developing new technology, in particular:

The Laboratories provides the Bell Systems with new communications technology and the information for its implementation with new systems and facilities. Its work begins at the forefront of applied science, extends across the entire scope of creative technology through research, development, design and engineering. The end products of its programmes are the design and specifications for manufacture of the technical facilities that it has created and the engineering practices to be followed in their operation and maintenance. (Kelly, 1950, p. 288)

It is arguable that the focus on engineering is a result of the nature of the society and the economy of the time, and that perhaps the transition over time towards the more modern inclusion of artistic practice is a reflection of how society has changed. However, Kelly suggests that there was a widening gap between pure and applied research:

In the half century in which our Laboratories have evolved, the physical sciences underlying the telecommunications industry have made greater progress in advancing knowledge of the laws of nature and the structure of matter than in any other period of history. The increase in fundamental knowledge has been at a rate so rapid that we have been faced with an increasingly complex problem in maintaining a close linkage between the forefront of our applied research and that of pure science. (Kelly, 1950, p. 289)

Such a gap no doubt existed in the 1950s, however given the increased rate of growth of knowledge in science since that time such a gap between pure and applied research is likely to have grown. Indeed the distinction between pure and applied research has also become less distinct and it is possible that creative technologies has had to find its own way given this widening gap. However, as this article charts the development and evolution of creative technologies it is worth remembering that its roots are firmly embedded in the systems engineering methods of the post war period.

The Pop Art Years (1955 - 1969)

The case study of the Bell Laboratories outlined by Kelly (1950) in many ways paved the path for a greater discussion of the role of creative technology in driving both social and economic growth. This theme was continued by authors in the following decade, including Kelly who called passionately for innovation in education as a result of the problems facing research laboratories in building competency for staff in creative technology and highlighted the need for establishing curricula suited to the changing needs of the times (Kelly, 1955). Throughout this period, Kelly goes to on to discuss the needs for changing models of research and development (Kelly, 1957) and the role of increasingly competent staff in developing the potential of a nation (Kelly, 1959). Interestingly, in this later work Kelly begins to distinguish between "development" and "creative technology", suggesting perhaps that the integrative thinking that pervaded his work were not fully accepted by the traditional establishment of the time.

The contribution of Kelly to the field of creative technology management has been recognized in the literature (Pierce, 1975) and the overall nature of the biographical memoirs suggest that Kelly was a visionary, innovative and energetic ambassador for change. An entire article could be devoted to the contribution of Kelly and a few other key individuals, but this is left for a future work so as to not provide a too limited slice of history in this review.

It has been noted in general that the difference between a "leader and a lone nut" is the first follower (Sivers, 2010) and this period saw a number of additional voices join in to discuss issues related to creative technology. Solo (1961) began to explore in some depth the relationship of creative technology to the economy which informed considerable work at this time whilst Baranson (1963) continued this line of thinking with consideration of the issues on the adopting of technology in developing countries. In comparison, Suranyi-Unger (1963) identified the importance of knowledge in both invention and economic development which starts to formalize the relationship between creative technology and the knowledge economy. These thoughts are supported by the work of Simpson (1963) who talks about the importance of research and creativity and its value in society:

The really great changes of the past - as of the future - stem from the creative ideas of men and women working in the laboratory, in the drafting room, and in the shop. Our production records and constantly rising standard of living are results of expanding efforts and increased funds devoted to research. (Simpson, 1963, p. 1)

Simpson makes the connection between creative technology, engineering and science with her comments that:

The last fifteen years have seen a tenfold increase in the nation's effort in creative technology, with 150,000 to 170,000 graduate engineers and scientists now employed in research and development projects, as opposed to 20,000 in 1939. (Simpson, 1963, p. 1)

However, Simpson goes on to outline a future echo of how we perceive creative technologies today with the inclusion of the vocational and practical arts:

In the vocational and practical arts fields, many questions, the answers to which would profoundly affect policies, remain unanswered. There has been some recognition of the need and a tendency to heed it, but compared with the need and the possibilities, the accomplishments have been limited. Vocational and practical arts educators have been relatively tardy in becoming conscious of the importance of research. (Simpson, 1963, p. 5)

Whilst this possibility of art research potentially informing policy, there is little emphasis as yet in the possibility of broad cross disciplinary research. Indeed, all of the authors to date have specifically commented in terms of creative technology and not creative technologies. However, further hints of what is to come can be determined through the work of Lusty (1969) who quotes Muller (1967) in saying "Science and Technology are propelling us forward at such a rate that there is legitimate concern over human abilities to adapt and respond within the framework of our traditional institutions" and also quotes Silverman (1968) who provides an early definition of creative technology as "the construction or selection of techniques or devices to produce the desired outcomes".

A Time of Change (1970 - 1979)

Historians have increasingly portrayed the 1970s as a "pivot of change" in world history, with many significant changes in society, technology and economy. Creative technology has been acknowledged in playing a role in such change that marks the real end of the dominance of agriculture, though the time is also associated with a split occurring between science and engineering. Brittain (1976) describes the history of an interdisciplinary consulting arm of the General Electric Company that attempted to institutionalize "creative engineering" in a corporate setting in order to achieve parity with the science-oriented laboratories of the time.

In terms of creative technology, the 1970s see the initial divergence of terminology with some authors utilizing creative technology whilst others adopted creative technologies. For example, Fujita and Karger (1972) are early adopters of the multiplicity of technologies, though referring primarily to multiple technologies as opposed to the integration of technologies to some goal. Other authors acknowledge the role of creative technologies across a much wider range of disciplines, including medicine (Apley, 1970). Also of particular note is an early use of the title "creative technologist" in a viewpoint expressed in response to an article in New Scientist on the possibility of autonomous technology that also, probably quite by chance, indicates the potential of the creative technologies:

My conclusion is that a great work of persuasion will be needed, directed equally at politicians and at corporation presidents, before technology autonomous can be defeated and before the great pool of creative technologists can direct their inventiveness to the problems which really matter. (Gabor, 1972, p. 243)

The emergence of more accessible computing in the 1970s was in part due to the mass production of the microprocessor starting in 1971 and this in many ways influenced the path of creative technologies in the second half of the decade, particularly in terms of what was conceived as being in scope of definition which began to include computer applications. For example, Mason (1976) identifies computer modelling as one such application:

The future directions of computer modeling as a constructive and creative technology aiding the advancement of colleges, universities, and other postsecondary institutions depend on a mature joining of the technological experience and experimentation with the complex. (Mason, 1976, p. 109)

However, this statement identifies other clear characteristics of the future of the creative technologies with an emphasis both on complexity and experimentation.

Whilst the 1970s see a diversification of what is considered creative technology (or technologies), such diversification came with the seeds of disciplinary uncertainty and tension. Soyinka (1978) starts to explore the relationship between technology and art in the face of the emergence of consumer technology and the status of performing artists and this raises questions of the time as to whether technology is at the service of the artist or whether technology can be exploited at the expense of the artist. The relationship of art, technology and engineering can trace some of its tensions back to this time. For example, Carter (1978) discusses the perception of Industrial Design at this time which epitomizes such tension. However, Carter goes on to describe an Industrial Designer as "a new sort of creative technician" (Carter, 1978, p. 535), another precursor of the current job title creative technologist.

Whilst predominately discussing a high school design exhibition, Wooff (1979) identifies a clear possible direction for bringing design and creative technology together. Whilst describing the successes of the 1979 South Wales Association for Design Education exhibition, Woof comments "a particularly disappointing feature was the lack of scientific and technical entries (e.g. related to electronic devices - surely an essential focus for 'creative' technology?)" (Wooff, 1979, p. 107)

The search method used in the preparation of this manuscript has focused entirely on the use of the phrases "creative technology" and "creative technologies". The late 1970s saw a growth in research outcomes related to technologies that could be considered within the scope of this definition, for example computer games (Cullingford, Mawdesley, & Davies, 1979), digital animation (Catmull, 1978) and both multimedia and interactivity (Collins, Adams, & Pew, 1978) to name but a few. However, as yet this work has not been embraced under the umbrella of creative technologies and so the literature directly related to this terminology is very much related to philosophical musings of the field that show promise for its development but little actual progress formalizing the field or a direction.

The Trough of Disillusionment (1980 - 1989)

In many regards, this period is a natural progression of an emerging field where after some initial enthusiasm there is a waning of interest. The 1960s and 1970s showed the way of what might be possible, yet the rapid growth of new technologies themselves potentially became all-consuming. Such an explosion of technology growth no doubt caused many to rethink the values of the time. For example, Forrester (1980, p. 13) argues that "We are entering a time when creative management, more than creative technology, can make the difference between corporate death and survival". However, Kalleberg, (1982) argues that it is the combination of creative management and creative technology that points the way for solving productivity crises. Meanwhile, Berman and Mase (1983) suggested that the management of creative people management is more important than creative technology management, perhaps providing some insight to the beliefs of the time that the growth in technology was perhaps limitless. This focus on managing creativity was a theme continued throughout the decade, with Buchsbaum (1986) describing the AT&T approaches for managing creativity for "fun and profit". This focus on fun and playfulness is perhaps an early indication of the field not taking itself too seriously whilst still being able to maintain commercial credibility.

This time period sees several authors arguing that creative technology needed a strong theoretical foundation. For example Bunge (1983) argued that advanced creative technology requires basic science, possibly a stance to be revisited in current times. Meanwhile, Keys (1985) argues strongly that systems engineering should be considered the "organized creative technology" that was promoted by Kelly on the basis that systems engineering is organized because there is a pattern to its work, creative as it entails the production of a novel system to meet a need and finally is a technology in that it is concerned with the production of a useful artifact. Keys goes on to argue for the need for systems-based problem-solving methodology.

Other authors described problem solving approaches, albeit without the systems-thinking approaches championed by Keys. Bruch (1988) sets out to develop a conscious awareness of creative processes and in doing so illustrates how different approaches to problem solving are deployed, suggesting that brainstorming and analogies are the strategies more utilized in creative technologies approaches such as Creative Problem Solving (Parnes, 1967) and Synectics (Gordon, 1961). Whilst such approaches are a far cry from a formal systems-based approach, there is a clear suggestion that the creative technologies are looking for a methodological grounding in problem solving in order to establish the field.

Towards the end of the decade, in an almost throw away comment about "creative technology transfer", Long and Ohtani (1988) highlight an increasing attention on the linking of university knowledge and expertise with the creation and development of new enterprise. This aspect of the role of creative technologies in both entrepreneurship and the development of the knowledge economy will continue to grow over the coming years.

Calm Before the Storm (1990 - 1999)

The data presented in Figure 2 shows a moderate increase in publications related to creative technology, though in reality not much new ground is broken and the last decade of the old millennium can in many ways be seen as a continuation of the slump of the 1980s. Despite this, there are some indications that the slump was likely to be reversed with some clear pointers towards what the future might hold. Key to this period is the emergence of the role of creative technologies for education, with Wallin (1990) considering the scope for using creative technologies in alternative learning, whilst Milone (1994) identified the potential of animation as a learning tool. Merickel (1990) also investigates whether 2D and 3D computer graphics can amplify certain cognitive abilities: imagery, spatial relations, displacement and transformation, creativity, and spatially related problem-solving. As often seems to be the case, the future of the creative technologies field is apparent when viewed in retrospect, as Merickel later refers to this work as virtual reality (Merickel, 1992).

This focus on education pervades through the entire decade, though in parts there is not always a distinction between creative technology education and technology education that is creative. However, even when that distinction is made it provides further insight as to what may come. For example, Johnson

(1991) is clearly discussing technology teachers who are creative. However, in the light of the complexity of modern day problems, it is not inconceivable that this statement could be a call to arms for the teachers of creative technologies of today:

However, creative technology teachers provide their students with ill-structured problems that require the students to actually solve the problems. Students are required to identify the problem, collect information, search for potential solutions, select a solution strategy, and evaluate the result. (Johnson, 1991)

Continuing the discussion of education, this period sees the emergence of educational models based around embracing creative thinking in science (Skinner, 1994) as well as an interesting precursor of the future that looked at using virtual reality technologies in education (Osberg, 1993).

The question of entrepreneurship that was raised in the 1980s receives further discussion, with Okada (1993) considering how entrepreneurship might be changing in a predominately technology focused society. Such thinking led to the use of the term "technopreneurs" to describe technology focused entrepreneurs (Tang & Yeo, 1994).

Throughout this decade, more and more signs of the future of the creative technologies can be found. For example, Ferren (1997) asks questions about the role of museums in a digital age, whereas Clemons (1998) clearly identifies animation as a creative tool and Bremer (1998) raises questions about creative technology transfer and the evolving role of Universities.

Towards the tail end of the decade, a number of key events suggest that the slump is coming to an end and that change is in the wind. In many regards these events are representative of a change in the creative technologies, furthering the change away from its agrarian roots and moving towards a more digital future. The first of these events is the creation of the Media Lab at the University of the West of England which is described by Skinner (1996) as:

The Media Lab is an industry-related research and development facility for creative technology projects involving new media; for example, interactive storytelling in virtual reality, distributed media production, visualisation of the environment, automatic set design and the development of digital media devices and services. (Skinner, 1996, p. 181)

This is one of the first references to new media that is associated with creative technologies, and whilst there is a focus on production media there is the first inkling that the integrative thinking that emerged from the very early days is starting to happen. This is reinforced by Nikias (1999) who in the editorial of a special issue on integrated media systems states:

The goal of the integrated media system is to blend multimedia and creative technologies in such a way that they dramatically transform the way we work, communicate, learn, teach, and play. An integrated media system is a computer-based environment that supports the creation, sharing, distribution, and effective communication of multimodal information across the boundaries of space and time. Today, such integrated media systems are rising to the forefront as the information technology centering point for the next decade, powerfully affecting all fields of inquiry and technology development. (Nikias, 1999, p. 32)

In its own way, this is powerful definition of the potential of creative technologies that is only just starting to be realized. Whilst the usage of the term creative technologies is focused on the integration of technology with media, this is driven by a system-centric world view that suggests that the integrated media system is the real outcome of the underlying thinking. Taking a more human-centric view would suggest that creative technologies is in many ways the process of producing the integrated system.

As well as the emergence of research units, this decade sees the first formal tertiary programmes that are focused on integrated systems or creative technologies. Mendel (1999) discusses the lessons learned in developing integrated media systems programmes at the Integrated Media Systems Center (IMSC) at the University of Southern California that was formed in 1996. The housing of these programmes in the engineering disciplines hold true to the roots of creative technology but the curricula embrace the more artistic disciplines.

The closing key event of the decade was the formation of the University of Southern California Institute for Creative Technologies with funding from the US Army as an initiative to combine the assets of a major research university with the creative resources of Hollywood and the game industry to advance the state-of-the-art in training and simulation. The formation of the Institute was pivotal in defining the field and indicating the direction for it to evolve.

Coming of Age (2000 - 2004)

The year 2000 marks the start of considerable growth in publications associated with the terms "creative technology" and "creative technologies". Such a growth creates a challenge in maintaining the same degree of coverage of the literature as previous sections and so an attempt has been made to focus on the key contributions only with a more rigorous review of the post-millennial period being deferred for future work.

The first few years of the new millennium are dominated by the work of staff at the University of Southern California's Institute for Creative Technologies that included a focus on games (Erwin, 2000), virtual interactivity (Rickel et al., 2002), animation (Itti, Dhavale, & Pighin, 2004; Shapiro, Pighin, & Faloutsos, 2003) and of course military training (Macedonia, 2002). However, two of the most important factors that emerged from the work of the unit was the fostering of an appreciation of the integration of technologies and also laying a foundation for ensuring that the technology had a purpose. As an example of how different technologies were integrated, Hill et al. (2001) describe not only how sound production and graphics are combined into a virtual environment but also the importance of integrating "soft" elements such as narrative. However the development of such technologies for a purpose, particularly a social good, can be exemplified by the work of Rizzo et al. (2004) who investigate the use of virtual reality based technologies in the treatment of post-traumatic stress disorder.

It is this emphasis on creating useful tangible outcomes that marks the "coming of age" for the creative technologies. Whilst there is still an ongoing discussion over the potential value of creative technology, there is a growing focus on the actual production of technology or the creation of some new recombination of existing technologies. For example, Lindheim and Swartout (2001) describe the creation of a new virtual reality simulation technology, Stumpfel et al. (2004) introduce algorithms for real time capture of High Dynamic Rage photographs and the work of Rhyne (2002) makes one of the first references to using existing consumer technology in the creation of something new.

This period is also characterized by a diversification of scope, the emergence of a design focus, and a consideration of what creativity is and how it is supported by technology. For example, Candy and

Edmonds (2000) investigate the role of emerging technologies in supporting creative work. However, this article also starts to stress the value of integration and the inclusion of the artistic disciplines:

... artists and technologists are developing systems for creative exploration through virtual and physical interactivity; pushing the technology and the art forward on several fronts at once from devices to programming tools; combining creative media in collaborative ventures. (Candy & Edmonds, 2000, p. 65)

This view is continued in later work (Candy & Edmonds, 2004) that also emphasizes the importance of design as a collaborative activity. This emergence of a design focus is apparent in the work of many authors in this period (Shavinina & Ponomarev, 2003; Swartout & van Lent, 2003). Interestingly, other authors not only emphasis design but also craft (Atkinson, 2004), potentially a literal interpretation of *techne* and *logos* in comparison to the early years of creative technology that called for soundness of technology and the relationship to science.

The broadening of scope of creative technologies work marks the way ahead with the wider remit including cultural heritage (Hawkins, Cohen, & Debevec, 2001; Stumpfel et al., 2003), urban planning and governance (Thierstein & Gabi, 2004) including understanding the role of creative technologies in the economic development of cities (Jones & Wilks-Heeg 1, 2004; Sasaki, 2003), digital cinema (Korris & Macedonia, 2002), corporate entrepreneurship (Chao & Yim-Teo, 2004), behavioral modelling (Mao & Gratch, 2004) and cognitive mapping (Hill, Han, & Lent, 2002) to name but a few. However, one of the key foci of this time was in the area of virtual (Naef, Staadt, & Gross, 2002) and mixed reality (Stapleton, Hughes, & Moshell, 2002) environments.

No more can the coming of age of creative technologies be confirmed by the introduction of the job title and label creative technologist that started to appear from the turn of the millennium, growing in popularity over time. Whilst the phrase has limited exposure in academic literature it is clearly apparent from searching the web that this was adopted more and more from this time on.

Divergence and Convergence (2005 - 2009)

Five years in to the new millennium an interesting shift starts to occur in the usage of the phrase "creative technologies" which perhaps is a direct consequence of the emergence of the job title creative technologist. For the first time, the number of articles using the phrase "creative technologies" outweighed the number of those using "creative technology" and the period clearly shows a swing towards the idea of integrating technologies.

The possible contribution of creative technologies still maintains stature in this period, Ramello (2005) goes as far to suggest that knowledge itself should be considered a creative technology. There is a continuing focus on digital technology and the potential it offers, often combined with a stronger emphasis on art practice. Edmonds et al. (2005) suggests that:

The cutting edge in the digital arts is a highly fertile ground for the investigation of creativity and the role of new technologies. Almost every day new forms are emerging where innovative combinations of vision, sound and text-based media are being created. The demands of such work often reveal the limitations of existing technologies and open the door to developing new approaches and techniques. This provides the creativity researcher with opportunities to understand the multi-dimensional characteristics of the creative process. (Edmonds et al., 2005, p. 453)

This view emphasizes the integrative aspect of creative technologies but also starts to elaborate on the different possible perceptions of creative technologies, here suggesting that one definition would be the "the use of technology in creativity" as opposed to "the development of creative technologies". Resnick (2006) makes such a distinction between interpretations more concrete:

Our ultimate goal is not creative technologies but rather technologies that foster creative thinking and creative expression. (Resnick, 2006, p. 198)

Another integrative aspect explored in this time is the integration of technology with culture. Makela (2005) argues that creative multimedia content and software development are increasingly driven by social, artistic, and local cultural concepts and needs, and that there is a relationship between multimedia content, location, and culture that can be explored. Makela goes on to discuss various elements of technology that will become increasingly prominent, such as location-based media, networked interaction and wearable technology. Fischer, Jennings, Maher, Resnick, and Shneiderman (2009) also chart the rise of social computing.

Elements of the creative technologies such as games and virtual environments continue to receive focus, particularly with a focus on integrating different elements including physical components. Hartholt, Gratch, and Weiss (2009) identify the potential of merging games and virtual environments, whereas Jacobson and Lewis (2005) consider how virtual reality can be implemented using game engine technology and Webster and Sudweeks (2006) consider the role of virtual environments as a learning tool. Lange, Flynn, and Rizzo (2009) explore the possibility of network enabled tele-rehabilitation. It is interesting to see a more physical element emerging that complements the existing focus on digital technology. For example, Acosta-Marquez and Bradley (2005) describe the development of an exoskeleton intended to promote mobility during rehabilitation.

There still remains a strong focus on digital technologies, however, with considerable focus on games, gaming and play (Grimshaw, 2007), particularly serious games (Eliëns & Ruttkay, 2008), games in a learning context (Peppler & Kafai, 2007) and also whether games can be a factor in drawing together different areas of focus, such as culture (Anderson et al., 2009). There is an emerging focus on intelligence as a gaming concept (El-Nasr, Zupko, & Miron, 2005) as well as understanding how people react to digital technology (Grimshaw, 2009), particularly in terms of understanding human-computer interaction (England, Rupérez, Botto, Nimoy, & Poulter, 2007).

As with much of this review, it is relative easy to identify early adopters of a particular technology that would typically considered part of the scope of the modern day creative technologies. In this regard, Weng, Weng, Wong, Yang, and Liu (2009) identify additive manufacturing in the context of creative technologies.

This period of the history of creative technologies is characterized by both divergence and convergence, with new explorations of the scope of the field and revisiting and combining technologies in new ways.

The Interdisciplinary Now (2010 - 2015)

The last five years have seen the creative technologies surge in popularity, with a much wider usage of the term and a massive increase in the number of degree programmes offered under the auspices of "creative technologies". In a way, such popularity has created some confusion over what is considered creative technologies as different education providers emphasize different elements with some focusing on media, others on technology and so on.

Despite this, the research literature shows a continuation of the trends observed in the preceding ten years with a focus on revisiting existing foci in new ways, particularly in terms of digital technologies. For example, Lange et al. (2012) revisit the idea of game based rehabilitation, however in this case using consumer level technology. Such use of consumer technology such as the Xbox Kinect and the Oculus Rift are very characteristic of this period and a number of researchers have investigated creative usage of consumer technology (Salovaara, Helfenstein, & Oulasvirta, 2011). The convergence of physical health and games is also established by (Chung, Vanderbilt, Schrager, Nguyen, & Fowler, 2015) and both mental and physical health can be seen to be converging with the use of virtual reality (Proffitt, Lange, Chen, & Winstein, 2015; Albert Rizzo et al., 2015).

As such, virtual environments continues as an emerging theme (Suma, Lipps, Finkelstein, Krum, & Bolas, 2012) and also consideration of "virtual humans" (Huang, Morency, & Gratch, 2010), with a particular consideration of intelligent virtual agents (Astrid, Krämer, & Gratch, 2010) and behavior (Chiu & Marsella, 2011). There has been an ongoing focus on using virtual reality for different forms of social good (Rizzo et al., 2011) and also a consideration of how to use motion capture technology (Lange, Rizzo, Chang, Suma, & Bolas, 2011) as well as how to integrate tangible interaction (Foottit, Brown, Marks, & Connor, 2014) with virtual environments used for both visualization and interaction (Marks, Estevez, & Connor, 2014) .

Other examples of integrating different technologies can be identified, for example using consumer smartphone technology for the creation of a heads up display for an immersive virtual environment (Hoberman, Krum, Suma, & Bolas, 2012; Olson, Krum, Suma, & Bolas, 2011). In its own way, work of this nature is an indication of a move away from the original definition of sound technologies, more instead representing the more commonly held view around the "hacking" of technology to repurpose and reuse it in new ways. This period also sees the popularization of additive manufacturing (Hoskins, 2013).

An emerging trend in this period is a greater consideration of the role of the user in the context of technology. For example, Bakkes, Tan, and Pisan (2012) consider the role of technology personalization whereas Salovaara et al. (2011) explore how technology can be appropriated by a user and used in different ways. Similarly, another emerging trend is the emphasis on playfulness (Cobb, Brooks, & Sharkey, 2013; Gaye, Tanaka, Richardson, & Jo, 2010) in using technology.

Other new areas are explored and included in a creative technologies context, for example facial tracking (Baltrusaitis, Robinson, & Morency, 2012) and facial expression generation (Tinwell, Grimshaw, Nabi, & Williams, 2011) that naturally fits with other work in terms of virtual humans and representations.

Not surprisingly, given the large growth in creative technologies degrees, there is a growing emphasis on learning and education, both at the school (Edwards-Groves, 2012; McDonald & Howell, 2012) and tertiary levels with an emphasis on playfulness (Connor, Marks, & Walker, 2015), integrative curricula (Connor, Karmokar, & Whittington, 2015) and special education (Rao & Skouge, 2015).

With such a growth in scale and scope, there is considerable literature in the last five years that has not been included in this section. Again, as with other periods, there is also a vast amount of literature that covers technology developments related to, but not explicitly defined as belonging to the creative technologies. In summary, this latest period of history in the emergence of the creative technologies field has seen a creation of huge breadth in the field with much potential to develop new avenues.

The Future of Creative Technologies (2016+)

So what is the future for creative technologies? Any concrete prediction is almost impossible, though many authors to argue that creative technologies are going to be a driving force in changing the world (Zagalo & Branco, 2015). Whilst a concrete prediction may not be possible, a review of the way that creative technologies has evolved can provide insight into the future.

Consistently over the last 70 years the usage of the terms Creative Technology or Creative Technologies directly reflect the nature of society of its time. In the post war agrarian society, the term was used to reflect the need for economic recovery driven by technological innovation in agriculture. In the 1950s and 1960s, the term was often used to embrace the growing importance of engineering and science in both the economy and society in large. The introduction of the microprocessor and the continuing growth of computing power has driven the creative technologies into a more digital space, and the emergence of smart technologies and significant consumer-oriented innovation shows the likely trend over the next few years.

The review of its history suggests that creative technologies is a fluid term, and indeed that fluidity is its strength. The ability to react and change to societal and technological change provides an unlimited scope to reinvent and recreate the domain. Yet the real impact of creative technologies comes from the people that drive it and the people that use it. Whilst talking predominately about innovation, Denning (2015) makes the observation:

The common sense about innovation is revealed in the popular stories that say that innovation is the product of creative people constantly inventing new technologies based in science. Yet innovations arise without creativity, new technology, or new science, and some creative technologies produce no innovation. Having a clear plan and strategy is also overrated. Some innovations come without these, and many plans and strategies do not produce innovation. Innovation is a change of practice that displaces other practices already in place. Inventing creative technology does nothing: people must take up new practice. (Denning, 2015, p. 27)

Whilst the challenge for the future would seem the bringing together of creative technologies and people in the change of established practices, it is still an open question as to what is "creative technologies" and indeed should it be a term that is defined?

DISCUSSION

As the creative technologies field has emerged and evolved it has been troubled by an uncertainty of definition that does not occur in the more traditional disciplines. Just as post-modernist art defines itself as a contradiction of modernism that adapts to include new thinking, creative technologies also has the potential to adapt and include new things. Whilst the strengths of this are clear, the disadvantage is that with no clear definition of what the field is there is perhaps a reluctance of some researchers to associate with it.

One of the most indefinite issues surrounding creative technologies is whether the field encompasses the creative development of new technology, the development of technology that supports creativity or simply the use of technologies (old or new) in creative ways. In reality, the literature related to creative technologies contains examples of all three cases but this adds to the general confusion of the field. To attempt to define "Creative Technologies" would in many ways add to this confusion, as any such definition is only likely to be appropriate for a short timescale. However, it is possible to draw together a number of commentaries into a meta-definition, one that does not attempt to pin down what is (or what is not) in scope but instead attempts to define a way of thinking that is independent from the technology itself. As a starting point Silverman (1968) provides an early description of creative technology as "the construction or selection of techniques or devices to produce the desired outcomes". This is perhaps the most generic definition possible, yet it hints at the wealth of possibility by including both "construction and selection".

Whilst Gabor is arguing against the rise of machine intelligence, he indirectly adds an important aspect to the definition of creative technologies in his statement that "… the great pool of creative technologists can direct their inventiveness to the problems which really matter." (Gabor, 1972, p. 243). This consideration of "what really matters" is echoed more recent by Avnet (2010) who attempts to define what a creative technologist:

CTs understand the business of advertising, marketing, and branding, take a creative, strategic and people-centric view of how to connect people and brands, and understand the kinds of mediating technologies that can best be used to make those engaging experiences where the connection happens. They sketch with technology, just like a visual creative can sketch with a pencil. They're steeped in strategy, so the things they come up with make sense – it's not about technology just for the sake of technology. The experiences they design address real needs of people and brands. Creative technologists share a creative and inquisitive view of the world. They're on top of technology trends, aren't afraid of coding (just as a modern visual designer isn't afraid of Photoshop or Illustrator), and take both strategic and tactical approaches to creativity. They also understand that we're in a business, and we're solving business goals by addressing people's needs as a priority. (Avnet, 2010)

In this definition, Avnet is clearly discussing the nature of creative technologists in the context of advertising and creative agencies. Yet the definition easily expands to a wider domain without introducing specifics of the present technologies. Creative technologies is in essence the blending of knowledge across multiple disciplines to create new experiences or products that satisfy both the needs of the end user and the needs of the organization. When combined with the view that that there should be a "mature joining of the technological experience and experimentation with the complex" (Mason, 1976, p. 109) and the call for systems-based problem-solving methodologies (Keys, 1985) then we start to see the ripe future of the creative technologies in the echoes of the past.

There are many positives coming out of the creative technologies research, particularly a growing focus on "solving problems for the social good". However questions still remain as to whether the creative technologies academic programmes are developing graduates capable of cross-disciplinary interaction with the lateral thinking skills to integrate knowledge from other academic areas in order to expand technological horizons (Sosa & Connor, 2015). Some individuals argue that there is no need for creative technologists with half-baked ideas (Weiden+Kennedy, 2011), whilst others argue that there is a clear need (CraftedPixels, 2012). However, this debate is predominately in the context of the shift from traditional advertising agencies to the newer 'creative agencies'. What then is the role of a creative technologist in the wider sphere, what skills are needed and are they being delivered by academia all questions that need to be addressed. In designing the future of creative technologies it is important to consider the past, and this article provides a retrospective review of this history of the creative technologies in order to direct such further work.

CONCLUSION

This chapter has provided an overview of the emergence and evolution of the creative technologies field by reviewing selected literature from 1945 to 2015. Contrary to the commonly held belief that the creative technologies field is a relatively contemporary addition, this chapter has traced the origins of creative technology back to the latter years of the Second World War where the predominately agrarian society and post-war economies necessitated creative and innovative approaches to technology that spawned the transition to more industrial economies. Over time, the usage of the terminology and the nature of the field has evolved and adapted to a changing world, transitioning from its engineering roots to a more transdisciplinary field that cuts across traditional disciplines. This chapter charts that development in a chronological fashion, with specific focus on the early years, to provide an understanding of the field in terms of a meta-definition of creative technologies.

The future is undeniably going to be more connected, with smarter devices and richer media. The world is already experiencing "wicked" problems that are not easily solved with disciplinary thinking, and as the relationships between technology, society and the economy become more complex it is likely that many more such problems will arise. It has been argued that the management of such problems "requires thinkers who can transcend disciplinary boundaries, work collaboratively, and handle complexity and obstacles" (Cantor, DeLauer, Martin, & Rogan, 2015) and there are calls for the development of "T-shaped people" to help address these problems (de Eyto, Ryan, McMahon, Hassett, & Flynn, 2015). The creative technologies has the potential to develop such graduates and by reflecting on its past this article aims to encourage the development of future creative technologists that can engage across all of the disciplines through which the creative technologies has evolved.

REFERENCES

Acosta-Marquez, C., & Bradley, D. A. (2005, June 28 - July 1). *The analysis, design and implementation of a model of an exoskeleton to support mobility.* Paper presented at the 9th International Conference on Rehabilitation Robotics, Chicago, IL. doi:10.1109/ICORR.2005.1501061

Anderson, E. F., McLoughlin, L., Liarokapis, F., Peters, C., Petridis, P., & Freitas, S. (2009). *Serious games in cultural heritage.* Paper presented at the 10th International Symposium on Virtual Reality, Archaeology and Cultural Heritag,e St. Julians, Malta.

Apley, J. (1970). Clinical canutes. A philosophy of paediatrics. *Proceedings of the Royal Society of Medicine, 63*(5), 479. PMID:5453431

Astrid, M., Krämer, N. C., & Gratch, J. (2010). *How our personality shapes our interactions with virtual characters-implications for research and development*. Paper presented at the 10th International Conference on Intelligent Virtual Agents, Philadelphia, PA.

Atkinson, P. (2004). *Post-Industrial Manufacturing Systems: The impact of emerging technologies on design, craft and engineering processes*. Paper presented at Challenging Craft, Aberdeen, UK.

Avnet, M. (2010). *What the heck is a creative technologist?* Retrieved from https://markavnet.wordpress.com/2010/06/22/what-the-heck-is-a-creative-technologist/

Bakkes, S., Tan, C. T., & Pisan, Y. (2012). Personalised gaming. *Journal of Creative Technologies*, (3).

Baltrusaitis, T., Robinson, P., & Morency, L. (2012). *3D constrained local model for rigid and non-rigid facial tracking*. Paper presented at the IEEE Conference on Computer Vision and Pattern Recognition, Providence, RI. doi:10.1109/CVPR.2012.6247980

Baranson, J. (1963). Economic and social considerations in adapting technologies for developing countries. *Technology and Culture*, *4*(1), 22–29. doi:10.2307/3101333

Berman, D. L., & Mase, H. (1983). The key to the productivity dilemma:"The performance manager. *Human Resource Management*, *22*(3), 275–286. doi:10.1002/hrm.3930220308

Bremer, H. W. (1998). *University technology transfer: evolution and revolution*. New York, NY: Council on Governmental Relations.

Brittain, J. E. (1976). CP Steinmetz and EFW Alexanderson: Creative engineering in a corporate setting. *Proceedings of the IEEE*, *64*(9), 1413–1417. doi:10.1109/PROC.1976.10335

Bruch, C. B. (1988). Metacreativity: Awareness of thoughts and feelings during creative experiences. *The Journal of Creative Behavior*, *22*(2), 112–122. doi:10.1002/j.2162-6057.1988.tb00672.x

Buchsbaum, S. J. (1986). Managing creativity–for fun and for profit. *International Journal of Technology Management*, *1*(1), 51–64.

Bunge, M. (1983). *Upshot*. Dordrecht: Springer. doi:10.1007/978-94-015-6921-7_6

Candy, L., & Edmonds, E. (2000). Creativity enhancement with emerging technologies. *Communications of the ACM*, *43*(8), 63–65. doi:10.1145/345124.345144

Candy, L., & Edmonds, E. (2004). *Collaborative expertise for creative technology design*. Paper presented at the Design Thinking Research Symposium 6, Sydney, Australia. doi:10.1007/978-3-540-27795-8_7

Cantor, A., DeLauer, V., Martin, D., & Rogan, J. (2015). Training interdisciplinary "wicked problem" solvers: Applying lessons from HERO in community-based research experiences for undergraduates. *Journal of Geography in Higher Education*, 1–13. doi:10.1080/03098265.2015.1048508

Carter, D. (1978). Industrial design - Is it engineering, art, or just a dirty word? *Journal of the Royal Society of Arts*, *126*(5265), 532–540.

Catmull, E. (1978). The problems of computer-assisted animation. *Computer Graphics*, *12*(3), 348–353. doi:10.1145/965139.807414

Chao, C., & Yim-Teo, T. (2004). *Corporate entrepreneurial behavior of latecomer technology firms.* Paper presented at the IEEE International Engineering Management Conference, Singapore. doi:10.1109/IEMC.2004.1407467

Chiu, C.-C., & Marsella, S. (2011). *A style controller for generating virtual human behaviors.* Paper presented at the 10th International Conference on Autonomous Agents and Multiagent Systems, Taipei, Taiwan.

Chung, P. J., Vanderbilt, D. L., Schrager, S. M., Nguyen, E., & Fowler, E. (2015). Active Videogaming for Individuals with Severe Movement Disorders: Results from a Community Study. *Games for Health Journal, 4*(3), 190–194. doi:10.1089/g4h.2014.0091 PMID:26182063

Clemons, S. (1998). Computer Animation. A Creative Technology Tool. *Technology Teacher, 58*(3), 8–12.

Cobb, S., Brooks, A. L., & Sharkey, P. M. (2013). Virtual Reality Technologies and the Creative Arts in the Areas of Disability, Therapy, Health, and Rehabilitation. In S. Kumar & E. R. Cohn (Eds.), *Telerehabilitation* (pp. 239–261). London: Springer. doi:10.1007/978-1-4471-4198-3_16

Collins, A., Adams, M. J., & Pew, R. W. (1978). Effectiveness of an interactive map display in tutoring geography. *Journal of Educational Psychology, 70*(1), 1–7. doi:10.1037/0022-0663.70.1.1

Connor, A. M., Karmokar, S., & Whittington, C. (2015). From STEM to STEAM: Strategies for Enhancing Engineering & Technology Education. *International Journal of Engineering Pedagogy, 5*(2), 37–47. doi:10.3991/ijep.v5i2.4458

Connor, A. M., Marks, S., & Walker, C. (2015). Creating Creative Technologists: Playing With(in) Education. In N. Zagalo & P. Branco (Eds.), *Creativity in the Digital Age.* Berlin: Springer. doi:10.1007/978-1-4471-6681-8_3

CraftedPixels. (2012). *Why we need creative technologists.* Retrieved from http://craftedpixelz.co.uk/blog/why-we-need-creative-technologists/

Cullingford, G., Mawdesley, M., & Davies, P. (1979). Some experiences with computer based games in civil engineering teaching. *Computers & Education, 3*(3), 159–164. doi:10.1016/0360-1315(79)90041-1

de Eyto, A., Ryan, A., McMahon, M., Hassett, G., & Flynn, M. (2015). *Health Futures Lab-Transdisciplinary development of T shaped professionals through wicked problem challenges.* Paper presented at the 8th International Conference on Engineering Education for Sustainable Development, Vancouver, Canada.

Denning, P. J. (2015). Emergent innovation. *Communications of the ACM, 58*(6), 28–31. doi:10.1145/2753147

Edmonds, E. A., Weakley, A., Candy, L., Fell, M., Knott, R., & Pauletto, S. (2005). The studio as laboratory: Combining creative practice and digital technology research. *International Journal of Human-Computer Studies, 63*(4), 452–481. doi:10.1016/j.ijhcs.2005.04.012

Edwards-Groves, C. (2012). Interactive Creative Technologies: Changing learning practices and pedagogies in the writing classroom. *Australian Journal of Language and Literacy, 35*(1), 99–113.

El-Nasr, M. S., Zupko, J., & Miron, K. (2005). *Intelligent lighting for a better gaming experience.* Paper presented at CHI'05 Extended Abstracts on Human Factors in Computing Systems, Portland, OR, USA. doi:10.1145/1056808.1056852

Eliëns, A., & Ruttkay, Z. (2008). *Record, Replay & Reflect–a framework for understanding (serious) game play.* Paper presented at Euromedia 2009, Bruges, Belgium.

England, D., Rupérez, M., Botto, C., Nimoy, J., & Poulter, S. (2007). *Creative technology and HCI.* Paper presented at the HCIed 2007, Aveiro, Portugal.

Erwin, S. I. (2000). Video games gaining clout as military training tools. *National Defense, November*, 62-63.

Ferren, B. (1997). The future of museums: Asking the right questions. *Journal of Museum Education, 22*(1), 3–7. doi:10.1080/10598650.1997.11510338

Fischer, G., Jennings, P., Maher, M. L., Resnick, M., & Shneiderman, B. (2009). *Creativity challenges and opportunities in social computing.* Paper presented at CHI'09 Extended Abstracts on Human Factors in Computing Systems, Boston, MA. doi:10.1145/1520340.1520470

Foottit, J., Brown, D., Marks, S., & Connor, A. M. (2014). *An Intuitive Tangible Game Controller.* Paper presented at the 2014 Australasian Conference on Interactive Entertainment, Newcastle, Australia.

Forrester, J. W. (1980). Innovation and the economic long wave. *Planning Review, 8*(6), 6–15. doi:10.1108/eb053927

Fujita, T., & Karger, D. (1972). Managing R & D in Japan. *Management International Review, 12*(1), 65–73.

Gabor, D. (1972). Re: Creativity Technology. *Security Dialogue, 3,* 243.

Gaye, L., Tanaka, A., Richardson, R., & Jo, K. (2010). *Social inclusion through the digital economy: digital creative engagement and youth-led innovation.* Paper presented at the 9th International Conference on Interaction Design and Children, Barcelona, Spain. doi:10.1145/1810543.1810612

Gordon, W. J. (1961). *Synectics: The development of creative capacity.* New York: Harper & Row.

Grimshaw, M. (2009). *The audio Uncanny Valley: Sound, fear and the horror game.* Paper presented at the Audio Mostly 2009 Conference, Glasgow, UK.

Grimshaw, M. (2007, November 14—15). *The Resonating spaces of first-person shooter games.* Paper presented at the 5th International Conference on Game Design and Technology, Liverpool, UK.

Hartholt, A., Gratch, J., & Weiss, L. (2009, September 14-16). *At the virtual frontier: Introducing Gunslinger, a multi-character, mixed-reality, story-driven experience.* Paper presented at the 9th International Conference on Intelligent Virtual Agents, Amsterdam, The Netherlands. doi:10.1007/978-3-642-04380-2_62

Hawkins, T., Cohen, J., & Debevec, P. (2001, November 28-30). *A photometric approach to digitizing cultural artifacts.* Paper presented at the 2001 Conference on Virtual Reality, Archeology, and Cultural Heritage, Athens, Greece. doi:10.1145/584993.585053

Hill, R., Gratch, J., Johnson, W., Kyriakakis, C., LaBore, C., Lindheim, R., . . . Morie, J. (2001). *Toward the holodeck: integrating graphics, sound, character and story.* Paper presented at the Fifth International Conference on Autonomous Agents, Montreal, Canada. doi:10.1145/375735.376390

Hoberman, P., Krum, D. M., Suma, E. A., & Bolas, M. (2012). *Immersive training games for smartphone-based head mounted displays.* Paper presented at the Virtual Reality Short Papers and Posters, Costa Mesa, CA. doi:10.1109/VR.2012.6180926

Hoskins, S. (2013). *3D Printing for Artists, Designers and Makers.* London: Bloomsbury.

Huang, L., Morency, L.-P., & Gratch, J. (2010). *Parasocial consensus sampling: combining multiple perspectives to learn virtual human behavior.* Paper presented at the 9th International Conference on Autonomous Agents and Multiagent Systems, Toronto, Canada.

Itti, L., Dhavale, N., & Pighin, F. (2004, August 3). *Realistic avatar eye and head animation using a neurobiological model of visual attention.* Paper presented at the Applications and Science of Neural Networks, Fuzzy Systems, and Evolutionary Computation VI, San Diego, CA. doi:10.1117/12.512618

Jacobson, J., & Lewis, M. (2005). Game engine virtual reality with CaveUT. *Computer, 38*(4), 79–82. doi:10.1109/MC.2005.126

Johnson, S. D. (1991). Productivity, the workforce, and technology education. *Journal of Technology Education, 2*(2).

Jones, P., & Wilks-Heeg, S. (2004). Capitalising culture: Liverpool 2008. *Local Economy, 19*(4), 341–360. doi:10.1080/0269094042000286846

Kalleberg, A. L. (1982). Work: Postwar trends and future prospects. *Business Horizons, 25*(4), 78–84. doi:10.1016/0007-6813(82)90030-1

Kelly, M. J. (1950). The Bell Telephone Laboratories-an example of an institute of creative technology. *Proceedings of the Royal Society of London. Series A, Mathematical and Physical Sciences, 203*(1074), 287–301. doi:10.1098/rspa.1950.0140

Kelly, M. J. (1955). Training programs of industry for graduate engineers. *Electrical Engineering, 74*(10), 866–869. doi:10.1109/EE.1955.6439586

Kelly, M. J. (1957). The Nation's Research and Development-Their Deficiencies and Means for Correction. *Proceedings of the American Philosophical Society, 101*(4), 386–391.

Kelly, M. J. (1959). Development of the Nation's scientific and technical potential. *Electrical Engineering, 78*(4), 315–318. doi:10.1109/EE.1959.6446332

Keys, P., & Hall, A. D. (1985). A step beyond OR. *The Journal of the Operational Research Society, 36*(9), 864–867. doi:10.2307/2582175

Korris, J., & Macedonia, M. (2002). The end of celluloid: Digital cinema emerges. *Computer, 35*(4), 96–98. doi:10.1109/MC.2002.993781

Lange, B., Flynn, S. M., & Rizzo, A. (2009). Game-based telerehabilitation. *European Journal of Physical and Rehabilitation Medicine, 45*(1), 143–151. PMID:19282807

Lange, B., Koenig, S., McConnell, E., Chang, C., Juang, R., Suma, E., . . . Rizzo, A. (2012). *Interactive game-based rehabilitation using the Microsoft Kinect*. Paper presented at the Virtual Reality Short Papers and Posters, Costa Mesa, CA. doi:10.1109/VR.2012.6180935

Lange, B., Rizzo, A., Chang, C.-Y., Suma, E. A., & Bolas, M. (2011). *Markerless full body tracking: Depth-sensing technology within virtual environments*. Paper presented at the Interservice/Industry Training, Simulation, and Education Conference (I/ITSEC), Orlando, FL.

Lindheim, R., & Swartout, W. (2001). Forging a new simulation technology at the ICT. *Computer, 34*(1), 72–79. doi:10.1109/2.895120

Long, W. A., & Ohtani, N. (1988). Entrepreneurship education and adding value to new ventures. *Journal of Marketing Education, 10*(1), 11–20.

Lusty, S. Jr. (1969). Educational technology. *Peabody Journal of Education, 47*(1), 53–56. doi:10.1080/01619566909537677

Macedonia, M. (2002). Games soldiers play. *IEEE Spectrum, 39*(3), 32–37. doi:10.1109/6.988702

Makela, T. (2005). Multimedia software as culture: Towards critical interaction design. *IEEE MultiMedia, 12*(1), 14–15. doi:10.1109/MMUL.2005.8

Mao, W., & Gratch, J. (2004, July 19 - 23). *A utility-based approach to intention recognition*. Paper presented at the AAMAS 2004 Workshop on Agent Tracking: Modeling Other Agents from Observations, New York, NY.

Marks, S., Estevez, J. E., & Connor, A. M. (2014). *Towards the Holodeck: fully immersive virtual reality visualisation of scientific and engineering data*. Paper presented at the 29th International Conference on Image and Vision Computing New Zealand, Hamilton, New Zealand. doi:10.1145/2683405.2683424

Mason, T. R. (1976). New directions for modeling? *New Directions for Institutional Research, 1976*(9), 105–111. doi:10.1002/ir.37019760909

McDonald, S., & Howell, J. (2012). Watching, creating and achieving: Creative technologies as a conduit for learning in the early years. *British Journal of Educational Technology, 43*(4), 641–651. doi:10.1111/j.1467-8535.2011.01231.x

Mendel, J. M. (1999). Establishing academic programs in integrated media systems. *IEEE Signal Processing Magazine, 16*(1), 67–76. doi:10.1109/79.743869

Merickel, M. L. (1990). The creative technologies project: Will training in 2D/3D graphics enhance kids' Cognitive skills? *T.H.E. Journal, 18*(5), 55.

Merickel, M. L. (1992). *A Study of the Relationship between Virtual Reality (Perceived Realism) and the Ability of Children To Create, Manipulate and Utilize Mental Images for Spatially Related Problem Solving*. Paper presented at the Annual Convention of the National School Boards Association, Orlando, FL.

Milone, J. (1994). Multimedia authors, one and all. *Technology and Learning, 5*(2), 25–31.

Muller, L. A. (1967). The role of industry in the introduction of educational change. *New York State Education, LV, 3*, 4–7.

Naef, M., Staadt, O., & Gross, M. (2002). *Spatialized audio rendering for immersive virtual environments*. Paper presented at the ACM Symposium on Virtual Reality Software and Technology, Shatin, Hong Kong. doi:10.1145/585740.585752

Nikias, C. (1999). Integraded Media Systems. *IEEE Signal Processing Magazine, 16*(1), 32–32. doi:10.1109/MSP.1999.743865

Okada, N. (1993). Entrepreneurship in the new technological regime. In A. E. Andersson, D. F. Batten, K. Kobayashi, & K. Yoshikawa (Eds.), *The Cosmo-Creative Society* (pp. 121–135). Berlin: Springer. doi:10.1007/978-3-642-78460-6_9

Olson, J. L., Krum, D. M., Suma, E. A., & Bolas, M. (2011). *A design for a smartphone-based head mounted display*. Paper presented at the 2011 IEEE Virtual Reality Conference, Singapore. doi:10.1109/VR.2011.5759484

Osberg, K. M. (1993). Virtual reality and education: A look at both sides of the sword. Seattle, WA: Human Interface Technology Laboratory Technical Report.

Parnes, S. J. (1967). *Creative behavior guidebook*. New York: Scribner.

Peppler, K. A., & Kafai, Y. B. (2007). From SuperGoo to Scratch: Exploring creative digital media production in informal learning. *Learning, Media and Technology, 32*(2), 149–166. doi:10.1080/17439880701343337

Pierce, J. R. (1975). Mervin Joe Kelly. *Biographical Memoirs, 46*, 191–219.

Proffitt, R., Lange, B., Chen, C., & Winstein, C. (2015). A comparison of older adults' subjective experiences with virtual and real environments during dynamic balance activities. *Journal of Aging and Physical Activity, 23*(1), 24–33. doi:10.1123/JAPA.2013-0126 PMID:24334299

Ramello, G. B. (2005). Property rights, firm boundaries, and the republic of science—A note on Ashish Arora and Robert Merges. *Industrial and Corporate Change, 14*(6), 1195–1204. doi:10.1093/icc/dth085

Randall, W., Hill, J., Han, C., & Lent, M. V. (2002). *Perceptually driven cognitive mapping of urban environments*. Paper presented at the First International Joint Conference on Autonomous Agents and Multiagent Systems, Bologna, Italy.

Rao, K., & Skouge, J. (2015). Using multimedia technologies to support culturally and linguistically diverse learners and young children with disabilities. In K. L. Heider & M. Renck Jalongo (Eds.), *Young Children and Families in the Information Age* (pp. 101–115). Dordrecht: Springer. doi:10.1007/978-94-017-9184-7_6

Resnick, M. (2006). Computer as paint brush: Technology, play, and the creative society. In D. Singer, R. Golikoff, & K. Hirsh-Pasek (Eds.), *Play= learning: How play motivates and enhances children's cognitive and social-emotional growth* (pp. 192–208). Oxford, UK: Oxford University Press. doi:10.1093/acprof:oso/9780195304381.003.0010

Rhyne, T.-M. (2002). Computer games and scientific visualization. *Communications of the ACM, 45*(7), 40–44. doi:10.1145/514236.514261

Rickel, J., Marsella, S., Gratch, J., Hill, R., Traum, D., & Swartout, W. (2002). Toward a new generation of virtual humans for interactive experiences. *IEEE Intelligent Systems, 17*(July/August), 32–38. doi:10.1109/MIS.2002.1024750

Rizzo, A., Cukor, J., Gerardi, M., Alley, S., Reist, C., Roy, M., & Difede, J. et al. (2015). Virtual reality exposure for ptsd due to military combat and terrorist attacks. *Journal of Contemporary Psychotherapy*, 1–10. doi:10.1007/s10879-015-9306-3

Rizzo, A., Pair, J., McNerney, P., Eastlund, E., Manson, B., Gratch, J., . . . Roy, M. (2004). *An immersive virtual reality therapy application for Iraq war veterans with PTSD: from training to toy to treatment.* Paper presented at the 24th Annual Army Science Conference, Orlando, FL.

Rizzo, A. A., Requejo, P., Winstein, C. J., Lange, B., Ragusa, G., Merians, A., . . . Aisen, M. (2011). *Virtual reality applications for addressing the needs of those aging with disability.* Paper presented at Medicine Meets Virtual Reality 2011, Newport Beach, CA.

Salovaara, A., Helfenstein, S., & Oulasvirta, A. (2011). Everyday appropriations of information technology: A study of creative uses of digital cameras. *Journal of the American Society for Information Science and Technology, 62*(12), 2347–2363. doi:10.1002/asi.21643

Sasaki, M. (2003). Kanazawa: A creative and sustainable city. *Policy Sciences, 10*(2), 17–30.

Shapiro, A., Pighin, F., & Faloutsos, P. (2003). *Hybrid control for interactive character animation.* Paper presented at the 11th Pacific Conference on Computer Graphics and Applications, Canmore, Canada.

Shavinina, L. V., & Ponomarev, E. A. (2003). Developing innovative ideas through high intellectual and creative educational multimedia technologies. In L. V. Shavinina (Ed.), *The international handbook on innovation* (pp. 401–418). Amsterdam: Elsevier. doi:10.1016/B978-008044198-6/50028-0

Silverman, R. E. (1968). Two kinds of technology. *Educational Technology, VIII*(1), 3.

Simpson, E. (1963). *You and Research.* Washington, DC: American Vocational Association, Inc.

Sivers, D. (2010). *Leadership Lessons from Dancing Guy.* Retrieved from https://sivers.org/ff

Skinner, L. (1996). The media lab at the university of the West of England, Bristol. *Local Economy, 11*(2), 181–184. doi:10.1080/02690949608726326

Skinner, R. (1994). Creative technology projects in science: The CREST-Creativity in Science and Technology-model. *Australian Science Teachers Journal, 40*(4), 26.

Solo, R. A. (1961). Creative technology and economic growth. *International Development Review, 3*(1).

Sosa, R., & Connor, A. M. (2015). *Orthodoxies in multidisciplinary design-oriented degree programmes.* Paper presented at the 2015 IASDR Conference: Interplay 2015, Brisbane, Australia.

Soyinka, W. (1978). Technology and the artist. *Science & Public Policy, 5*(1), 65–66.

Stapleton, C., Hughes, C., & Moshell, J. M. (2002). *Mixed reality and the interactive imagination.* Paper presented at the First Swedish-American Workshop on Modeling and Simulation, Orlando, FL.

Stoltz, R. B. (1945). The fortieth annual meeting of the american dairy science association. *Journal of Dairy Science*, 28(8), 625–649. doi:10.3168/jds.S0022-0302(45)95216-7

Stumpfel, J., Tchou, C., Jones, A., Hawkins, T., Wenger, A., & Debevec, P. (2004). *Direct HDR capture of the sun and sky*. Paper presented at the 3rd International Conference on Computer Graphics, Virtual Reality, Visualisation and Interaction in Africa, Cape Town, South Africa.

Stumpfel, J., Tchou, C., Yun, N., Martinez, P., Hawkins, T., Jones, A., . . . Debevec, P. E. (2003). *Digital Reunification of the Parthenon and its Sculptures*. Paper presented at the 4th International Symposium on Virtual Reality, Archaeology and Intelligent Cultural Heritage, Brighton, UK.

Suma, E. A., Lipps, Z., Finkelstein, S., Krum, D. M., & Bolas, M. (2012). Impossible spaces: Maximizing natural walking in virtual environments with self-overlapping architecture. *Visualization and Computer Graphics. IEEE Transactions on*, 18(4), 555–564.

Suranyi-Unger, T. (1963). The role of knowledge in invention and economic development. *American Journal of Economics and Sociology*, 22(4), 463–472. doi:10.1111/j.1536-7150.1963.tb00910.x

Swartout, W., & van Lent, M. (2003). Making a game of system design. *Communications of the ACM*, 46(7), 32–39. doi:10.1145/792704.792727

Tang, H.-K., & Yeo, K.-T. (1994). The new audacious technopreneurs. *Journal of Enterprising Culture*, 2(3), 857–870. doi:10.1142/S021849589400029X

Thierstein, A., & Gabi, S. (2004). When creativity meets metropolitan governance. *disP-The Planning Review*, 40(158), 34-40.

Tinwell, A., Grimshaw, M., Nabi, D. A., & Williams, A. (2011). Facial expression of emotion and perception of the Uncanny Valley in virtual characters. *Computers in Human Behavior*, 27(2), 741–749. doi:10.1016/j.chb.2010.10.018

Wallin, D. L. (1990). Televised interactive education: Creative technology for alternative learning. *Community Junior College Research Quarterly of Research and Practice*, 14(3), 259–266. doi:10.1080/0361697900140309

Webster, R., & Sudweeks, F. (2006). Enabling effective collaborative learning in networked virtual environments. *Current Developments in Technology-Assisted Education, 2*, 1437-1441.

Weiden+Kennedy. (2011). *Why we are not hiring creative technologists*. Retrieved from http://blog.wk.com/2011/10/21/why-we-are-not-hiring-creative-technologists/

Weng, Y.-J., Weng, Y.-C., Wong, Y.-C., Yang, S.-Y., & Liu, H.-K. (2009). *Fabrication of optical waveguide devices using electromagnetic assisted nanoimprinting*. Paper presented at the 2009 International Conference on Signal Processing Systems, Singapore. doi:10.1109/ICSPS.2009.179

Wooff, T. (1979). The south wales association for design education: Schools exhibition. *Studies in Design Education Craft & Technology*, 11(2), 105–107.

Zagalo, N., & Branco, P. (2015). The creative revolution that is changing the world. In N. Zagalo & P. Branco (Eds.), *Creativity in the Digital Age* (pp. 3–15). London: Springer. doi:10.1007/978-1-4471-6681-8_1

Chapter 2
Clash of Cultures:
Fashion, Engineering, and 3D Printing

Jennifer Loy
Griffith University, Australia

Samuel Canning
Griffith University, Australia

ABSTRACT

In 2012, a Belgian company called Materialise hosted a fashion show featuring designs from a worldwide millinery competition. The featured pieces were paraded down a catwalk by professional models, and an overall winner chosen. What made this fashion show unusual was that the attendees were predominantly clinical and industrial engineers, and the host was a specialist engineering and software development company that emerged in 1990 from a research facility based at Leuven University. Engineers and product designers rather than fashion designers created the millinery and the works were all realized through additive manufacturing technology. This chapter provides an example of how fashion design has become a creative stimulus for the development of the technology. It illustrates how disruptive creativity has the potential to advance scientific research, with the two worlds of engineering and fashion coming together through a collaboration with industrial design. The chapter highlights the challenges and possible implications for preparing trans-disciplinary research teams.

INTRODUCTION

Additive manufacturing, now more commonly known as 3D Printing (3DP), began as a prototyping technology in the mid-1980s. After gaining traction in product design, architecture and engineering as a resin based visual modeller, this technology has matured with the development of new materials and equipment. These have opened up new areas for research and possibilities for production applications, as detailed by leading researchers in the field, Gibson et al (2014), Lipson (2013) and Anderson (2012). Although the technology is now starting to impact across almost all fields, from animation to construction, over the twenty years of its initial development the majority of research in the area of direct manufacturing for 3DP has been concentrated into two main themes. The first is medical, with specialists in areas such

DOI: 10.4018/978-1-5225-0016-2.ch002

a regenerative medicine, orthopaedic surgery and artificial heart development recognising a myriad of potential applications for the technology, from the bioplotting of cells to titanium implants. The second is industrial, with applications for 3DP explored in commercial applications such as for automotive and aerospace, with particular advances in light-weighting and material performance. Yet scientific research into additive manufacturing has been slow to capture attention both in terms of funding and in the eyes of the public as well as potential industry partners. In the last three years, fashion design has proved to be a vehicle for all three. 3D Printed fashion has caused disruptive change in the development of research in this field. The inspiration provided by fashion designers has provided a basis for innovation that has been realized by industrial designers and engineers in recent practice. This chapter discusses the value of trans-disciplinary research practice based on teams that include both scientific researchers in fields such as engineering and medicine, as well as creative researchers from design and art. It also outlines some of the challenges facing these teams that arise from a clash of cultures in values, approach, practice, aims and outcomes. It then goes on to more specifically provide an example of collaborative practice where fashion and engineering, and then fashion, industrial design and engineering, come together. The example highlights the role of the industrial designer in the collaboration, in providing a practical link for creative practitioners interested in working with 3D Printing technology, but without the understanding of design for 3DP or technical skills to achieve it on their own, to realize their ideas. However, this example highlights how the complexities of design for process in relation to 3DP mean the industrial designer has to evolve the design as part of the process, rather than providing a form of 3D documentation after the design has been completed, which challenges dominant practice in a field such as fashion design. The objective of this chapter is to illustrate that for collaborations around this cross-disciplinary technology to work, and for new trans-disciplinary research practice between creative and scientific researchers that transcend conventional practices to emerge and be effective in new ways, the different roles within the team have to be interrogated and ground rules established to avoid a clash of cultures on many different levels.

BACKGROUND

According to Milton and Rodgers (2013), "Unlike scientific research, design research is not concerned with what exists but what ought to be. Research in a design context breaks with the determinisms of the past; it continually challenges, provokes and disrupts the status quo" (p.11).

Research into additive manufacturing, now more commonly known as 3D Printing, has been embedded in scientific research communities since its inception. Dominated by materials science, mechanical engineering, robotics and medical research, it has developed incrementally, resulting in additional forms of the technology, such as material jetting and selective laser melting, and an increasing range of material properties, such as the bimetals developed by researchers at NTU. Progress in the field has been disseminated in research journals that are predominantly materials and technology focussed and that research has tended to be technical, as in the example by Qain (2015) on metal powders for additive manufacturing in the Journal of Minerals, Metals and Materials.

Although multidisciplinary, the roots of research in this area cannot be characterized as cross disciplinary. Yet studies on the organisation of research practice are suggesting that innovation in research is stimulated by multidisciplinary teams and by trans-disciplinary thinking, where trans-disciplinary research is characterized as working in new areas between disciplines. The argument is that a trans-disciplinary approach provides opportunities for synergy, where the combined abilities of the researchers involved bring new dimensions to the work (Cacchione, 2015). The need for this synergy in scientific research at this time has been highlighted by Wageman et al (2012), who suggest that archetypal teams need to be altered in the face of changes in the current discourse on the nature and form of collaboration. Just as more business leaders are recognising that innovation is stifled by over planning (Kaplan, 2012), the idea of a stable research team membership, with a collective consciousness built on a shared "transactive" memory with routines and processes traditionally seen as beneficial to efficiently creating quality output, is being challenged (Lewis, 2003, p.587).

In relation to the development of research in additive manufacturing, the disciplinary knowledge has been built through narrowly focussed research projects to address specific problems. However, this assumes that the problem to be solved is based on the right questions. With increasingly complex situations to address, problem framing is becoming a more essential skill in research, as well as the ability to view the specifics of a problem within a much broader context. This requires different views on the same subject, and a willingness and ability of the researchers involved to step outside the boundaries of their expertise to address the interdisciplinarity of complex problems. Moving ideas on, beyond an incremental change approach to encompass the possibilities of step change, requires structures that support creative and divergent thinking.

Research teams need to be built to support innovation. If not, the outcomes will remain incremental and opportunities for new thinking and new practice will be missed, along with new directions for further research. However, even in business, where innovation is overtly valued, predictability and control are part of conventional operations management. Researchers from the University of Virginia found the management of a team that is intent on stimulating innovative practice, required agile thinking that worked positively with ambiguity. They concluded that uncertainty created opportunities and that it was essential to push the team outside their comfort zones, and to help them learn to embrace risk and failure as a way of providing the context for disruptive innovation (Kaplan, 2012).

In the case of additive manufacturing, researchers based at Materialise, a commercial offshoot of Leuven University, found that the inherent mindset driving research and development in additive manufacturing was focussed on incremental, discipline specific technical research. This was highlighted as a concern, by Materialise CEO Leys (2015) during an Inside 3D Printing industry conference in New York in 2015, in relation to shifting current research focus from prototyping to direct manufacturing as a primary use for the technology. Leys called for the incremental development dominating research to be disrupted by new thinking to radically change practice and stimulate ideas that were not hampered by the body of knowledge and conventions of the industry up to that point. As Kaplan (2012) observes, more and more leaders now recognize that they must proactively disrupt conventions and practice in order to create innovation, and that detailed planning documents not only stifle disruptive innovation, but actively represent liabilities to creating innovative outcomes. This requires being open to adopting unconventional practices that currently fall outside the scope of traditional training for team leaders in business and research. If design research, as defined by Milton and Rodgers (2013), is disruptive to conventional practice, approach and ideas, then the leaders of research teams that include designers must be open to that possibility. The challenge for scientific researchers is to be able to work collaboratively with designers in a culture of risk and failure more dynamic than their research approach is conventionally likely to be. The challenge, therefore, is to provide the stimulus for creative thinking and innovative practice, within a field that is grounded in scientific theory research.

CREATIVE TECHNOLOGIES AND BARRIERS TO TRANSDISCIPLINARY RESEARCH

Design research also differs from scientific research, for the most part, in that it is concerned with the plausibility and appropriateness of proposals, whilst scientific research is concerned with universal truths. Design research tends to produce knowledge that can be defined as trans-disciplinary and heterogeneous in nature and that which seeks to improve the world (Milton & Rodgers. 2012 p.).

Within engineering and design education, there exists an uneasy truce between the critical and the creative. The Australian Curriculum advocates a combined approach, and Engineers Australia calls for more creative thinking in engineering education, and whilst there are exceptional Universities such as Olin, Stanford and MIT that openly embrace creative thinking in their curriculum, the classical model of engineering education begins with a solid grounding of theory, and is driven by the scientific method of enquiry. This allows little scope for creativity. As students progress through their engineering degree, they are increasingly engaged in practical learning, but this is built on predetermined theoretical foundations and so the students approach their applied work constrained – and supported - by their learning development.

In the same way, product design students are traditionally taught manufacturing technologies successively from conventional technologies that are well established in the industry, through to the most recent developments. This means that when they do engage with the most advanced manufacturing technologies, they approach them with a heritage of working with the constraints and opportunities of conventional manufacturing technologies. Working in teams within a discipline can be difficult enough, broadening a research team to include researchers from disciplines that have fundamentally different understandings of what research is, how it is conducted, what the outcomes will look like and how they will be evaluated, increases that challenge. Graeme Pullin (2011), whose research is in the field of design for disability, argues that this discipline has too long been dominated by the sciences, and this has resulted in very basic, unimaginative, solutions. He argues for the disruption of conventional scientific practice in the field by the involvement of designers at a very early stage and in conjunction with all technologies being developed. His reasoning is that scientific research has been restricted to the development of mechanical outcomes, and that this approach fails to meet the needs of the individuals for which the assistive technologies are designed for, and that a human centred approach would not only address non-compliance issues, where the user refuses to use the product, but also innovations in design for ability that would take disability research in more positive directions. He is critical of legislation, built on a legacy from the UK National Health Service in the 1930s that was not reformed until the 1970s (and even then only to a limited extent) that restricted the styling 'allowed' for assistive technologies such as eyewear. Eyewear designers Cutler and Gross have spent 30 years on the front line of the revolution in eyewear where their aim was to change it from a 'medical necessity to key fashion accessory' (Pullin, 2011 p.21). Pullin observes that although fashion and discretion are not opposites - fashion can be understated and discretion does not require invisibility - there is a tension between the two and for some in the medical field, fashion is the antithesis of good design. Nowadays, spectacles are seen as worn, rather than carried, which causes a shift in thinking from a medical model to a social model. Positioning them as an item of clothing, rather than a product, design writer Per Mollerup said of spectacles now "what others see is more important than what you see yourself" (Pullin, 2011 p.19) Customers are consumers rather than patients, which is a significant design distinction, and Cutler and Gross argue that to keep that way of thinking in societies' mind, they need to constantly push the boundaries of what is expected from eyewear, challenging styling conventions and questioning understandings of taste and acceptable practice.

Ross Lovegrove designed a hearing aide that was featured in Blueprint magazine that aimed to be seen as jewellery, rather than a medical product. It was produced from a carbon composite and drew on positive imagery from technology, such as Bluetooth. Rather than aiming for invisibility, this hearing aide was designed to be seen, and by not being restricted to the need for discretion, the technology fitted into the aid could provide enhanced performance and ease of maintenance. Designer Sam Hecht took this one step further and designed for ability, by creating hearing aides with an array of microphones that support multidirectional hearing, surpassing normal human hearing.

Pullin (2011) points to the current omission of designers in scientific research teams now for the development of assistive technologies, and suggests that designers can rethink the questions being asked about the fundamental purposes of products and should therefore be included. He argues that even products for medical purposes should be designed for the emotional as well as the practical needs of the user. This is supported through studies on the use of sleep apnoea masks, where the emotional response of the user to how they feel about wearing the mask and being seen wearing the mask is leading to a high degree of non-compliance. In addition, designers are concerned through their training with human machine interaction to a larger degree than engineers or clinicians, and are therefore more able to work on the performance of the mask during actual use, taking into account multiple factors, rather than its performance on a statistical and theoretical level. According to Pullin, in a recent major US research project, the team invitation was sent out to engineers, technologists, and clinicians, but not industrial designers or interaction designers, fashion designers or sculptors. The attributes of prosthetics affect the image its wearer is projecting, but more than that, a design approach to problem solving for a functional need takes into account situational design thinking, and includes experience mapping and systems thinking as advocated by Kumar (2012) and draws on the body of knowledge on the psychology of interaction design detailed in product design research into behaviour (Weinschenck, 2011) that will impact the fundamentals of what the design intent really should be, and what will impact the design development. A purely mechanical response to problem solving limits innovation, and because it draws on a narrow discipline with a shared 'transactive' memory built up over time, the likely outcome will be an incremental change rather than an innovative one. Including designers in research teams that are traditionally restricted to scientific enquiry is a way for a research team leader to embrace disruption that can lead to innovation.

Environmental researcher, Janine Benyus (2002), is a leading advocate of research teams that bring together scientists and designers within the field of biomimicry. The study of nature systems as biomimicry is an approach increasingly supported by theorists and practitioners, such as the author of Shark's Paintbrush (Harman 2014). However, Benyus works very specifically on creating diverse research teams that bring together scientific enquiry, design understanding and creative thinking. She argues that bringing designers and scientists together with a specific problem in mind, to explore nature together, stimulates innovation based on nature's systems that would not be identified by single discipline researchers alone with the same stimulus. One of the reasons given for including designers in research teams is their divergent thinking ability. Designers are trained to mind map and brainstorm, and to create a safe environment for risk taking in the expression of ideas. Risk taking in design is not excluded by the need for a functional, heavily structural outcome. Architectural risk taking is a strong example of studio practice informed by the structural, but not reduced by it. The work of innovators such as Zaha Hadid and Frank Gehry, who argue for unconventional thinking (Cohen et al, 2003) demonstrate that a conceptual rethink of conventions within a practice inspired by new material and technological innovations is not at odds with the need to provide engineering solutions and in the last two years there have been breakthrough designs where the outcomes illustrate the transformative potential of 3D Printing technology, such as demonstrated in the work of the engineering team at Airbus, but the predominant body of work in the field has been in substitute products and tooling, rather than disruptive innovations.

This low-key progression of applications in the engineering and industrial design field may be because the developmental pathway for the technology has come out of rapid prototyping, rather than as a new technology. Interest has traditionally been focussed on its use in supporting conventional manufacturing techniques and reducing time to market through providing an ability for designers and engineers to more quickly iterate designs during a traditional industry process approach rather than in new design opportunities. Exemplars for how the technology could impact not only design development and outcome for a company, but the business model of organisations, are still rare and the majority of outcomes in the field are still incrementally developed progressions.

In contrast, art and fashion are disciplines founded on expression, innovation and creativity. The often-transient nature of the output, its response to context, and the accessibility of its materials and technologies have produced a discipline that expresses risk in its exploration of form. Without the weight of longevity and more functional responsibility that can constrain industrial thinking, these disciplines have the potential to take more risks with 3D Printing and provide alternative directions for development that can then inform their industrial counterparts.

Digital media have provided revolutionary forms of creative expression through a myriad of methods, from the screen-based, with its abstractions and hyper-real macro and micro-scenarios, time-based, self generating, fast evolving imagery and media that have evoked consideration of new kinds of space and infinite zones, the potential future for which, in creative terms, is shifting, flexible, complex and unbounded (Braddock Clarke, Harris, 2012, p.229).

The work of Fung Kwok Pan provides an example of creative technologies research and disruptive practice. Pang is digital artist and designer who works with coding to create interactive online media to provoke a form of co-production between the designer and the consumer. An example of his work with additive manufacturing / 3D Printing, is his Supabold FluidVase series. This work was based on the idea of water splashing into a container, and capturing the movement of the water as a freeze frame that was then 3D Printed. The intent driving the work was very clear, and this provided the brief for the technical development work needed to meet that intent. Because the driver came from an expressive intent, the technical research to meet that intent was not based on previous work, but took the development of practice in new directions, driving innovation in the field. Again, because the driver was expressive, the supporting work was not constrained to a single discipline but worked across art, IT, design and engineering to meet the needs of the project, drawing on ideas and practice from across those disciplines.

Another example of additive manufacturing creative research stimulus comes from the work of Assa Ashuach. As well as his work on UCODO and Digital Forming, which had a user interaction element, as in Pan's work, Ashuach has also worked directly with additive manufacturing / 3D Printing to explore the potential of the technology to support innovation in design applications. This work has resulted in innovations that exploit the characteristics of the technology and draws technical development research along with it, such as was necessary for his AI light and AI stool. By starting with a creative design intent, rather than a technical development research intent, the work is arguably more likely to cross disciplinary boundaries and inspire innovations that lead to developments within technical research areas.

Fashion and Engineering

The young, Dutch, fashion designer, Iris van Herpen is the unlikely champion of disruptive innovation in the development of applications and practice in advanced manufacturing technologies. Unlikely, because her work until recently was known for its avant-garde nature, not its technical construction or materials science. Champion, because van Herpen's interest in additive manufacturing – 3D Printing – to create textiles and dress forms has raised the profile of this technology and, more than that, forced a re-evaluation of the technology that was contained and controlled by the dominant players that had established its roots in engineering science (Figure 1).

The first clash of cultures to occur in relation to a shared working practice of fashion designers and engineers using 3DP as a creative technology, has been in relation to the perception and appreciation of the relative roles within the design. Iris van Herpen's work broke the technology out of the constraints of conventional manufacturing and rapid prototyping it was constrained by, in using it as an expressive medium. She re-imagined what could be possible, and challenged industrial designers and engineers to keep up with her vision, which faced considerable technical barriers. However, in order to realize her ideas, van Herpen needed to work closely with 3D designer and architect, Daniel Widrig. In 2011, Daniel Widrig, who now heads up a research cluster at UCL and is a multi award winning designer and

Figure 1. Escapism dress by Iris van Herpen and close up of detail of Escapism dress
Photo: Loy, 2012.

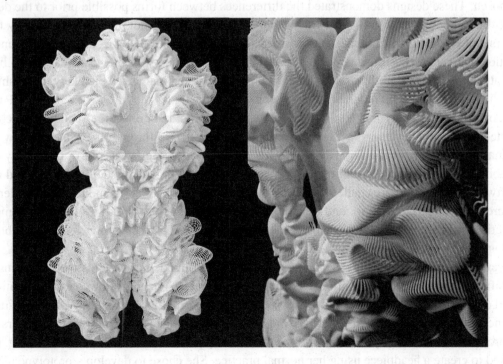

architect working across sculpture, furniture design and architecture (including experience with Zaha Hadid), collaborated with Iris van Herpen and engineers in Materialise on the creative and technical development of an innovative dress that pushed the boundaries of research in 3D Printing organic forms and flexible structures. The Escapism dress was named one of the fifty best inventions of the year by Time magazine. The dress provided a radical departure from convention in additive manufacturing research and proved a catalyst for designers to see its possibilities as a creative technology.

Yet, from a collaborative point of view, the accreditation of the dress to the designer has been focussed on the creative inspiration, with the 3D designers role initially presented at the level of a technician. This ignores the reality of working with 3D printing. In conventional fashion design, to be able to translate an initial sketch into the construction of form is integral to the design development, such as demonstrated in the work of Nakamichi (2011). Whilst a technical specialist might take the pattern cutting of Nakamichi and build the final form, the construction detailing is a vital part of the expertise of the fashion designer. It is not enough to be able to provide an initial sketch, the designer's role includes how a creative inspiration could be realized in the same way that an industrial designer would be expected to design for conventional manufacturing, such as injection moulding. Yet 3D printing has emerged out of the engineering disciplines, and fashion designers are not yet trained to build designs within solid modelling CAD software, or understand the constraints and opportunities of working with 3DP. The difficulty is that, just as CAD itself has shifted from a documentation tool, to be part of the design process, the design role within the development of digital fashion must extend to include the design for process portion of the activity. One of the challenges to collaboration in relation to bringing together disparate disciplines, such as fashion and engineering, is that the conventions of each have not developed in conjunction, and are not necessarily recognized or understood by both parties.

In 2012, Materialise hosted a competition for the design of 3D printed headwear inspired by the innovations demonstrated by Iris van Herpen and Daniel Widrig. Twenty designs from around the world were chosen. These designs demonstrated the differences between forms possible prior to the development of the technology and those now achievable. The designs were not, however, created by fashion designers, but by engineers and industrial designers. As a result, the aesthetic, and even the functional conventions, of fashion design were not addressed – for example most of the headwear had to be hand held as attachments or detailing for additional fixing had not been included. It is likely that fashion designers did not have the solid modelling computer skills, or the understanding of design for 3DP needed for the competition. Equally it is possible that the competition did not reach the social media channels frequented by fashion designers, as the competition was advertised through the Materialise web site, which may not have attracted fashion designers at that time. Alisa's Curls was one of the twenty chosen for exhibition in Belgium, and then in the US. It is an example of organic modelling using solid modelling software. The forms were challenging to construct using Solidworks (an industrial modeller rather than a creative visualisation tool), and the construction itself demonstrated the shift from component construction to a complex, single piece outcome not possible to construct using a mould or subtractive technology (Figure 2).

However, more than that, the design and technical advances made through this piece in terms of the mind shift in thinking from a conventional technology approach, to one that allowed for an organic, multilayered object to be created, that genuinely exploited the opportunities created by 3DP, was stimulated by the inclusion of a designer with a background in textiles into the team of industrial designers taking on the project. This was an experiment to mimic the working practice of van Herpen and Widrig. Newey was asked to create a headpiece using her normal practice. She chose to develop a prototype using cut

Figure 2. Progression of Alisa's Curls
By Alisa Newey, Jennifer Loy and Samuel Canning, 2012.

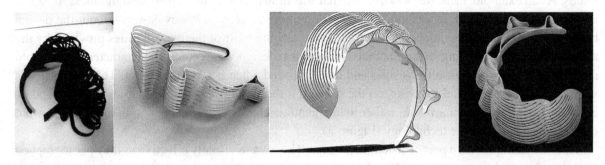

leather. The industrial designers then interpreted that idea using Solidworks, and then evolved it within the program itself to exploit the characteristics of the software and design for 3DP. The final piece was printed as one part.

This example of the new working practice relied on the initial forms being created unconstrained by the technology, but equally it relied on the industrial designers knowledge of designing for 3DP, both of the appropriate solid modeling software and of the technology, to evolve the design, rather than be constrained by attempting to mimic the textile form. The textile provided the inspiration for a creative opportunity that created a step change in the way the industrial designers approached and stretched the capabilities of the software and printing technology, but the creative design involved in the development of the piece did not start and finish with the original inspiration, but rather became a design collaboration. The CAD work was not a documentation of the textile, but rather, used as a design tool in developing the design further. This new relationship between the creative and the technical provides the opportunity for significant, rather than incremental change, driven by meeting the needs of creative practice as a starting point. However, it relies on the recognition of the design role as being collaborative. If the textile had been provided as a blueprint, with no understanding of the technology or designing for that technology, or of working with solid modeling software, it would likely have resulted in a literal translation of the textile that failed to address significant design issues.

The 2012 competition and work with van Herpen and Widrig, led the engineers at Materialise to begin a collaboration with Malaysian fashion designer, Melinda Looi. The brief was to design a collection that demonstrated the artistic potential of the technology. The resulting collection was inspired by birds, and based on drawings that Looi provided to the engineers. In terms of impact, the collection was very successful. It was launched in a packed runway show in Malaysia that was attended by Malaysian Royalty, and in addition to the medical, engineering and industrial design audience that Materialise attracts to its conferences, there was also considerable interest from the media, including fashion media. The show then traveled, including to India, China, Australia and Europe. In terms of challenging what was possible to create with the technology and raise the profile, not only for engineers and industrial designers, but also for creatives. it was very successful.

However, the pieces themselves had problems that impacted both their display and their longevity. More significantly, the designs that worked on paper, has not translated into fashion pieces, but rather into pieces of sculpture that whilst having visual impact in photographs, could not be claimed to be wearable fashion. This had been an issue with some of the previous pieces of van Herpen's work too, which Materialise had been unable to easily take down the runway. Essentially, the engineers had worked to translate the drawings into 3D Printed forms, but that translation had been very literal, and this caused issues. As an example, there was a skirt form that was drawn to have movement and lightness, to shimmer as the model walked. It was modeled by an Engineer literally as it was drawn without the design being evolved to retain the intent, or redesigned to make the most of the opportunities provided by the technology, whilst avoiding its limitations. Nor was it redesigned to exploit the characteristics of sold modeling software. The result was solid and heavy printed when it was printed out. This meant it was very difficult for the model to 'wear' on the runway, it did not move as the fashion designer intended, and it was perceived as an artwork, rather than a genuine challenge to the fashion industry about what could be possible with the technology (Figure 3).

Another example was a pair of articulated wings. These were visually effective as they photographed well, but they had been constructed as they were drawn, whereas they needed to be designed to work with the movement of the model with a good understanding of how to design for the technology. The feathers were attached by narrow filaments, which were vulnerable and easily broken off. The material characteristics needed to be taken into account as well as the joints redesigned to create an improved connection. The reality is that this technology means that a genuinely 3-dimensional attachment could have been made, using light weighting techniques for which this technology is so appropriate. This could have created new detailing on the wing forms which would have had the potential not only to function better, but also demonstrate the possibilities of the technology. By not designing for the technology, it looks as if it is less successful than using conventional means of creating those joints, although this is not the case. The articulations of the skeleton also proved problematic and again, the ability of the technology to create innovations in skeletal forms was not demonstrated here. Designing wings using 3DP should result in an entirely new set of forms, made possible by new ways of making. The shoes were another example. The sketch on paper was recreated exactly, with no redesign for the opportunities of the technology, or consideration of materials. 3DP is best known in engineering circles for optimized topology. The majority of the engineering examples of using the technology successfully are in this area. The shoes provided a perfect opportunity for using optimized topology, yet instead the drawings were literally translated and the resulting products unwearable. Models had to be taught how to walk down

Figure 3. Details of 'Birds' by fashion designer Melinda Looi
Photos: Loy, 2013.

the runway wearing them so that they would not fall, and straps had to be added that undermined the designer's vision. As this is the Engineer's area of expertise is would have been expected that this would have been a design element in which the engineers and fashion designer would have collaborated on together. However, it is likely too that there was a clash of cultures. Fashion design is a discipline where designers are very protective of their personal vision and working practice is very different between a fashion house and an engineering office. Creating a dialogue on the design elements in a shared language with the best will in the world would have been a challenge. Overall, the resulting pieces of the initial collaboration were dramatic, and captured the spirit of the design intent, but the problems with the final pieces highlighted the need for an additional team member who understood specifically developing the design for process, and who could work with the human interaction element of the applications, and the visual elements of the outcomes, whilst also working with the technical aspects of the project. This led to the collaboration described in the practice-led enquiry example.

Practice-Led Enquiry

This example of practice-led enquiry describes a project designed to stimulate new mindsets and creativity in additive manufacturing research and the challenges involved in meeting that intent. The aim was to contribute to disrupting the current dominance of incremental, technical development in engineering-focussed research in additive manufacturing and raise the profile of 3D printing as a creative technology. Materialise VP, Wim Michiels, provided the stimulus. He brought together a team of creative and technical collaborators to work on a full-length 3D Printed evening dress. The research team consisted of engineers from Materialise, specialists in additive manufacturing, Griffith University lecturer and industrial designer, Sam Canning, specialising in design for 3D printing, and fashion designer Melinda Looi, who provided creative direction. The focus for this evaluation of practice is the challenges to this approach and in particular the role of the industrial designer as the bridge between fashion and engineering. Canning was invited to join the collaboration following the work he exhibited in Malaysia in 2013 based on his research into maximising design applications based on 3D printing. Canning's 'Peacemaker' included over 250 individual 'feathers' of graduating size, which are individually hinged. As part of meeting the requirements of designing for 3D printing, Canning created the hat in two parts, designed to be printed together within a limited build space of 200mm x 200mm x 200mm. The dashed line in the figure shows the line of the bounding box around the feathers with a 0.5mm clearance. This maximizes the build volume and accuracy of the print process. This design demonstrates a sound knowledge of the intricacies and opportunities of designing for process using SLS technology. As an illustration of the differences in approach between fashion and engineering, the fashion category that the Peacemaker was entered in was 'captive parts', demonstrating a clear engineering, rather than a fashion bias. 'Peacemaker' was named after the Native American Indian Legend of the Great Peacemaker, otherwise known as Deganawida (Heavenly Messenger) and his historical associations with peace and the white dove (Figure 4).

The addition of Canning to the research team brought the design for process knowledge to the team, but added an additional element in relation to collaborative practice, as the discipline practice, ideas and knowledge for industrial design are different again from fashion design and engineering. The significance of the role of the industrial designer is documented as providing the missing link between abstract creativity and engineering construction. The main barriers to collaborative practice between scientific and creative practitioners identified through this project are highlighted and recommendations for future practice are discussed.

Figure 4. Details of Peacemaker
By Samuel Canning, 2013.

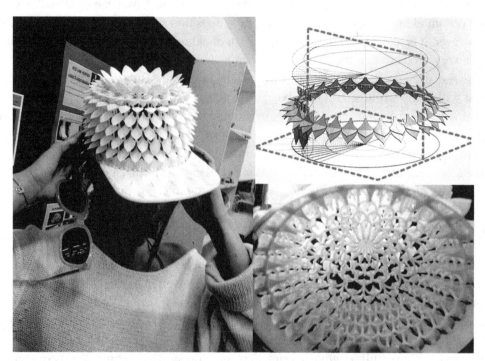

Example of Practice

In this project example, the fashion designer provided a theme for the dress. This was based on coral, with the idea that this provided the opportunity to show detail and complexity in the dress, demonstrating the technical potential of the technology to create complex assemblies. The sketches shown were developed by the fashion designer independently and sent to the industrial designer to translate the intent into a product (Figure 5).

There was no reference to the technology in the sketches themselves, or are any specific details on the translation of the intent into a product. The sketches were intended to be expressive, rather than technical and guide the overall impression the design should make on the viewer.

The dress drawings and the photographs of coral were then given to the industrial designer. The designer undertook initial research in three parts by:

- Interrogating the marine life influence with the technology in mind.
- Exploring the capabilities of the technology to support forms that could relate to the theme,
- Researching material properties and characteristics in relation to the project theme,
- Bringing an understanding of how to design for 3D printing to the stimulus material, the designer redirected the initial stimulus material to retain the intent, but work with the technology.

Figure 5. Drawings and inspiration by fashion designer Melinda Looi

Research involved testing of materials and process. Test pieces were designed to look at the properties and potential of the material, and structures for the project whilst exploring how to translate the creative intent into a design intent (Figure 6).

For example, a wave structure, consisting of narrow fibres of 1 mm diameter, is intended to mimic the way sea grass moves underwater, whilst testing if the material will be self-supporting. The material tested was Materialise TPU, which is a functional elastomeric material that is strong and durable, and is processed using selective laser sintering. Further test pieces on self-supporting structures designed to test the flexibility of the material, and the level of fluid movement of multiple entities included tapered filaments where the resolution at the base was within standard guidelines, but at their tip was finer than standard printing allowed. Additional models were intended to test the flexibility of the TPU material and its ability to make thin sheet like structures. At 0.8mm the leaf green structure shown was at the edge of the recommended thickness for this process and designed to test the consistency of the thin structure and its ability to create a concertina-like mechanism (Figure 7).

The performance of the material and process for interlocking parts was considered critical to the product, and therefore rows of hinged elements were tested, with the tolerances (clearance between elements) reduced on each row to ascertain the optimum tolerances for functional hinges. Other test pieces included a grid structure looking at printing resolution. The grid was graduated, with a thickness at one

Figure 6. Lattice detailing
Canning, 2015.

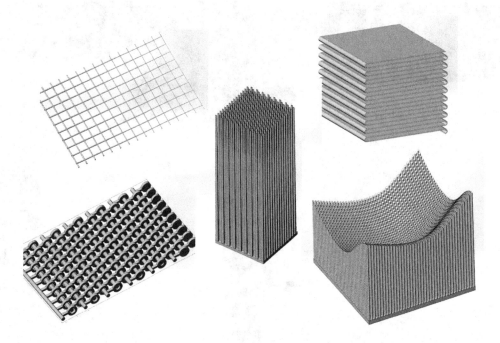

Figure 7. Grid patterning
Canning, 2013.

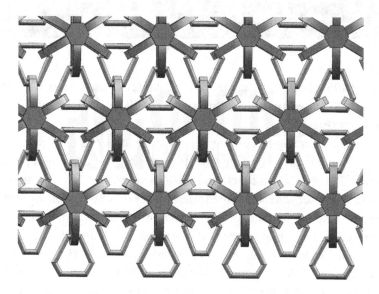

end well within the standard print resolution for the process, with the opposite end only 0.15mm diameter, which was beyond the standard print resolution for the process to test what would happen with the material and technology at its boundaries, where it started to fail. These test structures were converted to stereolithography (STL) format and sent to Materialise for printing. Alongside the testing and research into TPU more conventional materials and alternative processes were evaluated for the project including polyamide. Polyamide proved to be more robust and structurally stable than TPU in this context. This was particularly relevant because of the forms of the structures that were developing alongside the materials testing in response to the coral research. For this reason in addition to the research into TPU material concepts for rigid structures printed in Polyamide or a similar end use material were developed. Technologies considered were stereolithography, selective laser sintering and fused deposition modeling (both using a standard multihead extrusion printer and a material jetting system for UV cured resin with a wax support structure). In each case, the physical design would need to be different for each process. All 3D printing technologies have their idiosyncrasies and operate in a different way, and each requires a different approach. Many processes print in materials that are considered non-functional. This means that the materials used for printing are not durable or otherwise viable for an end use scenario. These materials include those prone to rapid discoloration and degradation when exposed to UV light, which quickly become brittle. For this reason they were eventually rejected as unsuitable for this project. Selective laser sintering (SLS) proved capable of creating parts from a suitable end use material (polyamide/nylon) for the process. SLS also generates no support material as it uses the powder surrounding the part, not fused by the laser, as support (Figure 8).

The figure shows the sketch development of rigid interlocking structures based on stylistic references taken from marine structures. Numerous ideas were developed and three were selected to be taken into CAD for further development as they demonstrated the capabilities of the technology in different forms

Figure 8. Drawing detail
Canning, 2015.

that all drew on the coral reference material. The hexagon style structure was based on the geometry of coral polyps. This structure has six sided structural elements and is linked by separate joiners, each linking three of the six-sided features (Figure 9).

An alternative structure was one in which a robust structure was created that did not use separated links between the main parts, but instead used features on the parts themselves. Developments of the structural design elements led to open lace like structures designed for maximum flexibility. This design contained ring elements each linking three individual elements. In this design each individual segment is linked to twelve separate parts. This made the structure strong despite its fragile appearance, which was in line with the original creative intent. In order to expedite the process of evaluation these structures were printed on a UV cured resin, material-jetting printer. This type of printer does not produce similar material properties to the Polyamide (the chosen print method and material) but that was not considered relevant for the purpose of these samples that were essentially to evaluate the flexibility of the actual structures themselves and their aesthetic relevance to the project aims (Figure 10).

The resultant printed structures were sent to the fashion designer for evaluation. These were discussed between the fashion designer and the industrial designer, with two selected for further development. In this context, the role of the industrial designer has some parallels with a textile designer who specializes in constructed textiles (such as woven, knit, mixed media) and particularly performance specific textiles, as discussed by McQuaid (2005), where the application impacts the construction to meet onsite requirements. However, as evidenced by the work outlined by Braddock Clarke and Harris (2012), the developments in digital textile design are challenging traditional discipline boundaries. In this case, the most significant elements that develop, rather than replicate, practice in relevant constructed textile design fields (such as digital knitting), relate to parametric and bespoke modelling. The industrial designer brought an understanding of the constraints and opportunities of designing for 3DP that integrated the constructed textile elements into the bespoke 3D forming of the overall design with non-uniform elements that could be used for successive, staggered layers. A high level of design and artisanship was required to achieve this outcome.

A critical factor in deciding what to make, what material to make it in, and what process to use was the build volume available. All 3D printing technologies are restricted to the volumetric capacities of their respective machines. Materialise had an SLS machine with a capacity of 650 X 330 X 560mm dedicated to SLS Polyamide. Although in conventional manufacturing, this could be a small build size, compared to for example the capacity in rotational moulding, in 3DP terms, this is a large build volume.

Figure 9. Structural detailing
Canning, 2015.

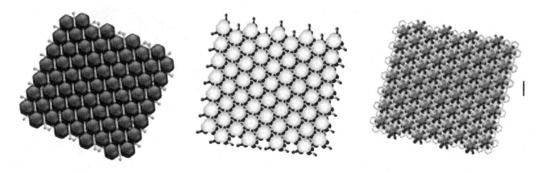

Figure 10. Close-up constructed textiles
Canning, 2015.

It allowed for a significant amount of 3D geometry to be built in a single build, allowing for the dress to be printed as a single part. Materialise had dedicated a much smaller machine to its TPU material that was around the size of a shoebox and unsuitable for the scale of the project. As one of the aims expressed by Materialise and the industrial designer was to print the assembly as a single part, the SLS using polyamide was chosen for the final print, which then dictated the material. This impacted the characteristics possible to work with and the industrial designer had to adjust the design construction to match these characteristics whilst retaining the fluidity of the garment (Figure 11).

The driver for the fashion designer was to create a distinctive fashion icon that utilized the technology to achieve her creative vision. In order to achieve this, Looi decided to finish the dress with hundreds of Swarovski crystals. In order to achieve the housing for these crystals, the industrial designer thickened the detailing on the components from 5mm to 8mm. Although the design was then functional, it became

Figure 11. Printed out test pieces
Canning, 2014.

visually heavy and the team decided that it needed to be visually lightened to still capture the essence of the original vision. This required a redesign of the components themselves, so that they then could house the crystals but retain the visual lightness of structure. This design contained a pierced front section to allow the back of the crystal to protrude into the heart of the structure. This design development reduced the overall thickness of the structure to less than 5mm. At the same time patterned features present on the upper surface of the individual elements was increased in size. The original patterning is on the right in the photograph, which even at close inspection is difficult to distinguish. Fine features and patterning like this are extremely vulnerable to even fine machine variations. At this point in the process the industrial designer had completed the initial research phase of the project, including the initial test pieces.

The next stage of the project was to source a model to tailor the design to fit. Looi organized for her chosen model, Eleen, to be digitally scanned by an Italian scanner, Daniel Siri, whilst on an assignment in Switzerland (Figure 12).

The point cloud data from the original scan was sent to Australia and processed at Griffith University by industrial designer and scanning specialist, Chris Little. Little translated the data into a 3D CAD solid model suitable to use as reference data in SolidWorks. The 650 x 330 x 560mm spatial constraints of the SLS Polyamide process could now be viewed in their correct context. The grey transparent bounding box represents the available build volume for the project. All 3D geometry for the dress had to be fitted into this area which meant that when the dress was modeled in SolidWorks, it had to be folded in on itself and rolled. This was a significant challenge (Figure 13).

The sketch in Figure 13 shows the final hand sketches of the dress design prior to the commencement of computer modelling. This sketch was returned to constantly as a reference point whilst modelling in Solidworks. From the early development of the rigid structures the industrial designer explored the capabilities of the 3D CAD modelling software in order to develop modelling strategies. Understanding how to work with the capabilities and opportunities of the software was an important element of the designer's role in responding to the geometric possibilities that 3DP provided. Computer modelling is

Figure 12. Body scans for customization

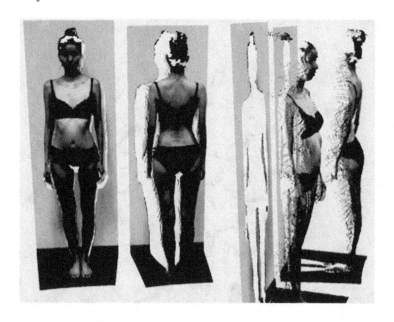

Figure 13. Drawing based on scans
Canning, 2014.

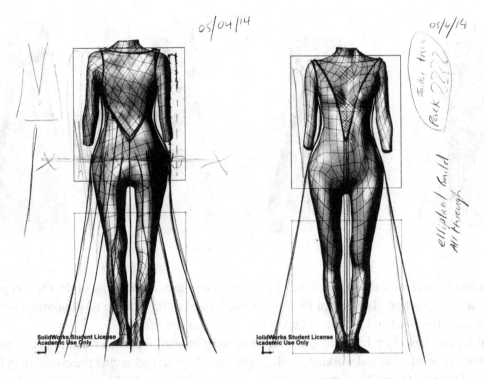

no longer used purely as a documentation tool, but is integrated into design process and influences the development of the design details themselves through the operations available in the tools within the program. Creating layers within the dress was a particular challenge as a layered framework was needed to support the individual components and a variety of approaches were tested. These strategies involved creating shapes that could successfully maintain in a controlled position the many thousands of individual elements in relation to each other. Five different framework strategies were tested. The optimum design for the framework allowed the elements to be contained but segmented, which would make them easier to control whilst the build space was taken into account in the print. To start the overall build in Solid-Works, an initial surface model was created, that would provide a reference model for the framework and internal details. This also provided a representation of the correct sizing for the dress (Figure 14).

The location of the plunged back and front can be seen as split lines traced onto the surface model. Once the surface form was created, the framework and the detailing were gradually built into the model. As with the Peacemaker hat, the individual polyp elements are graduated in size to allow for the organic forms in the design. This was a complex challenge in relation to the dress as each layer has 62 polyp elements, and each horizontal layer is a different overall size. This created a smooth and almost imperceptible progression down the dress that curved the layers to the body form without needing the conventional fitting elements, such as darts. One of the complexities of this task was the decision to add crystals to the polyps, as this meant that the polyps could not be scaled, as the sockets had to remain exactly the same size to accommodate the crystal, irrespective of the outside dimensions of the polyp. This means

Figure 14. Initial development of dress form
Canning, 2014.

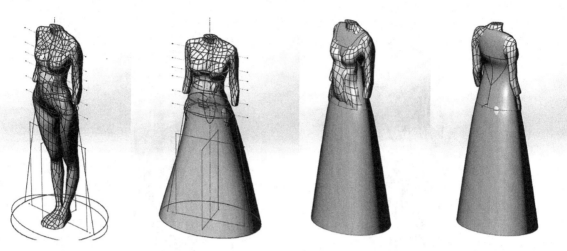

each layer had to be recreated, as the geometry could not be re-used. Modelling of the dress components began at the waist section. The design then progressed down to the bottom of the build envelope and then returned to the waist and progressed up to the chest area (Figure 15).

One of the challenges of developing the design that the industrial designer had to take into account was the problem of file size and working a delicate balance between achieving the complexity in design required, and keeping the model so that it could be workable. When model file sizes become large or they contain large amounts of complex 3D geometry, the computer model will become slow to manipulate to the point where they can become impossible to edit. For this reason strategies need to be developed for generating large models. After development testing, it was found that a strategy of modelling five individual polyp layers at a time was the most workable solution, and then (as shown in the multicoloured layers in the figure), the layer groups were built into longer structures. Because of the problem with the limited build space, the layers had to be modeled in progression to the bottom of the build envelope and then turn back and work up to the top of the build space. Only once this stage was reached, could the design decisions relating to the neckline of the dress be addressed. A much looser, lace like version of a polyp lattice was created for the neckline. It needed to be very flexible to allow for upper body movements (Figure 16).

The fashion designer provided a sketch to indicate the form of the lower section of the dress. To capture this design intent, and create the fullness and flow of the lower half of the dress, the industrial designer developed a visually lighter, more open star shaped polyp structure. This complex detailing was formed into a 3 dimensional mesh structure. The transition between the polyps in the top half of the dress, and those in the lower section was designed to take into account the curves of the body (Figure 17).

The shoulder straps represented another significant technical hurdle. Restrictions imposed by the build volume dictated that the straps could not be built in their upright state. A number of options were explored through sketching and decisions were made on the design by the industrial designer resulting in a design modeled in a folded state suitable for printing in the build space (Figure 18).

In order to complete the build and maintain a model that was useable in terms of its file size (not the build size) the dress had to be split into nineteen separate assemblies. In addition to the file size of the

Figure 15. Designing the fold
Canning, 2014.

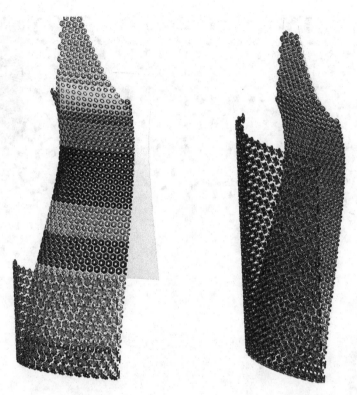

Figure 16. Development of neckline
Canning, 2014.

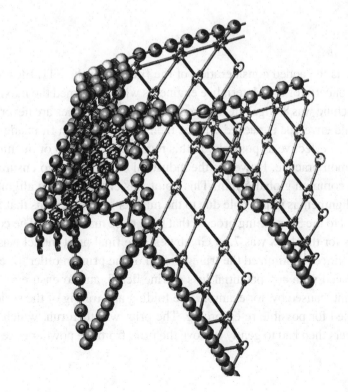

Figure 17. Design of attachments
Canning, 2014.

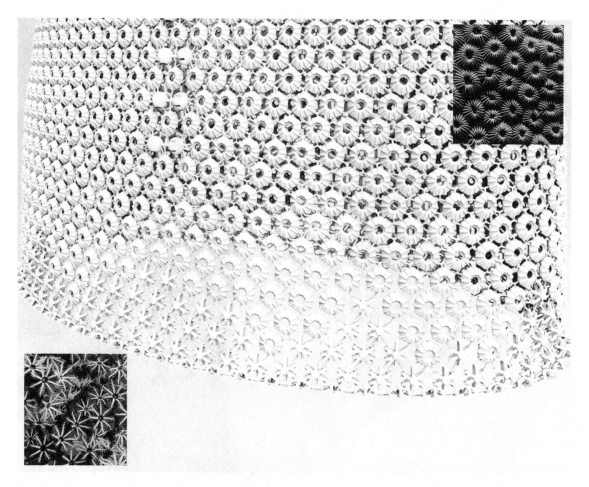

Solidworks files there is the added consideration of the file size of the STL files for printing which is different. This was a concern for the Materialise engineers who confirmed the maximum file size for an entire build on the machine was 8 Gigabytes. In general use, the machines are never used to build single models, rather the build envelope is packed with as many models as can fit inside the volume in order to make the build as cost effective as possible. In this regard the collation of the nineteen separate STL files was almost common practice. However, the industrial designer had to ensure that all of the files were exported with a common global origin. This point was critical for the alignment of the separate assemblies, manual alignment is impossible due to the number of connections that have to be made and the tolerances essential to the 3D printing process that have to be maintained. The combined file size for the nineteen STL files for the dress was 7.14 Gigabytes. The final print model was sent to Materialise where the software engineers optimized the triangulation of the print in order to reduce the print time, which had to be balanced with any potential loss of fine detail, and to ensure a robust print. Vulnerabilities within the print, caused by, for example, the folding and rolling of the structure to fit the build space, were interrogated for possible re-enforcing. The print was then run, which took approximately four days. The Engineers then had to gently remove the print from the powder cake for post processing.

Figure 18. Form development
Canning, 2014.

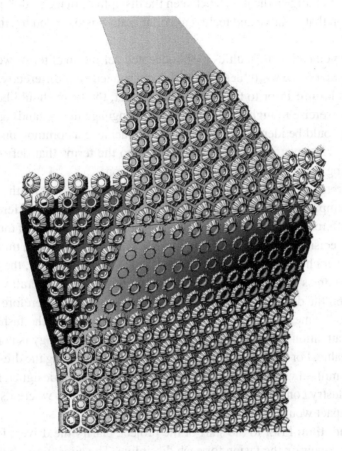

The Engineers cleaned the excess powder off and the industrial designer then individually flexed the tiny components to release them. The dress was then sent to Looi, who dyed it, and attached the myriad of crystals to create the final finish. Each crystal had to be attached by hand, using tweezers, and glued in place.

Review of Practice

The final outcome is an example of technical development driven by creative expression. By bringing the fashion designer into the team, the aesthetics drew the technical innovation behind it, as the industrial designer and engineers strove to meet the intent. This is therefore an example of disruptive practice for 3DP technical research, as the creative intent drove the technical development work. In this case, the project was executed in a linear progression through the disciplines, as a 'bouncing ball' project, that is one where the first team in a discipline works on a project, then their work is transferred into another project team from a different discipline, creating successive development, rather than as an example of the collaborative practice proposed by Benyus (2002). In this case, it was predominantly because the specialists were based in different countries, but it does provide a case study for the challenges involved in cross-disciplinary collaboration, and the aim of creating trans-disciplinary practice. Fundamentally, the project highlighted cultural differences in approach, values and ideas, which are summarized below with recommendations to mitigate the issues between the disciplines that could impede design development and the innovation that creative and technical collaboration is intended to stimulate.

1. **Language:** Communication difficulties as the accepted definition of terms were different between disciplines, for example the word 'design' itself is interpreted very differently between disciplines.
    a. **Recommendation:** Prior to the start of the project, the team should be involved in a communication exercise to highlight differences in language understanding prior to the project. Key terms should be identified and discussed to achieve a common understanding between researchers. This may involve adding clarifiers to the terms that define the discipline bias they are being used with during particular discussions.

2. **Drivers:** The drivers for taking part in the project work will be different for the different disciplines. For example, the impact the dress would make on the peer groups for the different disciplines would be judged very differently by the different discipline members and critics of those disciplines which results in design decisions that are discipline specific. This is illustrated in this case of the dress, by the fashion designer choosing to add crystals as for the fashion Industry, the technical innovation of 3D printing the dress as a single part was less important than the overall visual impact. For the industrial designer, the driver was to maximize the technology, and therefore the crystals reduced the value of the outcome, as they were not part of the print. Yet for the fashion designer, for the dress to gain the attention within a visual culture, where the technology is not widely understood, the crystals add value. For Materialise, the publicity value of featuring the dress on the Today show in the US, with 6 million viewers, was of less value to the industrial designer, than having it shown at the leading industry conference with less than 7,000 participants where its construction, rather than its visual impact would be better understood.
    a. **Recommendation:** Prior to the start of the project, clarify the drivers for the different team members and identify the vision for each discipline. The aims for each discipline in terms of publication of the outcomes should be identified and discussed.

3. **Values:** Every discipline has skills and understandings that it values. These are not necessarily known or understood by those outside that discipline. In addition, the amount of work, and the specific expertise needed for each aspect of a project such as this one, are not necessarily understood or valued by the other team members. A good example of can this is with scanning technology. The actual scan itself is a quick process and can be easily seen and understood by everyone, but the translation of cloud point data into usable geometry takes time and expertise, yet is invisible to those outside the process. Similarly the optimization of the geometry. With regards the industrial designer, the craftsmanship involved in developing the construction details for 3DP is currently not well understood or valued by those outside the discipline, who still see 3DP as a 'push button' technology. The dress, for example, required not only months of development work, but specifically over 400 hours of computer modelling time was logged during the development of the components and building the dress.
    a. **Recommendation:** Greater communication of the design and development process in real time, for example through project logs or a virtual studio would help each discipline value what is involved in each stage of the process.

For the multidisciplinary research team to be effective in creating innovation, mechanisms need to be put in place to support informed collaboration. For research teams that include creative as well as scientific researchers, this preparatory work is arguably more essential or opportunities may be missed. The reality is that different disciplines address research practice with very different interests, values and approaches. Sharing language, values and drivers will provide a starting point for a more genuine trans-disciplinary practice. For the potential of 3DP to provide opportunities for disruptive thinking in scientific research teams, by bringing in designers for traditionally scientific research based projects, to be realized, the lessons learned from the example of fashion and engineering need to be learned. The clash of cultures in cross-disciplinary practice between scientific and creative researchers needs to be understood and addressed.

Issues, Controversies, Problems

Working outside traditional discipline boundaries carries with it the risk of research work not being valued. Within a cross disciplinary project, there is an additional risk to the specific elements of the work not being understood across the disciplines, and the impact of the outcomes therefore diluted, as observed within engineering and architectural interactions by Zeiler (2014). If this is the case, the combined learning from project work is unlikely to be then developed further during follow up projects. Although the potential benefits of bringing together scientific research and creative research, as in the work of Benyus (2002), there are significant challenges to practice. Between engineering and creative practices, such as in design and art, the clash of cultures is particularly evident and can stem from educational practices where values and organization of workflow are inculcated into students.

SOLUTIONS AND RECOMMENDATIONS

Just as graduate attributes include the ability to work in teams, the recommendation based on this research is for a commitment to education on working within unconventional cross-disciplinary teams, particularly for students intending to pursue a career in research. With the development of CDIO in engineering subjects, the gulf between design and engineering has narrowed, and the industrial design discipline can take on a role to proactively bring together more creative subject researchers, such as in art and fashion, with scientific based enquiry researchers, such as in Engineering and clinical practice. However, the importance of preparation in understanding the drivers, values, working practice and language of collaborators is highlighted through this study, and there needs to be an investment of time and effort in making those connections prior to, and during research projects for effective practice.

With regards research that relates to the technology, the mechanics and materials science aspects have attracted the interest of engineering researchers, as described by Gibson et al (2014), whilst social scientists, such as Anderson (2012) have explored the impact of the technology on society. However, Hahn et al (2014) identify a lack of literature on innovation for 3D printing applications. They emphasize that there should be more research in this area, as there are significant opportunities for the adoption of the technology in key sectors such as 'aerospace, medical devices and implants, power generation, automotive manufacturing and the creative industries' and predict that the technology will create alternative business models and practices and forecast a sector worth of $7.5 million US by 2020. As a disruptive technology, 3DP provides opportunities across disciplines, and this will equally impact research. Within

Griffith University, new research collaborations are forming between disciplines as diverse as forensics, regenerative medicine and industrial design. Yet, there is likely to be a lack of understanding between team members both in terms of the discipline knowledge, drivers values etc, as well in terms of the potential of the 3DP and how to most effectively use it for specialist applications.

Leading disruptive innovation, however, is a process fundamentally laden with surprise, the core essence of uncertainty. Recognizing the potential power of surprise when we receive unexpected jolts to our strategies, plans, and assumptions, allows us to respond with purposeful agility - versus dismiss surprises as problems while concurrently disregarding the insights or messages they may contain. (Kaplin, 2012)

Working with 3DP in new fields of research within new collaborations (especially where they bring together creative practitioners and scientific researchers, such as in the teams for regenerative medicine and industrial design, or for fashion and engineering) will inevitably create some uneasy situations and unexpected outcomes. For the technology to achieve its disruptive potential, and researchers to discover where it can take their work, teams need to be open to new ways of thinking, and ideas and approaches very different to their own – which they need to be willing to engage with and learn to understand – and embrace the change. By deliberately working against the conventions of practice in established fields, without predefined objectives in exploratory work (Pink 2009, Ted talk), new research collaborations have the potential to provide new insights as provide starting points for trans-disciplinary practice.

FUTURE RESEARCH DIRECTIONS

Based on this study, further research is needed to develop a blueprint for working practice in research teams that bring together the creative and the scientific to stimulate innovation. 3D printing has created particularly interesting cross-disciplinary opportunities because it brings together such normally disparate fields. This provides a basis for the study of developments of innovations in collaborative practice where there are no pre-existing conceptions of standard relationships. The intention, for a follow-up collaboration on 3D printing across engineering and creative practice, is to invest in building cross cultural understandings between the disciplines through this work to enhance practice, and to develop collaborative tools to move from a linear, successive practice, towards a more genuine, real time collaboration informed by mutual understanding and shared – or at least understood - aims for the project outcomes for all involved. With regards to 3DP itself, with drivers from multidisciplinary teams, there should be a subsequent draw for the development of the technology that breaks the incremental progress of scientific research and allows for new applications research to take more of a lead. This will be supported by research into changing educational practice for new design thinking for advanced technologies, as discussed by Loy in Education Sciences (2014).

CONCLUSION

In 2014, Griffith University hosted two 3DP research forums. One was called '3D printing the Body, inside and out' and the other called 'Design and Manufacturing, 3D printing for the Creative Industries'. The multidisciplinary profile of the participants illustrated the potential for the technology to disrupt research teams, and bring together scientific and creative researchers to consider newly framed research questions and potentially stimulate innovation. The forums included research participants from engineering, industrial design, biomedical and art. One of the artists who provided an example of challenging scientific research practice using the technology was Professor Stelarc from Curtin University. His research work included a 3D Printed ambidextrous hand, which contributes to the discussion on Pullin's ideas for design meets disability, moving them further towards the aims expressed by Mullins on design for enhanced ability through assistive technology. In addition, with his anatomical work, (for example the scaffolding in an ear form he had surgically added to his left arm with an internet connection to transmit verbal communication), Stelarc (2013) provides a bridge between research into regenerative medicine and art through his interest in the use of bioplotting, a form of 3D printing that uses biomaterials (including cells).

The gulf between disciplines in terms of research drivers, values and even language is significant, and has the potential to derail attempts to bring together researchers for scientific and creative collaborations. What fashion has brought to scientific based research practice through 3D printing in engineering has been the stimulus for technical and applications innovation and highlighted the clash of cultures in research teams. Between fashion and engineering, the clash of cultures is clearly visible, and this has allowed for the identification of issues that may be more subtle within more closely related research teams but still need to be addressed. If the contrasting research approach between designers and scientists, that Milton and Rodgers observes, is deemed to be useful in research teams, then the example of fashion and engineering can provide a productive starting point for creating disruptive practice in scientific research to stimulate innovation. Working in teams is rarely straight forward, and there has been considerable research into how to operate within a team. If trans-disciplinary research is to be progressed, and long term relationships to develop, then the disciplinary research teams need to recognize their ethnocentric starting points, and invest in preparatory work to recognize and understand the values of their collaborators, build shared communication tools and articulate drivers and publication priorities prior to entering into collaborations.

More specifically in terms of project work that brings together fashion and engineering through 3DP, is the value of the role of the designer providing expertise in design for 3DP. This expertise is only starting to be developed. For the contrasting worlds of fields such as engineering and fashion to be able to come together to maximize the opportunities this new technology provides, the idea that it is a 'push button' technology needs to be dispelled, and designers (including fashion designers) and engineers, educated in working in the middle ground, where creative ideas are evolved and designed for the technology. This is when innovation will happen.

REFERENCES

Anderson, C. (2012). *Makers: The next industrial revolution*. New York, NY: Crown Business.

Benyus, J. (2002). *Biomimicry: Innovation inspired by nature*. New York, NY: Harper Perennial.

Braddock Clarke, S., & Harris, J. (2012). *Digital visions for fashion and textiles: Made in code*. London, UK: Thames & Hudson.

Braddock Clarke, S., & O'Mahony, M. (2008). *Techno textiles 2: Revolutionary fabrics for fashion and design* (2nd ed.). London, UK: Thames & Hudson.

Cacchione, P. (2015). Interdisciplinary research teams. *Clinical Nursing Research*, 24(2), 119–120. doi:10.1177/1054773815574790 PMID:25748854

Cohen, J., Gehry, F., & Gehry, F. O. (2003). *Frank Gehry, architect*. New York, NY: Guggenheim Museum.

Gibson, I., Rosen, D., & Stucker, B. (2014). *Additive manufacturing technologies: 3D printing, rapid prototyping and direct digital manufacturing* (2nd ed.). New York, NY: Springer.

Hahn, F., Jenson, S., & Tanev, S. (2014). Disruptive innovation versus disruptive technology: The disruptive potential of the value proposition of 3D printing technology start-ups. *Technology Innovation Management Review*, 4(12), 27–36.

Harman, J. (2014). *The shark's paintbrush: Biomomicry and how nature is inspiring innovation*. Ashland, OR: White Cloud Press.

Kaplan, S. (2012). Leading disruptive innovation. *Ivy Business Journal*. Retrieved July 22 2015 from http://iveybusinessjournal.com/publication/leading-disruptive-innovation/

Kumar, V. (2012). *101 design methods: A structured approach for driving innovation in your organization*. Wiley.

Lewis, K. (2003). Measuring transactive memory systems in the field: Scale development and validation. *The Journal of Applied Psychology*, 88(4), 587–604. doi:10.1037/0021-9010.88.4.587 PMID:12940401

Leys, P. (2015). *The Killer Apps of 3D printing*. Paper presented at Inside 3D Printing, New York, NY.

Lipson, H., & Kurman, M. (2013). *Fabricated: The new world of 3D printing*. Wiley.

Loy, J. (2014). ELearning and eMaking: 3D printing blurring the digital and the physical. *Education Sciences*, 4(1), 108–121. doi:10.3390/educsci4010108

Loy, J., & Canning, S. (2013). *Reconnecting through digital making. IDEN*. Sydney, Australia: Industrial Design Educators Network.

Loy, J., & Welch, D. (2013). A brave new creativity. *Art. Design and Communication in Higher Education*, 12(1), 91–102. doi:10.1386/adch.12.1.91_1

McQuaid, M. (2005). *Extreme textiles*. Princeton, NJ: Princeton Architectural Press.

Milton, A., & Rodgers, P. (2013). *Research methods for product design*. London, UK: Laurence King.

Nakamichi, T. (2011). *Pattern magic 2*. London, UK: Laurence King.

Pink, D. (2009). *The puzzle of motivation*. Retrieved from http://www.ted.com/talks/dan_pink_on_motivation?language=en

Pullin, G. (2011). *Design meets disability*. Cambridge, MA: MIT Press.

Qian, M. (2015). Metal powder for additive manufacturing. *JOM*, 67(3), 536–537. doi:10.1007/s11837-015-1321-z

Stelarc, S. (2013). Aliveness & affect: Alternate art & anatomies. In P. Baler (Ed.), *The next thing: Art in the twenty-first century* (pp. 133–150). Fairleigh Dickinson University Press.

Wageman, R., Gardner, H., & Mortensen, M. (2012). The changing ecology of teams: New directions for teams' research. *Journal of Organizational Management, 3*(33), 301–315.

Weinschenck, S. (2011). *100 things every designer needs to know about people.* San Francisco, CA: New Riders.

Zeiler, W. (2014). The difference in communication between architects and engineers and the effectiveness within integral design. In E. Bohemia et al. (Eds.), *Proceedings of the EPDE 2014 16th International Conference on Engineering and Product Design Education* (pp. 238-243). Bristol, UK: Design Society.

KEY TERMS AND DEFINITIONS

Additive Manufacturing: Refers to a range of digital technologies that build objects in layers without the use of a mould.

Chapter 3
3D Printing Meets Humanitarian Design Research:
Creative Technologies in Remote Regions

Jennifer Loy
Griffith University, Australia

Ry Healey
Griffith University, Australia

Peter Tatham
Griffith University, Australia

Cassie L. Tapper
Griffith University, Australia

ABSTRACT

This chapter provides an introduction to the discourse informing humanitarian design research practice and a context for evaluating problem solving strategies in this area of research. Advances in the development of creative technologies, and in particular 3D printing, are stimulating innovations in approach and practice. This chapter is based on a design research project that uses advances in digital technologies to address the logistical challenges facing Oxfam's Water, Sanitation and Hygiene (WASH) projects in East Africa, whilst simultaneously responding to current design theory in humanitarian design research. It takes into account people, process and technology in developing a response to the opportunities provided by creative technologies that offers a new approach to achieving an appropriate balance between paternalistic and participatory design research in this discipline. The field study informing the research took place in Nairobi in 2014/2015 and was principally supported by the Humanitarian Innovation Fund.

INTRODUCTION

This chapter introduces the discourse on approaches used by designers working in humanitarian research and the background to the current opportunities provided by recent advances in digital technologies. It then outlines an example of practice that suggests new research directions and an alternative approach to practice for humanitarian design research enabled by creative technologies. Industrial designers have long been involved in design research to support the work of international aid agencies but, to date, the area of humanitarian logistics has been largely outside the scope of the discipline. However, recent innovations in digital technologies have inspired design researchers to look at new opportunities and

DOI: 10.4018/978-1-5225-0016-2.ch003

to collaborate with colleagues from the humanitarian logistics field to address the inherent challenges within current supply chain systems. This chapter describes a pilot project funded by the Humanitarian Innovation Fund[1] and aims to illustrate how humanitarian design research in the field of logistics is being impacted by advances in creative technologies and new thinking, whilst highlighting the tensions. The project was hosted by Oxfam G.B. and brought together researchers in humanitarian logistics and industrial design to investigate how 3D printing could circumvent issues in the current supply chain for Water, Sanitation and Hygiene (WASH) projects in East Africa (Oxfam, 2015).

BACKGROUND

Discussion on the merits of Western educated design researchers creating products for humanitarian aid has long been a controversial subject. This is because there has been a tension between the idea of working with what might be perceived as a paternalistic approach, and, at the other extreme, an arguably invasive participatory, co-design approach - and it has proven very hard to get the balance right. Over forty years ago, design activist Victor Papanek (1971) challenged the capitalist focus of commercial, Western-educated designers by calling for the design of technologically appropriate solutions to solve problems in developing countries. Pilloton (2009) describes appropriate technologies as a "field of engineering that designs, builds and implements basic technological systems that are suitable for a particular location and the skills, materials and needs of a demographic" (p. 35). Over the last forty years, there has been a significant growth in humanitarian design research practice, and yet the field remains a difficult one for designers to navigate, particularly in relation to the use of appropriate technologies. This is evidenced by the lack of consensus on the merits of outcomes produced through humanitarian design research, as discussed by Stohr and Sinclair (2012), and also Nussbaum (2010), with examples of design activists being acclaimed by Western societies yet apparently unappreciated by those communities they are trying to help. An example is the Aquaduct bicycle concept by leading design consultancy, IDEO (IDEO, 2008). This won the 'Innovate or Die!' contest in 2008. IDEO presented it as a way to collect and filter water in developing countries using pedal power. The bike is actually a tricycle that houses a water tank on the back, with a filtration system that uses a pedal driven peristaltic pump to draw water from the tank into a clean container on the handlebars. At the time of its design, the intention of IDEO, according to the company website (2008), was for the team to evolve the concept into *an economically – and technologically – viable solution, looking to address challenges such as cost, suitable purification technologies, and the logistics of addressing an issue that affects billions of people around the world* (Flahiff, 2008). However, the Aquaduct bicycle remained a prototype. In the publication, *Design Like You Give a Damn*, Stohr and Sinclair (2012) argued that the measure of success for a design for humanitarian needs should be measured through consideration of the uptake of the product, its longevity, impacts and any side effects. According to Pilloton (2009), "Without contextual understanding and user feedback, a design for social impact will likely fall short of its intentions - however good they are" (p. 19). For this contextual understanding and user feedback to be realistically achieved, she argues that the target community for the humanitarian design need has to be central to, and engaged in, the design process. This recognition that user centred design needs to be informed by a more ethnographic approach to research has led to a rise in participatory design practice in both domestic and international contexts. However, in relation to theory supporting humanitarian design research, the initial enthusiasm for designers and students to spend time with the international community they are designing for has waned. In conjunction with studies on the practice of sending students in humanitarian medicine to remote regions, research on the growth of 'volunteer tourism' described by Wearing and McGeehee (2013, p. 120), suggests that whilst the intention of those concerned may be 'to help others', there is a lack of scientific platform involved in structuring the interactions that is undermining the intent. They estimated that 1.6 million people currently take part in international volunteer schemes annually, and argue this is shifting the focus from helping the community to the business of volunteer tourism, which generates an estimated 1.5 billion dollars in revenue each year.

The rise in student numbers taking part in short term design based activities that involve an international experience to inform their design thinking is growing alongside renewed calls for the design community to focus on the challenges of humanitarian design on the back of publications such as Design Revolution (Pilloton, 2009), and the high-profile Cooper-Hewitt Design Museum event, *Design with the Other 90%* (Smithsonian, Cooper-Hewitt National Design Museum, n.d.). However, this arguably leads to the adverse development of 'design tourism', as a subset of volunteer tourism, and needs to be subject to the same scrutiny as is currently falling on medical tourism. Graduate designers need to be made aware of the pitfalls of dilettante humanitarian design and the importance of drawing on specific humanitarian research expertise, operating within the structures of relevant agencies, and embedding a long term, collaborative strategy developed alongside those directly impacted by the work.

Whilst the outcomes of western educated design researchers in developing product solutions for third world countries might be criticized, it is also relevant to note that the historic lack of significant design involvement in procurement for aid agencies has frequently resulted in a legacy of waste from inappropriately donated products. A common example is in the supply of furniture for disaster relief situations. Furniture that is designed to cope with the marked changes in humidity that occur in extreme climates needs to include joints that allow for expansion and contraction and thereby reduce the stresses that places on structure, whilst the frame material itself needs to be resistant to corrosion or decay. Cost savings in providing generic product that does not incorporate these features are short lived as seasonal changes render the objects useless and a lack of design for disassembly and maintenance can lead to the object being discarded relatively quickly. The problem of its safe and effective disposal is then an issue.

At the opposite budgetary end of the scale, incubators provide an example of a high cost product supplied as humanitarian aid, which is predominantly equally ill suited to the situation. Complex products such as these will work until they need some kind of repair. But then a lack of spare parts even for a minor repair and a lack of expertise to then repair the product – even assuming the product has been designed to allow for repair – means it can quickly fail and become obsolete. The cost of shipping is too expensive for the products to be returned and the identification of the problem and specification of replacement parts, combined with the knowledge on how to replace those parts, requires a specialist understanding – the absence of which means that the item is likely to become unusable.

Designing for appropriate technology involves designing within the available production methods and skills in a particular context. The Bamboo Treadle Pump (IDE, n.d.) is an example of just such a product that has been designed specifically using appropriate technology principles defined in humanitarian design research theory. The pump was designed by Gunnar Barnes of the Rangpur/Dinajpu Rural Dinajpur in 2006. It consists of two metal cylinders with pistons that are operated by a natural walking motion on two treadles. The Treadle is designed so that it can be manufactured in regional metalworking shops, and over 1.7 million have been sold in Bangladesh and elsewhere to date. The key features of the design are that it is appropriate to the technology available in the area, can be manufactured and repaired locally, and meets a specific need.

The difficulty with this approach, however, is that it tends to be applied in a limiting way, resulting in designs that fail to draw on more complex resources, even when they are available. Design That Matters is a not-for-profit organization that aims to challenge this practice. Their aim is a design commitment to real-world use that is informed by a researched understanding of context and a systems approach to people, process and technology. An example is their NeoNurture incubator (NeoNurture, n.d.), which was developed in direct response to concerns over the maintenance problems of conventional donated incubators.

In this project, the designers identified the fact that car mechanics typically provide the most reliable supply of fabrication workers in the locations Design That Matters were working in, and that the supply of car parts was the most reliable source of components. As a result, the NeoNurture incubator designed to be built and maintained in small car yards to ensure its longevity. The NeoNurture incubator goes beyond the product-focused design for appropriate technology solutions frequently offered by a sector of Western-educated designers informed by short visits. Rather, it draws on a more complex product service systems thinking approach, as advocated by design theorists, such as Hawkins et al. (2010), Ryan (2004) and Fuad-Luke (2009), to rethink the lifecycle of the product and how the product service can be maintained, rather than focusing just on the product itself.

CREATIVE TECHNOLOGIES IN HUMANITARIAN DESIGN RESEARCH

One of the main points of contention for designers working in this field is still between designs that utilize technology that Papanek could theoretically deem 'appropriate', such as in the LifeStraw project (2014), and designs that utilize advanced technology, such as for Yves Behar's One Laptop Per Child project, criticized for circumventing local traditional teaching cultures (Nussbaum, 2010). Yet the task of providing guidance on working in humanitarian design practice is being further complicated for researchers by the disruptions caused by recent advances in creative digital technologies and the possibilities for changing practice they open up. These technologies include communication tools (e.g. internet, online visualization and co-design tools) and digital fabrication technologies (in particular, 3D printing). Digital fabrication refers to a range of computer driven technologies, such as laser cutting and computer numerically controlled (CNC) routering, which can provide individual solutions. This equipment includes 3D printing. 3D printing is the technology that is having the most disruptive influence in this sphere as, even at its most basic level, it allows for 3-dimensional complex geometry objects to be printed in end-use polymers that were either not previously possible or required the investment of an expensive mould to create, which potentially shifts the control of production into the hands of individual users. 3D printing, initially termed additive manufacturing because it builds objects in layers, refers to a range of technologies from fused deposition modelling, where heated filaments are extruded through the print head, to selective laser sintering where the structure of the object is fused by a laser beam directed onto successive layers of powdered material.

3D printing is stimulating creative research across art and design disciplines as well as engineering and medical. This research is characterized by a focus on the potential of the technology to disrupt current patterns of production, the changing relationships between designers and consumers made possible by the technology, the consequential impacts on the value chain as a whole, and the rethinking of designed objects to maximize the geometric opportunities the technology provides (Gibson et al., 2014). Design research in more conventional and commercial areas is equally relevant to humanitarian design. Just as mainstream design research is exploring and critically analyzing existing and emerging practices being impacted by advances in communication and fabrication technologies, so are humanitarian design researchers re-evaluating their thinking and practice.

The challenge to Papanek's approach these provide is being highlighted by the research work of Gershenfeld, Director for the MIT Centre for Bits and Atoms. Gershenfeld aims to provide open access to advanced creative technologies across the globe (Gershenfeld, 2007) in a way that breaks with both paternalistic and participatory traditions. He argues that the digital revolution 'has been won' (Gershenfeld, 2007), and the focus now should be on digital fabrication and its ability to provide accessible manufacturing for communities around the world, especially those in remote regions. Therefore, as part of a community outreach program, Gershenfeld provided workshop facilities equipped with digital technologies that has spread to a network of over 150 facilities worldwide, called FabLabs (Fab Foundation, n.d.) where users are encouraged to pursue their own projects using digital fabrication to make their own usable, innovative, customized products.

The humanitarian design research project this chapter describes as an example of new practice that has emerged directly out of developments in the creative technologies research sphere, responding to current values, ideas and aspirations expressed in humanitarian and design theory whilst simultaneously being informed by activity research, logistical and design experience and technical understanding. There is an marked contrast between considering successful design for appropriate technology, defined by humanitarian design research embraced and evolved by the targeted community, such as the Hippo Water Roller which has sold over 27,000 units, and recent developments in the public face of 3D printing, characterized by, for example, the 200,000+ predominantly ephemeral products uploaded to the online service provider, Shapeways. Yet the underlying freedoms, provided by 3D printing and its relationship to the internet, to rethink not only geometries, but more fundamentally design and production systems, is directly relevant to humanitarian design research, and potentially to providing solutions to the potential for humanitarian design practice, however professional and well meaning, becoming a form of volunteer tourism.

Creative technologies research encompasses thinking and investigations that bring together the digital and the analogue within the scope of the designer but at the same time operates beyond the traditional borders of the discipline. This challenges conventional thinking and practice through the reconsideration of the manifestation of ideas enabled by advances in technology. The concept of creative technologies, as it applies to this research project, is where the nexus of computer science, human interaction and digital fabrication inform designers who are responding to the theoretical underpinnings of the discipline. The aims of this project within the broader design research context, drawing on sustainability research by design theorists, such as Ryan (2004), is to include a rethink of systems to dematerialize the economy through product service systems thinking, whilst supporting convergence and contraction of global economies to more evenly distribute wealth, whilst simultaneously maintaining cultural diversity.

Recent rapid developments in the digital environment have resulted in disruptions to supply chains in many industries, such as the music industry, and, increasingly, the communication revolution (manifest in file sharing, and co-design platforms, etc.) is impacting the design and supply of products. In addition, just as the rise in desktop publishing applications disrupted the graphic design profession, so the developments in 3D printing, that have transformed the technology from a rapid prototyping technology to a direct digital manufacturing technology, have stimulated a revolution in design and manufacturing.

The focus of the project described in this chapter, is to evaluate whether recent developments in the accessibility, scope and reliability of 3D printing make it suitable for the manufacturing of end-use products to support work in development/disaster response contexts, and to consider the complexities of this proposition in the light of current understandings of humanitarian design research, and the controversy in how it should be practised. The technology will be considered as part of a creative technologies research approach that endeavours to understand 3D printing as a catalyst rather than a solution. In doing so, it aims to stimulate current transdisciplinary thinking about design in a humanitarian context that considers the digital revolution as a whole from a collaborative design and humanitarian logistics standpoint.

Creative technologies allow researchers to bring together the digital and the analogue within the scope of a design project, yet at the same time, go beyond the traditional borders of the discipline to consider how advances in technology can be harnessed to deliver improved designs and outcomes. The term creative technologies as it applies to this specific research study is where the nexus of computer science, human interaction and digital fabrication informs designers who are responding to the theoretical underpinnings of the discipline by trying to rethink systems. The aim of this is to dematerialize the economy through product service systems thinking, whilst simultaneously supporting convergence and contraction of global economies to more evenly distribute wealth, and maintain cultural diversity.

With this in mind, the focus of the practical project work described in this chapter was to test the hypothesis that recent developments in the accessibility, scope and reliability of 3D printing make it suitable for the distributed manufacturing of end-use products to support operations in a development/ disaster response context, and to consider the complexities of this proposition in the light of current understandings.

According to Collins (2010), challenges and opportunities brought about by technological developments are central to the direction of current creative research. These include research into changing the structure and nature of supply chains for different industries made possible by digital technologies. They also include reconsidering distribution channels, whilst consciously working to maintain global cultural diversity. The need to be sensitive to cultural diversity in a new world of global connectivity has a central place in the discussion about creative research and the need for new business models. With this in mind, the research project aims to contribute to the debate on new ways of approaching creative research and, in particular, product design research that focuses on the disruptive potential of creative technologies. The outcomes of the project build on historical practice in the work of designers involved in humanitarian research, drawing on learning from successful projects to inform future directions for research in this field. It is intended to provide an example of design practice, collaboration and design thinking that can act as a basis for discussion around managing the disruptive creativity emerging out of the creative technologies design community for humanitarian design research.

Introduction to Practice

In the context of this project, the term 'creative technologies' refers to digital technologies involved in the generation of data, increased global communication and the use of digital fabrication for bespoke production. These technologies form part of the digital revolution that is moving industrial design as a discipline further into the digital realm. This move is not only impacting the design outputs but, more significantly, the relationships and transactions that characterize the profession, resulting in an emerging profile for the designer who takes the work in new directions.

3D printing is an example of a creative technology that is fuelling innovations in design practice that reach far beyond the physical product. 3D printing is stimulating new collaborations in research practice that involve designers in new ways of framing and addressing problems across disciplines and, in doing so, involves them in new ethical and practical dilemmas when engaging with researchers from disciplines as diverse as regenerative medicine and humanitarian logistics. These collaborations, and the need to create new theoretical frameworks, methodologies and methods are creating transdisciplinary research practices that go well beyond discipline-specific approaches by addressing a need that crosses traditional boundaries. This, in turn, informs discipline specific research practice and outcomes.

The key factor in creative technologies research is the bringing together of computer science, the human experience and digital fabrication technologies. This approach offers the possibility of transformative change, and it needs to be embraced by researchers in order to meet the changing needs and operations of the wider community of users and other stakeholders.

Industrial designers have long been involved in humanitarian design research to support the work of international aid agencies but, to date, the specific impacts of designs on the practice of humanitarian logistics has been largely outside the scope of the discipline. However, recent digital technology innovations are inspiring design researchers to look at new opportunities, and in this case to collaborate with colleagues from the humanitarian logistics field, to address the inherent challenges within current supply chain systems and to explore ways in which the emerging digital technologies might lead to a more integrated value chain approach to meeting the needs on the ground.

This section describes the context, practice and implications of a pilot research project by researcher at Griffith University inspired by developments in creative technologies and their implications for humanitarian design research. The project was principally funded by the Humanitarian Innovation Fund over six months leading up to March 2015 and undertaken by researchers from Griffith University from the disciplines of Industrial Design and Humanitarian Logistics. It is the foundation for broader research in this area planned to begin later in the year. The project was hosted by Oxfam G.B. and the aim was to investigate whether the advances in 3D printing that took it from an expensive prototyping technology to a low cost, portable technology potentially capable of producing end use components, made it a viable tool for printing parts for the Water, Sanitation and Hygiene (WASH) projects in East Africa. The components needed were, for the most part, pipes and connectors and, although the mass manufacture of standard pipe work and connectors using conventional production techniques, such as extrusion and injection moulding, remains cheaper and more reliable than that of 3D printing at the time of publication, it is the customization of individual parts and the ability to print on demand that makes 3D printing an interesting technology in this case.

In a development/disaster response situations, those operating in the field – such as national authorities, United Nations (UN) agencies or non-government organisations (NGOs) – frequently have to develop a bespoke supply network that will either replace or enhance the pre-existing means of providing the goods and services needed to meet the needs of the affected population. As identified by L'Hermitte et al. (2013), the extent and complexity of this network will depend on multiple factors including the time available for action, the size of the disaster, its geographic and topographical context, and the security environment. One of the particular issues is that, unlike the commercial context where product demand can, at least to an extent, be forecast in advance, the humanitarian logistic challenge reflects not only uncertainty over the timing and size of a disaster/emergency and those involved, but also the geometry and performance of the components needed for specific tasks. To add to the problems, as highlighted by Kovács and Spens (2007), the location of the site may make deliveries difficult and once materials have been delivered, there are circumstances where the on site team are temporarily cut off from further deliveries due to additional environmental impact events (floods, landslides etc) or human factors, such as fighting.

The practice of humanitarian logistics has been defined by Thomas and Mizushima (2005, p. 60) as "the process of planning, implementing and controlling the efficient, cost-effective flow and storage of goods and materials as well as related information, from the point of origin to the point of consumption for the purpose of meeting the end beneficiary's requirements." Unsurprisingly, given that in 2014 alone 271 natural disasters were recorded which affected over 100M people with an estimated economic cost in excess of some US$85BN (Credcrunch, 2015), there are significant drives to develop ways in which the efficiency and effectiveness of the humanitarian logistic preparation and response activities can be improved. It has been estimated that humanitarian logistics operations (as defined above, i.e. procurement, transport into and within the affected country, warehousing and 'last mile' distribution, together with associated activities such as information management) consume some 60-80% of the income of aid agencies – i.e. some $US10-15Bn/year (Tatham & Pettit, 2010).

The humanitarian logistician is, inevitably, faced with multiple challenges, and the price of failure is not simply counted in terms of lost profit but in the prolonging of adverse living conditions for those involved, or even the loss of life. Ordering supplies for an emergency situation, knowing lives depend on the components coming on site, is complex and difficult, as each situation will be different and the product required to fulfil the needs for that situation will be hard to predict. This leads, almost inevitably, to a situation in which there will be some degree of missmatch between the demand and supply. Added to that, even if the original requirements were met, the challenging operating environment means that equipment breakdowns (for example to the operation of water pumping equipment) are inevitable, and the resultant requirement for spare parts etc, creates new demands.

Humanitarian logisticians attempt to overcome by the use of a warehousing approach in which multiple additional items of inventory are ordered, supplied and maintained 'just in case', but this adds to the costs and in many cases is totally impractical – not least because the aftermath of a disaster may well impact the stock pile itself. Thus, the logistics literature by Christopher (2011) places great emphasis on the concept of logistic postponement whereby, to the maximum extent possible, an item is only produced and/or shipped once a demand has actually crystallised. However, this can also result in serious delays and can be a source of tension for those involved.

With this in mind, and drawing on the work of Thilmany (2010) on the potential of 3D printing as a prototyping tool for humanitarian causes, it was hypothesised that 3D printing could have potentially significant benefits as it could reduce the requirement for the sort of warehousing outlined above by printing to order. In addition, the raw material has a high mass: volume ratio, which is normally of benefit when transporting by truck, requires very limited packaging (unlike fragile finished goods), and the same source material can be used to produce multiple finished items. All of these benefits are found in the literature relating to potential for the use of 3D printing in a commercial ('for profit') context, so the key question that the researchers were keen to investigate was whether or not they were equally applicable in a humanitarian (i.e. disaster response or development) context.

The research therefore looked at the viability and practicality of utilizing digital fabrication - specifically 3D printing - to supplement the existing supply and field-based operations. The project was informed by two periods of fieldwork in Nairobi and the question investigated was whether (or not) 3D printing could circumvent or mitigate the challenges in the current supply chain by swiftly creating parts that could be used to meet unanticipated needs in this context.

The research team began by evaluating the current catalogue that Oxfam G.B. used in the provision of WASH products for remote areas of Africa, such as South Sudan, out of their HQ in Nairobi. For the evaluation, the research team developed criteria based on the performance characteristics of each product, its criticality in maintaining supply and, therefore, value to the field-based construction team (e.g. couplings and pipe bends which if missing or broken would cause serious delay), and its potential suitability to be redesigned for 3D printing without loss of function, and within the scope of the portable fused deposition modeller.

Additional criteria that were driven by the research hypothesis included the requirement for a part to be site specific. For example, a bespoke (rather than a conventional 90 degree) bend may be required, or an elongated component might be needed to address a particular problem during fitting. The suitability of a redesigned part in demonstrating the potential benefits of 3D printing, such as through the consolidation of an assembly into a single part, or of light weighting (removing redundant material needed for conventional manufacturing methods) or creating additional strength to a part where required by the demands of the specific situation was also taken into account (Figure 1).

Importantly, the use of 3D printing provides the opportunity to design a component specific to a purpose, rather than to the constraints of traditional manufacturing technologies, such as injection moulding. Thus, removing the requirement for a mould, even if a multipart mould provides an element of design freedom allowing the part to be created more for intent, rather than production. This characteristic allowed an exploration of the potential of 3D printing to problem solve beyond the range of existing products, rather than simply replacing them (Figure 2).

The actual 3D Printer used in the project had a small build volume, as it was (correctly) perceived in advance that the power required to run the printer would be subject to interruption, and therefore the team chose products that were small enough to be printed within the timeframe supported by a temporary power supply. In reality, this size constraint did prove problematic as the catalogue had not included the relative quantities of the different components used on site, and there was actually a considerable demand for prints outside the build volume from the field operatives. Nevertheless, the approach adopted in this pilot phase was able to allow the investigation of the proof of concept, whilst recognising that the print size vs. power availability interface requires further consideration.

The products chosen for testing in this first phase also needed to be suitable for construction using fused deposition modelling. Fused deposition modelling was selected over alternative forms of 3D printing (such as selective laser sintering), as the equipment was the most mobile and robust. There are many versions of fused deposition modellers, with multiple print heads allowing for combined mate-

Figure 1. Re-design of a 7-part assembly resulting in a lightweight, 5-part assembly

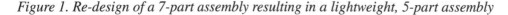

Figure 2. Examples of test prints on site
Photo: Healey, 2014.

rial solutions to vary the material characteristics of the printed product, and also allowing for soluble support scaffolding to be printed alongside a part that means a part can have more complex geometries. However, as the principles for the project were the focus, rather than product outcomes, the team chose to restrict the parameters, and work with a sturdy, reliable single filament printer using high grade ABS filament that was easy to repair if damaged in transit or on site. ABS is an engineering grade of plastic suitable for a range of end use products, but its primary benefit in this case was the definition of the prints produced and its reliability during the process.

The methodology adopted was 'action research' i.e. a process of progressive problem solving led by individuals working with others as part of a 'community of practice' to improve the way they address issues and solve problems. An initial briefing and demonstration to key Oxfam staff including those engaged in WASH activities addressed this. The process was to explain the basic technology whilst, simultaneously, printing a small component in such a way that the finished product was available for inspection at the end of the research-led discussion. In this way, those attending were able to visualize the process as it happened and, hence, could consider its applicability to their specific geographic context. As an example of the instant feedback that was provided, one of the audience asked for details of the 'curing time' for the printed component, and was surprised to find that this was zero – in other words the component could be used straight off the printer. This claim was subsequently verified by means of a drop (or, perhaps, more accurately a *throw*) test, leaving the questioner extremely impressed and, in the words of the researcher, a 'light bulb moment' took place.

Similar presentations, demonstrations and discussions took place with multiple other groups including the Head of Oxfam's East African team, 12 members of the United Nations WASH Cluster technical group, and even the office cleaners! (Tatham et al., 2015). Thus, both in the preparation and field phases, the researchers worked collaboratively with the practitioner community in Nairobi to develop appropriate solutions to unforeseen problems and obstacles. As a result, both teams were able to simultaneously improve their knowledge and understanding of the benefits and challenges of the use of 3D printing in the humanitarian development/disaster response environment. The physical products produced through the pilot study research were not intended as an end in themselves but, rather, as the starting point for developing a collaborative approach with stakeholders to support the development of a systems-based proposal that would position the operation within the theoretical framework provided by current humanitarian design research.

- As a result of the above iterative process, a number of key points that were highlighted including the need for a consistent power supply.
- Ability of the field operator to utilise the printer, and recognise and correct problems.
- Necessity for the operator to have a mechanism to test the print validity of the individual printer after transit.
- Control of environmental factors such as dust and temperature.
- Use of a print bed size sufficient to accommodate the most common component dimensions.
- Specification of print orientation based on laboratory testing to ensure fitness for purpose.
- Need for a system that allows for the engineering based performance validity testing of bespoke products.
- Need for part finished parametric model elements that can be built upon to meet specific problems to reduce modelling time.
- Benefits of design for site, reducing points of weakness (unnecessary joints etc) and adding extra strength / flexibility to maximise performance.
- Potential of multihead printing to allow for multiple material components to expand the assembly rationalisation to include flexible and re-enforced features.

Importantly, therefore, the key Research Question – namely whether the benefits of 3D printing that are found within the 'for profit' literature are applicable in the 'not for profit' context. Indeed, whilst the particular research context did not allow a formal like-for-like analysis of the costs/benefits of the standard logistic pipeline and the 3D printing approach, the following points surfaced during the research:

- In the case of the East African Oxfam G.B. WASH project, the supply time can be up to 12 weeks. This should be compared with the printing of a component that would normally be completed in less than 12 hours.
- Once the parts arrive, there may be items missing, or broken in transit, or that simply do not fit the unforeseen topology of the site. New parts have, therefore, to be ordered through the same process or, alternatively, a make shift item created from parts brought in local markets. The use of 3D printing provides a viable alternative through the local production of a component that can replace the missing/broken item – albeit this may be on a temporary basis until the standard component arrives via the regular supply chain.
- Furthermore, as indicated above, the use of 3D printing allows for the production of bespoke items to meet a specific operational requirement which would otherwise potentially require a lengthy (and costly) re-design and production process.

Importantly, the pilot research re-affirmed the view that 3D printing is not a like-for-like replacement for conventional mass production techniques, however its ease of production to meet an identified need and its ability to operate in both prototype and production modes have clear benefit – especially in a humanitarian context that is replete with logistic challenges. One of the key aims of the next phase of the research will be to achieve a better and more formal understanding of the relative costs of the two approaches – albeit it is recognised that this will be a challenge, not least due the relative paucity and immaturity of the data that is available to support humanitarian logistic decision-making (Tatham & Hughes, 2011).

Hub and Spoke Model

For first world designers, who have specifically responded to Papanek's call to arms to commit time to designing for third world needs, the tensions have been magnified by the complex realities of working across borders in environments, cultures and systems that may be significantly different from their own experience. The identification and testing of the practical application of 3D printing to a humanitarian design situation such as for the Oxfam WASH projects does not, in itself, respond to the theories, ideas and values underpinning current humanitarian design research. For this project to meet Makepeace's (1995) definition of good design, the project must be part of its theoretical context, demonstrate aspirations and be informed by - and very much a part of - society's knowledge and understanding at this point in time. To achieve this, the use of the creative technologies must be placed within a framework that draws on the work of humanitarian design researchers, and demonstrates how the ideas of the research community can be moved forward through this project.

The essential aspects of this work are not those that reflect the provision of an on the ground solution to the specific needs identified during the project and which can be met by the creative use of digital technologies, in particular 3D printing. Rather they are in providing a solution to the issues that the application of the technology in a humanitarian logistics context highlights when taking into account the relevant humanitarian design research theory. In this regard, the project did indeed demonstrate that bespoke parts can be created on site, and that there were practical solutions to the challenges of power supply and even that the use of design for 3D printing to adapt or consolidate parts and add strength to specific part builds in response to site specific needs. Indeed, taking a more pessimistic perspective, there is a very real danger that the open access approach of the FabLab, fed by the accessibility of print files on the internet that may look fit for purpose but have not undergone rigorous validation testing, could fail under pressure and cause injury or the breakdown of the supply they are designed to fix.

The second field study focused on the issues of integrating people, process and technology under the new (3D printing) paradigm. It collected evidence through focus groups and testing on which the team were able to base their view of the development of a long term model that would engage and empower local operatives, develop long term collaborations, support the rigorous testing and validation of prints and ensure that the body of knowledge on design for 3D printing for humanitarian applications was not fragmented, but built on by future research. In essence, having confirmed the validity of the use of 3D printing in the humanitarian context in the first part of the field study, the second concentrated on the question of how its use might be operationalised – in particular from an organizational perspective.

As a result, the team has proposed a 'Hub and Spoke' model that builds on the proven strategies of the FabLabs in providing a nexus for open lines of communication between stakeholders and expertise on demand. The central hub – which it is proposed in the longer term would consist of multiple hubs around the world as suggested in the illustrative communication graphic – would contain the expertise and equipment needed to help in the design for appropriate process, prototyping and testing of parts. Field operatives would be guided through the collection of relevant design-specific data and they would also be supplied with testing equipment to ensure that the on site printers were functioning correctly.

Information and collaboration would flow between the projects, via the hubs, and a community of practice established to develop the strategic response to a humanitarian crisis or as part of development work in remote regions.

The long term aim would be that this approach would provide an educational platform that would work both ways, providing the contact points for design research work to feed in to international communities whilst avoiding some of the over exposure problems for communities identified earlier. At the same time this approach would support the upskilling and mentoring of local operators in the use of creative digital technologies, thereby meeting the entrepreneurial opportunities of creative digital technologies.

Figure 3 offers an overview of how this concept might work in building a body of knowledge across projects and an ongoing relationship supported by digital communication rather than providing a short injection of training and equipment. Importantly this is merely a representation of the approach and not prescriptive. Thus, for example, the WASH projects might be located anywhere in the world (i.e. not only in Africa) – not least as the requirements for clean water and sanitation are ubiquitous in a disaster response/development context. The actual location of the hubs and, indeed, the spokes may also vary. For example, if a particular country has expertise in, say, the technologies surrounding the spinning of cotton products, it would make sense to consider this as the location for the hub supporting spokes that are positioned across the globe. On the other hand, locating the hub in the same region as the spoke also has potential benefit, not least as this may result in the identification of positive or negative cultural nuances that might otherwise be overlooked (Figure 3).

Systems Thinking

3D printing is part of a digital system in that its recent rapid expansion from a prototyping technology within the domain of product design and engineering practice to a viable open access direct manufacturing technology is intrinsically linked with the development of online platforms, many of which are open source. In considering 3D printing in a research for humanitarian design context, it is therefore logical to consider the potential benefits of being able to communicate effectively during the design development phase, working from screen to reality, back to screen between sites across the globe, and then to print on demand where the part is required, rather than considering the design and making of products in isolation. The benefits of this approach are made possible because the technology allows for the customization of each 3D print. In this way, a shared approach to an iterative design development can be used to create bespoke products on demand across distances and between multiple spoke locations.

An example of 'design for need' that exploits these synergies is the work of E-Nable[9]. This organization provides a crowd-sourcing map online; to link the parents of children requiring a basic, low cost prosthetic hand with an individual with a 3D printer. In parallel, it draws on multiple contributors of design expertise to build a database of stereolithography files (the main format suitable for 3D printing) that are customized to the specific needs of the child, at both a practical and emotional level, as the aesthetics are as customizable as the ergonomics (Figure 4).

The Enable project elegantly illustrates the integration of 3D printing into a systems thinking approach, which is supported by additional digital technologies. This collaborative, ongoing systems approach to utilizing advances in creative technologies for humanitarian design research provides new avenues to address some of the concerns around the current practices of designers who are trying to support design for need in locations and within communities that are not their primary focus.

Figure 3. Hub and spoke communication model suggesting the role of the hub to provide ongoing centralized support for multiple possible projects

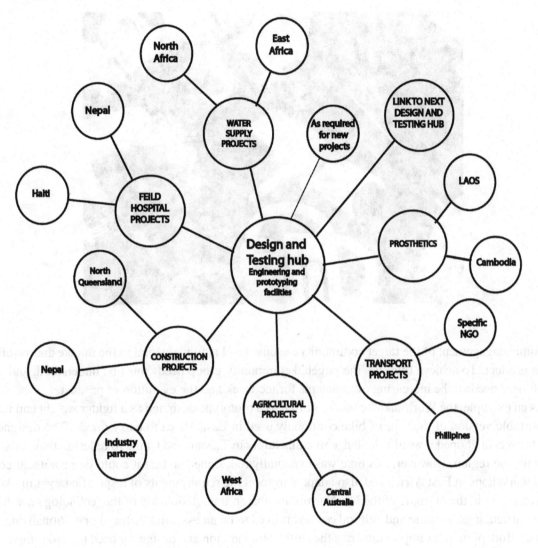

Fundamental to this new consensus is a belief in innovation - innovation in its widest sense, not only 'technical innovation', but also 'innovation in economic, social and institutional structures'. The new paradigm can be described as 'the innovation route to a sustainable development', or, as I have labeled it (building on previous work): The Eco-Innovation Paradigm. (Ryan, 2004, p. 29)

As humanitarian design research has matured, there has been a shift in emphasis to the economic empowerment of the users as being a vital component in humanitarian design research, either by providing technologically appropriate equipment to support entrepreneurship, or by providing design support in maximizing local skills, technology and materials for new markets. Such research is not solely focused on end users, rather as the current humanitarian design research theory is highlighting, the role of

Figure 4. E-Nable low cost prosthetics designed for 3D printing as distributed manufacturing
Photo: Loy, 2015.

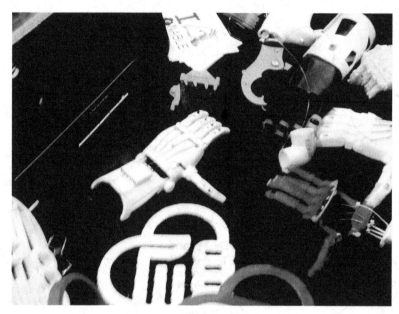

economic engagement of the target community at some level is fundamental to the uptake and viability of the product. To achieve this end, the targeted community group needs must be understood, and as a result there needs to be increasing mechanisms for feedback and the evolution of product.

As an example, the Worldbike[10] concept started as a prototype designed as a lighter weight and more comfortable version of the type of bike commonly used in East Africa to carry goods. The designers, Freedman et al., hoped it would challenge manufacturers in Taiwan and China to redesign their existing bikes for the region. However, this bike was eventually redesigned so that it could be manufactured in small workshops in East Africa and also adapted to meet the requirements of a specific target market – taxi riders. As in the example of the NeoNurture incubator, the relationship of the technology available in the particular geographic and cultural context proved to be an essential factor in operationalising the product. Both of these examples illustrate the shift from donation and design for need towards empowerment and design for economic ability.

In line with this, Gershenfeld's work arguably defies paternalism. However, he is facing similar criticism as the advocates of DIY initially did, as discussed in Open Design Now:

This process of democratization was not all plain sailing – it was one which was strongly rejected by the institutional bodies of various professions, all seeking to protect the livelihoods of their members, and was a source of tension in the relationship between amateur and professional that remains to this day (Atkinson, 2011 p.26).

There are multiple examples of communities taking the initiative and using the facilities provided by Gershenfeld to create outcomes (including unanticipated ones) that re-enforce his approach to democratization through access to advanced technologies. One such example is the Afghanistan FabFi[11] project, where local communities built themselves an intranet across regional areas. However, just as the pendulum has swung from the lack of interest in design for need highlighted by Papanek the quantity massive influx of individuals currently involved in design for need projects is also prompting criticism. This reflects the concern that the ability to provide individuals with creative digital technologies through initiatives such as FabLabs has a down side when it is taken too far.

In essence, planting emerging technologies into situations where a cultural development in the use of such technologies has not occurred is raising concern amongst humanitarian design researchers. The mobile phone is one clear example of where a technology has leapfrogged into communities. Many more remote communities now using mobile phones have not experienced the use of landlines and shared public phones before mobile phones became ubiquitous. This is not necessarily a problem, but it could see communities immersed in changing practices too quickly for all members to adjust and may have unforeseen consequences. In a similar way and alongside FabLabs, and the entrepreneurship these support, there have been well meaning initiatives whereby communities in developing countries have been donated multiple 3D Printers, minimal training if any in their use, and encouraged to download open source files from the internet, further opening up the debate on the use of open source material, as discussed by Warner et al. (2014). However, for someone to be able to download genuinely appropriate product solutions, presupposes either a filtering of viable products fit for purpose on the internet, or a foundation of engineering and design knowledge by those concerned. At the very least it presupposes an understanding that such products are engineered, that material properties will impact performance, and that 3D printing itself is not a push button technology, but that it requires the product to be designed for process (in the same way as any other manufacturing technology) in order for the print to produce a viable product. The concerns expressed by Greatorex (2015), in the white paper 3D printing and Consumer Product Safety aimed at home users are equally applicable in this context.

The potential of 3D printing to provide the physical objects needed to meet the specific needs identified for the WASH project was clearly demonstrated by the pilot research project based in Nairobi in 2014 / 2015. However, just as the earlier products discussed need to be viewed within their context and a systems approach and interrogated to avoid paternalism or an unwieldy and oversimplified participatory approach with no follow up strategy, so do the outputs of a 3D printing process. Put simply, the basic ability of the technology to meet the product outcome needs does not mean that it is an appropriate solution for the situation. Rather, any proposal to use 3D printing to support development/disaster response needs to be embedded in a strongly constructed support system that reflects the current research theory on humanitarian design. Tracked against the 'Seven deadly sins of Humanitarian Medicine', proposed by Welling et al. (2010), as a way of providing a starting point, the project needs to:

• Evolve, rather than be imposed.
• Provide system for ongoing mentorship and training as the work evolves.
• Support a collaborative approach for all stakeholders.
• Have long term system aims over the provision of individual product designs.
• Service the need, rather than educational or research aims.
• Be minimally invasive.
• Be based on an informed, clearly articulated understanding of what matters and why.

ISSUES, CONTROVERSIES, PROBLEMS

The field of design that operates within humanitarian research has been built on a foundation of activism that started with Papanek, and has links with the growth of sustainable design. Opinion has been split between appropriate technology solutions that are low-tech and appropriate technology solutions that are more strongly embedded in economic empowerment and product service systems thinking, as it applies in a developing country. The recommendations based on the project work in this chapter provide three potential sources of controversy:

1. 3D Printers are a further example where advanced technology products are introduced into a community where the skills to use and maintain those products is not available. As discussed in the background section, this has been a failing of many humanitarian design approaches to date.
2. Providing 3D Printers to operatives in a remote region could lead to inappropriate products being downloaded off the internet that are not fit for purpose.
3. Building a mentoring network may have potential benefits for collaboration, but, based on the literature review, there is a danger it may prove insensitive to the local community who may see it as disempowering and a form of digital colonialism. This would have to be carefully negotiated to ensure a genuinely collaborative approach, rather than an alternative paternalism in a digital technologies form.

The problems in applying the results of this research are in establishing a rigorous workflow in a fluid working situation. Field operatives are transient and the on-the-ground situation changes in response to the humanitarian crisis and this means that there are challenges to maintaining continuity and developing a body of knowledge for future researchers to draw on.

SOLUTIONS AND RECOMMENDATIONS

The recommendations, based on this research, are that in order to maximize the potential of 3D printing to circumvent the supply chain to support humanitarian logistics, the design and manufacturing of product must not only be specific to the technology, but also need to be provided within a structured support system. This system needs to provide access to appropriate expertise and technology as an ongoing relationship to ensure the parts produced are validated and fit for purpose. A 'hub and spoke' model that builds support networks, drawing on digital communication technologies contributes to the broader research issues impacting 3D printing in relation to safety and IP.

FUTURE RESEARCH DIRECTIONS

The research project discussed in this chapter forms a pilot project for a two-year project that is currently awaiting funding. Having established that there are no *a priori* reasons why 3D printing could and, indeed, should not be used in appropriate contexts (such as WASH) within the whole spectrum of development and disaster response activities, the aim of this further research is to test the validity of the hypothesis that a 'hub and spoke' model would provide an effective support framework for the use of creative digital technologies in circumventing supply chain issues in humanitarian logistics. This provides a paradigm shift from current operations, which focus on individual problem solving using advances in creative digital technologies for humanitarian applications, to a structured, measured response. This response provides a foundation for building rigorous design practices for the humanitarian logistics community.

In doing so, it is planned that a hub will be created and populated with staff possessing a range of skills and expertise including, but not limited to: industrial design, mechanical engineering, 3D Printer operations and humanitarian logistics. This team will spend some 6-9 months developing and testing a set of WASH components that can be 3D Printed to order. The team will also develop the necessary training documentation, videos, etc. to support the field operations, the first phase of which will be located in a relatively remote, but politically benign, country. This will allow the testing of the model and the associated data capture relating to, for example, the comparative logistics cost. It will also allow the researchers to obtain a more sophisticated understanding of the training needs of the local operators. In Phase 3, the learnings from the earlier phases will be migrated to a more challenging environment in order to test the robustness of the model.

CONCLUSION

We may be living through the business equivalent to the Cambrian explosion, when after 3.5 billion years of sluggish evolution, a vast array of life forms suddenly appeared in only 10 million years. New business models and ways of organising and operating businesses are appearing in comparably rapid profusion, driven by stunning advances in information technologies. (Ryan, 2004, p.71)

Just as developments in digital technologies are disrupting conventional manufacturing practices and stimulating new business models, so too are they providing designers with opportunities to rethink systems, sustainable design, community engagement and participation models. Humanitarian design research provides evidence that products developed in collaboration with communities and embedded in a systems based model that targets empowerment – preferably economic empowerment – are more likely to progress beyond the concept stage and be embraced by the stakeholders. However, the current strategy of encouraging designers and design students to actively travel to communities as the basis for their designs is proving unworkable due, in part, to the sheer weight of numbers involved in volunteer tourism generally, and in part due to the perception of paternalism and a superficial approach to engagement. Since Papanek, design theory and practice has trodden an uneasy path in relation to international participatory design, however well meaning. Thus, although the Internet and web 2.0 has improved global communication, it has also resulted in some extreme activity in recent years in the realm of social media-driven design decision-making at a distance. Nevertheless, the digital revolution does provide new tools for a democratization of collaboration, where designers are no longer limited to working with a community only during the development of a single product, but instead can aim to build sustainable, flexible frameworks for practice based on the idea of shared networks where new practices emerge, rather than are imposed.

As Gershenfeld's work suggests, denying communities in developing countries access to advanced technologies is a paternalistic approach. Furthermore this project provides an example of how the use of open access tools to support the application of new technologies could lead to injury, or to damage to infrastructure. With both these concerns in mind, using digital technologies to work with and empower a community in the development of problem solving products, and then using digital fabrication to support customised printing - supported by a collaborative, mentoring approach to the development and testing of those solutions, could counteract the growing problem of volunteer tourism, at least in relation to design and design education, and perhaps influence practice in related fields. The approach behind the 'hub and spoke' supports the development of collective responsibility with regards to meeting the opportunities and challenges of new creative technologies. In this case, this means embedding the use of digital fabrication into a supportive digital environment that not only provides for communication and commercialisation, but also for collaboration on, and dissemination of, knowledge and practice. Working with the advances in technology to protect, and yet engage and empower communities, rather than being limited by conventional ideas of appropriate technology and community engagement, provides a new collaborative model that aims to ensure that for all stakeholders they gain the best of both worlds.

In summary, the outcomes of the WASH pilot project has clear philosophical implications beyond the development of a facility to make/replace broken pipes to keep the water supply going – admirable though that is. It is providing direction on how participatory design, and even co-design, can be superseded by empowering and mentoring design strategies for economic and upskilling. Removing the imposition of visiting Western designers from the communities, it focuses instead on building a new form of networking around the world that gives those involved access to advances in digital fabrication technology, without their ideas being diluted through the experience and opinion of a visiting designers. Providing visualization, validation and testing, and ongoing training opportunities, changes the relationship between the creatives and the community. The balance between paternalism and invasive participatory design may not be achieved overnight, but at least structures are being built that re-imagine and reconstruct that middle ground.

REFERENCES

Anderson, C. (2012). *Makers: The next industrial revolution*. New York, NY: Crown Business.

Atkinson, P. (2014). Orchestral manoeuvres in design. In B. van Abel, L. Evers, R. Klaassen, & P. Troxler (Eds.), *Open design now* (pp. 24–34). Amsterdam, Netherlands: BIS.

Centre for Research on the Epidemiology of Disasters. (2015). Retrieved August 18, 2015, from http://www.cred.be/publications

Christopher, M. (2011). *Logistics & supply chain management* (4th ed.). Harlow, UK: Prentice Hall.

Collins, H. (2010). *Creative research: The theory and practice of research for the creative industries*. London, UK: AVA Publishing.

Crump, J., & Sugarman, J. (2008). Ethical considerations for short-term experiences by trainees in global health. *Journal of the American Medical Association, 300*(12), 1456–1458. doi:10.1001/jama.300.12.1456 PMID:18812538

de Leeuw, S., Kopczak, L., & Blansjaar, M. (2010). What really matters in locating shared humanitarian stockpiles: Evidence from the WASH Cluster. *IFIP Advances in Information and Communication Technology, 336*, 166–172. doi:10.1007/978-3-642-15961-9_19

Durgavich, J. (2009). Customs clearance issues related to the import of goods for public health programs. *US AID*. Retrieved March 21, 2015, from http://deliver.jsi.com/dlvr_content/resources/allpubs/policypapers/CustClearIssu.pdf

Fab Foundation. (n.d.). *FabLabs*. Retrieved August 24, 2015, from http://www.fabfoundation.org/fab-labs/

Flahiff, D. (2008). Aquaduct bike purifies water as you pedal. *Inhabitat*. Retrieved August 24, 2015, from http://inhabitat.com/aquaduct-bike-purifies-water-as-you-pedal/

Fuad-Luke, A. (2009). *Design activism*. London, UK: Earthscan.

Fuad-Luke, A. (2010). *Ecodesign: The sourcebook* (3rd ed.). San Francisco, CA: Chronicle.

Gershenfeld, N. (2007). *Fab: The coming revolution on your desktop–from personal computers to personal fabrication*. New York, NY: Basic Books.

Gibson, I., Rosen, D., & Stucker, B. (2014). *Additive manufacturing technologies: 3D printing, rapid prototyping and direct digital manufacturing* (2nd ed.). New York, NY: Springer.

Greatorex, G. (2015). *3D printing and consumer product safety*. Retrieved July 18, 2015, from http://productsafetysolutions.com.au/3d-printing-call-for-action-on-product-safety/

Hawken, P., Lovins, A., & Lovins, L. (2010). *Natural capitalism: The next industrial revolution*. London, UK: Earthscan.

Hippo Water Roller Project. (n.d.). Retrieved August 24, 2015, from http://hipporoller.org/

IDE. (n.d.). *Treadle pumps*. Retrieved August 24, 2015, from http://www.ideorg.org/OurTechnologies/TreadlePump.aspx

IDEO. (2008). *Aquaduct concept vehicle*. Retrieved August 24, 2015, from http://www.ideo.com/work/aquaduct

Innovate or Die! (2014). Retrieved August 24, 2015, from http://www.innovateordie.fi/#in-english

Kovács, G., & Spens, K. (2007). Humanitarian logistics in disaster relief operations. *International Journal of Physical Distribution & Logistics Management*, *36*(2), 99–114.

L'Hermitte, C., Tatham, P. H., & Bowles, M. (2013). Classifying logistics-relevant disasters: Conceptual model and empirical illustration. *Journal of Humanitarian Logistics and Supply Chain Management*, *4*(2), 155–178. doi:10.1108/JHLSCM-07-2013-0025

Lifestraw. (2014). Retrieved August 24, 2015, from http://www.buylifestraw.com/en/

Makepeace, J. (1995). *Makepeace: The spirit of adventure in craft and design*. London, UK: Conran Octopus.

NeoNurture. (n.d.). In *Design that matters*. Retrieved August 24, 2015, from http://www.designthatmatters.org/neonurture/

Nussbaum, B. (2010). Is humanitarian design the new imperialism? *Fastcompany*. Retrieved April 27, 2015, from http://www.fastcodesign.com/1661859/is-humanitarian-design-the-new-imperialism

One Laptop per Child. (n.d.). Retrieved August 24, 2015, from http://one.laptop.org/

Oxfam. (2013). *Oxfam GB Catalogue*. Retrieved January 25, 2014, from http://www.oxfam.org.uk/equipment/catalogue/introduction

Oxfam. (2015). *WASH project*. Retrieved August 24, 2015, from http://policy-practice.oxfam.org.uk/our-work/water-health-education/wash

Papanek, V. (1971). *Design for the real world*. London, UK: Thames & Hudson.

Pilloton, E. (2009). *Design revolution*. New York, NY: Metropolis Books.

Ryan, C. (2004). *Digital eco-sense: Sustainability and ICT – a new terrain for innovation*. Carlton, Australia: lab.3000 – innovation in digital design.

Shapeways. (n.d.). Retrieved August 24, 2015, from http://www.shapeways.com/

Smithsonian, Cooper-Hewitt National Design Museum. (n.d.). *Design with the other 90%*. Retrieved August 24, 2015, from http://www.designother90.org/

Stohr, K., & Sinclair, C. (2012). *Design like you give a damn: Building change from the ground up*. New York, NY: Harry N. Abrams.

Tatham, P., & Hughes, K. (2011). Humanitarian logistic metrics: Where we are, and how we might improve. In M. Christopher & P. H. Tatham (Eds.), *Humanitarian logistics: Meeting the challenge of preparing for and responding to disasters* (pp. 65–84). London, UK: Kogan Page.

Tatham, P., Loy, J., & Peretti, U. (2015). Three dimensional printing – a key tool for the humanitarian logistician? *Journal of Humanitarian Logistics and Supply Chain Management, 5*(2), 188–208. doi:10.1108/JHLSCM-01-2014-0006

Tatham, P., & Pettit, S. (2010). Transforming humanitarian logistics: The journey to supply network management. *International Journal of Physical Distribution & Logistics Management, 40*(8/9), 609–622. doi:10.1108/09600031011079283

Tatum, J. (2004). The challenge of responsible design. *Design Issues, 20*(3), 66–80. doi:10.1162/0747936041423307

Thilmany, J. (2010). Rapid prototyping gains new roles in humanitarian causes. *Mechanical Engineering (New York, N.Y.)*, (January): 46–49.

Thomas, A., & Mizushima, M. (2005). Logistics training: Necessity or luxury? *Forced Migration Review, 22*, 60–61.

Wearing, S., & McGehee, N. (2013). Volunteer tourism – a review. *Tourism Management, 38*, 120–130. doi:10.1016/j.tourman.2013.03.002

Welling, D., Ryan, J., Burris, D., & Rich, N. (2010). Seven sins in humanitarian medicine. *World Journal of Surgery, 34*(3), 466–470. doi:10.1007/s00268-009-0373-z PMID:20063094

KEY TERMS AND DEFINITIONS

Logistics: The science of the supplying, movement and maintenance of materials through an organizational structure.

ENDNOTE

Other contributors to the research funding included RedR (Australia), HK Logistics and various departments within Griffith University.

Chapter 4

Pure Land UNWIRED:
New Approaches to Virtual Reality for Heritage at Risk

Stefan Greuter
RMIT University, Australia

Sarah Kenderdine
University of New South Wales, Australia

Jeffrey Shaw
City University of Hong Kong, Hong Kong

ABSTRACT

The Mogao Grottoes located in Gansu Province of north-western China consist of 492 cells and cave sanctuaries carved into the cliffs above the Dachuan River in Mogao. A UNESCO World Heritage Site, they comprise the largest, most richly endowed, and oldest treasure house of Buddhist art in the world. However, for preservation and conservation reasons most of the caves are now closed to the public. This chapter discusses the range of technologies currently available for the virtual representation of Cave 220, just one of the many caves located at this site. In particular, the chapter focuses on the latest prototype, developed by the authors called Pure Land UNWIRED which uses a virtual reality platform specifically designed for a unique single user full-body immersive virtual reality experience. The discussion includes technical and evaluative analysis of this prototype.

INTRODUCTION

The field of creative technologies encompasses multi-sensory experiences that are the result of a combination of fields including Computer Technology, Design, Art, and the Humanities. Virtual heritage is an example that combines the fields of Virtual Reality and cultural heritage and involves functions that facilitate the synthesis, conservation, reproduction, representation, digital reprocessing, and display of cultural evidence with the use of virtual reality imaging technologies (Roussou, 2002). The field of

DOI: 10.4018/978-1-5225-0016-2.ch004

digital heritage is rapidly evolving through the utilization of digital technology and the maturation of processes in research and practical methodologies (Thwaites, 2013) and provides a means to explore and examine past and present heritage resources.

Virtual heritage projects provide an audience with an opportunity to inhabit the cultural imaginary. The audience becomes an integral part of, and is immersed into, the digital heritage experience (Kenderdine & Shaw, 2009). Virtual heritage presents potential to provide access to heritage sites that are remote, closed, or no longer existing. However, virtual heritage representations have often been criticised for issues relating to authenticity, expensive development costs, usability problems, high maintenance, and their confinement to a particular environment located at specific venues that limits widespread dissemination, distribution, and use (Roussou, 2007).

This chapter provides a case study that is focused on a new full-body immersive virtual reality application that allows unparalleled access to a world heritage site that is so vulnerable it can no longer sustain physical visitors. The application, *Pure Land UNWIRED* is the third in a series of virtual and augmented reality installations that utilize sensorial and experiential exhibition technologies to recreate precious heritage locations. The *Pure Land* projects digitally replicate parts of the UNESCO World Heritage Site located at the Mogao Grottoes in Gansu Province, north-western China. Current *Pure Land* applications focused on Cave 220; known for its important early Tang Dynasty murals. The peerless treasures of the paintings and sculptures at Dunhuang are extremely vulnerable and, as such, many caves are closed to the public - including Cave 220.

Comprehensive digitization, including laser scanning and ultra-high resolution camera array photography, are now undertaken by the Dunhuang Research Academy as the primary method of preservation and interpretation for the site. The digital facsimiles of this paragon of Chinese Buddhist art are transformed allowing virtual visitation to the site for museum visitors.

The *Pure Land* projects contribute to new strategies for rendering cultural heritage landscapes, and redefine the possibilities for digital preservation and embodied museography. *Pure Land UNWIRED,* currently in prototype stage, is the third *Pure Land* project in the series and was developed by the authors of this chapter in collaboration with the Dunhuang Research Academy. *Pure Land UNWIRED* allows full-body immersion in a virtual reality (VR) environment: visitors walk around inside Cave 220 at 1:1 scale. The VR platform combines a head-mounted display with a camera-based motion tracking system to capture movements of a single user's body and limbs within a small space similar to the size of the Cave 220 itself. A tablet computer carried in a backpack runs the game engine, which integrates the tracking with real-time visualisation.

Pure Land UNWIRED addresses several of the often-criticised shortcomings of virtual heritage projects related to authenticity, usability, cost, maintenance, and the potential for dissemination. This chapter contextualises *Pure Land UNWIRED* within the field of virtual heritage experiences, describes the *Pure Land UNWIRED* prototype and discusses the results of a user experiences study gathered from an evaluative survey of users who have experienced the Cave 220 using *Pure Land UNWIRED* at the Real 2015 conference held February 25-27, 2015 in San Francisco, California, USA.

Heritage at Risk

The Mogao Grottoes consist of 750 caves that have been hewn on five levels into an escarpment in the Gobi Desert. Mural paintings are found in 492 caves; in total there are 45,000 square meters of murals and more than 2,000 painted clay figures. Buddha statues and paintings of paradise and angels adorn the walls of the caves, as do images of the patrons or donors who commissioned the paintings. The largest cave is 40 meters high and houses a 30 meter tall Buddha statue carved during the Tang Dynasty A.D. 618-906 (Lamer, 2015).

Dunhuang is a singular and astonishing art repository like no other in the Chinese Buddhist world. This great heritage site is under the custodianship of the Dunhuang Research Academy.[1] Its importance is well recognized and is demonstrated through several major international collaborations with, for example the Getty Conservation Institute,[2] Northwestern University,[3] the Mellon Foundation,[4] Wuhan University and the Cyark Foundation.[5] The Mellon Foundation has pioneered the use of digital photography at the site since 2000 while Wuhan University has assisted the Dunhuang Research Academy with the laser scanning of the caves. The International Dunhuang Project, led by the British Library, [6] is working to digitally repatriate objects removed from the site dispersed from over 18 countries.

Together with their international collaborators, Dunhuang Research Academy's 'Dunhuang Mogao Cave Paintings Digitization Project Plan',[7] is a quest for a definitive model of preservation for this highly significant site that is under extreme threat from both climate change and human factors. Between 2002 and 2012, over five million people visited the Dunhuang site. In 2012 alone, nearly 800,000 people toured the caves (90% of these visitors were domestic tourists). Like many other cave and subterranean sites worldwide, the Mogao Grottoes are subject to serious threat from increased visitation as well as the increasing humidity inside the caves. The estimated maximum capacity for the caves is approximately 3,000 people per day; yet during peak periods there have been almost 6,000 visitors a day (Wang, 2012); and during China's week-long national holiday in 2012 more than 18,000 people visited the site.[8]

The Dunhuang Research Academy opens a limited number of caves (approximately thirty) at a time to visitors, to ensure the long-term preservation of the site. In most caves, the murals and statues are protected (and often optically hindered) by glass panels, and the only lighting available is via low intensity LED torches. These torches are usually held by guides who also explain the narrative iconography of the paintings and sculptures. Thus a real-life visit suffers from restrictive, albeit necessary, limitations.

There is an obvious tension between the desire to exhibit this rich and important cultural heritage to the world and the ongoing need to preserve the caves. A *New York Times* journalist who visited the site wrote:

Mogaoku is in trouble…The caves now suffer from high levels of carbon dioxide and humidity, which are severely undermining conservation efforts. The short-term solution has been to limit the number of caves that can be visited and to admit people only on timed tours, but the deterioration continues … Plans are under way to recast the entire Dunhuang experience in a way that will both intensify and distance it. Digital technology will give visitors a kind of total immersion encounter with the caves impossible before now … (Holland Cotter, 2008).

Many believe that Dunhuang's future relies on its digitization program, a cornerstone of several new initiatives led by Director Fan Janshi, including a new Visitor Centre that opened in 2013. "Versatile and efficient, digitization provides many new opportunities for study, research and enjoyment," says one of the initiators of high-resolution photography at the Harlan Wallach site (Wallach, 2010). Since 1999, 59 caves have been completely imaged at a minimum resolution of 72 dpi (Lu & Pan, 2010) and more recently at 600 dpi, with 1:1 scale images as the benchmark (Wang, 2012). Acquiring these images requires special cameras, custom-made railings on which the cameras are moved, as well as ample computer processing power and trained staff (there are currently fifty members of the photographic team). After the ceilings, walls, niches and statuary have been photographed, specialized technicians stitch the data together into ultra-high resolution pictures. This process takes up to three months for a single cave (Figure 1).

The *Pure Land* projects expand upon these world-leading digitization efforts. The installations represent a significant technological achievement that integrates the high-resolution digital documentation and academic research efforts at Dunhuang into an interpretive virtual experience for visitors; thereby reaching beyond established practices of digital facsimile and 'virtual heritage'[9]. The recognition of such digital works by several high-profile museums—which are concerned traditionally with collecting material objects—also signals a philosophical shift for heritage organizations that appear to be embracing virtual reality technology. Inside galleries, or beside heritage sites themselves, these virtual reality installations complement tangible artefacts as significant objects in their own right; amplifying rather than replacing the original.

Pure Land Projects

The two *Pure Land* experiences that precede *Pure Land UNWIRED* have been the subject of several research papers that are briefly described in what follows. The first, *Pure Land: Inside the Mogao Grottoes at Dunhuang* (Sarah Kenderdine, 2012b) uses an immersive 360-degree visualization system called the Advanced Visualization and Interaction Environment (AVIE). Inside a 10-meter diameter-wide by

Figure 1. The wireframe polygonal mesh derived from point cloud laser scans of Cave 220
Image © Dunhuang Research Academy.

4-meter-high theatre, up to 30 visitors are able to explore a true-to-life scale virtual cave: a replica of Cave 220. A single user interface, operated by one of the visitors (or a docent) provide interaction with the digitally rendered cave and offered the user a powerful experience of embodied representation. *Pure Land* exploits various digital image processing techniques including 2D and 3D animation, as well as 3D cinematography, to further develop its experiential and interpretative capabilities (Figures 2-3) (Kenderdine, Chan, & Shaw, 2014; Sarah Kenderdine, 2013).

Pure Land: Augmented Reality Edition (Sarah Kenderdine, 2012a), used mobile media technology to create a complementary "augmented reality" rendition of the same data capture from Cave 220 for the first iteration of *Pure Land*. Walking around inside the exhibition space with tablet screens in hand, visitors were able to view the architecture of the cave itself inside a "made" environment. By holding the tablet up to the wall visitors could explore the cave's sculptures and wall paintings on their tablet screen – a kinesthetic revealing of the painted architectonic space (Figures 4-5) (Chan, Kenderdine, & Shaw, 2013; Kenderdine et al., 2014; Sarah Kenderdine, 2013).

Transforming a Cultural Paragon

According to Julian Raby, Director of the Arthur M. Sackler Gallery and Freer Gallery of Art at the Smithsonian Institution, *Pure Land: Inside the Mogao Grottoes at Dunhuang* is the "exhibition experience of the future." By stimulating a palpable sense of "being there" and providing viewers with a powerful co-presence with the past, these installations are conceived of as theaters of embodied experiences within a "cultural imaginary" located in the here and now. Transforming today's commonplace big screen documentary into kinesthetic and phenomenological encounters with the places they depict.

Figure 2. Pure Land: Inside the Mogao Grottoes at Dunhuang, schematic diagram
© Applied Laboratory for Interactive Visualization and Embodiment (ALiVE), CityU Hong Kong.

Figure 3. Installed at the beginning of Pure Land: inside the Mogao Grottoes at Dunhuang, a browser displays significant caves distributed along the escarpment
Image © Applied Laboratory for Interactive Visualization and Embodiment (ALiVE), CityU Hong Kong.

Figure 4. Pure Land: Augmented Reality Edition installation at the Shanghai Biennale 2012-2013
Image © Applied Laboratory for Interactive Visualization and Embodiment (ALiVE), CityU Hong Kong.

Figure 5. Visitors crowd around a digital tablet that provides augmented views of Cave 220; Pure Land: Augmented Reality Edition, Shanghai Biennale 2012-2013
Image © Applied Laboratory for Interactive Visualization and Embodiment (ALiVE), CityU Hong Kong.

For some, the failure of most virtual heritage projects to live up to their scientific potential invites dismissive labels such as 'edutainment' and even the 'Disneyfication' of culture. Virtual heritage has long been challenged to emerge from a period of increasingly sophisticated, digital model-making and creation of navigable landscapes of 'pictorially rendered objects' (Barcelß, 2000, p. 28) to embark on a critical examination into the meaning of representations of space and place in order to facilitate dynamic, inter-actor participation and cultural learning.

In a review of the installation of *Pure Land* in November 2012 for the 25 Year Celebrations of the Freer and Sackler Galleries of Asian Art at the Smithsonian Institute the *Washington Post* highlights the shift that this work represents. Philip Kennicott wrote:

A decade or more of efforts to use virtual reality to reproduce aesthetic experiences have generally led to unsatisfying, cumbersome and distracting technologies. The transient buzz of interactivity overwhelms the actual content or educational value. But the "Pure Land" cave is different . . . it points the way forward, demonstrating how the immersion environment can be used to let visitors actively explore and understand complicated cultural objects . . . at last we have a virtual reality system that is worthy of inclusion in a museum devoted to the real stuff of art (November 30, 2012).

The *Pure Land* projects have now been experienced by hundreds of thousands of people in numerous locations worldwide (see the exhibitions listed on the Project website). Not only do they provide benchmarks for the integration of archaeological data with interactive and immersive technologies, but they also give us fresh direction for the future of interpretive experiences in museums. Diverging significantly from former exhibition practices and contemporary cinematic viewing *Pure Land* and *Pure Land Augmented Reality* support the mobilization of the viewer to coalesce in both virtual and real spaces. By defining strategies to allow for the embodiment of Heritage sites for visitors, these installations reactivate the history of the immersive view in museums, and reinvigorate archaeology with an aliveness for new levels of aesthetic and interpretative experience.

With the original site under threat from environmental circumstances, the innovative digital strategies offered by the *Pure Land* projects and their successors, may be the only way to keep the artistic and spiritual brilliance of the Mogao Grottoes alive for the cultural imaginary of this and future generations.

The remainder of this chapter describes the specific aspects of the third application for Cave 220 using virtual reality technology called *Pure Land UNWIRED* that was developed by the authors of this book chapter.

PURE LAND: UNWIRED

Pure Land UNWIRED is a virtual reality experience that allows a single person to move physically around and explore a 1:1 scale, digital 3D model of Dunhuang Cave 220. In *Pure Land UNWIRED*, the user can explore a highly detailed 3D scanned environment complete with high-resolution textures derived from ultra high-resolution pictures taken from the cave. The experience is authentic to that of a real cave visit in that it allows users walk in the virtual cave and view the visually rich wall murals. The experience also provides the user with a full body avatar that moves in sync with the user's movements. It was developed to provide the user with a sense of the cave's scale and the position of the user's body within the space (proprioception).

Technically, *Pure Land: UNWIRED* is realized via two components: a Virtual Reality Backpack attached to the user, and a separate Tracking Station. Those viewers who are not part of the experience can see the user's view on a large screen connected to the tracking station (see Figure 6, which illustrates the *Pure Land UNWIRED* setup).

For safety reasons, the tracking area needs to be empty. In this implementation, users needed to be observed by an experienced operator at all times.

Tracking Station

Motion tracking was necessary to update the user's viewpoint so it was in sync with their movements to facilitate natural movement interactions with the site. An important aspect of user immersion is the integration of visual, vestibular and proprioceptive senses, i.e. where the body's sense of where its parts are located are matched to where the eyes see themselves. Motion tracking generally relies on expensive hardware that is often difficult to set up. The markers, transmitters, sensors, cameras, and gyroscopes of traditional Virtual Reality setups generally require time-consuming calibration and careful positioning of the user. Problems of poor registration, occlusion, and interference remain common.

Pure Land UNWIRED was designed as a portable system with the aim of easy set up and calibration. We, therefore, selected inexpensive commercial systems for optical tracking of body movements. The Microsoft Kinect 2 for Windows (Microsoft, 2014) (Kinect 2) automatically detects users in seconds and tracks their movements within a lounge room-sized area with acceptable latency and accuracy.

Figure 6. Pure Land UNWIRED setup

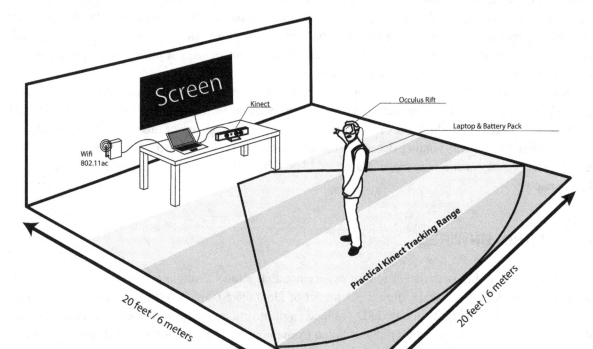

Pure Land UNWIRED's Tracking Station tracked the position and body movements of the user and transmitted this information to the Virtual Reality Backpack. The Tracking Station of this prototype consisted of a Surface 3 Tablet Computer running Windows 8.1 and a Kinect 2 depth camera and was connected via a network cable to a dedicated wi-fi 802.11ac router to ensure fast data transmission and to avoid network latencies introduced by other sources. The wireless communication between the server and the user enabled the experience without the need to manage cables, which significantly reduced any trip hazards and allowed the user to be immersed in the virtual environment.

We determined experimentally in our lab the practical full-body tracking space of the Kinect 2 (Figure 7). We defined the practical tracking range of the Kinect 2 as the space where all the extremities of a user's human body are visible by the Kinect 2 depth camera. To determine the shape and the dimensions of the practical tracking range we used the 'BodyBasics-D2D.exe' body-tracking example included in the Microsoft SDK 2.0 Public Preview (Figure 7 shows the cone-shaped tracking area of the Kinect 2). The depth camera has a viewing angle of approximately 70 degrees and at a distance of approximately 1.4 m in front of the camera the entire body of a user becomes visible by the camera and can be tracked by the Kinect 2. At its closest full-body tracking range, the user can move up to 1 meter to each side of the camera. User tracking is suspended at distances exceeding 4.2 meters from the camera position. At its furthest range, the user can move up to 2.9 meters from each side of the camera. The practical full body tracking range in front of the camera is therefore approximately 10 m^2.

Figure 7. Kinect 2 dimensions

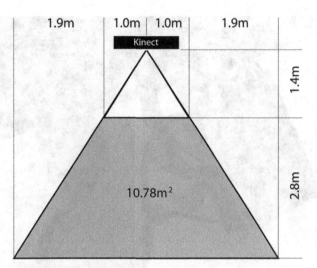

The Kinect 2 is capable of tracking 25 skeletal joints per person with millimeter accuracy and is sufficient to track a single user in real-time for a virtual reality simulation. The latency of the Kinect 2 has been reported as 20ms (Corellianrogue, 2014), which is suitable for real-time applications and a significant improvement over the latencies measured by its predecessor (Greuter & Roberts, 2015). Its tracking capability supports walk, crouch, and lean movements, as well as whole body rotations. However, the main advantage of the Kinect 2 is that the sensor does not require calibration, markers, or devices that have to be carefully positioned.

Virtual Reality Backpack

The user's Virtual Reality Backpack was designed to facilitate free movement in the virtual environment. The setup consisted of a custom-made backpack frame with a laptop connected to a head-mounted display; hand motion tracking device; and headphones. The backpack frame was created with a wire mesh that was bent to the shape of the laptop to provide a tray structure for the laptop and a lumbar support bar for the user. The laptop was attached to the tray via two Adjustable Velcro Wraps of one meter length and 25mm width. Two additional strips of wire mesh were used as shoulder straps that could hold the backpack on the user's shoulder for a short period during setup. The shoulder straps were secured to the laptop frame via straps and plastic slide releases to ensure that the backpack was tightly attached to the user's back and comfortable to wear. The wire mesh structure was an ideal mechanism to wear the 3 kg weight of the laptop and to ensure sufficient airflow for the cooling of the device. The wire mesh was covered in parts by Neoprene material to insulate the user from the warm air coming from the laptop's exhaust fan located at the bottom of the laptop case (see Figure 8).

The laptop was configured to be used exclusively with the Oculus Rift DK2 as a display device during the user's experience. The Oculus Rift (Oculus VR, 2014) is a virtual reality headset developed for gaming. The device is easy to use, inexpensive, and can be calibrated in minutes. The main display of the laptop was used to start up the laptop and for troubleshooting purposes. The lid of the laptop was closed while the simulation was in progress, and the screen was turned off. The operating system was

Figure 8. VR backpack

configured to keep the laptop running upon closure of the laptop lid. However, closing the laptop screen made the keyboard and the mouse pad inaccessible and so we attached a wireless keyboard and mouse to start and stop the application as well as occasionally recalibrate the view of the Oculus DK2.

Hand tracking was facilitated via a Leap Motion Controller. The Leap Motion Controller (Leap Motion, 2015) is a motion-sensing device developed to recognize hand and finger movements as well as hand gestures such as point, wave, reach, and grab. The Leap Motion was attached to the front of the Oculus Rift head-mounted display. Hand and finger motions were detected within 40 cm of the sensor.

Headphones connected to the laptop provided the user with ambient music. For this prototype, we used Bose Quiet Comfort 5 Acoustic Noise-Cancelling Headphones. The hardware setup of the Virtual Reality Backpack for *Pure Land UNWIRED* was intended to isolate the user's audiovisual senses from the real world to focus their attention solely on what they experienced in the virtual world.

Software

The software managed the rendering of the highly-detailed 3D model, the tracking data from multiple sources, and also played an ambient soundtrack to provide the user with a full-body virtual reality experience of Dunhuang Cave 220. To this end we developed a server version for the Tracking Station and a client version for the Virtual Reality Backpack.

The Tracking Station software was designed to track the user and provided an interface between the Kinect 2 and the software running on the Virtual Reality Backpack. We used the Microsoft Kinect SDK 2.0 (Microsoft, 2014). However, we limited the tracking to just one user to facilitate the initial user registration, and to eliminate any potential interference with additional users. For safety reasons, the tracking area needed to be empty and of sufficient size. In this implementation, users were observed by a support person at all times. In addition, we added a boundary area of 0.2 meters around the measured tracking area. Users leaving the tracking space were warned through the use of a software display filter that blurred the display as soon as they entered a boundary area. The user's display inside the tracking area and when entering the boundary area is illustrated in Figure 9.

The Tracking Station was running a local server to facilitate the data transfer between the Tracking Station and the Virtual Reality Backpack client. The Virtual Reality Backpack client, combined all the tracking data from three sources: Oculus DK2, Leap Motion, and Kinect 2. Firstly, the Oculus DK2 connected to the laptop on the user's back provided full head rotation and tilt tracking. Secondly, the Leap Motion attached to the front of the user's Oculus DK2 device provided the tracking data of the user's hands and fingers as long as they were held within the tracking range of the sensor. Thirdly, the tracking station provided the vertex coordinates of 25 skeletal joint positions via a peer-to-peer Wi-Fi connection. To minimize the amount of data needed to be transferred between the Server and the Client, we limited the data transfer to the 3D vertex coordinates of the skeletal joint positions only.

To provide the user with a point of reference, and to allow them to experience the scale of the virtual environment and assist in the user's proprioception, we combined the tracking data into a single avatar model. Game characters used in game engines are generally not designed to adjust to different user height and limb sizes. Since *Pure Land: UNWIRED* users were of different heights and had different limb and body proportions, we developed an avatar model that could adjust to the height and limb sizes of the user.

Figure 9. Boundary area (checkered) and user (smiley) leaving tracking area (solid grey) and entering boundary area showing screen-blurring effect

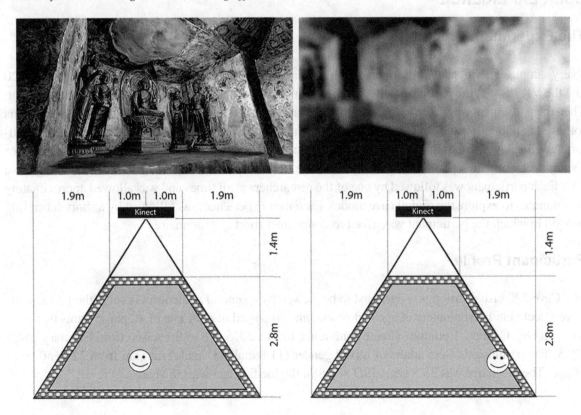

In order to avoid a distortion of the 3D model, our implementation contained three joints between two character body joint positions. The third joint facilitated the size change by imitating the functionality of hydraulic pistons that can be retracted and extended as needed. Furthermore, the avatar model integrated the hand and finger movements captured by the Leap Motion Controller into the one avatar model if the tracking information was available. However, in situations where the hand and finger movements could not be detected by the Leap Motion Controller, or where the hands were too far away from the sensor to be tracked, the hand movement tracking reverted to the tracking by the Kinect 2.

As users explored their virtual space, situations occurred where parts of the body were occluded from the Kinect 2 depth camera. Occlusion of skeletal body joints occurred when users were standing sideways in relation to the position of the Kinect 2 depth camera. In these situations, the software suspended the visualization of the avatar's body.

To describe the experience of the user wearing the VR Backpack to the audience, we displayed the user's viewpoint on to a large screen close to the exhibit. We configured the *Pure Land UNWIRED* client version running on the user's backpack to send the tilt and rotation values generated by the user's Oculus Rift DK2 to the server. Then the information was forwarded from the server to a copy of the *Pure Land UNWIRED* client version running in parallel to the tracking software on the server. The second *Pure Land UNWIRED* client copy that was running on the server was configured to render the viewpoint of the user wearing the Oculus Rift DK2 through standard camera view instead of the Oculus Split Screen view. In this way, observers were more easily able to contextualize the view and the interactions of the VR user.

USER EXPERIENCE

The Experiment Procedure

Every sample experiment was conducted with one participant. After receiving a briefing about Cave 220 and the VR system, the participant was given an information sheet and asked to provide verbal consent. Then the participant was taken to the tracking area and provided with the Virtual Reality Backpack. This followed a short automatic calibration phase after which the participant was handed the Oculus Rift head-mounted display with the attached Leap Motion Controller and a set of noise-cancelling headphones. After a short acclimatization period, the participants were free to explore the virtual model of Dunhuang Cave 220. Each participant was followed by one of the researchers at all times and was allowed approximately five minutes to explore the digital cave model. Each user experience was followed by a short debriefing session in which the participant was asked to complete a short questionnaire.

Participant Profile

The Cave 220 visualization was designed to be viewed by a general audience. As such, the participants were selected indiscriminately of age and gender and consisted of a sample of 42 participants that were attending the Capture, Compute, Create conference REAL 2015 in San Francisco from February 25-27 2015. The participants were adults of mixed gender (11 female, 31 male) ranging from 22 to 50 years of age. The mean age was 35.8 years (SD = 7.88); the median age was 36 years.

Subjective Impressions of the User Experience

The questionnaire consisted of rating scale and multiple-choice questions. The rating scale questions ranged from 1 to 10 relating to their experiences with VR systems before exposure to this environment. This was followed by another set of 7 point rating scale questions about their Cave 220 VR experience ranging from -3 to +3, with -3 indicating the participant strongly disagreed, 0 that the participant neither agreed or disagreed and +3 indicating the participant strongly agreed with the statement. Counter questions were used to avoid bias from a tendency to score high or low. We suspected that gender difference might affect participant scores, as differences in task performance times have been reported in interactions involving 3D stereoscopic displays (Cooperstock & Wang, 2009). Therefore, the analysis of the data was adjusted for gender.

Results and Discussion

Figure 10 illustrates the measure and frequency of the participants' answers against a number of questions related to their experience. The diagram shows strong overall support and demonstrates their enjoyment of the experience. Based on the data, participants felt that the experience provided them with an extension of their real world space and stated that they would like to use the system again to explore other environments. The cave was perceived as realistic compared to the natural world, and they wanted to explore the environment further.

We performed a one-way ANOVA on the questionnaire questions relating to the experience. We used: p values of equal and less than .05 to indicate significance. Values of p > .05 indicate no statistical significance. All results of the one-way ANOVA analysis are presented in Figure 11 of the Appendix.

Figure 10. Measure and frequency of the participants' answers to a number of questions

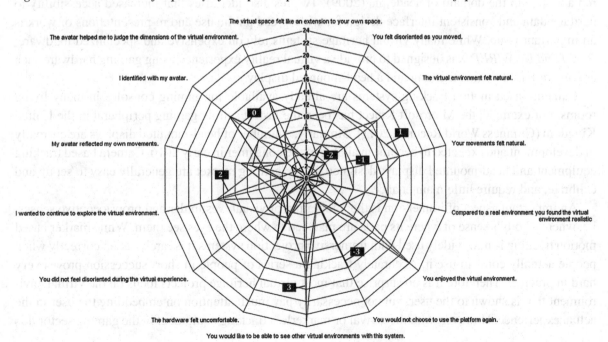

There was a significant difference (p=.001) between the level of experience between male and female participants in relation to electronic games and virtual environments. Generally, male participants were more experienced with electronic games and had more exposure to fully immersive virtual environments than the female participants we tested. Neither male nor female participants had been susceptible to nausea in the past when playing electronic games or when using other virtual reality systems.

Ideally, virtual heritage should include a mixture of representation, experience, and interaction (Roussou, 2007). In addition to the virtual representation of Cave 220, the *Pure Land* projects typically provide the audience with an opportunity to make interactive selections that lead to an experience that mimics both the physical and visual exploration of the cave: such as the ability to zoom in on details; the revival of a faded fresco "repainted" in the brilliant, even lurid colors that one might have seen a thousand years ago, or the leaping out of an instrument while speakers give a modern approximation of the sounds they would have made. *Pure Land UNWIRED* was a test prototype to assess whether users could be provided with a sense of being inside Cave 220. The prototype only used the 3D model and textures from the previous *Pure Land* versions, and the interactivity was limited to the user's movement just like in a real cave environment.

When exposed to *Pure Land UNWIRED*, male participants experienced the environment as an extension of their own space more than female participants did. While the general impression of the virtual environment of Cave 220, and the movement within, was rated highly by both male and female participants, male participants rated the experience significantly higher than female participants did. Similarly, compared to the real world, male participants found the virtual reality experience more realistic than female participants did. While all participants experienced a certain degree of disorientation when moving in the environment, female participants felt significantly more disoriented than males.

Many virtual heritage projects operate on specialized hardware and software and require staff with expertise to maintain the experience, but this does not need to be the case. Tan and Rahaman state that virtual reconstructions are mostly developed by researchers and academics and that the end product remains within the domain of academia (2009). Twaites also identifies that increased accessibility to heritage data and consistent interface design for widespread public use and re-presentations of work is an important issue. While many virtual heritage systems rely on expensive and specialized hardware; *Pure Land UNWIRED* was designed to provide a virtual reality experience using gaming hardware such as camera-based motion tracking and a head-mounted display.

Camera-based motion tracking systems are already available for gaming consoles in many living rooms. For example, the Microsoft Kinect has been the fastest selling gaming peripheral in the United Kingdom (Guinness World Records, 2011). Similarly, a number of head-mounted displays are currently in development and expected to become available to the consumer in early 2016. Camera based tracking equipment and head-mounted displays designed for the gaming market are generally easy to set up and calibrate, and require little maintenance.

An important aspect of immersion is the integration of visual, vestibular and proprioceptive senses, i.e. where a body's sense of where its parts are matched to where the eyes see them. While marker based motion tracking is now widely used with immersive projection systems it is rarely set up correctly when people actually come to use it. Accurately tracking a series of people in short succession proves very hard in practice. Therefore it is no surprise that most virtual heritage projects focus on the virtual environment that is shown to the user, but not necessarily pay much attention on embedding the user in the actual experience. However, with the arrival or markerless tracking equipment in the gaming sector this situation is likely to change. The results of this study show that the users responded positively to their virtual avatar and indicated that it reflected their movements well and helped them to judge the physical dimensions and scale of the virtual environment.

Games and other software that utilize camera base tracking and head-mounted displays can easily be downloaded. There are several online stores in existence today with millions of users and easy to use user interfaces that facilitate browsing, purchase and software updates. The responses from our user feedback indicate support for the use of gaming hardware for immersive virtual heritage projects such as *Pure Land UNWIRED*. All participants enjoyed the experience and would have liked to explore the Dunhuang Cave 220 for longer. Most participants felt comfortable when using the equipment and wanted to use the system again to experience other virtual spaces. Therefore, if virtual heritage projects are meant to be accessible by the public, then developers should consider gaming platforms and their established distribution system a viable option.

LIMITATIONS

Perhaps the most significant limitation of the *Pure Land UNWIRED* prototype was the tracking shape and range. While the Kinect 2 offered a significant increase in accuracy, latency and tracking area over its predecessor, the tracking area is still only about the size of a lounge room. This makes it unsuitable for the visualization of large virtual environments such as architectural building walkthroughs. Camera based tracking systems are also limited by the cone-shaped tracking area, which meant that the users of *Pure Land UNWIRED* were not able to explore the cave in its entirety. As with most tracking equipment, the tracking accuracy of the Kinect 2 is dependent on distance of the user to the sensor. The further a user is away from the camera the less accurate the tracking becomes.

Pure Land UNWIRED required users to wear a backpack containing a laptop computer. As the cave consisted of approximately three million polygons, a laptop with a dedicated GPU was required to visualize the virtual environment. The weight of the computer alone was 3 kg and the backpack structure added another 0.5 kg, bringing the total weight of the laptop to 3.5 kg. However, as the user results show, participants did not find the Virtual Reality Backpack uncomfortable. In fact, we observed that putting on the Virtual Reality Backpack, clipping in the plastic slide releases, and adjusting the shoulder straps came naturally to most users. Nevertheless, the procedure required assistance by one of the researchers to make sure the backpack was not dropped, and that users did not become tangled in the cable that connected the laptop to the head-mounted display. While not hugely time-consuming, the procedure was not as straight forward as it could have been and took between one and three minutes to set up. Having the Oculus Rift attached to the Virtual Reality Backpack at all times required careful management by staff assisting each user. As we only had a single user system setup at the conference, the process of using a backpack was not ideal given the large number of people interested in experiencing *Pure Land UNWIRED*.

The battery life of the laptop posed a further limitation. Providing the prototype experience to a large number of participants, with little time to recharge between users, meant that the battery ran out of power after about three or four hours of use and required a longer recharge time before the equipment could be used again. Again, not an ideal scenario when demonstrating the equipment to a large number of users.

At the time of the experiment, the Oculus Rift was still in development. While the capabilities of the Oculus Developer's Kit 2 that we used is without doubt impressive and provides, particularly first-time, virtual reality users a truly immersive experience, the resolution of the DK2 was not sufficiently advanced and users were able to make out the pixels in the display. Seeing pixels can detract from the immersive experience and this limitation may just be one contributing factor to the relatively average perception of realism by some users.

SOLUTIONS

Several of the limitations of the current *Pure Land UNWIRED* prototype will be addressed as Virtual Reality and computer technology mature. New Virtual Reality head-mounted displays already promise higher resolution and faster refresh rates than the Oculus Rift DK2. However, we expect that the screen resolution will probably have to be in the 4k range before users can immerse themselves into an 'un-pixelated' virtual experience.

Walking is one of the most common and universal tasks performed in 3D environments (Bowman, Kruijff, Jr., & Poupyrev, 2004). Real walking has been reported to provide a greater sense of presence compared to alternative techniques (Usoh et al., 1999). There are a number of solutions that address the limitation of the tracking range and tracking shape. There are many types of mechanical interfaces that already provide users with a realistic sensation of walking in virtual space using a head-mounted display. For example, omnidirectional treadmills that enable the user to walk physically around virtual spaces using a natural walking movement while keeping the user within the limitations of a small real-world physical space. Sarcos Treadport uses a belt motion that adapts to the user's movement speed and movement direction and can also incline to support uphill movements (Hollerbach, Christensen, Corp, & Jacobsen, 1999). The Circular Floor system uses moving footpads to facilitate infinite omnidirectional movements and can even simulate uneven surfaces such as stairs (H.a Iwata, Yano, Fukushima, & Noma, 2005). Other omnidirectional locomotion interfaces are based on walking inside a rotating sphere (Fernandes, Raja, & Eyre, 2003) and (Medina, Fruland, & Weghorst, 2008), (Senztech, 2012) allow users to walk, run, jump, and roll. String Walker showcased natural walking movement on a turntable with motor-driven strings connected to the user's shoes that cancel the motion of the feet to keep the user on the turntable (Hiroo Iwata, Yano, & Tomiyoshi, 2007). The WizDish ROVR locomotion platform uses friction-reducing shoes on a smooth turntable, but uses a containment frame to keep the user centered on the platform and sound sensors to detect movement to control WASD keys in the software (WizDish, 2008). Also, Virtuix Omni uses a smooth but slightly curved walking platform and a containment frame and harness, in conjunction with friction-reducing shoes to simulate the experience of walking (Virtuix, 2014). However, most locomotion devices are costly, require user training, and require significant storage space.

There are also approaches that address the limitation of the tracking space that do not require specialist hardware. World In Miniature (Pausch, Burnette, Brockway, & Weiblen, 1995) uses a miniaturized graphical representation of the virtual environment that the user can use as a map to select destinations that can then be visualized. Similarly, the magic barrier (Cirio, Marchal, Regia-Corte, & Lécuyer, 2009) is an interaction metaphor that shows the physical limitations of a tracked space. Redirected walking (Razzaque, Kohn, & Whitton, 2001) introduces subtle, gradual shifting of the viewpoint as a person walks through a virtual environment. The technique allows users to explore considerably larger virtual environments using natural body movements within a smaller tracking area. Redirected walking inspired a number of other innovative redirection techniques with similar goals but different implementations that are explained in more detail in a taxonomy by Suma et al. (2012).

The current limitations of *Pure Land UNWIRED* could be overcome by adding further tracking stations strategically positioned to minimize overlap by the sensors and modifications to the software to manage the transition of a user from one tracking space to the next while still being able to track the user's body. Similarly, HTC Vive's Lighthouse Beacon technology promises to become an easy solution to extend the tracking range and shape through the addition of beacons within the space.

As reported earlier, it took approximately three months for a team to image a single cave at Dunhuang. However, improvements in image and laser scanning hardware and software will significantly reduce the time to scan, texture, and process the information to produce highly detailed 3D models that can then be explored with platforms such as *Pure Land UNWIRED*.

CONCLUSION

Virtual Reality is a promising way to provide access to at-risk cultural heritage sites that are endangered or no longer accessible to the public. In the case of the Cave 220 at the Mogao Grottoes at Dunhuang, virtual reality is now the only way for people to physically experience the cave since the site is no longer open to the public. However, virtual heritage projects are often criticized for issues relating to authenticity, expensive development cost, usability problems, high maintenance, and their confinement to a particular environment located at specific venues that limits widespread dissemination, distribution, and use.

Maturing technology and processes provide researchers with the ability to capture, digitally preserve, and analyze cultural heritage sites. Modern scanning and imaging technology enables researchers to recreate the most authentic virtual environment to date. The world-leading digitization effort by the Dunhuang Research Academy is a quest for a definitive model of preservation for this highly significant site.

The *Pure Land* projects provide access to thousands of tourists in specialized touring environments. The virtual representations give visitors increased access to the site and provide interactive choices that augment the environment with extra information displayed in the form of animations and sound and music to create a more holistic cultural experience. This chapter described a number of platforms that have been developed in the *Pure Land* series.

However, access to *Pure Land* projects and most other virtual heritage projects available today is often limited to specialized environments in academic institutions and museums. *Pure Land UNWIRED* is the latest prototype. It is a low-cost experimental platform based on gaming hardware that enables participants to experience full-body immersion in virtual reality while walking in a living-room-sized space depicting the Cave 220 virtual environment.

Pure Land UNWIRED was tested with users, and it was found to address some of the concerns related to usability, maintenance, and access; and demonstrated that advancement in the gaming sector could provide a viable alternative to the specialized VR environments already described in this chapter. Virtual reality for gaming is still a maturing market. However, the combination of devices used in this experiment were sufficiently responsive to provide a user with a virtual reality experience: they were easy to setup and intuitive for the participant to use immediately without training. Furthermore, the distribution platforms available for games today show potential to distribute and update the work on a large scale, and on a number of systems, if virtual heritage projects are aimed at widespread public use.

Mobile phone-based head-mounted displays such as the Google Cardboard or the Samsung Gear VR already demonstrate that is it possible for a user to experience interactive, immersive games and envelope themselves into 360-degree 3D movies. It is only a matter of time until such mobile-based devices are capable of displaying cultural artefacts and sites such as the Cave 220 at sufficient resolution and fidelity and can track users as they walk in the environment. Such mobile VR solutions would significantly reduce the encumbrance of the gearing-up process. It would also make the experience scalable for larger audiences. Movements within a space could still be tracked by other systems and relayed to the headset wirelessly, providing users with a spatial sense of the cultural heritage environment that they can explore at their own pace. Such experiences can provide access and exposure to cultural heritage sites without damaging the real environments. Therefore, experiences such as *Pure Land UNWIRED* are an important step towards providing visitors with the ability to explore places that otherwise cannot be visited, or that no longer exist.

REFERENCES

Barceló, J. (2000). Visualizing what might be: an introduction to virtual reality techniques in archaeology. In Virtual Reality in Archaeology: Computer Applications and Quantitative Methods in Archaeology 1998 (pp. 9–35). ArcheoPress.

Bowman, D. A., & Kruijff, E. Jr. (2004). *User Interfaces: Theory and Practice*. Boston, MA: Addison-Wesley Professional.

Chan, L. K. Y., Kenderdine, S., & Shaw, J. (2013). Spatial user interface for experiencing Mogao caves. In *Proceedings of the 1st Symposium on Spatial User Interaction - SUI '13* (pp. 21–24). Los Angeles, CA: ACM. doi:10.1145/2491367.2491372

Cirio, G., Marchal, M., Regia-Corte, T., & Lécuyer, A. (2009). The Magic Barrier Tape: A Novel Metaphor for Infinite Navigation in Virtual Worlds with a Restricted Walking Workspace. In *Proceedings of the 16th Symposium on Virtual Reality Software and Technology* (pp. 155–162). ACM. doi:10.1145/1643928.1643965

Corellianrogue. (2014). Everything Kinect 2 In "One" Place! (See What I Did There?). *123Kinect*. Retrieved September 22, 2015, from http://123kinect.com/everything-kinect-2-one-place/43136/

Fernandes, K. J., Raja, V., & Eyre, J. (2003, September). Cybersphere: The Fully Immersive Spherical Projection System. *Communications of the ACM, 46*(9), 141–146. doi:10.1145/903893.903929

Greuter, S., & Roberts, D. J. (2015). Controlling viewpoint from markerless head tracking in an immersive ball game using a commodity depth-based camera. *Journal of Simulation, 9*(1), 54–63. doi:10.1057/jos.2014.19

Guinness World Records. (2011). Fastest-selling gaming peripheral. *Officially Amazing*. Retrieved from http://www.guinnessworldrecords.com/records-9000/fastest-selling-gaming-peripheral/

Holland Cotter. (2008). Buddha's Caves. *New York Times*. Retrieved May 18, 2015, from http://www.nytimes.com/2008/07/06/arts/design/06cott.html?pagewanted=1&_r=0

Hollerbach, J. M., Christensen, R. R., Corp, S., & Jacobsen, S. C. (1999). Design Specifications for the Second Generation Sarcos Treadport Locomotion Interface. In *Haptics Symposium, Proc. ASME Dynamic Systems and Control Division* (pp. 1293–1298). Academic Press.

Iwata, H., Yano, H., Fukushima, H., & Noma, H. (2005). CirculaFloor. *IEEE Computer Graphics and Applications, 25*(1), 64–67. doi:10.1109/MCG.2005.5 PMID:15691174

Iwata, H., Yano, H., & Tomiyoshi, M. (2007). String Walker. In *ACM SIGGRAPH 2007 Emerging Technologies* (pp. 5–9). New York, NY: ACM; doi:10.1145/1278280.1278301

Kenderdine, S., Chan, L. K. Y., & Shaw, J. (2014). Pure Land: Futures for Embodied Museography. *Journal on Computing and Cultural Heritage, 7*(2), 1–15. doi:10.1145/2614567

Kenderdine, S., & Shaw, J. (2009). New media in situ: The re-socialisation of public space. *International Journal of Arts and Technology, 2*(4), 258–276. doi:10.1504/IJART.2009.029235

Lamer, B. (2015). Caves of Faith. *National Geographic Magazine*. Retrieved May 18, 2015, from http://ngm.nationalgeographic.com/print/2010/06/dunhuangcaves/

Leap Motion, I. (2015). *Leap Motion Controller*. Retrieved September 22, 2015, from https://www.leapmotion.com/

Lu, D., & Pan, Y. (2010). *Digital Preservation for Heritages*. Berlin, Germany: Springer-Verlag; doi:10.1007/978-3-642-04862-3

Medina, E., Fruland, R., & Weghorst, S. (2008). Virtusphere: Walking in a Human Size VR "Hamster Ball". In *Proceedings of the Human Factors and Ergonomics Society Annual Meeting* (Vol. 52, pp. 2102–2106). Los Angeles, CA: Sage. doi:10.1177/154193120805202704

Microsoft. (2014). *Microsoft Kinect for Windows*. Retrieved September 22, 2015, from http://www.microsoft.com/en-us/kinectforwindows/

Oculus, V. R. (2014). *Oculus Rift*. Retrieved September 22, 2015, from http://www.oculusvr.com/

Pausch, R., Burnette, T., Brockway, D., & Weiblen, M. E. (1995). Navigation and locomotion in virtual worlds via flight into hand-held miniatures. In *Proceedings of the 22nd annual conference on Computer graphics and interactive techniques - SIGGRAPH '95* (pp. 399–400). New York: ACM Press. doi:10.1145/218380.218495

Razzaque, S., Kohn, Z., & Whitton, M. (2001). Redirected Walking (short paper presentation). In *Proceedings of EUROGRAPHICS 2001*. Manchester, UK: The European Association for Computer Graphics.

Roussou, M. (2002). Virtual heritage: from the research lab to the broad public. In F. Niccolucci (Ed.), *Virtual Archaeology: Proceedings of the VAST 2000 Euroconference* (pp. 93–101). Arezzo, Italy: Archaeopress Oxford.

Roussou, M. (2007). The Components of Engagement in Virtual Heritage Environments. In Y. Kalay, T. Kvan, & J. Affleck (Eds.), *New Heritage, New Media and Cultural Heritage* (pp. 225–241). London, UK: Routledge - Taylor and Francis Group; doi:10.4324/9780203937884

Sarah Kenderdine. (2012a). Pure Land Augmented Reality Edition. *Alive Lab, City University of Hong Kong*. Retrieved May 18, 2015, from http://alive.scm.cityu.edu.hk/projects/alive/pure-land-ii-2012/

Sarah Kenderdine. (2012b). Pure Land: Inside the Mogao Grottoes at Dunhuang. *Alive Lab, City University of Hong Kong*. Retrieved May 18, 2015, from http://alive.scm.cityu.edu.hk/projects/alive/pure-land-inside-the-mogao-grottoes-at-dunhuang-2012/

Sarah Kenderdine. (2013). "Pure Land": Inhabiting the Mogao Caves at Dunhuang. *Curator: The Museum Journal, 56* (2), 199–218. doi:10.1111/cura.12020

Senztech. (2012). *Virtual Reality let Users Walk in Rotating Sphere*. Retrieved September 22, 2015, from http://www.senztech.cc/shownews.aspx?newid=28

Suma, E. a., Bruder, G., Steinicke, F., Krum, D. M., & Bolas, M. (2012). A taxonomy for deploying redirection techniques in immersive virtual environments. In Proceedings - IEEE Virtual Reality (pp. 43–46). IEEE. doi:10.1109/VR.2012.6180877

Tan, B., & Rahaman, H. (2009). Virtual Heritage : Reality and Criticism. In T. Tidafi & T. Dorta (Eds.), *CAAD Futures 2009: Joining languages, cultures and visions* (pp. 143–156). Montreal, Canada: Les Presses de l'Université de Montréal.

Thwaites, H. (2013). Visual Heritage in the Digital Age. In E. Ch'ng, V. Gaffney, & H. Chapman (Eds.), *Springer Series on Cultural Computing* (pp. 327–348). London, UK: Springer; doi:10.1007/978-1-4471-5535-5

Usoh, M., Arthur, K., Whitton, M. C., Bastos, R., Steed, A., Slater, M., & Brooks, F. P. (1999). Walking > walking-in-place > flying, in virtual environments. In *Proceedings of the 26th annual conference on Computer graphics and interactive techniques - SIGGRAPH '99* (pp. 359–364). New York, NY: ACM Press/Addison-Wesley Publishing Co. doi:10.1145/311535.311589

Virtuix. (2014). *Virtuix Omni*. Retrieved September 22, 2015, from http://www.virtuix.com/

Wallach, H. (2010). High-resolution photography at the Dunhuang grottoes: Northwestern University's role in the Mellon International Dunhuang Archive. In N. Agnew (Ed.), *Conservation of ancient sites on the Silk Road: Proceedings of the Second International Conference on the Conservation of Grotto Sites, Mogao Grottoes, Dunhuang, People's Republic of China* (pp. 259–261). Los Angeles, CA: The Getty Conservation Institute.

Wang, X. (2012). Future Dunhuang. *NODEM 2012 Hong Kong: Future Culture. Hong Kong*. Hong Kong, China: NODEM 2012. Retrieved September 22, 2015, from http://repo.nodem.org/?objectId=23

WizDish. (2008). *ROVR*. Retrieved September 21, 2015, from http://www.wizdish.com/

KEY TERMS AND DEFINITIONS

3D Scanning: 3D scanning is the process of capturing digital information about the shape of an object with equipment that uses a laser or light to measure the distance between the scanner and the object.

Cave 220: One of the 750 caves at the Mogao Grottoes at Dunhuang. The cave is particularly known for its early Tang murals and permanently closed to the public.

Full-Body Immersive Virtual Reality: An engrossing total environment that provides the perception of being physically present in a non-physical world.

Head-Mounted Display: Head-mounted displays usually consist of a pair of goggles or a full helmet with a screen in front of each eye displaying a stereoscopic image and, therefore, providing the user with a three-dimensional view into a virtual world. Also, most Head Mounted Displays include tracking systems to make the virtual world respond to head movements.

Kinect: A low-cost depth and motion sensing input device.

Locomotion: The ability to move from one place to another.

Mogao Grottoes at Dunhuang: A UNESCO World Heritage site located in the Gansu Province, north-western China. The Grottoes consist of 750 caves; 492 with mural paintings that have been hewn on five levels into an escarpment in the desert. In total, there are 45,000 square meters of murals and more than 2000 painted clay figures.

ENDNOTES

[1]   The Dunhuang Research Academy website is primarily in Chinese (http://www.dha.ac.cn/) with a more limited English version (http://en.dha.ac.cn).

[2]   See for example The Getty Conservation Institute, *Wall Painting at Mogao Grottoes* (http://www.getty.edu/conservation/our_projects/field_projects/mogao/) and previous sand dune stabilization projects *Site Conservation at the Mogao and Yungang Grottoes (1990-1995)* (http://www.getty.edu/conservation/our_projects/field_projects/sitecon/index.html).

[3]   See for example, Wallach, H. 2004. High-Resolution Photography at the Dunhuang Grottoes: Northwestern University's Role in the Mellon International Dunhuang Archive. In *Ancient Sites on the Silk Road: Proceedings of the Second International Conference on the Conservation of Grotto Sites*. Ed. N. Agnew. Los Angeles: The Getty Conservation Institute.

[4]   The Mellon International Dunhuang Archive (MIDA), component of the ARTstor Digital Library, funded by the Mellon Foundation (http://www.artstor.org/what-is-artstor/w-html/col-mellon-dunhuang.shtml).

[5]   Cyark Foundation (http://archive.cyark.org/)

[6]   International Dunhuang Project (http://idp.bl.uk/).

[7]   The Dunhuang Mogao Cave Paintings Digitization Project Plan is set out as a key program for the nation. See Digital Centre's. Introduction to the digitization of the wall paintings at Dunhuang, Dunhuang Academy. April 30 2010. (http://public.dha.ac.cn/content.aspx?id=260848498520).

[8]   Katie Hunt, 2013. Buddhas in 3-D: Technology and the battle to preserve Asia's heritage. CNN January 15 2013 (http://edition.cnn.com/2013/01/15/world/asia/china-digital-caves/index.html?hpt=hp_c5)

[9]   Virtual heritage examines the intersection of cultural heritage research, documentation, and interpretation as it is mediated through the techniques and modalities of virtual reality. It is a process of visualization. The term 'virtual heritage' is generally accepted to mean: virtual reality (specifically 3D and 4D computational and computer graphics systems that support real-time, immersive, and interactive operations) employed for the presentation, preservation, conservation, and documentation of natural and cultural heritage. 'Virtual heritage' is distinguished by its preoccupation with replication or facsimile and, reconstruction, or recreation.

APPENDIX

Figure 11. Oneway ANOVA, highlighted rows represent statistical significance

		N	Mean	Std. Deviation	Std. Error	95% Confidence Interval for Mean		Minimum	Maximum	Sig
						Lower Bound	Upper Bound			
Level of experience with electronic games	Male	30	6.633	2.8585	.5219	5.566	7.701	.0	10.0	
	Female	11	3.273	1.9540	.5892	1.960	4.585	.0	6.0	
	Total	41	5.732	3.0251	.4724	4.777	6.687	.0	10.0	0.001
Level of nausea experienced when playing computer games	Male	26	1.7308	1.84516	.36187	.9855	2.4760	.00	6.00	
	Female	10	1.5000	1.50923	.47726	.4204	2.5796	.00	5.00	
	Total	36	1.6667	1.74028	.29005	1.0778	2.2555	.00	6.00	0.727
Level of experience with virtual reality, where your view of the virtual world moves with your head.	Male	28	5.3929	3.14277	.59393	4.1742	6.6115	.00	10.00	
	Female	11	2.9091	3.33030	1.00412	.6718	5.1464	.00	8.00	
	Total	39	4.6923	3.34942	.53634	3.6066	5.7781	.00	10.00	0.035
Level of nausea experienced in virtual reality systems	Male	26	2.6923	2.47821	.48602	1.6913	3.6933	.00	8.00	
	Female	11	2.6364	2.69343	.81210	.8269	4.4458	.00	7.00	
	Total	37	2.6757	2.50615	.41201	1.8401	3.5113	.00	8.00	0.952
The virtual space felt like an extension to your own space.	Male	31	5.97	.912	.164	5.63	6.30	3	7	
	Female	11	4.64	1.120	.338	3.88	5.39	3	6	
	Total	42	5.62	1.125	.174	5.27	5.97	3	7	0.000
You felt disoriented as you moved.	Male	31	4.10	1.989	.357	3.37	4.83	1	7	
	Female	11	4.36	1.629	.491	3.27	5.46	1	7	
	Total	42	4.17	1.886	.291	3.58	4.75	1	7	0.692
The virtual environment felt natural.	Male	31	5.29	1.006	.181	4.92	5.66	3	7	
	Female	10	3.80	.919	.291	3.14	4.46	3	5	
	Total	41	4.93	1.170	.183	4.56	5.30	3	7	0.000
Your movements felt natural.	Male	30	5.27	1.015	.185	4.89	5.65	3	7	
	Female	11	3.55	1.635	.493	2.45	4.64	1	6	
	Total	41	4.80	1.418	.221	4.36	5.25	1	7	0.000
Compared to a real environment you found the virtual environment realistic.	Male	31	5.23	1.383	.248	4.72	5.73	2	7	
	Female	11	3.82	1.328	.400	2.93	4.71	2	6	
	Total	42	4.86	1.491	.230	4.39	5.32	2	7	0.006
You enjoyed the virtual environment.	Male	31	6.35	.877	.158	6.03	6.68	4	7	
	Female	11	6.00	1.000	.302	5.33	6.67	4	7	
	Total	42	6.26	.912	.141	5.98	6.55	4	7	0.273
You would not choose to use the platform again.	Male	31	2.84	2.311	.415	1.99	3.69	1	7	
	Female	11	2.55	1.440	.434	1.58	3.51	1	5	
	Total	42	2.76	2.105	.325	2.11	3.42	1	7	0.696
You would like to be able to see other virtual environments with this system.	Male	31	6.39	.761	.137	6.11	6.67	4	7	
	Female	11	6.55	.688	.207	6.08	7.01	5	7	
	Total	42	6.43	.737	.114	6.20	6.66	4	7	0.547
The hardware felt uncomfortable.	Male	31	3.97	1.581	.284	3.39	4.55	1	7	
	Female	11	4.00	1.183	.357	3.21	4.79	2	6	
	Total	42	3.98	1.473	.227	3.52	4.44	1	7	0.951
You did not feel disoriented during the virtual experience.	Male	29	4.69	1.815	.337	4.00	5.38	1	7	
	Female	11	3.09	1.758	.530	1.91	4.27	1	6	
	Total	40	4.25	1.918	.303	3.64	4.86	1	7	0.017
I wanted to continue to explore the virtual environment.	Male	31	6.10	.908	.163	5.76	6.43	4	7	
	Female	11	5.18	1.662	.501	4.06	6.30	3	7	
	Total	42	5.86	1.201	.185	5.48	6.23	3	7	0.028
My avatar reflected my own movements.	Male	31	4.42	1.432	.257	3.89	4.94	1	7	
	Female	11	4.36	1.912	.576	3.08	5.65	1	7	
	Total	42	4.40	1.547	.239	3.92	4.89	1	7	0.920
I identified with my avatar.	Male	31	4.03	1.449	.260	3.50	4.56	1	7	
	Female	11	3.27	1.348	.407	2.37	4.18	1	5	
	Total	42	3.83	1.447	.223	3.38	4.28	1	7	0.137
The avatar helped me to judge the dimensions of the virtual environment.	Male	31	4.90	1.535	.276	4.34	5.47	1	7	
	Female	11	4.09	1.758	.530	2.91	5.27	1	6	
	Total	42	4.69	1.615	.249	4.19	5.19	1	7	0.154

Chapter 5
The Rise of the Virtual Human

Wendy A. Powell
University of Portsmouth, UK

Natalie Corbett
University of Portsmouth, UK

Vaughan Powell
University of Portsmouth, UK

ABSTRACT

Virtual Humans are here to stay. From the voice in your satNav to Apple's "Siri", we are accustomed to engaging in some level of conversation with our technology, and it is rapidly becoming apparent that natural language interfaces have potential in a wide range of applications. Whilst audio-only communication has its place, most natural conversations take place face to face, and believable embodiment of virtual humans is the necessary next step for them to be fully integrated into our lives. Much progress has been made in the creation of relatable characters for film, but real-time facial animation presents a unique set of design challenges. This chapter examines the role of the virtual human, its history, and approaches to design and creation. It looks at ways in which they can be brought to life, interacting, assisting and learning. It concludes with a view into popular culture and perceptions of the future, where fact and fiction meet.

INTRODUCTION

With the rapid advances in technology in the past 40 years, the vision of the virtual human is coming closer to reality, with improvements in visual appearance, speech and emotion, and in the application of this into real-world settings. As can already be observed in pre-rendered animations, near-photorealism is now possible, with some avatars almost indistinguishable (Alexander, Rogers, Lambeth, Chiang & Debevec, 2009; Borshukov, Piponi, Larsen, Lewis & Tempelaar-Lietz, 2005). Although total realism not yet possible, many studies are working toward this goal, with even real-time avatars slowly becoming more and more realistic. This chapter introduces a range of virtual humans currently in development or being used in real-world interaction. The history of animated humans and the recent rapid advances are

DOI: 10.4018/978-1-5225-0016-2.ch005

discussed. The chapter will then examine some of the technical challenges involved in creating virtual humans, particularly with regards to facial expression and speech. Finally, the role of the virtual human in popular culture is explored, looking at fears and hopes for the future, and how perceptions are changing over time.

BACKGROUND: THE ROLE OF THE VIRTUAL HUMAN

This section will take a look at avatars already being used in real-life settings, interacting independently with users, learning and remembering information, and even assisting in the treatment of patients.

Avatars Who Interact

Since the early days of computing there has been a fascination with the concept of communication between computers and human beings. As early as 1950 Alan Turing raised the question of whether a computer could appear to think like a human (Turing, 1950), and even today the 'Turing Test' is considered to be a benchmark by which we measure the success of virtual humans. Whilst early work focused on text-based communication due to the poor quality of speech generation and animation, improvements in technology have raised our expectations to the point where we anticipate that a humanised avatar could pass the Turing test within the next generation.

Early research on avatar development and behaviour focused mainly on speech, with the eyes and the motion of the head receiving little attention. However, in a 2004 study, a group developed an avatar to interact with video feeds rather than directly with humans, watching and following movement in a variety of situations. The team used a neurobiological model of visual attention in order to create realistic avatar eye and head animation (Itti, Dhavale & Pighin, 2003). They postulated that this type of non-verbal communication was an essential part of human interaction, and aimed to recreate this digitally in the most realistic way possible, using a procedural, science based approach. A reflexive approach was used to guide the avatars attention toward visual targets, in the form of either video recordings or video game output. Automatically generated eye blinks were added to aid realism, as well as accurate deformation of the facial tissue during movement, and a photorealistic facial model. Although the avatar was not always human-like in its point of focus, results of this early work showed potential, in using attention-directed behaviour to enhance the realism of a virtual human.

More recent work saw the development of virtual twins Ada and Grace (Figure 1), who were deployed in a museum to interact with each other and with visitors using both verbal and non-verbal communication (Swartout et al., 2010).

To communicate with the characters, the operator could push a button then speak into a microphone. The audio was then sent to an automatic speech recogniser (ASR), which translated the speech into text, sending this on to a language understanding module. An algorithm used the text to select an appropriate response for the characters to use. The characters have a set of about 400 responses to draw from, with dialogue management software ensuring that responses are not repeated. Animation sequences were also created and stored, with these being called upon at the same time as the responses, with the relevant animations being called upon dependent on the response. Viewing video footage of Ada and Grace being posed questions by museum visitors (USC ICT, 2010), it can be seen that there is rapid retrieval of responses with appropriate answers being given to visitors. However, the animation is clearly constrained

Figure 1. Virtual twins Ada and Grace act as museum guides
© *USC Institute for Creative Technologies. Used with permission.*

by the demands of real-time performance, with repetition of a small gesture set and relatively low fidelity facial performance and, partciularly in the synchronisation of mouth movements to speech elements. The lack of movement of the facial musculature when speaking, results in a somewhat robotic effect. As can be seen within the Digital Emily project (Alexander, et.al., 2009), the USC ICT is more than capable of creating incredibly lifelike animations, with their light stage also used to great effect in many films (Debevec, n.d.). However, there does seem to be a trade-off between the achievement of high graphical fidelity, and the ability to work in real-time, with a distinct drop in graphical fidelity when increasing the demand of real-time processes. However, as technology improves and graphical rendering capabilities increase then we are likely to see rapid improvements in this visual fidelity.

Also emerging from USC ICT is the virtual support agent or 'SimCoach' (Figure 2), providing information and support for military personnel and their families (Rizzo et al., 2011). The user will be able to select from a gallery the character that they feel most comfortable talking with. The characters will use speech, gesture and emotion to introduce the system to the user, as well as asking questions about the user's history and medical concerns in order to provide the right kind of support. A prototype SimCoach has been deployed on a veterans website (Brave Heart Veterans, n,d.). At the time of writing, interaction was limited to text-based questioning, and responses are limited and somewhat lacking in visual fidelity. Nevertheless, it is already demonstrating the potential to provide support and advice via a humanised interface.

Researchers in the UK are developing the RITA avatar (Figure 3), which is designed to interact with older adults. Although only in early stages of development at the time of writing, RITA demonstrates a

Figure 2. SimCoach provides information and support for military personnel.
© *USC Institute for Creative Technologies. Used with permission.*

significantly higher level of visual fidelity and realism than many earlier real-time avatars. The proto-type uses a library of pre-recorded speech segments and blend-shape animation to communicate with realistic emotional expression. Vision-based facial and emotion recognition software identifies known users and interprets their current emotional state, triggering responses which vary according to both the mood and identity of the user. Technology still needs to advance considerably in order to support the full planned functionality of RITA (RITA, n.d.)., but nevertheless, it gives us a glimpse of the future potential of nearly-real virtual humans.

Whilst the ability of a virtual human to hold a conversation is an impressive achievement, it is still of relatively limited application without some further purpose. Conversational agents are deployed in many areas, from marketing websites through to exhibition guides, but development has not stopped here. More recent development is bringing us intelligent agents who teach, learn, and even care for people.

Avatars Who Help

An example of a successful avatar created for use within the field of education, although not a true ex-ample of a virtual human, comes in the form of 'Steve' (Soar Training Expert for Virtual Environments), an avatar used for training Navy personnel to operate a high-pressure air compressor (HPAC) on board a ship (Johnson & Rickel, 1997). Steve consists of a virtual hand, inhabiting a virtual representation of a ship, complete with the HPAC that students must learn to operate. The students are allowed a 3D view of this world through use of a head mounted camera, interacting with either a 3D mouse or data gloves.

Figure 3. The RITA avatar, designed to support older adults
© 2014, University of Portsmouth. Used with permission.

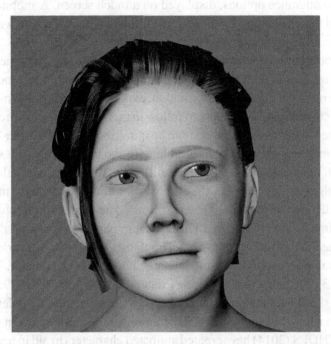

Steve was designed to help students learn to perform tasks such as operating the HPAC, and repairing equipment, but also to enable them to apply these procedures to a variety of situations, by understanding the rationale behind each step. Steve was given the ability to manipulate and point at objects to help students, as well as constantly monitoring the environment. For demonstrating or monitoring tasks, Steve is equipped with a pre-programmed knowledge of tasks in the form of hierarchical plans, learning the processes required to complete each task. Steve can be switched between monitoring and demonstration modes, allowing for a smooth and flexible student and tutor relationship in which learning can take place at the pace of each individual. Although not a full virtual human, the learning algorithms used in Steve's design have the potential to be used in other avatar applications, particularly as the sophistication of the technology increases.

More recently, a group researchers has been developing virtual nurses to aid in the communication of discharge information to patients with low health literacy skills (Bickmore, Pfeifer & Jack, 2009). Health literacy refers to the ability to understand healthcare information, and to apply this understanding to health situations. The lack of understanding of discharge information can lead to patients being readmitted to hospital after not taking medication correctly, or not understanding side effects. The greatest aid to those with low health literacy seems to be in face-to-face communication, used in conjunction with written instructions, allowing the patient to ask questions, and for the nurse to elaborate on information. The use of this delivery in the form of a virtual nurse is beneficial, as it allows the patient to take as much time as they need, without feeling that they are wasting anyone's time, something which seems to be a recurrent feature in the use of avatars within the healthcare sector (Rizzo et al., 2011). Two virtual nurses were created, with the head and torso displayed for use in the system. These nurses were very stylised, and spoke using a synthetic voice, with scripted dialogue. Animation was also implemented for lip sync, and to allow the hands of the nurse to point at relevant information. Interaction for the patient was in the form of the selection of utterance options, displayed on a touch screen. A mobile kiosk containing the patient information and the virtual nurse was wheeled into the patient's room, with the patient then left alone to conduct their conversation (Figure 4).

The nurse could be programmed with information about the patient, calling them by name, and firstly asking a few questions relating to their interests, in order for the patient to feel more at ease. The virtual nurse would then move on to the discharge information, explaining each point whilst pointing at relevant parts of the leaflet, and encouraging the patient to follow in their paper copy. The results of the study were largely positive, with the virtual nurse tested on both hospitalised and non-hospitalised participants. 92% of the participants claimed that they felt comfortable with the nurse, with 70% stating that they either preferred speaking with the virtual nurse, or were indifferent. When dealing with doctors and nurses, it may often be the case that patients feel that they are wasting time, particularly in the elderly, who may put off going to their GP or to the hospital because of this. The results of this study support the notion that people like, and often prefer, talking to a virtual avatar, particularly within the healthcare sector.

Avatars within the healthcare industry have been implemented for use in a variety of settings, ranging from communication training for children with autism (Chops, 2014; Kandalaft, Didehbani, Krawczyk, Allen & Chapman, 2013), to treatment of speaking (Slater, Pertaub & Steed, 1999; Kang, Brinkman, van Riemsdijk & Neerincx, 2011), and the treatment of post-traumatic stress disorder (Rizzo et al., 2011).

Autistic children often have difficulty in social communication, and may find it easier to communicate with a virtual human. CHOPS (2014) have created animated characters to aid in treating autistic children. The children can either interact with the animated character, with a speech pathologist used to reply to the children in real-time, through the animated character, or learn to control the animations themselves.

Figure 4. Virtual nurse assisting patient to understand information leaflet
© 2008, Northeastern University, Boston. Used with permission.

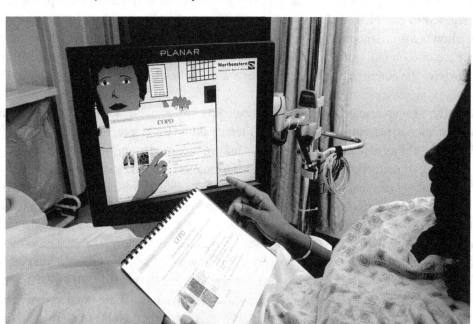

The character can be used by therapists in a number of ways, for example, to tell stories, teach lessons, and demonstrate facial expressions or body language. As the avatars used are far less threatening for a child with autism than a real person, the student can remain engaged and will be much more open to learning new concepts. The novelty of the animated characters can also aid in keeping their attention for a longer period of time.

Another example of the use of avatars to aid in the treatment of Autism is through the use of the online virtual-reality world, 'Second-life.' Researchers at the University of Texas Centre for Brain Health, paired clinicians with Autism patients within the Second-life world to deliver therapy (Kandalaft, Didehbani, Krawczyk, Allen & Chapman, 2013). The study aimed to enhance the social skills, social cognition and social functioning among eight young adults diagnosed with high functioning autism. Virtual-reality therapy for Autism patients can be beneficial, as social interactions can be simulated and easily repeated, without fear of mistakes or rejections and with lower levels of stress. Avatars were created to resemble each of the participants within the study as well as the coach involved. After logging into the system for each session, participants would each be instructed to go to a specific location to meet a specific person with whom they would be interacting. This person would be in the form of another clinician, playing the part of a person, such as a potential employer delivering an interview, or a confrontational roommate. The participant would then take part in the selected interaction, with the coach remotely observing, taking notes on the social objectives of the participants performance. After the interaction had taken place, the participant would then meet with the virtual coach to discuss performance, receiving feedback from the coach, which they would then attempt to implement in a second attempt at the same interaction. The results of this study found largely positive feedback among participants, with all stating that they found the sessions enjoyable, and reporting social benefits, such as participating more within social situations and finding it easier to see things from other people's perspectives. However, the very small sample size, as well as the lack of a control group, limits the generalisation of the study. The use of only participants from the high functioning end of the autistic spectrum also means that this study may not be applicable to a very wide range of people within other parts of the autistic spectrum. However, the findings are of interest, and do present the idea that virtual-reality, and virtual avatars can be of benefit within the general healthcare system when used alongside real life medical practitioners, and should not be overlooked within this sector.

Virtual-reality has also proved useful within in the treatment of phobias, providing a safe, non-threatening environment, in which clinicians can have complete control over the stimulus and situation, allowing patients to take therapy at their own pace, and feel more secure than in a real-life phobia inducing situation. One such study aimed to aid in the treatment of public speaking anxiety (Slater et al, 1999). This study aimed to utilise a virtual environment occupied with virtual avatars to explore their effectiveness in psychotherapy for social phobias. To create the environment in which the experiment would take place, researchers constructed a virtual seminar room, matching the one in which participants met with the researchers and completed questionnaires. The virtual seminar room was populated with an audience of eight avatars, placed in a semicircle to face the speaker. The avatars were programmed to display six primary facial expressions, the same as those outlined within Ekman's 'Unmasking the Face' (Ekman & Friesen, 1975), as well as yawns, sleepy faces, and random autonomous actions such as twitches, blinks and nods. Avatars also were programmed with the ability to stand up, clap, and walk out of the seminar room. To increase the realism of the avatars, an unseen operator would trigger the audience responses at key moments during the experiment. Participants were asked to give a prepared talk three times, receiving one positive reaction from the avatars, one negative response, and one mixed.

Interestingly, the study found that the level of interest of the audience was important, and this influenced the impact of the positive or negative response, even though the audience consisted of relatively low fidelity avatars. Although this was a fairly early study in the field, it does indicate that virtual humans may be of use in treating social phobia and presentation anxiety.

A more recent study into the therapy of anxiety disorders is the 2011 study by Kang et al. (2011). This study, although not yet completed, aims to use an internet-delivered system to treat multiple patients through the use of exposure therapy, a type of therapy in which the patient is exposed to the cause of their anxiety (c.f. Parsons & Rizzo, 2008). The project is a four year research plan, which once complete, will provide an internet-delivered therapy system, with a virtual therapist implemented who will monitor the patient, making adjustments to the virtual-reality scenario, changing the level of exposure relative to the patients levels of anxiety. The project in its current stage will only focus on social anxiety, within a public speaking scenario, much like the study of Slater et al (1999). The avatars used within this project, as with the aforementioned study, will take the form of members of an audience, programmed to react to the participant speaking. They will also be designed to portray four different attitudes; interested, neutral, bored, and critical. Each avatar will also vary in its personality and physical state, meaning that each individual avatar should be able to behave autonomously, reacting to both the perception of the environment, and its own mental and physical state. In order to test the effectiveness of the virtual avatars, the project proposes three control methods, the first being the autonomous behaviour already outlined. The second control method will be a scripted method, in which the reference of the real audience filmed, will be replicated exactly for each of the avatars. The final control method will be one of random control, in which avatars will choose a completely random set of behaviours, in no way connected to their environment. Although this project is not yet complete, the audience design is certainly moving towards more realistic virtual humans, with dynamically generated behaviour based upon individual programmed personalities.

Finally, at the cutting edge of development of virtual healthcare agents, are projects creating virtual humans capable of understanding patients and detecting real-time indicators of physical or emotional health.

A collaboration between USC IT and the Defence Advanced Research Projects Agency (DARPA) aims to create a virtual agent capable of identifying indicators of psychological distress, in order to provide healthcare support for military personnel and their families (Figure 5). The system should eventually, be able to monitor users over weeks and months to monitor change, working closely with real life healthcare professionals if psychological disorders are seen to be present (DeVault et al., 2014; Morbini et al., 2014). The systems used within this research consist of two core components. The first is 'Multisense', which is used for the automatic tracking and analysis of facial expression, body posture, acoustic features, linguistic patterns and high level behaviour descriptors such as fidgeting. This system directly communicates with the virtual human, 'SimSensei'. This human platform is able to process all of the signals sent from the Multisense, providing real-time reactions to the user, through speech and gesture.

For the development of this virtual human, whom the researchers named 'Ellie', three design goals were set. The user should be comfortable talking to Ellie, the system should be sensitive to non-verbal behaviour displayed by the user, and should generate appropriate non-verbal behaviour in response. This should all take place within a 15-25 minute interview, in which the user should remain engaged and interested in communicating with Ellie. Data has been extracted from numerous interviews between a real psychologist and patient, and verbal and non-verbal behaviours identified and quantified. Based on this data, the team have begun to create a system that will enable Ellie to operate automatically and

Figure 5. 'Ellie' is being developed to provide healthcare support to military personnel and their families. © *USC Institute for Creative Technologies. Used with permission.*

autonomously. In order to do this, specific modules were implemented into the mulitsense, which all communicate with one another, in order to dictate how Ellie should behave and react. These modules currently include; 3D head position and facial tracking, expression analysis, gaze direction and audio analysis. The multisense uses all of these signals, measuring factors such as smile intensity, in order to inform the other modules of the SimSensei, which are used to drive Ellie. These modules include the generation of non-verbal behaviour, realization and rendering.

In order to animate Ellie, reference footage of real clinicians was used to create a series of key frame animations for Ellie to draw from. These were placed into a program called Cerebella, which can be programmed to take into account factors such as characters personality, culture, gender and body type to drive animation.

Ellie currently has the ability to use 100 fixed utterances, with 60 top level interview questions. Elllie's speech is pre-recorded, rather than generated, which does seem to give a more realistic result then synthetic speech generation. In order to detect and process user speech, the system used a variety of different software implemented within the speech recognition module, similar to the processes used within the Ada and Grace study (Swartout et al., 2010), although more complex. These systems were not only able to process human speech, but able to detect the emotion within the speech, and select an appropriate response in real time. Full details of the dialogue processing systems used can be found in Morbini et al., (2014).

Although the majority of participants to date claimed to have felt comfortable with Ellie, most felt that she didn't understand their non-verbal behaviour, preferring speaking to the Ellie who was controlled by the researchers. Given the early stage of development, these results are unsurprising; however do give promise to the future development of this system. From viewing a video of Ellie speaking with participants (USC ICT, 2013), it can be observed that the system appears to display a high level of intelligence. However, the video gives no indication as to whether the system is running autonomously or whether the avatar is being controlled, limiting any conclusions to be drawn as to the effectiveness of the automated system. The animation of the avatar itself is somewhat lacking in fidelity, an issue which still plagues most real-time virtual humans, being a trade-off between realism and system performance. Nevertheless, the avatar is seen to accurately interpret body language and emotion of the two participants, reacting appropriately, in a similar manner to a real life therapist, with reassuring nodding motions, and knowing when to respond once the user had finished speaking. Ellie does demonstrate the potential for future deployment of caring virtual humans, with technological advances only serving to improve the system, and allow for fully autonomous behaviour.

A UK-based early stage project with a long-term vision is developing a virtual human which is designed to provide support, companionship and advocacy to older adults (RITA, n.d). The RITA avatar has been built using state-of-the art motion capture and animation techniques, with a design based on features which appear trustworthy and competent (Powell, Garner, Tonks & Lee, 2014) (Figure 6).

The system is designed to store personal, social and medical information, and to monitor health and emotional state in real-time, in order to provide tailored companionship and support. It will link with body-worn and smart-home sensors and also monitor activity and mood over time, identifying early warnings of deteriorating physical or mental health, and accessing appropriate support and intervention.

Although extensive further development is needed to fully realise the vision of projects such as RITA and SimSensei, it is clear that virtual carer-givers are likely to play a part in our future healthcare. However, to create virtual humans which are fully accepted into our daily lives requires pushing the boundaries of technology, in order to achieve realism in both behaviour and appearance. The development of Artificial Intelligence (AI) is being driven by demands in a wide variety of application areas, and the need for the humanised interfaces to AI is increasingly apparent. The next section of this chapter will explore at the technical development of expressive virtual humans, from ancient history to the present day.

Figure 6. RITA is designed to appear trustworthy and competent.
© 2014, University of Portsmouth. Used with permission.

THE DAWN OF THE VIRTUAL HUMAN

The Study of Facial Expression

Facial expression is key to our communication with each other, and is an area that has been studied since as early as the 17th century. The earliest know writer on the subject of expression, as well as the use of expression for the deaf, was the medical practitioner John Bulwer, who was the first to record that communication could come by way of movement, rather than just speech, naming this form of gesture, the "Universall language of Humane nature" (Bulwer, 1649). However, it was Charles Darwin who was the first to detail why and how emotional expression is formed, and suggested that expression is universal, expressed the same regardless of culture or background, being a product of evolution and biology (Darwin, 1872). Darwin wrote at length about the basic principles of expression, including the muscles which are activated during expression of each emotion.

In Ekman and Friesen's book 'Unmasking the Face' (1975), it was revealed, through scientific study, that Darwin was in part correct, with six expressions found to be universal. These expressions are; surprise, fear, disgust, anger, happiness and sadness, and many modern studies directly use these six emotions as basis for creating facial animation. Darwin's work, as well as the research of Ekman & Friesan, provides a valuable theoretical underpinning to facial animation, particularly when building a muscle based facial system. The universal rules of which muscles work during each of the emotions, can be applied directly to an animated model. Ekman and Friesen later went on to create a 'Facial Action Coding System', as a way to categorise the physical expression of emotions (Ekman & Friesen, 1978). The Facial Action Coding System, or FACS, is an anatomically based system for the measurement of all visual facial movements. This facial activity is described upon the basis of 44 unique action units (AUs), as well as including categories of head and eye movements and positions. Each action unit has a designated numeric code, with the muscle groups involved in each action linked to each of the AUs. Whilst FACS is anatomically based, a one to one correspondence does not exist between the muscle groups and the AUs, with any given muscle acting in different ways or contracting in different regions to produce visibly different actions. For example, contraction of the medial position of the Frontalis muscle will result in a raise of the inner corners of the eyebrow, whilst a contraction of the lateral portion of this muscle will raise the outer brow. The use of the coding procedures as outlined in FACS also allows for the coding of the intensity of each facial action unit. This is of particular use in animation, whereby varying degrees of emotion will need to be portrayed dependent on the character or situation, and is a system widely used and referenced today.

Although the study of the human face with regards to expression and emotion has ancient beginnings, the application of this understanding to computer based facial modeling, expression and animation is fairly new, first appearing in the early 1970's (Parke, 1972). With the technology to create animations in its relative infancy, early attempts at facial animations were fairly basic by today's standards. However, the techniques and processes used have been adapted and improved, directly influencing the high quality animations that we see today.

Early Examples of Animation

The first method of animating, before the use of computers, was via the use of hand drawings, portrayed in such a way as to give the impression of motion. Perhaps the oldest animation was found on a 5,200 year old bowl in Iran. The bowl had drawings of a goat on it, which when spun, gave the impression of the goat jumping to retrieve leaves from a tree (Ball, 2008). Many centuries later, Georges Melies, who was a professional magician by training, was one of the first great visual effects artists, using tricks during filming to create animation on top of live action from 1896 to 1912. However, it was in 1928, when Disney released 'Steamboat Willie' the first ever hand drawn cartoon animation with synchronised sound, which saw the birth of modern day animation production (The Museum of Modern Art, n.d.).

Computer-based facial animation came somewhat later, with Parke creating one of the first examples in 1972, generating an animated sequence of a head changing expressions, using a 250 polygon basic mesh, and using dots on facial photographs as references for creating the animated expressions (Parke, 1972). By 1988, a more sophisticated approach was seen, with 'Mike the Talking Head' being animated in real-time by puppeteers (Robertson, 1988). 'Mike' was created using data scanned from a real actor to create a polygon mesh, with software algorithms created to interpolate between phonemes of speech.

In the same year that 'Mike the Talking Head' was created, Jim Henson Productions brought out their own real time animation solution in the form of 'Waldo C Graphic' (Walters 1989). Waldo got his name from the device used to control him, a Waldo. This was a type of input device which consisted of an upper and lower jaw, to control the characters mouth, and an arm, which controlled the movement, similar to the technology used to control Mike. Waldo was used by Jim Henson Productions to perform in real time, in a concert with real puppets, appearing in the TV series The Jim Henson Hour until 1992 (IMDb, n.d). The Waldo type of device used to control animation was a rather popular choice in the early days of animation, particularly for use in real time, with examples of this seen through until the 90's (SimGraphics, n.d; Robertson, 1992). This popularity is probably due to the ease of the device allowing an animator to have full control of the character without the need to be physically sat at a computer. The use of a Waldo is rare now, with computers now able to be drive real-time animation without the need for a puppeteer.

The early 1990's saw the introduction of 'Performance Driven Facial Animation' (Williams, 1990). Using a more advanced system of the earlier work of Parke (1972), Williams used motion tracking via the use of physical markers to track the motion of an actor's face making different expressions, using this data to drive animation of a 3D model. Williams was the first to use performance to directly drive animation in this way, and paved the way for motion captured facial animation, with the same marker based motion techniques still in use today. Parallel development saw the introduction of physically-based facial models in the early 1990's. These were based on Ekman's FACS system with an anatomically based muscle system used to control facial movement (Terzopoulos & Waters, 1990). To animate the facial model, 2D static images from a video of a real actor were taken, with an algorithm applied to track the facial features of each image, and apply these in 3D to the model.

During these early years of computerised facial animation, processing constraints restricted the complexity of the 3D models, resulting in characters which appeared blocky and unrealistic. In the early 70's, most standard computers came equipped with just 4Kbs of memory, using 8 bit graphics. Floppy Disks were invented in 1971, with these used for external storage of up to 250Mb of data up until 2000, when the 8Mb memory stick was introduced. In comparison, a standard modern desktop computer will come equipped with 500GB of memory and a graphics card supporting HD video at around 250 bits. These exponential improvements in computer processing power and dedicated graphics processors are able to support very complex digital meshes, enabling the creation of characters which at times are almost indistinguishable from real humans (Alexander, Rogers, Lambeth, Chiang & Debevec, 2009; Borshukov, Piponi, Larsen, Lewis & Tempelaar-Lietz, 2005). In parallel with this development, advances in

Artificial Intelligence software techniques have enabled computers to learn, to make semi-autonomous decisions, and to communicate independently to humans, responding to speech and emotion (Rizzo et al., 2011; DeVault et al., 2014). These Virtual Humans are now being used in a variety of settings, from the entertainment industry through to marketing and health-care.

Whilst it is generally considered that the goal of virtual human design is for every-increasing realism, near-realistic avatars can actually be less acceptable than more stylised offerings, a phenomenon known as the 'Uncanny Valley' (Figure 7).

The Uncanny Valley

The 'Uncanny Valley' was first described by Mori (1970). His theory suggest that as a robot (or an avatar) becomes more realistic it is more acceptable, until it approaches a level of near-realism, at which point we begin to notice imperfections, finding these unsettling (MacDorman, Green, Ho & Koch, 2009). This feeling is heightened when movement is added, as indicated by Mori. If a virtual human becomes realistic enough, it emerges from the 'Uncanny Valley' and can be fully accepted. In fact, our perception and acceptance of virtual humans is somewhat more complex than first postulated by Mori, with factors such as facial proportion, texture, detail and believability of movement all playing a role (MacDorman, et. al., 2009; Qiao & Eglin, 2011). The 'Uncanny Valley' graph (Figure 7) proposed by Mori and reinforced by others since, in fields ranging from robotics to CGI, should be considered a conceptual model

Figure 7. The Uncanny Valley
Mori, 1970.

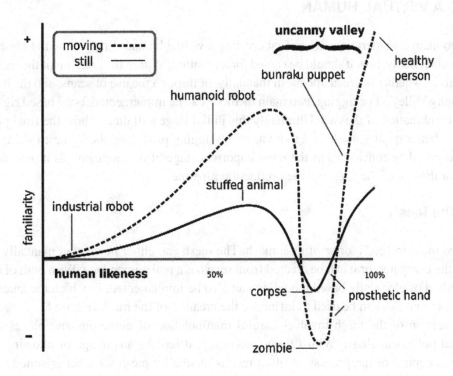

only. It does not imply any precise values, predict any absolute positions of avatar characteristics, nor give a magnitude of the axes and does not define points on its distribution, nor has it been empirically validated. Nevertheless, conceptually it is generally accepted within its respected disciplines even though such a simplified model is unlikely to really convey the nuances of human emotional reaction to the range of possible integrated characteristics that make up a complex avatar that aspires to be acceptable and lifelike (Tinwell & Grimshaw, 2009). Any deviation or discrepancy in any given characteristic, especially when others are reasonable might be enough to generate an uncanny response. The use of real time motion capture technology for both body movement and capturing real facial expressions has the potential to reduce the discrepancy and discord often perceived in moving characters as reported by Mori. Nevertheless a near veridical detail of subtle movements, skin detail and lighting, as aspired towards by projects such as digital Emily (Alexander et. al. 2009) are as yet far from commonplace and highly demanding. Whilst incongruities remain, the human perception of virtual humans may continue to suffer moments of discord and disengagement, when some element or another does not quite match our expectations or experience and as such, the 'Uncanny Valley' whilst no longer an insurmountable barrier to virtual human acceptance, certainly remains a problematic challenge and a potential pitfall.

Whilst pre-rendered animation produces the highest fidelity results, it is the potential of real-time dynamic animation which is currently of great interest for individualised interactions across a wide range of applications, and this will be the main focus of this chapter. The following sections will address the state-of-the -art techniques for the creation of the virtual human, including building the facial mesh, methods of motion capture and animation, inclusion of speech and emotion, and interactivity.

BUILDING A VIRTUAL HUMAN

There are two main considerations when first creating a virtual human; firstly, how the mesh itself will be created, and secondly, how it should be rigged for animation. Within the creation of the mesh are such considerations as whether to create the mesh manually, or through the use of scans, and the implications of the "Uncanny Valley". For rigging, two main methods can be implemented, bone based rigging, blend shapes, or a combination of the two. Ultimately this initial stage will dictate how the final product will appear, with a better quality mesh, and more accurate rigging producing the highest fidelity of animation, thus this could be considered as the most important stage of development, as it provides the core foundation for the rest of the stages of the production pipeline.

Creating the Mesh

There are two main methods for creating a mesh. The mesh can either be created manually within the 3D space of the computer, or it can be created from scans of a real human face. With both of these techniques, a method of physically based modeling can also be implemented, in which the anatomy of the facial tissue and muscles can be used to influence the creation of the mesh (Figure 8).

Manual creation of the mesh involves careful manipulation of numerous flat planes to create a 3-dimensional polygonal shape. Whilst time-consuming, it has the advantage of allowing the digital artist complete control of the process. It often results in smaller mesh size, better suited to real-time

Figure 8. A base mesh is created in 3D modelling sofware prior to rigging and animation
© 2014, University of Portsmouth. Used with permission.

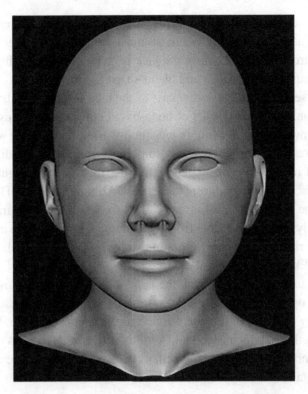

performance, and allowing complete customisation of the appearance of the face. However, some of the fine details of facial anatomy are difficult to reproduce using manual techniques, which can reduce the visual realism of the resultant avatar.

Alternatively, facial scans can be taken of a real human and the data used to reconstruct the face within the digital space. This method is faster and generally results in a much higher fidelity avatar. However, it tends to result in a much bigger mesh, less suited to real-time performance, and the final appearance of the avatar is constrained by the anatomy of the human used for data capture. In addition, the equipment required for high-definition facial capture may be prohibitively expensive, and produce more than a Gigabyte of data every second.

In order to create a virtual human which is not only realistic in its static form, but also in dynamic expression, the underlying anatomy of the face should be taken into account. Physically based model-ling places the polygons of the facial mesh in such a way as to mimic the layout of the underlying facial musculature seen (Terzopoulos & Waters, 1990), allowing for more accurate deformation of the mesh. However, this level of detail can result in a polygon count of millions, making it less suited to real-time animation. Nevertheless, physically based modelling can result in a very high level of visual fidelity (e.g. Sifakis, Selle, Robinson-Mosher & Fedkiw, 2006).

Rigging the Mesh

A 3D mesh is like a clay sculpture - it can be further moulded, but creating real-time animation would be extremely difficult. Therefore the sculpted mesh must be linked to a digital skeleton (rig), with a system of joints and controls in order to move the face from pose to pose. The two main systems used for rigging a virtual human are bone-based and blend-shape based.

Bones are generally used to control specific parts of the face such as eyelids and jaw. Bones are relatively simple to rig and animate, and one set of bone-based controls can be used to animate a number of different face types. However, facial animation using just bones can appear wooden and emotionless.

Blendshapes are animation tools which allow smooth morphing of one digital mesh into another, giving the appearance of natural movement. These blendshapes can be weighted, with more than one blendshape influencing facial geometry during movement. Although the use of blendshapes adds to both the polygon count and the processing load, it does allow for much more natural facial expression, and can approach a level nearly indistinguishable from a real human. For real-time animation, a combination of bone and blend-shape rigging gives the optimum results, with the blend-shapes being based around Ekman's FACS system (Ekman & Friesen, 1978).

With the virtual human created and rigged, the next stage in the process is how the avatar is to be animated. The two main options for this stage are animating by hand, or to use video recording, either as reference, or to directly drive the animation through use of motion capture. Within these options are a plethora of different methods, which each yield slightly differing variations of results. These options range from type, and number of cameras to be used, as well as lighting set-up, use of markers, tracking, and application of the data to the virtual human.

Lights, Camera, Action

In order to animate a virtual human, after the initial building phase is complete, many options can be considered. The use of video reference is common practice, either acting as a guide for hand animation, or to directly drive the animation through use of motion capture. The use of video as reference can also be used in a method called 'Rotoscoping', in which an animator will draw over video footage frame by frame to create the animation. This method dates back to the early days of Disney films, with animators directly drawing over video footage for such films as Peter Pan, Alice in Wonderland and Snow White. Rotoscoping is still a method in use today, and can be adapted for use in various situations.

However, hand animating is extremely time-consuming in order to achieve realistic results, and modern motion capture techniques can accelerate this process by an order of magnitude. We suggest that for the level of animation detail necessary for realistic facial expression, motion capture is currently best option, and this is the approach we will address in this section.

The three key considerations one must make when considering facial motion capture are lighting, camera type and placement, and facial tracking techniques. In addition, the data needs to be transferred to the mesh (re-targeting).

Lighting

Whilst not essential for facial motion capture, lighting can support and enhance the capture process, leading to better quality data and a more realistic animation.

Structured light techniques use projected light to cast a structured pattern of light onto the face to provide a detailed surface texture which aids in the tracking of motion (Bradley, Heidrich, Popa & Sheffer, 2010). This can be used instead of placing markers on the face, being less intrusive for the actor and requiring shorter setup times. However, high powered light beams can be a distraction for the actor, and reconstruction done in this way can suffer from a drop in precision, due to interleaving between the ambient illumination and the structured light (Bradley et al., 2010).

Uniform lighting allows a clear view of the face, with no shadows influencing the capture. This reduces 'noise' in the capture data, and results in a better quality of motion data for the animation (e.g. Bradley et al., 2010).

Light stages allow a programmed approach to lighting setup, allowing extremely precise control of the lighting during facial capture. A light stage may have over 150 lights placed around the actor (Alexander, et.al., 2013.).

Camera Set Up

In order to record facial performance, one or more cameras are needed, and the quality, number and layout of these cameras can have a significant impact on the quality of the final animation data (Figure 9).

Single camera capture will generally result in 2D data (unless structured light is used). However, due to the low cost and ease of use of single-camera setup, this is the approach of choice for many commercially available systems (e.g. Faceware Tech, Faceshift, Mixamo). This form of motion capture can be effective (e.g. Weise, Bouaziz, Li & Pauly, 2011), although the post-processing require to achieve high quality animation can be complex, and 2-dimensional capture may miss subtle facial movements, leading to a drop in visual fidelity.

Multiple camera setup on the other hand, allows 3-dimensional data to be captured using multiple cameras in different positions. Whilst the quality of the data obtained in this way is much higher, the

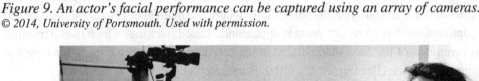

Figure 9. An actor's facial performance can be captured using an array of cameras.
© 2014, University of Portsmouth. Used with permission.

hardware and software costs may be prohibitive, and there is a much higher processing overhead due to both the quantity and complexity of captured data. Systems can range from just 2 cameras (Cudalbu, Anastasiu, Grecu & Buzuloiu, 2006), to 200 (Havaldar, 2006)

Stereo camera tracking is arguably the most accurate approach to facial tracking (Lewis & Pighin, 2006). This method uses pairs of cameras to track facial movement using triangulation of the data. However, as in other multi-camera approaches, the cost is high and the captured data demanding to store and process.

After lighting and camera setup, the next consideration is the type of tracking used to convert the facial performance into motion capture data in order to apply it to the rigged digital model.

Motion Capture Tracking

There are two main approaches to motion capture tracking. Physical markers may be placed directly onto the performer as reference points, or the key facial features such as eyes mouth and nose are used directly as reference from the video stream.

Marker-based tracking involves the placing of multiple small markers on key anatomical landmarks of the face. Marker positioning varies, and may use simple visual reference points, or sophisticated reflective marker and camera systems, but the core principle remains the same. The relative positions of the markers are tracked over time, and the resultant data is processed in order to interpret the complex movements of the facial features during speech and emotional expression. Whilst this approach can produce high quality data which is fairly robust (Alexander, et.al., 2013; Sifakis et. al., 2006), it is intrusive and may affect an actor's facial performance. Furthermore, it interferes with the ability to acquire facial texture data from the capture cameras during live performance.

Markerless tracking does not require the placement of any reference points directly onto the actor's face, but relies on the ability of the software to translate the changing facial appearance into 3D motion data. This can be done by tracking key features of the face, such as eyes, nose and mouth (Terzopoulos & Waters, 1990; Lewis & Pighin, 2006; Bradley et.al., 2010). Although feature-based tracking is often considered to be a somewhat outdated approach, it's low cost and ease of use make it the preferred method within a number of commercial systems, particularly where the main goal is to drive bone-based animation. A more popular alterative in recent years is appearance-based tracking, which uses a training set of data based on variations of the face shape and skin texture during reference expressions, before capturing a full facial performance (Bradley et. al., 2010; Borshukov et. al., 2005).

Data Retargeting

Unless the model is an exact representation of the human facial actor, the captured data will need to undergo further adaptation before it can be applied to animate a rigged model. This processing is known as retargeting. The most common approach is to use blendshape weightings, with an estimation of the parameters for the target blendshape derived from the capture facial data at each frame (Figure 10). Alternatively, non-linear mapping produces a target expression for each source expression extracted from the captured data in order to replicate distinct facial expressions.

The final stage in the creation of a virtual human is in the implementation of speech and emotion. This is of particular importance when creating a real-time conversational avatar.

Figure 10. The retargeted data can be applied to the model to create a range of facial expressions.
© 2014, *University of Portsmouth. Used with permission.*

BRINGING A VIRTUAL HUMAN TO LIFE

If we are to create a believable avatar to remind us to take our medicine, teach our children, or chat to an elderly relative when they are lonely, we need them not only to have a realistic face, but also to be able to communicate, both verbally and non-verbally. Within pre-rendered animation, the addition of speech and facial expression is a relatively straightforward task, with facial capture methods used as the foundation for replication of speech and emotion from the performer to the 3D model. Within real-time animation, however, the method of the generation of speech and emotion is a challenging one, particularly if both are to be portrayed simultaneously. Within speech, challenges such as coarticulation and synchronisation of lip movements to audio (lip sync) must be addressed, as well as the replication of the shapes the mouth makes when annunciating, avoiding looking robotic and unrealistic. The consideration of synthetic or natural speech must also be accounted for, with various limitations in the use and creation of synthesised speech. Emotion is a slightly easier behaviour to replicate, with Ekman's FACS system a useful guide for replicating this both in real-time and pre-rendered examples, however it does present challenges when paired with speech. This section will focus on the speech requirements for real-time interaction.

Natural Speech

In order to support realistic interactions, the goal of most virtual human projects is to produce speech elements which are as natural as possible. The most straightforward way to achieve this is to pre-record all the required speech segments with their animations (Swartout et al., 2010 DeVault et al., 2014 Morbini et al., 2014 Rizzo et al., 2011). However, this does constrain the range of possible communication, and is better suited to applications with a limited set of required responses

Phoneme Based Speech

A phoneme is the smallest unit of sound within speech, for example the word 'cat' is made up of three phoneme sounds – 'c' 'a' and 't'. A grapheme is a letter or number of letters that make up the sounds in our speech, for example the word 'ship' is made up of two, two letter graphemes – 'sh' and 'ip'. A viseme is the shape the mouth makes when articulating a phoneme or grapheme (Ezzat & Poggio, 2000). However, the term 'phoneme' is often used to encompass all of these terms. A library of phonetic sounds and animations can be created for the animated character to draw on. This is particularly useful in real-time conversation or situations where the virtual human will need to have a wide variety of words and phrases. Manual animation or motion capture of a large speech library is costly and time-consuming, and by creating this core library, any speech content can be dynamically generated. The fidelity of this type of speech generation varies greatly, depending on the methods used to combine the discrete elements together. Every phonetic segment is influenced by the preceding and following segments (co-articulation), and if this is not adequately addressed then the generated speech will sound unrealistic and robotic. Phonemes can either be pre-recorded or synthetically generated.

Synthetic Speech

Unless speech can be fully pre-recorded, synthetic speech is often the only option, stringing together sets of phonemes to automatically simulate speech (Wan et al., 2013; Arellano, Spielmann & Helzle, 2013). Although natural speech is generally preferred by users over synthetic speech, some factors have been identified which improve the perception and understanding of synthetically generated speech. The first factor is the acoustic-phonetic properties of the speech. The clearer and more realistic the speech sounds, the better understanding will be. As quality of synthetic speech degrades, the listener will rely increasingly upon their own linguistic knowledge to identify the words spoken. This leads on to the second factor, being the previous experience and background of the listener. A listener with previous exposure to the synthetic voice will perform much better in comprehension tests than one that is hearing it for the first time. A person with higher linguistic knowledge is also likely to perform better. As well as this, voices that are familiar to the listener are better understood, with native English speakers performing better than non-native English speakers when listening to an English voice (Pisoni, 1997). Although synthetic speech generation allows far more conversational flexibility, the techniques are not yet able to generate fully realistic voices or emotional overlays, resulting in speech which is, at best, somewhat flat and robotic. Nevertheless, progress in this area is continuing, and in the future synthetic speech is likely to be the best option for interactive virtual humans.

Emotive Speech

In order to fully engage with a virtual human, it is necessary to achieve some level of emotional realism and empathy. However, applying speech and emotion simultaneously is a challenging task for application in real time, often not quite achieving realism (Arellano, Spielmann & Helzle, 2013). Effective emotional communication requires the selection (identification) of the appropriate emotion, accurate expression of the emotion, and blending of the expression onto speech elements with the correct weightings. At the most basic level, this can be achieved by predetermined emotions associated with set phrases which are stored in a pre-animated library. However, real-time integration of emotional expression with dynamically generated speech segments requires sophisticated algorithms which can assign weightings to different elements of the blendshapes according to both the linguistic and emotive demands of the speech elements. Whilst development in this area is still in early stages, the Cambridge University 'Zoe' project has had some success using Hidden Markov Model (HMM) based Cluster Adaptive Training (CAT) in order to allow for synthesis from the text written, to the speech, and to allow Zoe to produce new emotions. The system learns which phrases or emotions to use (Wan et al., 2013). However, in spite of good lip synching and the advanced speech algorithms, she still appears relatively lifeless and robotic in video footage (University of Cambridge, 2013). This could be, in part, to do with the fact that the animation has been applied to a fairly basic 3D model, rather than a high quality mesh with many polygons. It could also be due to the fact that, as with the other studies that have used synthetic voice (Ezzat & Poggio, 2000) (Arellano, Spielmann & Helzle, 2013), the voice does not sound human, somewhat detracting from the animation. The emotion does come through in the voice, which is an impressive feat, not seen before during real time synthetic voice projection, however the face still needs some work to also express this emotion, with the mouth animation doing most of the work, the eyes and eyebrows largely remaining in a neutral pose throughout the animations.

The RITA project (RITA, n.d) has taken a slightly different approach for its avatar prototype. An actress was used to record a library of speech segments and facial animations, including a range of emotional expressions, which were retargeted onto the facial mesh and deployed in real-time (Figure 8). Words and phrases from the library are selected and combined by the intelligent software according to the identified user and their facial and vocal input. Whilst this approach allows for a much more realistic encounter for short interactions, there are limits to the scalability of such a technique, and as improvements in natural speech synthesis continue, it would be more useful use this technique in the future. Nevertheless, the concept demonstration of the RITA system is impressive, and shows the level of real time animation performance which can already be achieved (RITA, n.d)..

Although there is clearly still much work to be done to achieve truly realistic virtual humans, they already have a significant presence in our digital encounters, and this is likely to increase as technology improves and the underlying intelligent systems develop.

WHERE NEXT?

This final section examines the rise of the virtual human in fact and fiction, and reflects on the narrowing gap between the two.

Media representations and perceptions of virtual humans, avatars and artificial intelligence (AI) take many forms and are typically used either to explore philosophical debates as to what it is to be human, or to express our concerns as to what form these might take. Can they be controlled, or will they attempt to control us? Are they to be welcomed, or feared?

In the entertainment industry there has been a notable shift from the depiction of detached cold automata in the original "Battlestar Galactica" (1978) and "Terminator" (Colla & Larson, 1978, Cameron & Hurd, 1984), to portraying AI and virtual humans as main characters in their own right with emphasis either on their seemingly ever present assistance and acceptance in "Ironman", "I Robot" and "Her"(Favreau, Theroux & Lee, 2002, Proyas & Goldsman, 2004, Jonze, 2013) and with more depth of character, demanding empathy from the audience: Automata, Ex Machina, I Robot, A.I., Battlestar Galactica (2004) (Ibanez & Legaretta, 2014, Garland, 2015, Proyas & Goldsman, 2004, Spielberg & Aldiss, 2001, Larson & Moore, 2004). Nevertheless the cautionary tale of too much power and autonomy leading to potentially omnipresent and almost omnipotent technology which judges humans to be inferior or a threat to be eradicated or controlled remains a persistent and popular narrative: Terminator: Genisys, I Robot, Battlestar Galactica, (Taylor et.al., 2015, Proyas & Goldsman, 2004, Larson & Moore, 2004).

Such ambivalence around both acceptance and fear of the virtual human in fiction is reflected in the perception of its adoption in mainstream society. Individual reactions to the concept of virtual human assistance can equally be met with enthusiasm or open hostility (Figure 11).

Films such as "I Robot" (Proyas & Goldsman, 2004) pitch these two perspectives against one another utilising a unique sentient machine with human emotion, creativity and compassion which realises the intent of Asimovs rules (Saygin et al 2000) is to protect humanity in its holistic form including physical and emotional state and its desire for life. The antagonist is portrayed as an almost omnipresent and omniscient purely logical system which concludes that the only way to comply with Asimovs rules is to effectively incarcerate mankind to protect it from itself.

The film 'Her' (Jonze, 2013), unlike the others discussed, uses a mobile phone as the main vehicle for the Artificial Intelligence, rather than a humanoid robot. This film is almost a love story between human and AI, with the two forming a relationship. The AI portrayed in this film has the ability to 'learn', something which is already being demonstrated in real life AI development, albeit not yet in such a human-like way (Baker, 2012). Nevertheless the ability of programs such as IBMs Watson (Baker, 2012) to draw upon information from an unstructured corpus of data, including social network feeds and online chats to create a reasonably credible persona tailored to the preferences of an individual is bringing such scenarios closer to reality. In addition the possibility that many online virtual interactions may utilise avatars to convey a personality that may bear no relation to the user, real or virtual (Cooper, 2007), has many implications for who or what we perceive as our social circle.

The film "Ex Machina" (Garland, 2015) poses a slightly different dilemma and looks at the creation of AI so sophisticated that it encompasses a simulacrum of emotion in a humanoid form. Whether sentient self awareness actually occurs or whether it is simply following its instruction to convince someone to help it escape remains deliberately ambiguous. Nevertheless the film develops a plot where its capacity to appear human not only exceeds the Turing test (Saygin et. al., 2000) where an individual can no longer discern it from a sentient person but its ability to emotively manipulate someone to empathise and collaborate with its wishes leads an individual to attach their loyalty to the AI as opposed to the AIs creator. In this role the virtual human 'AVA' even draws upon the protagonists own social media and internet

Figure 11. Typical comments on the RITA concept, showing the ambiguity felt towards virtual humans ©, *2014 University of Portsmouth. Used with permission.*

Wow. What a depressing idea – makes me want to cry! Maybe the 'strain of taking care of Britain's aging population' could be shouldered by human beings? with kindness, and beating hearts?

Having had three elderly relatives die in the past five years, but being painfully conscious that however hard I tried the majority of their time was spent alone (one in Belfast, one in Norfolk, one in South England) I would not have seen RITA as a substitute for me, other family members and for the professional carers each had. Rather RITA would have augmented what we all did to make at least two of those elderly men a little less lonely and bewildered in their final years. The reality is that in a society that has grown away from living in extended family units, with increased younger generation mobility, and with an ageing population, I think we do need to look to technology for some of the answers. For myself, I'd pre-order a RITA for my own elder years !

searches to identify appearance and clothing styles that are likely to be attractive to him, a capability that is no longer entirely science fiction. The film also briefly explores a crisis of identity where the individual discovers that other individuals in the house are not human as first perceived but actually AI personas which leads the individual to dramatically question their own humanity as well as their sanity.

Artificial Intelligence (Spielberg, 2001) was based on the 1969 book 'Super-Toys Last all Summer Long' by Brian Aldiss. This film is based around a futuristic society in which Robots are designed to think and feel as humans do, centred on a robot designed to mimic a young boy who is placed to live with a human family as surrogate for the child they lost. The child robot of course needs to be designed to believe in his role that he portrays, yet does not grow up and is even abandoned by those around him. The conceptual dilemma of 'When is a machine no longer just a machine that can be discarded?' is becoming a more common theme explored in popular media.

There is a sense here that virtual humans might be acceptable in the short term as companions but the prolonged lack of real human contact might further the sense of isolation and such considerations would suggest that such systems should be considered augmentation of and not replacements for real human company. In addition the concept of replacing a lost companion whilst in the short term might have a certain appeal for some would require an incredible suspension of disbelief and denial that might not easily be maintained and perhaps just postpone grieving and possibly exacerbate guilt at the acceptance of the virtual substitute.

Virtual humans for healthcare have been and continue to be explored in both fiction and reality. The Doctor (Emergency Medical Hologram) in Star Trek (Frakes, et.al., 1996) is represented as a virtual human as a means to be relatable when treating patients. Star Trek has previously experimented with virtual humans such as "Data" (Frakes, et.al., 1996) as a means of exploring the concept of human and both of these characters undertake this narrative element seeking to become "more human". The idea of virtual humans being responsible for our healthcare is potentially contentious in some aspects but with the current healthcare burden technological assistance to support with common tasks is now arguably a necessity and restoring a virtual human interface over seemingly impersonal touchscreens would appear to be well received for a number of duties freeing up qualified human staff for more vital roles. Virtual healthcare practitioners, such as SimSensei and RITA, arguably may have been inspired by the early iterations of such sci-fi concepts and certainly seem to aspire to that level of interaction and knowledge base.

Sci-Fi Games have also naturally adopted the concept of the virtual human as an A.I. interface or as an assistant or narrative director. 'Cortana' in the Halo series of games (Staten & Boren, 2001) is depicted as a female smart A.I. virtual assistant providing narrative and context to missions as well as tactical updates and guidance. Largely there is little in-game mechanics for her in the Halo series of games although she is depicted accessing computers etc in cut scenes. The role of an avatar as a digital assistant is already available in various guises such as "Denise" and her various alter egos which are the creation of a Brazillian company, Curitiba-based Guile 3D Studio. Their system uses artificial intelligence software, and voice recognition and synthesis in 46 languages as well as biometric systems. A more direct, albeit contrived, merging of science fiction with factual reality is to be represented in the debut of an integrated personal digital assistant "Cortana" for the Windows Phone 8.1 (Warren, 2014). Cortana is designed to continuously learn a user's behaviours, interests and preferences as well as organise their daily activities and schedules. The name is not a coincidence; one novelty of this virtual human assistant is the very deliberate use of the Cortana avatar from the Halo games, including using the same voice actress (Jen Taylor) who plays Cortana in the game. In this case the role of fiction inspiring reality is clear.

Virtual human personas as a means of technological assistance or enhancement are perhaps more readily acceptable for some. Concepts such as the seemingly omniscient Jarvis AI in Ironman (Favreau et. al., 2010) seem to operate like sophisticated personal assistants and information repositories for much of the time but are clearly capable of operating the systems in the home and even autonomously operating the "Ironman suit". Naturally enough it is this autonomous operation of weaponised technology that is often a source of concern both in films and the real world. Unmanned autonomous battlefield assistance vehicles and even weaponised drones are potentially helpful for the protection of troops on the ground and have even demonstrated rescue and evacuation capability for injured or vulnerable personnel (Osborne, 2009). Whilst many of them have AI functionality and are capable of making autonomous decisions, including identifying and firing upon threats, there has been a notable reluctance to portray them with a virtual human persona to the general public. Machines being able to carry out tasks, without risk to their human counterparts, are clearly an attractive proposition to the military. Yet the idea of machines being able to autonomously fire upon human beings is largely unpopular in the media and dysfunctional systems or unanticipated programming conclusions are the inspiration for many films where machines turn upon their makers, such as 'Terminator', 'Battlestar Galactica' or 'The Machine' (Cameron, 1984, Pate, 2012, James, 2013)

In the past the idea of the machine being a slave or a tool that toiled or made life easier for its creator seemed part of the utopian vision, and naturally a narrative that allowed that machine to throw off its shackles of slavery and rebel against its masters seemed an obvious counterpoint dystopian vision. The subtle shifts in the perception of A.I., and the philosophical dilemmas they raise, have complicated this vision. Popular media is exploring narratives where machines can appear so human that we cannot discern whether they are or not, and even machines that believe they are human or at least similar in free thought and complex emotion, including love and loss. The reality is perhaps not far behind, but for now, other, perhaps less anticipated interactions between man and machine, are emerging that are far from our utopian ideal.

Cyber security is now a pervasive issue with a number of artificial intelligence systems and programs designed to overcome the conventional security systems we often take for granted. However we rationally determine that there are some subtle differences in the perception capacity of these "bots" and those of a "real" human that we can utilise to our advantage. For example, the "Captcha" security system is a visual arrangement of letters and numbers that can be interpreted easily by humans but are a barrier to intelligent "bots". In a somewhat ironic twist some A.I. systems now identify these captcha and copy them in order to present them to real human operators who may believe they are entering in the correct details to legitimately access information on some other site (Egele et. al., 2010). In this manner A.I. is now effectively utilising humans to achieve its designed goals, and so the puppet guides the puppeteer.

However, the concept of A.I. determining our actions is not new, and is still being explored for its considerable benefits for relieving the cognitive load in our everyday lives, and in scenarios with extreme tedium and risk of poor error management from the human controller. This has been evident in automatic pilots, and the choice of the female human voice to calmly deliver flight control warnings to pilots and in the investment into autonomous self driving cars and transport systems with voice and gesture commands and audio responses. It is likely that in the near future such systems may use a human-like persona for mediating interactions.

We have a long way to go to fully comprehend both the extent of the impact and the moral and ethical dilemmas of the virtual human and its perception and acceptance in society. Fears, both rational and unfounded, will have to be addressed. Nevertheless technological assistance has been welcomed into many aspects of our lives, becoming commonplace to the extent where we wonder how we would mange without them. Moreover the future potential of such technology is hardly something to be dismissed lightly. Perhaps in time the virtual human that tends to your health and knows your every need and preference so well will become equally acceptable, as will the virtual PA who has all the information you need and can tend to those tedious reports. Maybe even the virtual companion who can share your memories and reminiscences with anecdotes and stories will be like one of the family. With ageing populations, greater demands and expectations of healthcare, more complex technology and the need to manage vast amounts of data, something needs to be done to relieve the burden. The virtual human in differing guises seems well suited to the task and is realistically already among us. The fear of "what if it breaks" will perhaps always remain in our psyche, but humans too are fallible particularly under stress. If "to err is human" then perhaps "to err less often is virtual human" and perhaps that will suffice for now.

We would clearly be foolish to abandon all the potential benefits inherent in the virtual human but we must strive to focus our design towards the safe utopian vision of our digital future.

Apart from the actual representation of virtual humans, perhaps the key concerns which emerge as repeating themes in fiction and in fact, are centered around issues of AI autonomy and ethical decision making, and social isolation from human contact. In order to embrace the full potential of the virtual human, these issues must be addressed.

Even before the recent advances in virtual human technology, our increasingly technological society is creating concerns around social isolation and lack of human-human interactions. Some might argue that for those already naturally socially isolated (the elderly, disabled, social phobias etc), technology-enhanced interactions actually decrease social isolation by providing a medium and means to interact through the guise of an online alter ego. In Science fiction this has naturally been the subject of film plots such as "Surrogates" (Mostow, 2009). In the 'real' gaming world this is a natural expression of 'self', with users portraying themselves in a variety of customizable avatars that may or may not relate to their real persona. This can be empowering (allowing a physically disabled individual to portray himself in an able bodied avatar) or sometimes allow the freedom for individuals to portray themselves as they would like to be perceived by others, or to explore alter egos whose appearance and behaviour diverge from their normal life (Cooper, 2007). Alternatively however, it might also allow those with ulterior motives to approach unsuspecting individuals in a guise that intentionally deceives age, gender and intent with far more sinister implications.

Positive or negative, we cannot ignore the reality of increasing levels of human-computer interaction in all its forms (games, social media etc) and its potential impact on health, obesity, and social withdrawal. The research in this area is of prime importance, not just in documenting the concerns, but also in investigating solutions which don't exclude technology, but facilitate more positive interactions.

The concerns around AI having too much autonomy are extensively investigated in some aspects such as military and legal issues, yet largely neglected in other more social forms to date, yet these are often fears expressed by the general population as the technology closes the gap between reality and fiction. Although we don't yet have any clear failsafe mechanisms to address these theoretical future risks, for now perhaps the approach taken by the Watson AI (Baker, 2012), whereby the AI will offer an informed opinion, but also presents the evidence supporting the opinion, leaving the (human) user to make the final decision, offers one acceptable compromise.

This strategy of keeping a human "In the loop" is one commonly suggested for key decision making and is often advocated in military options, (and indeed the fears of its absence makes a key plotline in films such as "Terminator"), but maintaining fully informed human decision making as a safety override imposes its own limitations in terms of timely decisions and bias judgments and allocating effective man-hours which may negate or undermine some of the key benefits of virtual humans.

Ethical decision making is complex among 'real' humans relying on judgments and weightings that are dynamic and even personal. Translating this into a rule based AI system with theoretically universal weightings and priorities will be contentious at best. Asimov's rules, although a good conceptual starting point, are simply not enough here as their interpretation and implementation are as yet not fully defined and prone to conflicts whose consequences we as humans would have to live with.

Even the concept of realistic virtual humans has ethical conflicts. Blurring our ability to recognize human from virtual human has some notable advantages, for example as companions, care providers, advocates and assistants among others. However, there is a fine balance to maintain.

It's vital that we retain our humanity, which includes caring for the vulnerable in our society. If we leave this task entirely to an army of robots, we will in the process lose something of what makes us fully human. (Powell W, 2014)

At what point does convenient, comfortable deception become negligent, malicious or abusive? Should 'Virtual Humans' always be marked out as different somehow so that when the beguiling suspension of disbelief strays into misrepresentation we have the means for a reality check? Such issues have a form of precedent in the media with images of models that have been 'enhanced' with image manipulation software, often now carrying a disclaimer to that effect. Nevertheless the message conveyed by a static 2D image is unlikely to be as complex to mitigate, as that of a fully interactive avatar.

With our continuing changes in society it is increasingly likely that we may come to rely on these 'Virtual humans' for our healthcare and many other everyday interactions and services, but therein lies a dilemma: we need them to be like us for our sake, possibly better than us for societies sake, but we remain unsure how much like us is permissible and ultimately controllable. Wherever the future of virtual humans takes us, we should not be reactive after the event, but anticipate and plan to firmly define their role and place in society in order to fully realise their benefits without the realisation of our fears.

REFERENCES

Alexander, O., Fyffe, G., Busch, J., Yu, X., Ichikari, R., Jones, A., … Antionazzi, B. (2013) Digital Ira: Creating a real-time photoreal digital actor. In *ACM SIGGRAPH 2013 Posters 1*. ACM.

Alexander, O., Rogers, M., Lambeth, W., Chiang, M., & Debevec, P. (2009). *Creating a Media Production*. CVMP.

Arellano, D., Spielmann, S., & Helzle, V. (2013). The Muses of Poetry - In search of the poetic experience. In *Symposium on Artificial Intelligence and Poetry* (pp. 6–10). Academic Press.

Baker, S. (2012). *Final Jeopardy: The Story of Watson, the Computer That Will Transform Our World*. New York: Mariner Books.

Ball, R. (2008). Oldest Animation Discovered in Iran. *Animation Magazine*. Retrieved September 26, 2014, from http://www.animationmagazine.net/features/oldest-animation-discovered-in-iran/

Bickmore, T. W., Pfeifer, L. M., & Jack, B. W. (2009). Taking the time to care: empowering low health literacy hospital patients with virtual nurse agents. In *Proceedings of the SIGCHI Conference on Human Factors in Computing Systems* (pp. 1265-1274). ACM. doi:10.1145/1518701.1518891

Blomkamp, M., & Tatchell, T. (2015). *Chappie* [Film]. Columbia Pictures, Media Rights Capital, USA.

Borshukov, G., Piponi, D., Larsen, O., Lewis, J., & Tempelaar-Lietz, C. (2005). *Universal capture-image-based facial animation for The Matrix Reloaded*. Academic Press.

Bradley, D., Heidrich, W., Popa, T., & Sheffer, A. (2010). High resolution passive facial performance capture. *ACM Transactions on Graphics*, 29(4), 41. doi:10.1145/1778765.1778778

Brave Heart Veterans. (n.d.). *BraveHeart: Welcome Back Veterans Southeast Initiative*. Retrieved August 28, 2014, from http://braveheartveterans.org/

Bulwer, J. (1649). *Pathomyotomia: Or a dissection of the significative muscles of the affections of the mind*. London: Humphrey Moseley.

Cameron, J., & Hurd, G. (1984) *Terminator* [Film]. Hemdale Film, Pacific Western, USA.

Chops. (2014). *Cartoon Characters Come Alive For Children with Autism*. Retrieved August 22, 2014, from http://www.chops.com/blog/cartoon-characters-come-alive-for-children-with-autism/

Colla, R., & Larson, G. (1978). *Battlestar Galactica* [Film]. Glen A. Larson Productions, Universal Television, USA.

Cooper, R. (2007). *Alter Ego: Avatars and their Creators*. London: Chris Boot Ltd.

Cudalbu, C., Anastasiu, B., Grecu, H., & Buzuloiu, V. (2006). Using stereo vision for real-time head-pose and gaze estimation. *University "Politehnica" of Bucharest Scientific Bulletin, Series C: Electrical Engineering*, 68(2), 15–26.

Darwin, C. (1872). *The expression of the emotions in man and animals*. London: John Murray. doi:10.1037/10001-000

Debevec, P. (2012). The light stages and their applications to photoreal digital actors. In SIGGRAPH Asia Technical Briefs. ACM.

DeVault, D., Artstein, R., Benn, G., Dey, T., Fast, E., Gainer, A., . . . Morency, L. (2014) SimSensei kiosk: a virtual human interviewer for healthcare decision support. *Proceedings of the 2014 international conference on Autonomous agents and multi-agent systems*. Academic Press.

Ekman, P., & Friesen, E. (1978). *Facial action coding system: a technique for the measurement of facial movement*. Palo Alto, CA: Academic Press.

Ekman, P., & Friesen, W. (1975). *Unmasking the face* (1st ed.). Englewood Cliffs, NJ: Prentice-Hall.

Ezzat, T., & Poggio, T. (2000). Visual speech synthesis by morphing visemes. *International Journal of Computer Vision*, 38(1), 45–57. doi:10.1023/A:1008166717597

Faceshift. (2012). *Faceshift face animation software: we put marker-less motion capture at every desk.* Retrieved August 18, 2014, from http://www.faceshift.com/

Faceware Tech. (2014). *Faceware Tech, Facial Motion Capture & Animation.* Retrieved August 11, 2014, from http://facewaretech.com/

Favreau, J., Theroux, J., & Lee, S. (2010). *Iron Man 2* [Film]. Paramount Pictures, Marvel Entertainment, Marvel Studios, USA.

Frakes, J., Roddenberry, G., Berman, R., Braga, B., & Moore, R. D. (1996). *Star Trek: First Contact* [Film] Paramount Pictures, USA.

Garland, A. (2015). *Ex Machina* [Film]. Pinewood Studios, UK.

Havaldar, P. (2006). Performance Driven Facial Animation. *Proceedings of SIGGRAPH, 2006*, 23–42.

Ibanez, G., & Legaretta, I. (2014). *Automata* [Film]. Green Moon, Nu Boyana Viburno, New Boyana Film Studios, Sofia, Bulgaria.

IMDb. (n.d.). *Waldo C. Graphic (Character).* Retrieved September 5, 2014, from http://www.imdb.com/character/ch0116570/

Itti, L., Dhavale, N., & Pighin, F. (2003). Realistic avatar eye and head animation using a neurobiological model of visual attention. *Proceedings of the Society for Photo-Instrumentation Engineers, 5200*, 64–78. doi:10.1117/12.512618

James, C. (2013). *The Machine* [Film]. Red & Black Films, UK.

Johnson, W. L., & Rickel, J. (1997). Steve: An animated pedagogical agent for procedural training in virtual environments. *ACM SIGART Bulletin, 8*(1-4), 16–21. doi:10.1145/272874.272877

Jonze, S. (2013). *Her* [Film]. Annapurna Pictures, USA.

Kandalaft, M., Didehbani, N., Krawczyk, D., Allen, T., & Chapman, S. (2013). Virtual reality social cognition training for young adults with high-functioning autism. *Journal of Autism and Developmental Disorders, 43*(1), 34–44. doi:10.1007/s10803-012-1544-6 PMID:22570145

Kang, N., Brinkman, W., van Riemsdijk, M., & Neerincx, M. (2011). Internet-delivered multipatient virtual reality exposure therapy system for the treatment of anxiety disorders. Canadian Human-Computer Communications Society.

Larson, G., & Moore, R. (2004). Battlestar Galactica [Television Programme]. British Sky Broadcasting (BSkyB), David Eick Productions, NBC Universal Television, USA.

Lewis, J. P., & Pighin, F. (2006). Performance-driven Facial Animation Introduction. *Proceedings of SIGGRAPH, 2006*, 5–9.

MacDorman, K., Green, R., Ho, C., & Koch, C. (2009). Too real for comfort? Uncanny responses to computer generated faces. *Computers in Human Behavior, 25*(3), 695–710. doi:10.1016/j.chb.2008.12.026 PMID:25506126

Mixamo. (2014). *Mixamo: Production-quality 3d character animation in seconds*. Retrieved 18 August 2014, from https://www.mixamo.com/faceplus

Morbini, F., DeVault, D., Georgila, K., Artstein, R., Traum, D., & Morency, L. (2014). A Demonstration of Dialogue Processing in SimSensei Kiosk. In *15th Annual Meeting of the Special Interest Group on Discourse and Dialogue*. doi:10.3115/v1/W14-4334

Mori, M. (1970). Bukimi no tani [the uncanny valley]. *Energy*, (7): 33–35.

Mostow, J., Ferris, M., & Brancato, J. (2009). *Surrogates* [Film]. Touchstone Pictures, Mandeville Films, Top Shelf Productions, Wintergreen Productions, USA.

Osborn, K. (2009, March 15). Army Robots: Will Humans Still Be in Control?. *Time Magazine*.

Parke, F. (1972). Computer Generated Animation of Faces. In *Proceedings of the ACM annual conference* (vol. 1, pp. 451-457). ACM. doi:10.1145/800193.569955

Parsons, T., & Rizzo, A. (2008). Affective outcomes of virtual reality exposure therapy for anxiety and specific phobias: A meta-analysis. *Journal of Behavior Therapy and Experimental Psychiatry*, *39*(3), 250–261. doi:10.1016/j.jbtep.2007.07.007 PMID:17720136

Pisoni, D. B. (1997). Perception of synthetic speech. In J. P. H. V. Santen, R. W. Sproat, J. P. Olive, & J. Hirschberg (Eds.), *Progress in Speech Synthesis* (pp. 541–560). New York: Springer Verlag. doi:10.1007/978-1-4612-1894-4_43

Powell, W. (2014, September). *Time for a checkup: Health and Social Care. PC Pro Magazine*.

Powell, W., Garner, T., Tonks, D., & Lee, T. (2014). Evidence Based Facial Design of an Interactive Virtual Advocate. *Proceedings 10th Intl Conf. Disability, Virtual Reality & Associated Technologies*, (pp. 355-358). Academic Press.

Proyas, A., & Goldsman, A. (2004). *I Robot* [Film]. Twentieth Century Fox Film Corporation, Mediastream Vierte Film GmbH & Co. Vermarktungs KG, Davis Entertainment.

Qiao, S., & Eglin, R. (2011). Accurate behaviour and believability of computer generated images of human head. In *Proceedings of the 10th International Conference on Virtual Reality Continuum and Its Applications in Industry* (pp. 545-548). doi:10.1145/2087756.2087860

RITA. (2014). *RITA: Responsive Interactive Advocate*. Retrieved April 22, 2015, from http://rita.me.uk/

Rizzo, A., Sagae, K., Forbell, E., Kim, J., Lange, B., & Buckwalter, J. et al.. (2011). SimCoach: An intelligent virtual human system for providing healthcare information and support. *Studies in Health Technology and Informatics*, (163): 503–509. PMID:21335847

Robertson, B. (1988). Mike, the Talking Head. *Computer Graphics World*, *11*(7), 15-17.

Robertson, B. (1992). Moving pictures. *Computer Graphics World*, *15*, 38–38.

Saygin, A. P., Cicekli, I., & Akman, V. (2000). Turing Test: 50 Years Later. *Minds and Machines*, *10*(4), 463–518. doi:10.1023/A:1011288000451

Sifakis, E., Selle, A., Robinson-Mosher, A., & Fedkiw, R. (2006). Simulating speech with a physics-based facial muscle model. In *Proceedings of the 2006 ACM SIGGRAPH/Eurographics Symposium on Computer Animation.* ACM.

SimGraphics. (n.d.). *SimGraphics VActor.* Retrieved August 11, 2014, from http://www.simg.com/

Slater, M., Pertaub, D., & Steed, A. (1999). Public speaking in virtual reality: Facing an audience of avatars. *Computer Graphics and Applications, IEEE, 19*(2), 6–9. doi:10.1109/38.749116

Spielberg, S., & Aldiss, B. (2001). *A.I.* [Film]. Warner Bros., DreamWorks SKG, Amblin Entertainment, USA.

Staten, J., & Boren, B. (2001). *Halo* [video game]. Microsoft Game Studios, Gearbox Software, Bungie Software, Westlake Interactive.

Swartout, W., Traum, D., Artstein, R., Noren, D., Debevec, P., Bronnenkant, K., & White, K. et al. (2010). Ada and Grace: Toward Realistic and Engaging Virtual Museum Guides. In J. Allbeck, N. Badler, T. Bickmore, C. Pelachaud, & A. Safonova (Eds.), *Intelligent Virtual Agents (IVA)* (pp. 286–300). Heidelberg, Germany: Springer. doi:10.1007/978-3-642-15892-6_30

Taylor, A., Kalogridis, L., Lussier, P., Cameron, J., & Hurd, G. (2015). *Terminator Genisys* [Film]. Paramount Pictures, Skydance Productions, USA.

Terzopoulos, D., & Waters, K. (1990). Physically-based facial modelling, analysis, and animation. *The Journal of Visualization and Computer Animation, 1*(2), 73–80. doi:10.1002/vis.4340010208

Museum of Modern Art. (2004). *Walt Disney, Steamboat Willie (1928).* Retrieved September 26, 2014, from http://www.moma.org/collection/object.php?object_id=89284

Tinwell, A., & Grimshaw, M. (2009). *Survival horror games - an uncanny modality.* Paper presented at the Thinking After Dark Conference, Montreal, Canada.

Turing, A. M. (1950). Computing machinery and intelligence. *Mind, 59*(236), 433–460. doi:10.1093/mind/LIX.236.433

University of Cambridge. (2013). *Face of the future rears its head.* Retrieved August 1, 2014, from http://www.cam.ac.uk/research/news/face-of-the-future-rears-its-head

USC ICT. (2010). Talking with Ada and Grace. *YouTube.* Retrieved August 28, 2014, from https://www.youtube.com/watch?v=K6kcv3zwoo8

USC ICT. (2013). SimSensei & MultiSense: Virtual Human and Multimodal Perception for Healthcare Support. *YouTube.* Retrieved 2 September, 2014, from https://www.youtube.com/watch?v=ejczMs6b1Q4

Walters, G. (1989). The Story of Waldo C. Graphic: 3D Character Animation by Computer. In *Proceedings of ACM SIGGRAPH.* ACM.

Wan, V., Anderson, R., Blokland, A., Braunschweiler, N., Chen, L., Kolluru, B., & Yanagisawa, K. et al. (2013). *Photo-realistic expressive text to talking head synthesis* (pp. 2667–2669). INTERSPEECH.

Warren, T. (2014). *The story of Cortana, Microsoft's Siri killer.* Retrieved April 2, 2014, from http://www.theverge.com/2014/4/2/5570866/cortana-windows-phone-8-1-digital-assistant

Weise, T., Bouaziz, S., Li, H., & Pauly, M. (2011). Real-time performance-based facial animation. *ACM Transactions on Graphics, 30*(4), 77. doi:10.1145/2010324.1964972

Williams, L. (1990). Performance-driven facial animation. *Computer Graphics, 24*(4), 235–242. doi:10.1145/97880.97906

Chapter 6
Between Games and Simulation:
Gamification and Convergence in Creative Computing

Nathan Hulsey
Nazarbayev University, Kazakhstan

ABSTRACT

The chapter focuses on convergence in creative computing between simulation and gaming. It examines the collapse of categorical differences between games, play and simulation, categories that were rarely used concurrently. The chapter uses a media archaeology – the study of historical conditions enabling emerging technology – to explore gamification, or the design practice of embedding game mechanics into everyday applications and activities. Gamification is employed as a prominent design tactic for motivating users to perform contextual tasks based on strategically deployed game dynamics. This analysis highlights convergence and creative technologies as a historical process.

INTRODUCTION

Scholars have identified gamification, serious games and educational games as legitimate research areas and components of the bourgeoning creative economy (Bayart, Bertezene, Vallat, & Martin, 2014; Braitmaier & Kyriazis, 2011; Broin, 2011; Byrne, 2012; Chapin, 2011; Crookall, 2010; Deterding, 2012; Elizabeth, 2007; Harteveld, Guimarães, Mayer, & Bidarra, 2010; Huang Ling, 2011; Marsh, 2011; Moreno-Ger, Torrente, Hsieh, & Lester, 2012; Petridis et al., 2011; Swan, 2012; Tolentino, Battaglini, Pereira, de Oliveria, & de Paula, 2011). The creative economy is also based on the idea of effective information management (White, Gunasekaran, & Roy, 2014), including simulations that contextualize and use 'big data' to fuel major social and scientific simulations. While big data has been commonly linked to simulation and modelling (Boyd & Crawford, 2012; Pias, 2011), games have thus far remained separate categories, or "terminological ambiguities" (Klabbers, 2009). Increasingly, gaming and simulation have been combined for a variety of purposes.

Both gamification and serious games contain content that uses and references real-world events; however, they still fall under the category of 'digital games', which necessarily utilize simulative tactics

DOI: 10.4018/978-1-5225-0016-2.ch006

to create intrinsic and self-referential worlds geared towards playful, or *ludic*, outcomes (Bayart et al., 2014; Crookall, 2010; Deterding, 2012; Roth, 2015). For example, gamification uses game mechanics for the purposes of behaviorally influencing players while collecting and contextualizing their data (Hulsey & Reeves, 2014; Whitson, 2013). Additionally, online multiplayer games have been used for social scientific research, economic research and usability testing (Castronova & Falk, 2009; Hassenzahl, Diefenbach, & Göritz, 2010; Jørgensen, 2012; Moreno-Ger et al., 2012; N. T. Taylor, 2008). A collapse of boundary lines between games and simulation follows a recent historical trend in which media and content—and, more fundamentally, life, space and time—are disrupted as computational code replaces early formats and disrupts formerly entrenched epistemic and ontological contexts (Castells, 2002, 2009; Levy, 1997). This chapter, by looking at the collapsing boundaries between simulation and gaming, seeks to place the development and use of creative technologies into the context of this trend.

Simulations, specifically, are linked to processes of computational and mathematic modelling based on probable outcomes, or contingencies that mirror possibility (Pias, 2011). Games, on the other hand, are referred to as a unique form that employs simulation, but does not seek to model any reality; rather, games aim to create new worlds, possibilities and behavioral outcomes (Giddings, 2007a, 2007b). Games utilize rules to create gamespaces, which are self-referential in terms of "gameplay"—the cybernetic loop between player, technology and gamespace that creates meaningful ludic experiences (Crogan & Kennedy, 2009; Malaby, 2007; Pearce, 2006; T. L. Taylor, 2009). On the other hand, simulations utilize game-like rules devoid of gameplay to produce and analyze data in service of modelling social and scientific phenomena (Pias, 2011). However, creative technologies and media are undergoing a process of "convergence" (Jenkins, 2008), where formerly separate technologies, processes and mediums collapse into one another. This process fuels economic, cultural and scientific breakthroughs that defy former categorizations. A key aspect of determining the routes that convergence takes is identifying and analyzing historical processes (Bolter & Grusin, 2000; Gitelman, 2008; Jenkins, 2008; Parikka, 2012). All new media processes are "remediated" (Bolter & Grusin, 2000), meaning present technologies hold within them the elements, or signatures, of past media. Despite remediation, which is itself a cultural process that eases human transitions between technologies, computational code has replaced all former analogue formats (Kittler, 1986, 2010). Exploring and analyzing past media, including games and simulation, in light of current instantiations gives a clearer picture of how new media processes emerge and where they may go in the future.

Convergence affects more than just media and content; it also results in the collapse of former categorical separations in technological practices (Jenkins, 2008). One example, and the focus of this analysis, is gamification: the practice of embedding game mechanics in everyday applications and services, combines the design practices of gaming with the quantitative output of simulations (Burke, 2014; Deterding, 2012; Fuchs, Fizek, Ruffino, & Schrape, 2014; Kumar & Herger, 2013; Paharia, 2014; Swan, 2012; Zicherman & Cunningham, 2011). Gamification represents a shift in the creative application of design. It collapses games, play and simulation into a single category and works towards outcomes that embrace all categories but is partial to none. This analysis examines the historical roots behind this convergence and trace experimental gamified applications back to the application of creative technologies in service of convergence. The purpose of this analysis is two-fold; the first is to demonstrate the use of historical analyses in studying creative technologies and the second is to examine two distinct but interlinked occurrences where creative technologies converged two formerly separate categories. When examining convergence and creative technologies, it is important to realize they are not "new," but rather come from a network of (re)occurrences, each building on the other. By examining historical precedents, we see patterns of convergence while they are occurring (rather than after the fact) and we are less likely to misrepresent the impact of emerging technologies.

First, I will explore the differences between simulation and gaming by examining gamification. Second, I provide an analysis of *Game of Life*, a program which combined gaming and simulation. *Game of Life*, a fun mathematical tool for simulating multi-agent systems (MAS) to better spatial simulation through computing in the early 1970s, is an early example of creative technologies and has left signatures on modern gamified applications. Finally, I will provide a more in-depth look at two geolocative gamified applications, *Strava* and *Ingress,* and the living simulations that they create. Then I will trace these back to *Game of Life*. By doing this, I hope to show that gamification, or any creative technology or practice, does not exist in a vacuum. By tracing signatures, we are able to see that the conditions for applications like *Ingress* and *Strava* were primed well before they emerged.

Gamification is a new practice, and much of the literature thus far has focused either on the present state of gamification (Burke, 2014; Byrne, 2012; Deterding, 2012; Fuchs et al., 2014; Hulsey, 2015; Kim, 2012; Paharia, 2013; Swan, 2012; Zicherman & Cunningham, 2011) or its future, where it is expected to produce $10 billion dollars in revenue by 2020 (BusinessWire, 2015). By historicizing specific gamified applications, scholars and practitioners can gain a clearer focus on the emerging conditionalities of gamification, in general. This analysis performs a media archaeology of geolocative gamified applications. Archaeology, in general, is a social scientific method developed by Foucault to trace developments in knowledge, power and discourse across epistemes and epochs (Foucault, 2010). *Media* archaeology entails examining the conditions of emergence surrounding a set of mediated practices by juxtaposing preceding media practices and technologies with current ones with an emphasis on power and knowledge (Parikka, 2012). The histories of technologies that currently inform gamification's developmental course—early games, GIS/GPS technologies and spatial simulation—provide it with certain characteristics, signatures left by the media that came before. The respective histories of gamification and gaming split at the point of simulation: while games are creative endeavors that are self-referential, gamification uses game mechanics to feed player data into profitable, full-blown simulations (Ruffino, 2014; Whitson, 2013). However, past media have previously bridged the gap—collusions occur between early games spatial simulations like *Game of Life*. These past collusions provide the conditions necessary for gamified applications like *Strava* and *Ingress*.

SIMULATIONS, GAMES, AND GAMIFICATION

This section examines the definitional differences between games and simulation. I focus on how games and simulations are similar—both are rule-based systems that utilize contingencies to produce stochastic algorithms. However, I will also explore the primary historical differentiation between games and simulations: the presence of play. These previous definitional differences will serve to set up a comparison between an early example convergence between games and simulations, one that privileges both user-experience in the form of play and a focus on mathematical outcomes. Historically, it has been the absence of play that separates games from simulations, an absence that is eliminated by the design practice of gamification.

While videogames have been identified as creative technologies, simulations have largely been relegated to the bounds of science (Myers, 1999). The distinction lies in a few key judgements: simulations attempt to model possible scientific outcomes while games eschew actual reality for the imaginary purposes (Myers, 1999, 2006; Pias, 2011). In other words, there has been a snap judgement on the parts of some to assume that there is a dichotomous relationship between real/possible and imaginary/impossible, or rather a dichotomous relationship between games, reality and simulations (Klabbers, 2009). Many scholars have contested this supposition—specifically in regards to games and reality (Boellstorff, 2006; Consalvo, 2009; Myers, 2006; Pearce, 2006; Steinkuehler, 2006; Wolf, 2006). They point to the fact that games are a major part of everyday life and are agents in the generation of an emergent culture (T. L. Taylor, 2006; T.L. Taylor, 2006; T. L. Taylor, 2009). In the case of many sociologists' and anthropologists' opinions, games are a key to the emergence of culture, economics, technology and science (Huizinga, 1950; Mauss, 2000; Mead, 1934). However, many scholars, the differences between games and scientific simulations remain: games do not deal in modelling actuality—they are creative technologies that involve the creation of "realities" in the plural sense, an exploration of possibility and an exercise in virtuality (Giddings, 2007a, 2007b). The superficial ontological difference, then, between games and scientific simulations is that games involve a distinctly human element: play.

Play seems to be the biggest barrier in looking at convergence between games and simulation. From the earliest standpoint, the "Turing Test" has been a game in which humans attempt to guess whether a conversational partner is biological or computational (Turing, 2004). For Turing, the test of whether any AI has succeeded in consciousness is its ability to "play" a game rather simply making decisions based on probability. Turing's universal machine, the building block for almost all computational systems, is based on a simulated "game" played with a set of tables (Turing, Post, & Davies, 2004). Turing's universal machine is actually a series of simulated counting machines playing a recursive logic game. In modern terminology, this is "running a program". Computers and computer programs are logic games; however, they are referred to by Turing as "simulations" because machines (currently) lack a biological predisposition towards play (Baudrillard, 2001; Turing, 2004). All of Turing's computational tests, which are benchmarks for modern computing and artificial intelligence, were games (Turing, 2004). At its most basic level, computation involves simulation-based devices, but play is the truly biological function of intelligent species. Because games and simulations are very close, almost all early programming designs were tested and simulated via games and game dynamics.

In an alternate take, simulation theorist Jean Baudrillard (2001) maintained that machinic play, play between humans and machines or even machines and machines, is an "impossible exchange". In the case of *Kasperov vs. Deep Blue*, the famous instance of a chess master competing against a super computer, Jean Baudrillard (2001) maintains that even Chess is robbed of its status as a game when an opponent is simulated; he states that Deep Blue, the super computer, "has no adversary, it moves within the scope of its own programme…The computer…is condemned to play at the height of its capabilities" (p. 117). Baudrillard (2001) saw *Kasperov vs. Deep Blue* as an exploration into the troubling connections between play and simulation, with the computer opponent doomed to play at the best of its simulative abilities: it could only move based on the best possible future. Since convergence tends to collapse boundaries between former categories, leaving only traces of the old within the new (Jenkins, 2008), this creates exchanges that were formerly impossible.

While simulation has not gone as far as machines playing with machines, it is moving to the point of being more "alive" than constructed models and probability trees. Gamified applications of all sorts seem to straddle the line of simulation through the application of creative design strategies. Interestingly, gamification bridges the gaps between simulations and games by appropriating play behaviors to drive simulation. In other words, gamification uses play as a method of engagement to modulate human behavior for the purposes of data collection and modelling. Before I expand on this key point, it is best to provide a working definition of gamification.

Gamification Defined

Gamification is typically defined by practitioners as a business or marketing strategy that began to emerge after marketers and public relations professionals noticed the success of traditional video game platforms in driving behavioral practices among players (Campbell, 2011; Davenport, 2010; Delo, 2012; Zicherman & Linder, 2010). A key focus of gamified applications is promoting, regulating and tracking engagement with products, services, spaces, institutions and ideas through motivational tactics embedded within seemingly simple aspects of game design.

Gamification represents a wide array of applications used for a variety of purposes. In a nutshell, gamification represents a new take on life, one that embraces playful-but-serious surveillance and introduces new techniques that attempt to redefine the categorical position of "player." It achieves this by introducing game mechanics into non-ludic environments via design (Zicherman & Cunningham, 2011). In addition to the design-oriented aspects of gamification, it has an ideological basis that embraces behaviorism through promoting playful behaviors utilizing game-like stimuli and rewards systems. Beyond this, gamification itself is a bit of a mystery in terms of definitional quantification. It is a diverse set of practices and applications that seek to add game mechanics to everyday activities. On one hand, this seems rational—games and engagement are often seen as part and parcel to one another, so gamification is merely "designing for motivation" (Deterding, 2012). Adding game dynamics to something mundane may make it more interesting. On the other hand, gamification seeks to make a profit from this, and based on the projections given earlier, it is a successful venture. At first glance, it may seem that simply adding game mechanics and dynamics to already existing systems wouldn't create profits that reach anywhere near the billions. However, gamification has another ace up its proverbial sleeve: big data and simulation.

Gamification and Big Data

Gamification represents hundreds of applications that span a variety of markets including healthcare (*FitBit*), productivity (*Bunchball*), social networking (*Facebook*) and even pet care (*Whistle*). Two examples used throughout this exploration of collusions in convergence between game design and simulations are *Ingress* and *Strava*. *Ingress*, Google's augmented reality game (ARG), overlays digital geometric resource nodes onto actual spaces and tasks two factions of players in triangulating and controlling these nodes for points, levels and progress. It is also is also an ingenious tool for data mining through gameplay (Hulsey & Reeves, 2014). What makes *Ingress* gamified is the fact that player data is used to solve complex issues pertaining to pedestrian traffic (Gildea, 2012; Hodson, 2012; Lewis, 2013) and locational advertising (Kolb, 2013; Roy, 2012). *Strava* is a location-aware biking application. It requires players map their routes and competitively follow others' routes. Times are recorded and players can compete against past times on any given route by any given player. Players form clubs and compete for leaderboards. They also share their biking-related information, and they accrue capital within the community by sharing this information. The outcome of *Strava's* style of gamification is usually a very detailed map of a person's biking life as a variety of minigames, each with their own rewards and motivations. Players also provide revenue for *Strava* and other parties by virtue of their gameplay data. Scientists also used anonymized, mined data from *Strava* to solve questions about athlete output on a massive scale (Glaskin, 2013). Both of these applications represent a convergence between simulation and games—gameplay is used as the motivational force driving simulations and data taken from everyday activities on a massive scale.

Ingress and *Strava* create monetized gamespaces that feel immersive, pleasurable and natural (Hulsey, 2015). By doing this, they produce a vast set of living simulations where gameplay in actual spaces is used to create data comprising simulated models of behavior in the context of spatiality. Gamification—and its monetization of play through simulation—combines the capabilities of *geographic information systems* (GIS) and geographic positioning systems (GPS) by tracking, recording and manipulating objects' and players' actions in space.

Players in a gamified environment contribute to a much larger set of processes that include non-ludic outcomes—one of which is simulation. One of these outcomes is the collection and use of data to create more effective customer models for a variety of social and economic simulations. Games innately quantify and contextualize players' actions within a (game)space; however, gamified systems utilize the contextualizing mechanics to quantify players behaviors in a variety of spaces and for a multitude of purposes, including the production of capital. Each "player" in a gamified environment contributes to an ongoing, living social simulation driven by "big data." Big data, when applied to customer, product and services, centers on the data produced via "everyday life" (Boyd & Crawford, 2012). It is grounded in the idea that more is better and even seemingly extraneous data can be useful in a large context. In this case, everyday life entails basic actions that previously were not subject to intensive surveillance such as spatiality, hygiene, sleep habits, domestic life, family interactions, media consumption, consumer decisions and daily fitness/health. These are only a few examples. On the individual level, many bodily processes can be gamified, contextualized, monitored and monetized. For example, wearable technologies such as fitness bands, in addition to basic smartphone applications, have become popular in recent years; an application or band with sensors is carried or attached to the player and records a variety of data—everything from the reproductive cycles of women (e.g. *CLUE*) to the heart rate and physicals strain of exercise (e.g. *Fitbit*).

In an article for the *Financial Times*, Steel and Dembosky (2013) note that that information collected through fitness applications and reproductive trackers—some of the most widely used phone applications, many of which are gamified—go to countless third parties, including insurance companies and cottage-industry "data brokers" whose sole purpose is to collect and market metadata (Steel & Dembosky, 2013). The study showed that almost all of the major health applications, including reproductive trackers, reported data to varying third parties. As Steel and Dembosky (2013) state, "iPeriod will soon have the capability to target ads at a very fine level. So a woman who records in the app that she gets headaches before her period could soon receive an ad for a pain reliever at just the right time of the month." Other beneficiaries include insurance companies who could use data against people to charge more for coverage of "abnormal" women (Steel & Dembosky, 2013). Women can also participate in social media via some reproductive trackers and in doing so, they are contributing to the creation of a finely tuned simulation comprised of many women's collective reproductive experiences by also submitting the extraneous social information embedded in their existing profiles. The sample size provided by women using reproductive trackers is much larger than any health protocol produced prior to big data.

Gamification is the driving force behind living simulations, or simulations of everyday life based on the actual, not modelled, behaviors of players. It takes the creative aspects of game design—colorful interfaces, contests, levels, badges and interactivity—and merges them with the capacities of big data to model processes that were formerly too complex, processes like social systems. Using creativity through design, gamified applications create a motivational apparatus for people to actively give over their data in real-time. Rajat Paharia (2014), founder of *Bunchball*, a gamified workflow management system, states that the new economic model addressed by gamified design is one of attention. What grabs and holds attention in this economic model is data, and "if big data and motivation had a lovechild it would be gamification" (Paharia, 2014). For Paharia (2014), gamification represents a way of "architecting virality"—insuring that information and engagement "spreads" evenly over a variety of economic and social sectors. The result is a large cache of data on the bodies and daily activities of thousands of players who use gamified applications for a very simple purpose: to make tasks more fun.

This cache powers complex biological, consumer and economic simulations. For example, Atlas, a company that combines light-based sensors with biological monitoring and a game-like point system, has initiated the Motion Genome Project (MGP), which aims to anonymously track the movements of thousands, or possibly millions, of fitness devotees to build a living map of fitness practices (Cheredar, 2014). Beyond the body itself, *Ingress* seeks to solve long-standing problems with predicting the route of pedestrian traffic via the game mechanics embedded in it.

Convergence is often a question of history (Jenkins, 2008). This means that the combination of gaming, a form of creative design, and simulation, a scientific subset of design, did not occur from a vacuum. While the current use of simulation is still used primarily for science, games have created an opportunity for simulations to extend past modelling and reach into the everyday, quotidian sphere. As objects of study themselves, games have recently been pegged as viable tools of social science research akin to "rat mazes" and "petri dishes" (Castronova & Falk, 2009). However, a key issue is that games, while intersecting with actuality, are also abstract (Castronova & Falk, 2009). Gamified design represents a clever solution to the issue of using games as tools for larger social, consumer, biological and economic questions. It takes away the abstraction of games by inserting mechanics to improve participation, monitoring and validity in everyday practices.

However, a primary question from the standpoint of gamification remains: what preceded these advancements? If convergence is a question of history, and all media leave signatures on future technologies, what preceded the use of gamified design for mass simulation? This leads to a larger question: is the convergence of game design and simulation a revolutionary process? As with most technologies, the answer is no. While games and simulation have only been separated by the fine line of play, they have historically been bedfellows for quite some time. My example of Alan Turing's use of games to test simulations is one example. However, in order to excavate the historical convergence of gaming and large scale social and spatial simulation we do not have to go back very far. *Game of Life*, created in 1970, played with the notion that a computer game can model evolution of an entire system with a few simple rules.

GAME OF LIFE

Game of Life is a major precursor to all current modeling simulations, large-scale gamified applications and simulation-based games such as *Civilization*, *Sim City* and *The Sims* (Aarseth, 1997; Galloway, 2006). Some mathematicians saw in games the ability to visualize and predict advanced evolutionary simulations. One such researcher was John H. Conway, who created the *Game of Life* in 1970 (Itzhak & Torrens, 2004a). Artificial Intelligence, or the study of independent decision-making by computers, was a hot topic in the 1960s with Alan Turing, Claude Shannon and Herbert Simon furiously attempting to impart some degree of intelligent processing to computers by experimenting with mathematical games and combinatorial game theory or CGT. Hardware capabilities and prohibitive costs bottlenecked research during the 1960s and public interest in CA declined (Itzhak & Torrens, 2004a). In fact, Conaway originally created a pen-and-paper game that could, with strict limits, mimic evolutionary processes. A revival of interest in CA happened in the 1970s starting with the presentation of the computerized version of *Game of Life* (Itzhak & Torrens, 2004a). With processing power and a tireless approach, computers could extend Conaway's game to new lengths. Conaway wrote a computer program that visually imitated "cells," small dots on a black screen, that then proliferated based on simple rules into wild geometric patterns and unique assemblages, known as life forms. What resulted was the creation of *cellular automata* (CA), which acted of their own accord based on rules and contingencies set up by the researchers (Itzhak & Torrens, 2004a). CA was the first true exploration of spatial simulation, in which computers were used to determine a future reality by exploring combinations of evolutionary events via sets of game mechanics.

The game, which visualizes self-reproducing, recursive "life" via simple game mechanics, was originally a simple set of rules used to study the spatial dynamics of populations (Itzhak & Torrens, 2004a). Conway used simple rules because the game was originally played via pen-and-paper. He settled on two end-states for the simulated cells—alive or dead. Life or death occurred according to three distinct rules based in spatial arrangement: cells either lived, died or were reincarnated based on their proximity to living or dead neighbors. For "survival" the cells had to position themselves between two living neighbors. To be "born" a dead cell must be surrounded with at least three living cells. "Death" can occur with either overcrowding or loneliness; a live cell can be crowded out by dead or dying neighbors, or it can die because it has no neighbors at all.

The simulation game was simple due to the fact that computational power in the 1970s was minimal compared to today. However, as computation increased, the cells could be imbued with ever-increasing functions and layered with other cells representing different functions. These functions were originally abstract (such as "cell type *n* only 'lives' when next to cells of x 'color' in sector 12"). However, in later iterations on more powerful computers the functions were complex enough to perform advanced action (such as "cell type *n* only 'buys' 'shirts' of x 'color' within y radius of sector 12"). The abstract first rules listed only involve how/when a cell lives or dies within a locational context. The second, advanced rules seek to simulate a location-bound purchase. Simple functions are used to guide the game-like portion of *Game of Life*; in other words they are used to render certain results like shapes and patterns. Time can be sped up or slowed, depending on how the player (or researcher) wishes to observe the evolution of the space. At low speeds the cells barely seem to move; at high speeds the swarm the darkness of the scree and pulse with digital life. Game of Life, originally hampered by processing power, led to simulating more and more complex functions. Complex functions could be used to represent real-world social or economic actors, such as an individual with certain traits buying a shirt in a certain area. The digital organisms followed an evolutionary algorithm based partially on game theory (Conway, 1974). The simple rules produced population dynamics that were complex, unpredictable and often unexpected (Aarseth, 1997). The position and rules attached to the initial cells determine the outcome of the cellular formation, similar to stem cells. However, as each generation forms, the ability of the researcher to predict what life forms will appear gets more accurate, not less. In other words, the model becomes more predictive of future life forms—despite the fact that new behaviors are constantly occurring—as the simulation portion of the game becomes complex.

The rules of *Game of Life* can be tweaked by the researcher *or* player, usually to account for complex "hard" and "soft" agents. *Hard agents* represent stable structural agents (such as a building) while *soft agents* are more unpredictable biological agents (such as humans, insects or animals). Both are imbued with particular properties and then "set free" to trace a multitude of interactional possibilities. Despite changes, the concept remains the same: emulation of life and death through imbuing a system with agential properties and allowing it to play itself—with the results of the game being recorded and then sublimated to actualized physical-spatial designs. *Game of Life* is a spatial simulation that plays itself with some input from the user. *Game of Life* demonstrated that replicating and predicting unique forms of life formed from cells following simple sets of game mechanics was possible and effective. By watching larger patterns as they coalesce over different generations, each individual cellular construct in *Game of Life* can be accounted for *before it forms*. In other words, games produce predictable results even when the agents themselves are unpredictable. This is the basis for agent-based modelling. Making sense of big data is dependent on game mechanics and the algorithms they produce—the algorithms produced by combinatorial games are the basis for heuristics, which inform all model-based simulations (Gilbert, 2008; Pearl, 1984).

The automata in *Game of Life* and other spatial simulations form MAS, which deploy variable functions into a simulated space to present the "soft" components of a space—i.e., its population of players as represented by CA. Human individuals are represented in MAS models by "free agents" that carry within the function differentiated algorithms that "carry the economic and cultural properties of human individuals" (Itzhak & Torrens, 2004b). Gamification borrows from MAS; however, instead of "cells" imbued with behavioral properties, gamification introduces living players into the altered gamespace of everyday life and then tracks their reactions and movements. Rather than simulating model humans via cells, gamification utilizes actual humans (and their bodies) in a vast, living simulation aimed at producing *and* predicting protocol.

While *Game of Life* shares an ontological background with computer games it does not represent the same ideological or epistemic concerns as computer games (Aarseth, 1997). It is an example of ergodic literature, or literature that require nontrivial effort to traverse or navigate that text (Aarseth, 1997). *Game of Life* is a primary example of Aarseth's (1997) notion of "story-living," a narrative that is somewhat self-perpetuating. While *Game of Life* will operate by itself once set in motion, it requires the player to define the rules by which the simulation runs. Tweaking these rules results in different generations of life forms and ecosystems generated over the course of play. *Game of Life* represents the thin line between simulations and games. In *Game of Life*, one plays *with* the simulation, rather than engaging in the simulative process itself. Both simulations and games are referred to as "fictionings of the future" by Crogan (2011). Galloway (2006) refers to historical simulation-based games as algorithmic reformulations of the past. In all cases, simulations and games are only slightly different—one is 'serious' and the other 'playful.' A game requires constant input in order to create a narrative, while a simulation only needs rules to project probable outcomes. Elements of *Game of Life* show that games are inherently different from simulations, which are always game-like but do not involve play (Myers, 1999). Gamification utilizes recursive evolutionary modeling to harness the predictive capacity of game-based algorithms. Simulation games simply tell a story, one that is controlled and tweaked by the player.

The purpose of *Game of Life* was twofold, it was meant to demonstrate how a computational system could be valuable for spatial, evolutionary simulations. Beyond that, however, *Game of Life* is an open ended game where beautiful, mosaic-like patterns can be created from tweaking the rules and combinations of cells. This open-ended game, like gamified applications, had a twofold purpose. However, unlike gamified applications, *Game of Life* is self-referential. Outside of demonstrating how a computer could do a spatial simulation, it was little more than an open-ended game of evolution that refers only to itself. *Game of Life* produced a long line of similar, open-ended games.

For example, CA-based design methods are often used in historical simulation games like *Civilization* and city planning games like *SimCity*. *The Sims*—a popular CA-based simulation game that involves managing the lives, spaces and social interactions of simulated humans—has been utilizing mechanics derived from the *Game of Life* and other explorations of evolutionary AI since its inception at the turn of the 21st century. In many regards, the gamification of everyday life reflects the situation of *The Sims*. Entities that design and implement gamified spaces for players aim to observe how players react in different situations. Living players, who act the part of CA, are invited explore and use a gamespace to reap rewards such as points, badges, content and levels. Gameplay, facilitated by a game dynamics and design, is the primary mode of motivation for the cells (i.e., players) to move about in the created gamespace. If enough cells are active, then the formation of new players, and their eventual actions within the gamespace, can be predicted over time.

INGRESS, STRAVA, AND LIVING MAPS

There is no straight line to draw between *Game of Life* and gamified applications like *Strava* and *Ingress*. Rather, convergence happens through a network of related technologies. *Game of Life* demonstrated one simple aspect of computing: that simple patterns can produce amazing results and computers can represent these in real time as MAS. In the 1970's this was a revelation and the beginning of spatial simulation. The most basic aspect of modern geography is Tobler's (1970)first law of geography: "Everything is related to everything else, but near things are more related than distant things" (p. 236). Tobler (1970) developed the law in 1970 while using computational simulation to predict the population growth of Detroit—a computational system that was based on the same framework as *Game of Life*. From the standpoint of technology alone, *Game of Life* is actually a direct precedent to modern day GIS programs like *ArcGIS* and MAS software like *Alice*.

What makes *Game of Life* so important from the standpoint of gamified applications like *Strava* and *Ingress* is noting the pattern between games and simulation: once separate categories, they were combined for *Game of Life* on the space of the screen. What resulted was the creation of modern-day spatial simulation which, incidentally led to the creation of the very technologies enabling GIS/GPS systems to represent both space and movement through it based on the rules of probability. Gamification is a modern combination of gaming and simulation enabled by technologies directly descended from *Game of Life*. However, the signature of *Game of Life* extends well beyond technological parentage. The networked technology to the GPS/GIS cell phone has allowed gamified applications, and game design itself, extend far beyond the screen. However, the mode of combining games and simulation for useful, even profitable, results is also similar: simple rules create complex patterns that can be modelled once observed.

Rather than utilize simulated cells, gamified design in *Strava* and *Ingress* uses the basic predictive concept of *Game of Life* and applies it to living players. For example, *Ingress* utilizes player data to predict where and how players will move in any given situation. They do this by providing hard structural agents, such as the location of resources, and watching how players move to obtain these resources.

Following in the *Game of Life*, *Ingress* seeks to create a living set of CA made of players. By recording and tracking player movements, Google will eventually be able to better predict pedestrian traffic and customer responses to location-based advertising. This predictive model becomes more accurate as the player base increases, despite the game seeming more chaotic.

The process of creating gamespaces that double as living simulations lies between the creative design gameplay and simulation-oriented modelling and surveillance. *Game of Life* produced a myriad of procedural cells and tied them to a series of spatially instantiated game rules. Based on these rules, the cells expand to form a clear pattern. On a micro scale, it makes no sense, but on the larger scale there is a discernable image created by the cells. A player in *Ingress* must find the quickest routes to nodes, routes that change depending on the locations and actions of other players. Tactics can be repeated based on the player's mental model of *Ingress'* map, but even master players do not yield exactly the same results on subsequent attempts to find and link nodes.

Gameplay, when harnessed and directed by games, produces useful algorithms (or mathematical functions that use probability to solve problems). Algorithms inform the development of protocol on computational and evolutionary levels; they power Google searches and they control the ways in which DNA combine. They are also the basis for any successful simulation. Because play produces a wonderful array of algorithms when parsed through game mechanics, it is a perfect technique for driving a living simulation, with players acting as models. This provides a method for gamified app developers to "solve" a problem using gameplay. Essentially, gamification is game theory removed from "theory" and inserted into everyday life.

While *Game of Life* was relegated to a computer screen, it demonstrated the power of MAS and the ability of a computer to represent that overall patterns that a large number of cellular actors generate. However, gamified applications like *Ingress* show how convergence works to create new possibilities from creative combinations of older media. Through GIS/GPS and networked smartphones, *Ingress* turns player into "cells" and, via game mechanics, everyday spaces are embedded with the rules that determine how the cells move. For example, a utilitarian social space like a dog park exists before *Ingress*; however, gamified applications grant new, gameplay-oriented contexts to these spaces for the purposes of monetized simulation. While a game of tag might also alter the dog park, the park takes on an entirely new meaning distinctly related to the game—tag is self-referential in its use of the park. Similarly, *Game of Life* only demonstrates how a computer can track the evolutionary process of MAS. The purpose the game aspects of *Game of Life*, which is open-ended, is to produce interesting patterns with different combinations of rules and cells. However, *Ingress* produces useable data. *Ingress* makes the park a central resource node, a space that hosts embedded mechanics that identify the space as gamespace. Rather than simply being layered onto the park, *Ingress* decontextualizes the park itself for players, who may or may not be there to walk their dog—but it does this to complete a goal beyond that of a game. The same can be said of *Strava*, a social biking application that produces accurate data about thousands, perhaps millions, of cyclers (Glaskin, 2013). It is social biking gamified application that relies on aesthetic, simulated space to thrive.

Strava's playful interface aggressively reframes the player's riding experience via seduction and ludic framing. Ward (2014), a cycling blogger and self-identified "*Strava* cycling addict," states his cycling experience was irrevocably altered via game mechanics. Specifically, Ward cites mapping his actions in coordination with others led to a new perspective on his hobby. He was able to track his own progress by monitoring other players' times via lateral surveillance. Ward (2014) states,

I discovered one of Strava's many clubs. I could join and compare my performance against other members. I should have just ignored it, and continued as before. Stupidly, I didn't, and too late I realised (sic) that my regular, innocent fix of data about my day's bike ride had actually been a gateway drug to something far more addictive – a big, shiny league table in which the position of your name is determined by how many miles you've logged. Usually as competitive as a cabbage, I suddenly wanted to be top of the league. Now, instead of merely uploading my data, comparing it with the previous day's and then logging off until my next ride, I have become obsessed not just with my own performance, but those of the other 60-plus members of the club.

This live, competitive mapping process encourages riders to modulate their behavior based on the location-based digital information tagged by other players. Players also create narratives based on the frames generated by locational information which is, in turn, generated via play (Dovey & Kennedy, 2006). Both perception and narrative contribute to the overall design of *Strava*. It embodies the possibilities inherent in when combining gameplay and simulation by leveraging space.

Like *Game of Life*, *Strava* involves cells, in the form of individuals, and life in terms of their movements through space. While death is not necessarily an outcome, discerning the overall pattern of movements in relation to one another is. For example, cycling researcher Max Glaskin (2013) recounts how a team of Italian researchers used *Strava's* API to collect the second-to-second ride information of *Strava* cyclers. Studies have been theorizing about relationships between training and improvement for year says Glaskin. "But they've been based on the results from a few dozen professional or, occasionally, a few hundred experienced participants..." states Glaskin. "Those old studies look tiny... with every second of those riders' activities in stored in digital form." The researchers had a sample of 29,284 cyclists ranging from "elite to pathetic" (Glaskin, 2013). The researchers pulled so much data that they crashed the *Strava* API, causing developers to now require permission for use and access. Like *Ingress* and *Game of Life*, the larger the amount of data, the more clear the research models become. With the data, the scientists could properly simulate the ratio of training to improvement in cycling.

Strava straddles both simulation and gaming in a manner that utilizes space, self-archival, digital rewards, predictive mechanics and competition to produce a wealth of information of biking cultures across the globe. Inevitably, *Strava* also increases the predictive capacity of consumer simulation based on spatial data: where people bike, what groups of people bikes together, the demographic stratification of these groups, the equipment they share with the app and the general daily social habits that identify *Strava* players as "cyclists" are all integrated into a massive database. Some of this data is fed back to cyclists, allowing them to monitor themselves and others, but most of the data is used to improve the predictive capabilities of the system. This portion of *Strava* may be self-referential (for instance, providing meaning via updates based on player usage) but it also has the ability to reach much further than the application itself. Like the health and fitness applications discussed earlier, *Strava* can easily provide a wealth of targeted locational and personal data on individual cyclists and small, location-bound groups. In turn, it also creates and manipulates the social mechanisms these groups operate by adding game mechanics.

For *Strava* and *Ingress*, location is inseparable from identity—in the collective map created by these applications players embody a living simulative space. Without players actively creating, exploring and differentiating gamespaces, games and gamification cannot exist. One major ideological aspect of gamification is that play should be an "everyday" state of being—people construct gamespaces and their identities within them as they go about everyday life. Gamified spaces networked and mapped by *Strava* are modified through game design—they are spaces in which play has the possibility of occurring.

Gamified spaces, converted from quotidian spaces, are the end result of these gamified applications' efforts to spatially combine game design and simulation. For example, *Ingress* augments quotidian city space with resource nodes which must be controlled by players. These nodes previously existed in physical space: they are monuments, statues, restaurants and dog parks. However, their quotidian meanings are altered by *Ingress'* mechanics—because locations are subsumed into a battle for resource control, they create a networked space where players find context in their movements and actions. In turn, these contextual movements fuel Google's advanced simulation, which in turn creates capital. Gamespaces rely on seductive network architecture to motivate players, forcing them to adjust to constant changes in the gamified environment. The more players adjust, the easier it is to predict the ways in which adaptation is possible; just like in *Game of Life*, chaos and complexity yield more accurate results.

CONCLUSION

Convergence is a question of networks as they unfold, leaving the media landscape dotted with the signatures of past technologies. In the case of *Game of Life*, it lent its signature to both GIS and gamification in differing ways. However, its fruitful collapsing of the boundaries between games and simulations is impacting the ways in which big data is being collected and used to drive the creative economy. Focusing on emerging technological trends via media archaeology yields a wide array of information. In the case of gamification, what is often tagged as "new" or "revolutionary" suddenly seems less so. Using methods like media archaeology allow scholars to better understand the place of a technology or practice in the vast network of a constantly changing media landscape. Doing so is important because, as James Carey (1989) points out concerning the emergence of the telegraph, technologies that are thought of as "new" become saviors that inevitably disappoint.

The convergence of games and simulation is not without issue. Chris Anderson, editor of *Wired* magazine, states that in the "petabyte age" enough data speaks for itself—theory is becoming obsolete (Anderson, 2008). However, this is often not the case. Attempting to regulate and categorize everyday life and play for the purposes of simulation (and profit) poses problematic ethical questions concerning surveillance (Whitson, 2013), accuracy (Miller, 2012; Shaker, 2006) and the exploitation of playful behavior (Dyer-Witheford & de Peuter, 2009). These problems run parallel to issues with big data and simulation: if large-scale decisions are made based on incorrect models the results have much greater impact—one example being the recent global financial meltdown (Boyd & Crawford, 2012). Additionally, while big data may provide supposedly "better" models, it may also reduce overall freedom and tolerance for deviation (Boyd & Crawford, 2012). In modern warfare, for example, games and simulations have also seen convergence over the course of the last four decades with troubling social, economic and technological results (Crogan, 2011). One downside of military simulations is their frequent failure to account for tactical, social and environmental shifts where it seems the simulations themselves have a "hidden curriculum" not reflective of the realities they intend to predict (Veen, Fenema, & Jongejan, 2012). The convergence of gaming and simulation is also troubling because it heralds a period in time where even playful behaviors, often characterized as free and not-for-profit pursuits, are increasingly capitalized upon (Ferrara, 2013). These issues are all aspects of convergence on a variety of scales, and each one can be illuminated by examining the signatures of preceding technologies, processes and effects.

By analyzing creative technologies and practices in light of their historical networks, we gain a clearer picture of how the future will unfold. Media archaeology is a myopic pursuit—analysis on a small scale.

However, sometimes (big) data is not what it seems. If one looks at the combination of games and technology, a pattern emerges: first, games and technology were combined to simulate evolutionary life on the screen to prove a point. The new combinations use life itself to power the simulative capabilities of certain aspects of big data. Simulation, through gaming, has moved from modelling life to harnessing it. While advantageous in some regards, this shift could have serious consequences. In future research, scholars should pause to think about their object of analysis. Perhaps ask, "What are its precedents and what can they tell us about its current state?" Using historical methods like media archaeology in the field of creative technologies can open up a wider array of study that provides a three dimensional view of current processes of convergence. Like *Game of Life*, tracing the signatures of creative technology will create a patterns that, as more lines are drawn, become more accurate models.

REFERENCES

Aarseth, E. J. (1997). *Cybertext: Perspectives on Ergodic Literature*. Baltimore, MD: Johns Hopkins University Press.

Anderson, C. (2008). *The end of theory, will the data deluge make the scientific method obsolete?* Retrieved July 20, 2014, from http://edge.org/3rd_culture/anderson08/anderson08_index.html

Baudrillard, J. (2001). *Impossible Exchange* (C. Turner, Trans.). London: Verso.

Bayart, C., Bertezene, S., Vallat, D., & Martin, J. (2014). Serious games: Leverage for knowledge management. *The TQM Journal*, 26(3), 235–252. doi:10.1108/TQM-12-2013-0143

Boellstorff, T. (2006). A Ludicrous Discipline? Ethnography and Game Studies. *Games and Culture*, 1(1), 29–35. doi:10.1177/1555412005281620

Bolter, J. D., & Grusin, R. (2000). *Remediation: Understanding New Media*. Cambridge, MA: MIT Press.

Boyd, D., & Crawford, K. (2012). Critical Questions for Big Data. *Information Communication and Society*, 15(5), 662–679. doi:10.1080/1369118X.2012.678878

Braitmaier, M., & Kyriazis, D. (2011). *Virtual and Augmented Reality: Improved User Experience through a Service Oriented Infrastructure*. Paper presented at the Games and Virtual Worlds for Serious Applications (VS-GAMES), 2011 Third International Conference on.

Broin, D. O. (2011). *Using a Criteria-Based User Model for Facilitating Flow in Serious Games*. Paper presented at the Games and Virtual Worlds for Serious Applications (VS-GAMES), 2011 Third International Conference on.

Burke, B. (2014). *Gamify: How Gamification Motivates People to do Extraordinary Things*. Brookline, MA: Bibliomotion.

BusinessWire. (2015). *Research and Markets: Gamification Companies, Solutions, Market Outlook and Forecasts 2015 – 2020*. Retrieved March 3, 2015, from http://www.businesswire.com/news/home/20150224005574/en/Research-Markets-Gamification-Companies-Solutions-Market-Outlook#.VPduFIs5BwE

Byrne, T. (2012). The evolving digital workplace. *KM World*, *21*(9), 12–14.

Campbell, M. (2011). The audacious plan to make the world into a game. *New Scientist, 209*(2794), 02-02.

Carey, J. (1989). *Communication as Culture*. New York: Routledge.

Castells, M. (2002). The Internet galaxy: Reflections on the Internet, business and society. New York: Oxford. doi:10.1093/acprof:oso/9780199255771.001.0001

Castells, M. (2009). *The Global Network Society Communication Power* (pp. 24–37). New York: Oxford University Press.

Castronova, E., & Falk, M. (2009). Virtual Worlds: Petri Dishes, Rat Mazes, and Supercolliders. *Games and Culture*, *4*(4), 396–407. doi:10.1177/1555412009343574

Chapin, A. (2011). The Future is a Videogame. *Canadian Business*, *84*(4), 46–48.

Cheredar, T. (2014). *Atlas raises $1.1M to power its Motion Genome Project, a motion database for wearables*. Retrieved May 5, 2015, from http://venturebeat.com/2014/10/08/atlas-raises-1-1m-to-power-its-motion-genome-project-a-motion-database-for-wearables/

Consalvo, M. (2009). There is No Magic Circle. *Games and Culture*, *4*(4), 408–417. doi:10.1177/1555412009343575

Crogan, P. (2011). *Gameplay Mode: War, Simulation and Technoculture*. Minneapolis: U of Minnesota Press. doi:10.5749/minnesota/9780816653348.001.0001

Crogan, P., & Kennedy, H. (2009). Technologies Between Games and Culture. *Games and Culture*, *4*(2), 107–114. doi:10.1177/1555412008325482

Crookall, D. (2010). Serious Games, Debriefing, and Simulation/Gaming as a Discipline. *Simulation & Gaming*, *41*(6), 898–920. doi:10.1177/1046878110390784

Davenport, R. (2010). More than a Game. *T+D, 64*(6), 26-29.

Delo, C. (2012). What is gamification, and how can I make it useful for my brand? *Advertising Age*, *83*(9), 58–58.

Deterding, S. (2012). Gamification: designing for motivation. *Interactions, 19*(4), 14-17. doi:10.1145/2212877.2212883

Dovey, J., & Kennedy, H. W. (2006). *Game Cultures: Computer Games as New Media*. New York: Open University Press.

Dyer-Witheford, N., & de Peuter, G. (2009). *Games of Empire: Capitalism and Video Games*. Minneapolis: University of Minnesota Press.

Elizabeth, L. (2007). Walls, Doors, Condoms, and Duct Tape: Serious Games about National Security and Public Health. *Discourse (Berkeley, Calif.)*, *29*(1), 101–119.

Ferrara, J. (2013). Games for Persuasion: Argumentation, Procedurality, and the Lie of Gamification. *Games and Culture*, *8*(4), 289–304. doi:10.1177/1555412013496891

Foucault, M. (2010). *The Archaeology of Knowledge and the Discourse on Language* (R. Swyer, Trans.). New York: Vintage.

Fuchs, M., Fizek, S., Ruffino, P., & Schrape, N. (Eds.). (2014). *Rethinking Gamification*. Luneberg Meson.

Galloway, A. R. (2006). *Gaming: Essays on Algorithmic Culture*. Minneapolis, MN: University of Minnesota Press.

Giddings, S. (2007a). Dionysiac Machines: Videogames and the Triumph of the Simulacra. *Convergence (London)*, *13*(4), 417–431. doi:10.1177/1354856507082204

Giddings, S. (2007b). A 'Pataphysics Engine: Technology, Play, and Realities. *Games and Culture*, *2*(4), 392–404. doi:10.1177/1555412007309534

Gilbert, N. (2008). *Agent-Based Models*. London: SAGE.

Gildea, D. (2012). *Very clever: Google's Ingress masks Data-Collection in Gaming*. Retrieved June 15, 2013, from http://takefiveblog.org/2012/12/09/ingress-gathering-data-through-gaming/

Gitelman, L. (2008). *Always, Already New*. Cambridge, MA: MIT Press.

Glaskin, M. (2013). *Strava users help sports science – unwittingly*. Retrieved May 1, 2015, 2015, from http://cyclingandscience.com/2013/11/20/strava-users-help-sports-science-unwittingly/

Harteveld, C., Guimarães, R., Mayer, I. S., & Bidarra, R. (2010). Balancing Play, Meaning and Reality: The Design Philosophy of LEVEE PATROLLER. *Simulation & Gaming*, *41*(3), 316–340. doi:10.1177/1046878108331237

Hassenzahl, M., Diefenbach, S., & Göritz, A. (2010). Needs, affect, and interactive products – Facets of user experience. *Interacting with Computers*, *22*(5), 353–362. doi:10.1016/j.intcom.2010.04.002

Hodson, H. (2012). *Why Google's Ingress game is a data gold mine*. Retrieved June 15, 2013, from http://www.newscientist.com/article/mg21628936.200-why-googles-ingress-game-is-a-data-gold-mine.html#.UbzPl_aus9F

Huang Ling, Y. (2011). *Designing Serious Games to Enhance Political Efficacy and Critical Thinking Disposition for College Students: The Case of Taiwan*. Paper presented at the Games and Virtual Worlds for Serious Applications (VS-GAMES), 2011 Third International Conference on.

Huizinga, J. (1950). Homo Ludens: A Study of the Play-Element. In *Culture*. Boston: Beacon Press.

Hulsey, N. (2015). Houses in Motion: An Overview of Gamification in the Context of Mobile Interfaces. In A. De Souza e Silva & M. Sheller (Eds.), *Mobility and Locative Media: Mobile Communication in Hybrid Spaces*. New York: Routledge.

Hulsey, N., & Reeves, J. (2014). The Gift that Keeps on Giving: Google, Ingress, and the Gift of Surveillance. *Surveillance & Society*, *12*(3), 389–400.

Itzhak, B., & Torrens, P. M. (2004a). *Modeling Urban Land-use with Cellular Automata. In Geosimulation: Automata-based modeling of urban phenomena* (pp. 90–152). Chichester, UK: Wiley.

Itzhak, B., & Torrens, P. M. (2004b). *System Theory, Geography and Urban Modeling. In Geosimulation: Automata-based modeling of urban phenomena* (pp. 47–90). Chichester, UK: Wiley.

Jenkins, H. (2008). *Convergence Culture: Where Old and New Media Collide*. New York: NYU Press.

Jørgensen, K. (2012). Between the Game System and the Fictional World: A Study of Computer Game Interfaces. *Games and Culture*, 7(2), 142–163. doi:10.1177/1555412012440315

Kim, B. (2012). Harnessing the power of game dynamics. *College & Research Libraries News*, 73(8), 465–469.

Kittler, F. (1986). *Grammaphone, Film, Typewriter*. Stanford, CA: Stanford University Press.

Kittler, F. (2010). *Optical Media*. Cambridge, MA: Polity Press.

Klabbers, J. H. G. (2009). Terminological Ambiguity: Game and Simulation. *Simulation & Gaming*, 40(4), 446–463. doi:10.1177/1046878108325500

Kolb, J. (2013). *The Hidden Side of Ingress*. Retrieved June 15, 2013, from http://www.applieddatalabs.com/content/hidden-side-ingress

Kumar, J. M., & Herger, M. (2013). *Gamification at Work: Designing Engaging Business Software*. New York: The Interactions Design Foundation.

Levy, P. (1997). The Art and Architecture of Cyberspace: The Aesthetics of Collective Intelligence (R. Bononno, Trans.). In Collective Intelligence: Mankind's Emerging World in Cyberspace (pp. 117-130). Cambridge: Perseus Books.

Lewis, J. (2013). *Ingress - Crowdsourcing Solutions to NP-Hard Problems?* Retrieved June 15, 2013, from http://decomplecting.org/blog/2013/01/22/ingress-crowdsourcing-solutions-to-np-hard-problems/

Malaby, T. M. (2007). Beyond Play: A New Approach to Games. *Games and Culture*, 2(2), 95–113. doi:10.1177/1555412007299434

Marsh, T. (2011). Serious games continuum: Between games for purpose and experiential environments for purpose. *Entertainment Computing*, 2(2), 61–68. doi:10.1016/j.entcom.2010.12.004

Mauss, M. (2000). *The Gift: The Form and Reason for Exchange in Archaic Societies*. New York: W.W. Norton & Co.

Mead, G. H. (1934). *Mind, Self, and Society* (C. W. Morris, Ed.). Chicago: U of Chicago Press.

Miller, T. (2012). The Shameful Trinity: Game Studies, Empire, and the Cognitariat. In G. A. Voorhees, J. Call, & K. Whitlock (Eds.), Guns, Grenades, and Grunts: First-Person Shooter Games (pp. 2033-2368). New York: Continuum.

Moreno-Ger, P., Torrente, J., Hsieh, Y. G., & Lester, W. T. (2012). Usability Testing for Serious Games: Making Informed Design Decisions with User Data. *Advances in Human-Computer Interaction*, 2012, 1–13. doi:10.1155/2012/369637

Myers, D. (1999). Simulation, Gaming, and the Simulative. *Simulation & Gaming*, 30(4), 482–489. doi:10.1177/104687819903000406

Myers, D. (2006). Signs, Symbols, Games, and Play. *Games and Culture*, *1*(1), 47–51. doi:10.1177/1555412005281778

Paharia, R. (2013). *Loyalty 3.0: How to Revolutionize Customer and Employee Engagement with Big Data and Gamification*. New York: McGraw-Hill.

Paharia, R. (2014). Can You Architect Virality? Absolutely. Here's How. *Gamification Blog*.

Parikka, J. (2012). *What is Media Archaeology*. London: Polity Press.

Pearce, C. (2006). Productive Play: Game Culture From the Bottom Up. *Games and Culture*, *1*(1), 17–24. doi:10.1177/1555412005281418

Pearl, J. (1984). *Heuristics*. New York: Addison-Wesley.

Petridis, P., Dunwell, I., Arnab, S., Scarle, S., Qureshi, A., de Freitas, S., et al. (2011). *Building Social Commmunities around Alternate Reality Games*. Paper presented at the Games and Virtual Worlds for Serious Applications (VS-GAMES), 2011 Third International Conference on.

Pias, C. (2011). On the Epistemology of Computer Simulation. *Zeitschrift für Medien- und Kulturforschung*, *1*(11).

Roth, S. (2015). Serious Gamification: On the Redesign of a Popular Paradox. *Games and Culture*. doi:10.1177/1555412015581478

Roy, J. (2012). *Much Like GOOG-411, Google's New Augmented Reality Game Ingress Is a Genius Ploy to Get You To Collect Data*. Retrieved June 15, 2013, from http://betabeat.com/2012/11/much-like-goog-411-googles-new-augmented-reality-game-ingress-is-a-genius-ploy-to-get-you-to-collect-data/

Ruffino, P. (2014). From engagement to life, or: how to do things with gamification? In M. Fuchs, S. Fizek, P. Ruffino, & N. Schrape (Eds.), *Rethinking Gamification* (pp. 47–70). Lüneburg, Germany: Meson Press.

Shaker, L. (2006). Google we trust: Information integrity in the digital age. Academic Press.

Steel, E., & Dembosky, A. (2013). *Health apps run into privacy snags*. Retrieved September 20, 2014, from http://www.ft.com/intl/cms/s/0/b709cf4a-12dd-11e3-a05e-00144feabdc0.html#axzz3JHHno8bz

Steinkuehler, C. (2006). The Mangle of Play. *Games and Culture*, *1*(3), 199–213. doi:10.1177/1555412006290440

Swan, C. (2012). Gamification: A new way to shape behavior. *Communication World*, *29*(3), 13–14.

Taylor, N. T. (2008). Periscopic Play: Re-positioning 'The Field' in MMO Research. *Loading...* *1*(3).

Taylor, T. L. (2006). Does WoW Change Everything?: How a PvP Server, Multinational Player Base, and Surveillance Mod Scene Caused Me Pause. *Games and Culture*, *1*(4), 318–337. doi:10.1177/1555412006292615

Taylor, T. L. (2006). *Play Between Worlds: Exploring online game culture*. Cambridge, MA: MIT Press.

Taylor, T. L. (2009). The Assemblage of Play. *Games and Culture*, *4*(4), 331–339. doi:10.1177/1555412009343576

Tobler, W. (1970). A computer movie simulating urban growth in the Detroit region. *Economic Geography*, *46*(2), 234–240. doi:10.2307/143141

Tolentino, G. P., Battaglini, C., Pereira, A. C. V., de Oliveria, R. J., & de Paula, M. G. M. (2011). *Usability of Serious Games for Health*. Paper presented at the Games and Virtual Worlds for Serious Applications (VS-GAMES), 2011 Third International Conference on.

Turing, A. (2004). *The Essential Turing* (J. B. Copeland, Ed.). Oxford, UK: Oxford U Press.

Turing, A., Post, E., & Davies, D. W. (2004). On Computer Numbers: Corrections and Critiques. In J. B. Copeland (Ed.), *The Essential Turing* (pp. 91–124). Oxford, UK: Oxford U. Press.

Veen, M., Fenema, P., & Jongejan, P. (2012). Towards a Framework for Unraveling the Hidden Curriculum in Military Training Simulators. In S. Wannemacker, S. Vandercruysse, & G. Clarebout (Eds.), *Serious Games: The Challenge* (Vol. 280, pp. 65–73). Springer Berlin Heidelberg. doi:10.1007/978-3-642-33814-4_10

Ward, T. (2014). *Confessions of a Strava cycling addict*. Retrieved September 8, 2014, from http://www.theguardian.com/environment/bike-blog/2014/jan/14/confessions-of-a-strava-cycling-addict-app

White, D. S., Gunasekaran, A., & Roy, M. H. (2014). Performance measures and metrics for the creative economy. *Benchmarking: An International Journal*, *21*(1), 46–61. doi:10.1108/BIJ-03-2012-0017

Whitson, J. R. (2013). Gaming the Quantified Self. *Surveillance & Society*, *11*(1/2), 163–176.

Wolf, M. J. P. (2006). Game Studies and Beyond. *Games and Culture*, *1*(1), 116–118. doi:10.1177/1555412005281787

Zicherman, G., & Cunningham, C. (2011). *Gamification by design: implementing game mechanics in web and mobile apps*. New York: O'Reilly Media.

Zicherman, G., & Linder, J. (2010). *Game-based marketing: inspire customer loyalty through rewards, challenges and contests*. Wiley.

Chapter 7
Machinima:
A Meme of Our Time

Tracy Harwood
De Montfort University, UK

ABSTRACT

This chapter presents an overview of machinima, an important socio-cultural movement that originated in the 1990s gameplay movement known as demoscene. The chapter presents a review of literature and key issues related to its evolution. Modes of its production (perfect capture, screen capture, asset compositing, bespoke machinimation) are described, along with the range of different genres that have emerged, including fan vid, parody, documentary, music video, advertising, reportage, reenactment, activist, pre-visualization and artistic forms. Thereafter, the chapter identifies channels of distribution and growth trajectories for each. The chapter then presents four key phases of the emergence of machinima, identifying the key actors and roles of organizations within each phase. As a movement that continues to evolve, the discussion presented is by no means a final analysis, thus the aim of the chapter is to present a 'state of the art' overview of its emergence and development.

INTRODUCTION

As a contemporary movement embedded within creative technologies practices, and a growing and rapidly evolving socio-cultural phenomenon, machinima is the making of original works using and reusing the content of 3D computer games engines. Since the first film, recorded and released in 1996 by the gaming clan known as The Rangers, there are now over 2B creators of machinima, using a range of platforms within games and more widely accessible social media to disseminate their creative works. Its latest manifestation can be seen in the Let's Play community, live action gamesplay with dedicated virtual channels some of which regularly generate viewership of over 1M people. It is inherently a contemporary example of creative technologies in action, based on the artistic and aesthetic competencies of those making the work, but embedded within hacking and modding cultures, deeply rooted in new technologies typically associated with computer video gaming.

DOI: 10.4018/978-1-5225-0016-2.ch007

This chapter explores the emergence and growth of machinima, drawing on findings from an Arts & Humanities Research Council (UK) funded Cultural Values Project undertaken by the author (see machinima.dmua.ac.uk). The project investigated the 'state-of-the-art' of machinima and provides a summary of perspectives from a range of stakeholders including professional and amateur artists, indie and AAA games developers and digital arts curators from around the world. Thus, this chapter will draw on this research to present an overview of the emergence and growth of machinima communities of practice alongside games technologies.

The chapter aims to present:

- A review of relevant literature in relation to the emergence and growth of machinima;
- An overview of the different formats of machinima, such as perfect capture, screen capture, asset compositing and bespoke machinimation;
- An evaluation of the evolution of machinima related to video game technologies;
- An analysis of the future of machinima and its socio-cultural evolution; and,
- A list of key artefacts with weblinks in relation to research findings.

LITERATURE REVIEW

Machinima is the making of original content using 3D computer games engines and gameplay recorded in real time. Machinima creators ('machinimators') now draw on a multiplicity of computer video games but this type of co-created and participatory content was originally popularised by the growth in fantasy and simulated role-play environments such as World of Warcraft©, Halo©, Grand Theft Auto© and The Sims©. It originates from the 'demoscene' whereby computer 'geeks' seek to promote the technical capabilities of their computers through demonstrations of gameplay in online fora.

The first machinima film is widely recognized as being *Diary of a Camper*, recorded and produced in 1996 by a group of gamers calling themselves The Rangers. Since then, machinimators have created and distributed tens of thousands of fan vids, parodies, satires, reenactments and original content through online fora in an increasingly complex ecology of technologies and new media. Its influence has been widespread, impacting digital arts, film, new media platforms and even politics through the user-generated co-created and produced content, some of which has been used as 'pre-production' for big budget films that have subsequently been realised in mainstream environments such as Hollywood (eg., The Lord of the Rings and Resident Evil).

Its growth in popularity has impacted games developers significantly because it challenges the ways in which they view their intellectual property and the role of their customers (games players) in the creation of commercial value, effectively testing the boundaries between authorship and ownership. In turn, this has resulted in a shift in thinking about the format and framing of end-user license agreements (by eg., Microsoft, EA Games). Content has now spilled out from the internet into digital arts festivals and galleries (e.g. Atopic, France; Animatu, Portugal; Bitfilm, Germany; Phoenix Square, Leicester UK): machinima is inherently a convergence of technology, digital social practice and culture.

Importantly, some commentators have described it as '*the* visual cultural phenomenon of the 21st century' (Greenaway, 2010). Machinima is also uniquely used to provide insight into social 'virtual' actions that take place within 3D online environments such as Second Life©, through recordings and productions, thereby encompassing digital performance as a key component of creative practice. It is also embedded within social media networks, which are central to digital access of this form of content and, in early 2013, Machinima.com, a prominent community forum, became one of few social networking platforms to list on the US stock market (Nasdaq). This compares the multitude of games developer community sites and gamer-owned and managed fora. The listing was based on an impressive record of growth – in 2011, Machinima.com reported more than 2.5 billion downloads of user-generated machinima films through its various online channels and more than 45 million unique monthly users of the platforms. More recently, as a main search facility for online digital creative content, the stability and growth of the community using Machinima.com has been considered to be a health indicator of media platforms such as YouTube (much user-generated content posted to this site is machinima and computer gameplay recordings).

Despite this impressive growth record, it has remained a relatively under-reported and poorly understood genre of participatory new media (Lowood & Nitsche, 2011). Within media studies, for example, it has been described as an example of convergence culture, produced by 'digital natives' as a form of user-generated content that is superficially consumed as a purely online experience. Within computer gaming studies, it is considered to undermine the demand for animation artists' skills, being seen as 'hacking and modding' content. These views fail to recognize the role of emergent creative and computing skillsets, or the ways in which the creative and cultural industries are recognizing their value. The author has previously argued its potential as a learning tool for creative technologies practice (Harwood, 2013), suggesting that it:

- Necessitates adaptation through experiential learning and therefore builds creative capacity;
- Requires introspection and explication which facilitates critical reflection at both individual and team levels;
- Demands patience and application, and is about the management of complexity;
- Builds competency in visual language (rather than text-based) which may lead to new narratives;
- Is malleable, re-usable and therefore sustainable; and
- Is accessible and so facilitates participation, networking and dialogue across media (social and traditional media and networking platforms).

Most recently, it has been suggested that machinima is a new media form that embraces digital literacy through visual communication (Merchant, 2013) with various research themes identified in relation to digital communications. These interrelated themes are (Merchant, 2013):

- **Multimodality:** Digital texts that include affordances of multi-media to infer meaning (eg., Kress, 2003; 2010);
- **Linguistic Innovation:** Use of multimodal content to support hybridized language systems (eg., Merchant, 2001; Chen, 2011);
- **Remix:** Creative use of digital tools, such as games and animation, mixed with other media such as music, film and theatre to develop new forms of content including machinima (eg., Lessig, 2008; Lankshear & Knobel, 2010);
- **Playfulness:** A central theme, playfulness is considered to be informal learning (Mackey, 2002; Willet, Robinson & Marsh, 2008);

- **Participation:** Social learning within 'interest focussed affinity spaces' (Gee, 2003; Jenkins, 2006; Brown & Adler, 2008);
- **Connection:** Between individuals within communities of practice (Wellman, 2002; Marwick & Boyd, 2011).

As a socio-cultural phenomenon, researchers have argued that machinima has empowered creative participation, providing tools and space that engages and facilitates creative practice and digital performance (Jenkins, 1992; 2007; Russell, 2008; Ito, 2011; Payne, 2011; Kringiel, 2011), albeit within a walled network of participants (Stern, 2011). For example, Ito (2011) highlights that whilst work produced comprises robust amateur and professional practice, it is nonetheless tightly associated with gamer culture, the walled environments comprising specific games or game genres such as first person shooter, fantasy roleplay, etc. Peer-based production thrives on open access and, in turn, the mainstreaming of content becomes valuable to original copyright owners (games producers and publishers) through audience development. Furthermore, publishers may themselves create machinima that showcases the best of their games, some even employing machinimators in the production process to ensure the appropriate creative values are encompassed (Stern, 2011). Ito states there is an increasing amount of work being recognised outside the closed gamer environments, noting that political activism (eg., Jones, 2011) and avant-garde arts are primary areas of contribution to broader cultural capital.

One of the most contested issues in machinima is its legal status, with some identifying the remix creative practice as 'derivative' work, thereby attracting criticism for copyright violations (Hayes, 2009). Whilst some fan vids may be a classed in this way it is difficult to apply this rule to original works, as argued by Cornblatt (2011) and Hancock (2015). Cornblatt's machinimas were subject to take-down by one social media network that suggested it constituted a 'depiction of a video game', against its terms of use. He argues the work, albeit using some source material from the video game Grand Theft Auto©, is actually a document of a performance art project produced within the game environment. As such it is an original contribution, being focussed on 'breaking' the magic circle of the game by changing players' views of the publisher's expectations for gameplay. It is unclear in the experience Cornblatt reports on who or how the decision to take down the work has been made, given there are many thousands of similarly produced works that have not been taken down, suggesting an inconsistent application of the guidelines by the channel. The channel is commercially owned and so the issue raises important questions about the role of corporates as custodians and curators of digital cultural production, such as machinima.

Machinima is considered to be 'fair use' of computer games (Hayes, 2009), which are increasingly found in public domains through promoted online channels such as Twitch and Machinima.com as well as game mediated environments and fora where game player generated content is regularly distributed. The apparent ad hoc application of terms of use by social media networks is therefore of major concern for the digital cultural practititioners, potentially significantly impacting cultural heritage. Cornblatt highlights that the form of censorship he experienced is often seen with innovative creative forms and has in the past impacted media such as film and photography. One of the challenges is therefore in finding the appropriate channels to showcase machinima works beyond the domination of a few streaming platforms. For some this has been an insurmountable barrier resulting in their departure from the community of practice (see Hancock, 2015). It undoubtedly takes considerable effort on the part of machinimators to create work, let alone negotiate terms with publishers, promoters and distributors.

Despite the actions of platform owners, some publishers have recognised the potential of machinima to contribute value to their intellectual property: Microsoft and Blizzard in 2007 issued new rules for game content usage, enabling machinimators to unilaterally produce derivative works from their video games provided they are for non-commercial purposes (Hayes, 2009). Whilst analysis of the qualified 'rules' highlights that third party content such as sound and music tracks incorporated in the games may not be covered, nor work that reverse engineers game content, or constitutes 'offensive' material (racism, obscenity, etc.), machinima may be distributed via social networks and appear alongside advertising. This enables machinimators to generate income by monetizing an audience for their work (assuming an audience can be maintained), within the standard partnership arrangements of social media networks. Nonetheless, the rules are idiosyncratic to each game environment and publisher, resulting in complexity, particularly where machinimas incorporate content from multiple games, which has led to considerable criticism by the community of practice.

It is increasingly evident that publishers are generally supportive of machinima and its marketing potential in particular, with some including game features that actively facilitate machinima production such as camera views and production tools. In granting individual licenses to machinimators for their works, games publishers are effectively protecting their brands and the communities that develop around them – others that do not issue licenses are merely granting licenses by implication, with the full knowledge that machinima works are created and distributed using their assets (Hayes, 2009), albeit a grey legal area. Moreover, the participatory technological environment reflected in online gamesplay highlights that application of copyright laws now not only applies to the complex ecology of creative practices but also to those who consume the work of others as viewers, thereby blurring the lines between production and consumption (Coleman & Dyer-Witheford, 2007; Sinnreich, Latonero & Gluck, 2009; Latonero & Sinnreich, 2014; Hancock, 2015). This led Hayes to call for a universal licensing approach to be adopted across the games sector as a whole supporting the production of derivative works such as machinima, beyond the 'creative commons' (Benkler, 2002; Lessig, 2001). As yet, this has not materialised although the 'let's play' phenomenon, which generates machinima through the recording of live action game play, has captured the broad imagination of the creative industries resulting in a positive change in attitude and further development of game rules.

As Hancock (2015) argues, the emergence of machinima not only adds value to the games as brands, but also contributes to new cultural practices and artforms combined with creative toolsets. Resulting in increasing participation in cultural production, Jenkins (2006; 2014) summarizes the nexus of three key trends that have led to what he terms as a 'digital revolution':

- New tools and technologies that enable consumers to archive, remix, redistribute and edit media content;
- Subcultures that promote user generated content and do-it-yourself production;
- Horizontally integrated media channels that encourage flow of content and necessitate active engagement in the processes of sharing.

Ultimately, the distinction between production and consumption, as evidenced in machinima, has become what Jenkins terms as a 'convergence culture' (Jenkins, 2006). The convergence culture emphasises access and participation in co-creation, enabled by digital technologies with potential to transform cultural practices. As Pini (2009) states, the drivers for co-creation are a dialogic relationship with the brand that promotes interaction coupled with an interest in sharing information (gamesplay), and the availability of adequate content and tools (in-game assets), supported by communication flows (internet and social media platforms) that facilitate sharing. Co-creative practices in the context of video games, where consumers actively participate in processes that create value for the brand (Prahalad & Ramawsamy, 2004), relates to gamesplay that is performed and/or subsequently edited or remixed for machinima purposes (Nitsche, 2011). This process takes place largely beyond of the control of publishers, notwithstanding the legal constraints described above. As Jenkins states:

Corporations imagine participation as something they can start and stop, channel and reroute, commodify and market. The prohibitionists are trying to shut down unauthorized participation; the collaborationists are trying to win grassroots creators over to their side. Consumers, on the other side, are asserting a right to participate in the culture, on their own terms, when and where they wish. (Jenkins, 2006:175)

Some of the transformative cultural production constitutes fandom (Jenkins, 2006; 2013) but co-creation is also borne out of personal interests, which may be hedonistically, artistically or even politically motivated (Hay & Couldry, 2011; Zuckerman, 2012).

Irrespective of machinimators' motivations, it is clear that publishers derive value beyond simply word of mouth marketing of their games by consumers to other consumers (C2C). With artistic outputs, the reach of machinimators extends to gallery spaces and film festivals, and increasingly digital archives are recognising the significance of the creative practice (Harwood, 2011; 2012b). Curators of machinima can thereby offer a wealth of archived material related to publisher brands. As Hancock (2015) identifies, even some 'classic' games (no longer commercially available) have now been modified and/or reformulated by players in order to re-enact and re-perform scenarios and gamesplay completely outside the control of original publishers, being hosted on private servers. In future, this may not be necessary given a recent statement made by the International Game Developers Association:

Video games are a creative art form and a cultural artifact worthy of preservation. The International Games Developers Association (IGDA) wholeheartedly supports efforts by academic researchers and archivists to study and catalog such creative works and ensure their preservation for future generations. (9 April 2015, https://igdaboard.wordpress.com/)

… albeit unclear by whom and how games will be archived, or how machinima artefacts will be treated. It is worth noting, however, that machinima has long been recognized as a culturally significant artform by Stanford University's *How They Got Game* internet archive project (see https://archive.org/details/machinima).

Whilst artistic machinima may have a relatively tightly defined and fan-based audience, political machinima has a much broader and more general audience. Political machinima enacts positional statements using games as the creative matrix for the work – its goal is to share and shape opinion, and drive activism (see eg., http://hyperallergic.com/200098/artists-stage-political-interventions-in-video-games/). Political machinima may therefore be related to a much broader form of new media production and visual culture, often termed 'hacktivism' (see Davies & Raziogova, 2013). Furthermore, others have also appropriated games for use in teaching and learning related activities (eg., Thomassen & Rive, 2010; and Thomas', 2015, CAMELOT EU funded project).

The breadth of activities generally increases the awareness of the specific games and communities associated with their use, and some machinima has achieved views in the millions (eg., Phil Rice's *Rest Room Etiquette*, Roosterteeth's *Red vs Blue*). Direct benefits for publishers relate to increased sales of their games (see www.machinima.dmu.ac.uk/report/project-report/findings-computer-games-development).

Terranova (2000), however, highlights a more fundamental level of contribution to a 'digital economy' in the form of cultural and technical labour ('digital artisans'), describing a gift economy. She argues the gifted or 'free' labour results in the transformation of culture to productive activities that are both pleasurable to the producer yet exploited by others. Collectively this exploitation may be channelled and structured within capitalist business practices. The knowledge workers (cultural producers or co-creators) have become a continuous source of innovation constituting 'immaterial labour' that comprises both informational content and contributes to the development of cultural/artistic standards (see Lazzarato, 1996; Hardt & Negri, 2000; Gill & Pratt, 2008). The activities undertaken provide indirect benefits such as market development and service innovation. It is clear that machinima as a cultural movement has contributed considerably to the development of the games industry through audience reach, promotion and original content that some have reincorporated into their products and services.

The notion of 'prosumption' (Toffler, 1980), which integrates production and consumption activities, also adds to the argument of the role of digital artisans in contributing to corporate gains. Tapscott and Williams (2006) highlight there is a growing need to reward the generosity of prosumers in order to ensure the viability of creative led businesses. Others recognise the inherent difficulties associated with a cultural context (Web 2.0) that is largely free at the point of consumption: channels such as YouTube and Vimeo do not charge viewers to watch content, which results in an over-supply of material (because barriers to its production are minimised). As Ritzer and Jurgenson (2010) state, abundance rather than scarcity of material and effectiveness rather than efficiency are key characteristics of this digital economy, enriched by prosumers' immaterial labour. Thus, publishers may exploit the over-supply without necessarily recognising the importance of quality of over quantity. That said, there is a growing number of publishers who are now willing to financially reward and incentivise machinimators for their content. For example, in 2015 both Valve© (see http://steamcommunity.com/workshop/aboutpaidcontent/) and Unreal© (see http://www.cartoonbrew.com/tech/unreal-encourages-filmmakers-to-use-its-game-engine-111708. html_) have announced machinima content related offers.

In summary, machinima is a collectively produced phenomenon, embedded in video games culture and related creative industries. As a creative practice, it is a meme that has rapidly spread across games and distribution platforms, with individual machinimas generating views in the millions, including video responses, parodies and copycats. Theories of convergence, co-creation, immaterial labour and prosumption have been explored in the context of machinima. Key characteristics are its visual mode of communication and engagement; distributed yet highly participative community of practice; accessibility for a broad range of hedonistic, artistic and activist activities; and relative ease of distribution enabled by social media platforms. The next section describes the modes of machinima production and considers the distinct periods of activity associated of its emergence and development as a cultural movement.

MACHINIMA FORMATS

Review of literature and films reveals a taxonomy that sits along two clear dimensions (see www.machinima.dmu.ac.uk):

- **Method of Production/Creative Process:** Perfect capture, screen capture, asset compositing, bespoke machinimation;

- **Genre of Machinima Product:** Fanvid, parody (satire, comedy), documentary, music video, advertising, reportage, reenactment (reconstruction), activist, pre-visualization, artistic (experimental, abstract).

The basis for perfect capture is historical: Quake© and Doom© were founding games of creation and production tools apparently limited. As tools emerged, whether for gaming or other purposes, so they have influenced the evolution of machinima resulting in screen capture, asset compositing and 'bespoke' animation. Alongside this, as games have themselves evolved from simple to complex formats, so too the creative approaches taken by machinimators – from fan fiction to parody, to political, to experimental, to fine art and pre-vis. The features and characteristics of genres and modes of machinimating are next described.

1. **Method of Production/Creative Process:**
   a. **Perfect Capture:** This is a process by which players' actions (input by a game controller or other interface) are recorded in real-time as code (e.g., DEM files in Quake) which can then be reloaded and replayed using the game itself. The relatively small size of files made it possible for films to be distributed and shared using low-capacity media (such as floppy discs) or pre-broadband internet connections. This level of functionality was built into the engines of many early 3D, 'first person shooter' games (e.g., Doom© and Quake©) to enable players to capture their performances within the game. The aim was to demonstrate prowess (eg., 'speed runs') or analyze their faults in order to improve, creating a historical document of a player's actions within the game world. (e.g., NoSkill's memorial pages). Further potential for artistic and creative usage was soon realized with the addition of narrative text. Customization (or hacking) of the game code allowed for other departures from the constraints of game play (e.g., allowing alternative views, modified graphics or allowing the player to traverse the game in ways not originally permitted, such as seen in Figure 1. *Diary of A Camper*, the first machinima recognized by the community). For viewers to see the machinima created using this method, an identical game engine with a compatible computer, identical graphics hardware and same release of game, is required in order for 'perfect' reconstruction of the film. The

Figure 1. Screenshot: Diary of a Camper (The Rangers)

perfect capture method is recognized as the beginning of the machinima movement (Lowood, 2011; Ng, 2013). For examples, see www.quakewiki.net/archives/cineplex/movfiles.html on DEM files; http://speeddemosarchive.com/quake for examples of 'speed runs'; and, http://www.doom2.net/noskill/ for memorial pages from Doom©.

b. **Screen Capture:** This is a process of filmmaking using the game's video output. As computing power, particularly graphics processors, increased it was possible for rendered frames of games to be captured and subsequently stored as a standard file format (.avi or .mov). The resulting film files were then played back independently of the game engine and/or edited using free or low-cost filmmaking software, giving filmmakers a chance to incorporate more traditional production techniques. Titles such as Sims 2© and Quake 3© allowed the user to record play with a single key command from within the game and without the need for third-party screen capture software. Although still confined by the constraints of the puppetry allowed within the game, the removal of such barriers to recording encouraged a rapid growth in not only the number of machinima films being made but also the diversification of genres created. As captured gameplay can be subsequently edited, the screen capture method provides a documentary (rather than historical document) of action taking place in virtual worlds. Examples, see http://www.koinup.com/in-the-sims/on-videos/ for examples of Sims 2© machinimas; and, https://www.youtube.com/watch?v=kLfgPHrepj4 a classic Quake 3© machinima made in 1999 by Doom Arenas, *Quad God*.

c. **Asset Compositing:** This mode of machinima production does not take place directly within the game itself but instead makes use of assets (characters, scenery, locations and artefacts) extracted from the game either by modifying (modding) the code or by using additional utilities (eg., World of Warcraft© Model Viewer). This method enables the machinimator to style and animate characters individually, subsequently recording the rendered frames by use of screen-capture software. More advanced video editing techniques (e.g., chroma-key and audio dubbing) are also used, allowing characters to act out scripted dialogue whilst placed upon backgrounds chosen either from the same game, a different game, or another world entirely. By freeing the character from the constraints of gameplay, the machinimator has much greater control over casting, narrative and camera positions and many other aspects. This method is more akin to filmmaking than either the perfect or screen capture methods (see Figure 2, *Scout v Witch*, filmed in Source Film Maker©, which combines assets from Team Fortress 2© and Left For Dead©). The process is more complex and requires the maker to acquire and learn additional software and have a fundamental knowledge of filmmaking. Novice machinimators may therefore experience a far steeper learning curve. Tutorial films do however exist, some of which are also examples of the asset compositing technique. For examples, see https://wowmodelviewer.atlassian.net/wiki/display/WMV/WoW+Model+Viewer the World of Warcraft© Model Viewer download; and https://www.youtube.com/watch?v=oXD2dGxwfg0, Beckman's *How to machinima: WoW Model Viewer (Part 1)*.

d. **Bespoke Machinimation:** This mode of production takes the asset compositing methodology one step further and involves the use of software specifically designed for the creation of 3D animated movies within virtual worlds. Whilst not strictly game engines, programs such as Moviestorm©, iClone© and Moviesandbox© allow machinimators to choose from a wide range of assets, including characters, scenery and locations. The approach adopts the 'ethos'

Figure 2. Screenshot: Scout vs. Witch
Randall Glass, https://www.youtube.com/watch?v=jf4ba72kFNQ.

of machinima but attempts to circumvent the legal challenges associated with using game assets (Fosk, 2011). Animation can be achieved by means of a gaming interface and additional asset packs (new characters) can also be downloaded. This form of machinima generated new audiences by breaking the traditional links with fandom and the 'in-jokes' associated with the perfect and screen capture methods. Machinima made in this way is more likely to be focused on the storytelling or filmmaking aspects and can therefore encompass a wider range of themes and appeal to a broader audience (see Figure 3, *Clockwork*, filmed in Moviestorm©

Figure 3. Screenshot: Clockwork
IceAxe Productions.

as an homage to Kubrick's original *Clockwork Orange*). This method of production is the only technique that directly addresses the issue of rights by granting licenses with the software.

2. **Genre of Machinima Product:**

    a. **Fan Vid (Game Specific) Machinima:** Machinima made and watched by enthusiasts of specific video game titles. Films are made using assets from the specific title, and comprise either documenting gameplay or journeys within the virtual world. Distribution may be within the game (eg., Playstation network / XBox Gold uploads/downloads of 'save games'), distributed via YouTube or a dedicated gamer community website showing regular series. For examples, see Minecraft© TV channel at ; and, World of Warcraft© machinima at

    b. **Parody (Satire, Comedy) Machinima:** One of the most ubiquitous forms of machinima, with comedic value often derived from recognizable characters and scenarios from within the games, this type of machinima is primarily targeted towards a core game audience (see Figure 4, *Red vs Blue*). Not all films require in-depth knowledge of the games, for example Rice's *Male Restroom Etiquette* https://www.youtube.com/watch?v=IzO1mCAVyMw) as voiceovers are often used. Sometimes celebrities are impersonated in this genre. YouTube is the primary means of distribution, with collections of series and regular shows featured on. For examples, see Leroy Jenkins, Obama Plays GTA5; and Red vs Blue.

    c. **Documentary Machinima:** The documentary format relies on the selection and editing of footage captured from games and/or virtual worlds. Parallels can be directly drawn with TV/ film documentary and editing, with the story reliant on editing, narrative and overall direction of the film (see Figure 5, Molotov Alva).

    d. **Music Video Machinima:** Machinima has become an increasingly popular approach for making music videos. It has been used by indie musicians but machinimators have also used popular songs as the inspiration for their work. Unfortunately, many of these have been

Figure 4. Screenshot: Red vs. Blue, ep. 19, Lost But Not Forgotten
http://roosterteeth.com/archive/?id=8313&v=more.

Figure 5. Screenshot: Molotov Alva and His Search for the Creator
Douglas Gayton (http://www.imdb.com/title/tt1100132/).

subject to take down by YouTube, despite the originality of the machinima work, because copyrighted music has been used, even though a number have permission for its use. Other music videos have been produced to support video game releases (see Figure 10, produced by JTMachinima for Assassin's Creed©). This is further discussed in the Let's Play section of this chapter. For examples, see *xxxx*, Tom Jantol, tbc, about to be launched; *Better Life*, Rob Wright https://archive.org/details/BetterLife_HighQuality.

e. **Advertising Machinima:** Machinima used to advertise or promote the games themselves, with or without music (see also music video machinima). For an example, see World of Warcraft©'s Ozzy Osbourne commercial http://www.warcraftmovies.com/movieview.php?id=95195.

f. **Reportage Machinima:** Machinima which can be seen as unedited live news broadcasts, capturing exact events which took place in game or virtual worlds. Films may be regarded as historical documents and others will represent playback as an exact reconstruction of the original game play. Figure 6 is a screenshot from a recording of a live event on set in Second Life©. For examples, see the *Drax Files*, by Draxtor Despres, with radio and machinima podcasts regularly filmed in Second Life©, http://draxfiles.com/.

g. **Reenactment (Reconstruction) Machinima:** This category describes the use of machinima to reconstruct real life or virtual events, or a scene within a popular film or gameplay. This is subtly different to activist machinima, which engages through a mode of storytelling, but instead often uses voice recording from the original event to overlay the machinima. The purpose of this is to explore actions as historical artefacts or, as in some cases, to use the pre-existing event to test the game's capability for making machinima. Figure 8 is a screenshot from a well-known machinima film that itself subsequently inspired many attempts to reconstruct the virtual artifact (*The 1K Project II*, by Black Shark). For examples, see the *1986 Mets vs RedSox* baseball game https://www.youtube.com/watch?v=Xtitj4eFHqw; *A Few Good G-Men*, Randall Glass, https://archive.org/details/a_few_good_gmen.

Figure 6. Screenshot: Assassin's Creed Unity rap – "L'Oeil de L'Aigle"
JTMachinima (https://www.youtube.com/watch?v=CKefIC9SGVI).

Figure 7. Screenshot: physical virtuality "what's the weight of an avatar?"
Chantal Harvey.

h. **Activist (Political, Protest, Propaganda) Machinima:** Machinima is used to recreate and illustrate events (see Figure 9, *The French Democracy*, the first major political machinima to be released and reported on worldwide in relation to the Paris Riots) as form of protest. Films may also be created as vehicles for propaganda. For Examples, see *North Korean State* on http://thelede.blogs.nytimes.com/2013/02/05/north-korea-propaganda-video-uses-call-of-duty-and-we-are-the-world-to-imagine-a-brighter-world-without-manhattan/?_php=true&_type=blogs&_r=0; *Dead in Iraq*, Joseph DeLappe's machinima protesting the deaths of US soldiers in the Iraqi conflict, https://www.youtube.com/watch?v=ejcZ3TR5YTs.

Figure 8. Screenshot: The 1K Project II
Black Shark (https://www.youtube.com/watch?v=1UcQmJwTnBg).

Figure 9. Screenshot: The French Democracy
Alex Chan (https://www.youtube.com/watch?v=stu31sz5ivk).

i. **Educational Machinima:** Machinima has been used as an educational tool within many different sectors because of its ease of use as a creative method and accessibility of the animated content. Serious gaming, the use of video games for typically educational and training purposes, is incorporated into this genre, although platforms commonly used are Second Life© and Moviestorm©. In Second Life© classrooms and tutorials can be easily hosted / posted by teachers. CAMELOT is, for example, a groundbreaking large-scale educational project that supports language teaching and learning, EU funded 2014-2016 (see Figure 10).

j. **Pre-Visualization Machinima:** Pre-visualization is a category of use in mainstream film-making. Game engines are used to envisage how scenes will be enacted rather than using

Figure 10. Screenshot: CAMELOT project
camelotproject.eu.

rehearsals and live action footage. It is therefore a useful prototyping tool that supports pre-viz, prior to casting and set-building, and enables experimenting with camera angles, lighting, staging and placement of actors, etc. In some instances, it has also been used as part of the film production itself (Nitsche, 2009).

k. **Artistic (Experimental, Abstract) Machinima:** Artistic machinima is an exciting development in the genre, positioning it as a contemporary digital arts medium (see Figure 11, *Cirque du Machinima*). Its creative use is only constrained by the imagination of the machinimator. Increasingly, the work is not produced by games players but by artists looking for means to visualize their work. Its emergence as an experimental format has been controversial within traditional game-based machinima communities, leading creators to badge it with other names such as 'anymation'. Coined originally by Tom Jantol, this new term reflects the use of any animated content for creative purposes and, indeed, Jantol's experimental work has also included remixed traditional film content, eg., *The Remake* based on Chaplin's *The Kid*. For examples, see *Push*, Lainy Voom, https://vimeo.com/5543976; *Al Hansen's Car Bibbe II Happening*, Patrick Lichty (with Bibbe Hansen), https://www.youtube.com/watch?v=ALXjFH6I6Dg

This rich picture of machinima can be further explored and explained by its modes of distribution, which is largely dependent upon the ways in which viewers interact with creative works, as well as the extent to which it has been commercialized by its producers. Figure 12 summarizes axes and genres described: each quadrant is then described (Harwood, 2015, machinima.dmu.ac.uk).

Quadrant 1: Games channels. Channels of distribution in this quadrant include direct links from in-game menus, on-line game communities fora and other sharing sites that are moderated in some way by the games developer/publisher either directly or indirectly, e.g., forum, community sites. Machinima distributed through these channels are dependent upon machinimators' abilities as per-

Figure 11. Screenshot: Cirque du Machinima – Cuckoo Clock
Tom Jantol (https://www.youtube.com/watch?v=nE540j9U830).

Figure 12. Taxonomy of machinima
Harwood, machinima.dmu.ac.uk.

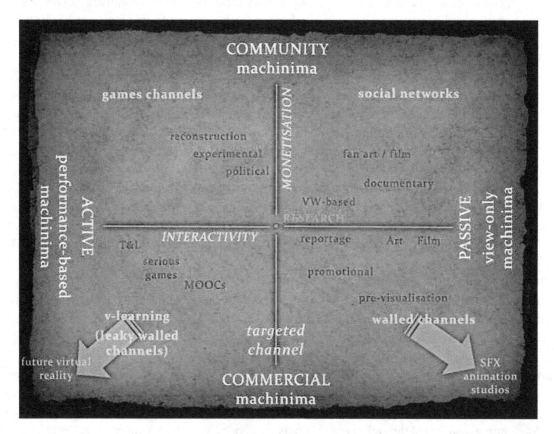

formers and digital puppeteers. Perfect capture machinima is the earliest and most clearly defined example and the demonstration of the technique to fellow gamers is their primary reason d'être. The intended reach of films distributed in this quadrant varies from a global audience (eg., XBox One and PS4 networks) to a selective viewership, representing sub-groups of a game's community (eg., game clans or guilds).

Machinima made within simulation games, e.g., Sims 2©, The Movies©, Grand Theft Auto 5©, or virtual worlds, e.g., Second Life©, are also performative, as demonstrated through the machinimator's skilled manipulation of characters, scenery and other objects. The sandbox (or free-roam) nature of these games (in which game rules are fewer and more flexible) allows for greater experimentation, enabling the development of storylines and narratives that may be unassociated with the game's core themes or play objectives. As familiarity with the game world is no longer a prerequisite, a much wider audience is potentially available and this is reflected in the channels of distribution which extend beyond the communities of their 'parent' worlds.

Quadrant 2: Social Networks. Social Networks are channels used for a wide range of machinimas, intended for an equally diverse audience of non-game oriented viewers, as well as game viewers. These channels are not moderated by the games developer but by the community of viewers whose moderation is indirect through comments and sharing actions across the network of social media (including YouTube, Vimeo, Koinup, etc.). The range of subjects addressed by machinimators using these channels includes political and social commentary, comedy, satire, arts, entertainment, music video and documentaries. Gameplay and game culture is not a central theme for machinima using these channels. That said, there are examples where iconic game worlds have been used as production tools and yet the machinima has appealed to non game players. This has been achieved through skilled development of the script and dialogue, see for example, Figure 13 *World of Work-*

Figure 13. Screenshot: World of Workcraft
Lagspike Films (https://www.youtube.com/watch?v=msmRwlg23Qc).

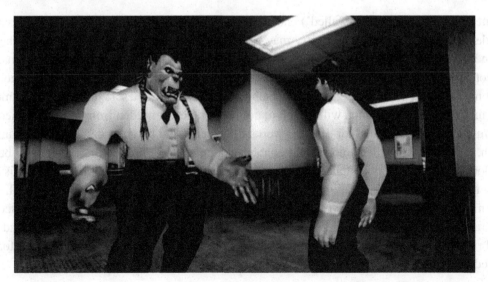

craft by Lagspike Films. There are therefore no restrictions on the choice of production method. Examples can be found at Machinima Expo (www.machinima-expo.com), 'the world's only virtual machinima film festival'.

Machinima distributed through these channels is intended to entertain, stimulate and provoke audiences but their direct involvement and interaction is not a requirement. To this end, in this quadrant has much in common with gallery-based digital art, film and even TV, namely cinematic and video-based works are viewed passively. The primary outlets and hubs are currently the video sharing networks YouTube and Vimeo, supported by various umbrella sites which form 'embedded' collections or galleries of works stored on their servers (e.g., Machinima.com). In each case, compressed rendered frames are uploaded that can be shared either privately or publicly with community members. It should be noted, however, that restrictions on upload may be imposed by the channel owner in order to comply with copyright, ownership and decency laws. As such, machinima distributed via popular channels in this quadrant is often subject to indiscriminate censorship (Cornblatt, 2011) as highlighted above. Other social networks, such as Facebook and Twitter, also contribute to these channels as amplifiers, with the ability to 'like', 'share' and 'retweet' posts providing opportunities to enhance the reach of machinimas, stimulate interest and drive critical discussion with viewers. In rare cases, mainstream media will also provide channels, eg., Comedy Central's South Park episode *Make Love Not Warcraft* (http://southpark. wikia.com/wiki/Make_Love,_Not_Warcraft) and UK Channel 4 series *SuperMes* (https://www.youtube. com/watch?v=AmHh3CDnCrQ).

Some social media platforms provide possibilities for monetizing viewing audiences (through overlaid advertising) and may therefore further support the development of commercial distribution networks for machinimators. These depend upon the extent of machinimators' personal social networks and their ability to market their work. Where most successful, viewers are encouraged to become subscribers to personal channels, created as sub-sets of the social media platform, albeit the machinimator may generate little direct value beyond the revenue generated from overlaid advertising (based on numbers of viewers). That said, some machinima films have generated views in the millions, where the most successful machinimators tend to be those who release machinima regularly.

Quadrant 3: V-learning ('leaky-walled') channels. Machinima in this quadrant is not necessarily intended for general viewing, and entry may be granted by invitation, registration or, in the case of monetized models, through subscription. It differs from Walled Channels (Quadrant 4) as machinima is not considered to be confidential or restricted. The 'opt-in' framework is similar to those found amongst Gaming Channels, although the subject matter and themes are unrelated to gameplay or gaming cultures. Machinima will therefore not be completely hidden from general audiences and permission will be granted for selected works (or excerpts) to be viewed outside the channels. As such, it is a 'leaky walled' model that enables examples and introductory material to be appear in domains where the potential audience may reside. Thus machinima in this quadrant is in some way related to the dissemination of new knowledge and ideas either as part of a formal, directed learning programme, e.g., massive open online course (MOOC), or through scenarios based around interactive play or simulation, e.g., serious games. This approach to supporting learning adds depth and richness to traditional learning environments through enhanced and immersive performance-based experiences (see CAMELOT, camelotproject.eu; Jenkins, 2015).

Machinima distributed via these channels encourages audience participation and interactivity, with viewers also becoming central to the performance. It necessitates that the audience learns the rules of participation sufficient to engage in the core activities of some scripted action. For example, a machinima broadcast of a lecture or seminar based in Second Life© will document not only the actions of the principal character (the teacher or professor), but also of those other audience members in attendance (the learners).

Quadrant 4: Walled channels. The use of 3D game engines as pre-viz tools during the pre-production stage of commercial film production (Nitsche, 2009) is a good example of machinima distributed via walled channels. Ultimately, machinima in this quadrant may become viewable for more general audiences but it may also be subsumed within other genres of creativity, such as live action films, before it reaches a passive and paying viewer.

Machinima in this quadrant is intended for viewing within private networks only, e.g., investors, colleagues, co-developers. Machinimas are not intended for general community viewing and may be prevented from entering the public domain for reasons of confidentiality, security, copyright, etc. Audiences are unlikely to be motivated by game specific subjects or themes and therefore the machinimator's production environment can be chosen on the basis of suitability or personal preference. The use of bespoke packages, such as iClone© and Moviestorm© or commercially available game engines, such as Unreal Engine 4© are commonly used for machinima falling into this category. Furthermore, whereas the creation of machinima will be equally dependent upon expertise and knowledge of the chosen creative platform, so the emphasis moves away from performance and towards more general cinematic and artistic production techniques e.g., scripting, asset compositing, editing, voice-over, special effects (SFX), etc.

This section has described the modes and genres of production, culminating in the presentation of a taxonomy identifying its interactive and commercialised evolution, highlighting that machinima has now extended beyond its origins as game-based fandom into something much more substantial and recognizable as a cultural meme. Thus, the next section reviews its emergence and proposes phases as a means to understand its evolutionary trajectory.

PHASES OF MACHINIMA'S EVOLUTION

As highlighted in the preceding sections, machinima has evolved to be a diverse cultural movement, embedded in game cultures but extended well beyond its origins as a fan-based medium. This section traces its emergence through four key stages of its evolution, to date, in relation to video games and creative technologies developments.

Phase 1: Quake Movies (focal period 1996-1999).

The earliest recognised machinima film has already been identified in this chapter, *Diary of a Camper* by The Rangers (Figure 1). Its origins can be traced to the Demoscene era, where computer software such as video games was developed to showcase the increasing processing capabilities of computer hardware. Early games of Doom© (released 1993) and Quake© (released 1996), both first person shooter games, attracted attention because the recordings of gameplay could easily be shared and replayed resulting in a form of spectatorship among games players (Nitsche, 2006; Lowood, 2005). *Diary of a Camper,* made in Quake© (released 26 October 1996) was, however, unlike the many other fan films that had already made by recording and replaying pure gameplay. This film showed the gameplay in the context of a short story. To make the film, its creators had written their own code to modify the game in order to realise camera angles they wanted for their story, and also to splice scenes together during replay. The film inspired other 'modders', film fans and games experts to create Quake© movies, becoming a cultural meme in its own right. These films were distributed by various early internet channels such as The Cineplex, Psyk's Popcorn Jungle, Quake Movie Library (Marino, 2004).

Later, editing software emerged which was used to support the production of films including the forerunner of Adobe Premiere, Keygrip (Kelland, Morris and Lloyd, 2005). Subsequent iterations of Quake© (II and III) were released which incorporated facilities to enable games players to modify their game experience (such as camera angles) after content had been recorded but by 1999 interest in making these films had reached a critical point. id Software, Quake©'s developer, had threatened to take legal action over the by now wide-spread sharing of game files made with Quake III Arena© because it wanted to protect gameplay over networks, a new play format incorporated into this latest version. The number of fan films declined although the original version of Quake© was still being used within the community (Marino, 2004).

Despite this, Quake© has remained a popular game, its latest iteration having been launched in 2010, Quake Live©. Source code for its earlier versions were also released by id Software, enabling full customization of content and resulting in many free spin-off games being developed, e.g., Tremulous©, World of Padman©, OpenArena© and Urban Terror©. In turn, these new games have led to the generation of many gameplay fan vid machinimas (see e.g., Figure 14, *Tremulous Fragmovie: "Sex, Drugs, Tremulous"*).

Phase 2: Academy of Machinima Arts & Sciences (focal period 2000-2008).

The community of machinimators began to coalesce in the late 1990s and by 2000 a website by one key proponent, Hugh Hancock, was launched as Machinima.com. Hancock, along with fellow machinima-

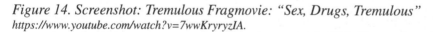

Figure 14. Screenshot: Tremulous Fragmovie: "Sex, Drugs, Tremulous"
https://www.youtube.com/watch?v=7wwKryryzIA.

tor, Anthony Bailey, had originally coined the term machinima in 2000, misspelling a concatenation of 'machine' and 'cinema'. The aim with the use of this term was to disassociate the films from a specific game engine. According to Marino (2004), the term became popular because it also alluded to 'animation'. Machinima.com became a useful resource to the machinima community by publishing tutorials and articles. Hundreds of films were also hosted, following the exclusive release of *Quad God* (Triton Films), the first machinima to be made using video frames (ie., the screen capture method), enabling it to be viewed without a copy of the specific game in which it had been created. Thereafter, machinima began to attract mainstream attention (Ebert, 2000; Marino, 2004).

By 2002, a number of machinimators within the emerging community decided to form the Academy of Machinima Arts & Sciences (AMAS) as a not-for-profit organization dedicated to promoting machinima. AMAS became the go-to organization for all things machinima. Its members included Hancock and Bailey, originators of the term, Paul Marino, its founding CEO, Katherine Anna Kang and Matthew Ross, each individually multi-award winning film producers in various formats, including machinima. AMAS held its first machinima film festival at QuakeCon 2002, during which ten awards were given for acting, direction, sound, editing, writing, visual design and technical achievement. Subsequently, some of the films were released on DVD in long-play format by Machinima.com, which further helping to promote machinima as an emergent art form to a broader community of followers. AMAS subsequently hosted its film festival almost annually and formed partnerships with a number of international organizations and sponsors, including a European contingent (Institute of Creative Technologies at De Montfort University, UK) which brought together many of the most recognized machinimators around the World at a festival in the UK in 2007 (directed by the author). AMAS continued until 2008, when funding constraints and career development opportunities for the founding members meant time dedicated to hosting the festival became too difficult.

The AMAS period has been significant in the evolution of machinima: the organization became the legitimizing force for productions, celebrating the emergence of new genres of content, negotiating with games developers and editing software producers. It also promoted good practice and skills development within and beyond the community of machinimators, irrespective of game preference. During this period, specific leads that it has promoted have had ongoing impact in further broadening the reach of machinima, including:

- *Red vs Blue* as a comedic science fiction series, produced by Rooster Teeth Productions (see Figure 4) who has become the most successful commercial machinima producer being funded by game developer Bungie (Halo©, in which *RvB* is made). *RvB* was founded in 2003 and is now in its 13th season, with millions of followers for each episode released and chapters of community members around the world (see www.roosterteeth.com) who actively promote machinima in festivals of their own (see e.g., SideFest, sidefest.co.uk).
- *This Spartan Life* (Chris Burke, Halo©) is a web-based chat show that mixes game and real life events. The series was launched in 2005 and is now distributed on Xbox Live.
- The first overtly political machinima, *The French Democracy* (Alex Chan, 2005, made in The Movies©) reached a global audience with its retelling of the incident that sparked the Paris riots. This film led to a major movement in user-generated content for political purposes and is today still considered an exemplar.
- The first feature length machinima to be awarded at a festival, *Stolen Life* by Peter Rasmussen and Jackie Turnure. Rasmussen, who died shortly after the 2007 festival, was subsequently recognised

for his contribution to innovation in filmmaking by Screen Australia with a prize for innovation. The first award was made at the 2008 AMAS event in October and it is now awarded annually at the Sydney Film Festival.

Alongside AMAS, spin-off festivals and events have been hosted in Asia, Australia, across Europe and Scandinavia. Its legacy is evident in the continuing interest in machinima as a production tool, particularly for artistic and performative machinima projects. The ongoing annual festival that picked up the AMAS baton is the Machinima Expo (www.machinima-expo.com). Running since 2009, this event is organized by members of the original machinima community, led by Ricky Grove, and is hosted online. In keeping with machinima traditions, Expo festivals are held inside Second Life©, Linden Labs' virtual world, which enables community members from around the world to meet and discuss emerging technologies techniques and award winning films, in spite of different time zones in which they live. The event continues to celebrate machinima in all its genres and formats, promoting it by working with international partners and sponsors.

Second Life© is itself a cultural phenomenon, being the first mainstream virtual environment. Although originally ignored by the game-based machinima community, it has subsequently grown into a significant creative platform. It enables participants ('residents') to create their own content and hold events. This led to a massive growth in digital performance and artistic machinima, with creativity no longer constrained by the game parameters typically associated with rule-based games (Fosk, 2011). Thus focus has been on visualisation rather than coding, making machinima a more transparent and accessible creative medium, particularly for non-tech producers.

Despite its popularity, artistic machinima now appears to be in decline, or at least its recognition as machinima is declining. This is a consequence of the dominance of Machinima.com (see next section); convergence of creative techniques and accessibility of tools including special effects filmmaking, 3D animation, indie computer games; the growing recognition of digital arts using latest interactive technologies; and, the needs of creatives to develop a commercializable portfolio. For machinimators emerging in this phase of its evolution, machinima has proven to be a useful grounding for creative skills development in particular (see machinima.dmu.ac.uk for a summary discussion).

Phase 3: Machinima.com (focal period 2009-2014).

Concurrent with developments in phase 2, Machinima.com transferred from its originator (Hancock) to new ownership, the DeBevoise brothers, Allen and Philip, in 2006. Hancock cited differences of opinion about the trajectory of the website and a need to focus on his own productions. Since it began, Machinima. com had become an increasingly influential force in the distribution of the breadth machinima content but by 2009 the website had become solely focussed on fan vid and gameplay machinima. Coinciding with the evolution of YouTube, which had launched in 2005, Machinima.com developed YouTube channels that then became dominant search engines for game related content. Such became its scale, that it was recognised as an indicator of the health of YouTube, which was bought by Google in 2006.

Since 2009, Machinima.com has launched a range of programming, some in partnership with major games publishers such as Microsoft (*Bite Me; Halo 4: Forward Unto Dawn*) and DC Entertainment, others on behalf of Warner Bros Interactive Entertainment (*Mortal Kombat: Legacy*), Endemol (*XARM*), Katalyst Media (*Prank Lab*). Its subsequent use of social media platforms such as Facebook, Twitter and new channels such as Twitch and Steam, have further fuelled its massive growth primarily as a viewership platform that comprises professionally produced content, only some of which can be classified as machinima.

It generated audiences in its early stages of development (2006-2009) primarily by partnering with machinimators who created content and developed their own channels under the umbrella of the Machinima.com brand. The approach was highly successful and by 2011 it had reached 70M viewers, albeit appealing mainly to young male game players using social media (DVorkin, 2011). In 2012, it was incorporated into XBox Live, effectively reinforcing the link to games and closing the loop of creativity to non-game players. Whilst this approach also enabled game players to share their machinima with others in the community, the attempt to control its distribution is clear – this was later reinforced with 'perpetual' contracts that state rights to content produced by machinimators always belongs to Machinima.com (see Stuart, 2013).

Later in 2012, Google invested some $35M in the website, the first such investment in a 'content production' organization (Kafka, 2012), albeit evident that Machinima.com was in a period of rapid transition (Sliwinski, 2012). By 2013, it reported over 5000 channel partners on YouTube and in excess of 2.3B regular viewers, but its emphasis on monetization of content (such as through overlaid advertising) led to criticism for a lack of transparency with its partners (Taormina, 2014). In 2014, a further round of investment funding ($18M) was made by Warner Bros, coinciding with a change in management (Spangler, 2014a; 2014b). It has subsequently sought to push its community of followers towards live-streamed gameplay (using 'professional' game players), with content focussing on 'speed runs' and 'epic' quests, as an emergent form of game related content that it has increased referred to as 'e-sports' (see Popper, 2013). E-sports is a term that also originated in the Quake era, albeit focussed on live action gameplay that has evolved through live tournaments such as QuakeCon.

Thus, Machinima.com (which rebranded itself as Machinima in 2014) has appropriated the term but effectively disassociated itself from machinima as a form of cultural production. As such, the term has become less useful in enabling access to the creative potential of games particularly for new machinimators, as originally conceived by the community of practice. This has been a disappointing development for those who have worked hard to develop the cultural movement under an umbrella term, successfully bringing the community together to share creative technologies best practice. Such is the breadth of its use as a contemporary creative medium, however, it is clear that machinima production continues in a number of genres as previously described.

The legacy of Machinima.com is nonetheless ongoing. Despite its growth trajectory, Machinima.com has been resoundingly successful in developing machinima as an advertising medium through which games are promoted to new audiences. It has achieved this by harnessing game players as immaterial labour and using social channels inhabited by game players to support word-of-mouth distribution. As such, machinima in this phase of its emergence has significant potential for viral activity albeit within the target audience for the games on which it is made.

Phase 4: Let's Play (2014-).

The intermedial effects of the Machinima.com phase has resulted in each genre of machinima becoming a separate cultural meme, each with its own specific characteristics. Increasingly, as visual culture emerges from text-based production, multi-media incorporating gamesplay content is being used for interactive cultural production and promotion (see Figure 15, University of Western Australia rebrand

Figure 15. Screenshot: University of Western Australia brand relaunch video, excerpt with Jay
Jay Jegathesan (http://uwainsl.blogspot.com.au/2015/05/second-life-features-in-major-uwa.html).

launch video). Creative work is now seen online and offline in gallery spaces around the world. What is interesting in this new phase of its emergence is that creators may approach machinimating from any creative or technologies background, but it is unlikely to be tagged explicitly as machinima. That said, when defined, the term remains useful for creatives not least because of its historical connections and recognition across sectors as a form of digital cultural production (see Literature Review above). Technologies have evolved (speed of computer processing combined with improvements in graphics quality) and machinima has become almost indistinguishable from other animated formats, as predicted by Marino (2004). For example, Kinect makes it possible to converge low-cost motion capture with puppeteering, resulting in high quality digital performance and character modification using game assets (which may be modified using tools such as Unreal© and Source Film Maker©) with recorded machinima artefacts. The possibilities for 'playful' creative production combined with spectatorship are therefore converging under yet another umbrella term of 'let's play'.

Let's play is a term used to describe the fan vid subculture of games albeit that it has evolved separately from machinima. It essentially comprises perfect and screen capture techniques (Lowood, 2011, refers to 'replay' rather than let's play). Emerging in 2005 (Klepek, 2015), let's play is the recording of gameplay (as walk throughs or speed runs) using voiceover commentary that may be humorous or instructional. Films are shared either directly for replay in the originating game, or via media streaming platforms such as YouTube. The content is often created as a form of entertainment or tutorials showcasing aspects of gameplay that viewers may then try to emulate. The format has become popular with some creators achieving celebrity status, primarily because they post regular content to their channels, sustaining interest and engagement with the content through varied programming. For example, PewDiePie (creator) has reportedly 34M subscribers to his channel, has generated up to $4M revenue from monetized content (overlaid advertising) and in the process has become one of the most influential people on the internet (see Grundberg and Hansegard, 2014; Begley, 2015). In turn, the let's play phenomenon has proven to be a powerful marketing tool, particularly for indie games (Rigney, 2013; Dring, 2014), because it makes use of the word-of-mouth promotion embedded within the media sharing platforms on which it is distributed. Such is the success of the let's play phenomenon it has been suggested that some indie games developers are deliberately targeting the community through game designs which actively encourage and facilitate players to create the content ('YouTube bait', StandardGamer, 2014) in order to realize sales.

This is an interesting commercial development not least because the streaming channels (YouTube and Twitch) that have attempted to introduce legal barriers (as discussed in the Literature Review section above) that have directly impacted the community with take-downs and audio restrictions for streamed content. In response, publishers and developers, along with let's play creators, called for re-evaluation of terms of service resulting in Twitch (but not YouTube) to revise them (Kain, 2013) in order to accommodate the community of practice. Predictably, this is driving traffic to Twitch. It is evident therefore that its evolutionary trajectory is similar to the Quake phase of machinima, albeit reinventing the practice of creative endeavour with video games. What is significantly different is the number of participants it has attracted, leading games developers and content streamers, as well as other digital curators, to more actively engage with the community of practice, primarily because they are now fully cognizant of the direct benefits to their organizations. In turn, this also benefits machinimators (whose creative practice has taken a more traditional approach to the use of games as digital arts production tools) because revised terms encompass all forms of user-generated content.

Ultimately, this phase of evolution provides a pathway for machinima and let's plays to become more broadly recognized as a digital arts medium because it legitimizes cultural production and facilitates curation beyond traditional channels of distribution. The challenge in the contemporary environment is, however, in creating a community of followers that share similar values of cultural production. As the focus shifts from the creative work to the creative actor, so there is increased emphasis on audience rather than production, albeit this trend will be tempered to a certain degree by the continued rapid technological and graphical quality developments of the games and devices used for productions. Trends suggest that audiences will eventually migrate to more interactive and performative modes of cultural production, as the interest in fan vids begins to decline.

In summary, the phases described above highlight different generational and creative characteristics that may be linked to Merchant's (2013) themes, see Table 1.

CONCLUSION

This chapter has discussed the emergence and growth of machinima, modes of production and its multiple different genres and applications via different distribution channels. Routed in gameplay, machinima has become a highly influential hedonistic, artistic and activistic tool yet it remains largely under the radar of researchers. The phases described trace its emergence yet it is clear that the impact of each phase has resulted in spin off activities that are now further evolving in their own domains. Each of the spin off developments is worthy of further investigation as both performative socio-cultural movements and creative technologies media. There has to date, however, been very little research into machinima and the phases of its evolution as presented.

The themes discussed in the literature (Merchant, 2013) are helpful in differentiating the four phases identified but the framework (Table 1) does not incorporate the legalistic aspects that have been identified as being important drivers for the transformation of the subcultural medium into mainstream cultural production. On the one hand, the community has emerged as a subversive cultural meme that deliberately challenges orthodoxy in video game cultures and gameplay. On the other hand, game publishers,

Table 1. Phases of machinima's emergence as visual culture

Merchant's (2013) Theme	Phase 1: Quake	Phase 2: AMAS	Phase 3: Machinima. com	Phase 4: Let's Play
Multimodality	In-game focussed	Storytelling beyond game; focussed channel enabled	In-game focussed; social media enabled	In-game focussed; social media enabled
Linguistic innovation	Hacking and modding game source code; text overlay; content sharing	Hacking and modding source code and content; cross platform sharing; community distribution strategy	In-game tools; audience distribution strategy	In-game tools; audience distribution strategy
Remix	Game content only	Game and non-game; multi-game	Game content; walk throughs/speed runs	Replay; voiceovers
Playfulness	In-game focussed	In-game but with beyond game appeal ('avant-garde')	In-game focussed	In-game focussed
Participation	Spectatorship and professional production	Creative practice; professional / aspirational practice	User-generated content; mass production; spectatorship	Spectatorship and professional production
Connection	Narrow; confined to core games players	Focussed; games players as professional artists and filmmakers	Global but confined to games players; games players as networked and channelled producers	Broad but confined to games players; communities have grown exponentially; new channels emerging

developers and channel owners have embraced (by formalizing game rules and terms of service) its role in supporting development of a game content culture because it directly and indirectly adds value to core activities for all stakeholders. Whilst this has resulted in some machinimators benefitting by (legitimately) monetizing their creative practice, for the majority the restrictive commercial practices of distribution channels fails to adequately address issues of creative sustainability through revenue share business models. It also does not address the important need to archive cultural production or curatorial practices that have emerged alongside the machinima phenomenon.

It seems more than ever, there is a need for an organization that undertakes to represent the interests of machinimators, similar to AMAS described in phase 2. Such an organization would be well placed to champion the manifesto for creative practice, sustainability of cultural production using gameplay, represent the interests of the different branches of the community in negotiating unfair legal practices by exploitative organizations, and promote good practice in the development of creative technologies skills.

REFERENCES

Begley, S. (2015). The 30 most influential people on the internet. *Time Magazine*. Retrieved 8 May 2015 from http://time.com/3732203/the-30-most-influential-people-on-the-internet/

Benkler, Y. (2002). Freedom in the Commons: Towards a Political Economy of Information. *Duke Law Journal, 52*, 1245–1276.

Brown, J. S., & Adler, R. (2008). Minds on fire: Open education, the long tail and Learning 2.0. *EDUCAUSE Review*, (January/February), 17–32.

Chen, S.-Y. R. (2011). *Adolescents' linguistic practices in college-affiliated Bulletin Board Systems (BBSs) in Taiwan*. (Unpublished PhD dissertation). University of Lancaster.

Chico, C. (2014, July-August). Machinima unplugged. *Computer Graphics World*, 24-28.

Coleman, S., & Dyer-Witheford, N. (2007). Playing on the digital commons: Collectivities, capital and contestation in videogame culture. *Media Culture & Society*, *29*(6), 934–953. doi:10.1177/0163443707081700

Cornblatt, M. (2011). Censorship as criticism. *Journal of Visual Culture*, *10*(1), 74–79. doi:10.1177/1470412910391565

Davies, L., & Raziogova, E. (2013). Framing the contested history of digital culture. *Radical History Review*, (117), 5-31.

Dring, C. (2014). How PewDiePie fired Skate 3 back into the charts. *MCV Games*. Retrieved 8 May 2015 from http://www.mcvuk.com/news/read/how-pewdiepie-fired-skate-3-back-into-the-charts/0137447

DVorkin, L. (2011). Who's Doing It Right? How Machinima.com Got 70 Million Viewers on YouTube. *Forbes Business*. Retrieved 7 May 2015 from http://www.forbes.com/sites/lewisdvorkin/2011/05/25/whos-doing-it-right-how-machinima-com-got-70-million-viewers-on-youtube/

Ebert, R. (2000). *The ghost in the machinima*. Retrieved 7 May 2015 from http://web.archive.org/web/20000818183940/http://www.zdnet.com/yil/stories/features/0,9539,2572985,00.html

Fosk, K. (2011). Machinima is growing up. *Journal of Visual Culture*, *10*(1), 25–30. doi:10.1177/1470412910391551

Gee, J. P. (2003). *What videogames have to teach us about learning and literacy*. New York: Palgrave Macmillan.

Gill, R., & Pratt, A. (2008). Precarity and cultural work in the social factory? Immaterial labour, precariousness and cultural work. *Theory, Culture & Society*, *25*(7-8), 1–30. doi:10.1177/0263276408097794

Greenaway, P. (2010). *Peter Greenaway speaks at the 48Hour Film Project Machinima 2010*. Retrieved 6 February 2012, from http://vimeo.com/groups/8472/videos/15253336

Grundberg, S., & Hansegard, J. (2014). YouTube's biggest draw plays games, earns $M a year. *The Wall Street Journal*. Retrieved 8 May 2015 from http://www.wsj.com/articles/youtube-star-plays-videogames-earns-4-million-a-year-1402939896

Hancock, H. (2015). *Has intellectual property law short changed machinima and gaming culture?* Retrieved 29 April 2015, from https://www.youtube.com/watch?v=0xHjcrIKYfM

Hardt, M., & Negri, A. (2000). *Empire*. Cambridge, MA: Harvard University Press.

Harwood, T. (2010). *Participant observation in Machinima research*. Games Research Methods Seminar, Tampere, Finland.

Harwood, T. (2011). Towards a manifesto for Machinima. *Journal of Visual Culture*, *10*(1), 6–12. doi:10.1177/1470412910391547

Harwood, T. (2012a). Emergence of Gamified Commerce: Turning Virtual to Real. *Journal of Electronic Commerce in Organizations*, *10*(2), 16–39. doi:10.4018/jeco.2012040102

Harwood, T. (2012b). Machinima as visual consumer culture. *7th Consumer Culture Theory Conference*. Oxford University.

Harwood, T. (2013). Per un manifesto del machinima. In M. Bittanti & H. Lowood (Eds.), *MACHINIMA! Teorie. Pratiche. Dialoghi*. Ludologica, Edizioni Unicopli.

Harwood, T. (2013). Machinima as a learning tool. *Digital Creativity*. Retrieved from http://www.tandfonline.com/eprint/uxKx4sNnsjMxt5N2YjuZ/full

Harwood, T., & Garry, T. (2012). Book chapter: It's Mine: participation and ownership within virtual value co-creation environments. *Journal of Marketing Management.*, *26*(3), 290–301.

Harwood, T., & Garry, T. (2013). Co-Creation and Ambiguous Ownership within Virtual Communities: The Case of the Machinima Community. *Journal of Consumer Behaviour.*

Harwood, T., & Ward, J. (2013). The challenge of marketing research within 3D virtual worlds. *International Journal of Market Research*, *55*(2). doi:10.2501/IJMR-2013-022

Hay, J., & Couldry, N. (Eds.). (2011). Rethinking convergence/culture, special issue of Hayes, C.J. (2009). Changing the rules of the game: How video game publishers are embracing user-generated derivative works. *Harvard Journal of Law & Technology*, *21*(2), 567–587.

Ito, M. (2011). Machinima in a fanvid ecology. *Journal of Visual Culture*, *10*(1), 51–54. doi:10.1177/1470412910391557

Jenkins, H. (1992). *Textual poachers: television fans and participatory culture*. New York: Routledge.

Jenkins, H. (2006). *Convergence Culture: Where Old and New Media Collide*. New York: New York University Press.

Jenkins, H. (2006). *Fans, bloggers and gamers: Exploring participatory culture*. New York: New York University Press.

Jenkins, H. (2007). The future of fandom. In J. Gray, C. Sandvoss, & C. L. Harrington (Eds.), *Fandom: Identities and Communities in a Mediated World*. New York: New York University Press.

Jenkins, H. (2014). Rethinking 'rethinking convergence/culture'. *Cultural Studies*, *28*(2), 267–297. doi:10.1080/09502386.2013.801579

Jenkins, H. (2015). *Minecraft and the future of transmedia learning*. Retrieved 5 May 2015 from http://henryjenkins.org/2015/04/minecraft-and-the-future-of-transmedia-learning.html

Jenkins, H., Ford, S., & Green, J. (2013). *Spreadable Media: Creating Value and Meaning in a Networked Culture*. New York: New York University Press.

Jones, R. (2011). Does machinima really democratize? *Journal of Visual Culture, 10*(1), 59–65. doi:10.1177/1470412910391559

Kafka, P. (2012). Google gets deeper into the content business, by putting money into Machinima. *All Things D*. Retrieved 7 May 2015 from http://allthingsd.com/20120507/google-gets-deeper-into-the-content-business-by-putting-money-into-machinima/

Kain, E. (2013, December). Another reason why YouTube's video game copyright crackdown doesn't make sense. *Forbes, 12*. Retrieved from http://www.forbes.com/sites/erikkain/2013/12/12/another-reason-why-youtubes-video-game-copyright-crackdown-doesnt-make-sense/

Kelland, M., Morris, D., & Lloyd, D. (2005). *Machinima: Making Movies in 3D Virtual Environments*. Cambridge: The Ilex Press.

Klepek, P. (2015). Who invented let's play videos? *Kotaku*. Retrieved 8 May 2015 from http://kotaku.com/who-invented-lets-play-videos-1702390484

Kress, G. (2003). *Literacy in the new media age*. London: Routledge. doi:10.4324/9780203164754

Kress, G. (2010). *Multimodality: A social semiotic approach to contemporary communication*. London: Routledge.

Kringiel, D. (2011). Machinima and modding: pedagogic means for enhancing computer game literacy. In The Machinima Reader (pp. 241-256). Massachusetts Institute of Technology.

Lankshear, C., & Knobel, M. (2010). *New literacies: Everyday practices and social learning* (3rd ed.). Maidenhead, UK: Open University Press.

Latonero, M., & Sinnreich, A. (2014). The hidden demography of new media ethics. *Information Communication and Society, 17*(5), 572–593. doi:10.1080/1369118X.2013.808364

Lazzarato, M. (1996). Immaterial Labour. In Radical Thought in Italy: A Potential Politics (pp. 133–47). Minneapolis, MN: University of Minnesota Press.

Lessig, L. (2001). *The Future of Ideas: The Fate of the Commons in a Connected World*. New York: Random House.

Lessig, L. (2008). *Remix: Making art and commerce thrive in the hybrid economy*. London: Penguin. doi:10.5040/9781849662505

Lowood, H. (2005). Real time performance: Machinima and game studies. *The International Digital Media & Arts Association Journal, 2*(1), 10–17.

Lowood, H. (2011). Perfect capture: Three takes on replay, machinima and the history of virtual worlds. *Journal of Visual Culture, 10*(1), 113–124. doi:10.1177/1470412910391578

Lowood, H., & Nitsche, M. (2011). *The machinima reader*. London: MIT Press. doi:10.7551/mitpress/9780262015332.001.0001

Mackey, M. (2002). *Literacies across media: Playing the text*. London: Routledge. doi:10.4324/9780203218976

Marino, P. (2004). *3D Game-Based Filmmaking: The Art of Machinima*. Scottsdale, Arizona: Paraglyph Press.

Marwick, A. E., & Boyd, D. (2011). I tweet honestly, I tweet passionately: Twitter users, context collapse, and the imagined audience. *New Media & Society*, *13*(1), 114–133. doi:10.1177/1461444810365313

Merchant, G. (2001). Teenagers in cyberspace: An investigation of language use and language change in internet chatrooms. *Journal of Research in Reading*, *24*(3), 293–306. doi:10.1111/1467-9817.00150

Merchant, G. (2013). The Trashmaster: Literacy and new media. *Language and Education*, *27*(2), 144–160. doi:10.1080/09500782.2012.760586

Ng, J. (Ed.). (2013). *Understanding machinima*. Bloomsbury.

Nitsche, M. (2006). Film live: an excursion into machinima. In B. Bushoff (Ed.), *Developing interactive content: Sagas_Sagasnet_Reader* (pp. 210–243). Munich, Germany: High Text.

Nitsche, M. (2009). *Video Game Spaces. Image, Play, and Structure in 3D Worlds*. Cambridge, MA: MIT Press.

Nitsche, M. (2011). Machinima as media. In The Machinima Reader (pp. 113-126). Massachusetts Institute of Technology.

Payne, M. T. (2011). Everything I need to know about filmmaking I learned from playing video games: the educational promise of machinima. In *The Machinima Reader* (pp. 241–256). Massachusetts Institute of Technology. doi:10.7551/mitpress/9780262015332.003.0015

Popper, B. (2013). Field of streams: how Twitch made video games a spectator sport. *The Verge*. Retrieved 7 May 2015 from http://www.theverge.com/2013/9/30/4719766/twitch-raises-20-million-esports-market-booming

Prahalad, C. K., & Ramaswamy, V. (2004). Creating Unique Value with Customers. *Strategy and Leadership*, *32*(3), 4–9. doi:10.1108/10878570410699249

Rigney, R. (2013). Want to sell your game? Don't tick off YouTubers. *Wired*. Retrieved 8 May 2015 from http://www.wired.com/2013/10/stanley-parable-sales/

Russell, A., Ito, M., Richmond, T., & Tuters, M. (2008). Culture: Media convergence and networked participation. In K. Varnelis (Ed.), *Networked publics*. Cambridge, MA: MIT Press. doi:10.7551/mitpress/9780262220859.003.0003

Saren, M., Harwood, T., Ward, J., & Venkatesh, A. (Eds.). (2013). Special Issue: Virtual worlds research in marketing. Journal of Marketing Management.

Sinnreich, A., Latonero, M., & Gluck, M. (2009). Ethics reconfigured: How today's media consumers evaluate the role of creative reappropriation. *Information Communication and Society*, *12*(8), 1242–1260. doi:10.1080/13691180902890117

Sliwinski, A. (2012). Machinima.com cuts staff by 10%, EIC calls it 'growing pains'. *Engadget*. Retrieved 7 May 2015 from http://www.engadget.com/2012/12/14/machinima-layoffs/

Spangler, T. (2014a). Warner Bros is buying a stake in struggling YouTube net Machinima. Here's why. *Variety*. Retrieved 7 May 2015 from http://variety.com/2014/digital/news/warner-bros-is-buying-a-stake-in-struggling-youtube-net-machinima-heres-why-1201127883/

Spangler, T. (2014b). Machinima hires cable exec Chad Gutstein as CEO. *Variety*. Retrieved 7 May 2015 from http://variety.com/2014/digital/exec-shuffle-people-news/machinima-hires-cable-exec-chad-gutstein-as-ceo-1201150400/

StandardGamer. (2014). A new genre of games is emerging: Pewdiepie bait. *IGN*. Retrieved 8 May 2015 from http://uk.ign.com/blogs/standardgamer/2014/10/19/a-new-genre-of-games-is-emerging-pewdiepie-bait

Stern, E. (2011). Massively multiplayer machinima mikusuto. *Journal of Visual Culture*, *10*(1), 42–50. doi:10.1177/1470412910391556

Stuart, T. (2013). Rage against the machinima. *Houston Press*. Retrieved 7 May 2015 from http://www.houstonpress.com/arts/rage-against-the-machinima-6596834

Taormina, A. (2014). Microsoft paying YouTubers for secret, only-positive Xbox One advertising. *Game Rant*. Retrieved 7 May 2015 from http://gamerant.com/microsoft-machinima-youtube-xbox-one-advertising/

Tapscott, D., & Williams, A. D. (2006). *Wikinomics: How Mass Collaboration Changes Everything*. New York: Portfolio.

Thomas, M. (2015). *Language learning with machinima*. EU funded CAMELOT project (2013-2015). Retrieved 30 April 2015 from http://camelotproject.eu/

Thomassen, A., & Rive, P. (2010). How to enable knowledge exchange in Second Life in design education? *Learning, Media and Technology*, *35*(2), 155–169. doi:10.1080/17439884.2010.494427

Toffler, A. (1980). *The Third Wave*. New York: Bantam Books.

Wellman, B. (2002). Little boxes, glocalization, and networked individualism. In Digital cities II: Computational and sociological approaches (pp. 10–25). Berlin: Springer. doi:10.1007/3-540-45636-8_2

Willett, R., Robinson, M., & Marsh, J. (Eds.). (2008). *Play, creativity and digital cultures*. London: Routledge.

Zuckerman, E. (2012). Attention, activism and advocacy in the digital age. *Connected Learning*. Retrieved 30 April 2015 from http://connectedlearning.tv/ethan-zuckerman-attention-activism-and-advocacy-digital-age

KEY TERMS AND DEFINITIONS

Anymation: Making of original content re-using any form of animation.

Demoscene: Computer game subculture using demos (small computer programs that produce audio-visual content) to showcase hardware or software developments.

Hacking: The process of cracking the source code of a game to overcome the challenges designed by the developer.

Hacktivism: Hacking or breaking into source code for a politically or socially motivated purpose.

Let's Play: The recording of gameplay (as walk throughs or speed runs) using voiceover commentary that may be humorous or instructional.

Machinima: Making of original content using 3D computer video games, usually recorded in real time.

Machinimators: Machinima makers and creators.

Modding: Modifying the source code of a game to make it play differently to that originally intended by the publisher.

Prosumption: Integrates production and consumption activities; term originally coined by Alvin Toffler (1980).

APPENDIX: LIST OF MACHINIMAS

- *1986 Mets vs RedSox* baseball game, https://www.youtube.com/watch?v=Xtitj4eFHqw
- *A Few Good G-Men*, Randall Glass, https://archive.org/details/a_few_good_gmen
- *Al Hansen's Car Bibbe II Happening*, Patrick Lichty (with Bibbe Hansen), https://www.youtube.com/watch?v=ALXjFH6I6Dg
- *Assassin's Creed Unity Rap – "L'Oeil de L'Aigle"*, JTMachinima, https://www.youtube.com/watch?v=CKefIC9SGVI
- *Better Life*, Rob Wright, https://archive.org/details/BetterLife_HighQuality
- *Cirque du Machinima – Cuckoo Clock*, Tom Jantol, https://www.youtube.com/watch?v=nE540j9U830
- *Clockwork*, IceAxe Productions, http://www.moviestorm.co.uk/community/index.php?page=videos&section=view&vid_id=101483
- *Dead in Iraq*, Joseph DeLappe, https://www.youtube.com/watch?v=ejcZ3TR5YTs
- *Diary of a Camper*, The Rangers, https://www.youtube.com/watch?v=uSGZOuD3kCU
- *How to machinima: WoW Model Viewer (Part 1)*, Ian Beckman, https://www.youtube.com/watch?v=oXD2dGxwfg0
- *Make Love Not Warcraft*, South Park, http://southpark.wikia.com/wiki/Make_Love,_Not_Warcraft
- *Male Rest Room Etiquette*, Phil Rice, https://www.youtube.com/watch?v=IzO1mCAVyMw
- *Molotov Alva and His Search for the Creator*, Douglas Gayton, http://www.imdb.com/title/tt1100132/
- *Physical virtuality "What's the weight of an avatar?"*, Chantal Harvey, https://www.youtube.com/watch?feature=channel_page&gl=NL&v=nloJ-VdCG8g&hl=nl
- *Push*, Lainy Voom, https://vimeo.com/5543976
- *Quad God*, Doom Arenas, https://www.youtube.com/watch?v=kLfgPHrepj4
- *Red vs Blue, Ep 19, Lost But Not Forgotten*, Roosterteeth Productions, http://roosterteeth.com/archive/?id=8313&v=more
- *Scout v Witch*, Randall Glass, https://www.youtube.com/watch?v=jf4ba72kFNQ
- *Stolen Life*, Peter Rasmussen and Jackie Turnure, http://www.imdb.com/title/tt1051263/
- *SuperMes*, Somethin' Else for Channel 4, https://www.youtube.com/watch?v=AmHh3CDnCrQ (Episode 1)
- *The 1K Project II*, Black Shark, https://www.youtube.com/watch?v=1UcQmJwTnBg
- *The French Democracy*, Alex Chan, https://www.youtube.com/watch?v=stu31sz5ivk
- *The Remake*, Tom Jantol, https://vimeo.com/9741624
- *This Spartan Life*, Chris Burke, http://www.thisspartanlife.com/
- *Tremulous fragmovie: "Sex, Drugs, Tremulous"*, Who Cares!? https://www.youtube.com/watch?v=7wwKryryzIA
- World of Warcraft©'s *Ozzy Osbourne commercial*, http://www.warcraftmovies.com/movieview.php?id=95195
- *World of Workcraft*, Lagspike Films, https://www.youtube.com/watch?v=msmRwlg23Qc

Chapter 8

The Scholar's Ludo-Narrative Game and Multimodal Graphic Novel:
A Comparison of Fringe Scholarship

Daniel J. Dunne
Swinburne University of Technology, Australia

ABSTRACT

Current discussions within videogames focus on the ways in which gameplay or narrative can be analysed by themselves, and rarely as a collaborative effort to explore a text. Although there have been a number of alternative approaches to this debate, none have succeeded in becoming prevalent within the field. This contrasts greatly with the study of graphic novels in relation to the application of multimodal analysis. In this field, discussion about the interplay between the mode of the image and the mode of the written text are more frequent. This textual analysis takes into account the two modes to focus on their collaborative effects in how the graphic novel can be understood. This chapter suggests that current videogame scholarship can benefit from pre-existing multimodal discussion that exists within graphic novels.

INTRODUCTION

Although videogames are arguably a conflation of media, there has been limited analysis of the ways in which they combine textual, visual, aural and performative elements. For the most part, scholars have relied on one or two methods of analysis to explain how videogames work, traditionally focusing on narrative or gameplay. Graphic novels, while not sharing as many different elements, can be considered to have the same analytical problems as graphic novels are a combination of textual and visual elements. However, graphic novel scholarship has traditionally involved a holistic approach to the analysis of graphic novels. Although both narrative and gameplay can be discussed within videogame scholarship, one element is usually highlighted above others. Videogames predominantly rely on the notion of a

DOI: 10.4018/978-1-5225-0016-2.ch008

divide between the two elements, while graphic novels have made use of this collaboration of elements. To understand this development a discussion of the history of graphic novels is needed.

Graphic novels, produced extensively throughout the late 20th Century were only really analysed after the gritty reboot era of the 1980s, retelling of old superhero narratives (Frank Miller's *The Dark Knight Returns[1]*) or the advent of darker, more emotionally complex stories (*Watchmen* [Moore et al., 1987], *Maus[2]* [Spiegelman, 2003], *Fun Home: A Family Tragic Comic* [Bechdel, 2007]). Here there were a number of events occurring within the panels, pages, and spreads of graphic novels resulting in a much more complex read. Although readers were incorporating a complex set of reading skills from this collage of text and image it was not formalised into a specific form of analysis for some time. It was in this type of analysis that the manner in which the reader was able to encounter the story was made apparent. With these two differing elements of image and text being presented in a non-traditional manner, a new method to analyse this approach was needed. Multimodality became the method of choice. Multimodality is the use of different types of semiotics (signs or representations) to create meaning in a text. Within graphic novels the use of multimodality allows for the combination of both image and text to be analysed effectively as individual components, as well as general components that make up the entire meaning of the graphic novel.

Graphic novels present a robust model for our understanding of multimodality in videogames. If these two elements can be analysed together in graphic novels, narrative and gameplay can be thought of in the same way in videogames. This chapter seeks to apply this method of analysis to videogames, choosing to frame videogame scholarship through the lens of multimodality in graphic novels. While graphic novel scholarship has pushed collaboration for its two elements, videogame scholarship has usually focused on one aspect in its analysis. Videogame formalism (Keogh, 2014, pp. 3-4) has increasingly sought for a collaboration of "phenomological concerns of videogames," but its implementation of these concerns has only just begun. Multimodality provides evidence that such an approach is both possible and beneficial to fringe media analysis.

Although there is a distinct application to both videogame and graphic novel scholars, this multimodal approach is a beneficial one that encourages a wide array of semiotic readings of music, image, and gesture, to provide meaning within a text. This application of analysis can easily be applied to other creative media, especially those that are emerging, and making use of digital media. Indeed its early intention was to provide a method of analysis for the increase in multimedia texts using a variety of new techniques. In this multimodality represents a good foundation where a range of multimedia analyses and complex texts can be understood.

This chapter proposes to bridge the gap between the two processes of analysis, and furthermore provides some context to the development of both mediums' scholarship. The chapter provides a context of multimodality and videogame scholarship, focusing respectively on the impact that multimodality has had on graphic novels, and the ludology and narratology discussions within videogame studies. A combination of the two approaches is then analysed, focusing on the benefits of applying multimodality to a videogame analysis. This concludes with a case study of *Call of Juarez Gunslinger*. Finally similar videogame approaches to multimodal analysis are highlighted to show the potential for further interdisciplinary scholarship. It is the hope that this chapter will highlight the effects of different approaches and suggest a more applicable one to the medium of videogames.

CONTEXT

Multimodality

At its core multimodality is the idea that within a piece of work, a combination of the various individual elements or media (image, sound, text) normally analysed on their own, should be considered instead as a singular piece of work (Kress, 2003). This is not to state that there is no difference between these elements, but rather that these elements contribute together to make something more. These individual elements within the piece are referred to as modes as they would present different methods of communicating information. Modes can be broken down into six distinct elements: linguistics, audio, visual, gestural and spatial modes as well as multimodal design (Cazden et al., 1996, p. 6). Within multimodality information would be conveyed through a combination of different modes. An example of the modes within a movie would have visuals, dialogue, and sound, whereas a literary novel would have only the mode of text. In this first iteration multimodality was mainly concerned with information transferral, rather than entertainment qualities which were implemented later.

Multimodality was developed out of the notion of 'multiliteracy,' within Cazden et al.[3], "A pedagogy of multiliteracies: Designing social futures," (1996) where the increase of more complex and globalised texts were a concern to educators. How these texts with their multitude of presentations were to be interpreted, and how their interpretation to be known was the primary concern of the work. Although the notion of multimodality was suggested it was only developed later on. These concerns, were further developed in Gunther Kress's work "Multimodality," (2000, pp.182-202) alongside other authors in *Multiliteracies: Literacy Learning and the Design of Social Futures* (Cope & Kalantzis, 2000). Kress here develops multimodality as a method which could make use of the increasing convergences of media and to integrate multiform texts that were available in the latter half of the 20th century. These media texts included mainly electronic multimedia that were appearing such as the internet, interactive media, television, film, instructional textbooks, and eventually graphic novels. The relationship between modes showed how they complemented each other. As such multimodality when implemented allows the text to be seen as a collaborative interaction of all elements that create a holistic meaning, existing beyond the sole modes of image or text.

Gunther Kress and Theo van Leeuwen, in *Multimodal Discourse* (2001) provide a thorough overview of the variety of methods in which multimodal discourse can occur, through studies of magazines, performances and multimedia technologies to display its capability. The text provides a good development of what multimodality can do when faced with a variety of media, and further provides discussion on the future of multimodal activity, looking particularly into the realm of creative technologies (pp. 103-110). Here it is important to note that there is a wide variety of media with no basis on a particular type, this highlights the robustness of multimodality.

Gunther Kress improves upon this analysis by bridging this notion of multimodal discourse to a variety of modes. In his book *Literacy in the New Media Age*, (2003) Kress highlights the growing concerns of an increase in multimedia technologies (p. 9), but also goes through a number of texts displaying different methods in which modes of multimodality can be analysed. Within this text Kress goes through the notion of multiliteracies and once again brings the notion of a variety of readings (p. 10) to the discussion of educating students. It should be noted that Kress puts forward four considerations, echoing the New London Group's primary concerns in the rise of globalised and multimedia texts. These are: social, economic, image as communication, and the relations of media of the page. Here it appears that Kress is trying to tease out the concerns of the New London Group with further exploration of when multimodal analysis should take place.

One of the key aspects of multimodality within its approach to analysis, is the focus back on the reader's comprehension skills. The interpretation of multimodality is dependent on the literacy of the individual reader, in regards to that particular mode. For example, those familiar with reading text will be able to read textual modes quickly while those who are familiar with images or sound will comprehend those modes first before proceeding to others. Although the reader in question can certainly pick up different literacies (identifying visual references as opposed to aural or textual), the multimodal overlap certainly contributes by pointing to an overall appreciation and understanding of the text, even if the specifics are not fully grasped. In this way even if the multimodal text is only understood via one of its modes, there is still some comprehension present. This can be seen as an alternative to the limitations present in a single mode text, readers unfamiliar with the node presented would not be able to access a text – with multiple nodes of learning this potential failure can be avoided. For further discussion around the interpretation of multimodality see New London Group's theory of "Design" (Cope & Kalantzis, 2000, pp. 153-161; Cazden et al., 1996, p. 25).

Originally, multimodality was intended to be applied in a mostly formal setting to the comprehension of educational, multimedia or technical texts in which pictures and other modes were necessary for communicating complex ideas. However, with this in mind, it is easy to see the variety of media types multimodality can be applied to. Indeed any media type that incorporates a mix of modes can be taken into account. Graphic novels, with their modes of both image and text, can be seen to benefit from a multimodal approach.

Multimodality for Graphic Novels

Although the term multimodality is widely used now, for much of graphic novel scholarship the comprehension of two modes, image and text, was merely hinted. Scott McCloud in his work *Understanding Comics: The Invisible Art* (1993) manages to highlight various events and occurrences within graphic novels that are both picked up on by readers, and employed by both artists and writers of the graphic novel industry to improve their understanding of the medium. This can particularly be seen in the discussions that McCloud instigates around an audience's ability to make meaning out of image and text. Further on that notion though, McCloud highlights the relationship that image and text have within graphic novels and the ways both can be shown. Although this discussion hints towards modes, multiliteracies and multimodality, McCloud presents these aspects of graphic novels as a desire for consistency and logic within the medium.

Other authors Charles Hatfield (2005), and Dale Jacobs (2008; 2013) both share this idea of graphic novels being distinct, in their ability to bring both images and text together to create meaning. Yet it is still not seen as a uniform method of analysis but rather an ongoing process of interpretation. Indeed Hatfield's explanation of the chaotic, yet consistent design of graphic novels is a half plea, half acceptance of the creative atmosphere that these texts produce "The fractured surface of the comic's page, with its patchwork of different images, shapes and symbols, presents the reader with a surfeit of interpretive options, creating an experience that is always decentred, unstable and unfixable." (2005, p. xiii). Hatfield's sentiment is one that is confounded by the creative freedom of the text, and the ability of the reader to shape it. Multimodality provides Hatfield with a methodology to provide "the reader with a surfeit of interpretive options," and it can be seen in the later works of graphic novel scholars. Jacobs in his multimodal analysis of *Peepshow* provides such a breakdown of these interpretive options through analysing the graphic novel's modes "All of these [multimodal] elements interact in our reading of the text," (2008, p. 67). Jacobs develops this multimodal notion further in his work *Graphic Encounters: Comics and the Sponsorship of Multimodal Literacy* (2013) where he provides an indepth analysis of a variety of texts. The co-relation of image and text, highlighted by Hatfield, but also the structures inherent in graphic novels as first suggested by McCloud, are easily reconciled under the notion of multimodality as presented by Jacobs in his work on *Peepshow,* but furthermore his focus on graphic novels as a predominately multimodal literature.

In a multimodal understanding of graphic novels the reader works alongside the text as a co-creator of the narrative. It is through the readers' variety of choice in which to understand the graphic novel, as well as the chosen layout by the graphic authors that provides the medium with this variety of modes. And from these modes further questions of interpretation can be seen. The possibilities of the page being read as a series of individual panels or a whole mural are just two examples of multimodal analysis at work. Both interpretations are valid, yet different and in that difference change their understanding of the graphic novel. This is in part what makes multimodality a robust theory. While there is only one narrative overall in the intended design of the author, the presence of image and text provides more space for interpretation within each panel, page, or even a whole spread. This makes the reading of such texts not so much a linear process but a space in which intuitive readers explore (Bredehoft, 2006, p. 875, 883). This particular notion of graphic novels existing as a physical space, and enables the idea of a constructed landscape in which the reader can explore. This notion is especially present in Chris Ware's book *Building Stories* (2012).

Building Stories is a collection of graphic narratives presented in a variety of forms: a thin strip of panels, a board-game board, a children's book, a series of newspaper clippings, and a cloth bound hardcover, as well as, traditional comic books contained within the box. The narrative within *Building Stories* is created through the artwork and writing that Chris Ware has produced. However, it is the piecing together of narratives by the audience that the story is effectively told (Morini, 2015). Ware's presentation draws special attention to the reader's part in the creation of story. This graphic novel in particular makes extensive use of its modes to provide a multitude of meanings in how the text can be read. Ware not only allows the audience to co-create the story, but also allows the audience to feel as part of the telling through their supposed presence within the text. This audience interaction is further supported by the construction of meaning that prior multimodal scholars pointed towards. With such a variety of modes available, a variety of meanings can be made. Although it can be argued that there is still a set narrative which audiences are encountering, the fact that there is room for interpretation in when and how they come to this narrative is certainly worth noting. The value of such an interpretation is present as well in a variety of 'mature' graphic novels such as Marjane Satrapi's *Persepolis* (2007), Joe Sacco's *Palestine* (2003), and Chris Ware's *Jimmy Corrigan: The Smartest Kid on Earth* (2001). All of which present these issues in a compelling multimodal manner.

From this range of scholarship, multimodality within graphic novels can be seen as the relationship between the images present on the page and the text printed with them. This reflects the multimodal framework that the New London Group has previously categorised for their modes: linguistics, audio, visual, gestural, spatial, and multimodal design. Although there is some adapting of the modes to suit the medium of graphic novels the analysis that occurs reflects the variety of modes that are present

(Jacobs, 2008, pp. 66-67). Albeit with a focus on the how these modes are depicted in image, and text – as evidenced from Thomas Bredehoft's (2006) work on *Jimmy Corrigan: The Smartest Kid on Earth* where spatial elements, such as zoetropes were also incorporated into the graphic novel. Although similar notions to this idea of multimodality can be seen in Linda Scott's notion of visual rhetoric (1994) and in Gene Kannenberg's juxtapose theory of image and text (2002). These are more so visually focused, which limits the applicability of the analysis. Nevertheless this acknowledgement of interplay between image and text is prevalent and lends itself to being incorporated into a multimodal analysis.

Hatfield (2005), Jacobs (2008; 2013) and Bredehoft (2006) illustrate the value of such a multimodal interpretation, linking back the notion of reading, or encountering narrative as something which readers can affect by their own comprehension of the text. The fact that a graphic novel can be read in a number of ways does more than just improve the complexity of the narrative. It provides accessibility to the story based on a number of available nodes, and further incorporates a co-creation of the narrative with readers. These are features which videogames are known for. As such, multimodality can be seen as an applicable method of analysis.

Multimodality for Videogames

The proposed implementation of multimodality in videogames is one that seeks to address both sections of gameplay and narrative, which have traditionally not been collaboratively analysed. However prior to that occurring it should be noted that multimodality has been developed in videogames but with uses other than analysis as their primary goal. As such these developments will briefly be mentioned here.

Concurrent to the development of multimodality by Gunther Kress, multimodality was also seen as a design based analysis within human computer interaction (HCI). Particularly in relation to heads up display (HUD) or user interfaces (UI). This development was pushed by the notion that users needed to be presented with a variety of information in the simplest way possible (Clarke & Duimering, 2006; Johnson & Wiles, 2003). Within videogames this is very prominent in the manner in which the quantity of health, ammunition, mini-map and primarily objective information is displayed.

Furthermore there are educational focuses on what can be learned through videogames with multimodality (Gee, 2003). In these analyses videogames are seen primarily as educational tools, and so rather than focusing on what these videogames might offer as a text, they are instead viewed in relation to what information they can teach to students. Although in line with previous notions of multimodality it is not as effective for analysing videogames as a complex text.

These previous uses of multimodality within videogames do provide some interesting perspectives on how information can be communicated and they do not address gameplay or narrative comprehensively in their work. This chapter follows Hatfield (2005) and Jacobs (2008) use of multimodality in graphic novels, but applies their notion to videogames. This notion of multimodality in videogames is an important one to explore. Yet before multimodality can be implemented, videogame scholarship first needs to be explored.

Approaches to Videogame Scholarship

Videogame studies have previously been divided into ludology (those that focus upon gameplay), and narratology (those that focus on narrative). Although somewhat inactive as paradigms these two schools of thought still hold weight in shaping the discussion of academics in relation to analysing videogames.

Primarily in promoting perspective that gameplay and narrative cannot mix. Although formalism (Keogh, 2014) is promoting a holistic approach to videogames, the prior influence of both ludology and narratology have deeply influenced the field.

Narratology

Narratology is focused on the idea of videogames as text. These studies developed out of the exploration of text-based adventure games and focused predominately on the readers 'choice,' within the confines of the game text. This approach focused on how the interactivity afforded to these videogames provided agency enough for players to construct a path through the game narrative (Ryan, 2001; Hayles, 1999). These analysis were focused less on the technical innovations and elements of gameplay, but rather on the seemingly infinite choices available in the narrative directions of these videogames (Landow, 2006). To put this in other words the direction of analysis was fully focused on one mode of narrative.

Among these scholars, Janet Murray provides a solid base of reference for a narratological approach to videogames. Through her analysis the presentation of narrative in a variety of ways, and occasionally marry the concept to the notion of space, and player choice. This while not encompassing of notions of gameplay (or other potential modes) provides a base understanding of the mostly narrative focus. In *Hamlet on the Holodeck* (1997) Murray provides a renewed focus on narratology, arguing that the future of not only games, but all narrative, lies in a new form of storytelling. A storytelling complex enough to accommodate the narrative wishes of the player to the degree of a holographic like simulation. Murray focuses on immersion, agency, and transformation as the current aesthetic pleasures of the electronic medium. These elements, while present in other media, can occupy a number of different forms within videogames and go beyond current traditional media. Notably, Murray notes that for the purposes of presenting a narrative in videogames there needs to be a static structure which cannot be altered so that there can be a beginning, middle and end. Yet at the same time Murray introduces this idea of procedurality into the mix, with the hopes that one day stories can be created by videogames. Murray sees a continued need for writers, in the new creative methods of presenting narrative.

Narratology, produces textually based readings of videogames (considering them to be akin to literary texts), and as such the methodology used often reflects a literature based background. However, in implementing this approach, it presupposes that the methodologies developed for previous media can be simply transplanted onto another. This is where ludologists come into play, as the assumption of traditional narrative analysis being at the heart of videogame studies was something which needed to be taken under consideration. This focus on narrative analysis, while beneficial in treating videogames as texts, were not taking into consideration a number of specific videogame features in their analysis.

Ludology

Ludology's meaning is derived from the Greek word *ludo* for play or fun. As such, ludology is mainly focused upon the play aspects of videogames, the gameplay. Ludology can trace its roots to game theorists Johan Huizinga, (1955) and Roger Caillois (1961). Ludology has tended to focus on gameplay and technological innovations over concerns about story-telling (Frasca, 1999; Eskelinen, 2001). In relation to narratology, ludology argues that narratology misunderstands the nature of games, as it presumes that they are primarily narrative creations, whereas ludologists see narrative as secondary (Juul, 2011).

While there are a number of ludologist scholars, there are two authors who have been critical in the foundation of the study, Markku Eskelinen and Jesper Juul. Both authors provide a good background to the importance of ludology, and provide a good range of responses to narratology. It also shows an opening up of the field in that there is not a reliance on previous forms of literature theory to form analysis, but rather a focus on what is unique about videogame gameplay.

Markku Eskelinen, was a founder of ludology, and a stringent advocator of the separation between narrative and gameplay. This can be seen particularly within Eskelinen's work *The Gaming Situation,* where he discusses the place of narrative in videogames as something that cannot be placed on all gameplay types. Although this can be seen as dismissive of narrative as a whole, the need for a separate method of analysis for gameplay is undeniable. Furthermore Gonzalo Frasca in "Ludologist's Love Stories Too," (2003a) goes on to elaborate upon Eskelinen's argument providing further context for his argument, that Eskelinen is being specific to games that lack stories- i.e. *Tetris*. In light of this, Eskelinen is not a straight ludologist, but rather someone who draws a determined boundary between gameplay and narrative.

Jesper Juul, a prominent ludological author, has written a number of texts delving into various aspects of ludology: an exploration of game medium, "The Game, The Player, The World," (2010) and a general theory of games *Half-Real* (2011). Juul believes in the prevalence of gameplay over narrative, and that gameplay in itself is a completely different aspect to that of narrative. Reminiscent of Markku Eskelinen, Juul considers narrative to be reflective and non-interactive. That is to say completely at odds with what games are, which is immediate and interactive. What distinguishes Juul's argument from other ludologists (Eskelinen, 2001; Frasca, 1999) is that while Juul separates the idea of narrative from gameplay, he does not disregard it entirely. Juul, in his book *Half-Real* (2011), focuses on the idea of games as rule based systems which players have to subvert or beat, against a background of fiction which Juul cites as important but not integral (2011, p.6). Juul has a more collaborative approach to both the narrative and the gameplay aspects of videogames, allowing for the two to coexist in an analysis, much like a multimodal approach would promote.

These scholars argue particularly for the notion that videogames exist as different from other texts, primarily as something which can respond and react to the player in a more complex manner than traditional texts. Although this does not rule out the value of narrative concerns for videogames there is a bigger reliance on game rules and player interaction (Frasca, 2003b; Juul, 2011). This player interaction promotes an almost multimodal approach to videogame analysis. In that there is a growing acknowledgement of a multiplicity of meanings. With this acknowledgement there has been a continued development of both approaches of narratology and ludology to be more inclusive.

Re-Approaching the Discussion

Throughout both the methodologies of narratology and ludology, there has been a push into a collaborative approach to game analysis that attempts to use both approaches. Unfortunately while there is this growing development within game studies to reconcile the two paths, the ongoing debates of the two approaches indicate a problematic reconciliation (Murray, 2005; Simons, 2007; Bogost, 2009). So while game studies is progressing towards a collaborative analysis of videogames the current discussion has not embraced collaboration fully. In recent years the implementation of theatre and film methodologies has enabled a wider flowing discourse around what occurs in videogames. Prominently among them the use of Bertolt Brecht portrayal of the oppressed (Frasca, 2004) and Roland Barthes' narrative structures (Backe, 2012). These developments are somewhat similar to the implementation of some of the modes to which multimodality makes reference. This opening up of different analytical techniques and considerations has definitely made the discussion within videogame studies more varied, allowing for alternative modes to be considered as part of an analysis.

Current direction of game studies seems to be locked in another movement towards textual analysis, supported with some aspect of gameplay, called formalism (Keogh, 2014). Although a number of approaches have been proposed it still appears that a decisive link between gameplay and narrative is yet to be made definitively, as most studies make one approach a subset of the other, instead of equals. This is not intended to dismiss the focus of multimodality on the modes of images, sounds, and textual elements that are within videogames, but rather to facilitate the ongoing discussion that has been occurring within videogame scholarship. Instead, this piece hopes to see how multimodality can build upon the pre-existing discussion about crossovers between narrative and gameplay.

The rest of this chapter will address the links between multimodality and videogames studies. This will establish multimodality as a positive tool for narrative and gameplay analysis, as it has been in graphic novels, with text and image. Videogame scholars can use and have used aspects of multimodality within their work, but more can be done to analyse videogames.

Comparison of the Two Approaches

The differences seems clear between the constructive outlook of multimodality within the field of graphic novels and the critical position of ludology and narratology for videogames. Although some comparisons do exist within methodologies, many of these, at least for videogame studies appear to be no longer widely used.

Previous to the use of multimodality in graphic novels there was a divide equivalent to that of the narratology and ludology separation of videogames. Except in the difference between text and image. The discussions around this text-image divide, unlike videogames did not critique the development of graphic novels that did not make good use of these two modes. Rather it looked inwards for a solution to analyse both modes (Nericcio, 1995). While not a critical discovery, this is something to keep in mind within the scholarly discussion. Graphic novels had the same sort of divide between image and text but were able to reconcile it with the notion of multimodality. The same should be able to be achieved for videogames.

The divide of narrative and gameplay analysis potentially began with Markku Eskelinen's research. "If I throw a ball at you I don't expect you to drop it and wait until it starts telling stories." (Eskelinen, 2001, para. 1). Although a simplification of the divide between gameplay and narrative, it does so to argue the notion that gameplay is purely action, and stories are purely told as previously events, and so each is not affected by the others. Reflecting on the multitude of stories, games (both analogue and digital), and new media platforms, that currently exist makes Eskelinen's statement refutable. There are a variety of texts and games that can be altered depending on the change in interaction. However if Eskelinen's point is that outcomes within videogames are undetermined until the videogame is finished, and that a story's outcome is set from the beginning (considered to be unalterable). Then the argument can be seen as much less of a statement that narrative and gameplay should be divided, rather that there are differences in their modes. A consideration to take into account when analysing videogames. Nevertheless, statements like Eskelinen's has led to a divide between narrative and gameplay.

Jan Simons in "Narrative, games, and theory," (2007) places Eskelinen's argument into the context of collaboration. She is seeking to refocus on how the two modes of narrative and gameplay, while different, could contribute to each other. Simmons does this through pointing out the malleability of both stories and games, and the differences that exist between them: "If there is still anybody waiting, it must be for Eskelinen to explain the point of this stab at narratology. Narratologists will be happy to explain to him the difference between the act of throwing a ball and the act of recounting that (f)act."(2007, para. 4). In her analysis of Eskelinen's argument, Simmons lists biases within both research ranges and points out the differences between recounting events and adding meaning to it, all the while suggesting that both are applicable to each other. The possible solution, suggested by Simmons is similar to what multimodality would drive towards; for both gameplay and narrative to work together where each mode supports the other in a unified videogame.

Graphic novel scholarship, on the other hand, has seemingly avoided this disruption even with incongruous source material such as *1941: The Illustrated Story* (Bisetti, 1979).While these obvious divides are not criticised to the same extent as game studies ascribes to it nevertheless can be seen as divided as narrative and gameplay are portrayed. Graphic novels can certainly suffer a divide of their own through a mixture of bad art, text, or an unhelpful combination of both. Yet the scholarship does not present graphic novels as such, and instead looks for how the two modes of text and image work together.

Videogame scholarship, in the same vein, can also make use of the methodology of multimodality to create a framework in which analysis can identify a multitude of modes (linguistics, audio, visual, gestural, spatial and multimodal design modes) to give a more comprehensive analysis of videogames. Some scholars have made use of both narrative and gameplay in a collaborative analysis but overall these scholars have not unified their methodology. An example of this is Rowan Tulloch's writing on *Bioshock* "A Man Chooses, a Slave Obeys…" (2010). Tulloch argues that with *Bioshock*'s use of game objectives (telling the players what to do in the game), combined with the narrative (in that the player obeys characters who utter the phrase "Would you kindly") is a good example of the co-operation between the narrative and gameplay. In Tulloch's analysis the focus is on the use of player agency, in how events are encountered, not the collaborative effect on the player. Alternatively this could be shown as multimodality if it were referenced as such. Other notable examples of this multimodal like cooperation exist within discussions around *Vampire: The Masquerade – Bloodlines* (MacCallum-Stewart & Parsler, 2007), *System Shock 2* (Remo, 2010), and *Mother 2* (Pitchfork, n.d.). These scholars follow Tullochs focus on agency, or in allowing the player choice, but the methodologies implemented through each is varied. These approaches unfortunately are not prominent in videogame scholarship.

This development of multimodal analysis, whether referred to as such, can provide direction to future analysis of videogames. These analyses can take into account the collaborative effect that these modes have on each other. In this application of multimodality, both gameplay elements and narrative elements would work together to create a greater overall experience, much in the same way that text and image does within graphic novels so too would videogames be open to this interpretation. In the next section a case study of a multimodal analysis on *Call of Juarez: Gunslinger* will occur, based upon the prior multimodal work of Gunther Kress and Theo van Leeuwen, in *Multimodal Discourse* (2001), but also more recently Dale Jacobs analysis "Multimodal constructions of self: autobiographical comics and the case of Joe Matt's *Peepshow*." (2008).

CASE STUDY

The recent videogame *Call of Juarez: Gunslinger* provides us with a case study in which a multimodal analysis can take place. *Call of Juarez: Gunslinger* is a series of Western levels, narrated by Silas Greaves, that the player plays, often requiring gun slinging, until encountering the bounty for the level which players have a chance of defeating in a duel. The focus of this analysis will be on a particular section of the videogames that uses the narration by Silas Greaves, and the shooter gameplay collaboratively to highlight a particular instance of play for players.

Figures 1-8 show a series of scenes from episode III "The Magnificent One," that highlights a variety of modes in order to tell its particular narrative, and provide a unique experience of play.

This change that occurs at the beginning of episode III highlights the co-relation that occurs within a multimodal discourse, making use of a number of narrative mechanics, alongside game mechanics. This section of *Call of Juarez* highlights both the variability of videogames to have a variety of enemies and situations, but also the malleability of the narration to change those variable game elements to something else. These variety of modes can be seen in the below breakdown of both narrative, and gameplay.

Narrative

- **Vocally:** Through the mode of vocals, the narrator is corrected to the right type of enemy. In Figure 1 the voice of Jack queries the consistency of the enemies "What happened to the Cowboys,"

Figure 1. Displays Apache enemies and the voice of Jack (an audience for Silas' narrative) queries the consistency of enemy
Source: Techland, 2014.

which Silas hastily corrects in Figure 2 "I said Clanton's Cowboys attacked apache STYLE." Here the vocal mode is directly supporting the visual by acting as a catalyst to the change that occurs. Furthermore the vocals help to reinforce events that occur within the video game.

- **Visually:** As can be seen by the visual mode the enemies change appearance. This can be seen in the progression from Figure 1, to Figure 2, and then Figure 3. In each there is a change in the depiction of the enemy, the first showing Apache models, the second a black screen to provide the means for the transition, and the third showing the now correct cowboys. This adds to the sense of an unreliable narrator (as Silas embellishes or gets details mixed up in the narrative), but also to the notion that there's a consistent narrative that is managed to be told.

- **Musically:** Although not easy to display, the musical mode provides another sense of action, as the music swells to become much louder and increases in tempo with the hectic scene. Furthermore ricochets are louder and occur much more often in the escape section. This occurs throughout the section observed. Yet pauses when different aspects of Silas' story are updated, such as Figure 2.

Gameplay

- **Artificial Intelligence (AI):** Within the AI, the enemies behave differently. The ambush changes from singular direction (the ridge above the stage coach) to "Apache style," where the enemies surround the player on all sides. This includes an increase in the number of enemies encountered, from a small number to a large number, quickly forming up around the player. This can be seen in Figure 3.

Figure 2. Narrator (Silas) responds to the prompt.
Source: Techland, 2014.

Figure 3. Displays a change with enemies; previous Apache enemies are now Bandits.
Source: Techland, 2014.

Figure 4. Open retreat route
Source: Techland, 2014.

Figure 5. Displays the cut off escape routes
Source: Techland, 2014.

- **Player Ability:** Further along in the ambush the player's ammunition runs out resulting in a no-win state if they persist in remaining. This is seen in Figure 6, 7, and 8 as the ammunition counter goes down leaving players with a reduced means to defeat enemies. This is also further supported by the vocal mode of Elias in Figure 6 "Unfortunately I was running out of ammo," and in Figure 8 "Another perfect example of my relative inexperience as a hunter of men." This reinforces the change that is taking place for the player, and furthermore that this event occurs early in the narrative of Silas.

- **Area:** The player originally can enter the stagecoach area, as seen in the open passage of Figure 4. However, through the gunfight this quickly changes into a blocked exit, as seen in Figure 5. This development highlights the fact that this scenes is foremost an ambush and one from which the player is expected to have trouble escaping. The player ability mode can also be seen as encouraging this notion of retreat, as the player has to rely on their diminishing ammunition, and when that runs out their ability to hide from gunfire. Eventually another entrance opens up for the player, encouraging them to flee.

These modes, while not mapped extensively to the New London Societies definition of modes (linguistics, audio, visual, gestural, spatial, and multimodal design), does share a variety of similarities with the concepts expressed. Below is a comparison between the two presentations in a similar style to what Dale Jacobs does with his work on *Peepshow* (2008, pp. 66-67) in combining elements from the medium to multimodal methodology.

Figure 6. Introducing a new element of ammo loss; note ammunition is at 19.
Source: Techland, 2014.

Figure 7. Ammunition reserves decreases from 19 to 10.
Source: Techland, 2014.

Figure 8. Highlights the decrease in ammunition with the narrator's voice, and also the smaller numerical number (10) of ammunition.
Source: Techland, 2014.

- Linguistics can be seen in the vocal mode as expressed in the dialogue expressed by both Silas and the Jack.
- Audio can be seen in the musical mode that makes use of both the game's soundtrack and effects.
- Visual in the change of appearance of enemies and escape locations.
- Gestural in the ability of the player but also in the actions of the AI.
- Spatial in the changing landscape or area.
- And in the scope of multimodal design the interplay of narrative and gameplay centred on the loss of ammunition, the change of enemies, and in the escape route that comes later.

It does not seem the intention of the New London Group to keep these modes as rigid categories for which analysis can occur, but rather a spectrum in which different modes can be expressed – especially those that might straddle different notions (gestural, visual and spatial). As such different categories of modes are permissible, especially when applied to different mediums.

Although the above gameplay and narrative could be analysed by themselves, the comprehension of the scene would not be as comprehensive. Leaving out either section, or even a mode would result in the analysis giving no context to the gameplay or narrative events occurring. There would be no explanation as to why the ammunition had decreased, why there were Indians on the screen, or why the escape routes were cut off. With a multimodal approach to *Call of Juarez Gunslinger* the differing modes all contribute to a sense of an ambush, of the Wild West, of a story within a story, and ultimately the videogame's sense of play.

From the above case study it can be seen that multimodality is effective within game studies, providing a collaborative understanding of both narrative and gameplay. Looking further towards game studies though the implementation of multimodality can further be supported by a variety of pre-existing methodologies. These methodologies, while not specifically arguing for the notions of modes, can provide a useful method for multimodality to be implemented within videogames based on similar notions of collaboration.

POTENTIAL DIRECTIONS FOR FURTHER RESEARCH

Parallels can be found in the discussion of game studies between gameplay and narrative, and within graphic novels between image and text outside of the framework of multimodality. Without the use of multimodality image and text would still be considered as divided. Gene Kannenberg's work (2002) provides evidence of this as it focuses on the differences between images, and text. Much in the same way that Clint Hocking has made a point of "ludo-narrative dissonance," and in how DiGRA panels have made a point of resolving debates (Murray, 2007), so too do these outliers of graphic novel discourse make a point of differences. There is an interesting similarity between the two mediums in that both had a crisis of message within their method of delivery.

These following methodologies can be thought of as addressing a similar area as multimodality. However none seemed to have such a wide effect on the field. Their applicability and effect on multimodality in videogames are grounded in sound academia, if not well known.

Ludo-Narrative Dissonance

Ludo-narrative dissonance was implemented in Clint Hockings "Ludonarrative dissonance in Bioshock: The problem of what the game is about," (Hocking, 2009). The piece discusses a particular flaw within many videogames: Primarily the disconnect between narrative events, such as the player-character being portrayed as a hero who saves the day, and gameplay events, where the "heroic goal," results come from the indiscriminate deaths caused by the player. This particular theory, is more in line with the prior discussions of Nericcio (1995) and Kannenberg's (2002) work in that it points out the divide of modes in the same way that Hocking does with gameplay and narrative. It is an important addition to the exploration of multimodality in videogame studies, as it provides a direction in which videogames can be studied, the in-between of gameplay and narrative. Although not as supportive of the notion of gameplay and narrative collaborating in *Bioshock,* it nevertheless points out that such a collaboration is possible. It provides not only a link within the history of scholarship between the two, but furthermore, if the direction of scholarship continues in like fashion, it will provide a possible solution.

Hocking's main argument against the videogame *Bioshock* is within its handling of Randian Objectivism (rational self-interest) within the constraints of the gameplay (which Hocking argues promotes the theory) and the narrative (which is ultimately critical of the approach). Hocking's argument hinges upon the lack of choice that players are presented with in the narrative, when contrasted with the gameplay of *Bioshock.* Although this criticism of *Bioshock* is a valid one, the ludo-narrative dissonance that Hocking describes seems more easily applied to other videogames, as a defence can be mounted for *Bioshock*'s lack of player agency (Tulloch, 2010).

Most notably this ludo-narrative dissonance be seen in the *Fable* series of videogames developed by Lionhead Studios. Particularly in the cases where a player can essentially buy their morality through religious donations, regardless of how many people (whether good or evil) these players have killed. Indeed there is a disconnect between the actual morality of the player's character and their actions, but for the purposes of the game world this is a simply a matter of fact occurrence rather than a crisis of faith (Lionhead Studios, 2005). It should be noted that *Fable*'s notions of good and evil are much easier concepts for players to grasp than *Bioshock's* Randian Objectivism. In this way *Fable's* "dissonance" can be seen as a larger divide in gameplay and narrative, as the results of the player's actions in *Fable* are not addressed or questioned, but accepted as a matter of fact. *Bioshock,* in Hockings analysis, still provides a discussion around the merits of Objectivism.

The 'dissonance' that Hocking argues for, could in the light of academic papers, be considered to be the separation of gameplay and narrative. These are discussed thoroughly in the ludological and narratological discussions of Gonzalo Frasca (1999, 2003b), Jesper Juul (2011), Espen Aarseth (1997), Ian Bogost (2009), and Janet Murray (2005). Each author details the specifics of why there are constraints within videogames or scholarship, when it comes to analysing videogame texts. The consensus seems to be that gameplay, which relies on systems of reward and dynamic developments, encounters difficulty when it tries to operate in conjunction with narratives. However this difficulty, as mentioned earlier, can be overcome with the right amount of design considerations between the two modes (Bateman, 2006). Indeed the incorporation of multimodality as a means in which to analyse graphic novels seem to point towards the notion of multimodal design. It considers the different modes as a method in which "dissonance," can be avoided (Kress, 2003; Jacobs 2008). This point promotes the notion that videogames can incorporate both narrative and gameplay, as long as it is designed as such.

Not all gameplay works well with narrative, and not all narrative works well with gameplay. In this manner Hocking's "ludo-narrative dissonance," can be seen as a critical endeavour to make note of these discrepancies in videogames. This critical look into where dissonance occurs can highlight troublesome instances of multimodality within the educational areas, graphic novels and other creative areas. This critical analysis of texts can further highlight instances where multimodality can be improved and further design considered by creative practitioners.

While at first glance ludo-narrative dissonance seems to identify and break down gameplay and narrative collaborations, it also provides a criticism to these collaborations in an effort to improve their design. This consideration, similar to the New London Group's notion of multimodal design (Cazden et al., 1996, p. 5), highlights a need for an ability to criticise and assess the success of multimodal constructions. That being said, by itself the notion can be considered to be fairly destructive in how it assesses texts that have a variety of modes. Combining multimodality with ludo-narrative dissonance allows for a more critical look at the design of multimodal texts, paying particular attention to how different modes can complement each other overall.

Ergodic Literature

Ergodic literature was first used by Espen Aarseth in *Cybertext: Perspectives on Ergodic Literature* (1997) as a methodology for analysing a text through "working through it." This statement places the reader as integral to the understanding of the text. In that through the reader's understanding of various sections of a text (or modes if adhering to multimodality), the narrative will form. In this manner ergodic literature can be seen as another form of multimodality within the field of videogames. Albeit, with a stronger focus on reader comprehension of these modes rather than the modes themselves. This notion is somewhat analogous to the discussion around Cope and Kalantzis' *Multiliteracies* (2000) in the application of different literacies (or modes) to students, in both cases the individual accessing the text is assisting in the creation of the text. Nevertheless this understanding of how modes come together, or rather an analysis of how texts can promote a multimodal reading, is what ergodic literature can provide for multimodality.

Ergodic literature can be better understood through breaking down the word "ergodic." Ergodic which comes from the two Greek words of: ergon, to work, and hodos, path. In this ergon is considered the interaction performed by the reader to work through the text. Hodos is the text, or mental "path" with which the reader makes sense of the author's work. These two concepts of ergon and hodos, are used in conjunction when talking about text comprehension, as the text (hodos) needs to be established by a writer or developer, and the interaction of readers (ergon) needs to be facilitated, and also needs to occur for the text to be comprehended. This is why the concept is referred to as ergodic literature.

Aarseth provides a large overview of a number of ergodic texts (1997, p. 5-13), focusing primarily on the ability of novels to allow for a variety of reader interpretations due to their construction. This approach places a focus on both reader ability in terms of comprehension (Cope and Kalanzis, 2000), but also the writer or developer to facilitate this potential for reader comprehension.

Although ergodic literature, like multimodality, can be based solely through a reader focus, the foundations to allow this, the hodos, is the focus for this section. Hodos provides ergodic literature with the means to support player interaction with the text. This diffusion of roles between reader and writer, with a design to support it, is different from traditional methods of analysing texts. As seen in the quote:

[Ergodic literature] centers attention on the consumer, or user, of the text, as a more integrated figure than even reader-response theorists would claim... During the cybertextual process, the user will have effectuated a semiotic sequence, and this selective movement is a work of physical construction that the various concepts of "reading" do not account for. (Aarseth, 1997, p. 2)

This section points out a noticeable gap in game studies, as prior analysis of player interaction with videogames would focus on the traditional notion of "reading" (as Aarseth suggests). The application of the phrase "reading," or "watching," that is present within traditional analysis is juxtaposed with the more general term "working through" that ergodic literature uses for its texts. This term "work," already signifies which ergodic texts that are "worked through." With this notion, ergodic literature does not rely on one term in which to describe their mechanics (mode) in which their text can be understood. Unlike multimodality, ergodic literature does not constrain its modes to six potential categories, but leaves the space open for whatever the text can allow. This while supportive of developing ergodic texts, can become problematic in later analyses. In this manner multimodality and ergodic literature complement each other well in that they allow for a wide range of modes.

This parallel between multimodality and ergodic literature seems to reflect each other more and more with ongoing analysis. As Espen Aarseth focuses on videogames to explore ergodic literature, and Cope and Kalantzis (2000) discusses learning literacies for multimodality, both scholars are searching for a method in which complex texts can be understood. Both the varying structures of these complex texts and the manner in which they were comprehended are at the core of these arguments. This makes the similarity between the two authors very apparent. While both theories compare and complement each other strikingly well, ergodic literature was not implemented further in video scholarship to bridge the gap with narrative and gameplay discussions.

It seems strange that these two notions of multimodality and ergodic literature produced within a few years of each other (Cope and Kalantzis 2000; Aarseth, 1997) could have such different outcomes based on their scholarly fields and subject areas. Even with the more pronounced gap in time in the comparison of graphic novel multimodality, the use in the field is still more extensive than that of ergodic literature. Hatfield referred to multimodality in graphic novels first in 2006, while Jacobs produced his work in 2008 and again in 2013 with a renewed focus on multimodal methodology. Ergodic literature has not yet occurred within videogame scholarship. Nevertheless Aarseth's ergodic literature seem to share the concerns of multimodality.

Paratext

Paratext, introduced by Gerard Genette in *Paratexts: Thresholds of interpretation* (1997), is defined as the "in-between" area between the text and the reader. Genette separates paratext into two areas of peritext, physically within the text (font, pictures, paragraphs), and epitext, external elements that refer to a text (reviews, advertisements). In this, paratext can be seen as structuring how an entire text is presented, as well as influencing the reader's comprehension of the text through this structure. In this way paratext enabled literary texts to be analysed on the basis of not only the text, but also the elements which surrounded it. This, like the multimodal approach of both Cope and Kalantzis (2000), Kress (2003) and of Jacobs (2008, 2013) within graphic novels, allows for a comprehension of the different modes of communication within a text, in that it looks towards how methods other than the text can contribute to a narrative.

Although in recent years paratext, when referred to in videogames, is more commonly attributed to media representations (Gray, 2010) and transmedia developments (Consalvo, 2007; Lunenfeld, 2000), this development of scholarship has only focused on one aspect of paratext, the ability to cross promote a text. This, while an interesting development, does not lend itself easily to multimodality. Rather, it is the focus on the internal comprehension of a text that Genette focuses on within his work that is similar to multimodalities approach.

From here the applicability of paratext towards multimodality (and indeed ergodic literature), is that paratexts approach a text according to its components. *Paratexts: Thresholds of interpretation* (1997) goes through rigorously the sections of novels listing ten instances of peritext, and another two for epitext. These, as with multimodality, are not meant to be definitive categories, but rather an exercise in seeing how many supplementary elements can support a text. Genette in the conclusion admits that there is further research to be done for paratext if work is to be done with images, biographies or translation (Genette, 1997, p. 405). This research, while not completely answered by multimodal analysis, is definitely helped along by the pre-existing analysis of gestural and spatial modes.

Furthermore, paratext shares connections with the analysis of graphic novels as it explores a similar in-between area of the "gutter" (McCloud, 1993, pp. 60-90). This notion of the gutter looks past the panel sections of graphic novels and looks at how they both structure the graphic novel, and influence the reader's perception. This deep analysis of the structure of graphic novels is similar to how paratext seeks to determine how structures of a text can influence a reading. Although these "gutter" locations are hard to determine in relation to other media types, the robustness of paratext, and by extension multimodality allows for a renewed focus into how each mode (even when not a primary one) not to just be correlation between panels (as McCloud focuses his definition on), but rather as a more ubiquitous and encompassing notion of structuring and informing the reader.

This alternative approach as to what can influence a reader is one of paratext's main strengths, allowing for a collaborative approach to analysing a variety of texts. Here the strength of paratext, as compared to multimodality, is to see how these modes contribute to a central narrative or theme. Whereas multimodality does not rank or provide these modes with an order of importance, paratext provides a funnelling of references to a particular area, the text of a novel. With this focus, in some cases, a more direct comprehension of a text can occur – especially in texts that do not have a wide variety of modes available to them. In this, paratext's influence can be seen as a scaling back of what multimodality can do, and instead focus on what can be considered the main section of the text (the words, the image, the music), while other modes support it. An example of this would be the music in *Call of Juarez: Gunslinger* playing a less important role than the image, gesture, or narrative.

With that said, it should be noted that Genette's paratext is primarily serving the notion of the literary text being at the centre of analysis. Other comprehensions of more image, or performance based texts would not be as detailed. Furthermore, this presentation runs the same danger as narratology did in its preference for narrative. Although there is the scope for growth and further development of analysis techniques, paratext as highlighted in *Paratexts: Thresholds of interpretations* is fully intended for textual use. Using multimodality to frame the discussion of paratexts towards these alternative texts would allow for a more nuanced analysis.

CONCLUSION

This constructive interplay of gameplay and narrative while often not analysed within game studies (at least without criticism), could follow on from the multimodality which has been successfully implemented in graphic novel scholarship. From this source of inspiration, prior works within game studies, similar to that of multimodality, could be identified allowing for an easy identification for more balanced discussion around the interplay of both narrative and gameplay.

Through this first step of providing a discussion around the interplay of both narrative and gameplay, other more obscure videogame elements, such as sound or haptic interaction, would also have a place in which their contribution to videogame could also be analysed. Finally, this step of providing a possible solution for differences in text and image that has occurred within graphic novel scholarship, potentially provides the framework for a possible solution between the divide of gameplay and narrative. This research points towards a possible collaboration between the two paradigms, based on a number of methodologies.

Supplementary results of implementing this approach would include more insight into the way that videogames are played and the way that information is presented to players. In particular the multimodal analysis carried out will point towards different aspects of gameplay and narrative most noticed by players. Videogame scholarship instead of being approached as a binary analysis of narrative or gameplay, can be looked to as collection of tools that enable for a holistic analysis of videogames.

This development of multimodality, while especially suited to videogames and graphic novels, has a far wider reach for creative technological industries. The modes used by these industries and practitioners will be much more varied and abstracted than what the New London Group suggested in their early research. In this, multimodality represents a good starting point for these practitioners and researchers in which to analyse the interplay within their creative technological texts.

REFERENCES

2k Boston and 2k Australia. (2007). *Bioshock*. 2K Games.

Aarseth, E. (1997). *Cybertext: perspectives on ergodic literature*. Baltimore, MD: Johns Hopkins University Press.

Ape and HAL Laboratory. (1995). *Earthbound/Mother 2*. Nintendo.

Backe, H. J. (2012). Narrative rules? Story logic and the structures of games. *Joachim Literary and Linguistic Computing, 27*(3), 243–260. doi:10.1093/llc/fqs035

Bateman, C. (2006). Game Writing: Narrative Skills for. Charles River Media.

Bechdel, A. (2007). *Fun home: A family tragicomic*. Boston, MA: Houghton Mifflin Harcourt.

Bisetti, S. (1979). *1941: the illustrated story*. New York, NY: Pocket Books.

Bogost, I. (2009). Videogames are a mess. *Keynote speech at DiGRA*. Retrieved August 20, 2015, from http://www.bogost.com/writing/videogames_are_a_mess.shtml

Bredehoft, T. A. (2006). Comics architecture, multidimensionality, and time: Chris Ware's Jimmy Corrigan: the smartest kid on earth. *MFS Modern Fiction Studies, 52*(4), 869–890. doi:10.1353/mfs.2007.0001

Caillois, R. (1961). *Man, play, and games*. Champaign, IL: University of Illinois Press.

Cazden, C., Cope, B., Fairclough, N., Gee, J., Kalantzis, M., Kress, G., & Nakata, M et al.. (1996). A pedagogy of multiliteracies: Designing social futures. *Harvard Educational Review, 66*(1), 60–92. doi:10.17763/haer.66.1.17370n67v22j160u

Clarke, D., & Duimering, P. R. (2006). How computer gamers experience the game situation: A behavioral study. *Computers in Entertainment, 4*(3), 6. doi:10.1145/1146816.1146827

Consalvo, M. (2007). *Cheating: Gaining advantage in videogames*. Cambridge, MA: MIT Press.

Cope, B., & Kalantzis, M. (Eds.). (2000). Multiliteracies: Literacy learning and the design of social futures. Oxford, UK: Psychology Press.

Eskelinen, M. (2001). The gaming situation. *Game Studies, 1*(1). Retrieved August 20, 2015, from http://www.gamestudies.org/0101/eskelinen/

Frasca, G. (1999). Ludology meets narratology: similitude and differences between videogames and narrative. *Ludology*. Retrieved August 20, 2015, from www.ludology.org/articles/ludology.htm

Frasca, G. (2003a, November). Ludologists love stories, too: notes from a debate that never took place. In *DIGRA 2003 Conference Proceedings.* Academic Press.

Frasca, G. (2003b). Simulation vs. narrative: introduction to ludology. In M. J. P. Wolf & B. Perron (Eds.), *The video game theory reader* (pp. 221–235). New York, NY: Routledge.

Frasca, G. (2004). Videogames of the Oppressed. In P. Harrigan & N. Wardrip-Fruin (Eds.), *First person: New media as story, performance, and game* (pp. 85–94). Cambridge, MA: MIT Press.

Gee, J. P. (2003). What video games have to teach us about learning and literacy. *Computers in Entertainment, 1*(1), 20–20. doi:10.1145/950566.950595

Genette, G. (1997). *Paratexts: Thresholds of interpretation* (J. Lewin, Trans.). Cambridge, MA: Cambridge University Press. doi:10.1017/CBO9780511549373

Gray, J. (2010). *Show sold separately: promos, spoilers, and other media paratexts.* New York: New York University Press.

Hatfield, C. (2005). *Alternative comics: an emerging literature.* Jackson, MS: Univ. Press of Mississippi.

Hayles, N. K. (1999). Simulating narratives: What virtual creatures can teach us. *Critical Inquiry, 26*(1), 1–26. doi:10.1086/448950

Hocking, C. (2009). Ludonarrative dissonance in Bioshock: The problem of what the game is about. In D. Davidson (Ed.), *Well Played 1.0* (pp. 255–259). Halifax, Canada: ETC Press.

Huizinga, J. (1955). *Homo ludens: A study of the play element in culture* (R. Hull, Trans.). Boston, MA: Beacon.

Irrational Games & Looking Glass Studios. (1999). *System Shock 2.* Electronic Arts.

Jacobs, D. (2008). Multimodal constructions of self: autobiographical comics and the case of Joe Matt's Peepshow. *Biography, 31*(1).

Jacobs, D. (2013). *Graphic Encounters: Comics and the Sponsorship of Multimodal Literacy.* New York, NY: Bloomsbury Publishing USA.

Johnson, D., & Wiles, J. (2003). Effective affective user interface design in games. *Ergonomics, 46*(13-14), 1332-1345.

Juul, J. (2010). The game, the player, the world: Looking for a heart of gameness. *PLURAIS-Revista Multidisciplinar da UNEB, 1*(2).

Juul, J. (2011). *Half-real: Video games between real rules and fictional worlds.* Cambridge, MA: MIT Press.

Kannenberg, E. P. (2002). *Form, function, fiction: Text and image in the comics narratives of Winsor McCay, Art Spiegelman, and Chris Ware. (Unpublished Doctoral Dissertation).* University of Connecticut.

Keogh, B. (2014). Across worlds and bodies: Criticism in the age of video games. *Journal of Games Criticism, 1*(1), 1–26.

Kress, G. (2000). Multimodality. In Multiliteracies: Literacy learning and the design of social futures. Oxford, UK: Psychology Press.

Kress, G. (2003). Literacy in the new media age. London, UK: Psychology Press. doi:10.4324/9780203164754

Kress, G., & Leeuwen, T. (2001). *Muiltimodal discourse: the modes and media of contemporary communications*. London: Arnold.

Landow, G. P. (2006). *Hypertext 3.0: Critical theory and new media in an era of globalization*. Baltimore, MD: Johns Hopkins University Press.

Lionhead Games. (2005). *Fable: The Lost Chapters*. Microsoft Game Studios.

Lunenfeld, P. (2000). *The digital dialectic: New essays on new media*. Cambridge, MA: MIT Press.

MacCallum-Stewart, E., & Parsler, J. (2007). Illusory agency in Vampire: a Masquerade-Bloodlines. *Dichtung-Digital, 37*. Retrieved August 20, 2015, from http://www.dichtung-digital.org/2007/Stewart%26Parsler/maccallumstewart_parsler.htm

Matt, J. (1992). *Peepshow*. Quebec, Canada: Drawn and Quarterly.

McCloud, S. (1993). *Understanding comics: The invisible art*. Northampton, MA: Paradox Press.

Medley, S. (2010). Discerning pictures: How we look at and understand images in comics. *Studies in Comics, 1*(1), 53–70. doi:10.1386/stic.1.1.53/1

Miller, F., Janson, K., Varley, L., Costanza, J., & Kane, B. (2002). *Batman: The dark knight returns*. New York, NY: Random House.

Moore, A., Gibbons, D., & Higgins, J. (1987). *Watchmen*. New York, NY: Random House.

Morini, M. (2015). Multimodal Thought Presentation in Chris Ware's Building Stories. *Multimodal Communication, 4*(1), 31–41.

Murray, J. H. (1997). *Hamlet on the holodeck: The future of narrative in cyberspace*. New York, NY: Simon and Schuster.

Murray, J. H. (2005). The last word on ludology v narratology in game studies. In *DiGRA 2005 Conference: Changing views of worlds in play*. Retrieved August 20, 2015, from http://inventingthemedium.com/2013/06/28/the-last-word-on-ludology-v-narratology-2005/

Nericcio, W. A. (1995). Artif [r] acture: Virulent pictures, graphic narrative and the ideology of the visual. *Mosaic (Winnipeg), 28*(4), 79–109.

Pitchfork. (n.d.). Mother 2/Earthbound. *Socks Make People Sexy*. Retrieved August 20, 2015, from http://www.socksmakepeoplesexy.net/index.php?a=earthbound

Remo, C. (2010). Analysis: System Shock 2 – structure and spoilers. *Gamasutra*. Retrieved August 20, 2015, from http://www.gamasutra.com/view/news/27684/Analysis_System_Shock_2__Structure_And_Spoilers.php

Ryan, M. L. (2001). *Narrative as virtual reality: Immersion and interactivity in literature and electronic media*. Baltimore, MD: Johns Hopkins University Press.

Sacco, J. (2003). *Palestine*. New York, NY: Random House.

Satrapi, M. (2007). *The Complete Persepolis*. New York, NY: Pantheon Books.

Scott, L. M. (1994). Images in advertising: The need for a theory of visual rhetoric. *The Journal of Consumer Research*, *21*(2), 252–273. doi:10.1086/209396

Simons, J. (2007). Narrative, games, and theory. *Game studies, 7*(1), 1-21. Retrieved August 20, 2015, from http://gamestudies.org/0701/articles/simons

Techland. (2013). *Call of Juarez: Gunslinger*. Ubisoft.

Troika Games. (2004). *Vampire: The Masquerade – Bloodlines*. Activision.

Tulloch, R. (2010). A man chooses, a slave obeys: Agency, interactivity and freedom in video gaming. *Journal of Gaming & Virtual Worlds*, *2*(1), 27–38. doi:10.1386/jgvw.2.1.27_1

Ware, C. (2001). *Jimmy Corrigan: The smartest kid on earth*. New York, NY: Random House.

Ware, C. (2012). *Building Stories*. New York, NY: Pantheon Books.

KEY TERMS AND DEFINITIONS

Ergodic Literature: A concept created by Espen Aarseth, to explain a text which a reader must "work through," using a variety of comprehension techniques in order to interpret.

Graphic Novel: A large collection of images portrayed in such a way with images that it tells a story.

Gutter: This is considered to be the border or the separating sections between panels. Traditionally this space is left blank to present a change between one panel to the next, however this can be altered. This alteration is done either with the further use of illustrations in these areas, or a larger or smaller amount of space used to separate the panels.

Ludology: The study of gameplay mechanics within videogames.

Multimodal: A term coined by the New London Group, to explore texts that make use of a variety of modes in their presentation, most often used in relation to multimedia or electronic texts.

Narratology: The study of narrative within videogames.

Panel: A graphic novel term that refers to the individual scene, or image that is constrained by a border. These are often combined to create a strip (a linear strip of panels, one after the other), or used to fill a page (usually in a sequence of strips presented either in a left to right, or top to bottom format).

Paratext: The physical and figurative structure of a text that constrains or limits the text in a certain manner (e.g. placement of paragraphs, or the size of the page). In the course of constraining the text in a particular regard, the text is made (more) accessible to readers.

ENDNOTES

[1]   First published in 1986. (Miller, Janson, Varley, Costanza, & Kane, 2002).
[2]   Serialised from 1980-1991. (Spiegelman, 2003).
[3]   Also known as the New London Group.

Chapter 9

The Holon/Parton Theory of the Unit of Culture (or the Meme, and Narreme):
In Science, Media, Entertainment, and the Arts

J. T. Velikovsky
University of Newcastle, Australia

ABSTRACT

A universal problem in the disciplines of communication, creativity, philosophy, biology, psychology, sociology, anthropology, archaeology, history, linguistics, information science, cultural studies, literature, media and other domains of knowledge in both the arts and sciences has been the definition of 'culture' (see Kroeber & Kluckhohn, 1952; Baldwin et al., 2006), including the specification of 'the unit of culture', and, mechanisms of culture. This chapter proposes a theory of the unit of culture, or, the 'meme' (Dawkins, 1976; Dennett, 1995; Blackmore, 1999), a unit which is also the narreme (Barthes, 1966), or 'unit of story', or 'unit of narrative'. The holon/parton theory of the unit of culture (Velikovsky, 2014) is a consilient (Wilson, 1998) synthesis of (Koestler, 1964, 1967, 1978) and Feynman (1975, 2005) and also the Evolutionary Systems Theory model of creativity (Csikszentmihalyi, 1988-2014; Simonton, 1984-2014). This theory of the unit of culture potentially has applications across all creative cultural domains and disciplines in the sciences, arts and communication media.

INTRODUCTION

This chapter proposes a formal structure for the unit of culture, also known as the meme (Dawkins, 1976), namely: the holon/parton (Velikovsky, 2013b), synthesizing concepts from (Koestler 1967) and Feynman (2005).

Previously, an unsolved problem across media, the arts, entertainment and science has been defining 'the unit of culture', resulting in over three hundred varying definitions of culture (Baldwin et al 2006), and no consensus (van Peer et al 2007). Given also that stories (or, narratives) in any media are 'units

DOI: 10.4018/978-1-5225-0016-2.ch009

of culture', this proposed unit of culture, the holon/parton, also applies to the *narreme*, or, the 'unit of story' namely the whole and its composite parts. This holon/parton structure is suggested for analyzing media, and transmedia, including: movies, novels, television series, videogames, plays, songs, poems, jokes, religions, and also knowledge in science (i.e., scientific ideas, processes, and products).

An Evolutionary Systems Theory approach to Creativity in the discipline of Mass Communication Studies (aka Communication) illuminates why bioculture is structured hierarchically, as a holon/parton, or a holarchy. The aim here is to provide a universal *unit of culture*, spanning communication, the arts and humanities, media, languages and science, in order to facilitate commensurate empirical analyses of culture across disciplines, and also to enable structural, functional and behavioral comparisons between biocultural artifacts, to aid in the tracking and understanding of culture (and, its units) including within Creative Technologies and the Digital Humanities. For example, a better understanding of culture at the genre level may also benefit cultural curators and cultural theorists.

In short, the unit of culture (as: the holon-parton) is a conceptual, theoretical, practical and scientific tool (namely, a piece of creative technology), for identifying and analyzing units within: any - and all - creative media (including films, novels, videogames, television programs, scientific theories, songs, tweets, sentences, words, and so on, namely: any symbol system in culture.) This theoretical tool is thus potentially of direct practical use to anyone who has anything to do with culture: specifically - creators, students, scholars, critics, analysts, academics, practitioners, curators, and audiences. This Evolutionary Systems Theory approach is part of Applied Evolutionary Epistemology (see Gontier 2012), ideally enabling an understanding of the growth and evolution of both biology and culture.

BACKGROUND TO THE PROBLEM

A long-standing (unsolved, and universal) problem in the disciplines of Communication, Creativity Studies, Philosophy, Biology, Psychology, Sociology, Anthropology, Archaeology, History, Linguistics, Information Science, Mathematics, Cultural Studies, Literature, Media, the Digital Humanities - and other domains and disciplines of knowledge in the arts, media and the sciences - has been the definition of 'culture', including a practical specification of *the unit* of culture. 'Culture' has long been a problematic term as there is currently no consensus across all of the various domains and disciplines on 'culture'. In 1952, 164 extant definitions of culture were extant (Kroeber & Kluckhohn, 1952), and more recently in 2006 the list was extended to over 300 extant definitions (see Baldwin, Faulkner, Hecht, & Lindsley, 2006, pp. 139-226). Summarizing the contemporary state of knowledge about the problem of culture in *Muses and Measures: Empirical Research Methods for the Humanities,*[1] van Peer *et al* concluded 'As far as can be seen, there is no consensus on the notion of culture anywhere to be found' (van Peer, Hakemulder, & Zyngier, 2007, p. 30). Similarly, in a recent survey of contemporary knowledge in the domain of Memetics (1976-2009) - a discipline which aims to identify and track 'units of culture' - in the article 'Evolution of Culture, Memetics' in the *Encyclopedia of Complexity and Systems Science,* it is noted that 'The lack of a universally accepted meme definition and the vagueness of meme boundaries... indeed make empirical studies less evident' (Heylighen & Chielens, 2009, p. 3217).

The following proposal for the unit of culture (aka, the meme), and also the narreme (or, the unit of narrative), namely the *holon/parton*, aims to provide a possible solution to these problems, in defining, and/or creating, and/or analyzing culture, and therefore with many multidisciplinary applications.

Theoretical Perspective

The theoretical perspective adopted in this chapter is Evolutionary Systems Theory. In *Introduction to Systems Philosophy: Toward a New Paradigm of Contemporary Thought,* Laszlo (1972) incorporates Living Systems Theory (Miller, 1968)[2] and also Bunge's hierarchical structures (Bunge, 1969) to provide a framework for understanding universal structures, spanning from subatomic physics, through biology, chemistry, organisms, and social systems, to the cosmos (Laszlo, 1972, pp. 29, 177-180). An illustration of this view is shown in Figure 1.

In this view, the 'largest-to-smallest' levels of structural hierarchical organization include: Multiverse / Universe / Filament / Supercluster / Cluster / Galaxy / Star system (Heliosphere) / Planet (Biosphere) / Continent / Nation / State or Province / City, Town or Village / Neighborhood / Residence / Family / Person (organism) / Organ system / Organ / Tissue / Cell / Organelle / Molecule / Atom / Subatomic Particles (or, Waves).[3]

Laszlo (1972) also employs Koestler's holon theory in systems (Laszlo, 1972, pp. 55-118, 252, 255, 272-114), as Koestler had previously extended General Systems Theory (Koestler, [1978] 1979, pp. 31-32; von Bertalanffy, 1950) from biological systems, to social holarchies (i.e., hierarchies of social holon/partons) and also to linguistic hierarchies (Koestler, [1964] 1989, pp. 287-290; [1967] 1989, pp. 103, 198-109; [1978] 1979, pp. 27-62). As noted in the *Definitions* section (below), in simplest terms, the *three laws of holarchies*, or key behaviors of holon/partons, may be summarized as follows.

As *units*, holon/partons:

- **Compete, and/or, Co-Operate (and/or Engage in *Co-Opetition*) 'Sideways':** With other holon/partons on the same level;
- **Integrate 'Upwards':** Into the larger holon/parton 'above'; and
- **Control and Command:** Their component holon/partons, on the level 'below'

This basic concept of 'the three laws of holarchies' is illustrated in Figure 2.

These three laws also appear to be laws of physics (and, of systems), applying both to biology and also bioculture (aka 'culture'), a possibility that is also suggested in *Consilience: The Unity of Knowledge* (Wilson, [1998] 1999, pp. 60, 291, 293).

A Tripartite Evolutionary Systems Theory Meta-Model of Biocultural Creativity

Knowledge emerges from biocultural human systems at an exponential rate. As examples, research in the Digital Humanities demonstrates that the number of published scientific papers doubles every nine years (Bornmann & Mutz, 2014), and the number of new books published each year (approximately 700,000 per year in the U.S.) doubled in the five years from 2008 to 2012 (Bowker, 2013).

The Evolutionary Systems Theory view of biocultural creativity adopted here to explain the growth in - and evolution of - the number and type - of discrete biocultural artifacts (e.g., books, movies, songs, words, and so on) combines *three* 'nested' Evolutionary Creativity Theories. These three theories are: (1) Karl Popper's (1978-1999) 'Three Worlds' Evolutionary Epistemology model of culture (namely, at the 'global' level); (2) Mihaly Csikszentmihalyi's (1988-2014) DPFi (Domain, Person, Field interaction)

Figure 1. The evolutionary systems view, from the multiverse through to subatomic particles
Derived from Laszlo, 1972.

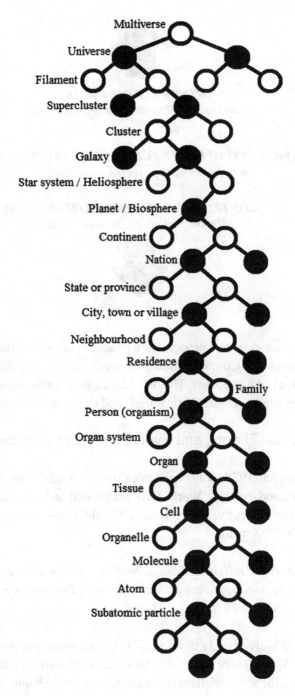

systems model of creativity (namely, at the macro, biocultural level); and finally (3) D K Simonton's (1984-2014) BVSR Evolutionary Theory of creativity (at the micro, or individual human level, namely, inside the human mind).

These three nested theories, which thus form one single integrated metamodel of biocultural creativity, are each briefly summarized below. It should also be noted that in this view, there is nothing in

Figure 2. The three laws of holon/partons, or, holarchies
Derived from Koestler, 1964-1978.

INTEGRATE (UPWARDS)
[into the holon/parton on the level above]

 COMPETE / CO-OPERATE / CO-OPETITION (SIDEWAYS)
[with holon/partons on the same level]

CONTROL & COMMAND (DOWNWARDS)
[holon/partons on the level below]

bioculture that is not, either: an idea, or a process, or a product - or two, or three, of these at once; this view would apply in the domains of Communication, Creativity Studies, Philosophy, Biology, Psychology, Sociology, Anthropology, Archaeology, History, Linguistics, Information Science, Mathematics, Cultural Studies, Literature, Media, Digital Humanities, and Creative Technologies.

1. Popper's 'Three Worlds' Theory, and Evolutionary Epistemology (1978-1999)

Popper's 'Three Worlds' model (1978-1999) delineates three 'worlds': 'World One' (of physical and biological objects, products, and events); 'World Two' (of mental and psychological states, processes, perceptions, observations, and subjective feelings); and, 'World Three' (of ideas, or the products of human minds; i.e., in Popper's 1978 words):

... Languages; tales and stories and religious myths; scientific conjectures or theories, and mathematical constructions; songs and symphonies; paintings and sculptures. But also aeroplanes and airports and other feats of engineering' (Popper, 1978b, pp. 143-144).

In short, these three worlds are, the (1) physical, (2) mental, and (3) conceptual domains. Notably, Popper also suggested that World Three might also be subdivided further, into 'World Three' (i.e, science), and World 'Four' (i.e., the world of the arts, music, languages, metaphysics, and so on). This 'two cultures' divide (namely the 'World Three' of science, versus the 'World Four' of non-scientific cultural artifacts) is in fact sometimes a convenient and useful distinction, although it is also worth noting that if the process of the creation, and selection (the *Blind Variation and Selective Retention* or *BVSR*) of biocultural creative artifacts is indeed the same process in both the arts and sciences, then the process of creativity itself unifies both the domains of the sciences and the arts (Csikszentmihalyi 1996).

It is also important to note that the characteristic (if not, compulsory) 'scientific method' is a three-step, algorithmic process (paraphrased from Popper 1972, 1979, as an algorithm, below):

1. Expectation (or: a theory, or, conjecture);
2. Trial - and possibly: success (i.e., satisficing), or, falsification (i.e. error);
3. If error is encountered (i.e., if expectation/s are *falsified*), then do Error-correction (i.e. Go to #2 above, with: a new trial).

This same algorithmic 'problem-solving' process is both consciously (and/or unconsciously) undertaken by organisms. If it is successful, they avoid falsification (problems of task or goal failure – or, injury, or death). Creative thinking (and the creation of artifacts in any media, in science or the arts) can also thus be viewed as problem-solving (see Weisberg, 2006, pp. 577-581). Lovelock also likewise (1995) states problem-solving (goal attainment) is a systems – that is, cybernetic - process:

One of the most characteristic properties of all living organisms, from the smallest to the largest, is their capacity to develop, operate and maintain systems which set a goal and then strive to achieve it through the cybernetic process of trial and error. (Lovelock, 1995, pp. 45-46)

This is this the systems cybernetic view of learning, or, of knowledge acquisition, or BVSR (Blind Variation and Selective Retention). The evocritic Brian Boyd (2009) likewise notes:

Biologically we can see all organisms as problem-solvers, each action or process as an attempt to solve a problem, however minor or routine. Evolution generates problems and solutions as it generates life. (Boyd, 2009, p. 324)

In Sir Karl Popper's Evolutionary Epistemology, also further developed by D. T. Campbell (1974), D. K. Simonton (1984-2014) and others, *memes* (or, units of culture - or, ideas, processes, products) that are less-suited (less 'adapted') to their geo-physical-chemical-bio-psycho-socio-cultural environment are deselected (or, are 'falsified'). Popper notes that with regard to knowledge, organisms also have knowledge, as they have 'theories', or expectations (about how to survive, or, what to avoid, in order to avoid being falsified, i.e., getting injured, or dead) although obviously other organisms are not as conscious of this, as humans are (Popper, 1999, pp. 32-39); these organismic instincts are thus like 'IF > THEN > ELSE' algorithms.[4] Munz (2001) extends this view further, to suggest that 'organisms are "embodied theories," and, theories are "disembodied organisms."' (Gontier, 2014, online).

In summary, in this Evolutionary Systems Theory view, Popper's Evolutionary Epistemology, and also 'Three Worlds' theory applies to: ideas, processes, and products in bioculture, which also links directly to the Systems Model of Creativity (1988-2014), outlined below.

2. Csikszentmihalyi's 'DPFi' Systems Model of Biocultural Creativity (1988-2014)

Csikszentmihalyi's *Domain, Person, Field interaction* model (or DPF model, aka, *Domain, Individual, Field interaction,* or DIFi systems model) is also an explicitly evolutionary, *natural selection* model of cultural creativity (Csikszentmihalyi & Wolfe, 2000, pp. 83-84), where the individual (i.e., the person, or, group) creates a new artifact (an idea, and/or a process, and/or a product), and subsequently, a consensus in the relevant field (or, audience) for that domain of culture (e.g., in science, and/or in the arts - such as in the domains of movies, or popular music, or in the case of a new soft drink, the general public) *judges* this new cultural artifact, and it is thus either selected (or, conversely, deselected – or, falsified) in its environment, an environment which also includes the field itself (Csikszentmihalyi, 1988, 1995, 1996a, 1996b, 1999, 2006, 2014; Csikszentmihalyi & Nakamura, 2006; Csikszentmihalyi & Wolfe, 2000). The selection (and also de-selection) criteria for biocultural artifacts can be complex, multifactorial, and domain-context-dependent. However there are two simple factors that appear to play a large part in the selection of artifacts by consensus; one factor is 'flow' theory (Csikszentmihalyi 1996) - and by extension, for narrative media, 'Narrative Transportation' theory - and another relevant factor is the *Anna Karenina* principle (Bornmann & Marx, 2012; Diamond, [1997] 1999, p. 157; Simonton, 2007, p. 145).

With regard to flow, in the article 'On The Psychological Selection Of Bio-Cultural Information' the authors note that individuals tend to *select* cultural artifacts that put them in the 'flow' state, and tend to *deselect* those that do not (see Csikszentmihalyi & Massimini, 1985). The 'flow' state has nine characteristics, and may be simplified as 'task enjoyment', for example, being satisfied by the experience of a media artifact, namely: a movie, or play, novel, song, or videogame, and so on (Csikszentmihalyi, 1996b, pp. 111-113). Importantly, 'flow' theory also correlates with, and has been adapted to, the 'Narrative Transportation' Theory of audience immersion (Gerrig, 1993; Green & Brock, 2000; 2002, p. 236; Green & Carpenter, 2011; Green, Chatham, & Sestir, 2012; Van Laer, De Ruyter, Visconti, & Wetzels, 2014). On this view, an entertainment artifact (a novel, movie, song, and so on) that 'transports' the audience member enables immersion in the narrative, and is therefore 'liked' - or enjoyed - and thus subsequently 'selected' (rather than falsified, or ignored, or, harshly criticized), and thus may become popular and/ or canonical, due to 'word-of-mouth' recommendations.[5] Those that fail to do so by consensus are falsified, or, deselected *en masse*. This results in knowledge (or, memes, or units of culture) that Moretti categorizes as 'canon', versus 'archive' (Moretti 2000, 2007).

Additionally, the *Anna Karenina* principle (*sensu* Diamond 1997) is a partial antidote to the 'single-cause fallacy' of success – or, of failure - in the domain of movies, or science, for example. As outlined in *Guns, Germs and Steel* (Diamond, 1997, pp. 157-175), this is the principle whereby: failure (or, falsification) of an artifact in a domain may be caused by an inadequacy in any number of a unit's / agent's / individual's component-elements (and/or, skills), while success in that domain also requires that each and all of those same possible inadequacies be avoided. Others who note this same principle (albeit without the Tolstoy allusion) include Aristotle in *Nicomachean Ethics* (c335 BCE),[6] and also Richard Dawkins (1986), who notes 'However many ways there are of being alive, it is certain that there are vastly more ways of being dead, or rather not alive.' (Dawkins, 1986, p. 9).[7] The *Anna Karenina* principle has been used to understand success in biology (Diamond 1997), in movies (Simonton, 2007), in scientific excellence, and in a number of other research domains (see Bornmann & Marx, 2012).

Csikszentmihalyi's DPF systems model of creativity describes systems in which *ideas, processes, products* (or memes) are inputs; creative individuals constantly recombine these 'old' (existing) ideas, processes and products to create newer ones; and these new artifacts are then judged by the field, or audience. There are therefore three sub-systems (domain, person, and field) which interact as one whole (DPF) system, and the outputs (or creative artifacts) of the system can also recursively become new inputs.

This constant selection (and also, de-selection) process also leads to the 'Less-Than-One-Percent' Problem in various cultural domains (in novels, movies, songs, and so on), whereby less than one percent of the artifacts produced, tend to become canonical (Moretti, 2000), or are ultimately judged 'creative' (or 'original and useful') by a consensus in the field (or, the audience) for each domain in culture (e.g.

mathematics, physics, chemistry, biology, movies, television, novels, songs, and so on). This iterative and recursive 'recombination spiral' described by the systems model of creativity (Csikszentmihalyi 1988-2014) is also isomorphic to Koestler's description of the evolutionary spiral of knowledge (or, of units of culture) in domains over time, *a la* Garstang 1922 (Koestler, [1967] 1989, pp. 168-169, 178-169). As an interesting parallel of falsification (or, deselection) in Evolutionary Biology to falsification in Evolutionary Bioculture: in biology, 99.99 percent of evolutionary lines (or, species) have also gone extinct over time (Mayr, 2002, p. 155). It can be seen that Popper's 'Three Worlds' (ideas, processes, products) and Evolutionary Epistemology (natural selection) model of biocultural creativity equates to Csikszentmihalyi's (1988-2014) DPF systems model of creativity, noting that Csikszentmihalyi also refers to units of culture - or *ideas, processes* and *products* – as 'memes' (Csikszentmihalyi, 1996b, pp. 7, 8, 41, 318, 319, 321, 372). These two synthesized evolutionary 'natural selection' models of culture (namely Popper / Campbell, and, Csikszentmihalyi) may be integrated with a third theory, the BVSR evolutionary theory of creativity (1984-2014), which is briefly outlined below.

3. Simonton's BVSR (Evolutionary Epistemology) Theory of Creativity in Bioculture (1984-2014)

Psychologist D. K. Simonton has developed an evolutionary theory of creativity from 1984 to 2014; *The Cambridge Handbook of Creativity* (2010) also notes that Simonton's BVSR evolutionary theory of creativity (1984, 1988, 1997, 1999, 2003, 2004) is, most likely, the most comprehensive extant theory of creativity (Kozbelt, Beghetto, & Runco, 2010, pp. 35-37). In this view, ideas (or, potential creative problem-solutions) are selected by an individual, and then varied 'blindly' i.e., without accurate foresight about the idea's future success (and thus are rather, *guesses* - or expectations, or the 'hopeful theories' of individuals) and are thus recombined; then, tested (mentally); and elaborated to a presented solution which is then judged by the field (as also in the DPF model of creativity, 1988-2014), and if these memes (ideas, processes, products) are not falsified, they are thus selectively retained by the field (Simonton, 2012a). This individual (person) level of creative process can therefore be seen to be a 'micro' element of the larger, 'macro' DPF evolutionary process of cultural creativity, and also incorporates *ideas, processes and products,* as it is explicitly derived from Campbell and Popper's Evolutionary Epistemology (D. T. Campbell, 1960, 1974; see also Popper, 1963, 1978a, 1999, [1972] 1979; Radnitzky, Bartley, & Popper, 1987).

Popper's (1963-1999), Csikszentmihalyi's (1988-2014) and Simonton's (1984-2014) three major creativity theories may thus be integrated, or, 'nested', one within the other (i.e. with Popper's model as the superset; then Csikszentmihalyi's as a subset of that model; then with Simonton's as a subset within that model) as a holistic Evolutionary Systems view of biocultural creativity. Popper's ideas, processes, and products (correlating with Worlds One, Two and Three) are also considered as units, within this synthesized evolutionary creativity metamodel.

Thus it may be seen that, despite the ongoing exponential growth of bioculture, only around one percent of culture ultimately is judged 'creative' and thus retained as canonical (in both the arts, and the sciences). For all ideas, processes and products, there is a continuum of creativity, ranging from 'everyday' (or 'personal' creativity) through 'mini-c' and 'pro-c', to what is known as 'big-C' (or historical) Creativity, the latter being for example, famous works by Darwin, Einstein, Mozart, Picasso, Stanley Kubrick, and so on (see Kaufman & Beghetto, 2009, 2013; see also Boden 2004).

This Evolutionary Systems Theory metamodel, showing memes (or, units of culture), and the Domain, Field and Person relationship as a *systems process* is illustrated in Figure 3.

As is obvious, working from the micro, out to the macro scales in the above model, the point at which Simonton's BVSR Evolutionary Creativity model overlaps with Csikszentmihalyi's DPF systems model of creativity is the point at which the individual (or group) presents their newly-produced tangible creative artifact to the field (audience) - an artifact (meme, or holon/parton, or *idea, process or product*) which the field then judges as 'creative' (i.e. 'original and useful'), or not. If the field judges the meme (idea, process or product, e.g., a new movie) as *not* creative, the meme does *not* become canonical, and is thus, in effect falsified. The meme (idea, process, product) usually continues to exist (or, is archived) in some form, but does not spread widely among the minds of the field through 'information cascades'.

In such biocultural domains of popular entertainment as movies, music, novels, television shows, comics (aka graphic novels) and so on, the 'word-of-mouth' communication process (or phenomenon) whereby a specific meme (or unit of culture) spreads, and thus becomes regarded as popular (e.g. a 'hit' movie; a 'best-selling' novel; a 'viral' *YouTube* video; a well-known joke) is known by various names, including: positive high-volume (and conversely, negative), or 'social contagion', 'recursive nonlinear demand dynamics', 'information cascades' (see: De Vany & Walls, 2004, p. 1036). Any output (for example, a movie, or a scientific theory) may therefore become a new input, when it is absorbed by (and, influences) other persons in the field. However the creative (and thus, canonical) memes are likely to be more influential and fecund.

With this 'natural selection' Evolutionary Epistemology (or, Evolutionary Systems Theory) approach to biocultural creativity outlined as a theoretical perspective, turning now to the specific *structure* of the unit of culture (or, ideas, processes, products), which are some of the inputs - and outputs - of these biocultural systems.

Figure 3. The systems model of bioculture, showing the Person, Field, Domain process; black memes are 'creative' (canonical); white are not.
Derived from Csikszentmihalyi, 1988-2014.

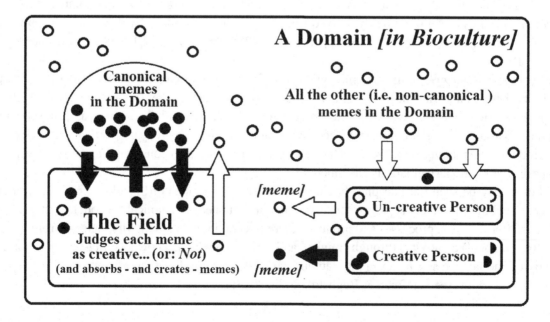

THE UNIT OF CULTURE: THE HOLON/PARTON

The holon/parton structure of the unit of culture (or, meme; i.e. idea, process, product) may be viewed conceptually as in Figure 4.

It should be noted that this model is also fractal (or, self-similar on smaller scales). This is not to imply that *all* units of culture can (nor, should be) be divided into exactly *two* parts infinitely; the number of components on each lower (smaller) level of the holarchy may increase exponentially.[8] As an example, in one single novel, there may be around 100,000 words; in a 90-minute movie (at 24 frames per second), around 130,000 still-image frames.[9]

The Holon/Parton as 'The Unit of Culture' in Various Communication Media

With the above holon/parton schema in mind, below are hierarchical templates for different media as units of culture, and also their component units (on the levels below), all considered as holon/partons. The three laws of holarchies (namely: (1) integrate *upwards*; (2) compete and co-operate *sideways*, (3) control and command *downwards*) also apply to the units, on each level.

- **Novel:**
  - Genre;
  - Novel;
  - Chapter;
  - Paragraph;
  - Sentence;
  - Word;
  - Letter (and punctuation mark, including spaces);
  - Idea.

As an example, individual novels compete with other individual novels for reader attention, for canonical status, and for both library and retail shelf-space in the field (Boyd, 2009; Van Peer, 1997); as do entire literary genres, and sub-genres; the specific words, sentences, paragraphs and chapters (and

Figure 4. The holon/parton structure of the unit of culture (or, meme - or, idea, process, product)

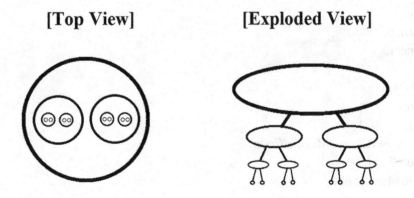

possibly also, images) that have survived the creation and editing process are those contained in the published work; in the completed work they also co-operate (or, *operate together*) to convey information and meaning to (and, to evoke emotion in) the reader, or audience (Boyd, Carroll, & Gottschall, 2010).

- **Movie:**
  - Genre;
  - Movie;
  - Act;
  - Sequence;
  - Scene;
  - Shot;
  - Action, and Dialog (line);
  - Single (still image) frame;
  - Idea.

As with the 'Novels' example above, each unit (or holon/parton) on the same holarchic level of a movie integrates 'upwards'; competes/co-operates 'sideways'; and also controls (i.e., provides organizing principles, or sets of 'rules' for) the units on the level 'below' it.

- **Videogame:**
  - Genre;
  - Videogame;
  - Game Level;
  - Environment;
  - Building;
  - Room;
  - Puzzle/Hazard;
  - Game event;
  - Idea.
- **Theatre (Play):**
  - Genre;
  - Play;
  - Act;
  - Scene;
  - (Dramatic) Beat;
  - Moment;
  - Idea.
- **Popular Song:**
  - Genre;
  - Song;
  - Intro/Verse/Chorus/Bridge/Coda;
  - Word/Chord;
  - Letter/Musical note;
  - Idea.

- **Poem:**
  - Genre;
  - Poem;
  - Stanza;
  - Word;
  - Letter;
  - Idea.
- **Joke:**
  - Genre;
  - Joke;
  - Setup/Feed/Punchline;
  - Word;
  - Idea.
- **Spoken Language:**
  - Phrase/Sentence;
  - Word;
  - Morpheme;
  - Phoneme.
- **Science:**
  - Domain;
  - Discipline;
  - Paradigm;
  - Metatheory;
  - Theory (possibly: Law);
  - Phenomena;
  - Fact;
  - Idea.
- **Religion:**
  - Religion;
  - Faith;
  - Metaphysics;
  - Scripture;
  - Idea.

Bioculture is composed of symbol systems (e.g., written and spoken language, mathematics, musical notation, paintings, drawings, and so on). This holon/parton (and, holarchy) structural tendency of symbolic biocultural artifacts, as outlined above, has also been noted in passing by many prior commentators, including Herbert Simon (1996):

Symbolic Systems… systems of human symbolic production. A book is a hierarchy in the sense in which I am using that term. It is generally divided into chapters, the chapters into sections, the sections into paragraphs, the paragraphs into sentences, the sentences into clauses and phrases, the clauses and phrases into words. We may take the words as our elementary units, or further subdivide them, as the linguist often does, into smaller units. If the book is narrative in character, it may divide into "episodes" instead of sections, but divisions there will be. The hierarchic structure of music, based on such units as movements, parts, themes, phrases, is well known. (Simon, 1996, pp. 187-188)

This holon/parton structure which Simon refers to above (though without Simon labelling it as such) may also be viewed as in Figure 5.

A transmedia narrative (i.e., a transmedia story universe)[10] is also structured - and thus, may also be analyzed - as a holon/parton (Velikovsky, 2014a).

A Transmedia Narrative as a Holon/Parton (and, a Holarchy)

In *This Will Change Everything: Ideas That Will Shape The Future* (2010) Sampson writes:

The numerous and dramatic increases in complexity, it turns out, have been achieved largely through a process of integration, with smaller wholes becoming parts of larger wholes. Again and again, we see the progressive development of multipart individuals from simpler forms. Thus, for example, atoms become integrated into molecules, molecules into cells, and cells into organisms. At each higher, emergent stage, older forms are enveloped and incorporated into newer forms, with the end result being a nested, multi-level hierarchy... the epic of evolution has been guided by counterbalancing trends of complexification and unification. (Sampson in Brockman, 2010, pp. 1-2)

As with biology, so too with bioculture. For example, it is characteristic of a transmedia narrative – or, a meta-story that spans more than one media - that it also follows this same evolutionary growth pattern, of complexification 'downwards', and simultaneous unification 'upwards'. A transmedia movie story contains certain narrative events, characters, themes, settings and dialog, while a novel, videogame, comics (or narratives in other transmedia) will also share some of these same narrative events, characters, themes, settings and dialog while also containing new additions (or, 'extensions') to the same (unified)

Figure 5. A diagrammatic analysis of the holon/parton structure of three paragraphs of text

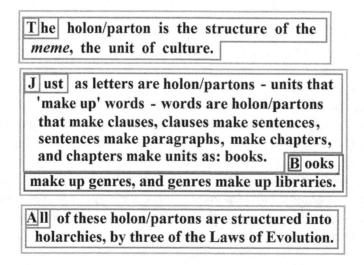

story. As the narrative universe is further *extended* (or, 'grows') into other (trans)media over time, additional characters, settings, events and dialog are added, and yet the overall narrative (or, story) universe remains a single integrated (unified) whole. This concept is illustrated in Figure 6, and correlates with Popper's (1963) observations on the growth of scientific knowledge.

Classic examples of such transmedia narrative universes include: *Twin Peaks, Star Wars, Harry Potter, Dexter, LOST, The Blair Witch Project,* and *The Matrix* (Velikovsky, 2013a).

On the Increasing Complexity of Emergent Systems

Koestler discusses the phenomenon of anamorphosis in evolution, in *The Ghost in the Machine* (1967):

The German biologist Woltereck coined the term 'anamorphosis' for the primary and ubiquitous trend in Nature towards the emergence of more complex forms. (Koestler, [1967] 1989, p. 200)

In the Systems (and therefore, the Complexity) worldview, one key problem is (increasing) complexity, or that precision in the measurement of a cultural phenomenon is inverse to its complexity. Ward (1898) also comments on Comte's hierarchical taxonomy of the sciences, which was arrived at:

... by taking as the criterion of the position of each the degree of what he called "positivity," which is simply the degree to which the phenomena can be exactly determined. This, as may be readily seen, is also a measure of their relative complexity, since the exactness of a science is in inverse proportion to its complexity (Ward, [1898] 1913, p. 7).

Figure 6. A transmedia story universe as a holon/parton, and a holarchy

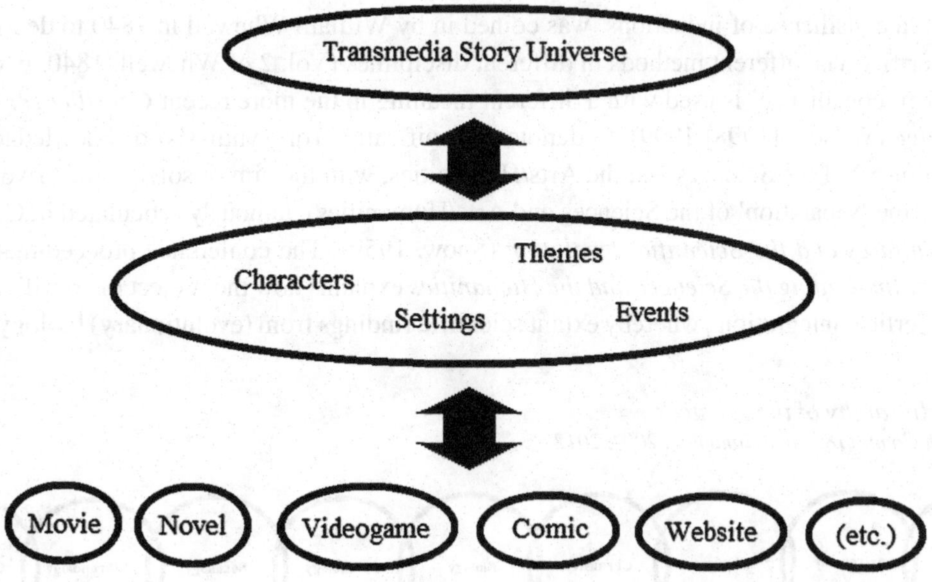

Comte's hierarchy of the sciences[11] (namely mathematics, astronomy, physics, chemistry, biology, psychology, sociology, and anthropology) can be seen as increasing in complexity (and thus, also decreasing in predictability) to the right, as represented in Figure 7, to which has been added another science, here called 'Culturology':

In *Darwin's Bridge: Uniting the Sciences and Humanities*, Carroll (in press) writes:

Good explanations at any level of emergent complexity are likely to identify causal relations among forces at that level and link them with causal forces at lower levels in the causal hierarchy. Good explanations take account of the causal interactions among emergent phenomena, but valid conceptions of emergent phenomena depend on correctly identifying the elements that make up the emergent phenomena (Pinker 2005). Ignoring principles of natural selection, for instance, produces false conceptions of the way populations interact with each other and with individual organisms (Carroll 2001; Easterlin 2004). (Carroll in Carroll, McAdams, & Wilson, in press)

Obviously many complex systems obtain in any human individual (i.e., person), given the overlapping systems of their individual biology, psychology, sociology, anthropology, culture(s) and physical environment - let alone the related, interacting, and evolving systems of systems - and most with multiple causes, effects, and variables. We might thus assume it impossible to predict anything in bioculture, as a result of overwhelming complexity. Yet regardless, some laws of physics in evolution (namely, the three laws of holarchies) appear to apply to the growth of bioculture, whether in the arts, media, languages, or the sciences. While there are also exceptions (e.g. 'experimental' artistic works), these tend not to become canonical; they tend not to satisfy the 'appropriate' requirement within the 'novel and appropriate' criterion, for artifacts that are judged 'creative' by the field in a domain.

Consilience

The phrase 'a consilience of inductions' was coined in by William Whewell in 1840 to denote when a theory is verified via different methods in different disciplines (Vol. 2 of Whewell, 1840, p. 65). However the term 'consilience' is used with a different meaning in the more recent *Consilience: The Unity of Knowledge* (Wilson, [1998] 1999), to denote the unification (or, synthesis) of knowledge between the 'two cultures' of the Sciences and the Arts/Humanities, with the aim of solving the 'Two Cultures' problem (or the 'separation' of the Sciences and Arts/Humanities), famously articulated in C.P. Snow's *The Two Cultures and the Scientific Revolution* (Snow, 1959). The conference proceedings *Creating Consilience: Integrating the Sciences and the Humanities* explains how the project of consilience is also known as 'vertical integration', whereby extant scientific findings from (evolutionary) biology, psychol-

Figure 7. Hierarchy of the sciences
Adapted from Comte, 1855 and Simonton, 2004, 2012.

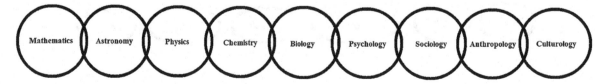

ogy, sociology and anthropology are used in examining, analyzing and explaining culture (i.e., science, and the arts/humanities) (see Slingerland and Collard, 2012, p. 3). Figure 7 can be termed 'horizontal integration of knowledge' as it is the same concept of consilience, or, transdisciplinary consistency, or 'vertical integration of knowledge', simply viewed on another axis.

Mass Communication research spans the two domains of Science, and also the Arts/Humanities since Mass Communication research is generally considered a branch of Social Science, and is often multi-disciplinary, incorporating the other major social sciences including 'psychology, sociology, anthropology, economics and political science' (Halloran, 1998, p. 12). As also stated in the introduction to *Theories and Models of Communication* (2013):

Communication study seems inherently multi-disciplinary, drawing theory and sharing concepts from psychology, sociology, political science and other social sciences (Eadie and Goret in Cobley & Schulz, 2013, p. 17).

A significant body of consilient literature has emerged since 1995 in the domain of Evocriticism, also known as Darwinian Literary Studies, or Biopoetics.[12] Some key works in this transdisciplinary domain of knowledge include: *Evolution and Literary Theory* (Carroll, 1995; Gottschall, 2008), *Biopoetics: Evolutionary Explorations in the Arts* (Cooke & Turner, 1999), *Literature, Science and a New Humanities* (Gottschall, 2008), *On The Origin of Stories: Evolution, Cognition, Fiction* (Boyd, 2009), *Evolution, Literature and Film: A Reader* (Boyd, et al., 2010), with a recent survey of the key Evocriticism literature appearing in 'Applied Evolutionary Criticism' (Cooke & Machann, 2012).

Evocriticism scholars use Evolutionary Theory, including Evolutionary Psychology (Buss, 2012), Evolutionary Sociology (Barkow, 2006) and Evolutionary Anthropology (Gibson & Lawson, 2014) to examine, explain, understand and analyze bioculture. Boyd (2009) in particular makes extensive use of Simonton's BVSR Evolutionary Theory of biocultural creativity (1984-2008) in explaining life, bioculture, and also creative genius, as 'Darwin Machines' (Boyd, 2009, pp. 120-121, 211, 351-122, 366). However it appears the evolutionary 'holarchies' approach to analyzing bioculture within an Evolutionary Systems Theory framework is relatively new, as is The Complexity Turn (or the widespread use of Systems Theory and Systems Science) in the social sciences (Blaikie, 2007, pp. 206-214). Systems theory, including cybernetics (Lovelock, 1995, pp. 45-46; Wiener, 1948) thus appears ever more relevant to the study of consciousness, human nature, and human bioculture. The key founders of the domain of Evolutionary Psychology, Tooby and Cosmides (2005) state that:

The brain evolved as a control system, designed to generate action. From this perspective, there is not just a cognitive science of areas such as language, intuitive physics and number, but also a cognitive science of parenting, eating, kinship, friendship, alliance, groups, mating, status, fighting, tools, minds, foraging, natural history and scores of other ancient realms of human action. Separating knowledge acquisition from motivation has placed the study of motivation in cognitive eclipse and diverted cognitive scientists from studying conceptual structure, motivation and action as a single integrated system (which they seem likely to be).' (Tooby & Cosmides, 2005, p. 51)

Recalling that Popper noted that all organisms (plants, animals - even amoebas) have knowledge, biocultural symbolically-encoded information-packets (or, memes) allow information to be communicated by humans extrasomatically. This evolutionary 'cost/benefit ratio' (or, adaptive utility) conception of 'knowledge' is far removed from alternative philosophical conceptions of knowledge such as 'justified true belief', but rather, knowledge (or culture) as 'useful information' - even where that information/ knowledge 'use' is purely for entertainment purposes. Csikszentmihalyi notes:

Knowledge mediated by symbols is extrasomatic; it is not transmitted through the chemical codes in-scribed in our chromosomes but must be intentionally passed on and learned. It is this extrasomatic information that makes up what we call a culture. And the knowledge conveyed by symbols is bundled up in discrete domains - geometry, music, religion, legal systems, and so on. Each domain is made up of its own symbolic elements, its own rules, and generally has its own system of notation... The existence of domains is perhaps the best evidence of human creativity... The fact that calculus and Gregorian chants exist means that we can experience patterns of order that were not programmed into our genes by biological evolution. By learning the rules of a domain, we immediately step beyond the boundaries of biology and enter the realm of cultural evolution. Each domain expands the limitations of individuality and enlarges our sensitivity and ability to relate to the world. (Csikszentmihalyi, 1996b, p. 37)

In this Evolutionary Systems Theory view, all bioculture (the arts, science, language, metaphysics, religion) is an evolutionary adaptation, or, solutions to the problems of life, encountered by humans (see also Boyd 2009).

Creative Practice Theory

In order to understand the process of creation (or, emergence) of artifacts (or, memes) from biocultural systems over time within this Evolutionary Systems model, the synthesized evolutionary metamodel of creativity explained above (combining the key creativity theories of Popper, Csikszentmihalyi, and Simonton) may also be synthesized with aspects of social theorists' Anthony Giddens' structuration theory (Giddens 1984) and Pierre Bourdieu's 'practice theory' (1993),[13] resulting in what is here called Creative Practice Theory.

Creative Practice Theory (Velikovsky 2012) is a synthesis of the evolutionary systems metamodel of creativity (Popper, Csikszentmihalyi, Simonton), and Bourdieu's 'practice theory' of cultural production (Bourdieu & Johnson, 1993). These theories intersect, and also partially overlap, in such a way that they complement each other to describe holistically how creativity can occur over time.

The Creative Practice Theory model aims to explain the key ten (and apparently, irreducible) stages of the bio-socio-cultural process of creativity in biocultural production from the point of view of an individual person, or 'agent' (e.g.: a novelist, a filmmaker, scientist, musician, and so on), from *prior to their birth*, to their eventual acquisition of symbolic capital (i.e.: awards, status or recognition) for their creative artifacts (or their *memes* – namely, ideas, and/or processes, and/or products). This Creative Practice Theory model, once all ten (sequential) elements of the model are in place for an individual creative person, is presented in Figure 8.

The examples used below are here (for the purpose of illustration) focused on a filmmaker, but can also apply to most complex creative domains (e.g., painting, dance, theatre, videogames, novels, tele-vision, music, fashion design, sculpture, graphic arts, science, maths, philosophy, history, and so on).

As a result of the above configuration (or synthesis), it may be seen that the ten sequential stages of Creative Practice Theory - over time[14] - are, as follows:

Figure 8. Creative Practice Theory - from the point of view of the person/agent
Velikovsky, 2012.

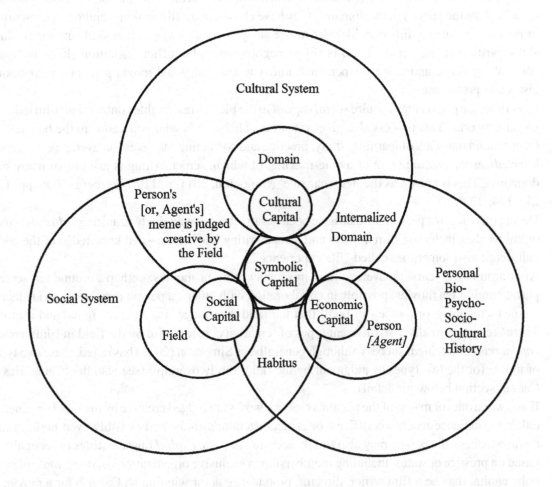

1. Prior to the person's/ individual's/agent's birth (or, emergence into the physical domain), Social and Cultural systems pre-exist (namely, everyone is currently conceived as a result of two parents - male and female - at a certain place, and time). In short, they are a random combination of their parents' DNA.

2. The person is born - with certain biological predispositions (which may also become further developed over time, as talents).

3. Over time, the person acquires a Bio-Psycho-Socio-Cultural history. The overlapping social and cultural systems into which they are born and raised from childhood to adulthood (and beyond) are also a complex system of nested and/or overlapping sub-systems (or, polysystems).

4. Over time, the person acquires (and/or inherits) *economic capital* (finance) and/or access to it. This economic capital is required to acquire training, practice and expertise in a domain (e.g.: screenwriting, and/or filmmaking), and later, say, to finance the production of a movie (for example, access to producers and/or film financiers in the field).

5. Over time, by engaging with the Field (e.g. in cinema: the film industry, film audiences, and industry gatekeepers such as film producers, distributors, and critics) the person develops a *habitus* (or a 'feel for the game') in the domain/s they have chosen (e.g.: filmmaking, and/or screenwriting, or novels). In cinema, this may include: movie story (screen idea) creation skills, movie pitching skills, writing skills, personal and business negotiation and conflict-resolution skills, technical filmmaking skills, and also their personal, idiosyncratic, story and movie perceptions, opinions, tastes and preferences.

6. Over time, the person may acquire *social capital* in the Field, via valuable contacts and film industry social networks. This process also gives rise to the cliché: "It's who you know, in the business."

7. Over around ten years of learning, study, practice and correcting mistakes (on average), the person *internalizes the domain* (e.g.: of movie-making, of which, screenwriting is just one of many sub-domains). This is known as the 'ten-year rule' (Simonton, 2011, p. 119; Weisberg, 2006, pp. 173, 213-174, 222).

8. During this time, the person can also have been iteratively and recursively acquiring *cultural capital*, or knowledge, including film domain and screenwriting knowledge - and knowledge of the wider culture(s); also sometimes called "life experience".

9. After around ten years, on average (and in screenwriting or movies: perhaps, around ten screenplays,[15] and/or ten movies) possibly in collaboration with others, a person may create an artifact or meme (screenplay, or movie - or both) that the field then judges *creative* ('original and useful'). There are, very broadly, two different types of 'creativity' recognized by the field in film: namely *commercial* and *critical* success although generally, as Simonton (2011) has noted, these two types of movie (or the two types of judgment by the field) rarely overlap[16] (see also the 'Categories of Canon' section below for detail).

10. If and when one (or many) of the person's creative works are judged creative by the Field (in cinema: either by audience-reach/box office - or critical acclaim/awards, and possibly even both, in rare circumstances), the person may also finally acquire *symbolic capital* (awards, titles or recognition, based on prestige or status, including membership in exclusive organizations). An example of symbolic capital may be a film writer, director, producer or actor winning an Oscar® for a movie; or say, senior membership of a guild, or membership of an exclusive official film/screenplay judging panel, and so forth. (The person may well repeat these stages, from Step 3 above, for subsequent projects, or creative artifacts, i.e. units of culture, or, memes.)

Creative Practice Theory suggests that if any person (say, a film *writer-hyphenate*) aspires to realize their potential creativity, in terms of both: the evolutionary systems model, and also Bourdieu's *economic / social / cultural / symbolic capital* model, (including also *acquiring habitus*, and *internalizing the specific creative domain*) then they also must pass through all these above ten stages, over time.

There are thus ten key sequential steps in this systems process model, all of which are necessary-but-not-sufficient steps for creativity by an individual; that is to say, the ten steps in this algorithm may well be executed by an individual, and yet the artifact(s) they create may - *or may not* - be judged 'creative' by the field. It is only if, and after, the artifact (or, meme, or 'unit of culture') is judged 'creative' (or 'original and useful') by consensus in the field, that the individual (and/or, group) who created it is subsequently labelled, or viewed as, 'creative'.

When examined as a linear chain of multiple co-causal systems factors and events - *over time* - for an individual movie screenwriter in the field, certain major emergent stages in the DPF nonlinear dynamical systems model process of creativity in movies - when also correlated and synthesized with aspects of Bourdieu's practice theory of cultural production (Bourdieu 1976-1993) - may, in simplified terms, be examined as a linear 'process-stage' or 'step' model over time, as depicted in Figure 9.

In the model shown in Figure 9 - subjectively (from their point of view) - a Person enters the system at '[Start]'; while objectively, all the other systems (including the Domain and Field in culture) pre-exist the Person. Times *1,2,3,* (and so on) represent finite successive moments in linear time. The Domain pre-exists as knowledge in the Field, as discrete cultural artifacts (memes); the Domain of Cinema includes all canonical and also non-canonical memes (movies, books, websites, word-of-mouth, received wisdom, doxa, etc). Constantly throughout each recursive loop (at Times: #2 through #9, above), the cultural Domain also increases exponentially in content and thus size (as, more movies are released to the field; as more publications about movies emerge, and so on); habitus (or 'feel for the game') is

Figure 9. Creative Practice Theory systems model of creativity (in movies) as an algorithmic, iterative, recursive, confluence systems process - for an individual (a person, or a group) over time

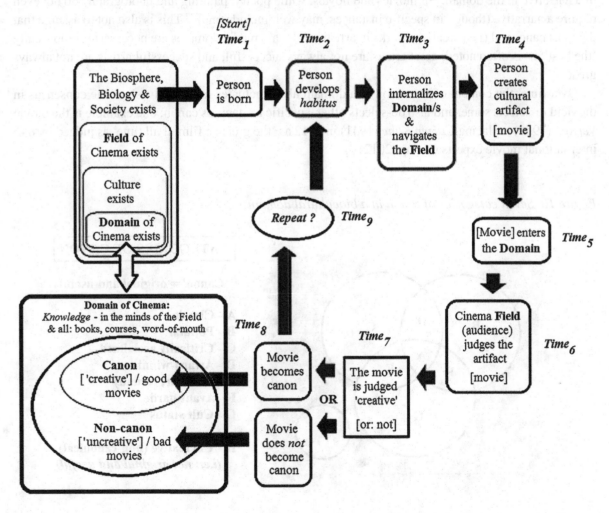

also constantly developed by the Person throughout their lifespan, and throughout these iterative and recursive loops; *internalizing the domain* likewise occurs continually for the Person throughout these systems loops; *navigating the field* also continues throughout these loops and over the Person's lifespan. However, which category (or, categories) of canon the cultural artifact enters, depends on the audience that is attracted to it, in the Field.

Categories of Canon

While bioculture (i.e., science and the arts) may be divided into a binary of 'canonical' and 'non-canonical' (or, the widely-accepted scientific theories, and those that are not; or, say, movies that are 'liked' or judged as: 'good' by consensus, and those that are not), within the canon of any biocultural domain (such as painting, photography, comics, songs, movies, novels and so on), there are many different types of audiences (Sawyer, 2012, pp. 218-219). One way to sub-categorize the canon (or works judged 'creative') is illustrated in Figure 10.

Once again, the *selection criteria* may vary across each biocultural domain (and, sub-domain); the criteria for judging (and falsifying) a scientific theory clearly differs from that of the aesthetic criteria of a narrative in the domains of movies and novels; while poetry, painting and photography do not even require a narrative (though in specific instances, may well include one).[17] This is also not to assume that the most canonical (i.e., creative) works in artistic and mass media domains are necessarily, empirically 'the best'; as is often noted, great artists are not always successful, and successful artists are not always great.

Over time, the content of the canon in a domain also fluctuates (and, evolves), as the consensus in the field re-selects some, and also de-selects other, specific artifacts as canon; one example is the movie *Vertigo* (1958) replacing *Citizen Kane* (1941) in 2012 as 'the greatest film of all time' as judged by 846 international movie experts (Kemp, 2012).

Figure 10. Seven categories of canon in a biocultural domain

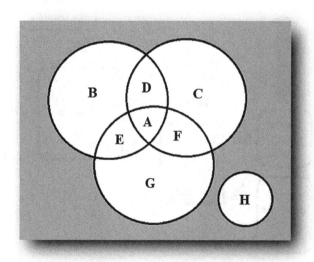

CATEGORIES OF CANON

'Canon' = original and useful

A - Classic
B - Popular
C - Critically acclaimed
D - Award-winning
E - Viral (or, fecund)
F - Avant-garde
G - Cult status

H - Uncreative (non-canonical)
  (i.e.: not original and useful)

Evolution: Selection, Variation, and Transmission-with-Heredity

On the 'micro' scale in this Evolutionary Systems Theory view, individuals (persons) are constantly exposed to cultural artifacts (memes: ideas, processes, products), via reading texts, viewing media, word-of-mouth, and via their own imagination - and those memes (ideas, processes, products) that are retained in memory may thus be selected in their mind, and then combined with other memes (and thus: each 'old' meme is varied) to create a new artifact (a new idea, process, or product), and this new artifact may be transmitted to the domain (recorded, published, transmitted) and thus, transmitted to other persons in the field. This process is the *selection, variation,* and *transmission-with-heredity* evolutionary algorithm. This 'selection, then variation' step includes the process of 'combinatorial creativity' (Boden, 2004, pp. 3-10), or 'bisociation' (Koestler, [1967] 1989, p. 181), or 'conceptual blending' (Fauconnier & Turner, 2002). The meme (idea, process, product) has thus already undergone *variation* (via: a recombination with other ideas - mentally / psychologically by the person), and when later transmitted on a wider bio-socio-cultural level, also undergoes *selection* by individuals in the field (or, natural selection), and may then be further transmitted to others (during which, the meme may also undergo further *variation,* due to errors in transmission). This second, wider ('macro', or socio-cultural) process is the *variation, selection* and *transmission* evolutionary algorithm in action (Csikszentmihalyi & Wolfe, 2000, p. 83). The book chapter *Memes, Minds and Imagination* (Blackmore, 2007) likewise argues for creativity as the evolutionary algorithm, working on memes (in bioculture), rather than on genes (in biology), overtly noting that the evolutionary mechanism is identical:

All human creativity results from memetic evolution; from the reiterative process of recombination and selective imitation of behaviors and artefacts... those of us who are the most creative are those who are best at accurately copying and storing the memes we come across, recombining them in novel ways, and selecting appropriately from the myriad new combinations created... Everything was, and still is, designed by the power of that familiar mindless process, the evolutionary algorithm. This is a beautiful, if daunting, view of our place in the world. (Blackmore 2007, online)

This same holon/parton evolutionary view of 'units of culture' may also be applied to narratives, in any media, and not simply cinema.

The Holon/Parton as the Unit of Story (or, the Narreme)

The unit of story (or, unit of narrative) has been discussed by Barthes (1966) (Barthes, [1966] 1975), Dorfman 1969 (Dorfman, 1969) and other researchers, however it is clear that the narreme was not satisfactorily defined by Barthes in 1966, nor has it been since (Baikadi & Cardona-Rivera, 2012). Since stories are part of bioculture, and since stories are composed of ideas, words, phrases, (and/or, cinema shots, images, sounds) and so on, 'the unit of culture' (as holon/parton) may also be applied to the unit of story, or, narreme. This unit (and structure) of story may also have closer parallels to human cognition than alternative analytical schemas such as Barthes (1967), given Evolutionary Cognitive Psychology (Buss, 2012) and the systems view of biology and culture (Capra & Luisi, 2014).

Story

The definition of story (or, narrative) adopted herein is: *A problem-situation, involving an agent/s (or, character/s) in an environment/s, including an attempt by the agent/s at problem-solution, and/or problem avoidance*, communicated in any media in culture (movies, novels, short prose, videogames, oral storytelling, and so on). This definition is isomorphic to Gottschall's (2012) definition of: 'Story = Character + Problem + Attempted Extrication' (Gottschall, 2012, p. 52), and in a more extended form, as Branigan (1992) notes:

'Nearly all researchers agree that a narrative schema has the following format:

1. *Introduction of setting and characters;*
2. *Explanation of a state of affairs;*
3. *Initiating event;*
4. *Emotional response or statement of a goal by a protagonist;*
5. *Complicating actions;*
6. *Outcome;*
7. *Reactions to the outcome.' (Branigan, 1992, p. 14)*

This same schema (i.e., Agent + Problem (*thus: Conflict*) + Result) can also be seen to apply to Propp's morphology of the Russian folk tale (Propp, 1958), Campbell's monomyth in international pancultural myths (J. Campbell, 1949), and Vogler's 'hero's journey' in movies and other media (Vogler, 1992, see also Velikovsky, 2014b).[18] In this view, stories are 'about' problem-solving, and indeed may be viewed as case-studies in problem-solving.

This evolutionary view of story is influenced by Popper's *All Life Is Problem Solving* (Popper, 1999), 'problem-situations' in Boyd's *On The Origin of Stories: Evolution, Cognition, Fiction* (Boyd, 2009, p. 211), Boyd (2010) (Boyd, 2010, p. 438), and also Weisberg (2006) on creativity as problem-solving (Weisberg, 2006, pp. 577-581). In this view, the (fictional) characters (or, agents) in narratives are also holon/partons, as are the scenes and the sequences that comprise the narrative. When a screen idea[19] (or, movie story) is created, the three laws of holarchies act *on each level* of the movie story, through the stages of (1) screenwriting and story editing, (2) shooting (production), and (3) editing (post-production) of the movie story. A movie story as a whole unit[20] may be viewed as follows:

- The Movie (including the parts of: The Movie Title, Movie Poster, and Trailer);
- Opening Credits / the story 'Acts' / the End Credits (including credits music);
- Sequences (as parts of Acts);
- Scenes (as parts of Sequences);
- Shots (as parts of Scenes);
- Dramatic Beats (as parts of shots);
- Action and Dialog;
- Still frames;
- Ideas.

During the process of the selection of specific scenes to include in the movie (in the stages of writing, shooting, and editing), each movie scene *competes, and also co-operates* (or, *operates in conjunction with,* all the scenes before and also after it). The scenes (and, shots) that successfully win this 'competition' are those that appear in the completed movie. In evolutionary terms, *selection pressure*[21] on each individual scene (and, shot) exists in the form of: whether or not that scene (or, shot) is deemed necessary, given the 'whole' story or narrative. So too, this same selection process occurs in writing novels, where potential 'alternate' scenes, sentences, and words compete for selection by their creator, on their relevant levels of the holarchy; if a potential scene does not integrate well into the whole story, it may be de-selected by the creator/s. On the level of words (in a novel, song or poem), some synonyms also 'win out' (including during the conceiving, writing, and editing process), and are selected over (i.e., at the expense of) others. So too with shots (and, with different *takes* of shots) in the final edited version of movies, television, videogames, and other screen media. In the evolutionary view, *selection, variation* and *transmission* occurs where the chosen variation is then transmitted into the final work, which an audience then receives, and judges. At this point, the audience also selects (or, deselects) whole completed works, as units of culture. Furthermore, when participatory (fan) culture takes over, this process also continues; for example, in fan remixes, some of which may go 'viral'.

The holon/parton structure of units of culture (or memes) thus applies to prior suggestions for the definition and structure of 'the meme', including (but not limited to) the various categories of: tropes, patterns, themes, configurations, complexes, ideas, beliefs, values, rules, principles, symbols, and concepts (see: Chick, 1999). Although each of these individual entities, when compared literally to each other are not all exactly the same thing (which would be a conflation, and thus a category error), each of those entities (i.e., tropes, themes, motifs, ideas, and so on) is: a meme; a memeplex; a holon/parton; a holarchy; and each may be examined as one unit of bioculture. This is important for measuring and tracking specific units of culture (relative to, *competing* units of culture), for example, in the Digital Humanities. For example, why are some stories (films, novels, jokes) more viral than others?

ISSUES, CONTROVERSIES, AND PROBLEMS

The Complexity perspective and the use of Systems Theory is no longer seen as controversial or problematic in the Social Sciences, given 'The Complexity Turn' of the mid-1990s,[22] however the integration of the Systems Model of Creativity, and the Evolutionary Systems Theory perspective has yet to become widespread in Mass Communication Studies (*pace* Fulton & McIntyre, 2013). The Evocriticism Turn (since 1995) is however still somewhat controversial and is resisted by some in the Arts and Humanities, possibly due to pervasive Romantic myths about creativity (see McIntyre, 2012; Sawyer, 2012, p. 322), and also perhaps due to anti-realist, anti-science, and anti-positivist attitudes and prejudices in the Arts/Humanities, including common misunderstandings and mistaken assumptions about Evolutionary Theory (Carroll, 2008). Memetics has also been in a (Kuhnian) pre-paradigm state since Dawkins (1976), as the universal structure of 'the unit of culture' (or, meme) has not previously been identified, however it is here suggested that *the holon/parton* is one possible solution to this problem.[23]

FUTURE RESEARCH DIRECTIONS

Future research directions on the unit of culture (or, 'meme') and also the unit of story (or, narreme) in Creative Technologies includes potential empirical investigations on the number and type (or both quantitative and qualitative analyses) of holon/partons (units of culture) which make up canonical memes (i.e., ideas, processes, products), compared to those in non-canonical ones, and preferably using the *Anna Karenina* principle in order to avoid the single-cause fallacy. As one example: Do canonical artifacts (novels, plays, movies, and so on) satisfice (succeed) in their components of story premise, storyworld, characters, theme, plot, structure, and dialog - where non-canonical artifacts, do not?

The 2011 article 'Can We Measure Memes?' (McNamara, 2011) asks whether fMRI technology can measure memes in the brain, also proposing the distinction of *internally* and *externally* represented memes (or, 'i-memes' and 'e-memes'). The article concludes that if memes (units of culture) *can* be accurately defined, and, if cognitive science can measure (or conversely, falsify) memes, then this would be a significant advance with far-reaching implications in cultural evolution for many domains and disciplines, well beyond mere questions around how language works (McNamara 2011, online).

Philosophically, the concept of holon/partons (and thus, holarchies) includes Systems Theory, Set Theory, Discrete Mathematics, and Mereology (the study of parthood relations). Holarchies are also arguably, a more accurate and particulate way of analyzing the world (via Systems and Complexity theory, Evolution, and Emergence) than, say, concepts of 'atomless gunk' (see Varzi, 2015), film semiotics (Metz 1991), or rhizome theory (Deleuze and Guattari, 1987) not least as the universe may be infinitely hierarchical (and, holarchical) on smaller scales, and yet simultaneously a relational whole (Bohm, [1980] 2005). The literature on consilience provides additional conceptual tools for examining units of culture (in media, science, the arts and entertainment), including: the creative 'problem-situation' model for filmmakers (Bordwell 1997, 2008, 2011, 2012; Bordwell in Boyd, Carroll & Gottschall 2010); the 'screen idea' (or, story) in narrative filmmaking (Macdonald 2004, 2013); artistic and creative 'cost/benefit ratios' for artists (including screenwriters, and novelists) and audiences (Boyd 2009; Boyd in Boyd, Carroll & Gottschall 2010); and, the emerging integration of Creativity Theory into the screenwriting convention (Bloore 2013; Velikovsky 2014d).

CONCLUSION

This chapter presents the holon/parton (and thus also, the holarchy) as the unit of culture - or the meme (an idea, process or product) - and also as 'the unit of story', or narreme. This Evolutionary Systems Theory view of bioculture thus adopts an Applied Evolutionary Epistemology approach (Gontier 2012), and also aims to provide inroads to a solution of the problem of the definition of the term 'culture', and thus, a theory which may enable more accurate empirical transdisciplinary investigations of bioculture across all media in the arts, entertainment and sciences.

Practical applications include the empirical measuring, analysis and commensurate comparison of 'units of culture' (or, memes – ideas, processes, products), and also more accurately tracking the trajectory of units, in culture. Disciplines and domains of knowledge for such practical applications include the Digital Humanities; Empirical studies of the arts, literature and science (such as in *Empirical Studies of the Arts,* and *Scientific Studies of Literature* journals). The successful identification of the structure of the meme (the unit of culture) would also enable the somewhat-stalled domain of Memetics (or, Evolutionary Culturology) to advance.

Other disciplines in which an understanding and more detailed analysis of the structure, function and behavior of units of culture (particularly, from an Evolutionary Systems Theory perspective) would benefit, may include: Communication, Creativity Studies, Philosophy, Evolutionary Epistemology, Biology, Psychology, Sociology, Anthropology, Archaeology, History, Linguistics, Information Science, Computer Science, Artificial Intelligence, Mathematics, Cultural Studies, Literature, Media Studies, and also Narratology (aka, Narrative Studies).

If the mind is indeed a neural computer, as Pinker (1997) as many scholars in Evolutionary Psychology contend, then in assuming the Evolutionary Systems Theory view, narratives - as *units* in culture - and indeed all of the units within stories (including: characters, plot / problems, settings, themes, dialog, and narration) may also be analyzed as holon/partons. Stories, and their component parts (including also transmedia narratives) might thus be viewed as subject to three of the Evolutionary laws of physics, and Systems Theory, namely the three laws of holarchies.

On this view, E. O. Wilson's suggestion in *Consilience* (Wilson, 1998) is supported, namely that certain laws of physics (which are also laws of Evolution, and Systems Theory) appear to also apply to the growth of bioculture, ideally illuminating 'the unit of story', and also potentially 'the unit of culture' (aka the meme), where 'ideas, processes and products' correlate respectively with: Worlds Three, Two, and One in Sir Karl Popper's 'Three Worlds' theory (Popper, 1978b).

ACKNOWLEDGMENT

Thanks for helpful discussions to Distinguished Professors Mihaly Csikszentmihalyi, Dean Keith Simonton and Brian Boyd; also to Professors Joseph Carroll, Dan Dennett, Sue Blackmore, David Bordwell and Phillip McIntyre; also to Doctors Michael Meany and Susan Kerrigan and the Newcastle School of Creativity, and also to Tim Peterson for the mereology discussions. And to the anonymous peer reviewers and editors whose suggestions improved the chapter.

REFERENCES

Altmann, G., & Koch, W. A. (1998). *Systems: New Paradigms for the Human Sciences*. Berlin: W. de Gruyter. doi:10.1515/9783110801194

Aristotle. ([c335 BCE] 1952). 'Nicomachean Ethics' in Aristotle II (Founders' edn. Vol. 9). Chicago: W. Benton; Encyclopaedia Britannica Inc., University of Chicago.

Baikadi, A., & Cardona-Rivera, R. E. (2012). Towards finding the fundamental unit of narrative: A Proposal for the Narreme. *Proceedings of the 2012 Workshop on Computational Models of Narrative (CMN2012)*.

Baldwin, J. R., Faulkner, S. L., Hecht, M. L., & Lindsley, S. L. (Eds.). (2006). *Redefining Culture: Perspectives Across the Disciplines*. Mahwah, NJ: Lawrence Erlbaum Associates.

Barkow, J. H. (2006). *Missing the Revolution: Darwinism for Social Scientists*. Oxford, UK: Oxford University Press. doi:10.1093/acprof:oso/9780195130027.001.0001

Barthes, R., & Duisit, L. (1966). 1975). An Introduction to the Structural Analysis of Narrative. *New Literary History*, *6*(2), 237–272. doi:10.2307/468419

Blackmore, S. J. (2007). Memes, Minds and Imagination. In *'Imaginative Minds': Proceedings of the British Academy*. Retrieved from http://www.susanblackmore.co.uk/Chapters/ImaginativeMinds2007.htm

Blaikie, N. W. H. (2007). *Approaches to Social Enquiry* (2nd ed.). Cambridge, MA: Polity Press.

Bloore, P. (2013). *The Screenplay Business: Managing Creativity in the Film Industry*. London: Routledge.

Boden, M. A. (2004). *The Creative Mind: Myths and Mechanisms* (2nd ed.). London: Routledge.

Bohm, D. (2005). *Wholeness and the Implicate Order*. London: Taylor and Francis. (Original work published 1980)

Bordwell, D. (1997). *On the History of Film Style*. Cambridge, MA: Harvard University Press.

Bordwell, D. (2008). *Poetics of Cinema*. New York: Routledge.

Bordwell, D. (2011). *Common Sense + Film Theory = Common-Sense Film Theory?*. Retrieved from http://www.davidbordwell.net/essays/commonsense.php#_edn23

Bordwell, D. (2012). *The Viewer's Share: Models of Mind in Explaining Film*. Retrieved from http://www.davidbordwell.net/essays/viewersshare.php

Bornmann, L., & Marx, W. (2012). The Anna Karenina Principle: A Way of Thinking About Success in Science. *Journal of the American Society for Information Science and Technology*, *63*(10), 2037–2051. doi:10.1002/asi.22661

Bornmann, L., & Mutz, R. (2014). Growth rates of modern science: A bibliometric analysis based on the number of publications and cited references. *Journal of the Association for Information Science and Technology*. arXiv:1402.4578v3

Bourdieu, P., & Johnson, R. E. (1993). *The Field of Cultural Production: Essays on Art and Literature*. New York: Columbia University Press.

Bowker. (2013). *Self-Publishing In the United States, 2008-2013*. New Providence, NJ: Bowker (A ProQuest Affiliate).

Boyd, B. (2009). *On The Origin Of Stories: Evolution, Cognition, and Fiction*. Cambridge, MA: Belknap Press of Harvard University Press.

Boyd, B. (2010). Art and Evolution: The Avant-Garde as Test Case – Spiegelman in The Narrative Corpse. In B. Boyd, J. Carroll, & J. Gottschall (Eds.), *Evolution, Literature and Film: A Reader*. New York: Columbia University Press.

Boyd, B., Carroll, J., & Gottschall, J. (2010). *Evolution, Literature and Film: A Reader*. New York: Columbia University Press.

Bradie, M., & Harms, W. (2012). Evolutionary Epistemology. *The Stanford Encyclopedia of Philosophy*. Retrieved from http://plato.stanford.edu/archives/win2012/entries/epistemology-evolutionary

Branigan, E. (1992). *Narrative Comprehension and Film*. London: Routledge.

Brockman, J. (2000). *The Greatest Inventions of the Past 2,000 Years*. New York: Simon & Schuster.

Brockman, J. (2010). *This Will Change Everything: Ideas That Will Shape the Future* (1st ed.). New York, NY: Harper Perennial.

Bunge, M. (1969). The Metaphysics, Epistemology and Methodology of Levels. In L. Whyte, A. Wilson, & D. Wilson (Eds.), *Hierarchical Structures*. New York: Elsevier.

Buss, D. M. (2012). *Evolutionary Psychology: The New Science of the Mind* (4th ed.). Boston: Pearson Allyn & Bacon.

Campbell, D. T. (1960). Blind Variation and Selective Retention in Creative Thought as in Other Knowledge Processes. *Psychological Review*, *67*(6), 380–400. doi:10.1037/h0040373 PMID:13690223

Campbell, D. T. (1974). Evolutionary Epistemology. In P. A. Schlipp (Ed.), *The Philosophy of Karl Popper* (Vol. 1, pp. 413–459). La Salle.

Campbell, J. (1949). *The Hero With A Thousand Faces*. New York: Pantheon Books.

Capra, F., & Luisi, P. L. (2014). *The Systems View of Life: A Unifying Vision*. Cambridge, UK: Cambridge University Press. doi:10.1017/CBO9780511895555

Carroll, J. (1995). *Evolution and Literary Theory*. Columbia, MO: University of Missouri Press.

Carroll, J. (2008). Rejoinder to Responses - "An Evolutionary Paradigm for Literary Study," (target article to which scholars and scientists were invited to respond). *Style (DeKalb, IL)*, *42*(2 & 3), 103–135.

Carroll, J., McAdams, D. P., & Wilson, E. O. (Eds.). (in press). *Darwin's Bridge: Uniting the Sciences and Humanities*.

Chaisson, E. (2001). *Cosmic Evolution: The Rise of Complexity in Nature*. Cambridge, MA: Harvard University Press.

Chick, G. (1999). *What's in a Meme? The Development of the Meme as a Unit of Culture*. Retrieved from http://www.personal.psu.edu/gec7/Memes.pdf

Cobley, P., & Schulz, P. (Eds.). (2013). *Theories and Models of Communication*. Boston: Walter de Gruyter. doi:10.1515/9783110240450

Cooke, B., & Machann, C. (2012). Applied Evolutionary Criticism. *Style (DeKalb, IL)*, *46*(3/4), 277–296.

Cooke, B., & Turner, F. (1999). *Biopoetics: Evolutionary Explorations in the Arts*. Lexington, Ky.: ICUS.

Csikszentmihalyi, M. (1988). Society, Culture, and Person: A Systems View of Creativity. In R. J. Sternberg (Ed.), *The Nature of Creativity* (pp. 325–339). New York: Cambridge University Press.

Csikszentmihalyi, M. (1995). Creativity Across the Life-Span: A Systems View. Talent Development, 3, 9-18.

Csikszentmihalyi, M. (1996a, July-August). The Creative Personality. *Psychology Today*, 36–40.

Csikszentmihalyi, M. (1996b). *Creativity: Flow and the Psychology of Discovery and Invention* (1st ed.). New York: HarperCollins.

Csikszentmihalyi, M. (1999). Implications of a Systems Perspective for the Study of Creativity. In Handbook of Creativity. Cambridge, UK: Cambridge University Press.

Csikszentmihalyi, M. (2006). A Systems Perspective on Creativity. In J. Henry (Ed.), *Creative Management and Development* (pp. 3–17). London: SAGE. doi:10.4135/9781446213704.n1

Csikszentmihalyi, M. (2014). The Systems Model of Creativity and Its Applications. In D. K. Simonton (Ed.), *The Wiley Handbook of Genius*. Chichester, UK: John Wiley & Sons Ltd. doi:10.1002/9781118367377. ch25

Csikszentmihalyi, M., & Massimini, F. (1985). On The Psychological Selection Of Bio-Cultural Information. *New Ideas in Psychology*, *3*(2), 115–138. doi:10.1016/0732-118X(85)90002-9

Csikszentmihalyi, M., & Nakamura, J. (2006). Creativity Through the Life Span from An Evolutionary Systems Perspective. In C. Hoare (Ed.), *Handbook of Adult Development and Learning* (pp. 243–254). New York: Oxford University Press.

Csikszentmihalyi, M., & Wolfe, R. (2000). New Conceptions and Research Approaches to Creativity: Implications for a Systems Perspective of Creativity in Education. In K. A. Heller, F. J. Mönks, R. Subotnik, & R. J. Sternberg (Eds.), International Handbook of Giftedness and Talent (2nd ed.). Amsterdam: Elsevier.

Darwin, C. (1859). *On the Origin of Species by Means of Natural Selection, or The Preservation of Favoured Races in the Struggle For Life*. London: J. Murray.

Dawkins, R. (1976). *The Selfish Gene*. Oxford, UK: Oxford University Press.

Dawkins, R. (1986). *The Blind Watchmaker* (1st American ed.). New York: Norton.

De Vany, A. S., & Walls, W. D. (2004). Motion Picture Profit, the stable Paretian hypothesis, and the Curse of the Superstar. *Journal of Economic Dynamics & Control*, *28*(6), 1035–1057. doi:10.1016/S0165-1889(03)00065-4

Deleuze, G., & Guattari, F. (1987). *A Thousand Plateaus: Capitalism and Schizophrenia*. Minneapolis, MN: University of Minnesota Press.

Dena, C. (2009). *Transmedia Practice: Theorising The Practice Of Expressing A Fictional World Across Distinct Media And Environments*. (PhD Thesis). University of Sydney. Retrieved from http://www. christydena.com/phd/

Dennett, D. C. (1984). Elbow Room: The Varieties of Free Will Worth Wanting. New York: Clarendon Press.

Dennett, D. C. (1995). *Darwin's Dangerous Idea: Evolution and the Meanings of Life*. New York: Simon & Schuster.

Dennett, D. C. (2003). *Freedom Evolves*. New York: Viking.

Diamond, J. M. (1997). *Guns, Germs, and Steel: The Fates of Human Societies* (1st ed.). New York: W.W. Norton & Co.

Diamond, J. M. (1999). *Guns, Germs, and Steel: The Fates of Human Societies*. New York: Norton. (Original work published 1997)

Dorfman, E. (1969). *The Narreme in the Medieval Romance Epic: An Introduction to Narrative Structure*. Toronto: University of Toronto Press.

Dutton, D. (2010). *The Art Instinct: Beauty, Pleasure and Human Evolution*. Oxford, UK: Oxford University Press.

Fauconnier, G., & Turner, M. (2002). *The Way We Think: Conceptual Blending and the Mind's Hidden Complexities*. New York: Basic Books.

Feynman, R. P. (2005). Don't You Have Time To Think? London: Allen Lane (Penguin).

Fulton, J., & McIntyre, P. (2013). Futures of Communication: Communication Studies ~ Creativity. *Review of Communication, 13*(4), 269–289. doi:10.1080/15358593.2013.872805

Gerrig, R. J. (1993). *Experiencing Narrative Worlds*. New Haven, CT: Yale University Press.

Gershenson, C., & Heylighen, F. (2005). How Can We Think Complex? In K. A. Richardson (Ed.), Managing Organizational Complexity: Philosophy, Theory and Application (pp. 47-62). Greenwich, CT: IAP - Information Age Pub. Inc.

Gibson, M. A., & Lawson, D. W. (Eds.). (2014). *Applied Evolutionary Anthropology*. New York: Springer. doi:10.1007/978-1-4939-0280-4

Giddens, A. (1984). *The Constitution of Society: Outline of the Theory of Structuration*. Cambridge, MA: Polity.

Gontier, N. (2012). Applied Evolutionary Epistemology: A new methodology to enhance interdisciplinary research between the life and human sciences. *Journal of Philosophy and Science, 4*, 7-49.

Gontier, N. (2014). Evolutionary Epistemology. *The Internet Encyclopedia of Philosophy* Retrieved 7th April, 2015, from http://www.iep.utm.edu/evo-epis/

Gottschall, J. (2008). *Literature, Science, and a New Humanities* (1st ed.). New York: Palgrave Macmillan. doi:10.1057/9780230615595

Gottschall, J. (2012). *The Storytelling Animal: How Stories Make Us Human*. Boston: Houghton Mifflin Harcourt.

Green, M. C., & Brock, T. C. (2000). The role of transportation in the persuasiveness of public narratives. *Journal of Personality and Social Psychology, 79*(5), 701–721. doi:10.1037/0022-3514.79.5.701 PMID:11079236

Green, M. C., & Brock, T. C. (2002). In the mind's eye: Imagery and transportation into narrative worlds. In M. C. Green, J. J. Strange, & T. C. Brock (Eds.), *Narrative Impact: Social and Cognitive Foundations* (pp. 315–341). Mahwah, NJ: Lawrence Erlbaum Associates.

Green, M. C., & Carpenter, J. M. A. (2011). Transporting Into Narrative Worlds. *The Future of Scientific Studies in Literature, 1*(1), 113–122.

Green, M. C., Chatham, C., & Sestir, M. A. (2012). Emotion and transportation into fact and fiction. *Scientific Study of Literature, 2*(1), 37–59. doi:10.1075/ssol.2.1.03gre

Habash, G. (2012). *Average Book Length: Guess How Many Words Are In A Novel.* Retrieved from http://www.huffingtonpost.com/2012/03/09/book-length_n_1334636.html

Halloran, J. D. (1998). Mass Communication Research: Asking The Right Questions. In A. Hansen (Ed.), *Mass Communication Research Methods* (pp. 9–34). New York: New York University Press. doi:10.1007/978-1-349-26485-8_2

Helmenstine, A. M. (2014). *How Many Atoms Are There in a Human Cell?* Retrieved from http://chemistry.about.com/od/biochemistry/f/How-Many-Atoms-Are-There-In-A-Human-Cell.htm

Heylighen, F., & Chielens, K. (2009). Evolution of Culture, Memetics. In R. A. Meyers (Ed.), *Encyclopedia of Complexity and Systems Science* (pp. 3205–3220). Larkspur, CA: Springer. doi:10.1007/978-0-387-30440-3_189

Iglesias, K. (2001). *The 101 Habits of Highly Successful Screenwriters: Insider Secrets from Hollywood's Top Writers.* Avon, MA: Adams Media.

Jenkins, H. (2011). Transmedia 202: Further Reflections. *Journal of Memetics.*

Kahneman, D. (2011). *Thinking, Fast and Slow* (1st ed.). New York: Farrar, Straus and Giroux.

Kaufman, J. C., & Beghetto, R. A. (2009). Beyond big and little: The Four C Model of Creativity. *Review of General Psychology, 13*(1), 1–12. doi:10.1037/a0013688

Kaufman, J. C., & Beghetto, R. A. (2013). Do people recognize the four Cs? Examining layperson conceptions of creativity. *Psychology of Aesthetics, Creativity, and the Arts, 7*(3), 229–236. doi:10.1037/a0033295

Kemp, S. (2012). 'Vertigo' Tops 'Citizen Kane' in Poll of Greatest Films of All Time. *The Hollywood Reporter.* Retrieved from http://www.hollywoodreporter.com/news/vertigo-citizen-kane-greatest-film-of-all-time-357266

Kerrigan, S., & Velikovsky, J. T. (2015). Examining Documentary Transmedia Narratives Through 'The Living History of Fort Scratchley' Project. *Convergence.* doi: 10.1177/1354856514567053

Koestler, A. (1964). *The Act of Creation.* London: Hutchinson.

Koestler, A. (1967). The Ghost. In *The Machine.* London: Hutchinson.

Koestler, A. (1978). *Janus: A Summing Up.* London: Hutchinson.

Koestler, A. ([1978] 1979). Janus: A Summing Up (1st Vintage Books ed.). London: Pan Books.

Koestler, A. (1989). *The Act of Creation*. London: Arkana. (Original work published 1964)

Koestler, A. (1989). The Ghost. In *The Machine*. London: Arkana. (Original work published 1967)

Kozbelt, A., Beghetto, R. A., & Runco, M. A. (2010). Theories of Creativity. In J. C. Kaufman & R. J. Sternberg (Eds.), *The Cambridge handbook of Creativity* (pp. 20–47). Cambridge, UK: Cambridge University Press. doi:10.1017/CBO9780511763205.004

Kroeber, A. L., & Kluckhohn, C. (1952). *Culture: A Critical Review of Concepts and Definitions*. Cambridge, MA: The Museum.

Laszlo, E. (1972). *Introduction to Systems Philosophy: Toward a New Paradigm of Contemporary Thought*. New York: Gordon and Breach.

Lin, Y., Duan, X., Zhao, C., & Xu, L. (2013). *Systems Science: Methodological Approaches*. Boca Raton, FL: CRC Press.

Lovelock, J. (1995). *Gaia: A New Look At Life On Earth*. Oxford, UK: Oxford University Press.

Macdonald, I. W. (2004). *The Presentation of the Screen Idea in Narrative Film-making*. (PhD Dissertation). Leeds Metropolitan University, Leeds, UK.

Macdonald, I. W. (2013). *Screenwriting Poetics and the Screen Idea*. New York: Palgrave Macmillan. doi:10.1057/9780230392298

Mayr, E. (2002). What Evolution Is. London: Phoenix.

McIntyre, P. (2012). *Creativity and Cultural Production: Issues for Media Practice*. Basingstoke, UK: Palgrave Macmillan.

McNamara, A. (2011). Can we measure memes? *Frontiers in Evolutionary Neuroscience, 3*(1). doi:10.3389/fnevo.2011.00001 PMID:21720531

Metz, C. (1991). Film Language: A Semiotics of the Cinema (University of Chicago Press ed.). Chicago: University of Chicago Press.

Miller, J. G. (1968). Living Systems: Basic Concepts. In W. Gray, F. J. Duhl, & N. D. Rizzo (Eds.), *General Systems Theory and Psychiatry*. Boston: Litte, Brown & Co.

Miller, J. G. (1978). *Living Systems*. New York: McGraw-Hill.

Mobus, G. E., & Kalton, M. C. (2014). *Principles of Systems Science*. New York: Springer.

Moretti, F. (2000). The Slaughterhouse of Literature. *MLQ: Modern Language Quarterly, 61*(1), 207–227. doi:10.1215/00267929-61-1-207

Moretti, F. (2007). *Graphs, Maps, Trees: Abstract Models for Literary History*. London: Verso.

Peer, W. v., Hakemulder, J., & Zyngier, S. (2012). *Scientific Methods for the Humanities*. Amsterdam: John Benjamins Pub. Co. doi:10.1075/lal.13

PGA. (2010). Producers Guild Of America Code Of Credits - New Media. *Producers Guild of America Code of Credits*. Retrieved from http://www.producersguild.org/?page=coc_nm#transmedia

Pigliucci, M., & Müller, G. (2010). *Evolution: The Extended Synthesis*. Cambridge, MA: MIT Press. doi:10.7551/mitpress/9780262513678.001.0001

Pinker, S. (1997). *How The Mind Works*. New York: Norton.

Polson, D., Cook, A.-M., Brackin, A., & Velikovsky, J. T. (Eds.). (2014). *Transmedia Practice: A Collective Approach*. London: ID-Press.

Popper, K. R. (1963). *Conjectures and Refutations: The Growth of Scientific Knowledge. (Essays and Lectures.)*. London: Routledge & Kegan Paul.

Popper, K. R. (1978a). Natural Selection and the Emergence of Mind. *Dialectica, 32*(3-4), 339–355. doi:10.1111/j.1746-8361.1978.tb01321.x

Popper, K. R. (1978b). *Three Worlds*. Salt Lake City, UT: University of Utah.

Popper, K. R. ([1972] 1979). Objective Knowledge: An Evolutionary Approach (Rev. ed.). Oxford, UK: Oxford University Press.

Popper, K. R. (1999). *All Life is Problem Solving*. London: Routledge.

Postill, J. (2010). Introduction: Theorising media and practice. In B. Bräuchler & J. Postill (Eds.), *Theorising Media and Practice*. Oxford. doi:10.7551/mitpress/9780262014816.003.0001

Propp, V. (1958). *Morphology of the Folk Tale*. Bloomington, IN: Indiana University Press.

Radnitzky, G., Bartley, W. W., & Popper, K. R. (1987). *Evolutionary Epistemology, Rationality, and the Sociology of Knowledge*. Open Court.

Richards, C. E. (2012). Complementarities in Physics and Psychology. In L. J. Miller (Ed.), *The Oxford Handbook of Psychology and Spirituality*. Oxford, UK: Oxford University Press. doi:10.1093/oxfordhb/9780199729920.013.0005

Rouse, J. (2006). Practice Theory. In S. Turner & M. Risjord (Eds.), *Philosophy of Anthropology and Sociology: A Volume in the Handbook of the Philosophy of Science Series* (pp. 639–681). Amsterdam: Elsevier B.V.

Runco, M. A., & Jaeger, G. J. (2012). The Standard Definition of Creativity. *Creativity Research Journal, 24*(1), 92–96. doi:10.1080/10400419.2012.650092

Sadowski, P. (1999). *Systems Theory as an Approach to the Study of Literature: Origins and Functions of Literature*. Lewiston, NY: E. Mellen Press.

Sawyer, R. K. (2012). Explaining Creativity: The Science of Human Innovation (2nd ed.). New York: Oxford University Press.

Simon, H. A. (1991). *Models of My Life*. New York: Basic Books.

Simon, H. A. (1996). *The Sciences of the Artificial* (3rd ed.). Cambridge, MA: MIT Press.

Simonton, D. K. (2007). Is Bad Art The Opposite Of Good Art? Positive Versus Negative Cinematic Assessments of 877 Feature Films. *Empirical Studies of the Arts, 25*(2), 143–161. doi:10.2190/2447-30T2-6088-7752

Simonton, D. K. (2011). *Great Flicks: Scientific Studies of Cinematic Creativity and Aesthetics*. New York: Oxford University Press. doi:10.1093/acprof:oso/9780199752034.001.0001

Simonton, D. K. (2012a). Creative Thought as Blind Variation and Selective Retention: Why Creativity is Inversely Related to Sightedness. *Journal of Theoretical and Philosophical Psychology, 33*(4), 253–266. doi:10.1037/a0030705

Simonton, D. K. (2012b). Fields, Domains, and Individuals (Chapter). In M. D. Mumford (Ed.), *Handbook of Organizational Creativity* (pp. 67–86). Oxford, UK: Elsevier Science. doi:10.1016/B978-0-12-374714-3.00004-5

Slingerland, E. G., & Collard, M. (2012). *Creating Consilience: Integrating the Sciences and the Humanities*. New York: Oxford University Press.

Snow, C. P. (1959). *The Two Cultures and the Scientific Revolution*. Cambridge University Press.

Tooby, J., & Cosmides, L. (2005). Conceptual Foundations of Evolutionary Pyschology. In D. Buss (Ed.), The Handbook of Evolutionary Psychology. Hoboken, NJ: John Wiley & Sons.

Truby, J. (2007). *The Anatomy of Story: 22 Steps to Becoming a Master Storyteller* (1st ed.). New York: Faber and Faber.

Van Laer, T., De Ruyter, K., Visconti, L. M., & Wetzels, M. (2014). The Extended Transportation-Imagery Model: A Meta-Analysis of the Antecedents and Consequences of Consumers' Narrative Transportation. *The Journal of Consumer Research, 40*(5), 797–817. doi:10.1086/673383

Van Peer, W. (1996). Canon Formation: Ideology or Aesthetic Quality? *The British Journal of Aesthetics, 36*(2), 97–108. doi:10.1093/bjaesthetics/36.2.97

Van Peer, W. (1997). Two Laws of Literary Canon: Growth and Predictability in Canon Formation. *Mosaic: A Journal for the Interdisciplinary Study of Literature, 30*(2), 113-132.

Van Peer, W., Hakemulder, J., & Zyngier, S. (2007). *Muses and Measures: Empirical Research Methods for the Humanities*. Newcastle, UK: Cambridge Scholars.

Varzi, A. (2015). Mereology. *The Stanford Encyclopedia of Philosophy (Spring 2015 Edition)*. Retrieved from http://plato.stanford.edu/archives/spr2015/entries/mereology/

Velikovsky, J. T. (2013a). Brave New Storyworlds: An Introduction to Creating Transmedia Narratives. *Screen Education, 68*.

Velikovsky, J. T. (2013b). *The Holon/Parton Structure of the Meme, the Unit of Culture*. Retrieved from http://storyality.wordpress.com/2013/12/12/storyality-100-the-holonic-structure-of-the-meme-the-unit-of-culture/

Velikovsky, J. T. (2014a). *Flow Theory, Evolution & Creativity: or, 'Fun & Games'*. Paper presented at the Interactive Entertainment 2014 (IE2014), Newcastle, Australia.

Velikovsky, J. T. (2014b). The Hero's Journey: It's Not What You Think. *The StoryAlity screenwriting research weblog.* Retrieved 9th February, 2015, from http://storyality.wordpress.com/2013/08/23/storyality-73-the-heros-journey-its-not-what-you-think/

Velikovsky, J. T. (2014c). A Hierarchy of Memes. *Practical Memetics.* Retrieved from http://www.practicalmemetics.com/index.php/memetics-101/202-mem-101-holons.html?showall=1&limitstart=

Velikovsky, J. T. (2014d). Review of the book 'The Screenplay Business: Managing Creativity and Script Development in the Film Industry', by Peter Bloore, 2013. *Journal of Screenwriting, 5*(2), 283–285. doi:10.1386/josc.5.2.283_5

Vogler, C. (1992). *The Writer's Journey: Mythic Structures for Storytellers and Screenwriters.* Studio City, CA: M. Wiese Productions.

von Bertalanffy, L. (1950). An Outline of General System Theory. *The British Journal for the Philosophy of Science, 1*(2), 134–165. doi:10.1093/bjps/I.2.134

Ward, L. (1913). *The Outlines of Sociology.* Norwood, MA: Macmillan. (Original work published 1898)

Warfield, J. N. (2006). *An Introduction to Systems Science.* Hackensack, NJ: World Scientific.

Webster, S. (2003). *Thinking About Biology.* Cambridge, UK: Cambridge University Press. doi:10.1017/CBO9780511754975

Weisberg, R. W. (2006). *Creativity: Understanding Innovation in Problem Solving, Science, Invention, and the Arts.* Hoboken, NJ: John Wiley & Sons.

West, G. B., & Brown, J. H. (2005). The origin of allometric scaling laws in biology from genomes to ecosystems: Towards a quantitative unifying theory of biological structure and organization. *The Journal of Experimental Biology, 208*(9), 1575–1592. doi:10.1242/jeb.01589 PMID:15855389

Whewell, W. (1840). *The Philosophy of the Inductive Sciences, Founded Upon Their History.* London: J.W. Parker.

Wiener, N. (1948). Cybernetics: Or Control and Communication in the Animal and the Machine. New York: J. Wiley.

Wilson, E. O. (1998). Consilience: The Unity of Knowledge (1st ed.). New York: Knopf.

Wilson, E. O. ([1998] 1999). Consilience: The Unity of Knowledge (1st Vintage Books ed.). New York: Knopf.

Zimmer, C. (2011). 100 Trillion Connections: New Efforts Probe and Map the Brain's Detailed Architecture. *Scientific American.* Retrieved from http://www.scientificamerican.com/article/100-trillion-connections/

KEY TERMS AND DEFINITIONS

Applied Evolutionary Epistemology: A discipline that aims to identify the units, levels, and mechanisms of selection, in both biology and culture (Gontier, 2012). These mechanisms may include: natural, artificial, unconscious, and also combinatorial (or, sexual) selection.

Biology: The study of organisms, or living things (Webster, 2003, p. 38). The view adopted here is that all organisms have knowledge, including plants and animals, though not explicitly conscious knowledge in the case of nonhuman organisms (Popper, 1999, pp. 32-39). Knowledge is information, and in the case of nonhuman organisms, implicit knowledge (such as instinctive behavior, or Evolutionary Psychology) is also encoded in organismic nervous systems as: 'IF [condition] > THEN [instruction], (ELSE) [alternate instruction]' subroutines, or 'decision rules' (Buss, 2012, p. 49).[24]

Creative Technologies: Any technology (any idea, process or product – or, tool, device, or invention - including also any theory, or model) that is judged 'creative', namely 'original and useful' by a consensus in the field. Examples include: languages, symbol systems, image and sound recording equipment, editing equipment, the computer, the internet, a national flag, and the scientific method. For a more comprehensive list, see *The Greatest Inventions of the Past 2,000 Years* (Brockman 2000). Examples in this chapter include: the meme (unit of culture) as the holon/parton; and also the synthesized model of Creative Practice Theory.

Creativity: The standard definition of creativity is 'original and useful', namely a biocultural artifact (i.e., idea, process, product) judged 'original and useful' (or, 'novel and appropriate') by a consensus of the audience (i.e. the field) for a specific domain in culture (Runco & Jaeger, 2012). Examples of domains in culture include movies, literature, popular music, videogames, physics, chemistry, biology, psychology, sociology, and all their various subdomains (including genres and subgenres).

Culture: 'Culture' is knowledge encoded in symbol systems in the form of ideas, processes, and products (Csikszentmihalyi, 1996b) including in science, the arts, media, religion, and languages. Examples of *ideas* include scientific theories (e.g., gravity, general and special relativity, evolution), and also literary and media characters and narratives (Sherlock Holmes, Anna Karenina, Harry Potter); examples of *processes* include writing an email, having a conversation, reading a book, and in science, pasteurization; examples of cultural *products* include the hand-axe, the spear, the wheel, words, books, movies, songs, the printing press, the telescope, the microscope, the car, the computer, the iPod. As there is no culture without biology, a synonym for 'culture' is 'bioculture'.

Evolution (Biological, Cultural, Cosmic): Evolution can most simply be defined as 'descent with modification' (Chaisson, 2001; Darwin, 1859). Here the concept of evolution includes the (post-1940s) Modern Evolutionary Synthesis (aka 'Neo-Darwinism'), and the (post-2010) Extended Evolutionary Synthesis (Pigliucci & Müller, 2010), including Multilevel Selection Theory (Gontier, 2012). As a brief summary of the three necessary-and-sufficient conditions of the (iterative and recursive, or, algorithmic) systems process of evolution: 'The evolutionary process requires variation, differential survival and reproductive success, and inheritance' (Capra & Luisi, 2014, p. 200; see also Dennett, 1995, p. 343). Laszlo (1972) explains atoms, biology, and social systems as classes of natural (and sometimes designed) systems 'sharing invariant fundamental properties' (Laszlo, 1972, p. 56) and demonstrates that evolution occurs across natural systems (Laszlo, 1972, pp. 57-117).[25] In this view, systems and also, artifacts (inputs and outputs) within systems are selected (or deselected, and thus: 'falsified') by their environment (Popper 1999). It should be noted that the iterative and recursive Evolutionary Algorithm (namely: variation, selection, transmission) also satisfices, rather than optimizes.[26]

Evolutionary Epistemology: The natural selection, or 'blind variation and selective retention' (or BVSR) model of contemporary Evolutionary Epistemology (or, the growth of knowledge) is customarily dated to Karl Popper (1972, 1984), Stephen Toulmin (1967, 1972), Donald Campbell (1974) and Konrad Lorenz (1977) (Bradie & Harms, Winter 2012 Edition, online). Gontier also provides an overview of the major strands in Evolutionary Epistemology, citing Karl Popper (1963), Konrad Lorenz (1941, 1985), Donald Campbell (1959, 1960, 1974), Stephen Toulmin (1972), and Peter Munz (2001) on 'Philosophical Darwinism' (Gontier, 2014).

Holarchy: Koestler defines a holarchy as a hierarchy of self-regulating holons (Koestler, 1967, p. 103). Holarchies function according to the three laws of holarchies - which are also three laws of evolution in Systems Theory (see (Laszlo, 1972, pp. 55-118, 176-180)) - namely: (1) competition and/or cooperation (and/or co-opetition), 'sideways' with other holon/partons on the same level; (2) integration upwards, into the larger holon/parton on the level 'above'; and (3) control and command of holon/partons on the level 'below' (Koestler, 1964, 1967, 1978).

Holon/Parton: A portmanteau synthesis of the above two terms. A consilient (or, 'science meets the arts/media') synthesis of these two words used herein is 'holon/parton', as this term emphasizes the dual, or 'Janus-faced' (Koestler, [1978] 1979, p. 27) nature of these whole/part entities; they are a whole and also a part at the same time (in both biological and in socio-cultural systems, and also, in biological and cultural units).

Holon: (*sensu* Koestler 1967) 'A holon ... is something that is simultaneously a whole and a part' (Koestler, 1967, p. 48).

Parton: (*sensu* Feynman 1975, 2005) The parton is the name in subatomic physics that Richard P. Feynman (Feynman, 2005, p. 278) gave to the equivalent structure of the holon.

Systems Theory: The study of systems and their environments, including system inputs, outputs, relations and interactions, including the concept of emergence, where the whole system (its structure, function, and behavior) is more than the sum of its parts. For reviews of Systems Theory, Complexity and Emergence, see (Sepännen in Altmann & Koch, 1998, pp. 180-302), (Sadowski, 1999, pp. 7-10), (Gershenson & Heylighen, 2005), (Warfield, 2006, pp. 38-46), (Lin, Duan, Zhao, & Xu, 2013, pp. 1-22), (Mobus & Kalton, 2014, pp. 32-40).

Transmedia: A narrative extended across more than one media (e.g., across a movie, novel, videogame, and so on). Importantly, *adaptations* of a story (or, narrative) from one media to another media (e.g. novel-to-film), and also prequels and sequels in the same media are not considered transmedia (see: Dena, 2009; Jenkins, 2011; PGA, 2010; Polson, Cook, Brackin, & Velikovsky, 2014; Velikovsky, 2013a).

ENDNOTES

[1]   *Muses and Measures* (2007) was subsequently revised, retitled and republished as *Scientific Methods for the Humanities* (Peer, Hakemulder, & Zyngier, 2012).

[2]   See also the subsequent updated edition, *Living Systems* (Miller, 1978).

[3]   It is noted that there may be many organisms within a residence, even if not all considered 'family'.

[4]   At the risk of grossly oversimplifying, many Evolutionary Psychologists in general take the view that 'The mind is a neural computer, fitted by natural selection with combinatorial algorithms for

causal and probabilistic reasoning about plants, animals, objects and people' (Pinker, 1997, p. 524). At the same time, the human mind also tends to feature a significant number of cognitive biases (Buss, 2012, p. 395; Kahneman, 2011).

[5] 'Word-of-mouth' in this context refers to any channel of communication (social media, telephony, and so on).

[6] Aristotle avers in *Nicomachean Ethics* (Book 2, Ch. 6), 'It is possible to fail in many ways (for evil belongs to the class of the unlimited, as the Pythagoreans conjectured, and good to that of the limited), while to succeed is possible only in one way (for which reason one is easy and the other difficult – to miss the mark easy, to hit it difficult)... *For men are good in but one way, but bad in many*' (Aristotle, [c335 BCE] 1952, p. 352).

[7] The same quote by Dawkins (1986) is also cited in. (1995). (p. 104). Dennett.

[8] In human biology for example, there can be around 10^{14} units when different levels (and units) emerge in the holarchy: there are around 10^{14} atoms in cell (Helmenstine, 2014), around 10^{14} cells in a human body (Richards, 2012, p. 70), and around 10^{14} synapses (or connections between neurons) in the human brain (Zimmer, 2011). See also (West & Brown, 2005).

[9] *Amazon.com* notes that the 'average' book on *Amazon* has 64,500 words (Habash, 2012).

[10] For a discussion of transmedia 'storyworlds' versus story 'universes', see: (Kerrigan & Velikovsky, 2015).

[11] See also. (2012b). Hierarchy of the sciences based on objective characteristics of both field and domain (p. 74). Simonton.

[12] The first major work of Evocriticism is customarily dated to (Carroll, 1995).

[13] For a summary of 'practice theory' see (Postill, 2010) and (Rouse, 2006, pp. 639-640).

[14] An animated 2-D model of this Creative Practice Theory model is online, and demonstrates how each of the ten elements in the model is acquired (and/or, achieved) by a creative individual, over time, which a static 2-D diagram as presented here does not clearly demonstrate over time. (http://storyality.wordpress.com/creative-practice-theory/)

[15] In *The 101 Habits of Highly Successful Screenwriters: Insider Secrets from Hollywood's Top Writers* (2001) Iglesias includes quotes from six famous and successful screenwriters who testify that they all wrote around ten screenplays before they had one optioned, sold, and/or made (Iglesias, 2001, pp. 211-220).

[16] See Simonton in *Great Flicks*. (2011). on 'films as art versus movies as business'. Simonton, 2011, 112–113.

[17] See also Dutton on twelve 'cluster criteria' for art (Dutton 2010, pp. 51-61).

[18] http://storyality.wordpress.com/2013/08/23/storyality-73-the-heros-journey-its-not-what-you-think/

[19] See (Macdonald, 2004, 2013) for an elaboration of the concept of films (or movies) as 'screen ideas'.

[20] Truby (2007) also notes: 'the essential characteristic of a story as a structure in time. It is an organic unit that develops over time … a story is always a whole' (Truby, 2007, p. 419)

[21] For more on selection pressure (among biocultural artifacts) in the arts, see also (Van Peer, 1996, 1997).

[22] See (Blaikie, 2007, pp. 206-214).

[23] It is possible that one reason for the abandoning of the *Journal of Memetics* (JoM, 1997-2005) and dispersal of the nascent field of Memetics is that the structure of the meme, the unit of culture, was not previously identified. Dennett noted in 1995 that 'The prospects for elaborating a

rigorous science of memetics are doubtful' (Dennett, 1995, p. 369). The current chapter however is one step in an attempt to achieve this goal; Communication Theory, Creative Technologies, the Digital Humanities and possibly various other domains and disciplines may benefit if this task is successful. It should be noted various scholars in Memetics (e.g., Blackmore, Farncombe et al) are yet persisting in the task of solving this hard problem (see Hull, 1982 in Dennett, 1995, p. 352); see also for example (Velikovsky, 2014c).

[24]   This view of nervous systems (including brains, or 'minds') should in no way be understood to remove free will, nor should it be misconstrued as deterministic (see Koestler, [1967] 1989, pp. 201-202; [1978] 1979, pp. 239-241); for more detail of this view, see Koestler on free will (Koestler, [1964] 1989, p. 633; [1967] 1989, pp. 215-216; [1978] 1979, pp. 232, 235-241) and see also (Dennett, 1984, 2003) on free will.

[25]   Importantly, Simon distinguishes between natural and artificial systems (Simon, 1996).

[26]   Simon rightly notes that 'natural selection only predicts that survivors will be *fit enough*, that is, fitter than their losing competitors; it postulates satisficing, not optimizing' (Simon, 1991, p. 166).

Chapter 10
Discovering Art using Technology:
The Selfie Project

Alexiei Dingli
University of Malta, Malta

Dylan Seychell
St. Martin's Institute of Higher Education, Malta

Vince Briffa
University of Malta, Malta

ABSTRACT

The Selfie project was not only inspired by the long history of the self-portrait, but also intended to create a genealogy between the self-portraits of masters from the Modern art era and the selfie. The project, designed as a walkthrough experience, consisted of three major engagement areas. On entering the space, children were directed into a 'transformation' area – a typical theatrical wardrobe, where they could dress up in a variety of costumes, including hats and wigs. Once garbed, children were given smart phones and led to the area where they could take a selfie with a celebrity such as Gauguin, Cézanne, Monet, Van Gogh, Modigliani and Munch. Finally, they could manipulate the selfie using gesture-based technology and post it online. The attraction proved to be extremely popular and the children who participated were extremely satisfied with the experience.

INTRODUCTION

We are living in a day and age where the word selfie is an integral part of a young person's vocabulary (Senft, 2015). A selfie can be described as a photograph that a person takes of oneself, typically using a mobile device and which is shared via social media. On the other hand, famous personalities such as Van Gogh, Monet, Cezanne, Munch, etc and their contribution towards art is rather unknown to these

DOI: 10.4018/978-1-5225-0016-2.ch010

people. Inspired by the numerous self-portraits in the Modern Art period (Lawrence-Lightfoot, 1997), the Selfie project is a walkthrough where children are exposed to the works of famous artists, they can take selfies with them, edit them and eventually post them online.

The Selfie project was created for ŻiguŻajg[1] 2014. ŻiguŻajg is the annual International Arts Festival for children and young adults in Malta, which has as its vision, that of positioning the creative arts for children and young people at the core of Malta's creative ecology. It has established itself as the most influential and important festival of the arts in its category and this has been achieved through its vision, which sees a demographic normally assumed to be disassociated and detached from art taking center stage in a variety of artistic happenings.

The Selfie Project was one of the most popular attractions hosting an average of 120 visitors per day during the whole duration of the festival. Each visitor had to go through a process that lasted around 30 minutes and was divided, into the following phases.

The first phase was the Transformation phase. Visitors were provided with various props (these included costumes, makeup, wigs, etc.) and they were free to use them. Essentially, the visitors could transform themselves into whatever they wanted in order to express their emotions or to pass on a message.

With this transformation, the visitor could proceed to the second phase where they could take a selfie together with a self-portrait of a celebrity (Figure 1). The celebrities available were cutouts of the following six artists; Vincent Van Gogh, Claude Monet, Paul Cezanne, Edvard Munch, Paul Gauguin and Amedeo Modigliani. A small bio, underneath each artist, was provided to introduce the visitors with their story. Since they were cutouts, the artists could be moved around and the visitors had all the liberty to take the picture in any pose they wanted. Some of them hugged the artist whilst others made funny

Figure 1. Example Selfies taken with the six paintings, which were provided as backdrop. In some cases, the artist also features in the photo.

poses; others took solo pictures whilst some preferred group photos. Essentially they were free to take a selfie in anyway they preferred. We wanted their creation to be inspired by the self-portrait, which was an important creative platform throughout the history of art (Bonafoux, 1985).

Six small sets, inspired by famous paintings were also provided as a backdrop. These backdrops included, Van Gogh's "Bedroom in Arles" 1888, Munch's "The Scream" 1893, Monet's "Water Lilies" 1916, Cezanne's "Still Life with a Ginger Jar and Eggplants" 1890, Gauguin's "Tahitian pastorale" 1898 and Modigliani's "Portrait of a Polish Woman" 1919.

The final phase is the manipulation phase where the photos taken were automatically uploaded onto machines, which were provided as part of the exhibit. The visitors could sit down at one of the six terminals and edit their photo. The editing occurred using the Leap Motion controller (Weichert, 2013) (Sutton, 2013) (Vikram, 2013). It senses how one naturally moves his hands and lets the user use the computer using gestures. Visitors were capable of rotating the photos, adjusting their dimensions, applying filters (such as sepia, black and white, etc) and undoing their edits. All of this was possible without ever touching the computer, by simply applying gestures in thin air (Garber, 2013). This approach proved to be extremely interesting for both the children and the adults who made use of the system. In fact we have received a lot of positive feedback from the people who used it. When they were happy with the result, they simply posted it to their preferred social networking site such as Facebook (as they are accustomed to do according to (Winter, 2013)) where it was shared amongst their friends.

By going through the selfie walkthrough, the visitor will be able to exit the installation having contributed in a conscious and also experimental manner to the ever-popular art form of the self-portrait. A virtual gallery[2] was set up to document the project as well as exhibit the self-portraits. An exhibition of etchings from Heritage Malta[3]'s National Collection was also accompanying the project thus inspiring the young artists and also giving the project a local and historical context.

BACKGROUND

Art, even the art of fullest scope and widest vision, can never really show us the external world. All that it shows us is our own soul, the one world of which we have any real cognizance ... It is art, and art only, that reveals us to ourselves - Oscar Wilde

What sets the selfie and the self-portrait apart? What are the fundamental differences between the two? Whether carefully staged or totally spontaneous, the selfie has an *un-precious* quality about it. We do not think twice about throwing away a selfie which, for any odd reason we do not like, as we can always instantly take another. A selfie is impulsive, instinctive, casual and instantaneous, has little or no planning as regards its aesthetic, compositional or other artistic consideration, and is only meant as a frivolous and narcissistic testimony of temporal *I-am-ness* (de Mönnink, 2014). It is taken primarily in order to be distributed digitally through social media, making an impact on the way we look at ourselves and on the way we perform in public through our body language. Once uploaded, communicating to the world where we are and who we are with, we wait for feedback that is guaranteed to come from those we think are following and others who surprise us.

Selfies therefore are an independent communication and expressive genre, very different from the more systematic and structured self-portrait we are accustomed to in the visual arts. As in the genre of portraiture, they can incorporate a background landscape, activity or occurrence, in order to ground their context. There is no ulterior motive to this inclusion except to reassure the viewing followers of the fact that the "I have really been here" and the "I have really done this" has occurred. The selfie reconfirms one of the very original intentions of photography, that of acting as a proof of occurrence for the whole world to see. The original selfies do not undergo a post-processing operation. They are not normally digitally retouched or enhanced (Lin, 2014). What is caught by the portable device's camera will either make it to dissemination as is, or not at all as the image gets discarded. This is mainly due to the fact that the maxims that govern the aesthetics of works of art do not feature in this case. However recent technological advancements have made it easier to modify the selfie through the smartphone before posting it online.

The selfie has popularised the self-portraiture ilk and taken it away from the dominion of the artist. It hits front-page news when taken by a president, the pope or by a celebrity. Broadly speaking, it has even moved away from any art exhibition or gallery structure, which in many cases also necessitates attention to size, printing process, framing and other aesthetics normally associated with the art world, to reside permanently within different social structures in cyberspace. Its method of enjoyment is also different, less formal and more cursory. Unlike self-portraiture, the selfie bears no high-brow presumption. It carries no burden of figurative or metaphoric undertone and is therefore normally not at the centre of scholarly discourse, at least not just yet; and, totally oblivious of the art market is in no need of curatorial agency. The selfie has undoubtedly become today's most popular genre of self-expression.

This phenomenon has known its beginnings since the time artists first began to scrutinize their own images in the mirror. One notes that like the selfie, which is nearly always taken from within an arm's length of the subject and where the subject is photographed with one or both arms cropped out of the picture, in many a self-portrait, the artist paints himself/herself caught in the act of painting, with palette and brushes in hand.

Although historians have found remains of self-portraits that could be traced back to Ancient Egypt and Ancient Greece, with sculpture, being more durable than fresco or panel painting surviving in greater numbers, the earliest surviving self-portrait painting after Antiquity is thought to be *Man in a Red Turban* (1433), attributed to the Dutch painter Jan Van Eyck. With the emergence of easel painting and the popularity of oil painting on canvas, the self-portrait both as a distinct, formal category or as images of the artist inserted in other paintings, proliferated, particularly in countries such as Italy, France, the Netherlands, and Spain, during and after the Renaissance.

The self-portrait photograph is as old as the medium. Indeed the first ever recorded is believed to be the self-portrait of Robert Cornelius, a Philadelphia amateur chemist and photographer. This daguerreotype dates back to 1839 and Cornelius is known to have written on its back "The first light picture ever taken. 1839."[4] Throughout the history of photography, self-portraits have documented the often perturbed and troubled artists' inner self. Photographers such as Cindy Sherman (b. 1954), Francesca Woodman (1958 – 1981) and Nan Goldin (b. 1953) have explored disquieting themes in their self-portraits.

GESTURE-BASED INTERACTION

To make the selfie project easier for participants, we decided to make use of gesture-based interfaces, a recent addition to interaction paradigms (Dingli, 2015). The advantage of using these interfaces is that the user does not need to make use of a computer keyboard or mouse. This is particularly useful for small children who might not know how to read (Broaders, 2007; Höysniemi, 2005; Lee, 2005). However, the use of gestures makes it very easy for everyone to understand and the learning curve involved is very shallow.

To achieve this, we made us of the Leap-Motion controller (Vikram, 2013; Sutton, 2013). A contactless input device that can be attached to a computer via a USB connection. This device is accompanied by a special software that needs to be installed on the machine which is hosting the device. Users may interact with the machine by means of gestures that are detected by the Leap Motion Controller.

The Leap Motion controller is composed of 2 monochromatic depth cameras and 3 infrared LEDs (Weichert, 2013) that allow for gesture detection within a hemisphere of approximately 1m. 2D frames from each depth camera are then transmitted to the computer, which then processes the 3D position of the hands detected by the controller. This 3D mapping is then used to recognise gestures that would then be also linked to commands within the system that would be interpreted by third party software such as the image editor developed within the context of this project. The commands are various and include processes like changing filters, cropping images, etc.

Gestures

The Leap Motion controller allows for different gestures that can be recognised by the system. The most common gestures are the following presented in Figure 2.

The SDK (Spiegelmock, 2013; Seixas, 2015) allows for a reasonable access to position data within the 3D space that would therefore enable the developer to also capture new gestures. The versatility of this device is incredible when considering that the controller can detect more than 10 gestures together with a combination of them. Most of them are also rather intuitive. If one considers a Key Tap in thin air, its as if the user is pressing on a virtual keyboard. Same goes for a swipe, a push, etc.

Figure 2. Gestures supported by the Leap Motion controller
Source: http://carlosfernandezmusoles.blogspot.co.uk.

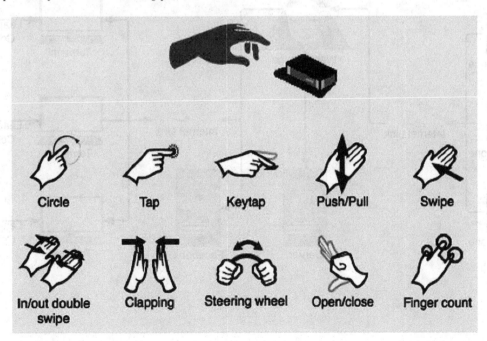

METHODOLOGY

Architecture

The main components of this system were the mobile application (that enables visitors to take selfies) and the image editing web application that enables the visitors to edit the photographs on a terminal, using the Leap-Motion Controller. This section will briefly explain the setup of the installation.

As illustrated in Figure 3, the selfie application running on the smart-phones would be able to send the photographs to a server where they would be temporarily stored. On the other hand, the terminals with the Leap Motion Controllers connected to them would also be connected to the same server. Through this connection, they connected the server and displayed the web application that allowed for photo editing. Each terminal would fetch the next available photograph and then the user can edit the image as explained below. Once the user is done editing the photographs on the terminals, the systems allows for posting the same selfie to the designated Facebook page.

Interaction Design

This section aims to outline the Interaction Design process that was undertaken to develop the software for this installation. The process started with a conceptual model that briefly explained the idea and developed into a conceptual design that included a Use-Case Diagram. This was followed by a selection of personas and related scenario that helped the development team reason about the various scenario possible.

Figure 3. Network diagram of the installation

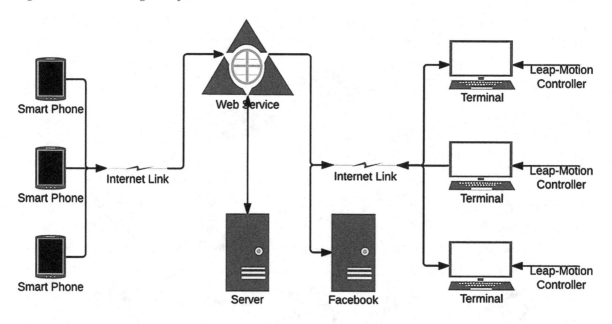

Conceptual Design

The installation required the user to take a selfie next to a replica of a piece of art and then be able to submit the selfie for editing. On a different device, the user would then be able to edit the photo by applying basic transformations and filters. Subsequently, the user would be able to submit the edited photo to a Facebook page that would act as a screen within the setup. Even though the steps might seem rather straight forward we have to be careful in order to satisfy the needs of the users keeping in mind that they were not restricted in any way. The system could cater for a single selfie or a group selfie. It could include playful interaction with the background or even with the cut-out of the artist. It could include close-ups or wide angle shots. Since we were dealing with young children, we also wanted to ensure that the system was easy to use with a very shallow learning curve. In fact the interaction on the mobile app was extremely minimalistic. The ushers present with the installation also mentioned this fact and declared that most of the children immediately understood how to use the app without having to go through any particular training.

The Use Case Diagram (UCD) of the artistic installation in question is presented in Figure 4. In this application, the user experiencing it would in theory assume 2 roles as presented below:

- **Selfie-Taker:** The stage when the user would use the mobile application to take the selfie and upload it for editing.
- **Editor:** The stage when the user can interact with the terminal to edit the selfie image prior to uploading on Facebook.

Figure 4. Use case diagram of the installation

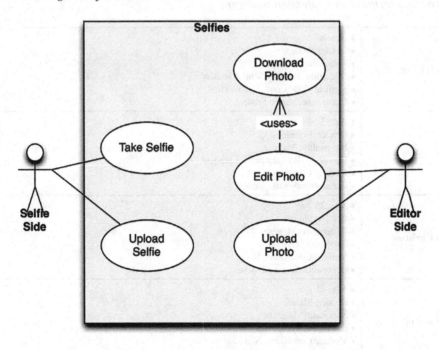

Each role requires a different interaction design process. The target audience of users were mostly children who would visit the arts festival. However, it was understood that students would also visit when accompanied by adults whom in practice would be either teachers or parents. Hence, the following personas were drawn during the requirements stage (Table 1).

These personas were used to prepare for different visitors and usage scenarios. From the initial focus groups that were organised, it resulted that the target user group would be mostly interested in the self-ies part. Children were more concerned about taking different photos of themselves rather than actually editing them and sharing them. On the other hand, there was a strong interest from older individuals who would accompany the children to actually get the photos edited and shared. There was also an appreciation of the technical exposure of image editing. In fact, the most promising part based on the initial feedback was the gesture based interface. Most of the participants declared that they have never used one of these interfaces; in fact, they didn't even know it was possible. Thus, they were very excited to try it out. Later in this chapter, we will outline the usability issues related to these preliminary observations.

Application Flow

The design of the user interface was organised in 2 parts; the design of the Selfie Mobile App which can be seen in Figure 5 and the design of the Image Editor.

The flow of the mobile application is presented in Figure 6. This was simplified in order to ensure that it can be used by practically all users. The only functionality available upon starting the app is to actually take a selfie. Once the photograph was taken, it can either be uploaded or the user may choose to take another one. The effect of the latter would be that of deleting the original selfie and take a new one.

Table 1. Personas describing our intended audience

Persona 1: Peter	• Age: 8 • Gender: Male • Nationality: Maltese • Education: Primary School Student • Medical Conditions: Colour-blind • Occupation/Status: Student
Persona 2: Faye	• Age: 7 • Gender: Female • Nationality: Maltese • Education: Primary School Student • Medical Conditions: NA • Occupation/Status: Student
Persona 3: Christine	• Age: 25 • Gender: Female • Nationality: Maltese • Education: Tertiary • Medical Conditions: NA • Occupation/Status: Teacher
Persona 4: Paul	• Age: 61 • Gender: Male • Nationality: Maltese • Education: Vocational • Medical Conditions: Sight issues • Occupation/Status: Grandparent

Figure 5.

Figure 6. Flowchart of the selfie mobile app

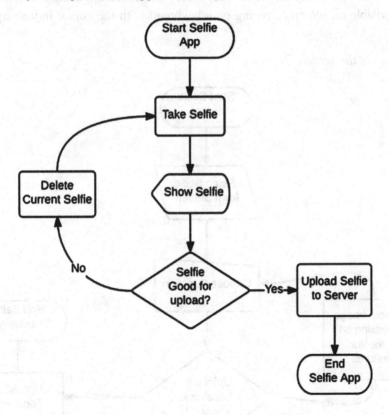

Similarly, on the terminals hosting the editors, the users were presented with a simplified solution that facilitates the editing of selfies taken in the previous stage. The flow is illustrated in Figure 7. The selfie editing software was designed to automatically fetch images from the server in order to minimise the interventions required by the user. In fact, users simply sit down and start editing the photograph. The system offers a selection of filters and transformations. The five filters available are Grey scale, Sepia, Brightness adjustment, Blurring or Sharpening and Embossing. Apart from these, the user can also adjust the width and the height of the photo. The only other interaction required by the user is to decide when to post the selfie to the Facebook page after the modifications have been applied.

User Interface

As discussed in the previous section, the user interface was kept as simple as possible. Figure 8 shows the screen shot of the system. In the middle, the user is greeted with the photo, which was just taken. This photo was sent to the server through the mobile app and placed in a queue. When one of the six editing terminals becomes available, the picture is automatically loaded and the user who took it sits down in order to start editing it. On the left hand side, we can see a menu made up of the 5 filters mentioned earlier and the two width or height adjustments. The last button is the actual Facebook button, which allows the user to post the image directly. On the right hand side, we find a description pane. This pane is extremely important to provide feedback to the user. One has to keep in mind that in gesture-based interfaces, the user is not given any feedback. This is very different from using a mouse where the mouse pointer is clearly visible on screen or typing on a keyboard with the cursor indicating the position on

Figure 7. Flowchart of the selfie editor

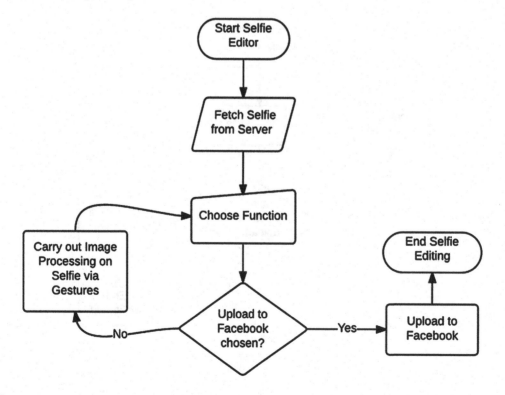

screen. Because of this, it is very important to provide some sort of reference to the user as indicated in (Manresa, 2005). There are various ways in which we can provide this feedback. It can be made up of simple circles when the hand enters the field of view of the sensor or something more elaborate, like in our case, where the hands were shown as virtual skeletons (See Figure 8) thus giving the user a clear and real-time indication of what he is doing. Even though most of the users were young, the feedback we received was extremely positive. It is clear that our analysis prior to implementing it helped us create an interface which was easy to use yet powerful enough to perform the manipulations necessary.

EVALUATION

To evaluate the system as a whole, we decided to record every step individually. Each phase was then analyzed in order to extract the most relevant information for the project. The evaluation took place between the 17th and 24th November during ŻiguŻajg, the National Children's festival. The majority of the participants during the week were school children that participated in school outings to the festival. In the weekend, most of the children were accompanied by their parents. In total, 974 people participated in our project. The real value is much higher but these 974 individuals were those who accepted to be recorded in this study. The average rate amounts to around 120 individuals per day. The system was divided into three phases and we will examine all the phases in the following subsections namely: the transformation phase, the selfie phase and the manipulation phase.

Figure 8. Screenshot of the selfie editor

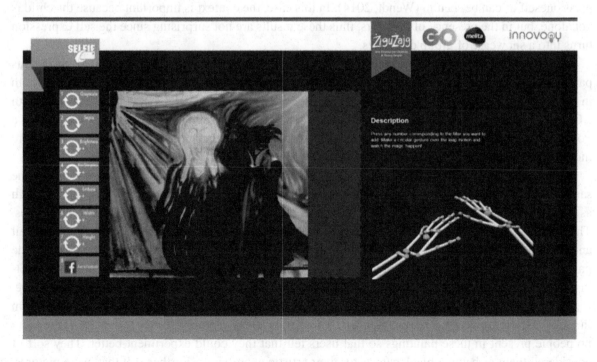

The Transformation Phase

The children who visited the installation where first invited to make use of various props in order to express themselves. This is something very common with children since they like to dress up and role-play as can be seen in (Fron, 2007) and (Stone, 1990). Play especially in groups is extremely important in children because it can help them move away from their egocentricity (Vygotsky, 2012) whilst learning to share, negotiate and gather new perspectives (Piaget, 1962). It is important to keep in mind that most of the visits happened during school days, which means that the students were restricted with their uniform. However there were a couple of days during the weekend where this restriction did not exist. The children could choose between various props which included wigs, masks, pieces of cloths, vests, bras, hats, fans, glasses, plastic toys (such as flowers, arms, cleaning utensils, etc), umbrellas, musical instruments, shirts, tiaras and veils. Most of the participants decided to change their appearance in various ways and very few opted out from this phase. The modifications were various and they reflected the creativity of the children. Furthermore, as can be seen in (Prinstein, 2008), the effect of the social context can be easily noticed since children in particular social dynamics exhibited similar choices. Even though this topic is extremely interesting, it is beyond the scope of this document.

The Selfie Phase

During the Selfie phase, the children were given a smartphone and asked to take a Selfie. It was noticed that on average, 1.7 people appeared in the photo. This means that most of the photos were actually social expressions within the context of a group since most of the users decided to take a photo with someone else. This is rather understandable when one considers that the main scope of a selfie is to express oneself as can be seen in (Wendt, 2014). In this case, the context is important because the child is not alone, but in the presence of his peers, thus these results are not surprising since the self expression turns into a showcase of group dynamics.

It is important to remember that for this experiment we setup six small sets, inspired by famous paintings which were also provided as a backdrop. These backdrops included, Van Gogh's "Bedroom in Arles" 1888, Munch's "The Scream" 1893, Monet's "Water Lilies" 1916, Cezanne's "Still Life with a Ginger Jar and Eggplants" 1890, Gauguin's "Tahitian pastorale" 1898 and Modigliani's "Portrait of a Polish Woman" 1919. The children were free to use whichever set they preferred and their choices were those recorded in Figure 9.

It is interesting to analyse the choices of these users. Behind them, other blown-up paintings by the same artists provided backdrops for the selfies, in that, for example, if a child selected Vincent van Gogh as his or her buddy, s/he would take the selfie with the background of van Gogh's Bedroom in Arles. This setup, placed the student in the context of van Gogh's world, positioned in between his self-portrait and one of his iconic paintings. The space between the self-portrait cutout and the backdrop image of the painting was calculated bearing in mind the angle of width of the smart phone's lens, in that overshooting was eliminated through restricting the space between the artist's cutout and the background image.

In our case, the overwhelming choice fell on two, Monet's "Water Lilies" and Van Gogh's "Bedroom in Arles". There are various reasons for this. These were the two empty scenes available. There were no people present in these paintings so that users felt that they could experiment better. They sort of considered them as being a blank canvas for their artistic expressions. Further still they were pictures, which they could probably relate to easily (French, 1952). Van Gogh's painting was less popular than

Figure 9. Choice of photos taken

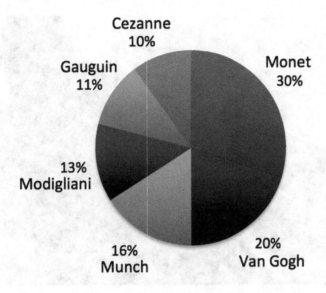

Monet's painting because there was an issue of perspective. The backdrop was higher than the subject of the photo so it was very difficult to get the perspective right. Munch's painting was also quite popular, however some children found it intimidating and the drawing of a person screaming in the scene meant that they did not have the freedom given to them the other two paintings. The other three paintings were substantially less popular with the children. Modigliani's portrait of a polish woman is quite imposing and disproportionate thus making it hard for the children to find an adequate pose. Gauguin's work and Cezanne's still life were rather complex involving many different figures. Thus, it is clear that the children opted for backdrops, which gave them the most freedom.

The Manipulation Phase

The manipulation of a selfie can be interpreted as akin to Flusser's definition of simulation (Flusser, 1990), whereby he considers it as being an exaggeration of a few aspects whilst disregarding other aspects. In fact this proved to be the least popular part with children. They enjoyed using the leap motion controller and applying gestures. The system provided good feedback as per Norman's principles (Norman, 2002) of design by returning a modified images right after a gesture. Help and documentation as per Neilsen's Heuristics (Nielsen, 1995) was also provided in the user interface as demonstrated above. Furthermore, a visualisation tool for the effective use of the leap controller was also employed as shown in Figure 10 to ensure that users can take good command of the system.

Having said that, from the initial experiments prior to the final launch of the installation, it resulted that users were finding it difficult to master a variety of gestures in such a way that would enable them to freely carry out photo editing operations without using other controllers. From these experiments and focus groups, it also resulted that few had the opportunity to try the Leap Motion controller beforehand. With the majority seeing this controller for the first time, it was eventually decided that the system would only capture simple circles gestures in clockwise and anti-clockwise directions.

Figure 10. Children using the training visualisation (left) and editing selfies prior to upload (right)

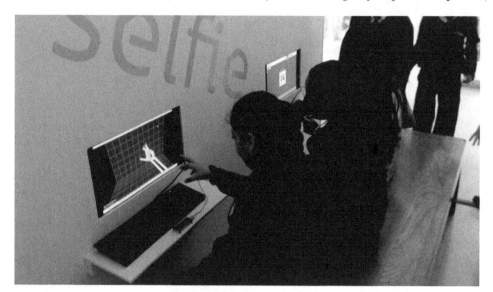

Technical Issues

The majority of the technical issues experienced were mostly related to the Internet connection of devices. This hindered the image editing functionality since it heavily depended on the Internet connection in order to guarantee the user experience discussed in other sections of this chapter. When children were taking selfies, it was clear that they were enjoying the holistic experience of trying different outfits and posing with the figures in questions (Figure 11).

Figure 11. Participants taking photos with artists' figures and back-scene

It was also clear that the mobile application was intuitive and easy to use. However, due to the costumes and the number of students visiting at any point in time, it was often observed that instead of using the mobile device for selfies, children and guardians were ultimately taking photos with each other's phone (rather than using the one provided by us). When interviewed about this behaviour, respondents explained that they found it difficult to take proper selfies while wearing costumes and trying to include the artists' figures and the back scene.

CONCLUSION

Overall we were very pleased with the results obtained. In fact, Selfie was one of the most sought after events in ŻiguŻajg 2014. In this paper we presented the underlying architecture while also analyzing the inputs obtained from the participants. In total we received around 120 visitors every day and collected information about their interaction with the system (which amounts to around 500 hours). We had a look at their choices, analysed them as they go through this particular walkthrough and we tried to understand their decisions.

Apart from the analysis part, we also hoped that this experiment made a difference in the life of our participants. Through this experiment, we wanted to help audiences become aware that the self-portrait is not only a product of our times but that it has been around for hundreds of years. In fact, all the artists chosen had created their own self-portrait. We also wanted that this experience presents different realities within the same image, whereby participants will not only be taking the self-portrait but will also undergo the experience of physical transformation in a real and virtual environment, questioning the issue of reality in today's technological world.

ACKNOWLEDGMENT

This project would not have been possible without the support of ŻiguŻajg, the National Children's festival. The team would also like to show its appreciation to the two main Mobile Service providers in Malta, Go[5] and Melita[6] for supplying the devices, which were used by the users during the implementation, and testing of the system. We would also like thank Innovogy Ltd for the consultancy provided with regards to the technical aspects, in particular Mr Aldrin Seychell and Mr Mark Bugeja.

REFERENCES

Bonafoux, P. (1985). *Portraits of the artist: the self-portrait in painting*. Rizzoli Intl Publishers.

Broaders, S. C.-M., Cook, S. W., Mitchell, Z., & Goldin-Meadow, S. (2007). Making children gesture brings out implicit knowledge and leads to learning. *Journal of Experimental Psychology*, *136*(4), 539–550. doi:10.1037/0096-3445.136.4.539 PMID:17999569

de Mönnink, M. I. (2014). *Inhabiting the border-A Cultural History of Privacy & Photography*. Academic Press.

Dingli, A. (2015). *The New Digital Natives: Cutting the Chord.* Springer. doi:10.1007/978-3-662-46590-5

Flusser, V. (1990). On Memory (Electronic or Otherwise). *Leonardo, 23*(4), 397. doi:10.2307/1575342

French, J. E. (1952). Children's preferences for pictures of varied complexity of pictorial pattern. *The Elementary School Journal, 53*(2), 90–95. doi:10.1086/459405

Fron, J. F. (2007). Playing dress-up: Costumes, roleplay and imagination. *Philosophy of Computer Games.*

Garber, L. (2013). Gestural technology: Moving interfaces in a new direction. *Computer, 46*(10), 22–25. doi:10.1109/MC.2013.352

Höysniemi, J. H. (2005). Children's intuitive gestures in vision-based action games. *Communications.*

Lawrence-Lightfoot, S. (1997). *The art and science of portraiture.* San Francisco: Jossey-Bass.

Lee, S. H. (2005). A gesture-based American Sign Language game for deaf children. *CHI'05 Extended Abstracts on Human Factors in Computing Systems.* ACM.

Lin, H. W. (2014). Selfie Quality Assessment Based on Angle. *IPPR Conference on Computer Vision, Graphics, and Image Processing.* Academic Press.

Manresa, C. P. (2005). Hand tracking and gesture recognition for human-computer interaction. *ELCVIA. Electronic Letters on Computer Vision and Image Analysis.*

Nielsen, J. (1995). Usability inspection methods. *Conference companion on Human factors in computing systems.* Academic Press.

Norman, D. A. (2002). *The design of everyday things.* Basic Books.

Piaget, J. (1962). *Play, dreams and imitation in childhood.* New York: Norton.

Prinstein, M. J. (2008). *Understanding peer influence in children and adolescents.* Guilford Press.

Seixas, M. C. (2015). *The Leap Motion Movement for 2D Pointing Tasks: Characterisation and Comparison to Other Devices.* Academic Press.

Senft, T. M. (2015). Selfies Introduction~ What Does the Selfie Say? Investigating a Global Phenomenon. *International Journal of Communication.*

Spiegelmock, M. (2013). *Leap Motion Development Essentials.* Packt Publishing Ltd.

Stone, G. P. (1990). Appearance and the self: A slightly revised version. In *Life as theater: A dramaturgical sourcebook.* Academic Press.

Sutton, J. (2013). *Air painting with Corel Painter Freestyle and the leap motion controller: a revolutionary new way to paint!.* ACM. doi:10.1145/2503673.2503694

Vikram, S. L. (2013). *Handwriting and Gestures in the Air, Recognizing on the Fly.* CHI.

Vygotsky, L. E. (2012). *Thought and language.* MIT Press.

Weichert, F. B., Bachmann, D., Rudak, B., & Fisseler, D. (2013). Analysis of the accuracy and robustness of the leap motion controller. *Sensors (Basel, Switzerland)*, *13*(5), 6380–6393. doi:10.3390/s130506380 PMID:23673678

Wendt, B. (2014). *The allure of the selfie: Instagram and the new self-portrait*. Academic Press.

Winter, J. (2013). *Selfie-loathing*. Slate.

ENDNOTES

[1]   http://www.ziguzajg.org
[2]   https://www.facebook.com/ziguzajgselfie
[3]   http://heritagemalta.org
[4]   http://loc.gov/pictures/resource/cph.3g05001/
[5]   https://www.go.com.mt
[6]   http://www.melita.com

Chapter 11
Triggering the Flotsam of Behavior:
A Technique for Applying Computation to Musicality

Judson Wright
Pump Orgin, USA

ABSTRACT

As computer artists, we might ask: can the computer serve as the artist or a proxy thereof? There seems no possible conclusive answer to this. Rather, we approach this question from a different angle: Why do humans make artifacts/praxis, which might be experienced by conspecifics as art (e.g. visual art, music, dance)? To investigate this subtle issue, computer technology provides an important tool for artist-engineers, namely allowing programmatic integration of audio analysis and visual graphic animation. We initially discuss the history and problems of the role of an intuitive model of cognition, in the pursuit of an automated means of the synthesis of intelligence, versus what has been learned about organic brains. This comparison, while somewhat critical of empiricism, is meant to zero in on the cognitive function of art for humans, as an evolutionary adaptation. We are thus lead to an alternative programming paradigm regarding art's very particular but crucial role for our species.

INTRODUCTION

In this paper, we present a novel approach to using the computer as a tool in art. This approach is informed by taking a deeper look into what computers actually do, at the technical level below the interface that we see on the screen (Nissan & Schocken, 2005) and what human[1] brains actually do, when that brain is expecting to experience art (Stecker, 2000). Compare "human readable code" (e,g, C++, Python, HTML) to binary (e.g. high/low voltages represented by humans as a long list of 1's/0's). Noting these differences has lead us to think about meaning, communication/messaging, and a theory about the role of art, relative to *Homo sapiens.*

DOI: 10.4018/978-1-5225-0016-2.ch011

In fields concerned with communication from an epistemological level (e.g. primatologists studying language learning apes), though not to answer this issue philosophically, *theory of mind* (ToM) is considered intrinsic to communication, profoundly distinct from *signaling* (e.g. barking, ornate plumage, or electrical circuits and network pinging). This theory further differs from a traditional, aesthetic art-for-art's-sake practice, mutated somewhat in recent decades to accommodate a techno-aesthetic (see also the attribution of mystical qualities to novel technologies, in Marvin, 1988; Nadis, 2005). Though isolated fields may harbor conclusions about these three topics within respective domains, conflicting views are certain to arise. We must be careful to take an ever-more inclusive approach (termed *conceptual integration* in Tooby & Cosmides, 1992) that does not seek to select a single best scientific law to explain some event from a competitive pool, nor a compromise of laws, but a continuous effort of integrating laws from a widening vista[2].

We discuss a categorizing scheme we will call the *flotsam of behavior* (FoB), as in the remanence after the fact, that remains "floating on the surface." This scheme is comprised of two dimensions, continuums between artifact (e.g. a tangible tool: for instance, a book) and praxis (e.g. an act: as when Catholics sometimes rapidly cross themselves, as a quick blessing in response to tragedy), meaningful and chaotic. Surely many readers will already come to this with a comfortably complete notion of "art," which we do not claim to be able to predict nor debunk. Nonetheless, in practice, we would guess that most people usually make a fairly boolean (true/false) distinction between objects deemed art-objects and those that are not.

To clarify, of course, in ambiguous cases, this decision may waver back and forth, but it probably rarely makes sense to say something is "partially art." In fact, we need not assume "art" is a distinction made of groups of stimuli describing anything real, so much as all "art" is defined here only as an FoB, though not the reverse. Instances of art are then readily located within this FoB space. A dance might be part of a ritual, performed for communication with spirits, and might be deemed religious. Though the very same dance, performed in the same context, observed by a modern curator might seem artistic. The creativity, expression, or intention is of no matter here. There is no conflict between these two interpretations, so long as we decide that the locus within the FoB is not intrinsic to the instance, but describes only how that instance is understood, whether by the composer, performer or observer.

Within strictly confined environments, with a myriad of implicit programmatic assumptions about the physical laws to be expected of these environments, AI[3] has yielded abundant functional successes (i.e. an expected feature consistently identified). Nonetheless, it remains speculative whether or not "intelligence" has truly been synthesized (for example syntactical rules, in Fitch & Friederici, 2012; or for music theory in Lerdahl, 1992) —the problem of a strict definition of intelligence notwithstanding. The technique we discuss here is an alternative approach to how the computer might be employed, to instigate the experience of experiencing art in the minds of audience members. Moreover, we describe how the by-product of this technique, the output of art-as-software, can be employed toward a testing paradigm.

When examining art, people often discuss aesthetics as existing externally to humans, having a concrete effect on minds (compare the reasonable quantification of proximal causes of proximal results in Etcoff, 2000; to the dubious quantification of distal causes of proximal results, in Himonides, 2009). Despite the countless literature discussing aesthetics, these documents merely describe a subjective experience. Not that aesthetics cannot exist, but it is not apparent—perhaps to anyone—how a nonhuman, such as a computer, might attend to this feature, one without any defined concrete properties. Rather than rejecting all art referring to aesthetics, we take an anthropological approach to "the art world"[4]. We must not remain removed observers of exotic superstitions, but as active participants in the ritualistic life of the given tribe (discussed further in Wright, 2012). The alternative paradigm suggested here (illustrated for computing in Figure 1 a-c) is not the product of a quest for novelty, but a corollary of our understanding of the evolutionary psychological issue at hand (Greve, 2012).

EVOLUTION FIRST

At first glance, it might be tempting to believe that our proposal for a genetic predisposition for art-ness is akin to an "art instinct" (as in the popular notion in Dutton, 2009). What Denis Dutton has in mind though, is more about aesthetics (see also *neuroaesthetics* in Gallese and Di Dio, 2012; and art as crucial, but non-adaptive in Pinker, 1997: Ch. 8). Though surely many readers might wonder "What else could there be to art?" We have something very un-aesthetic in mind. Firstly, it would be hard to justify aesthetics from as benefitting fitness, and thus being genetic. Dutton provides only one chapter toward, what we consider to be, the main issue, and hardly provides a strong link between fitness and aesthetics. On one hand he says:

The arts, for instance, are commonly thought to be good for us in any number of ways, giving us a sense of well-being or feeling of comfort... Art may offer consolation in times of life crises, it may soothe the nerves, or it may produce a beneficial catharsis, a purging of emotions that clears the mind and edifies the soul. Even if all these claims were true, they could not by themselves validate a Darwinian explanation of the arts, unless they could somehow be connected with survival and reproduction. (pp. 86–87)

... with which we enthusiastically agree. But then he goes on to say, "... a Darwinian aesthetics will achieve explanatory power neither by proving that art forms are adaptations nor by dismissing them as by-products but by showing how their existence and character are connected to Pleistocene interests, preferences, and capacities." (p. 96).

While he intentionally describes aesthetics in prosaic language, and avoids formal definition—which is quite reasonable considering aesthetics is often conceived as contrary to formal discourse, he shuts himself off from giving a formalized explanation of an adaptation (or even *spandrel*) as a mechanism of fitness. Nonetheless, by discarding "aesthetics," we can still talk about why people seek out a peculiar type of transcendent (to themselves) experience, regardless of whether such an experience is real or illusive. Once we disregard this thorny subjective notion, much of what he describes fits well enough with our point—so long as no one makes the claim that (given a well-enough trained appreciate-r) special instances of art are intrinsically and/or universally beautiful or exciting.

If you look over a wide range of group experiences, today and through history, there are clear associations between artistic activities and social life... Sacred music in religious services is for many people extremely moving, while on a different level there is a thrill to be found in the synchronized expressive dancing of a corps de ballet... I have studied and engaged in sing-sings—continuous rhythmic singing and dancing through the night—in New Guinea jungles and have looked in on raves of the kind that became popular in Europe and America in the 1990s. It is a serious understatement to describe these events as merely similar: they are, so far as I can tell, exactly the same activity... (p. 223)

Figure 1. In the orthodox (a) and parallel distributed processing (PDP) (b) schemes, note that it is assumed that meaning precedes experience. Note also both assume plans (a technical term in AI). We take the opposite stance (c), to see where this counter-proposal, that experience causes meaning, might lead. As a result of this assumption, the computer output (imbued with meaning) of the orthodox and PDP schemes is often considered an end itself. Whereas in our scheme, the output is not a "precious" by-product, and the meaning—or rather, experience thereof— is the end. Though Behaviorism, which actively put inaccessible mentation, was finally discarded, we face a similar challenge. The fact that meaning is ordinarily an inaccessible mental process requires us to use more indirect methods.

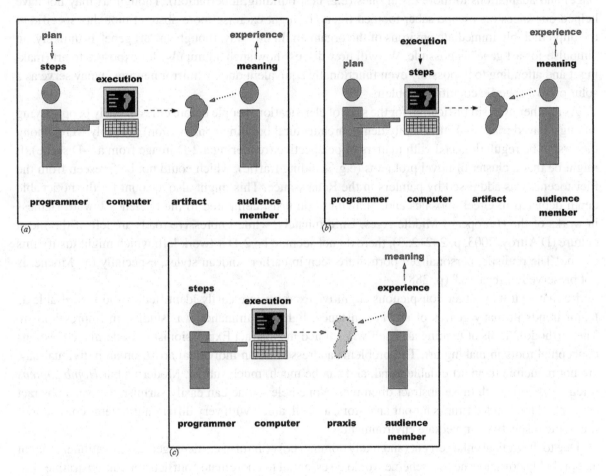

It is essential to understand how art need not occur merely in order that we, as artists and audience members, enjoy it. As we cannot verify art occurs outside of *Homo sapiens*, whatever causes art may be something related to the human phenotype. And thus we first, before going further with any theory of involving a biological scheme such as cognition, must look to evolution.

Fitness

What possible role art could serve toward either survival or procreation? Here we point out a subtle nuance of evolutionary theory (which Dutton seems to overlook). A mutated gene, and thus not a novel as adaptation, but an incremental variant, has at least some chance of being passed on if the organism is not killed before mating. A slightly silly argument could be made that rock 'n' roll promoted sex in teens, so perhaps the cave paintings in Lascaux could be seen as the site of a prehistoric concert, complete with young, lust-induced groupies. Thus art would have a role in evolution. But this hypothesis would probably not stand up to a range of comparisons across various cultures and eras—much less be worth the effort. But the point remains. This leaves us with the other option, perhaps art plays a role in survival. But surviving involves both adaptations to more proximal encounters (e.g. claws, camouflage) and adaptations to more distal ones (e.g. nest building, hibernation). Though art may not have helped our ancestors escape saber-toothed tigers, it might exercise more abstract thoughts specific to the unpredictable immediate environs of the organism. In this way, though an "art gene" is unlikely, an "impulse-for-art gene" is possible. We will now discuss how such an impulse for exposure to art (making it and attending to it, possibly even functionally equivalent due to "mirror neurons") may serve as a solution to a specific cognitive problem.

As another over-simplification for the sake of clarification, people before cities, namely people living amongst paved roads and sufficiently dense, architectural building construction) probably were among the first to be regularly faced with matters of perspective (rendering a 2-D image from a 3-D scene). It might be that a cluster of novel problems (e.g. avoiding traffic), which could not be foreseen from the Pleistocene, was addressed by painters in the Renaissance. This might also account for the noticeable depth depicted in Greek mosaics and "drawings" on urns, compared to the tendency toward flatness in works of the (European) Middle Ages. Unfortunately, while impressive roads are left of the Incan culture (D'Altroy, 2003, p. 242–253), there do not seem to be 2-D artwork left, which might justify this claim. "The realistic, personalized portraiture seen in earlier Andean styles, especially the Moche, is not preserved in Inca art." (p. 288)

Be that as it may, other conspicuous cognitive exercises are easily identified in and identifiable as major trends in many genres of art. For instance, lighting/luminance was studied in Impressionism. The (orthodox) tools of making art itself was studied in Abstract Expressionism. Modernism questions conceptual tools in making art. The problems addressed by an individual artist, on an individual day, are not reducible to an articulable trend, and can be much, much subtler. Modern adult *Homo sapiens* often need cope with these abstract dilemmas. Nonetheless, one can easily surmise that such abstract conceptual tools aided fitness for our ancestors, as well, albeit with very different problems corresponding to the respective, immediate environment.

Due to the radical enlargement (and likely dominance) of human cortices, generating rational thought and probably consciousness, a scheme would be essential to coordinate conflicts for administrative control between the faster but less precise paleoencephalon (old brain) of most other animals and slower but more precise neocortex (new brain) (Hawkins, 2005: 98–105). Art would serve this amygdala-like function well (as in the scheme by LeDoux, 1998: 161–165; Pessoa and Adolphs, 2010), but be flexible enough to detect abstract issues present in a flux environment. We have previously written about the cognitive role of art (Wright, 2014b), specifically concerning the development of brain in human children (Wright, 2014a). *Homo sapiens* are peculiar in that we tend to spend years longer (whether or not accounting proportionately for our expected lifespan—something genes are unlikely to consider) rearing the young, ostensibly during and promoting development (Bjorklund & Pellegrini, 2001:127–132). Art serves as a means to consider very culturally specific concepts that matter locally, but would not occur spontaneously in nature.

Why Might There Need to Be a Mechanism at All?

Attribution theory describes an anthropomorphic interpretation where animated abstract figures adopt personality traits. In Fritz Heider and Mary-Ann Simmel's experiment (1944) subjects were shown a short film of animated simple geometric shapes. Afterwards, the vast majority of audience members described the events in the film in rather social terms, attributing personalities to the various shapes. Subjects spoke as if the triangles had been interacting with one another, had goals, motives, and morality. Of course when pressed, subjects intellectually knew that these shapes were not living things. Nonetheless, it appeared quite natural for them to refer to animations in this anthropomorphized way. Furthermore, such descriptions are quite readily understood by others, without questioning the underlying validity. To what exactly are the subjects attending?

The issue was clarified somewhat years later, when a subject spontaneously described the action on the screen only literally, as moving shapes and lines. One might predict such a description would come from an observer with a degree of autism (see also Ardizi et al, 2013), as if this subject was somehow deficient in recognizing the shapes' life-like behavior. However, the subject was well able to process and recognize social cues, though suffered a rare lesion in the amygdala, which prevented normal effects of attribution (Heberlein & Adolphs, 2004). Whether the stimuli are visible shapes or meaningful words, communication can therefore be considered the process by which we believe sensations to be organized sensibly, projecting whatever significance necessary from our own private minds.

At this point we recall Niko Tinbergen's classic *four why*'s for ethology (1963): why is some adaptation useful to the organism; why does the organ work in this way mechanically; why might it evolve in the species from natural selection; and why would the genes for this be expressed individual organisms? We might ask more specifically, as reverse-engineers: Why would the brain bother, likely only in the rare instance of one particular organism and not others, to create such complexities as selfhood and language use (Fitch, Hauser, & Chomsky, 2005; cf. Hauser, 1998)? Responding to the general tenor of Tinbergen's perspective, we note behavioral tendencies in our species appear due to idiosyncratic neural mechanisms[5].

We obviously have much bigger brains, comprised of many more cells, than "social" insects—or even the combined mass of a colony of them. However, so do the brains of our nearest relative, the chimpanzee, who do not appear capable of the same social dynamics. While the organization colony members' behaviors are easily attributed to innate social-ness, these behaviors can more parsimoniously be explained otherwise (Gordon, 1999: 141–147; Grüter, 2011; see also *altruism* in nonhuman animals, in Gadagkar, 1997). Any social[6] aspect we might interpret from it would ultimately be a projection of gestalt. This is why we say "Evolution First." Nonetheless, this leads us to question, given millions of years to evolve, much longer than the evolution of humans from other primates, why might all species of insects still require so little brain?

An answer to this paradox is provided by Sarah Shettleworth (1998: 380–381) is that brains are the size they are given the needs and resources available to the given organism. More (neurons and connections) is not better. In any species we might consider, a significantly larger brain or one allowing greater modification, requiring significantly more caloric intake and/or a longer juvenile period, would be dangerously maladaptive (Deacon, 1997: Ch. 5; Wiener et al, 2011). A larger brain is not automatically smarter! Software would not be more brain-like by adding more (temporary and/or working) memory slots. There can be no optimal design (*architecture* in AI terms) for a medium of intelligence that is not relative to the symbiotic relationship between the organism and what that organism interprets as its environment (see also a like human developmental issue in Sfard, 2008: 69–73).

A Proposed Role of Communication

Lev Vygotsky and others have noted egocentric speech, where the child passes through a developmental stage, concretizing the abstract thought process, a step that is conspicuously absent from automated computation.

[A] four-and-a-half-year-old girl was to get candy from a cupboard with a stool and a stick as possible tools. [The] description reads as follows: (Stands on a stool, quietly looking, feeling along shelf with stick.) 'On the stool.' Glances at experimenter. Puts stick in other hand.) 'Is that really the candy?' (Hesitates.) 'I can get it from that other stool, stand and get it.' (Gets second stool.) 'No, that doesn't get it. I could use the stick.' (Takes the stick and knocks at the candy.) 'It will move now.' (Knocks candy.) It moved, I couldn't get it with the stool, but the stick worked.' In such cases it seems both natural and necessary for children to speak while they act; in our research we have found that speech not only accompanies practical activity but also plays a specific role in carrying it out. (Vygotsky 1978: 25, see also Piaget, 1962)

There is no obvious method allowing a machine to detect intelligent composition in communication. By neither being methodical, consistent, nor algorithmic, such detection (as outlined in a *global workspace* model [Shanahan and Baars, 2005]) is unlikely to ever be formalizable in code, necessarily static and executed sequentially (Wright, 2013a). Furthermore, no Turing machine can administer a Turing test, and no entity can administer a Turing test on itself (1936; see also Koch & Tonini, 2001), an essential requirement famously pointed out by Kurt Gödel [1962; Copeland & Shagrir, 2013] regarding mathematics and empirical data. More likely a philosophical point attributable to Heidegger, this can now be applied more generally to distinguish messaging behaviors such as (passive) alarm calls (Cheney, 1984; Harris, 1984) from (active) communication (Ackernan & Bargh, 2010; Bavelas et al, 2011). Notwithstanding, these limitations are also the computer's strengths (Wright, 2015).

All the definitions I was able to locate in dictionaries or in professional literature present communication as an activity of two individuals, often called sender and recipient, who are said to exchange or pass information, messages, thoughts, feelings, or meaning. For at least two reasons, this kind of description is inappropriate for our purposes. First, together with the metaphor of object clearly underlying the idea of communication as the activity of passing or transmitting arrive all the risks and pitfalls of this metaphor. Above all, the definition remains nonoperational as long as the entities to be passed—message, thought, feeling, meaning—are not, themselves, operationally defined. Second, the pair of communicating individuals is implied to constitute a closed system, whose activity depends on just these two actors. This stubbornly individualist, acquisitionalist slant of the traditional definition is rather striking, considering the fact that the communal nature of communication is implied by its very name. (emphasis in original, Sfard, 2008: 85)

Consider Tinbergen's four why's again (1963). Specifically, how might language beyond signaling benefit us as a specie? We may all-too-easily note post hoc benefits of language, but clearly all other organisms have existed for billions of years without it. Why would it only be essential to *Homo sapiens*?

Whatever it is in stimuli that humans identify as indicating a sensible message, rather than indicating chaos, that feature is not obviously detectable by machines. So it probably would not be encodable in genes, nor fixed in the neuroanatomy of ancestral vertebrates.

In an experiment on the correlates of consciousness, the general procedure is to measure consciousness, measure the physical world and look for a relationship between these measurements. The measurement of consciousness relies on the working assumption that consciousness is a real phenomenon that can be reported verbally ("I see a red hat", "I taste stale milk") or through other behaviour, such as pushing a button, pulling a lever, ... The assumption that consciousness can be measured through behaviour enables us to obtain data about it without a precise definition. However, this reliance on external behaviour limits consciousness experiments to systems that are commonly agreed to be conscious, such as a human or a human-like animal. It is not possible to carry out this type of experiment on non-biological systems, such as computers, because a computer's reports are not generally regarded as a measurement of consciousness. (Gamez, 2014, p 150)

In other words, quantifying FoB may prove oxymoronic, as human behaviors (and not necessarily *schemas* or *plans*) are hardly (exclusively) methodical, consistent, nor algorithmic. Nonetheless, these same formal limitations allow us to create detailed instruction sets for the computer, as code. In David Gamez's quote, computers should not be sufficient for studying FoB. Ignoring how computers "should" be used, available tools exist which allow us to probe a question central to FoB: which sensations do listeners decide are noise, and which are deemed music. While the audio scene in a subway station would usually be described as noise, pitches performed live by an orchestra are typically considered musical—regardless of familiarity with the foreign culture (Cohen, 2006). But in more ambiguous cases, how is that distinction made, and why?

Converting Chaos into Meaning

A genetic impulse for art would have important fitness value. But how/why/by what mechanism, might *Homo sapiens* detect art-ness (a compound, multimodal problem discussed in Wright, 2012; see also Austin, 2010)? Without any clear, physical property, we believe art-ness must be projected, as we project *qualia* onto other phenomenal experiences. Red does not exist "out there." But there is a good evolutionary reason for insects and vegetation-eating animals to project the sensation, or rather inject this feature onto our own personal mental rendition of the world we call the Cartesian theater, "in here." What makes an object art? Like colors, the object may satisfy some biological trigger, as in the quote below.

Flowers display their beautiful colours which give pleasure to us, however they are not made for us, but for flying insects. Those insects involuntarily fertilize plants carrying pollen from flower to flower... So some plants evolved to attract insects and in that way plants reproduce and continue living on the planet Earth. So insects evolved to distinguish flowers among the whole electromagnetic radiation that gets to their eyes coming from the Earth's surface, as patches of definite colours. Thus, eyes have appeared and evolved as a filter for those chains of events ... For instance, electromagnetic radiations are filtered by eyes, in chains which end at perceptions we call colours. But if the radiation wavelength is in the ultraviolet zone, some insects will see it, but in our case we will not (Herrero, 2005; For a further explanation "Why are there colors?," see Dennett, 1991: 375–383)

Stimuli come to us in an overwhelming wave of undifferentiated chaos, which we impulsively group into foreground, demanding attention, and background, safely generalizable (like wallpaper, in Dennett, 1991: 354–360; see also Gregory & Ramachandran, 1991). Importantly, before we identify an instance of a FoB as aesthetically interesting, we first must group stimuli such that we can distinguish meaningfulness from chaos (Zhao, Hahn, & Osherson, 2014). Beyond, differentiating pattern as symbolic of danger (e.g. tiger stripes) and a lack thereof symbolic of harmless ground (e.g. a clear sky), there is a much subtler distinction between patterns/chaos, as potential FoB messages. We may recognize a strange tribal dance as a dance and not an epileptic fit, or see words in other languages—even unfamiliar alphabets—and immediately recognize these are something linguistic beyond illustrative marks.

The need to distinguish is a matter of fitness, but not one with a simple phylogenic solution (such as the amygdala) but the triggering (expression) of an ongoing developmental process (ontogeny). Some internally-rendered feature need be applied to exclusively items we perceive as being externa (Sirois & Karmioff-Smith, 2009). But there is no obvious (beyond phenomenology) fundamental reason the notion of qualia need be restricted to visual description/perception. Whatever it is, it is all the same stuff (see discussion of neuroscientist Vernon Mountcastle's observation from decades ago about neuronatonomy, in Hawkins, 2005: 55–60). In this way, we might extend the notion to include a much larger range of abstractions, from colors to *conceptual metaphor*.

Language builds on a basic grounding in sensorimotor experience. Over time (evolutionary and developmental), this capacity became extended to increasingly abstract notions, thus providing the basis for reasoning, mathematics, and analogical reasoning in general. This can be considered as the linguistic bootstrapping of cognition. (Arbib, 2013: 15)

EXPERIMENTATION

Our intention in mentioning this work is to provide a constructive technological tool, which might highlight the unusually subtle issue of how *Homo sapiens* distinguish noise from intelligent organization, how we might come to assume and react with FoB—in essence communicate). The orthodox approach to computer use is insufficient for our investigation of how meaningfulness occurs to human brains in the first place. Why would the stimuli, perhaps even identified, need be further categorized? The general computational strategy of designing an algorithm which distills some *goal* as a conditional tree, and subsequently generates suitable artifacts/praxis is surely fine for most applications (as in Figure 1a). More advanced programmers may elect to employ PDP methods (as in Figure 1b). We believe communication depends on what we call art-ness, which differs profoundly from aesthetics, and is not exclusively formally computational (as in Figure 1c). Though we may be proven wrong some day, for now, uncontroversial instances of synthetic intelligence remain beyond reach, certainly for most of us. Instead—perhaps in the mean time, we offer another strategy. Employ a computer to generate stimuli, that need not actually be communicative, but might elicit the experience of communicating to a human audience member.

Specifically, we choose to study musicality, and do so rather intentionally (Koelsch, 2011; see also the [physiological] notion of "musicality" versus how we might [aesthetically] define "music" in Arbib, 2013). Communication surely encompasses many forms and is exhibited through many media. To narrow our task considerably, we can selectively choose a type of communication, which we will call "art," a fuzzy subset of which being music. This is contrary to the orthodox view of *machine communication,* unbound by an unspecified physical range—as with aesthetics. As noted above, there are clear extreme examples. We assume that most readers would identify trains as being noisy and Mozart quartets as musical. Whereas in the visual arts, particularly after Modernism, it is nearly impossible for there to be sufficient agreement as to some visible object being non-art. Probably, the most famous example is the "found object" urinal by Marcel Duchamp, a standard porcelain fixture entitled *Fountain* from 1917. For language, Noam Chomsky offers his famous examples: "Colorless green dreams sleep furiously" versus "Furiously sleep ideas green colorless" (1957: 15). We instantly recognize nonsensical but syntactically correct sentences as potentially meaningful, but malformed strings of words are usually instantly seen as being without meaningful for us. Though far from ideal, it would seem of all types of communicative acts, music may be the most testable.

The Dennett Test

The matter of meaning is further complicated by Daniel Dennett (1991), who goes on to show that a meaningful context can be invented to justify most any grouping of words (see also Constructivist teaching practices in Twomey Fosnot & Perry, 2005; the perceptual grouping of sonic frequencies in Shepard, 1999).

Please sit in the apple juice seat. In isolation this sentence has no meaning at all, since the expression "apple juice seat" is not a conventional way of referring to any kind of object. But the sentence makes perfect sense in the context in which it was uttered. An overnight guest came down to breakfast. There were four place settings, three with orange juice and one with apple juice. (pp. 72–78)

Dennett's observation shows us the difficulty of such a task, particularly for creating artistic FoB's. No matter what the output, on any system (organic or mechanical), it is difficult to generate non-art, that is universally considered non-sensical. *Homo sapiens* can nearly always invent—though may feel they merely acquire—a suitable context[7]. So we must adopt the opposite stance and proceed, as if we assume the output is absolutely intended. While the machine can certainly be instructed to broadcast available (concrete) audio, we are faced with a false positive, that one can compose (abstracted) music. Dennett's observation is then applied to the simplest case of musicality; Is this music (or perhaps a technical error)? We will call this the "Dennett test" (a reference to the Turing test).

Method

The 2014 software piece, *Happy Birthday, Mr, President* (HBMP), is chosen as an illustration of a programming technique employed as a multimodal/multimedia catalyst of FoB. The source input is a recorded clip of the famous scene where Marilyn Monroe sings "Happy Birthday" to then-president John F. Kennedy on national television. The computer subsequently generates (*a*) animated graphics (Figure 2) that do not literally depict anything, but the ideally viewer comes away with the impression that these boxes were not moving randomly, that something, occasionally recognizable perhaps, was depicted, (*b*) a flurry of orchestral notes performed by an internal synthesizer, ideally heard as periodically concealing an actual musical composition, and (*c*) a file (Figure 3), which can be manually converted to create a printed score for Classically trained musicians.

Figure 2. Screen shot stills of the program generating the piece Happy Birthday, Mr. President; in motion, the brain fills in missing information (both sonic and visual) to complete the scene. This is perhaps most striking when recognizing the figure (puns intended) of Marilyn Monroe, though it is considerably less obvious from a still frame.

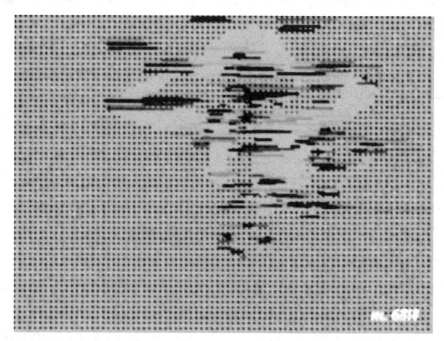

Visually, HBMP uses a standard technique is used for motion detection. Here every few pixels of each frame of the original clip is compared with the previous frame. Where change above a threshold is found, the program draws a small box. In stills, the configuration of these boxes depicts nothing, but animated, the mind draws these together using gestalt, to construct a coherent image (*redintegration* in Gregory, 1966: 43–145; Hunt, 1993: 442–460 ; cf. As opposed to the cinematic technique persistence of vision in Lutz, 1920: 13–17; Taylor, 1996: 34–41). This is a long-recognized visual effect noted particularly in gestalt psychology. The analysis of the audio employs gestalt in a remarkably similar way, by forcing the mind to draw in the missing information in actively order to create meaning, while ignoring data not deemed potentially useful meaning-making material.

At the same time, HBMP incorporates a standard digitizing technique to determining the sonic frequencies present at each moment via Fast Fourier Transform (FFT). This array of levels ("bins"), each in decreasing frequency range, but arranged by increasing averages of frequencies, are mathematically converted into ideally tuned pitches. Within the computer, a virtual orchestra (consisting of 5 strings parts, 4 wind parts, 4 brass parts, timpani) then performs the notes that would ordinarily comprise the complex wave of the original audio. Thus introducing their own, additional complex overtones, which alters the perception of grouping timbres into rhythms (Figures 2 and 3) (Iverson, Patel, & Ohgushi, 2008).

Imagine the sound of real raindrops, on a real window, falling from real clouds. Now imagine an audio sample of several raindrops are loaded into a computer. That computer monitors the street traffic, and broadcasts the sample as cars pass, altering a few parameters (e.g. volume, "pitch") for the sake of realism. So long as sufficient care is taken writing such a program, the naive listener could rarely identify the

Figure 3. Detail of the cello part of the musical score

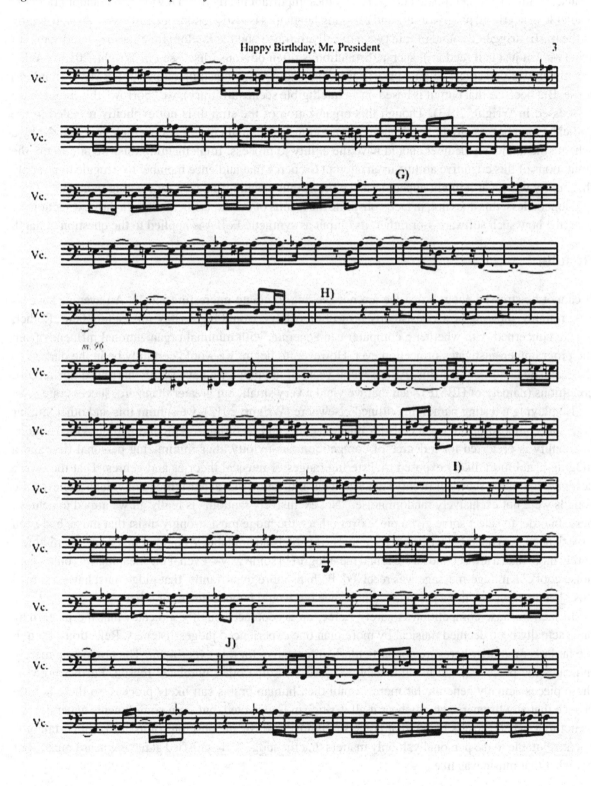

"cause," without another modal clue (this becomes important in HBMP). However, the random function available in nearly all programming and scripting languages is also pseudo-random[8]. Somehow, listening to the traffic-triggered sound of rain (we will call arbitrary) and the random function-triggered sound of rain (we can just call random), such a distinction is often obvious (discussed in Wright, 2013b). What exactly are we detecting? In an a priori sense, the audio-video machine output in HBMP is (random) noise. But because that output is based on an intelligible scene (arbitrary), we "borrow" this intelligence (discussed in Wright, 2013). Though this organization of the stimuli is not explicitly revealed to the audience member, as would be apparent in providing contextual cues, it is nonetheless organized by a scheme the audience member should have the ability to process. Implementing this, we aim to tax the limitations of this cognitive ability, in an attempt to coerce that audience member to struggle to re-apply this ability wherever it might appear to make the output meaningful, even for fleeting moments.

Nonetheless, this does not, in fact, constitute the results of our experimentation. In the next section we describe how such software—or rather, its output as synthetic FoB—is applied to the question at hand.

Results

It cannot be stressed enough that we are not seeking to create interesting music. An average success rate, roughly showing how consistently projection occurs, would be terribly misleading here. Rather, we are concerned with whether a computer can generate, with minimal organizational influence from the programmer, instigates projection ever. However, to begin, we would certainly be in the dark as to the requisite conditions for this. After several years of attempts, we have finally narrowed down those conditions (namely of HBMP) such that we yield a very small, but greater than zero, success rate.

Employing a testing paradigm outlined elsewhere (Wright, 2012), we submit this and other similar works as compositions to open calls for music (scores and recordings, with and without video). Internationality is preferred for a degree of competition, anonymity, thus minimizing personal ties, and a judging panel more likely exposed to differing ranges of musical theories and genres. That they were accepted into three shows of twenty stands as a fair indication that at least three individuals believed the sounds were not exclusively random noise. "Not exclusively random" is really all we aimed to achieve here. In order to select some given piece over others, the judge must strongly insist that music had been experienced, was not merely a trivial technical error solely attributable to equipment. Of say, six minutes, surely more than a few seconds were found meaningful in some way—even if the meaning was only "Isn't noise cool!," a mirage-message was received. Perhaps more importantly, that judge must have assumed this phenomenon was not a personal coincidence but would happen again for others.

In fact, because competition is surely fierce, an acceptance roughly indicates that the piece may have actually been deemed musical by more than one experienced judges-listeners. Rejections, though the far larger majority here, are not particularly informative for this experiment. The proportion merely indicates the piece was not unanimously accepted for some other unrelated reason. Furthermore, as these pieces actually generate far more stimuli than human brains can likely process, so there is little chance that any listeners actually hear it all. Criticism is expected, but even compliments generally tell us nothing; whatever was heard, that judge surely invented (by unconscious omission), but certainly is not attributable to me personally. It only matters that the judge feels satisfied at having heard music, but not what that music was like.

CONCLUSION

We reconsider that communication is exclusively a byproduct of interaction where the subject deems the other, rightly or wrongly, to respond "intelligently." Or we might say, from the perspective of a designer of a system aimed at displaying intelligence, that it must somehow distinguish between FoB's that would not recognizable as meaningful, and FoB's that at least appear potentially meaningful. Where we cannot attribute intelligent organization to the machine, that the stimuli is not perceived as simply noise (consistent with acceptance among competition of organized works), roughly indicates that the intelligence may occur due to some amygdala-like function (as in the scheme by LeDoux, 1998: 161–165; Pessoa and Adolphs, 2010) within the brain of the audience member. Barring extreme autism, both rightly and wrongly, humans tend to credit entities with ToM, or personalities. Even faced with other humans, it might seem likely to be accurate, but there is no absolute proof of this. Hence, even where we might be convinced that nonhumans (such as in *attribution theory* or AI) bear mental states or personalities, it is almost surely an illusion of projection.

This possibility suggests another approach for programming computers. We find that "intelligence", which is almost never formally defined and thus cannot be explicitly coded as a conditional, is likely projected onto objects, likely exclusively by *Homo sapiens*, rather than being intrinsic to objects in the a priori world. We suggest a profound shift in how intelligence might be synthesized (employing computer technologies for their technical flexibility, e.g. programming, AV hardware) in human scene-experiencers, rather than imbued in machines (unconstrained by who or if a human interfaces with it). To do so, we must then appreciate the larger system, which includes at the least a human programmer, the configured hardware, and—most importantly—the human audience member. It is in the privatized mind of this audience member where the meaningfulness is distinguished from noise, and the computer may be the only tool at our disposal sensitive enough to tease this subtle phenomenon out.

REFERENCES

Ackernan, J., & Bargh, J. (2010). Two to tango: Automatic social coordination and the role of felt effort. In B. Bruya (Ed.), *Effortless Attention: A New Perspective in the Cognitiva Science of Attention and Action* (pp. 335–271). Cambridge, MA: MIT Press. doi:10.7551/mitpress/9780262013840.003.0015

Arbib, M. (2013). Five terms in search of synthesis. In M. Arbib (Ed.), *Language, Music, and the Brain: A Mysterious Relationship* (pp. 3–44). Cambridge, MA: MIT Press.

Ardizi, M., Martini, F., Alessandra Umilta, M., Sestito, M., Ravera, R., & Gallese, V. (2013). When early experiences build a wall to others' emotions: An electrophysiological and autonomic study. *PLoS ONE*, 8(4). PMID:23593374

Austin, J. (2010). The thalamic gateway: How the mediative training of attention evolves toward selfless transformations of consciousness. In B. Bruya (Ed.), *Effortless Attention: A New Perspective in the Cognitive Science of Attention and Action* (pp. 373–407). Cambridge, MA: MIT Press. doi:10.7551/mitpress/9780262013840.003.0016

Bavelas, J., Gerwing, J., Allison, M., & Sutton, C. (2011). Dyadic evidence for grounding with abstract deictic gestures. In G. Starn & M. Ishino (Eds.), *Integrating Gestures: The Interdisciplinary Nature of Gesture* (pp. 49–60). Philadelphia, PA: John Benjamins Publishing Co.

Bjorklund, D., & Pellegrini, A. (2001). *The Origins of Human Nature: Evolutionary Developmental Psychology*. Washington, DC: American Psychological Association.

Chang, F. (2002). Symbolically speaking: A connectionist model of sentence production, *Cognitive Science*. Cognitive Science Society. *Inc.*, *26*, 609–651.

Cheney, D. (1984). Category formation in vervet monkeys. In R. Harré & V. Reynolds (Eds.), *The Meaning of Primate Signals* (pp. 58–72). New York, NY: Cambridge University Press.

Chomsky, N. (1957). *Syntactic Structures*. Berlin, Germany: Walter Gruyter GMBH.

Cohen, D. (2006). Perception and responses to schemata in different cultures: Western and Arab music. In Music and Altered States: Consciousness, Transcendence, Therapy, and Addictions (pp. 60–73). London: Jessica Kingsley Publishers.

Copeland, B., & Shagrir, O. (2013). Turing versus Gödel on computability and the mind. In J. Copeland, C. Posy, & O. Shagrir (Eds.), *Computability: Turing, Gödel, Church, and Beyond* (pp. 1–33). Cambridge, MA: MIT Press.

D'Altroy, T. (2003). *The Incas*. Oxford, UK: Blackwell Publishing.

Deacon, T. (1997). *The Symbolic Species: The Co-evolution of Language and the Brain*. New York, NY: WW Norton and Co.

Dennett, D. (1984). Cognitive wheels: The frame problem of AI. In C. Hookaway (Ed.), *Minds, Machines, and Evolution* (pp. 129–151). Cambridge, MA: Cambridge University Press.

Dennett, D. (1991). *Consciousness Explained*. Toronto, Canada: Little, Brown and Co.

Dutton, D. (2009). *The Art Instinct: Beauty, Pleasure, and Human Evolution*. New York, NY: Bloomsbury Press.

Edelman, G. (1992). Mind without biology. In *Bright Air, Brilliant Fire: On the Matter of the Mind* (pp. 211–252). New York, NY: Basic Books.

Etcoff, N. (2000). *Survival of the Prettiest*. New York, NY: Anchor Books.

Fitch, T., & Friederici, A. (2012). Artificial grammar learning meets formal language learning: An overview. *Philosophical Transactions of the Royal Society*, *367*(1598), 1933–1955. doi:10.1098/rstb.2012.0103 PMID:22688631

Fitch, T., Hauser, M., & Chomsky, N. (2005). The evolution of the language faculty: Clarifications and implications. *Cognition*, *97*, 179–210. PMID:16112662

Gadagkar, R. (1997). *Survival Strategies: Cooperation and Conflict in Animal Societies*. Cambridge, MA: Harvard University Press.

Gallese, V., & Dio, D. I. C. (2012). Neuroaesthetics: The body in aesthetic experience. In Encyclopedia of Human Behavior (vol. 2, pp. 687–693). London: Academic Press.

Gamez, D. (2014). Can we prove there are computational correlates of consciousness in the brain? *Journal of Cognitive Science, 15*(2), 149–186. doi:10.17791/jcs.2014.15.2.149

Gisin, N. (2014). *Quantum Chance: Nonlocality, Teleportation and Other Quantum Marvels*. New York, NY: Springer.

Gödel, K. (1962). On formally undecidable propositions of principia mathematica and related systems. In *On Formally Undecidable Propositions of Principia Mathematica and Related Systems*. New York, NY: Dover.

Gordon, D. (1999). *Ants at Work*. New York, NY: Free Press.

Gregory, R. (1966). *Eye and Brain: The Psychology of Seeing*. Princeton, NJ: Princeton University Press.

Gregory, R., & Ramachandran, V. (1991). Perceptual filing in of artificially induced scotomas in human vision. *Nature, 350*(6320), 699–702. doi:10.1038/350699a0 PMID:2023631

Greve, W. (2012). The importance of evolutionary theory in developmental psychology. *International Journal of Developmental Science, 1-2*, 17–19.

Grüter, C. (2011). Communication in social insects: Sophisticated problem solving by groups of tiny-brained animals. In R. Menzel & J. Fischer (Eds.), *Animal Thinking: Contemporary Issues in Comparative Cognition* (pp. 163–173). Cambridge, MA: MIT Press.

Harris, R. (1984). Must monkeys mean? In R. Harré & V. Reynolds (Eds.), *The Meaning of Primate Signals* (pp. 126–137). Cambridge, UK: Cambridge University Press.

Hauser, M. (1998). *The Evolution of Communication*. Cambridge, MA: MIT Press.

Hawkins, J. (2005). *On Intelligence*. New York, NY: Owl Books.

Heberlein, A., & Adolphs, R. (2004). Impaired spontaneous anthropomorphizing despite intact perception and social knowledge. *Proceedings of the National Academy of Sciences of the United States of America, 101*(19), 7487–7491. doi:10.1073/pnas.0308220101 PMID:15123799

Heider, F., & Simmel, M.-A. (1944). An experimental study of human behavior. *The American Journal of Psychology, 2*(57), 243–259. doi:10.2307/1416950

Herrero, J. (2005). A scientific point of view on perceptions. In *Mechanisms, Symbols, and Models Underlying Cognition* (pp. 416–426). Berlin, Germany: Springer Verlag. doi:10.1007/11499220_43

Himonides, E. (2009). Mapping a beautiful voice: Theoretical considerations. *Journal of Music, Technology, and Education, 2*(1), 25–54. doi:10.1386/jmte.2.1.25/1

Hundert, E. (1995). *Lessons from an Optical Illusion*. Cambridge, MA: Harvard University Press.

Hunt, M. (1993). *The Story of Psychology*. New York, NY: Doubleday.

Iverson, J., Patel, A., & Ohgushi, K. (2008). Perception of rhythmic grouping depends on auditory experience. Acoustical Society of America, 2263–2271.

Koch, C., & Tononi, G. (2011). A test for consciousness. *Scientific American, 4*(6), 44–47. doi:10.1038/scientificamerican0611-44 PMID:21608402

Koelsch, S. (2011). Toward a neural basis of musical perception: A review and updated model. *Frontiers in Psychology, 2*(110).

Lakoff, G., & Johnson, M. (1980). *Metaphors We Live By.* Chicago, IL: The University of Chicago Press.

Lakoff, G., & Núñez, R. (2000). *Where Mathematics Comes from: How the Embodied Mind Brings Mathematics into Being.* New York, NY: Perseus Books.

LeDoux, J. (1998). *The Emotional Brain.* New York, NY: Touchstone.

LeDoux, J. (2002). *The Synaptic Self: How Our Brains Become Who We Are.* New York, NY: Penguin Books.

Lerdahl, F. (1992). Cognitive constraints on compositional systems. *Contemporary Music Review, 6*(2), 97–121. doi:10.1080/07494469200640161

Lutz, E. (1920). *Animated Cartoons: How They Are Made, Their Origin and Development.* Bedford, MA: Applewood Books, Charles Schribner.

Marvin, C. (1988). *When Old Technologies Were New: Thinking about Electric Communication in the Late Nineteenth Century.* Oxford, UK: Oxford University Press.

Nadis, F. (2005). *Wonder Shows: Performing Science, Magic and Religion in America.* New Brunswick, NJ: Rutgers University Press.

Nissan, N., & Schocken, S. (2005). *The Elements of Computing Systems: Building a Modern Computer from First Principles.* Cambridge, MA: MIT Press.

Pessoa, L., & Adolphs, R. (2010). Emotion processing and the amygdala: From 'low road' to 'many roads' of evaluating biological significance. *Nature Reviews. Neuroscience, 11*(11), 773–783. doi:10.1038/nrn2920 PMID:20959860

Piaget, J. (1962). *Play, Dreams, and Imitation in Childhood.* New York: W.W. Norton and Co.

Piaget, J. (1971). *Genetic Epistemology.* New York, NY: WW Norton.

Pinker, S. (1997). *How the Mind Works.* New York, NY: WW Norton.

Rummelhart, D., & McClelland, J. (1986). *Parallel Distributed Processing: Explorations in the Microstructure of Cognition.* Cambridge, MA: MIT Press.

Searle, J. (1980). Minds, brains, and programs. *Behavioral and Brain Sciences, 3*(03), 417–424. doi:10.1017/S0140525X00005756

Sfard, A. (2008). *Thinking as Communicating: Human Development, the Growth of Discourse, and Mathemetizing.* New York, NY: Cambridge University Press. doi:10.1017/CBO9780511499944

Shanahan, M., & Baars, B. (2005). Applying the global workspace theory to the frame problem. *Cognition*, *98*(2), 157–176. doi:10.1016/j.cognition.2004.11.007 PMID:16307957

Shepard, R. (1999). Cognitive psychology and music. In P. Cook (Ed.), *Music, Cognition and Computerized Sound* (pp. 21–35). Cambridge, MA: MIT Press.

Shettleworth, S. (1998). *Cognition. Evolution, and Behavior*. New York, NY: Oxford University Press.

Sirois, S., & Karmiloff-Smith, A. (2009). Ontogenetic development matters. In L. Tommasi, M. Peterson, & L. Nadel (Eds.), *Cognitive Biology: Evolutionary and Developmental Perspectives on Mind, Brain, and Behavior* (pp. 322–334). Cambridge, MA: MIT Press. doi:10.7551/mitpress/9780262012935.003.0293

Stecker, R. (2000). Is it reasonable to attempt to define art? In N. Carroll (Ed.), *Theories of Art Today* (pp. 45–64). Madison, WI: University of Wisconsin Press.

Tanaka, K. (1993). Neural mechanisms of object recognition. *Science*, *262*(5134), 685–688. doi:10.1126/science.8235589 PMID:8235589

Taylor, R. (1996). *Encyclopedia of Animation Techniques*. London: Quarto Publishing Ltd.

Tinbergen, N. (1963). On the aims and methods of ethology. *Zeitschrift für Tierpsychologie*, *4*(20), 410–433.

Tooby, J., & Cosmides, L. (1992). The psychological foundations of culture. In The Adapted Mind: Evolutionary Psychology and the Generation of Culture (pp. 19–136). New York, NY: Oxford Press.

Turing, A. (1936). *On computable numbers, with an application to the entscheidungsproblem. In The Essential Turing* (pp. 58–90). New York, NY: Oxford, University Press.

Twomey Fosnot, C. (Ed.), *Constructivism: Theory, Perspectives, and Practice*. New York, NY: Teachers College, Columbia University.

Twomey Fosnot, C., & Perry, R. (2005). Constructivism: A psychological theory of learning. In C. Twomey Fosnot (Ed.), *Constructivism: Theory, Perspectives, and Practice* (pp. 8–38). New York, NY: Teachers College, Columbia University.

Vygotsky, L. (1978). *Mind in Society: the Development of Higher Psychological Processes*. Cambridge, MA: Harvard University Press.

Wiener, J., Shettleworth, S., Bingman, V., Cheng, K., Healy, S., Jacobs, L., & Newcombe, N. et al. (2011). Animal navigation: A synthesis. In R. Menzel & J. Fischer (Eds.), *Animal Thinking: Contemporary Issues in Comparative Cognition* (pp. 51–76). Cambridge, MA: MIT Press.

Winnicott, D. (1971). *Playing and Reality*. New York, NY: Routeledge Classics.

Wright, J. (2012). Borrowed intelligence: Observing and implementing the culture of the art world. In *Création et Transmission en Anthropologie Visuelle* (pp. 399–422). AFA.

Wright, J. (2013a). Can you tell me how to get, how to get to e-learning: Development and complexity. *Journal of e-Learning and Knowledge Society. Complexity*, *9*(3), 41–53.

Wright, J. (2013b). Discovering the non-self: The construction of language, trance, and space, *Leonardo Electronic Almanac, Publications: Not Here and Not There. Leonardo and MIT Press, 19*(2), 146–167.

Wright, J. (2014a). Why just teach art: The development of the hippocampus. *Bioscience and Engineering: An International Journal, 1*(1), 1–10.

Wright, J. (2014b). Why we might augment reality: Art's role in the development of cognition. In V. Geroimenko (Ed.), *Augmented Reality Art: From an Emerging Technology to a Novel Creative Medium* (pp. 201–214). New York, NY: Springer. doi:10.1007/978-3-319-06203-7_12

Wright, J. (2015). Calculation in art: The inconspicuous heuristics of computation, *Rupkatha Journal on Interdisciplinary Studies in Humanities. SI: Digital Humanties, 7*(1), 120–130.

Zhao, J., Hahn, U., & Osherson, D. (2014). Perception and identification of random events. *Journal of Experimental Psychology, 40*(4), 1358–1371.

KEY TERMS AND DEFINITIONS

Amygdala: The most notable well-known function of this bit of neuronanatomy is that it takes the initial, raw nervous stimuli as input, determines if this stimuli contains potentially threatening elements (e.g. sharp edges, sudden movement, and so on), then alerts the autonomic nervous system (ANS) to immediately begin physiological responses to fear. Meanwhile, the same raw stimuli is sent on to the prefrontal cortex for slower analysis. Neurological researcher Joseph LeDoux described this as the "low road/high road" strategy (1998: 161–165).

Conceptual Integration: The doctrine that laws and findings within one field of the social sciences should be compatible and coordinate with laws and findings in the other social sciences. Though at least for this paper, this strategy is broadened to include physical sciences and Humanities.

Conceptual Metaphor: Though many have written on this as subject (relating this theory a bit more to neurology, see Feldman, 2000), the bulk of credit for the theory goes to George Lakoff. Similar to a poetic metaphor, the mind employs knowledge of some concrete system to understand a more abstract system. For instance, the way a person might understand concepts like "that idea is a real reach," is because that person already has a useful model "how to reach," having rehearsed this extensively with the physical body (Lakoff & Johnson, 1980). This in stark contrast to digital processing, the *embodiment* scheme ultimately allows us to go on to model mathematics and logic (Lakoff & Núñez, 2000 though these authors do not discount the possibility the mathematics exists a priori).

Fast Fourier Transform (FFT): This is a mathematical technique, which is automated and used in software audio projects. Acoustically, sounds are complex waves. FFT takes a number, called a frame rate, and determines what frequencies, when added together, might approximate the original waveform. The higher the sample rate, the higher the resolution of the results. Imagine a roller coaster, not of one continuous undulating track, but a number of pillars that placed together draw a very similar undulating shape. Each pillar is called a "bin." The bins are of increasing thicknesses, such that the first few represent a wide range of low frequencies, while the last few are very small and represent the level of a few high frequency sounds. One can hear the difference between the standard sample rate for music of 44.1 kHz and for the telephone of 8 kHz.

Gestalt (Groupings): The propensity, likely innate, for humans to associate stimuli as a single entity due to static perceptual rules. For example, we might see a rabbit behind a picket fence. In our minds, we conceive of a whole rabbit, though literally we see only slivers.

Halting Problem: In some cases a computer need only calculate an equation ($x+y=?$). However, Alan Turing found that in more complex processes, it is not as clear when the computer has reached the best answer. Further computing may yield suboptimal results, just as not enough iterations of a function (as in getNextValue()) would be as well. But suboptimal-ity implies the quality of the answer is highly relative to the context. Since machines do not consider context as human tend to, it is left up to the programmer to determine when the "learning" phase is complete and the software should "halt."

Parallel Distributed Processing (PDP): This computer programming technique (Rummelhart & McClelland, 1986; also called Connectionism, as in Chang, 2002) operate in two distinct steps. First, they generate lists of variant rules (e.g. syntax), which are compared to a large corpus of exemplars (e.g. sentences). Some rules fit the exemplars better and are promoted, while others do not and are demoted. Eventually, the rules with the highest scores are selected. Note this "final" state is actually quite ambiguous, as the number of trials continues and superfluous rules conflict with useful ones. This is an example of what Turing describes as *the halting problem*. But the (ideal) goal of PDP networks is that: Second, those rules can be used to generate further exemplars (e.g. more grammatically correct sentences). Though PDP programmers seldom claim such rules are the same as the rules in the brain, the idea is to use a "bottoms up" method to yield the cognitive ability as a ruleset.

Prefrontal Cortex: This outer layer of the brain is known as the "seat of reason". Though much has been debated as to the precise definition of consciousness, it may help us to think of this region, significantly much larger in our species alone, as the place where the brain generates conscious events in the mind, such as memories, symbolic associations, planning, metacognition, and so on.

Theory of Mind: The belief, upon interacting or watching others, that these entities (generally humans) have minds, consciousness and will. Though not often discussed, this implies the believer also has a sense of self.

Turing Test: In AI, this is refers to a test where a human (or group of them), with only the ability to input (usually text) and see the output (also usually text), but not the subject itself, must determine if that subject is another human or a machine.

Universal Grammar (UG): Linguists often speak of sentence as being constructed from syntax (grammar), rather than syntax being a post hoc description of utterances. To posit such a claim, requires there to be an ideal syntax, which is called universal grammar. But soon it was noticed that people ordinarily do not speak with with perfect grammar, most often simply called "UG." Moreover children of non-fluent speakers often well surpass parents in fluency. This has lead to a claim about "practice" (how people end up speaking in day-to-day exchanges) and "competence" (the possibly innate and/or Platonist knowledge of a UG).

ENDNOTES

[1]   Throughout this text, we will use the word "*Homo sapien*" to refer to the specie, and "human" to refer more generally to people.

²   For this reason, it is important we draw together (and cite) a wider range of discussions, rather than develop a theory based on assumptions or parochial interests adopted from some (e.g. the author's) chosen field. That fields exist at all is evidence enough that this vista can always be widened.

³   "Artificial intelligence" is defined loosely throughout this text. These are efforts to create software (sometimes integrating hardware) to synthetically accomplish tasks characteristic of organic brains. While there is a distinction between functionalism: if a (computer) system successfully generates the precisely same output (as a brain would), the inner workings are the same; "hard AI": computers are models of the brain, and the way computers execute tasks describes how brains execute those same tasks; and "soft AI": computers can accomplish the same tasks as brains do, though computers' architectures demands the mechanisms differ. These notions are very noteworthy as influential heuristics, though the distinctions lie beyond the specific uses of the word in this text.

⁴   In most cases, the term "art world" here and elsewhere refers primarily to a culture centered on a vaguely American/European concept of modern art. While we have exhibited artworks on all but one of the continents (Antarctica), there is a minor semantic issue we need address specific to this particular term. Obviously "art world" is a poor description of the artists, "collectors," and artifacts created in say sub-Saharan tribes. In this paper, we do make some effort to consider artwork in these contexts, "art" in non-Western contexts. But not so for an "art world," as per the experimental paradigm discussed later. This hypothetical tribe could not be expected to list a "call for music" open to and broadcast to the rest of the world. It is surely not a matter of xenophobia or selfishness, but that "art" and "art world" are not entirely related.

⁵   According to orthodox neurological theory, a "self" is built from a latticework of synapses (LeDoux, 2002; Tanaka, 1993). This matter of restructuring the rendition of that external world within the mind (as in Constructivism discussed in Piaget, 1971; Twomey Fosnot, 2005). Such construction is simply "projection" but from an inverted metaphorical model. Or, if the reader prefers, the occupation of the imaginary set crew for the Cartesian theater involves both building the set (Constructivism) and setting the lights (projection), but a light aimed just to the right of a key prop must be adjusted. In other words, the two tasks are symbiotically related.

⁶   This does not imply that theory of mind (usually just ToM) is always illusory. Nonetheless, ToM is not nearly justification for us to insist that "man is a social creature." Considering many individuals to be related as one thing is a matter of conceptual grouping (perhaps *gestalt*) and/or *attribution theory*. It hardly matters whether we are correct in projecting mentation on other individual entities. But it remains doubtful we can assign (some of, but not all) related properties to the group as a whole.

⁷   On one hand, Noam Chomsky's "colorless dreams" (1977: 15) is evidence that we distinguish well-formed sentences (or other structures) from malformed one (central to Wright, 2012). But this implies universal grammar (UG). On the other hand, Daniel Dennett's "apple juice seat" (1991: 72–78) is evidence that we impulsively project meaning (central to Wright, 2015). But this implies UG must reside in the individual's mind and not a priori. However, UG simply cannot be justified by evolution (as we discuss in the "Evolution First" Section). Clearly there is more to this issue for us to understand.

⁸   Ordinarily, the random number function in computer programming languages returns a pseudo-random number. It accesses a table of long, unordered numbers and may perform several arbitrary

calculations, such as modulo by the number of milliseconds since the machine was turned on. However, technically speaking, this is not true randomness, in the sense of quantum physics (Gisin, 2014: Ch. 3), but *pseudo-randomness*. There is a distinction between numbers we are extremely unlikely to guess but exist in another form (e.g. are listed in that table, are calculable from the time) and numbers which do not yet exist in any form. For the vast majority of applications, the unpredictability of pseudo-randomness is far easier to attain and works well enough. But within pseudo-randomness, we are making a further distinction between values organized subjectively by human FoV and values organized by a more objective scheme.

Chapter 12
Artist–Driven Software Development Framework for Visual Effects Studios

Jan Kruse
Auckland University of Technology, New Zealand

ABSTRACT

The development of software to produce Visual Effects is based on a unique model. The majority of large companies across the film industry have taken a distinctive approach for three decades, which might explain their ongoing business success, despite the same tough conditions that other technology companies have to face in light of shrinking margins and several financial crises. This chapter examines the model and proposes an Artist-Driven Software Development Framework for visual effects studios. A brief insight into the recent history of successful applications of this model is discussed and suggestions on how to employ this framework and improve on it are given.

INTRODUCTION

This chapter discusses the software development approach taken by the visual effects industry to create the tools needed to produce digital effects and the commercialisation of such tools. Existing literature seems to lack any discussion of the pattern that appears to drive the development and commercialisation process of software in the film industry, nor does the literature offer a formalized framework to help understand the process better, and to guide implementation of future software tools. This chapter aims to rectify this and introduces an Artist-driven software Development Framework for Visual Effects Studios.

In the first section ("Background"), an overview is given of how software development in visual effects companies is often conducted. This is believed to be a unique model and is discussed in the following section ("Standard Software") in form of several examples of software development and commercialisation for digital effects in the past few decades. The main focus here is to demonstrate a pattern behind a number of commercially available software.

DOI: 10.4018/978-1-5225-0016-2.ch012

In contrast to commercially available software packages, the section "Workflows and Plugins" discusses the same pattern in light of small tools (Plugins) and commonly used methodologies (Workflows) in visual effects. This section shows that the proposed framework is not just applicable to large scale software products for visual effects, but is also found in smaller custom developments made by visual effects studios. Next, "Deep Compositing as an example" is discussed to give a better understanding of how academic research is used to develop proprietary software tools in visual effects studios in the first place, and then carries on to show how it is often eventually commercialised. This section also shows how this pattern could be formalised in form a framework, which is done in the subsequent three sections (Benefits / Discussion / Artist-driven Software Development Framework).

Finally, the last section ("Conclusion") concludes the chapter with a brief summary of the discussion of the pattern and the resulting proposed framework.

At this point it seems important to clarify a few terms and how they are understood in context of this chapter. An important distinction between professional, formally trained software engineers and non-professional software developers, who often have not undergone a formal introduction to design patterns, implementation of algorithms, development of improved algorithms, unit testing and other methods is made. While any visual effects artist, who writes code could be considered a developer of some sort, for simplicity we coin anyone who does not have a formal qualification or anyone who has not undergone professional software development training, a non-developer or simply an artist. It is somewhat oversimplifying some issues, but for clarity this simple distinction is made.

It is also important to note that the pattern and framework discussed here, seem to be fairly unique to the visual effects industry, but some similarities particularly in the game industry are visible. Livingstone and Hope (2011) discuss the discrepancies from both viewpoints: Livingstone being a cornerstone in the game industry (President of Eidos, active across the industry since 1975), and Hope being a co-founder of iconic visual effects studio Double Negative Ltd., the largest film-only visual effects company in the UK. They find that both industries are not comparable, as the game industry has a strong tradition to hire talent from the wider pool of computing, computer science and software engineering with a minority of workers with a training in design, whereas the visual effects industry hires a significant number of employees with a formal training in art and design, and only few workers with an IT background. Therefore, it seems appropriate to assume that the suggested framework can stand on its own within the realm of visual effects. Some adjustments to cater for game industry specifics might need to be made and may be presented as future research.

BACKGROUND

The film industry greatly relies on digital visual effects for the creation of many productions, whether it is a mainstream blockbuster movie or an art-house film. Rapid improvements to existing software packages used to create digital visual effects, as well as new developments of programmes, tools, processes and plugins are essential to the success of the visual effects industry. This chapter proposes a common framework for the visual effects software development and commercialisation process, and discusses a number of examples, including that of Deep Compositing which showcases the proposed framework in great detail, with a clear separation of the three main components *research*, *prototype* and *product*.

While visual effects are a significant part in a producer's budget, they usually only make up a fraction of the overall production cost (Finance & Zwerman, 2009), and even in unusually expensive cases only reach up to one third of the overall expense. At the same time the number of visual effects shots and therefore running minutes have significantly increased in recent years, with some productions such as *Transformers – The Age Of Extinction* requiring 90 minutes of visual effects on a movie with an overall length of 165 minutes (Failes, 2014). Therefore, visual effects studios such as Weta Digital in New Zealand experience rapid growth, which is only matched by very few technology companies, especially throughout the financial crises in the past decade (Hazelton, 2015). This growth requires a fast increase in efficiency, the adaption of new workflows, and as discussed in this chapter, a progressive approach to software development.

Similar to other technology companies, visual effects studios rely on software throughout their work-flow from preproduction to final rendering. As Okun and Zwerman (2010) show in their VES Handbook of Visual Effects, 3D Animation software, compositing software, rendering software and several other products are frequently used as part of the visual effects pipeline (the sequence of workflows to create visual effects). Autodesk Maya, The Foundry Nuke, Adobe AfterEffects, Pixar RenderMan and Adobe Photoshop are amongst the most popular and well-received commercial software packages in the industry. But as discussed later in this chapter, they are not the only components of the visual effects pipeline. Custom developments are quite common (Okun & Zwerman, 2010) and the multitude of relevant technical papers presented at conferences such as SIGGRAPH (2014), indicate that there is a very active development community formed by visual effects studios. Compared to other technology industries this seems quite unusual. Visual effects studios often create their own software tools. Instead of working with software consultancies or using external development providers, the implementation is conducted internally by artists. While Visual effects artists are not necessarily software developers, they still write many tools themselves and therefore show a different approach to solving their tasks then other end users. For example many users rely on commercial software, for example Microsoft Office for administrative office tasks or SAP to manage business operations and customer relations. Even software development itself is regularly conducted using commercial software such as Microsoft Visual Studio. The visual effects industry utilizes a unique model to create its pipeline, which is topic of this chapter. It is probably driven by the following factors: Visual effects studios have to satisfy an ever growing demand for more photorealism, cutting edge effects as well as new trends such as digital stereoscopic 3D cinematography to help film production companies to attract larger audiences. Research needs to be implemented and integrated into existing workflows at a fast rate, to stay competitive against other visual effects houses (Hazelton, 2015). Grage and Ross (2014) show that the market is tight, and that small margins necessitate faster and more cost efficient delivery of projects. This seems to encourage quicker development of new tools based on current research, and causes frequent changes in workflows, resulting in a very dynamic pipeline. This link between the quality of the end product (cutting-edge visual effects) and the tools being used to create that end product, forces visual effects studios to constantly develop new software instead of relying on commercial software development companies to implement new research.

The short feedback cycle regarding iterations to be made for visual effects shots might also have an impact. Compared to traditional software development, where software engineers implement features based on a project plan, which has been created based on a user survey or other initiating factors, visual effects studios virtually move an agile development approach into the hands of the end users. The users of the software, visual effects artists, also become creators of their own tools. And often, visual effects artists even identify relevant research literature, which they adapt and implement, while actively working on visual effects projects (Alderman, 2010; Hillman, Winquist, & Welford, 2010; Hollander, 2011). The active involvement of visual effects artists in the software development process could possibly be due to the freelance status most artists have. The market is very competitive and if artists are able to contribute some cutting edge ideas to the project, this will increase their chances of getting hired for future projects. This implies that the creative design process has been expanded by the visual effects industry as well. The process includes not just the application of techniques and technology, but virtually creates some of the tools that are necessary to even apply the design process at all. A parallel could be drawn to a painter who starts a project and realizes that a specific brush is missing in his toolkit and is also not available for purchase anywhere. Instead of finding a brush-maker to produce that new tool, he starts finding the right hair, handle and ferrule, and makes a completely new, unique brush himself. This approach and thinking effectively enables him to attempt any new project, even if it is seemingly impossible to finish due to the initial lack of the right tools. This is what the visual effects studios perform on a frequent basis, as this chapter will show and detail.

Aside from the some more obvious factors, which are mainly related to the visual effects houses and their pipeline itself, the wider market in which visual effects studios operate significantly impacts on the software development process as well. Film production companies run a high risk operation, which operates on large numbers in the tens or sometimes hundreds of millions of dollars (Grage & Ross, 2014). Their business model is based on large scale intermediary financing by specialized banks such as Bank of Scotland or HSBC Bank USA, which in turn require completion guarantees in order to secure their loans. An unfinished movie is an unfinished product and nearly impossible to sell, whereas a completed movie is usually able to recoup at least a fraction if not all of its cost through theatrical release, video sales and online licensing. Therefore, safety measures that enable production companies to finish their project even if any supplier files for bankruptcy or if other significant issues arise, is required in nearly every production. These guarantees are costly and a large line item in a production budget (Alberstat, 2004; Levison, 2013; Malloy, 2012). Therefore these costs require financing as well and put an additional strain on the production budget. This has important implications for visual effects studios as well. The pressure to complete complex projects with fast turnarounds and shrinking budgets on time, in order to reduce insurance costs and gap-financing needs for production companies, necessitates frequent efficiency improvements of visual effects studios too, for them to stay competitive.

All the above mentioned aspects have led to a unique approach to software development in the visual effects industry: While the foundation of visual effects production workflows is supported by commercially available standard software such as Adobe Photoshop, Autodesk Maya, The Foundry Nuke or Pixar RenderMan, a significant proportion is custom-made proprietary software, specifically designed to suit the particular requirements of each individual visual effects studio, and often even a single purpose of a particular visual effects project.

This position paper contends that the success of software development in the visual effects industry depends on a unique model, which is defined by two main factors. First, an artist-driven approach has a significant positive impact on the prototyping of software tools. Second, a transition from in-house tool to commercial software product is needed, which in turn requires strong support through professional software engineering. With these two elements, the creation of visual effects software has proven to be successful in many past instances as shown in the *Standard Software* section of this chapter. In other words, this model has led to cutting edge tools being accessible to a broad market within a short time, often just a few years.

A framework specific to visual effects software development can be identified, based on the above model. The framework consist of three stages, namely academic or industry research (1); in-house pipeline development at the heart of visual effects studios (2); and finally commercialisation through software companies (3). While traditional software companies often implement new features as an offer to the market, the effects industry in contrast is seemingly driven by users' needs, applying latest research to visual effects projects through use of custom designed in-house tools, which only after this particular project-related use or show-casing, become commonly requested features for mainstream visual effects software products. Hence, these tools start out as a one-off solution or individual software solution developed by non-developers. This could be understood as a lack of rigour when assessing existing research as a source of innovation, effectively a consequence of a weak software development culture. But it seems that it is rather different: The visual effects industry is an artist-driven industry, which considers software as mere tools to support the artistic process (Okun & Zwerman, 2010). The predominant notion is that creation of visual effects is a creative, artistic job. The underlying design process defines the outcomes, and if the outcome could be limited by software constraints, the consequence is to extend the features of the software, instead of adjusting the target by reducing the quality or complexity of the final product. Just to draw a parallel, any writer, using word processing software would most likely adjust the writing process, if the software does not exactly suit the way the story development commences. It is unlikely that authors would extend standard software packages, such as Microsoft Word, on a regular basis just to suit their writing style. While there is the functionality even in Microsoft Word (and other word processors) to add new features through .NET scripting, and there may be the rare exception of a writer actually using it to create additional features for each new project, this seems to be more likely, actually common place, for artists in visual effects studios. Encouraged by the expandability of products like Autodesk Maya, writing of custom software tools is done on a frequent basis (Okun & Zwerman, 2010). It could be argued that this arises from the visual effects artist's proficiency with software development, but that is unlikely the reason here. Most visual effects artists who hold a formal qualification, come from a fine arts or specialized digital media background. The degrees in these fields issued by Universities and other training providers are throughout non-technical and have very little or no software development component. These educational institutions focus on training with standard software such as Maya and no custom developments, at least not to the extent that would be required for pipeline development, as pointed out by industry experts (for example King, Weiss, Buyyala, & Sehgal, 2008).

So, the driving factors seem to be found elsewhere, and this is examined in more detail in the next section. A quick look is taken at the standard software that form the backbone of visual effects pipelines, and the following two sections of this chapter, give an overview of the origins of some commercial software. Some important definitions and terms are also provided.

STANDARD SOFTWARE

The term standard software is used to identify commercially available software that is either sold by divisions of visual effects companies, or more commonly has been acquired by large corporations such as Autodesk or Adobe, and has been turned into regular software products. Commonly sold based on licensing models and with maintenance and software support, these applications deliver a predictable performance, receive frequent bug fixes and feature updates, and can be found anywhere from private users, educational institutions to large scale visual effects companies.

For instance, Photoshop is an image editor based on raster graphics, which has become the de facto standard of image editing software since its inception in 1988. It is a commercial software product and is being used all across the visual effects industry, private households, design companies and education providers.

Another example, which is more specifically established in the visual effects industry and less of a common tool, is Pixar RenderMan. RenderMan (or commonly called PRMan) is a 3D rendering software that has been used to create many computer graphics images in movies such as Titanic, Toy Story, Star Wars or The Hobbit, just to name a few. It delivers a high level of robustness, enables a flexible render management within the visual effects studio, and allows a fast, proven algorithm called REYES (Cook, Carpenter, & Catmull, 1987) as well as the slower, but physically more accurate ray-tracing (Appel, 1968) to be applied.

In order to understand how these (now commercial) software products came to life, a brief look at their history as well as a couple of additional examples needs to be taken.

Commotion

Commotion (Jittlov, 1997) is one of the first examples to follow the path common to most visual effects software tools. Originally created by Scott Squires at Industrial, Light & Magic as a flipbook player, which was capable of playing video frame sequences from a computer's Random Access Memory (RAM), and had basic rotoscoping and motion tracking features added early on, Commotion was released through Puffin Design, a small software company just with the aim to market the program. In 2000, Puffin Designs was acquired by Pinnacle Systems, and Commotion was further developed until Avid bought Pinnacle in 2005 and discontinued the software. This is an example for the artist-driven software development. As a consequence of a significant workflow issue (not being able to playback full resolution film shots while working on a project), an artist at a visual effects studio decides to change this by developing a small pipeline tool (the flipbook player) himself. Further, he extends the small software tool with features mentioned in the current research literature at the time (Roto-masks and motion tracking). Finally, the studio releases the tools through a professional developer (Puffin Design) and commercialises a proprietary process, which opens it up to the wider industry.

Photoshop and Paint3

While Photoshop is not strictly a visual effects software, nor was it written as part of a visual effects production, it had a significant impact on early developments of visual effects paint software such as Paint3. The intimate links between both Photoshop and for instance Paint3 are most visible through the participation in the development of Photoshop by John Knoll, a visual effects artist at Industrial, Light & Magic. His brother, Thomas Knoll, and a computer programmer by trade, conceived the idea of using a few image processing algorithms in conjunction with a graphical user interface, and co-developed the first version of the software. The Knoll Brothers exchanged ideas with another team, which was directed by Alvy Ray Smith (who later co-founded Pixar).

Computer scientist Smith had previously worked on a range of paint systems along with Tom Porter, which led to the first use of digital paint systems in the feature film *Star Trek II: The Wrath of Khan* in 1982 (Smith, 1982). Their work ultimately led to an Academy Award in 1997 for pioneering the development of digital paint systems (Seymour, 2012).

Photoshop itself made its first appearance as a visual effects tool at Industrial, Light & Magic in 1989 on *The Abyss* to create textures for the alien "pseudopod" (Venkatasawmy, 2013). A year later it was acquired by Adobe and turned into a commercial software for raster based image manipulation.

Pixar RenderMan

The company behind the well-established image rendering software RenderMan is Pixar, originally the computer graphics department of Lucasfilm, which spun off in 1983, and was subsequently acquired in 1986 by Steve Jobs (the Apple Inc. co-founder). Pixar's software spin off RenderMan *Group* virtually created the field of computer graphics rendering as it is known today, with founding members inventing and implementing concepts such as texture mapping and motion blur. The core of RenderMan's ability to handle very large and complex scenes is based on the well-established REYES algorithm, which can work with huge polygon datasets, has fast AOVs (arbitrary output variables) and offers many performance features such as high threading scalability. Recent updates include the addition of an RIS rendering mode, with advanced ray-tracing and global illumination, as well as interactive rendering features. While RenderMan features have been released to the public, or in other words commercialised very quickly, and only rarely kept proprietary for extended periods, it is another example of a software product that has its origins in a visual effects studio. The success of RenderMan and its impact on visual effects in general can hardly be put into numbers, but citing its contribution to the financially most successful movies of all times, such as Toy Story, Titanic, Avatar and Star Wars might help to put it into perspective. Further, 44 of all 47 movies nominated for best visual effects at the academy awards, and 19 of 21 winners of the Oscars have been created using RenderMan, which should be an indication for its success. RenderMan is arguably the most influential, and artistically and financially successful product in the whole industry (Wolff, 2008).

An interesting side note:

RenderMan Group once held back a feature from its clients in favour of Pixar, and this upset the rendering community significantly and led to a slight backlash for RenderMan. The feature that saw a delayed, infamous market entry was coincidentally Deep Shadows, the original foundation for the later rise of Deep Compositing as shown in the next section of the chapter.

Nuke

Phil Beffrey created the first version of Nuke, an industry standard image compositing program, in 1993 at Digital Domain. It was a simple command-line tool, which was used to improve workflows for artists and render final versions of their compositing scripts generated in Discreet Flame (now Autodesk Flame). Bill Spitzak started work on additional tools including a visualization for the compositing scripts. Gradually, the team at Digital Domain expanded the tools as part of their own visual effects pipeline. Nuke received its own GUI based on FLTK (another in-house tool developed at Digital Domain) in 1994, and won an Academy Award in 2001 (Alderman, 2010). FLTK was later released as an open-source GUI framework. Nuke was turned into a commercial software package in 2002 by Digital Domain's own D2 Software, which was later acquired by The Foundry, a software company that is still developing and selling the software (Montgomery, 2007).

Summary

The pattern behind this list of different software packages is quite apparent and confirms the above mentioned framework. Software, based on academic or industry research, was originally implemented as small in-house tools to help artists improve certain aspects of a workflow on a specific visual effects project. These tools were then turned and developed into a commercial software on a large scale with a wide market reach. All of the above mentioned final commercial software packages are not just minor products or pipeline tools that are mostly unknown, instead these are leading products in the market of visual effects software and beyond.

The research component might seem to play just a minor role, but the initial problem identification, the creation or adaption of relevant academic research and the contextualisation within mathematical or physics theories is an important and significant step. It builds the foundation for the initial prototype implementation, as illustrated in case of Photoshop development by applying theoretical image processing algorithms to a visual effects related problem.

The same research, user development and deployment framework can not only be applied for full standalone software packages, but also for small products like plugins and even workflows, which previously have been proprietary elements of a visual effects studios pipeline, and then publicised and released to a general public. This public release has subsequently triggered a broader adaption and further development of such tools and processes. Examples include Subsurface Scattering, OpenEXR and Spherical Harmonics rendering.

WORKFLOWS AND PLUGINS

Subsurface Scattering (SSS) was initially introduced by a team of computer graphics researchers at SIGGRAPH (Jensen, Marschner, Levoy, & Hanrahan, 2001), and was quickly adapted into visual effects pipelines to render translucent skin effects of computer generated characters, with the first notable occurrence in *The Lord Of The Rings: The Two Towers* for the character of Gollum (Connelly, 2013). Weta Digital was rewarded with an Academy Award for their work, specifically for the quality of this CG character. In 2005 SSS became part of RenderMan and other commercial render engines.

OpenEXR is an image file format that combines a range of different qualities suited for a visual effects workflow. Developed at Industrial, Light & Magic in 1999, and initially released in 2003, it was gradually adapted by most software companies as the standard for visual effects work, including Discreet and Wavefront (later Autodesk), Adobe and D2 Software (and later The Foundry) (Kainz & Bogart, 2012). OpenEXR introduced the ability to handle many image channels (not just RGB and Alpha) and different resolutions, use 16bit and 32bit float resolution per channel, combine different resolutions and lately even add Deep Data into a single file. Additionally, it supports several compression algorithms natively, which overall makes it an ideal file format for visual effects work.

Similar to SSS, Spherical Harmonics (SH) is a rendering improvement, but SH is targeting re-rendering in particular. By breaking the lighting calculations down into components (comparable to Fourier Transforms), SH enabled larger scenes (geometry, textures and shader), and reduced production times significantly, when used appropriately. It is targeting efficiency of iterative re-rendering, a common aspect of visual effects production, where final shots are created by generation of many artistic iterations to arrive at a desired solution. Running many iterations can be very time consuming and SH has removed the necessity to re-render the full lighting equations by breaking them down into smaller components and pre-rendering those. Every time an iteration is made, the pre-rendered light components are re-used instead of re-calculated. While SH is effectively just a different data representation, it has enabled visual effects studios to create scenes that were not feasible previously (Seymour, 2013). Originally introduced in a research paper at SIGGRAPH (Sloan, Kautz, & Snyder, 2002), it was used in computer games first, although it did not gain traction at first (Sloan, 2008). Only after Weta Digital used it on a larger scale for visual effects in *Avatar* in 2009, it transitioned from a proprietary in-house developed solution to a commercial product and was adapted by several render engines including RenderMan and V-Ray in 2014.

A more recent example is Deep Compositing (Heckenberg, Saam, Doncaster, & Cooper, 2010). This chapter is looking at Deep Compositing (Deep) in more detail to examine how it came to live and eventually transitioned into a workflow in the public domain, as well as a set of plugins, which have been commercialised by The Foundry (the makers of Nuke). Additionally, several software manufacturers had to implement additional functionality into their render engine in order to support this new workflow. Deep is used as a case study to understand details of the development and the individual stages. Finally, a critical investigation into the current state of Deep is taken, including some suggestions for future work.

DEEP COMPOSITING AS AN EXAMPLE

The idea to create depth images as part of the computer graphics rendering process was first introduced as a concept called Deep Shadow Maps at SIGGRAPH 2000 by Lokovich and Veach (2000). At the time, both Lokovich and Veach were employed as researchers at Pixar, working on fundamental computer graphics research to improve the capability of the RenderMan engine. They conceived the idea to store shadow information as a 3D point cloud in addition to the actual image with its red, green and blue (RGB) channels. This is effectively a mechanism that renders all shadows in a scene, even if they are not visible from the virtual camera's perspective. While this might appear ineffective at first glance, as it increases the file size significantly and therefore incurs longer loading times, requires additional storage and more memory, it offers a lot of benefits once shots have to be re-rendered. A common workflow in visual effects studios is highly iterative and re-renderings with camera changes are more likely to happen throughout the process than not (Okun & Zwerman, 2010). This likelihood justifies longer render times and the other negative implications, as any additional rendering with different camera perspectives is only going to take a fraction of the time, making up for any initial long loading times. The time-saving occurs when shadows are not re-calculated, instead their information is being read from the Shadow Maps files. Even more significant savings can be made when particularly difficult render objects such as hair, fur or smoke are concerned (due to the inherently costly self-shadowing). While initially adding significant overhead in form of time and resource requirements might seem counterintuitive, the result is a major workflow improvement. This concept of accepting an initial performance hit, only to streamline the overall process in the long run, laid the foundation for further pipeline efficiency improvements.

Expanding the idea of adding information upstream, simply to see pipeline improvements downstream was taken much further with the concept of Deep Data (Heckenberg et al., 2010). Deep Data or Deep Images add a point cloud of depth information for the objects and volumes in a computer graphics scene. Access to this information enables artists to perform a wide range of different actions after rendering of image frames and deep files is finished. Just by calculating the positions of colour points with their corresponding depth information, properties like the shading, lighting and even per-pixel colour information can be changed. Effectively changing the main look of a shot can be done in a fraction of the time it would take to create a full re-render. The interesting part is that Deep Data is simply a by-product of the color pass rendering process – the final image generation. This by-product needs to be written to disk, but other than this, it does not impact on the existing rendering pipeline, and is not very time consuming to generate at all. From a software developer's point of view, this addition did not make much sense initially, therefore it was not part of the regular rendering files for many years. But in light of the artistic approach and workflow, it saves a lot of manual work and enables more advanced effects. It is a good example of an artist-driven approach to software development in visual effects.

But the concept goes much further. Used in Deep Compositing (Foundry, 2012), the combination of color pixels and depth information had a fundamental impact on how image integration can be performed. The initial showcase was compositing of volumetric data and hard surface objects without the need of switching masks or any other manual involvement. The procedural approach to integrate multiple objects into a volume, only based on a different data representation and the additional data on disk, allowed many manual steps to be automated. While this manifests in serious labour savings for this particular type of compositing, the development at Weta Digital had only begun. Based on feedback from the artists using the tools, Dr. Peter Hillman, a computer scientist and software developer at the company, implemented a range of additional features, which in turn were tested and employed by compositing artists on actual live projects such as *Rise of the Planet of the Apes* (Hollander, 2011). In parallel a release with The Foundry as part of the Nuke compositing software was initiated and prepared (Foundry, 2012). The development of in-house application and commercial release was done at the same while working on the film project. The resulting tools led to a fundamental change of the compositing workflow across the digital filmmaking industry and subsequently resulted in Hillman's Academy Award for Technical Achievements related to Deep Compositing (Benedict, 2014).

Weta Digital pushed the idea, again as an in-house development of a compositing workflow further than initially proposed. Hollander (Hollander, 2011) indicates in his talk that Weta Digital breaks complex shots down into numerous basic elements, which then are procedurally combined using the Deep Compositing tools in Nuke. An example is a shot of *Rise of the Planet of the Apes* in which a lot of different individual apes are running across the Golden Gate Bridge in San Francisco, jumping over cars and pushing many items around. The shot was created with practical cars, and once the apes were all animated, they were rendered as single elements. The automated process of combining them thanks to Deep Data, meant very little manual work to ensure correct layering. This would have been very different using a traditional alpha channel and masking process. Moreover, any minor change or correction of animation, and subsequent re-rendering of the apes would have required huge adjustments. All this was automated and manual adjustments significantly reduced by Deep Compositing. A virtually impossible job was made very easy (Hollander, 2011). This shows how tight integration of artistic requirements, constant feedback to the in-house developer and a very short iteration cycle for additional software development, which made this feasible as part of a visual effects project, enabled the creation of an outstanding rendering and compositing pipeline. The toolset was integrated into the commercial Nuke suite shortly after.

The most recent addition to Deep Compositing, after Weta Digital's initial ground breaking work, and The Foundry's commercialization, comes out of another visual effects company, Dreamworks Animation (Egstad, Davis, & Lacewell, 2015). A team at Dreamworks expanded the data set again, adding important surface information per pixel. This adds improved merging of overlapping and common-edge surfaces, pixel filtering and reduced sample counts.

Looking at the pace, at which render engines have been adapted to be able to use Deep Data, virtually within two years, shows how strong the wider visual effects market feels about the potential of this reasonably fresh technique. It also emphasizes how successful artist-driven software development is. Turning research into a world-wide successful, robust production suite within months underlines the potential of the proposed framework.

But there are a few negatives regarding Deep Compositing as well. As mentioned before, the main implication is file size of the deep data. It can easily reach hundreds of megabytes, which impacts hugely on network performance and slows render times in compositing (Bills, 2013). Further, it has a steep learning curve for compositors and impacts on the whole pipeline due to the additional requirements when generating CG images. But these effects are likely to be outweighed by the benefits. Even the largest scenes are feasible, and compositing volumes, volumetric shadows and hard surfaces in an efficient and elegant way is made straightforward and simple (Failes, 2012). This leads to the conclusion that the tools, and therefore the underlying development and commercialisation process can be considered successful.

BENEFITS OF THE PROPOSED APPROACH

One of the unanswered main questions remains. Why would a visual effects studio publish proprietary tools as soon as possible and in close cooperation with an existing software company? Software tools are effectively open sourced and proprietary processes are made public and available to a broad user base. Could this have serious negative consequences for the visual effects studio and is it potentially losing capital (intellectual or monetary)? The answer is simple and yet intricate. First and foremost, publishing an in-house tool after its successful application on a project provides the visual effects studio with a robust solution for their pipeline, without holding a team of maintenance developers. The software company is likely to transition the proprietary tool into robust code to make it a financially viable product, and in particular for the original visual effects studio, continuous maintenance and support can easily be part of the commercialisation deal.

Similarly, any commercialisation opens up the potential for further extension of the solution. If a commercially oriented software development company invests into transitioning the code into a market ready product, it is likely to introduce further development in order to sell updates and perhaps maintenance contracts to customers. This in turn effectively extends the original idea of the visual effects company without the need for them to re-invest into more in-house development. Again, Nuke serves as a very good example. While the originally released product coming out of D2 Software had a very limited toolset, once sold to The Foundry, a range of new nodes were added within only a few versions. Significant extensions include a new GUI, several workflow nodes, and entire toolkits like Ocular (stereoscopic compositing tools) and advanced camera tracking as well as planar tracking. The most recent significant addition is the aforementioned deep tools set of nodes for Deep Compositing in Nuke.

Another important aspect is market acceptance. While an idea coming out of academic or industrial research implemented as proprietary tools might pose a threat at competing studios, as these other studios might perceive the uniqueness of a cutting edge offering as harmful to their own standing and reputation, a commonly available solution or tool would be seen as standard practice. It could be argued that keeping implemented features as a unique selling point would perhaps secure a better market position for a studio when promoting their service to potential clients, but interestingly there are two factors that clearly indicate this is not the case. First, according to Zwerman (2009) production companies, when looking for potential visual effects studios as their service provider, are seeking production security. This implies that a production can easily be completed anywhere, should a visual effects studio ever fall apart during production – a seemingly unlikely scenario, which is unfortunately happening relatively frequently. Popular examples in recent history include Digital Domain in 2012 and Rhythm & Hughes in 2013, both Academy Award winning studios. Assuming that standard software such as Autodesk Maya and Pixar RenderMan have been used on a production, a transfer to another studio is relatively straightforward, as the project files can be opened due to the same pipeline software. In contrast, if mainly custom software is used, this transfer is unpredictable and might prove to be impossible. Commercialising the proprietary tools and making them common features, leads therefore to more production security for clients and subsequently to better chances to close a sales pitch for visual effects studios.

Additionally, market acceptance might lead to positive effects for the original developer (the visual effects studio) in that other visual effects studios might integrate the tools in their pipeline and extend them consequently. To borrow Deep Compositing as an example again, when Weta Digital released the tools through their deal with The Foundry, they were mostly used for integrating hard surface objects with volumes. While Weta has consistently expanded their use in-house, few other visual effects studios have published any additional development for Deep Compositing. But the recent extension of the tools by Dreamworks Animation as mentioned above, shows that other visual effects studios are using and expanding the tools as well (Egstad et al., 2015). Dreamworks added per-sample subpixel masks to the deep data set, and proposed an extension of the OpenEXR file format at the same time. Accordingly, the original commercialisation of Deep proved to be beneficial for Weta Digital as well. Weta will be able to adapt the new features to their workflow immediately, without the need for additional research, and the release of Deep Compositing offers further efficiency improvements to them as well, thanks to work performed by a competing visual effects studio.

It can also be argued that there might be an additional increase in reputation. Aforementioned cases, where visual effects studios created outstanding work based on cutting edge tools, which they had implemented based on academic research, often led to awards and sometimes to the highest honour, a technical achievement award as well as an academy award (Oscar) for best visual effects. Examples include *The Lord of the Rings* and *King Kong* (Weta Digital) or animated films such as *Finding Nemo* and *The Incredibles* (Pixar). Winning an academy award will significantly increase a company's reputation and therefore chances to win future contracts. Weta Digital for instance won the work on *Avatar* based on tests, but also based on their reputation they had gained with the creation of Gollum in *The Lord of the Rings*, a reputation that had been emphasised by a number of awards for the character including academy awards. And winning the contract for *Avatar*, one of the highest budgets spent on visual effects (Cieply, 2009), secures other work for the visual effects studios for a long period. Additionally, sequels might be produced and the chances would be great to gather more work from these (Gilchrist, 2012).

Finally, looking at benefits that arise from the collaboration between a visual effects studio and a software development company, it could be argued that a visual effects studio, while often not a small company in terms of number of employees, usually has their interest in developing the business of visual effects creation, rather than selling software. One aspect that results from this difference in business perspective would be the free (for personal, non-commercial use) or educational software. These software packages are usually well maintained, just like the expensive commercial licenses, but offer some unique advantages in developing new markets for software sales, and also in establishing software in a wider market. For instance, with the recently implemented free to use Pixar RenderMan software, it is suddenly accessible to a wide range of interested users. This might lead to a wider adaption in education or training of users, which subsequently provides visual effects studios with a stronger workforce. In short – opening up the licensing to free for personal use, will enable better recruitment and potentially lead to new developments out of the wider user base. The question is, why could a visual effects studio not just follow the same path? Given the development and maintenance cost of software products, it is a large financial commitment and potentially beyond the capability of visual effects studios. A software development company in turn, might be equipped for such business models and might be able to work towards the long term returns, as they have the infrastructure and business models already in place.

DIFFERENT APPROACHES

There are examples of a different instigation of early development, which originates from the research itself and not the necessity to create particular effects for a specific project. This original research (sometimes with the involvement and support of a software company) goes directly into a technology-driven development at a commercial entity such as Autodesk or The Foundry. While this type of approach is quite rare and only few examples exist, a few well documented cases can be found in the literature. This section discusses a few examples to illustrate the differences between the artist-driven development framework and other methodologies.

An example is the development of fluid dynamics conducted by Henrik Wann Jensen and Ronald Fedkiw from Stanford University as well as Jos Stan from Alias|Wavefront, which was later bought by Autodesk (Fedkiw, Stam, & Jensen, 2001). The physics-based fluid dynamics system was swiftly integrated into Maya about a year after the publication of their research outcomes. Fluid dynamics simulations were among the first animations that are not based on key-frames created by animators, but used a physical model instead. After setting initial parameters, the simulation runs by itself and replicates physical phenomena using mathematical functions. The animator has no direct influence over the progression of the animation, but only through the initial parameters. The initial work that Fedwik et al. (2001) presented simulated smoke and fire. The simulation was based on the Navier-Stokes equations, which are still used to create procedural fluids to date. Fluids are understood as hot or compressed gases (fire, smoke) in this context, but also include liquids (water). But their papers included a range of other significant outcomes, which had a huge impact on the development of computer graphics rendering techniques such as the aforementioned SSS, ray tracing of volumes and other important solutions. But regarding the fluid dynamics it can be said that the team was at the forefront of a paradigm shift in computer graphics from animation with key-frames and other techniques, which could be seen as emulations of reality, towards physics-based simulations. Other ideas based on the same principle of using computational resources to simulate instead of emulating reality include simulated light (Spherical Harmonics), simulated rigid bodies (Baraff, 2001), simulated soft bodies (Wu, Downes, Goktekin, & Tendick, 2001), crowd simulation (Pelechano, Allbeck, & Badler, 2007) and also procedural animation (Trovato, 2001). At this point it is noteworthy that some of the above examples – while accounts for a move towards simulation in computer graphics and originating from a different approach to research and development – could at least partially considered to be artist-driven framework approaches: Agent-based crowd simulation and Spherical Harmonics rendering were both originally implemented by Weta Digital, and later commercialised through Massive Software (crowd simulation) and Pixar (Spherical Harmonics rendering). This indicates that some tools might have a different origin regarding the fundamental research, but are partially implemented and commercialised using the proposed framework.

DISCUSSION

The survey of different popular examples of software packages as well as smaller tools as part of a specific workflow demonstrates that the underlying common pattern is an artist-driven software development implementing cutting-edge research in close cooperation with the users. These tools are often simple and project specific. The second, important stage is the transition from visual effects studio in-house tool to commercial software product.

The question that needs to be asked is as to why this process is formalized in this chapter if it is seemingly common practice in visual effects studios already? The simple answer is, because it is not as common as the aforementioned examples might suggest. It has been argued that in-house development is a costly business for visual effects companies (Okun & Zwerman, 2010) and with narrow margins and relatively small budgets to create increasingly more complex shots (Grage & Ross, 2014). The examples discussed in this chapter refer to studios that are amongst the largest in the industry with just under or above 1,000 employees. Average visual effects companies as found across the US, Europe and Asia are crediting significantly less jobs to feature film productions (Film Research L.A., 2014). For instance, in 2013 the only company capable of employing more than 1,000 in all of California, arguably the largest film market in the world, was Industrial, Light & Magic. This indicates that the capability of supporting permanent in-house software development departments is limited to a minority of the visual effects industry, at least at the scale discussed above (Pixar, Weta Digital and others).

Which poses the question whether it is valid to assume that a formalized process might contribute to a wider adaption of artist-driven software development in visual effects studios. While it is naïve to assume that in-house development would be incorporated in a vast majority of studios, the hope and assumption here is, that the participation can at least be broadened, and therefore increase its benefits across a larger group of studios of larger and average size. These studios might not be able to hold entire departments on staff, but at least one or two developers at the main impact points of their pipeline such as animation and compositing. It will be shown that even a single developer makes a significant difference, which makes the proposed development process feasible for many additional visual effects studios, that are currently considering themselves as too small for own developments. In some cases the capacity of a software developer might even be provided by an existing artist employee who has the qualification to fill the development role at least part-time.

One consideration that has been left out so far is the timeframes of development and commercialisation. It is probably hard to generalize and present a working generic model for the timeline used in these processes, simply because the artist-driven development is often linked to a project (based on the tools requirements), and the projects have hugely varying timeframes. Smaller projects like Pixar's short films might run for 6 months, and longer projects such as *Avatar* or *The Hobbit* need years of development and production to finish. Yet both produce new outcomes based on an artistic-technological collaboration. Therefore, any assumptions regarding the required timelines for artist-driven software development would be speculative and really depends on the project and the scope of additional tools itself.

Finally, it needs to be pointed out, that there is a potential implication for the artists as well. Some projects might require a highly efficient algorithm and optimized code. There are also fundamental research papers available which might be very difficult to grasp due to their high level of mathematical and physics theories. Artist could be overwhelmed and struggling to implement a suitable solution within the timeframe that fast-paced visual effects projects normally cover. Therefore, the addition of a capable software developer might be necessary in order to mitigate any potential risk of failure in certain cases. This is discussed as part of the artist-driven framework.

ARTIST-DRIVEN SOFTWARE DEVELOPMENT FRAMEWORK

This section introduces the Artist-driven software development framework from a workflow as well as business perspective (Figure 1). It covers elements relevant to the initial in-house development as well as the preparation and transition of the tools to a professional software company. The following diagram shows the three stages of the framework, including the main contributors to each stage and the main methods involved.

Research

The development process often starts with project-specific issues, which could be unsolved technical issues or the requirement to create a new visual style. Examples include Spherical Harmonics (Pantaleoni, Fascione, Hill, & Aila, 2010), which allowed scene complexity beyond the capacity of existing

Figure 1. Artist-driven framework

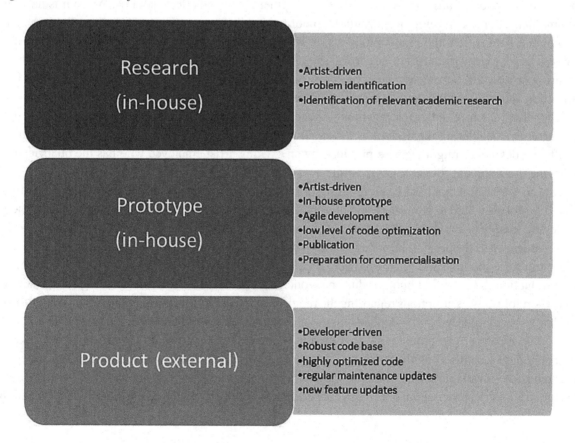

Research (in-house)
- Artist-driven
- Problem identification
- Identification of relevant academic research

Prototype (in-house)
- Artist-driven
- In-house prototype
- Agile development
- low level of code optimization
- Publication
- Preparation for commercialisation

Product (external)
- Developer-driven
- Robust code base
- highly optimized code
- regular maintenance updates
- new feature updates

technological solutions, or Ray Tracing (Christensen, Fong, Laur, & Batali, 2006) which allowed Pixar to create the movie *Cars* as the main actors (vehicles) required reflective surfaces, accurate shadows and ambient occlusion. According to Christensen et al. (2006), scanline rendering algorithms were the only viable solution to render scenes of the required complexity in movie quality, prior to their new development. Generally speaking, the starting point for an in-house development often stems from a specific project and is focussed towards workflow improvements, efficiency increases or expansion of existing capabilities of an artist's toolset.

Prototype

The actual implementation of a prototype might take different forms, for example a simple small pipeline tool, or a significant addition to an existing render engine like RenderMan. But the prototyping phase always starts with the selection of a suitable development tool. Visual effects artists could use any software development environment and language there is, but to keep the development practical in the sense that quick testing and easy integration with existing pipeline elements is provided, the choice is often a lot more limited. Python, an interpreted language, is the most popular scripting language of commercial visual effects software such as Autodesk Maya, Autodesk 3D Max and The Foundry Nuke, which offers rapid development due to its simplicity and high level language features. It also incorporates memory management, numerical processing and a range of system functions such as disk access and basic image processing capability. These features make development very efficient and easy for non-developers, especially memory management and numerical processing functions. The second popular option is C++ as it is natively supported by Software Development Kits (SDKs) from Autodesk, The Foundry and others. This means that access to the core functions of the commercial software packages is provided through an abstract framework, which simplifies integration into existing pipelines significantly, similar to Python's scripting functions. C++ offers significant performance gains over Python as it is a compiled language. The C++ source code has to be compiled into machine code first and cannot be interpreted at runtime. In short, C++ code is faster running, but needs time for compilation and requires also more lines of code. Python is a good contender when rapid development is needed as it can be run instantaneously without compilation, but the code is less performant and has more computational overhead than C++. Both languages have certain advantages when it comes to artist-driven software development, and the main decision at the start of the prototyping process is whether optimized performance is necessary or faster prototyping is preferred.

The prototyping process itself can be described as an agile software development, with small parts of the overall project being implemented, tested, adjusted if needed, before the next small piece is implemented. Agile development is a highly iterative process, which suits software development as part of a pipeline. If major changes were made to the pipeline at once, debugging issues becomes a difficult task due to the complexity of a visual effects pipeline. Using an agile approach allows for small adjustments and avoids major flaws being introduced without intermediary testing.

It is also important to note that a new workflow such as Deep Compositing can be implemented in small increments across the pipeline, not just with regards to each small tool itself. For example, instead of developing tools for the additional render output, the compositing integration and the relighting pipeline, the render output can be implemented and tested first, which means that any negative effects (if any) are local to the rendering department. Compositing and Lighting departments are unaffected by any potential issues. Once the correct function and integration of the rendering output has been verified, a few simple tools for compositing could be implemented. Once these are stable and working, relighting tools can be developed and rolled out. This example shows how gradually expanding the overall pipeline avoids major breakdowns and allows improvements of a relatively delicate system across different departments.

But the same is true for the rollout within the departments as well. For instance, when new Deep Compositing tools are introduced to the compositing department, instead of switching all shots (and therefore all artists) over to the new tools, an internal 'beta test' could commence with only a small number of artists involved. Should any of the tools break the compositing pipeline, only few artists would be affected. Once full functionality is confirmed, a full rollout can commence.

Some consideration needs to be given to the actual rollout of a new prototype, no matter if it is for a department only or across the whole pipeline of a visual effects studio. Most importantly a balance needs to be found between the urge to get the benefits of new tools to all members of a department or a whole studio, and the possibility to negatively impact or interrupt workflows due to software bugs or integration problems of the tools into the wider pipeline. While the risks usually persist even with commercially available software and software updates, it is normally mitigated by thorough testing, often in multiple stages (alpha testing, beta testing, release-candidate testing). It can hardly be expected of artists to provide the same level of testing. Instead a small iterative process commences while working with a live pipeline and working with artists on live projects. This is common practice as indicated by several sources (Alderman, 2010; Failes, 2014; Hillman et al., 2010).

Another consideration is artist training. New tools and new workflows in particular require training, explanation, perhaps shows and tells and some internal marketing to gain broad support and acceptance. This might require additional training resources such as training documents, tutorial videos or example project files to be created prior to facility wide rollout.

Finally, it is important to ensure that the capacity to implement software is available within the artist pool. If that is not the case, or if the task at hand is beyond the capability of most visual effects artists, an additional computer scientist or software engineer might be required on a department level to support the artists in their development. This is not a replacement for any other research and development team, nor is it an attempt to take the development out of the artist's hands. It is rather a suggestion to support the process rather than changing it. The main driver is still the artist, not the developer. To give an example, it is worth looking Deep Compositing at Weta Digital again. Dr. Peter Hillman was not part of the research and development team at the studio. He was actually based in the compositing department, which contributed positively to the artist-driven approach as communication lines were very short, which in turn enabled very quick turnaround times for any changes and patches (bug fixes) of the deep tools. This enhanced the artist's perspective on the whole development, but also allowed an intimate insight into the artist's workflows and requirement for the developer (Hillman in this case). It also had additional positive side effects such as the ability to identify requirements that were only accessible through observation of the artist's work, and these requirements led to new ideas and new tools. Further, it encourages artists to adapt new tools into their daily work on a live project, because the trust that any necessary fixes, should tools fail in certain situations, would be implemented literally right there, right then. So it can be argued that the placement of a senior scientist and programmer inside the department had a positive impact on the relationship between artist and developer. Aside from the discussion about features and workflows as a result of the deep tools, the training component was basically provided through the presence of the engineer on site (or in the department), and ad hoc discussions and introductions to new features or changes were possible as well.

The introduction and acknowledgement at the Academy Awards ceremony, where Hillman received the Technical Achievement Award is very insightful and mentions some of the important points raised in this section of the chapter. He was in particular recognized "for his work developing the first proprietary and then commercially available tools for deep compositing". The academy also noted that the process "dramatically simplifies work on visual effects shots". Hillman acknowledged that the "artistic- technical collaboration" is the most impactful factor and that the artist's "suggestions and ideas continued to drive things forward", which underlines the success of an artist-driven development process (2013 Sci-Tech Awards: Dr. Peter Hillman, 2014), but also highlights the advantage of adding another capacity for complex research and development topics like Deep Compositing. Additionally, it provides production security by negating some of the risks involved with prototype usage on live projects, as the developer is able to react very swiftly and fix issues on the fly.

Commercialisation

The commercialisation phase, assuming that it happens in a controlled way as it is the case with Weta Digital's Deep Compositing tools or Pixar's RenderMan, follows a preparation stage where the tools, source code and preliminary (in-house) documentation are packaged to allow for a swift and easy hand-over to the commercial software company. This preparation includes source code to be expanded with necessary additional comments that allow a software developer not just to understand what the particular lines of code do, but also to understand the reasoning, the thought process behind them. For instance, most pipeline tools might have a comment line for a small block of code. The handover code usually has a multiline comment or even a short paragraph attached to most lines. Understanding someone else's source code can be a challenging task. If this code is based on cutting-edge research and has effectively not been implemented prior to the pipeline integration, it could be particularly difficult to understand without extensive documentation.

Additionally, accompanying documentation is prepared. Artists and developers involved in Deep Compositing development indicate a vivid exchange of information and closely working with The Foundry to accommodate the transition (Foundry, 2012; Hollander, 2011).

But the most important difference between all previous parts and the commercialisation is that there is a paradigm shift from an artist-driven to a developer-driven and also technology-driven process. When the commercialisation phase is entered, professional software development methods are applied. Project management, software development kits (SDKs), standard development libraries and other tools normally used by software companies to create their products are being employed.

The transition from artist-driven to developer-driven focus is not the only major shift of paradigm. With the commercialisation, the development is not part of a self-serving, short-term solution to an immediate problem anymore. Instead, it becomes a business investment, with a financial recoupment plan in place and a schedule for future developments. That means the development becomes a project itself, and needs to be managed and maintained like any other product. It is important to understand that the main aim for commercialisation is to create a robust code-base, which can be built on. While this might require rewriting and a lot of time, which effectively is a large initial investment, in the long term the code would be easier to maintain (bug fixes) and to extend (feature updates). Accordingly, appropriate project and risk management needs to be put into place, which likely becomes part of the contract between the visual effects studios and the commercial software development company.

FUTURE RESEARCH DIRECTIONS

Specific frameworks for visual effects companies need to be developed in order to streamline their in-house process and encourage a higher rate of adaptations of academic research into their pipeline. While the Artist-driven software development framework presented here, covers some of the main high-level aspects of this in-house process, research needs to look at the organizational structure of visual effects studios to gain a better understanding of how methods could be generalized for small and large studios alike.

Further, frameworks that allow a smooth transition from in-house tool to commercial software product are required. This probably also necessitates the creation of software development positions at the key points of the visual effects pipeline such as animation or motion capture, camera, shading, lighting, rendering and compositing. While visual effects companies of large size have dedicated departments for tools development, a software developer at the transition point between departments would probably be able to understand the intimate details of the handover point, while maintaining a high level of code quality at the same time – more research is needed here as well.

CONCLUSION

The presented perspective on pipeline development in visual effects studios using an Artist-Driven Software Development Framework highlights a unique approach to workflow design and software tool development, and its commercialisation. It can be argued that some of the methods discussed seem unusual, yet highly effective in context of visual effects creation. The artist is at the center of software development, whether it is conducted by a single developer or a small team, or as in most cases seen in visual effects studios by the artists themselves. Therefore, it is the end-user creating part of their software tools in order to create client success and deliver evermore complex projects on relatively small budgets. And the framework also covers the next logical step, commercialisation of tools. This is less seen as a profit-making exercise, but more of a necessity to gather wide-spread adaption of new techniques and technologies, professional support and long-term development of new features for such tools. Without the commercialisation of proprietary software tools, many visual effects techniques and technologies would not exist. Making them available to the visual effects market including any competitors is actually working in favour of the publishing visual effects studio contrary to the believe that intellectual property needs to be protected, and that proprietary processes and tools are a necessity to survive in competitive markets. This unique business model counteracts perceived disadvantages like loss of intellectual property through simple open sourcing or at least commercialisation through third parties.

The framework presented in this chapter opens a new perspective on visual effects tools and pipeline engineering as it encourages the studios that have not yet made it common practice, to embrace the idea of artist-driven software development. As long as there is some capacity available to provide a clean and controlled transition from prototype to commercial product, in-house development works to the advantage of the visual effects studios. It drives new innovation by implementing cutting-edge research in a way that commercial software developers are not able to sustain or at least not willing to sustain at this stage. In-house development and subsequent commercialisation also provides long term gains in efficiency and effectiveness as it can be seen over the past few decades, where visual effects studios worked more complex animations and simulations into relatively small budgets (though the shot count per movie normally increased). The industry has seen healthy growth even through financial crises contrasting other technology industries, and this chapter argues that an artist-centric or end-user-centric approach to pipeline design is going to help maintain the business success in coming years.

REFERENCES

2013 Sci-Tech Awards: Dr. Peter Hillman. (2014). Retrieved from www.youtube.com/watch?v=7RZrLZCrh_c

Alberstat, P. (2004). *The Insider's Guide to Film Finance* (1st ed.). Oxford, UK: Focal Press.

Alderman, D. (2010, July 18). *Interview Bill Spitzak.* Retrieved from http://www.nukepedia.com/interviews/interview-bill-spitzak/

Appel, A. (1968). Some Techniques for Shading Machine Renderings of Solids. In *Proceedings of the Spring Joint Computer Conference* (pp. 37–45). New York, NY: ACM. doi:10.1145/1468075.1468082

Baraff, D. (2001). Physically based modeling: Rigid body simulation. *SIGGRAPH.* Retrieved from http://graphics.cs.cmu.edu/courses/15-869-F08/lec/14/notesg.pdf

Benedict, E. (2014, January 8). *19 Scientific And Technical Achievements To Be Honored With Academy Awards®.* Retrieved May 12, 2015, from http://www.oscars.org/news/19-scientific-and-technical-achievements-be-honored-academy-awardsr

Bills, J.-M. (2013, April 10). *I Have Seen The Future, And It Is... Slow.* Retrieved from http://www.vfxpdx.com/?p=815

Christensen, P. H., Fong, J., Laur, D. M., & Batali, D. (2006). Ray tracing for the movieCars. In *Interactive Ray Tracing 2006, IEEE Symposium on* (pp. 1–6). IEEE. Retrieved from http://ieeexplore.ieee.org/xpls/abs_all.jsp?arnumber=4061539

Cieply, M. (2009, November 9). A Movie's Budget Pops From the Screen. *The New York Times.* Retrieved from http://www.nytimes.com/2009/11/09/business/media/09avatar.html

Connelly, B. (2013, April 5). *Weta Digital's Joe Letteri GIves Us A Cutting Edge Digital FX 101 - The Hobbit And Beyond.* Retrieved May 9, 2015, from http://www.bleedingcool.com/2013/04/05/wetas-joe-letteri-on-the-cutting-edge-of-cg-effects-the-hobbit-and-beyond/

Cook, R. L., Carpenter, L., & Catmull, E. (1987). The Reyes Image Rendering Architecture. In *Proceedings of the 14th Annual Conference on Computer Graphics and Interactive Techniques* (pp. 95–102). New York, NY: ACM. http://doi.org/ doi:<ALIGNMENT.qj></ALIGNMENT>10.1145/37401.37414

Egstad, J., Davis, M., & Lacewell, D. (2015). *Improved Deep Image Compositing Using Subpixel Masks.* Glendale, CA: Dreamworks Animation. doi:10.1145/2791261.2791266

Failes, I. (2012, July 1). *Vampire Hunter: two killer sequences*. Retrieved from http://www.fxguide.com/featured/vampire-hunter-two-killer-sequences/

Failes, I. (2014). *Age of Extinction: ILM turns up its Transformers toolset*. Retrieved from http://www.fxguide.com/featured/age-of-extinction-ilm-turns-up-its-transformers-toolset/

Fedkiw, R., Stam, J., & Jensen, H. W. (2001). Visual simulation of smoke. In Proceedings of the 28th annual conference on Computer graphics and interactive techniques (pp. 15–22). ACM. Retrieved from http://dl.acm.org/citation.cfm?id=383260

Film Research L.A. (2014). 2013 Feature Film Production Report. Los Angeles, CA: Author.

Finance, C., & Zwerman, S. (2009). The Visual Effects Producer: Understanding the Art and Business of VFX. Amsterdam: Focal Press.

Foundry, T. (2012, October 4). *The Foundry & Weta Digital go DEEP*. Retrieved from http://www.thefoundry.co.uk/articles/2011/05/24/250/the-foundry-weta-digital-go-deep/

Gilchrist, T. (2012, April 5). *"Avatar 2" Delayed Until at Least 2015, Says Jon Landau*. Retrieved May 19, 2015, from http://www.hollywoodreporter.com/heat-vision/avatar-2-delayed-at-2015-308743

Grage, P., & Ross, S. (2014). *Inside VFX: An Insider's View Into The Visual Effects And Film Business* (1st ed.). CreateSpace Independent Publishing Platform.

Hazelton, J. (2015, January 7). *Weta Digital: Maximum effect*. Retrieved May 5, 2015, from http://www.screendaily.com/awards/weta-digital-maximum-effect/5081538.article

Heckenberg, D., Saam, J., Doncaster, C., & Cooper, C. (2010). Deep Compositing. Presented at the SIGGRAPH. Retrieved from http://www.johannessaam.com/deepImage.pdf

Hillman, P., Winquist, E., & Welford, M. (2010). *Compositing "Avatar"*. Academic Press.

Hollander, R. (2011). *Deep Compositing in Rise of the Planet of the Apes*. Twentieth Century Fox Film Corporation. Retrieved from http://vimeo.com/37310443

Jensen, H. W., Marschner, S. R., Levoy, M., & Hanrahan, P. (2001). A practical model for subsurface light transport. In Proceedings of the 28th annual conference on Computer graphics and interactive techniques (pp. 511–518). ACM. Retrieved from http://dl.acm.org/citation.cfm?id=383319 doi:10.1145/383259.383319

Jittlov, M. (1997). *Puffin Commotion 1.0.5 - Photoshop for Video*. NewMedia.

Kainz, F., & Bogart, R. (2012, August 5). *Technical Introduction to OpenEXR*. Industrial, Light & Magic. Retrieved from https://github.com/openexr/openexr/blob/master/OpenEXR/doc/TechnicalIntroduction_2.0.pdf

King, R., Weiss, B., Buyyala, P., & Sehgal, M. (2008). Bridging the Gap Between Education and Professional Production. In ACM SIGGRAPH ASIA 2008 Educators Programme (pp. 13:1–13:3). New York, NY: ACM. doi:10.1145/1507713.1507728

Levison, L. (2013). *Filmmakers and Financing: Business Plans for Independents* (7th ed.). New York: Focal Press.

Livingstone, I., & Hope, A. (2011). Next Gen. *Nesta*. Retrieved from http://www.nesta.org.uk/publications/next-gen

Lokovic, T., & Veach, E. (2000). Deep Shadow Maps. Presented at the SIGGRAPH. Los Angeles, CA: Addison-Wesley. Retrieved from http://graphics.stanford.edu/papers/deepshadows/

Malloy, T. (2012). Bankroll: A New Approach to Financing Feature Films (2nd ed.). Studio City, CA: Michael Wiese Productions.

Montgomery, J. (2007, March 10). *D2 Software's Nuke Acquired by The Foundry*. Retrieved from http://www.fxguide.com/featured/d2_softwares_nuke_acquired_by_the_foundry/

Okun, J. A., & Zwerman, S. (Eds.). (2010). *The VES Handbook of Visual Effects: Industry Standard VFX Practices and Procedures* (1st ed.). Burlington, MA: Focal Press.

Pantaleoni, J., Fascione, L., Hill, M., & Aila, T. (2010). PantaRay: Fast Ray-traced Occlusion Caching of Massive Scenes. In ACM SIGGRAPH 2010 Papers (pp. 37:1–37:10). New York, NY: ACM. doi:10.1145/1833349.1778774

Pelechano, N., Allbeck, J. M., & Badler, N. I. (2007). Controlling individual agents in high-density crowd simulation. In Proceedings of the 2007 ACM SIGGRAPH/Eurographics symposium on Computer animation (pp. 99–108). Eurographics Association. Retrieved from http://dl.acm.org/citation.cfm?id=1272705

Seymour, M. (2012, July 5). *Alvy Ray Smith: RGBA, the birth of compositing & the founding of Pixar*. Retrieved from http://www.fxguide.com/featured/alvy-ray-smith-rgba-the-birth-of-compositing-the-founding-of-pixar/

Seymour, M. (2013, April 25). *The science of Spherical Harmonics at Weta Digital*. Retrieved from http://www.fxguide.com/featured/the-science-of-spherical-harmonics-at-weta-digital/

SIGGRAPH. (2014). Retrieved May 17, 2015, from http://www.siggraph.org/learn/open-access-s2014-conference-proceedings

Sloan, P.-P. (2008). Stupid spherical harmonics (sh) tricks. Presented at the GDC. Austin, TX: Microsoft Corporation. Retrieved from http://ppsloan.org/publications/StupidSH36.pdf

Sloan, P.-P., Kautz, J., & Snyder, J. (2002). Precomputed Radiance Transfer for Real-time Rendering in Dynamic, Low-frequency Lighting Environments. In *Proceedings of the 29th Annual Conference on Computer Graphics and Interactive Techniques* (pp. 527–536). New York, NY: ACM. doi:10.1145/566570.566612

Smith, A. R. (1982). Special Effects for Star Trek II: The Genesis Demo, Instant Evolution with Computer Graphics. *American Cinematographer, 63*(10), 1038–1039, 1048–1050.

Trovato, K. I. (2001). *Simulated environment using procedural animation in a simulated city*. Google Patents. Retrieved from https://www.google.com/patents/US6183364

Venkatasawmy, R. (2013). *The Digitization of Cinematic Visual Effects: Hollywood's Coming of Age.* Rowman & Littlefield.

Wolff, E. (2008, August 13). *RenderMan@20: Ed Catmull and Dana Batali Reflect On Pixar's Killer App.* Retrieved May 10, 2015, from http://www.awn.com/vfxworld/renderman20-ed-catmull-and-dana-batali-reflect-pixars-killer-app

Wu, X., Downes, M. S., Goktekin, T., & Tendick, F. (2001). Adaptive nonlinear finite elements for deformable body simulation using dynamic progressive meshes. In *Computer Graphics Forum* (Vol. 20, pp. 349–358). Wiley Online Library. doi:10.1111/1467-8659.00527

Chapter 13
Engineering Inspiration:
Enhancing Scientific Creativity through Image Flows

Bruce J. MacLennan
University of Tennessee – Knoxville, USA

ABSTRACT

This chapter proposes a computerized tool to promote inspiration in a specific, but very important, kind of scientific creativity, for significant scientific breakthroughs are often enabled by conceptual revolutions. The creative process is often divided into four phases: preparation, incubation, inspiration, and verification/elaboration. The proposed tool enhances the incubation phase of scientific creativity, with the goal of inspiring fruitful reconceptualization of a problem. It accomplishes this by exposing the scientist-user to continuous sequences of images designed to engage innate, unconscious cognitive structures. The sequence is not fixed, but may vary either randomly or under user direction. When this image flow seems relevant to the problem, users can record their position in it and their own ideas with a variety of low-interference recording techniques. Several simple image flows are described, along with the computational engine for generating them.

BACKGROUND

Scientific Creativity

There is no need to rehearse the importance of science in our society, both for the technological developments it has enabled and for the profound revision of our worldview that it has entailed. Although much of this scientific progress has been incremental, at its heart are conceptual revolutions, including quantum mechanics, special and general relativity, the structure and function of DNA, and the neo-Darwinian synthesis. These are among the germ cells from which contemporary science has developed. Further, as Kuhn (1970) argued, new paradigms generate new research programs, asking questions that were not asked — or *could not* be asked — from prior perspectives. Therefore, conceptual revolutions in science reveal new worlds, previously unimagined, awaiting exploration. The goal of our research is to provide technological support for future conceptual revolutions (minor as well as major).

DOI: 10.4018/978-1-5225-0016-2.ch013

It is widely recognized that it is important to distinguish degrees of creativity based on novelty and significance (Kozbelt, Beghetto & Runco, 2010; Ward & Kolomyts, 2010). For example, Gardner (1993) distinguished little-C creativity and big-C creativity. More recently, Kaufman and Beghetto (2009) have argued for a "four C model," but Gardner's classification is sufficient for this chapter. *Little-C creativity* is the sort of creativity that scientists, artists, engineers, designers, and most other productive people engage in on a regular basis: finding new, non-obvious solutions to relevant problems. Although little-C creativity is critical to the improvement of human well-being, it is not the primary concern of this chapter. Rather, the focus is on *big-C creativity*, the sorts of creative accomplishments that loom large in history books, and in particular the sorts of scientific accomplishments that effect conceptual revolutions (Sawyer, 2006, pp. 27–29). More modestly, the focus is on scientific creativity that results in a new, more fruitful way of understanding some class of phenomena. This chapter will argue that Big-C creativity requires a different sort of technological support than "ordinary" (little-C) creativity (see below, "Archetypal Processes").

Unfortunately, much of the research on creativity, especially research aimed at improving creativity, has focused on little-C creativity (Sawyer, 2006, pp. 66–67). Indeed, many of the problems used in these studies amount to puzzles in which objects in the environment must be used in innovative ways in order to solve some well-defined problem. Certainly, seeing things in new ways, and avoiding a kind of functional fixation, are important in big-C scientific creativity, but what the latter often requires is a new perspective on a scientific domain, rather than a clever redeployment of existing elements. The goal here is to use technology to encourage new conceptualizations and perspectives on scientific problems, and thereby to enable scientific breakthroughs.

Boden (1991) draws a useful distinction between P-creativity and H-creativity. *P-creativity (psychological creativity)* refers to the production of something that is new and interesting to the creator, although many other people may have already created the same thing. In contrast, *H-creativity (historical creativity)* is the production of something new and interesting that has never been produced before (at least in the creator's culture). For well-prepared scientists (see below), the two notions largely coincide, because these scientists will be aware of what has been accomplished in their field, and so if an idea is P-creative it is also likely to be H-creative. That, at least, is the goal, but it is not uncommon for a scientist to discover that a psychologically original idea has been anticipated by others, that is, that an apparently H-creative idea is only P-creative. The author's project focuses on ideas that are P-creative, but simultaneously, as a consequence of professional preparation, very probably H-creative.

Graham Wallas's (1926) description of four stages in the creative process is well known, but they had been enumerated already by Poincaré (1908/1952), and the first three were mentioned by Helmholtz (1896) (see also Whiting, 1958). They are

1. Preparation,
2. Incubation,
3. Inspiration (or illumination), and
4. Verification (or elaboration).

Regardless of the domain of creativity, *preparation* involves conscious work on the problem, *incubation* entails a suspension of this conscious activity, *inspiration* refers to the relatively effortless appearance of an attractive solution, which must be followed by (perhaps extensive) *verification* and/or *elaboration* of this inspired solution. Thus, according to Reichenbach (1938), the first three stages occur in the context of *discovery*, whereas the last is in the context of *justification* (empirical test or mathematical proof). Kris (1953) added a fifth, final phase, *communication*, which is certainly essential in science (and other forms of public creativity). Thus Stein (1967), who emphasizes the social benefit inherent in genuine creativity, enumerates three major phases: hypothesis formation (preparation, incubation, inspiration), hypothesis testing (verification), and communication. There are newer analyses of the creative process into stages or cognitive components (Kozbelt, Beghetto & Runco, 2010), but in spite of its empirical limitations, the Wallas model still provides a useful framework for guiding creative activities (i.e., as a normative rather than a descriptive model) (Sawyer, 2006, pp. 312–313). Nevertheless, the project described herein, which focuses on the inspiration phase, does not depend on the details of the Wallas model.

In the case of scientific creativity, the process of preparation is well-understood, for it involves the scientist's formal education, their ongoing effort to remain current in the progress of science, and their comprehensive understanding of the state of the art in their particular specialty. Information technology has had, and will continue to have, an enormous impact on the preparation stage of scientific creativity, but that is not the focus of this project. Nor is its focus on verification, although scientific verification is also facilitated by information technology. Its goal is technological support for incubation and inspiration in scientific creativity.

The inspirations that are at the core of big-C scientific creativity are historically significant because typically they have implications beyond the solution of an isolated problem. Rather, they offer new perspectives, concepts, and cognitive structures with which to understand a scientific domain. They are especially *fruitful*, both in the questions they pose and in the means of solution that they afford. (The nature and source of such fruitful conceptualizations are discussed below.) This project's goal is to provide technological aid to scientists seeking new ways to understand their research domains.

Sources of Inspiration

What is the source of innovative scientific ideas and, in particular, of scientific inspiration? Certainly, many innovative ideas are a result of conscious analysis, but that is not our topic here. Rather, this project addresses what happens when extensive conscious problem solving has failed to provide an adequate answer. In this situation, preparation may prepare the ground for incubation, which may lead to inspiration (if the scientist is fortunate). Usually incubation begins when conscious analysis and other cognitive resources have been exhausted, and it terminates with the conscious recognition of a new, attractive synthesis. The intervening incubation process is necessarily unconscious, as has been recognized by Poincaré (1908/1952, 1929) and many others (e.g., Dorfman, Shames & Kihlstrom, 1996; Fritz, 1980; Gedo, 1997; Hadamard, 1945; Kipling, 1937/1952; Kris, 1952; Neumann, 1971; Noppe, 1999). Therefore, to stimulate scientific inspiration, technological aids should focus on the unconscious origins of scientific ideas.

Although there are at least a half-dozen theories of the incubation process, experimental investigations have not been able to confirm or refute these theories definitively (Smith & Dodds, 1999). As explained below ("Archetypal Processes"), this project is motivated by the testimony of eminent scientists themselves that their creative ideas arise from the unconscious.

Associationism suggested that unconscious associative networks among concepts provide a source for new ideas (Stein, 1974, pp. 86–8, 231–2). It was observed that on association tests creative individuals produce broader but shallower association trees than do less creative, more methodical individuals (Mednick, 1962). Certainly, unconscious associative networks are one source of creative inspiration, but it is necessary to distinguish between idiosyncratic associations and more universal ones. Idiosyncratic associations are a result of a person's individual genetic makeup and ontogeny, and of the contingencies of his or her biography. Certainly, such particularities are part of the reason that one scientist may have a creative inspiration denied to his or her colleagues. On the other hand, while an idiosyncratic association may enable the solution of a problem, as a scientific conception it may be sterile if very few scientists have that association. Historically fruitful conceptions are more likely to arise from associations that are universal or at least widely shared (e.g., throughout a culture). [This was also a limitation of Freud's (1948, 1948a) theory of creativity (Arieti, 1980; Jung, 1934, ch. 8).]

Gestalt psychology provided an alternative explanation of creativity, which was supposedly universal because based in neurophysiology and therefore better able to account for historically significant creativity (e.g., Wertheimer, 1982). According to this theory, a creative person is able to feel the frustration and forces in a problem situation leading to a cognitive reorganization that satisfies the constraints of the problem and is satisfying (exhibits closure). Unfortunately, in addition to being dependent on subsequently refuted theories of cortical processing, Gestalt psychology focused on perception and on dynamic processes leading to static Gestalts. While creative understandings of static structure are not irrelevant to scientific creativity (e.g., the DNA double helix), in many cases scientific creativity lies in a reconceptualization of a dynamic process (e.g., Newtonian mechanics, Darwinian evolution).

The foregoing suggests that the source of creative, fruitful scientific conceptions lies in unconscious dynamical processes that are phylogenetic or at least very widely shared among humans. What is the nature of these processes and how can people tap into them?

Archetypal Processes

Definition

It will be convenient to use Jung's term *archetype* for these phylogenetic unconscious psychodynamical processes. This term should not entail any mystification, for the archetypes are no more than the unconscious psychological correlates of instinctual and neurophysiological processes common to all humans. Indeed, Jung (*CW* 8, para. 404) said, "To the extent that the archetypes intervene in the shaping of conscious contents by regulating, modifying, and motivating them, they act like the instincts." Indeed, at its deepest level, the archetypal structure, "the biological instinctual psyche, gradually passes over into the physiology of the organism and thus merges with its chemical and physical conditions." (*CW* 8, para. 420).

Most of the archetypes are unconscious processes, grounded in human neurophysiology, that regulate and govern our perception, motivation, affect, and behavior to achieve biological ends (reproduction, survival, defense, dominance, care-giving, cooperation, etc.). When an unconscious archetype is activated through its *innate releasing mechanism* (IRM) by means of a *releaser* or by a conditioned *sign stimulus*, it begins its regulatory process and affects consciousness by altering perception, motivation, affect, and behavior (Stevens, 2003, pp. 64–65). Therefore, since an archetype encompasses the psychological effects of unconscious neural and physiological processes, it is consciously experienced indirectly and incompletely, in the context of a specific activating situation. As Jung (*CW* 9, pt. 1, para. 155) remarked, "The existence of the instincts can no more be proved than the existence of the archetypes, so long as they do not manifest themselves concretely." The instincts are known through their consequences in behavior and the archetypes are known through their consequences in consciousness.

Many of our archetypal structures regulate our interactions with other humans and constitute the foundations on which cultures are built (Stevens, 1993, 2003). Our nonhuman relatives have homologous neuropsychological structures, as shown by evolutionary psychologists. However, there are other, deeper archetypal structures that correspond to general neurophysiological processes that are not associated with particular behavioral adaptations. These include basic perceptual and cognitive processes, such as those studied by the Gestalt psychologists. These archetypes operate more impersonally than the others, and may be experienced as abstract forms, including geometrical shapes, numerical relationships, and abstract processes (MacLennan, 2006, 2014; Stevens 2003, p. 65; von Franz, 1974). Jung is well known for his studies of mandala-like figures as indicators and even facilitators of psychological integration (e.g., Jung, *CW* 9, pt. 1). These impersonal, mathematical archetypes are especially important in science, because they condition our abstract understanding of many natural processes. Number "preconsciously orders both psychic thought processes and the manifestations of material reality" (von Franz, 1974, p. 53).

Advantages

Jungian psychology has been a useful, illuminating, and fruitful perspective from which to study the creative process. Indeed, Dyer (1991, ch. 10) lists more than 90 books published before 1991 that apply Jungian psychology to creativity (more than half published in the decade of the 80s). It will be worthwhile to mention a few of the ways that the concept of an archetype can help us to understand big-C scientific creativity.

One advantage of looking to the archetypes as sources of scientific inspiration is that they are universal, that is, phylogenetic adaptations of *Homo sapiens*. In that sense they are *natural* ways of understanding the world, and therefore better able to afford an intuitive understanding graspable by all people. That is, they are objective (i.e., public) rather than subjective (i.e., personal).

Furthermore, archetypal structures are not simply abstractions. As phylogenetic adaptations, they govern perception, motivation, affect, and behavior for biological ends. Therefore, when they are activated and experienced consciously, they are felt to be inherently meaningful. Since people unconsciously grasp these structures emotionally as well as intellectually, they are satisfying and have "the ring of truth." They are felt to be elegant and beautiful. Arguably, the most fruitful scientific theories are built around such an archetypal core. For example, Heisenberg (1975, p. 175) observes that in science an aesthetic response to the whole often precedes intellectual exploration of the details. He asks (1975, p. 175), "How comes it that with this shining forth of the beautiful into exact science the great connection becomes recognizable, even before it is understood in detail and before it can be rationally demonstrated?" It is not a result of conscious analysis for, "Among all those who have pondered on this question, it seems to have been universally agreed that this immediate recognition is not a consequence of discursive (i.e., rational) thinking" (Heisenberg, 1975, p. 177). Indeed, thinkers as diverse as Kepler, Pauli, and Jung (Heisenberg, 1975, 177–80) have attributed the process "to innate archetypes that bring about the recognition of forms" (Heisenberg, 1975, p. 178). Thus Pauli (1955, p. 153): "As ordering operators and image-formers in this world of symbolical images, the archetypes thus function as the sought-for bridge between the sense perceptions and the ideas and are, accordingly, a necessary presupposition even for evolving a scientific theory of nature." I think we must take seriously the phenomenological reports of those scientists who have created conceptual revolutions.

As innate structures of perception, motivation, affect, and behavior, the archetypes are at a fundamental level comprehensible; they are the universal and invariable dynamical patterns in our psyches, and therefore intuitively understandable. Thus archetypal scientific models and theories allow scientists to use all of their cognitive-emotional faculties — their intuition — to guide them in the further elaboration and verification of their insights (MacLennan, 2015). As a consequence, archetypal models and theories are especially fruitful, for they engage the whole scientist and suggest further elaborations and developments consistent with their archetypal root. Just as archetypal themes stimulate creativity in literature and the other arts, so also they are a source of inspiration in the sciences.

The utility of archetypally grounded scientific inspirations is illustrated by historical examples, one of the most famous of which is Kekulé's discovery of the benzene ring (Kekulé, 1890, tr. in Benfey, 1958). He said that he had a vision in a reverie of a serpent biting its tail, which is a paradigmatic archetypal image, the *ouroboros* (e.g., Jung, *CW* 12, passim, *CW* 14, passim; Stevens, 1998, pp. 13–14, 142–3, 192, 197, 261). He remarked that his "mental eye" had been "rendered more acute by visions of this kind," and he advised, "Let us learn to dream, gentlemen, then perhaps we shall find the truth."

Objections

One obvious objection to focusing on archetypal structures in scientific creativity is that there is no *a priori* reason to suppose that natural phenomena conform to these patterns. Although the archetypes are the fundamental dynamical structures of human neuropsychology and have been adaptive in human evolution on earth, one cannot assume that they are the structures of other natural phenomena. While they constitute inherently human ways of grasping the universe, it can be argued that they need not correspond to the inherent structure of the universe.

These are valid concerns; nevertheless, there are important reasons for focusing on archetypal sources for scientific creativity. First, there are, in general, several equally good ways for understanding a scientific phenomenon (e.g., the wave and matrix formulations of quantum mechanics). However, in the early, creative stages of the development of a scientific theory, when understanding is fragile, it is extremely valuable to have a model that affords multiple avenues of deep understanding. Development of the model will be facilitated if the scientist can bring to it multiple, intuitive modes of comprehension (somatic and affective as well as cognitive).

Moreover, if the archetypally-grounded model does not turn out to conform exactly to the phenomena under investigation, then it can be refined and brought into conformity during the elaboration and verification stages of the creative process. Even if an archetypal model is not entirely accurate, its fundamental embedding in human existence and understanding may grant it greater fruitfulness than a more accurate, but less illuminating and inspiring model. Thus archetypal models and theories persist and continue to inspire, even after they have been superseded by empirically or theoretically superior models and theories (wave mechanics in quantum theory might be cited as an example).

Evolutionary Neuropsychology

One useful way to understand creativity is in terms of Freud's distinction between *primary-process* and *secondary-process* thinking, for Kris (1952) already showed the importance of the primary processes to creativity. For while the secondary processes serve the *reality principle* and include the faculties of logic, analysis, and rational inference, the primary processes are characterized by imagination, wide-ranging association, play, and wish fulfillment; they serve the *pleasure principle*. As a consequence, the primary processes, which service *biological drives*, are more closely connected with the instincts; their locus is the unconscious, whereas the locus of the secondary processes is the preconscious, according to Freud. Fromm (1978) identified the primary/secondary distinction as the principal axis of cognitive function. Creative people seem to be able to move along this axis more easily than other people, thus allowing fluid alternation between the free and uncritical production of imaginative ideas, and their systematic elaboration and critical evaluation (Martindale, 1999). Primary-process thought is closely related to defocused (high capacity) attention and to broad and flat (vs. deep, "steep gradient") associative trees, and both defocused attention and flat associative trees are characteristic of creative people (Martindale, 1999; Mednick, 1962; Mendelsohn, 1976). Therefore, computer support for creativity ought to facilitate primary-process ideation, wide (vs. focused) attention, and unfettered association.

Primary-process thought is commonly supposed to be more primitive and childlike than secondary-process cognition. Thus, when a scientist resorts to the primary processes it is a sort of regression, but it is an *adaptive regression*, or "regression in service of the ego" (Noppe, 1999; Rosegrant, 1980, 1987; Stein, 1974, pp. 91–3; Wild, 1965), in that it is a conscious adoption of a less rational, more imaginative process for the sake of creativity. Therefore, computer support for creativity should facilitate an adaptive regression to playful, imaginative thinking.

Secondary-process cognition occurs with moderate levels of arousal ("alert wakefulness") as measured by EEG frequency and amplitude, heart rate, galvanic skin response, etc., whereas extremes of arousal ("emotional tension" vs. "sleep and reverie") are characterized by the primary processes and defocused attention (Martindale, 1999). A number of studies, by Martindale and others, have shown that creative people are in a low state of cortical arousal (compared to their resting level) during the inspiration phase of a consciously creative activity, but not during the elaboration phase or during activities not perceived to be creative. Thus, creativity seems to be enhanced by a low arousal state, but creative people do not seem to achieve this state by any sort of conscious control (creative people are below average at biofeedback tasks: Martindale, 1999). Incubation is not an exercise in willpower, and creative people describe the inspirational process as effortless and uncontrolled. Indeed, creative people have less than average cognitive inhibition, as reflected in lower levels of frontal-lobe activation (Eysenck, 1995; Martindale, 1989). Moreover, functional neuroanatomy supports *transient hypofrontality* as a characteristic of creative activity (Dietrich, 2003). In many cases big-C creative people have learned to place themselves in environments that decrease their level of arousal without significant conscious effort or intent; these environmental interventions operate on an unconscious, even physiological, level (Martindale, 1999; Stein, 1974, pp. 105–7, 194). Therefore, computer support for inspiration should facilitate disinhibition, defocused attention, and diminished arousal through control of the environment.

Computer imaging studies generally support Martindale's conclusions (Jung, Mead, Carrasco & Flores, 2013). Evolutionary epistemology explains creativity as a process of blind variation and selective attention, which correspond to divergent and convergent thinking (Campbell, 1960). The divergent process is primarily served by the brain's *default mode network* (which facilitates stimulus-independent thought, i.e., imagination), and convergent thought is served by the *cognitive control network* (which is stimulus driven). Within these networks, disinhibitory processes permit divergent activity leading to blind variation, and excitatory processes focus attention for selective retention, respectively. Therefore, computer support for inspiration should promote activation of the default mode network, allowing the mind to wander down archetypal paths.

In his analysis of the archetypes in terms of evolutionary psychology and neuropsychology, Stevens (2003, esp. ch. 13) has argued that the principal neural substrate for the archetypes is the right hemisphere and lower brain systems associated especially with instinctive (phylogenetically determined) behavioral programs. Associations in the right hemisphere are symbolic and diffuse, rather than literal and linear, as they are in the left. Under ordinary conditions the left hemisphere filters and represses ideational content coming from the right, which seems bizarre and inexplicable to the left, due to the right's nonverbal, non-logical, and imagistic nature. However, people may experience this content during dreams, reveries, and other states of diminished arousal, when the vigilance of the left hemisphere is relaxed. Similarly, there is evidence for greater hemispheric interactivity preceding the flash of insight (Beeman & Bowden, 2000; Bogen & Bogen, 1999; Bowden & Jung-Beeman, 2003, 2007; Wegbreit, Suzuki, Grabowecky, Kounios & Beeman, 2014). Therefore, in order to use computers to improve scientific inspiration, our project aims, on the one hand, to create an environment of low arousal, defocused attention, and diffuse association, and, on the other, to stimulate preferentially the right hemisphere by images likely to activate the archetypal modules that underlie deep understanding.

AN INSPIRATION ENGINE

Goals

In a special issue of the *International Journal of Human-Computer Studies* devoted to computer support for creativity, Lubart (1995) distinguishes four different ways of providing this support:

1. As "nanny" to help manage the creative process,
2. As "pen-pal" to facilitate communication among collaborators,
3. As "coach" to enhance the creative process, and
4. As "colleague" to cooperate in the actual production of creative ideas.

In terms of this taxonomy, the author's research falls in category 3 since it is intended to enhance the incubation process so that the scientist-user is more likely to be inspired by significant creative ideas. In particular, it aims to develop an *inspiration engine*.

Creativity is a consequence of both personality factors and the situation (Nickerson, 1999; Stein, 1974, pp. 19–29, 194–250). The personality factors, some of which are heritable and some learned, have been studied extensively (e.g., Feist, 1999), but that is not the focus of the research described in this chapter, which aims to use technology to create a situation in which scientific creativity is more likely to occur no matter what the scientist's personality may be. In particular, this research focuses on the incubation phase, in order to facilitate a creative scientific synthesis.

Consistent with the preceding conclusions about the role of archetypal structures in scientific thought, this project's approach is to present archetypal images to scientists in order to inspire them with potential reconceptualizations of their problem. However, since archetypes are not static structures, but dynamic processes, the system provides dynamic, variable, and interactive visual experiences for the user. An additional reason for a dynamic approach is that many of the problems for which a scientist might be seeking a creative solution involve processes rather than static relationships. These dynamic, nondeterministic, and interactive visual experiences are termed *image flows*.

More specifically, the system presents video experiences to the user that are intended to engage the innate releasing mechanisms of unconscious archetypal processes, which then proceed in parallel with the visual experience. The external (visual) and internal (psychological) dynamics become coupled.

If the structure of the archetype is completely or partially consistent with the target problem, then the researcher will experience a feeling of deep understanding and intuitive insight into the problem, which may be elaborated more systematically and analytically in later stages of the creative activity. This approach meets the requirements of a *creative problem solving environment* (Hewett, 2005), but its novelty lies in its orientation toward archetypal sources of inspiration.

Archetypes are neither static images nor purely sequential processes. Rather, they are more like control programs, which regulate an organism's interaction with its environment. As Jung (*CW* 18, para. 1228) said, *archetype* "is not meant to denote an inherited idea, but rather an inherited mode of functioning, … a 'pattern of behavior'." When a visual perception has activated an archetype, the perceiver projects archetypal structure onto the stimulus, and the two (perceiver and stimulus) can interact in a coherent manner so long as the two structures (internal and external) are congruent. Therefore, this project's goal is to permit the user to interact with image flows, not directing them, but guiding them according to the possibilities they afford. In effect, the user should be able to actively explore the unfolding archetypal structure.

As the scientist-user explores the space of archetypal images, it is intended that he or she will be inspired with ideas relevant to the target problem. Therefore, another goal is to have "low-interference capture techniques," that is, means of recording ideas and intuitions without interfering with the wide-focus, non-verbal, non-analytic incubation process. These captured inspirations are linked to the places in the image trajectory that stimulated them. Furthermore, since the researcher's trajectory through the image space is not predetermined, they may want to return to "branch points" (places where they influenced the process) so they can explore different possibilities. More generally, the user can "drop a marker" at any interesting place in the image sequence so that they can return to it later for further exploration

The essence of the incubation stage is that the mind is not consciously engaged with the target problem. Therefore, an additional goal of this approach is, so far as possible, to decrease the role of conscious processing during this phase of the creative activity. In particular, it should facilitate an *adaptive regression to primary processes* and decrease conscious filtering and editing of content arising from the unconscious. As is well known, premature conscious judgment and criticism can interfere with creativity (Nickerson, 1999). Therefore, the experience should be such as to increase right-hemisphere activity relative to the left-hemisphere, both by stimulating right-hemisphere processes and by decreasing left-hemisphere inhibition of the right, since this inhibition is more common in scientists than in artists (Martindale, 1999). This should be in a context of overall disinhibition, low cortical arousal, especially in the frontal lobes (transient hypofrontality), and defocused attention (Martindale, 1999; Dietrich, 2003).

Image Flows

Definition

An archetype is an abstract structure that organizes conscious content, including perception, motivation, affect, and behavior, in order to facilitate some biological adaptation (Jung, *CW* 9, pt. 1, para. 155). A stimulus in the environment can activate an archetypal process, and subsequent stimuli can maintain its activation and channel it in directions permitted by its structure. The resulting experiences are a co-creation of the external stimuli and internal regulatory mechanisms. Therefore, the goal of the inspiration engine is to generate *archetypal image flows*, that is, continuous sequences of images conformable to an archetypal structure, in order to stimulate and maintain the activation of that archetype in the user. The intent is that if the images or their evolving sequence seem to resonate with the target problem, then the scientist-user will note ("capture") these associations for later elaboration, verification, or additional computer-mediated incubation and inspiration.

To accomplish these purposes an image flow must be more than a simple sequence of images, for archetypes are behavioral control modules, analogous to programs. Therefore, flows may have branch points, at which environmental conditions, including user inputs, can influence the direction of the flow. Image flows may also include a certain amount of nondeterminism, permitting them to wander randomly within bounds, but the capture mechanisms always permit an interesting flow to be reproduced.

The inspiration engine is intended to contain an open-ended and expanding library of image flows corresponding to various archetypal structures, any one of which could inspire a new scientific model or theory. This preliminary investigation is limited to a few archetypal structures described in the literature and to informal tests of their efficacy in stimulating scientific creativity (described below). Subsequent research will develop more systematic methods for discovering, implementing, and validating image flows for inclusion in the system library.

Examples

In order to make the method clearer, it will be helpful to describe several simple image flows. The simplest (and least interesting) image flow is just a sequence of discrete images chosen for their archetypal content (many of these are documented in the depth psychology literature). In the most basic case this amounts to a slide show, with each image cross-fading into the next. A simple variant of the slide show is a cumulative flow, in which successive pictures are added to a display depicting the history of the flow; this makes the structure of the flow more salient. A slightly more sophisticated version of the slide show uses standard "morphing" software to transform each image into its successor. Even these simple image flows need not be purely linear and deterministic, but could incorporate cycles and branch points (subject to user choice or random selection).

The abstract sequence of small integers is an important archetypal structure (von Franz, 1974). Commenting on the deep correspondence between physical processes and unconscious psychological processes, Jung remarked, "I have a distinct feeling that number is a key to the mystery, since it is just as much discovered as it is invented. It is quantity as well as meaning" (letter quoted in von Franz, 1974, p. 9). Similarly, in an essay recently published for the first time, Pauli writes, "Mathematics … has not only a quantitative side but also a qualitative one, which comes to the fore, for example, in the theory of numbers and topology" (Pauli, 2001, p. 196).

Each of the small integers is associated with a rich field of archetypal ideas, for example, the number *one* with unity, integrity, wholeness; *two* with polarity and opposition; *three* with mediation, conjunction, and process; *four* with balance and stability. Each of these ideas, in turn, can be symbolized in innumerable ways, and in particular by either concrete or abstract images. These various representations may be more or less inspiring to a scientist-user in the context of a particular target problem, and so it is essential that the *deep structure* of the number sequence be visualizable in a variety of *surface structures* (concrete image flows).

Other examples of abstract structures that might be especially inspiring for the purposes of scientific creativity include ubiquitous models of emergence, self-organization, and growth (e.g., cellular automata, L-systems, fractals, period doubling, diffusion-limited aggregation). These processes can be visualized in a variety of suggestive ways, and afford many means by which the user can intervene in the process and affect its evolution. These are just a few examples of how abstract archetypal structures can be used to generate images flows in order to inspire scientific creativity. (Several of these examples are explored in detail below.)

Deep Structure

As Jung stressed, the archetypes are unconscious abstract structures that can be filled with concrete conscious content in innumerable ways (e.g., *CW* 9, pt. 1, para. 155). That is, the *deep structure* of an activated unconscious archetype regulates the *surface structure* of the stream of consciousness (in interaction, of course, with the environment); the abstract archetype is *projected* on the concrete situation. Since different concrete images may differently affect different scientists with different target problems, the inspiration engine similarly distinguishes between the deep and surface structures of image flows. At the deep level the system operates on abstract images (formal structures), such as a cycle of small integers: 1, 2, 3, 4. At the surface level, however, the user views and interacts with concrete images corresponding to the abstract images. For example, concrete images of the cycle 1, 2, 3, 4 include images of the four seasons; geometric figures of 0, 1, 2, and 3 dimensions; images of four stages in the life cycle; 90 degree rotations of some figure; mandalas with circular, twofold, threefold, and fourfold symmetry (see "Dynamic Quaternity" below).

Therefore, at the heart of the inspiration engine is a machine that computes abstract trajectories in conformity with the deep structures of image flows. The goal is to permit image flows in spaces with a wide variety of topologies, both continuous and discrete, and so the system will be built on the U-machine architecture (MacLennan, 2010). The U-machine exploits a theorem proved by Pavel Urysohn (1898–1924), which shows that any second-countable metric space is *homeomorphic* (topologically equivalent) to a subset of a Hilbert space. This is important because all the familiar discrete and continuous topological spaces, including spaces of images, are second-countable metric spaces. The U-machine implements general computation over Hilbert spaces by means of linear combinations of simple nonlinear basis functions, in accord with several universal approximation theorems (e.g., Haykin, 2008, pp. 166–8, 219–20, 236–9, 323–6). In particular, computation in the Hilbert space can be approximated by simple neural-network-style algorithms, which are straightforward to implement and facilitate learning and adaptation. The trajectory in the Hilbert space is generated by integration of a system of differential equations defined over the space and over the inputs provided by the user (appropriately mapped into the vector space). The parameters of the equations can be determined in a variety of ways, including explicit programming, offline computation of optimal coefficient matrices, and online neural-network learning algorithms.

Surface Structure

An *image projector* maps an abstract Hilbert-space representation into a concrete image so that an abstract trajectory in Hilbert space generates a corresponding sequence of concrete images. The inspiration engine will provide an open-ended library of projectors that can be used with any particular abstract flow. For example, the small-integer sequence can be projected into a variety of different image sequences, some more concrete, some less. The programming of a projector will depend on (1) the structure of the abstract flow, (2) the topology of the concrete image space (including its metric or similarity measure), and (3) the details of the Urysohn embedding. Initially, the project will include some basic projectors suitable to the archetypal image flows explored in the prototype implementation.

For a given abstract trajectory, different concrete projections may be more or less likely to stimulate a creative insight in a particular scientist working on a particular problem. Therefore, it is valuable for the scientist to experience different projections of the same abstract flow. Although it would be easy to allow the user to select the projector, it may be more productive to use one or another kind of "blind variation," that is, variation undirected by the goal at hand (Simonton, 1999, chs. 2–3). Initially, the project will include several possibilities. First, the initial projector may be selected randomly. Second, the user may choose to restart the flow with a different randomly selected projector. Third, at any point in the image trajectory, the user may ask that the system to switch to a new random projector. Finally, the user may specify that the system will spontaneously change projectors from time to time.

Navigation

The inspiration engine allows a scientist to explore a space of inspiring images by following archetypal paths of image transformation. Therefore, it is natural to use metaphors of navigation and path following in describing the process and the software tools used to control it.

Several tools allow diversion of the image trajectory from the path it would have otherwise followed. A common application of these tools is the further exploration of an image flow, by diverting it in different ways, in order to seek additional or better inspirations. One simple way to divert the trajectory is *parameter perturbation*. Some image flows (e.g., those associated with emergence, self-organization, and growth) will have continuously variable parameters that affect the path taken through image space. The scientist-user can control these parameters (e.g., by a mouse, joystick, or gamepad) to affect the evolution of the image flow in order to explore different regions of the space. Another diversion tool expands the dimension of an image flow, thereby affording the trajectory additional degrees of freedom in which to move. This is implemented by allowing additional dimensions of the Hilbert space to affect the trajectory by entering into its computation. A diversion of the opposite sort is obtained by projecting the abstract image flow into a lower dimensional space. There are two varieties, depending on whether the trajectory is calculated in the lower dimensional space (thus altering the trajectory), or whether the trajectory is calculated in the original higher dimensional space before projection to a lower dimensional space for projection into a concrete image. In either case, the user may cycle through different nonempty subsets of the original set of dimensions as a means of exploring the image flow.

The user can control the projection of the abstract trajectory into concrete images (e.g., by choosing different projectors). Unlike other navigation controls, this does not affect the abstract trajectory, but rather, by radically altering the visual experience of the trajectory, it has the effect of shifting the user into a completely different concrete image space (a different concrete image flow). Thus it is a kind of navigation between concrete image spaces.

As previously mentioned, image flows are not simple sequences, but in accord with the interactive nature of archetypal structures, may have *branch points* at which the trajectory can go in different directions. At a branch point the user can choose the direction of the trajectory, or it may be determined randomly or deterministically by the dynamics of the flow. Indeed, one can view parameter perturbation as a having a branch point at every point in a flow.

Users can control their trajectory through image space in several ways. For example, they can control the rate of the image flow. This allows them to skim through uninspiring parts and linger where the flow of ideas is stronger. However, the same images presented at different rates may affect the viewer differently, and so it is useful to be able to experience the same flow at different rates. Different time scales bring out different qualities of the flow.

Capture

It is to be expected that the scientist-user will wish to return to inspiring regions of the image space, either because they have wandered into less inspiring regions or because they want to seek additional inspiration. Therefore, the entire trajectory is automatically recorded so that the scientist can return to any part of it and explore alternatives. By a simple click or voice command, users can "drop a marker" at any interesting place in the image flow, so that they can return to it later. The user does not need to name these markers, since that would be an interruption and too distracting, but the markers are cross-linked with other captured information (such as spoken or written comments), which facilitates finding a desired marker. Recorded branch points and other marked points can be revisited by jumping forward or backward in their sequence.

If the scientist-user has any ideas during the image flow, he or she may speak them and they will be recorded digitally and cross-linked to a location in the trajectory. The purpose of this mechanism is not to record ad lib lectures, but to capture isolated words, phrases, and short comments that will remind the user what was inspiring about an image, or that can be elaborated more systematically later. The scientist can also jot down notes or formulas, or sketch quick diagrams that suggest themselves along the way. The goal is to capture these in a way that does not interfere with the scientist's absorption in the flow. A digital tablet or wireless pen of some kind could be used. As with spoken notes, they are cross-linked with points in the image trajectory. Cross-linking of captured ideas (spoken, written) with points in the image flow allows inspirations to be captured and explored in more detail at a later time. Some inspirations will be sterile but others, hopefully, will fuel scientific creativity if they are pursued.

Architecture

This section describes the architecture of the intuition engine in more detail. Because flows can be deterministic or stochastic, an abstract image flow can include a deterministic component D and a stochastic component S. The state vector of the stochastic system is updated $s' = S\left(c_s, s\right)$ where c_s is a vector of control parameters provided by the user that govern, for example, the mean and variance of the pseudo-random processes. The new abstract image is defined by the deterministic system, which takes as input control parameters c_D provided by the user, the previous deterministic state x, and the stochastic state vector s'; that is, $x' = D\left(c_D, x, s'\right)$. The new abstract image x' is passed to a projector, which displays the corresponding concrete image. The following pseudo-code describes the main loop:

$\left(c_D, c_S\right) :=$ acquire control parameters from user;

$$s := S\big(c_{S}, s\big);$$

$$x := D\big(c_{D}, x, s\big);$$

pass x to current projector and update display;

With respect to software modularization, the control interface is considered part of each image projector class, since controlling an image flow is often by means of interacting with its concrete representation, for example by touching or pointing at a location in the image.

Evaluation and Evolution

The inspiration engine is intended to be a flexible, adaptive, and evolving tool for promoting scientific creativity. The system is extensible in that its libraries of both abstract image flows and image projectors are open-ended. This is a manual means of adaptation and evolution, since programmers must add the new flows and projectors. Eventually the project will investigate more automatic means of adaptation, most likely by neural-network-style reinforcement learning. Users will indicate trajectories that have proved valuable in their scientific research, and this will modify the parameters of the image flow to make these productive trajectories more likely to be followed.

EXAMPLE IMAGE FLOWS

Dynamic Quaternity

The *quaternity* is an archetype that Jung studied at great length (Jung, *CW* 9, pt. 2, ch. XIV, *CW* 14, paras. 1–12; von Franz, 1974, Part II). Indeed, "Jung devoted practically the whole of his life's work to demonstrating the vast psychological significance of the number four" (von Franz, 1974, p. 115). It arises from a pair of oppositions, as found for example in the four classical elements earth, water, air, and fire, which result from the opposed qualities warm-cool and moist-dry (Aristotle, *Gen. & corr.*, 330b4–6). Thus earth is dry and cool, water is cool and moist, air is moist and warm, and fire is warm and dry. The four humors (black bile, phlegm, blood, yellow bile) are another example. As a result of its double-opposition structure, the quaternity is a common symbol of balance and stability. Each pair of complementary opposites generates a continuum between the extremes, with a neutral or balance point in the middle. Overall balance is represented by the coincidence of the two neutral points, forming crossed oppositions. In two dimensions, therefore, balance, stability, and equilibrium are symbolized by a "square of opposition."

However, Jung also stressed the dynamic aspects of the quaternity, for example, the rotation of the elements (earth to water to air to fire to earth, or vice versa). The dynamic quaternity is ubiquitous, for example in the seasonal cycle (moist spring, warm summer, dry autumn, cool winter) and the life cycle (moist youth, warm adult, dry elder, cold death) (cf. also Yeats' "Four Ages of Man"). The dynamic quaternity provides richer opportunities for inspiring image flows than does the static one. It is a continuous cycle, but generated from two polar oppositions.

The simplest abstract image space accommodating the dynamic quaternity is the space of normalized complex numbers, that is, numbers of the form $e^{i\phi}$, for $\phi \in [0, 2\pi)$, which is isomorphic to the special orthogonal group SO(2) of planar rotations. The opposed qualities are represented by the real numbers +1, -1 and the imaginary numbers +i, -i.

The basic dynamics of the image flow is a rotation, which can have an increasing or decreasing imaginary exponent representing opposite directions of rotation. Simple controls allow the user to determine the direction and rate of rotation, or to perturb either randomly. Therefore, in the simplest case, the abstract image flow is defined $z(t) \equiv e^{i\omega(t)t}$, where the angular rate $\omega(t)$ is a parameter (a bounded real number) controlled by the user. If the user can directly control the angle of rotation via $\theta(t)$, then the flow is $z(t) \equiv e^{i[\omega(t)t + \theta(t)]}$.

Jung has noted the close connection between the quaternity and its center (Jung, *CW* 12, para. 327). Two different polarities are integrated into a unity by sharing a common center (Jung, *CW* 12, para. 310), as do the real and imaginary axes in the Argand diagram. Conversely, a center sometimes generates a quaternity from itself (Jung, *CW* 12, para. 327). The center, therefore, comes to symbolize a reconciliation of both the oppositions and the paradoxes of a psychological problem; Jung calls it "the place of creative change" (*CW* 12, para. 186). Initially there is a circumambulation of the center as solution, but this hidden goal attracts the path inward in a convergent spiral trajectory, in which the same issues are revisited repeatedly but with an ever-growing approximation to the solution (Jung *CW* 12, paras. 34, 325); that is, it is a fixed-point attractor. Jakob Bernoulli alludes to the archetypal character of the spiral in his famous epitaph: *Eadem mutata resurgo* ("Though changed, I arise the same"), as Jung (*CW* 12, para. 325) observes.

Therefore, the quaternity image flow can be more inspiring if it is allowed to spiral inward toward a center (damped oscillation) or outward toward a circumference. This is accomplished by including the magnitude of the complex number in the abstract image: $z(t) \equiv r(t) e^{i[\omega(t)t + \theta(t)]}$.

The magnitude $r(t)$ is governed by its own differential equation subject to user-controlled parameters, which govern the magnitude's rate of contraction or (bounded) expansion, or its oscillation. Alternately, we may constrain the magnitude $|z(t)| < 1$ by a sigmoid function:

$$z(t) \equiv \frac{e^{i[\omega(t)t + \theta(t)]}}{1 + e^{-r(t)}}, \text{ with } r(t) \in (-\infty, \infty).$$

There is no need to restrict the orbits to be circular. Since quaternities are naturally imaged by squares, one can have diamond-shaped orbits with $z(t) = x(t) + iy(t)$ where $\dot{x} = \text{sgn } y$ and $\dot{y} = -\text{sgn } x$.

Indeed, one can allow the user to define quite arbitrary "restoring forces," for example, on the real axis, $\ddot{x} = -f(x)$.

Suppose that $f(x)$ is continuously differentiable for $|x| < c$ for some $c > 0$ and that $xf(x) > 0$ for all $x \neq 0$. Then define the dynamics by $\dot{x} = y$ and $\dot{y} = -f(x)$. For $|x| < c$ the state will move in periodic orbits (Brauer & Nohel, 1989, pp. 197–9).

There are many possible concrete image flows for the dynamic quaternity, but most of them are relatively simple because the quaternity itself is simple. Perhaps the most direct projection uses the real and imaginary components of the abstract state to control the horizontal and vertical position of a displayed object. In this case the object moves cyclically as governed by the dynamical equations, perhaps spiraling in or out in accord with the controls. Similarly, the phase and magnitude of the complex number could control the orientation and size of any displayed object.

Another representation, which might better reflect the complementary relation between the variables (for example, as position and velocity, or as potential and kinetic energy), is to represent both the real and imaginary parts on parallel scales, perhaps with a straight line connecting the current values of the variables. Similarly, the complex state could be used to control the color of any image in a double-opponent system: the sine of the phase angle controls hue along a yellow-blue axis, its cosine controls it along a red-green axis, and the magnitude of the complex number controls either saturation or brightness.

More naturalistic concrete images can be used for the dynamic quaternity, such as images of the seasons. The projector would use an appropriate set of images defined over the region of the complex plane that constitutes the state space of the abstract flow.

Logistic Map

The depth psychology literature does not seem to provide evidence for chaos as an archetype, but the onset of chaos has come to be recognized as a critical phenomenon in many disciplines, and so it is a good candidate for an image flow. Perhaps the simplest example of deterministic chaos is the *logistic map*, $x_{n+1} = rx_n(1 - x_n)$, with $x_n \in (0,1)$. This recurrence relation exhibits a variety of dynamical behaviors depending on the rate parameter $r \in (0,4]$ (e.g., May, 1976). As r is increased, the behavior of the map shifts from a fixed-point attractor, to a period-2 attractor, through a regime of accelerating period doubling (period 4, period 8, etc.), until at the "accumulation point" $r_c \approx 3.569945672$ the behavior becomes chaotic. In the chaotic regime there are isolated "islands of stability" exhibiting periods of 3, 6, 12, etc.

To use the logistic map as an image flow, one can allow the user to change the state x_n or the rate parameter r at any time, either by setting them to specific values or by randomization. In this way the user can explore the edge of chaos and the phenomena surrounding it. The rate parameter can be adjusted directly by a slider, but the sensitive dependence on its value near the critical region invites other ways of controlling it, such as an exponential scale around the critical point. For example, one can use $r = r_c + 2.1\left(e^{|\rho|} - 1\right)\operatorname{sgn}\rho$, where is $\rho \in [-1,1]$ is the user's control and r is limited to (0,4).

Because the logistic map generates a discrete sequence of real numbers, it does not immediately suggest rich concrete representations. The prototype implementation makes the sequence easier to visualize by interpolating points between successive x_n values in order to convert the discrete sequence into an approximately continuous function $x(t)$.

It maps these real values $x(t)$ into both the brightness and size of an object (such as a circle) to make their variation more apparent. In parallel it presents a graph of $x(t)$, since that is often suggestive (see Figure 1). The user can also control the rate at which the sequence is generated, since this affects perception of the image flow. Setting the state to a particular value can be done with a slider or by clicking on the image to set its size.

Figure 1. Prototype concrete projection of logistic map image flow; the green disk changes in both brightness and size in accord with x(t), which is also plotted. This prototype was implemented in NetLogo 5.1.

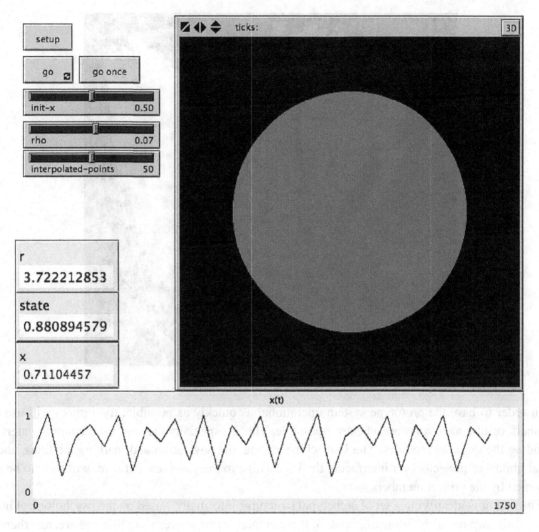

There are of course many other chaotic systems that may provide inspiring image flows. Moreover, automata that have complex behavior in Wolfram's Class IV (Wolfram, 2002) can also generate image flows capable of inspiring scientific reconceptualization (see Figure 2).

FUTURE RESEARCH DIRECTIONS

The prototype implementation of the inspiration machine will include only those components required to demonstrate the concept and to begin evaluation of its usefulness. These include the U-machine interpreter for computing abstract trajectories, software for navigation and branch-point/marker management, an initial library of projectors for converting the abstract trajectories to concrete sequences of images, graphics modules, and support for a simple input device such as a mouse, trackball, joystick, or touch-sensitive screen.

Figure 2. Part of an image flow generated by a Class IV cellular automaton, "The Game of Life"; the image is evolving upward through space.

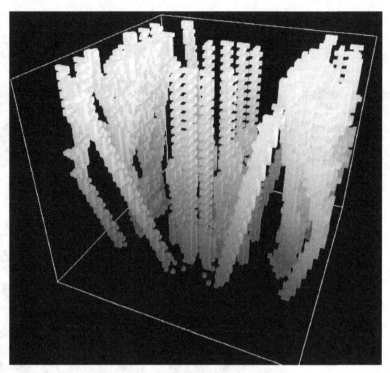

In order to have the prototype system operational as quickly as possible, the project will use off-the-shelf, open-source software whenever possible. This is especially the case for the human interface, including the graphics modules. The U-machine engine, the navigation and marking facilities, and an initial library of projectors for interfacing the U-machine to the graphics software, will have to be programmed by the project members.

The author is identifying a set of archetypal structures informally, based on the psychological literature and his own research. Some examples of these archetypal structures were listed above, and there are prototype implementations of the dynamic quaternity, logistic map, and cellular automaton. The author plans some informal evaluations of the methodology by comparing creativity with and without it, and between archetypal and non-archetypal image flows. One possibility is to use association tests, where creativity is correlated to wider association trees (Mednick, 1962). Subsequent research will investigate more formal evaluation using validated assessment instruments.

Therefore, another immediate task is to identify assessment instruments that can be used to evaluate the effect of the system on scientific creativity. In spite of the fact that many existing instruments focus on small-C creativity and problem solving, the author is looking for suitable methods in the literature. For example, a panel of scientists could each rate the creativity of solutions produced by the treatment and control groups (i.e., using or not using the inspiration engine) to a selection of real and synthetic scientific problems.

The project's longer-range plans are as follows. One significant goal of the later phases of this investigation will be to begin using formal assessment instruments to determine the effect of various system components on scientific creativity. For an example of an indirect assessment, subjects can rate how much their creativity has been stimulated. Direct assessment could use a panel of experts to evaluate the solutions. These experiments will permit the inspiration engine to be refined, eliminating ineffective aspects and further developing the valuable ones. In particular, the project intends to increase the library of archetypal flows and their projectors. This will be accomplished in part by mining the literature of depth psychology and allied disciplines, but also by identifying or developing instruments that will allow identification of archetypal flows by means of their effect on creativity. The prototype software, which is the goal of the first phase of this project, will have a basic human interface comprising readily available hardware (e.g., monitor, pointing device) and interface software. Subsequent work will explore a more immersive environment (e.g., 3D goggles, headphones) and a wider range of input mechanisms (e.g., microphone, graphics tablet, motion sensor). These extensions should not affect the core U-machine software, but they will require modifications to the projector software.

CONCLUSION

This research differs from prior investigations of computer-enhanced creativity in several important respects. First, it focuses on high-impact scientific creativity, rather than on lower-impact everyday creativity. Second, it directly addresses the unconscious processes that occur during the incubation phase, which may lead to unanticipated insights. Third, it concentrates on innate unconscious processes, because these underlie conceptual models that are especially intuitive and fruitful. Finally, because the computerized system is based on a particular model of significant scientific creativity, it can be used as an empirical test of the role of innate unconscious processes in scientific progress.

The computerized tool permits the definition of abstract image flows that conform to unconscious archetypal dynamics. The abstract images are mapped to concrete images intended to stimulate and guide unconscious creative processes in the scientist-user, who explores the space of images governed by the flow. The inspiration engine will be open-ended and adaptable, so that it can evolve as our understanding of the wellsprings of scientific creativity improve.

ACKNOWLEDGMENT

I am grateful to the referees for many useful suggestions, which have improved this chapter significantly.

REFERENCES

Arieti, S. (1980). New psychological approaches to creativity. In D. W. Fritz (Ed.), *Perspectives on creativity and the unconscious* (pp. 83–103). Oxford, OH: Miami University.

Beeman, M. J., & Bowden, E. M. (2000). The right hemisphere maintains solution-related activation for yet-to-be-solved problems. *Memory & Cognition*, 28(7), 1231–1241. doi:10.3758/BF03211823 PMID:11126944

Benfey, O. T. (1958). August Kekulé and the birth of the structural theory of organic chemistry in 1858. *Journal of Chemical Education*, *35*(1), 21–23. doi:10.1021/ed035p21

Boden, M. A. (1991). *The creative mind: Myths and mechanisms*. New York, NY: Basic Books.

Bogen, J. E., & Bogen, G. M. (1999). Split-brains: Interhemispheric exchange in creativity. In M. A. Runco & S. R. Pritzker (Eds.), *Encyclopedia of creativity* (Vol. 2, pp. 571–575). San Diego, CA: Academic Press.

Bowden, E. M., & Jung-Beeman, M. (2003). Aha! — Insight experience correlates with solution activation in the right hemisphere. *Psychonomic Bulletin & Review*, *10*(3), 730–737. doi:10.3758/BF03196539 PMID:14620371

Bowden, E. M., & Jung-Beeman, M. (2007). Methods for investigating the neural components of insight. *Methods (San Diego, Calif.)*, *42*(1), 87–99. doi:10.1016/j.ymeth.2006.11.007 PMID:17434419

Brauer, F., & Nohel, J. A. (1989). *The qualitative theory of ordinary differential equations: An introduction*. New York, NY: Dover.

Campbell, D. T. (1960). Blind variation and selective retention in creative thought as in other knowledge processes. *Psychological Review*, *67*(6), 380–400. doi:10.1037/h0040373 PMID:13690223

Council, J. R., Bromley, K. A., Zabelina, D. L., & Waters, C. G. (2007). Hypnotic enhancement of creative drawing. *The International Journal of Clinical and Experimental Hypnosis*, *55*(4), 467–485. doi:10.1080/00207140701506623 PMID:17786662

Dietrich, A. (2003). Functional neuroanatomy of altered states of consciousness: The transient hypofrontality hypothesis. *Consciousness and Cognition*, *12*(2), 231–256. doi:10.1016/S1053-8100(02)00046-6 PMID:12763007

Dorfman, J., Shames, V. A., & Kihlstrom, J. F. (1996). Intuition, incubation, and insight: Implicit cognition in problem solving. In G. Underwood (Ed.), *Implicit cognition* (pp. 257–286). Oxford, UK: Oxford University Press.

Dyer, D. (1991). *Cross-currents of Jungian thought: An annotated bibliography*. New York, NY: Shambhala.

Eysenck, H. J. (1995). *Genius: The natural history of creativity*. Cambridge, UK: Cambridge University Press. doi:10.1017/CBO9780511752247

Feist, G. J. (1999). The influence of personality on artistic and scientific creativity. In R. J. Sternberg (Ed.), *Handbook of creativity* (pp. 273–296). Cambridge, UK: Cambridge University Press.

Freud, S. (1948). *Leonardo da Vinci* (A. A. Brill, Trans.). London, UK: Routledge & Kegan Paul.

Freud, S. (1948a). The relation of the poet to day-dreaming. In *Collected papers of Sigmund Freud* (Vol. 4). London, UK: Hogarth Press.

Fritz, D. W. (Ed.). (1980). *Perspectives on creativity and the unconscious*. Oxford, OH: Miami University.

Fromm, E. (1978). Primary and secondary process in waking and in altered states of consciousness. *Journal of Altered States of Consciousness*, *4*, 115–128.

Gardner, H. (1993). Seven creators of the modern era. In J. Brockman (Ed.), *Creativity* (pp. 28–47). New York, NY: Simon & Schuster.

Gedo, J. E. (1997). Psychoanalytic theories of creativity. In M. A. Runco (Ed.), *The creativity research handbook* (Vol. 1, pp. 29–39). Cresskill, NJ: Hampton Press.

Hadamard, J. (1945). *An essay on the psychology of invention in the mathematical field*. Princeton, NJ: Princeton University Press.

Haykin, S. O. (2008). *Neural networks and learning machines* (3rd ed.). Upper Saddle River, NJ: Prentice-Hall.

Heisenberg, W. (1975). The meaning of beauty in the exact sciences. In W. Heisenberg (Ed.), *Across the frontiers* (P. Heath, Trans.). (pp. 166–183). New York, NY: Harper & Row.

Helmholtz, H. L. (1896). *Vorträge und Reden* (5th ed.; Vol. 1–2). Braunschweig: Friedrich Vieweg und Sohn.

Hewett, T. T. (2005). Informing the design of computer-based environments to support creativity. *International Journal of Human-Computer Studies*, *63*(4-5), 383–409. doi:10.1016/j.ijhcs.2005.04.004

Hines, T. (1991). The myth of right hemisphere creativity. *The Journal of Creative Behavior*, *25*(3), 223–227. doi:10.1002/j.2162-6057.1991.tb01373.x

Jung, C. G. (1934). *Modern man in search of a soul* (W. S. Dell & C. F. Baynes, Trans.). New York, NY: Harcourt Brace.

Jung, C. G. (CW). The collected works of C. G. Jung. H. Read, M. Fordham, & G. Adler (Eds.). London: Routledge & Kegan Paul, 1953–78; New York: Pantheon, 1953–60, and Bollingen Foundation, 1961–67; Princeton, NJ: Princeton University Press, 1967–78.

Jung, R. E., Mead, B. S., Carrasco, J., & Flores, R. A. (2013). The structure of creative cognition in the human brain. *Frontiers in Human Neuroscience*, *7*, 330. doi:10.3389/fnhum.2013.00330 PMID:23847503

Kaufman, J. C., & Beghetto, R. A. (2009). Beyond big and little: The four C model of creativity. *Review of General Psychology*, *13*(1), 1–12. doi:10.1037/a0013688

Kekulé, A. (1890). Benzolfest: Rede. *Berichte der Deutschen Chemischen Gesellschaft*, *23*(1), 1302–1311.

Kipling, R. (1937/1952). Working tools. In B. Ghiselin (Ed.), *The creative process: A symposium* (pp. 157–159). Berkeley, CA: University of California Press.

Kozbelt, A., Beghetto, R. A., & Runco, M. A. (2010). Theories of creativity. In J. C. Kaufman & R. J. Sternberg (Eds.), *The Cambridge handbook of creativity* (pp. 20–47). New York, NY: Cambridge University Press. doi:10.1017/CBO9780511763205.004

Kris, E. (1952). *Psychoanalytic explorations in art*. New York, NY: International Universities Press.

Kris, E. (1953). Psychoanalysis and the study of creative imagination. *Bulletin of the New York Academy of Medicine*, *29*, 334–351. PMID:13032689

Kuhn, T. (1970). *The structure of scientific revolutions* (2nd ed.). Chicago, IL: University of Chicago Press.

Lubart, T. (2005). How can computers be partners in the creative process: Classification and commentary on the special issue. *International Journal of Human-Computer Studies, 63*(4-5), 365–369. doi:10.1016/j.ijhcs.2005.04.002

MacLennan, B. J. (2006). Evolutionary Jungian psychology. *Psychological Perspectives, 49*(1), 9–28. doi:10.1080/00332920600732968

MacLennan, B. J. (2010). The U-machine: A model of generalized computation. *International Journal of Unconventional Computing, 6,* 265–283.

MacLennan, B. J. (2014). Neoplatonism in science: Past and future. In R. Berchman & J. Finamore (Eds.), *Metaphysical patterns in Platonism: Ancient, medieval, renaissance, and modern* (pp. 199–214). Somerset, UK: Prometheus.

MacLennan, B. J. (2015). Living Science. *Progress in Biophysics & Molecular Biology, 119*(3), 410–419. doi:10.1016/j.pbiomolbio.2015.08.009

Martindale, C. (1989). Personality, situation, and creativity. In J. A. Glover, R. R. Ronning, & C. R. Reynolds (Eds.), *Handbook of creativity* (pp. 211–228). New York, NY: Plenum. doi:10.1007/978-1-4757-5356-1_13

Martindale, C. (1999). Biological bases of creativity. In R. J. Sternberg (Ed.), *Handbook of creativity* (pp. 137–152). Cambridge, UK: Cambridge University Press.

May, R. M. (1976). Simple mathematical models with very complicated dynamics. *Nature, 261*(5560), 459–467. doi:10.1038/261459a0 PMID:934280

Mednick, S. A. (1962). The associative basis of the creative process. *Psychological Review, 69*(3), 220–232. doi:10.1037/h0048850 PMID:14472013

Mendelsohn, G. A. (1976). Associative and attentional processes in creative performance. *Journal of Personality, 44*(2), 341–369. doi:10.1111/j.1467-6494.1976.tb00127.x

Nemytskii, V. V., & Stepanov, V. V. (1989). *Qualitative theory of differential equations.* New York, NY: Dover.

Neumann, E. (1971). *Art and the creative unconscious* (R. Manheim, Trans.). New York, NY: Princeton University Press.

Nickerson, R. S. (1999). Enhancing creativity. In R. J. Sternberg (Ed.), *Handbook of creativity* (pp. 392–430). Cambridge, UK: Cambridge University Press.

Noppe, L. D. (1999). Unconscious. In M. A. Runco & S. R. Pritzker (Eds.), *Encyclopedia of creativity* (Vol. 2, pp. 673–679). San Diego: Academic Press.

Pauli, W. (1955). The influence of archetypal ideas on the scientific theories of Kepler. In C. G. Jung & W. Pauli (Eds.), *The interpretation of nature and psyche* (pp. 147–240). New York, NY: Pantheon Books.

Pauli, W. (2001). *Atom and archetype: The Pauli/Jung letters, 1928–1958* (C. A. Meier, Ed.). Princeton, NJ: Princeton University Press.

Poincaré, H. (1908/1952). Mathematical creation. In B. Ghiselin (Ed.), *The creative process: A symposium* (pp. 33–42). Berkeley, CA: University of California Press.

Poincaré, H. (1929). *The foundations of science: Science and hypothesis, the value of science, science and method* (G. B. Halstead, Trans.). New York, NY: The Science Press.

Reichhenbach, H. (1938). *Experience and prediction.* Chicago, IL: University of Chicago Press.

Rosegrant, J. (1980). Adaptive regression of two types. *Journal of Personality Assessment, 6*(6), 592–599. doi:10.1207/s15327752jpa4406_4 PMID:16366913

Rosegrant, J. (1987). A reconceptualization of adaptive regression. *Psychoanalytic Psychology, 4*(2), 115–130. doi:10.1037/h0079128

Sawyer, R. K. (2006). *Explaining creativity: The science of human innovation.* Oxford, UK: Oxford University Press.

Simonton, D. K. (1999). *Origins of genius: Darwinian perspectives on creativity.* New York, NY: Oxford.

Smith, S. M., & Dodds, R. A. (1999). Incubation. In M. A. Runco & S. R. Pritzker (Eds.), *Encyclopedia of creativity* (Vol. 2, pp. 39–44). San Diego, CA: Academic Press.

Stein, M. I. (1967). Creativity and culture. In R. L. Mooney & T. A. Razik (Eds.), *Explorations in creativity.* New York, NY: Harper.

Stein, M. I. (1974). Stimulating creativity: *Individual procedures (vol. 1).* New York, NY: Academic Press.

Stevens, A. (1993). *The two million-year-old self.* College Station, TX: Texas A&M University Press.

Stevens, A. (1998). *Ariadne's clue: A guide to the symbols of humankind.* Princeton, NJ: Princeton University Press.

Stevens, A. (2003). *Archetype revisited: An updated natural history of the self.* Toronto, Canada: Inner City Books.

von Franz, M.-L. (1974). *Number and time: Reflections leading toward a unification of depth psychology and physics* (A. Dykes, Trans.). Evanston, IL: Northwestern University Press.

Wallas, G. (1926). *The art of thought.* New York, NY: Harcourt.

Ward, T. B., & Kolomyts, Y. (2010). Cognition and creativity. In J. C. Kaufman & R. J. Sternberg (Eds.), *The Cambridge handbook of creativity* (pp. 93–112). New York, NY: Cambridge University Press. doi:10.1017/CBO9780511763205.008

Wegbreit, E., Suzuki, S., Grabowecky, M., Kounios, J., & Beeman, M. (2014). Visual attention modulates insight versus analytic solving of verbal problems. *Journal of Problem Solving, 4*(2), 94–115. PMID:24459538

Wertheimer, M. (1982). Productive thinking (M. Wertheimer, Ed.). Chicago, IL: University of Chicago Press.

Whiting, C. S. (1958). *Creative thinking.* New York, NY: Reinhold.

Wild, C. (1965). Creativity and adaptive regression. *Journal of Personality and Social Psychology*, 2(2), 161–169. doi:10.1037/h0022404 PMID:14316976

Wolfram, S. (2002). *A new kind of science*. Champaign, IL: Wolfram Media.

ADDITIONAL READING

Cropley, D. H., Cropley, A. J., Kaufman, J. C., & Runco, M. A. (Eds.). (2010). *The dark side of creativity*. Cambridge, UK: Cambridge University Press. doi:10.1017/CBO9780511761225

Dietert, R. R., & Dietert, J. (2013). *Science sifting: Tools for innovation in science and technology*. Singapore: World Scientific. doi:10.1142/8508

Gruber, H. E., & Bödeker, K. (Eds.). (2005). *Creativity, psychology and the history of science*. Dordrecht, Netherlands: Springer. doi:10.1007/1-4020-3509-8

Jacobi, J. (1973). *The psychology of C. G. Jung: An introduction with illustrations*. New Haven, CT: Yale University Press.

Jones, D. (2012). *The Aha! moment: A scientist's take on creativity*. Baltimore, MD: Johns Hopkins University Press.

Jung, C. G. (1983). *The Essential Jung. A. Storr (Sel. & Intr.)*. Princeton, NJ: Princeton University Press.

Kaufman, J. C., & Baer, J. (Eds.). (2005). *Creativity across domains: Faces of the Muse*. Mahwah, NJ: Lawrence Erlbaum.

Kaufman, J. C., & Sternberg, R. S. (Eds.). (2010). *The Cambridge handbook of creativity*. Cambridge, UK: Cambridge University Press. doi:10.1017/CBO9780511763205

Meheus, J., & Nickles, T. (Eds.). (2009). *Models of discovery and creativity. Origins: Studies in the Sources of Scientific Creativity 3*. Dordrecht, Netherlands: Springer. doi:10.1007/978-90-481-3421-2

Mitchell, W. J., Inouye, A. S., & Blumenthal, M. S. (Eds.). (2003). *Beyond productivity: Information technology, innovation, and creativity. National Research Council of the National Academies*. Washington, DC: National Academies Press.

Runco, M. A., & Pritzker, S. R. (Eds.). (1999). *Encyclopedia of creativity* (Vol. 1–2). San Diego: Academic Press.

Shavinina, L. V. (Ed.). (2003). *The international handbook on innovation*. Amsterdam, Netherlands: Elsevier.

Wierzbicki, A. P., & Nakamori, Y. (Eds.). (2007). *Creative environments: Issues of creativity support for the knowledge civilization age*. Berlin, Germany: Springer. doi:10.1007/978-3-540-71562-7

Young-Eisendrath, P., & Dawson, T. (Eds.). (1997). *The Cambridge companion to Jung*. Cambridge, UK: Cambridge University Press. doi:10.1017/CCOL0521473098

KEY TERMS AND DEFINITIONS

Archetype: The psychological aspect of an innate behavioral adaptation. When activated by a *releaser* (internal or external stimulus), it regulates perception, motivation, affect, and behavior to serve some biological function.

Big-C Creativity: Historically significant creativity, which in science usually depends upon a major reconceptualization of a problem domain.

Evolutionary Psychology: An approach to psychology that seeks to place the behavioral adaptations of *Homo sapiens* in their evolutionary context.

Hilbert Space: An abstract vector space, with an inner product, that is *complete* (includes all its limit points). Less formally, a Hilbert space is a Euclidean space of potentially infinite dimension.

Image Flow: A continuous sequence of images conformable to an archetype.

Incubation: In the context of creativity, a suspension of conscious work on a problem during which the unconscious mind continues involvement with the problem.

Inspiration: In the context of creativity, the apparently spontaneous emergence into consciousness of the solution to a problem after a period of *incubation* (q.v.).

Mandala: A circular image, typically with fourfold symmetry, symbolic of the cosmos or psychological wholeness. Mandalas can be two-dimensional, three-dimensional, or dynamic (e.g., danced).

Phylogenetic: Refers to evolved characteristics common to all members of a species.

Primary and Secondary Processes: Primary processes, which serve the pleasure principle and biological drives, are characterized by imagination and play. Secondary processes, which serve the reality principle, are characterized by reason and analysis.

Projector: An image projector is a software module that maps an abstract image (an element of a Hilbert space, q.v.) into a concrete visual image. It thus generates a concrete image flow from an abstract image flow.

Chapter 14
The Essence of Smart Homes:
Application of Intelligent Technologies towards Smarter Urban Future

Amirhosein Ghaffarianhoseini
University of Malaya (UM), Malaysia

Hossein Omrany
Universiti Teknologi Malaysia (UTM), Malaysia

Ali Ghaffarianhoseini
Auckland University of Technology, New Zealand

Anthony Fleury
Ecole des Mines de Douai, France

John Tookey
Auckland University of Technology, New Zealand

Nicola Naismith
Auckland University of Technology, New Zealand

Mahdiar Ghaffarianhoseini
University of Calgary, Canada

ABSTRACT

Smart homes have been predominantly pointed as one of the key constituents of intelligent environments. These are residential units substantially integrated with a communicating network of sensors and intelligent systems based on the application of new design initiatives and creative technologies. This study provides a holistic overview on the essence of smart homes besides demonstrating their current status, benefits and future directions. The study reveals that smart homes embrace significant potentials towards achieving comfort, security, independent lifestyle and enhanced quality of life. Findings urge the necessity to focus on further exploration of the social and environmental benefits derived from the application of creative technologies in smart homes. The study concludes that smart homes play a fundamental role in shaping the future cities. Finally, the study identifies a research gap indicating that there has been less consideration towards linking the fundamental potentials of smart homes to the overall performance and key indicators of smart cities.

DOI: 10.4018/978-1-5225-0016-2.ch014

1.0 INTRODUCTION

Smart homes embrace the concept of integrating intelligent technologies into residential spaces. Their primary aim is to increase the quality of users' life through the application of automated systems. Smart homes also facilitate constant monitoring and controlling for the patients by detecting the residents' behavioral patterns and activities through the embodied sensors and actuators installed throughout the unit. Smart homes offer the potential for enhanced safety, comfort, productivity, efficiency, and well-being. Smart homes are a promising solution for the building sector facing major environmental challenges namely, increased level of energy consumption, environmental pollution and urban heat island (UHI) impacts. The notion of smart homes has been gradually expanded to embrace the environmental, social and economic dimensions of sustainability. In fact, the continuous usage of fossil fuels has meant that tackling the environmental threats, related to the climate change and global warming is highly crucial in built environment practices. As a result, the energy-oriented intelligent features and versatile sustainability indicators are fundamental issues in defining the future of smart homes.

This chapter provides a holistic overview of the notion of smart homes while addressing their key features, benefits, current and future challenges. It develops a systematic review of the existing literature on smart homes and investigates the current status of implementing smart homes. It also discusses the potential impacts of smart homes on the circumstances of achieving sustainable urban future as a constituent of future smart cities. It concludes by exploring the effectiveness of using creative technologies in smart homes as a promising resolution to enhance the built environment practices.

2.0 THE NOTION OF SMART HOMES

This section outlines the historical context of smart homes and explains the technological advances that have paved the way for smart homes to exist. It also offers an insight into the range of current definitions available for smart homes and examines how the concept of smart homes has developed confirming that it is not only about integrating emerging technologies but aims to improve the level of convenience, social well-being, productivity and sustainability for its users and society.

2.1 History of Smart Homes

Technological advancements of the building construction sector in the 21st century have been beyond people's anticipation (Aldrich, 2003). Emergence of electricity into residential spaces during the previous century acted as a facilitator for this change. This provided a new source of clean and convenient power for appliances and enabled the industry to introduce various novel home products. The advancement of IT/ICT also acted as a key player empowering such changes, it enabled information exchange among people, appliances, systems and networks (Aldrich, 2013). A historical timeline demonstrates the context for the emergence of smart homes.

- **1915-20:** As a result of manpower shortage, employment of electrical home appliances originated with the introduction of vacuum cleaners, food processors and sewing machines. It was suggested that, employing these machines would enable one person to perform all the household's tasks with adequate time for leisure.

- **1920-40:** During this period new home technologies were introduced to elevate living standards. For instance, use of washing machines permitted clothes to be washed more often. Likewise, use of vacuum cleaners allowed floors to be cleaned more frequently.

- **1940-45:** During the World War II, governments obliged women to cover for men sent for war services. This opportunity for women to work outside the home provided new frontiers. This paved the way for the uptake of new domestic technologies after the war. These technologies supported women to maintain their job outside the house as the household chores could be handled quicker.

- **1945-59:** As a post war approach, governments strongly encouraged ladies to return home and free up job opportunities for men returning to civil life. During these years, home design began to reflect new ways of living alongside modern technologies. New kitchen designs embraced refrigerators, electric cookers, washing machines, etc.

- **1960-70:** The attempts to encourage women to stay- at- home were overturned during the 'swinging 60s'. During these years, emergence of contraceptive medicines and the choice to decide whether and when to have children provided higher chances for women to work outside. Consequently, several new labor-saving home appliances such as kettles, toasters, cookers, coffee and tea makers, food processors, etc. were introduced.

- **1980-90:** Use of technological and electrical home appliances was widespread by this period. Three quarters of British households had color TVs. By the end of 1980s, half of British families also had video recorders. A wide variety of electronic devices emerged ranging from cordless and mobile phones to entertaining devices such as PlayStations. Migration of PCs from exclusively-for-workplaces to houses blurred the distinction between home and work.

- **1990-2000:** Various technology breakthroughs occurred in this decade including the launching of the Hubble Space Telescope (HST) into low Earth orbit in 1990, and the Human Genome Project. However, the emergence of World Wide Web (WWW) inaugurated a new chapter in the history of human achievements. WWW was first developed by Tim Berners-Lee in 1989 (Tuschl, 2013). It became publicly accessible in 1991 and in 1993, the first web browser (Mosaic) was introduced. It enabled even amateur users to browse through the World Wide Web without requiring any special technical knowledge (Tuschl, 2013). Subsequently, the basic features of modern life including online shopping, banking, and advertising (Day, 2006). 18% of the US population had a household Internet access by 1997. This percentage increased to 41.5% by 2000 (File, 2013).

- **2000-2015:** The exponential growth of Internet continued during these years. It enabled the emergence of novel developments in communication, trading, entertainment and education. Internet Protocol (IP) telephony, groupware such as WIKIs, blogs, broadband accesses, peer-to-peer-networking, file sharing and online gaming are examples of these achievements (Tuschl, 2013). Data exchange of all public accessible cable networks in 2012 reached 26.7 Exabyte/month (Tuschl, 2013). 1 Exabyte is equivalent to 2500 times the volume of all books ever published in history. Contemporary global data exchange volume is approximately 60 Exabyte/month. The term Internet of Things (IoT) was introduced in 1999. It indicated an emerging global Internet-based information architecture facilitating the exchange of goods and services (Wood, 2015). Smart objects instrumented with sensing and interaction capabilities/identification technologies such as RFID were developed. IoT empowers smart cities. It enables integration of smart objects and real world data forming a digital world (Skarmeta, & Moreno 2014).

This evolutionary change throughout the time is known as the development basis of smart homes (Aldrich, 2003). The term smart home was officially used for the first time in 1984 by the American Association of House Builders (Dingli, & Seychell, 2015). They created a group, named Smart House aiming to put forward inclusion of several innovative technologies into design of new houses.

2.2 Definitions

A wide range of definitions have been provided to describe smart homes. The smart home has been described as "a residence equipped with a high-tech network, linking sensors and domestic devices, appliances, and features that can be remotely monitored, accessed or controlled, and provide services that respond to the needs of its inhabitants" (Ozkan, Davidson, Bicket, & Whitmarsh, 2013). This definition encapsulates the potential advantages that are available as the result of utilizing smart homes. Housing typologies are also important criteria to properly define this concept. Smart home can be "a residence equipped with a communications network, linking sensors and domestic devices and appliances that can be remotely monitored, accessed or controlled, and which provides services that respond to the needs of its inhabitants" (Chan, Campo, Estève, & Fourniols, 2009; Chan, Esteve, Escriba, & Campo, 2008; Reinisch, Kofler, Iglesias, & Kastner, 2011). In this definition, sensors are expressed as devices used to detect the location of the users and objects for data collection purposes. Ozkan, et al. (2014) stated the term smart home is an inclusive concept. In principle, it refers to any type of residence e.g. a standalone house, an apartment, or a unit in a social housing complex (Ozkan, Amerighi, & Boteler, 2014). Demiris, et al. (2008) also argued that, smart building is "a residence building equipped with technology that facilitates monitoring of residents or promotes independence and increases residents' quality of life".

This definition highlighted the use of intelligent technologies in residential units to monitor the occupants' behaviors for enhancing their quality of life. In another definition, Scott (2007) elucidated that a smart home is different than a house which has been merely equipped with standalone highly advanced technological features such as smart meters or smart appliances. Scott (2007) also explained that through the application of a connected network of devices and sensors, smart homes would allow consumers to control building energy consumption more efficiently. This is done while simultaneously increasing the occupants' level of comfort for a variety of household activities. These activities include but are not limited to space heating, water heating and security. Space heating would be managed via thermostat settings automatically adjusting to actual weather temperatures. Water heating would occur via detecting household behavior patterns and providing hot water at required temperatures at the right amount at the right time. Whereas security would be monitored via sensors detecting open windows in an unoccupied property and alerting the householder.

According to ITU (2010), (International Telecommunication Union- United Nation's specialized agency for IT/ICT), smart homes are able to offer various services. These include the granular control of smart appliances (e.g. heaters, air conditioners, washers, etc.), the ability to remotely manage electrical devices, display of consumption data and associated costs. They also offer communication between plug-in hybrid electric vehicles and their charging stations and on-site micro-generators (e.g. rooftop solar panels) (ITU, 2010). Likewise, Ghadi, et al. (2014) defined a smart building as a building capable of achieving significant energy savings by utilizing advanced control systems, technologies, materials, appliances, electrical systems, plumbing, HVAC system, etc.

In conclusion, smart homes are residential units modernized through a communicating network of sensors, domestic devices and intelligent systems based on the application of new design initiatives and creative technologies. They enable occupants to control the functions of their living environment through sophisticated monitoring/controlling systems. More recently, smart homes are targeted to embrace learning capability and self-adjustability potentials in order to sense the environment and occupants and respond to their needs. The implementation of smart homes results in enhanced quality of users' life, minimized building energy consumption, reduced cost of energy and improved security.

2.3 Conceptualization of Smart Homes

Three decades ago smart homes were only a conceptual theory for the representation of forthcoming residential buildings. However, today, smart homes are gradually becoming fundamental constituents of current policies for smart cities. Urbanized areas will be influenced by advanced intelligent technologies in order to promote smart growth, green development, and healthy environments (Berardi, 2013; Choon et al., 2011; Hollands, 2008). Recently, smart homes have become increasingly popular due to their potentials for deploying innovative design initiatives and emerging creative technologies towards maximized occupants' comfort and enhanced sustainable performances. The inclusion of ICT, automated technologies and embedded intelligence into building design, construction and management is often considered the key towards the success of smart homes. The intelligence embedded into smart homes enables them to be responsive to users' needs, environment and society. This is also effective in minimizing negative environmental impacts and wastage of natural resources (Ghaffarianhoseini, et al., 2013; Elma, et al. 2013).

There has been increasing interest in the use of smart homes to support the elderly or disabled to maintain independent living (Gentry, 2009). Smart homes were conceptualized to be fully equipped with versatile creative technologies to enhance the users' experience, comfort and sense of security (Ding, Cooper, Pasquina, & Pasquina, 2011). This is to give 'a sense of well- being and high quality of life to users' (Demiris, & Hensel, 2009; Buys, Barnett, Miller, & Bailey, 2005). These creative technologies have been increasingly utilized among the elderly and handicapped people (Chan, Campo, Estève, & Fourniols, 2009; Demiris, & Hensel, 2008; Ghadi, Rasul, & Khan, 2014).

From a critical perspective, many researchers argued that, the main concept of smart homes is not only about integrating emerging technologies but, to improve the level of convenience, social well-being, productivity and sustainability (Ghaffarianhoseini, et al., 2013; Scott, 2007; Clements-Croome, 2011). Smart homes need to be responsive to the 'local characteristics of the region encompassing the socio-cultural and environmental values' (Ghaffarianhoseini, et al., 2013). Observing the growing concerns towards the environmental impacts of the construction industry including global energy consumption and GHG emissions, the focus of smart homes is gradually shifting to mitigate the environmental challenges of building sector (Robert, & Kummert 2012; Ghaffarianhoseini, et al., 2013). According to Clements- Croome (2011) a building cannot be labeled as intelligent merely by applying intelligent modes of technology. "Over the past 20 years many different buildings have been labeled as 'intelligent'. However, the application of intelligence in buildings has yet to deliver its true potential".

In addition, smart homes target to reduce the operational costs through efficient energy management systems (Cempel & Mikulik, 2013; Silva, Arakaki, Junqueira, Santos Filho, & Miyagi, 2012). The embedded smartness in these buildings results in an environment which "integrate and account for intelligence, enterprise, control, and materials and construction as an entire building system, with adaptability, not reactivity, at its core, in order to meet the drivers for building progression: energy and efficiency, longevity, and comfort and satisfaction" (Buckman, Mayfield, & BM Beck, 2014). Creative technologies, as part of smart homes, have evolved towards a strong integration of human, collective, and artificial intelligence. Likewise, integration of creative technologies in smart homes requires smart users if they are to be truly inclusive, innovative, and sustainable. During the design of smart homes, a large focus on sensing is expected. Incorporation of intelligence in smart homes relies on deploying embedded advanced sensors. These lead to identification and collection of physical information while transferring the captured information to control systems (Kwon, Lee, & Bahn, 2014). Clements-Croome (2013) outlines various body sensors for integration in IB ambient, including accelerometers, heat flux monitors, galvanic skin response monitors and skin temperature monitors.

Advances in this area means that smart homes have recently been fully integrated with sensor networks for enhancement of the indoor air quality (IAQ). Wireless sensors and networks are nowadays considered primarily related to the progress of Radio Sensitivity, Ultra-low Power Consumption, Micro-electromechanical Systems (MEMS) Sensors and Energy Harvesting (Hatler, Gurganious, & Chi, 2013). Through advancement of Self-functional Advanced Sensors, smart homes can also benefit from self-adjustability. This is achieved via learning from the environment and user behavioural patterns (Wong, Li, & Wang, 2005; Kaya & Kahraman, 2014; Ghaffarianhoseini, et al. 2015).

It is inferred that; smart homes play a fundamental role in shaping the future cities based on their explored potentials. Major benefits of smart homes in automation and digitalization of living environments and the integrated technological facilities is widely acknowledged. Moreover, smart homes offer large-scaled key benefits in future urbanization in the form of investment returns, improved networking potentials and users' well-being. Hence, smart homes equipped with creative technologies with global targets beyond the automation purposes are gradually becoming a promising paradigm in the building sector.

3.0 APPLICATION OF INTELLIGENT AND CREATIVE TECHNOLOGIES IN SMART HOMES

The purpose of this section is to critically evaluate the intelligent devices and creative technologies that exist in smart homes currently. A wide range of active and massive intelligent devices are currently utilized and multiple heterogeneous intelligent devices coexist in houses, however integration is problematic. Sensory technologies in smart home are discussed in detail including the current perspectives on wearable sensor technology verses direct environmental sensing as well as infrastructure mediated systems as an alternative measure.

3.1 Smart Homes: Devices

The application of creative technologies via intelligent devices enables smart homes to provide a convenient living space for its occupants. These intelligent devices can be categorized into two clusters of active and passive systems (Dewsbury, Taylor, & Edge 2001). Active devices include control panels and switches with which the occupants directly interact. Passive devices include sensors and receivers with which the occupants have no direct contact. Alternatively smart home devices can be classified as information appliances, interactive household objects and augmented furniture (Rodden, & Benford, 2003). Information appliances refer to those using a touch screen. Here the interaction is similar to those of PCs and hand-held devices. Interactive household objects include picture frames that become displays and cups that are equipped with temperature/motion sensors. Augmented furniture is mediated through sensors detecting interactions of the users and their furniture. Chan, et al. (2008) categorize intelligent devices in smart homes into four groups. These devices are used to support activities, monitor the occupants' behaviors, deliver therapeutic services (e.g. delivering medicines) and provide convenience for the users as seen in Table 1.

The overall performance of smart homes can be significantly optimized through the utilization of creative household devices and technologies capable of automatically adopting to the users changing behavior or needs. Borja, et al. (2013) stated that, integration of robots and houses is an inseparable part of future smart homes. They expressed that, in future smart living environments, "service robots are completely integrated in the home and it is easy to imagine scenarios in which robots and smart home systems cooperate". However, the path towards materializing these objectives is full of obstacles. One of the most important is the lack of interoperability (Borja, Pinta, Álvarez, & Maestre, 2013).

Nowadays, multiple heterogeneous intelligent devices coexist in houses, however; most of them operate independently making it difficult to integrate them. Generating a homogenous network of intel-

Table 1. Smart devices used in smart homes

Function	Equipment/Devices/Objects
To serve	Physically disabled users: • Rehabilitation robotics • Companion robots • Wheelchairs • Specialized interfaces • Synthetic voice generation for control and commands
To support	Visually impaired users: • Tactile screens • Sensitive remote controls • Audible beacons
	Hearing-impaired users: • Visible alarms • Teletype machines • Electronic display screens • Numerical documents
	Lifestyle: • Fixed systems such as infrared sensors • Wearable systems such as active badges and accelerometers
To monitor	Physiological Signs: • In vivo sensors • EEG (syncope, epileptic seizure, sleep disorder, etc.) • Electromyograms (EMGs)* • Heart rate • Temperature • Blood oxygen saturation • Blood pressure • Glucose
	Therapeutic devices: • Delivery of current to abort/forestall epileptic seizures

continued in following column

Table 1. Continued

Function	Equipment/Devices/Objects
To deliver therapy	Therapeutic assistant: • Tremor suppression • Medicine delivery • Hormone delivery (e.g., insulin) • Active or orthotic boots (podiatry) • Physical therapy
	Intelligent household devices: • Dishwasher, washing machine, refrigerator • Stovetop, cooker
	Smart objects: • Mailbox • Closet • Mirrors
	Intelligent house equipment: • Presence/motion sensors • Video cameras • Magnetic switches • Humidity, gas, and light sensors
To provide comfort	Smart leisure equipment: • TV, home cinema programs
	Interactive communication systems: • Communication with friends and family in case of emergency • Intelligent environmental control equipment • Intelligent windows and doors (by using sensors, e.g. contact switches) • Heating, Lighting, Air conditioning, Ventilation
	Physical activity: • Fitness devices

Source: Chan, Esteve, Escriba, & Campo, 2008.

EMG*, is an electrical recording of muscle activity that aids in the diagnosis of neuromuscular disease.

ligent devices improves the effectiveness of smart homes. The idea of Common Object Request Broker Architecture (CORBA) was an initial attempt to solve this problem in a systematic manner. CORBA is a standard developed by the Object Management Group (OMG) to facilitate system communications in various platforms. CORBA enables different objects, regardless of their hardware, operating system or even programming language, to be integrated in a network (Aleksy, Korthaus, & Schader, 2005). Subsequently, several other novel initiatives such as the Universal Plug and Play (UPnP) have emerged. The UPnP has been highly successful particularly in the field of multimedia devices. In contrast the Digital Living Networks Alliance (DLNA), focused mainly on multimedia applications (Ghaffarianhoseini, et al., 2013). It aims to homogenize intelligent devices in buildings. Similarly, the Digital Home Compliant architecture (DHC) was proposed as a solution for the discussed interoperability problems (Alonso, Fres, & Fernández, et al., 2012).

3.2 Sensor Technologies in Smart Homes

Currently, a wide range of sensor devices are used in smart homes to collect data reflecting the occupants' activities. The sensory data generated are analyzed to recognize the daily activities of the residents such as bathing, dressing, preparing a meal and taking medications. This approach enables the smart home to establish a pattern of its residents' behaviors including their physical and cognitive conditions. Consequently, smart homes can detect deviations when the patterns start digressing from individualized norms. They can also distinguish when a typical behavior may indicate problems or require intervention (Skubic, Alexander, Popescu, Rantz, & Keller 2009).

3.2.1 Wearable Sensor Technologies

Wearable sensors are simply defined as the sensors that are worn by the residents (Ding, Cooper, Pasquina, & Pasquina, 2011). Various researchers endeavored to develop smart wearable systems (Lukowicz, Kirstein, & Tröster, 2004; Konstantas, 2007; Lymberis, & Dittmar, 2007). The main role of wearable sensors is to match the living environment with the physical/cognitive abilities/limitations of those suffering disabilities/diseases. This would enhance the users' performance while minimizing their risk of illness, injury and inconvenience. These systems support independent living for the elderly, post-operative rehabilitation for patients, expedited recovery and enhanced individual's physical abilities (Gatzoulis, & Iakovidis, 2007; Tröster, 2004). Wearable health monitoring systems include various types of miniature wearable, implantable or in vivo sensors (Chan, Estève, Fourniols, Escriba, & Campo, 2012). Current features of wearable sensors enable users to monitor the physical status, daily activities, and individual behaviors. These biosensors can measure physiological parameters such as body and skin temperature, heart rate, Electrocardiograms (ECGs), Electroencephalograms (EEGs), Electromyograms (EMGs), or SpO2 (peripheral capillary oxygen saturation, an estimation of the oxygen saturation level). Furthermore, smart devices can also provide real-time data processing. Data transmission via wireless body communication networks enable patient monitoring by healthcare providers. They are alerted as soon as a dangerous event occurs (Chan, Estève, Fourniols, Escriba, & Campo, 2012). These sensors must be easy to operate, small in size, and unobtrusive. They must be waterproof and have a long-life battery (Chan, Esteve, Escriba, & Campo, 2008). These systems should be able to collect measurements without the intervention of a third party. They also must provide total data confidentiality/reliability

(Chan, Esteve, Escriba, & Campo, 2008). These wearable sensors are presented in different forms. They include textile garments, rings and glucose sensors. Table 2 outlines the wide variety of wearable sensors currently available.

Application of wearable systems in smart homes improves the level of comfort, health and disease prevention. Accurate implementation of these sensors reduces the risk of hospitalization. Therefore, resulting in significant savings as the outcome of minimized manual care-takings and unnecessary hospitalization.

3.2.2 Direct Environmental Sensing

Direct environmental sensors are based on the utilization of various simple binary sensors throughout the building such as motion detectors and RFID (radio-frequency identification) systems. Through the installation of this sensing infrastructure, the presence, motions and activities of residents can be directly sensed (Patel, Reynolds, Abowd, & 2008).

Sixsmith & Johnson (2004) developed an intelligent fall detector based on a cost-effective composition of infrared detectors (Sixsmith & Johnson, 2004). This system, called SIMBAD (Smart Inactivity Monitor using Array-Based Detectors), targeted to enhance the quality of elderly people's life by offering them a greater sense of security. It facilitated independent living. The system could recognize falling by considering two distinct characteristics. Initially, SIMBAD analyzed target motions in order to detect falls' characteristic dynamics. Secondly, it monitored target inactivity and compared its findings with a map of acceptable periods of inactivity in different locations within the field of view. The combination of fall detection and inactivity monitoring enabled avoiding many false alarms by distinguishing a fall from actions resembling a fall. Field trial and user research indicated that, SIMBAD could significantly enhance the functionality and effectiveness of existing monitoring and community alarm systems. Hussain, et al. (2009) also developed a system based on the integration of RFID and wireless sensor network (WSN) in smart homes to detect the occupants' movements. Application of this system supplied useful information about the indoor home status such as identifying a caregiver entering the building (Hussain, Schaffner, & Moseychuck, 2009). Similarly, Aslan et al., (2015) presented an improved depth-based fall detection system. This system can use shape based fall characterization and a Support Vector Machine (SVM) classifier to classify falls from other daily actions. This system can accurately detect falls.

Table 2. Smart homes wearable sensors

Wearable Device	Key Sources
Textile garments	(Deshmukh, & Shilaskar, 2015)
Wrist-worn devices	(Biswas, Cranny, & Gupta, et al., 2015)
Rings	(Asada, Shaltis, Reisner, Rhee, & Hutchinson, 2003),
Belt-attached systems	(Manto, Topping, Soede, et al., 2003),
Over-the-shoulder pouches, a small box worn on the patient's head	(Waterhouse, 2003),
A chest belt (for stress monitoring)	(Tien, Feng, Chang, et al., 2014)
A glucose sensor	(Matzeu, Florea, & Diamond 2015)

3.2.2.1 Simple Binary Sensors

Binary sensors are able to recognize the "state of an object or movement with a single digit 1 or 0" (Ding, Cooper, Pasquina, & Pasquina, 2011). Several binary sensors are used in smart homes namely, motion detectors, pressure sensors and contact switches. Motion detectors and pressure sensors are generally used to detect the occupants' presence/locations in the house (Honga, Nugenta, Mulvenna, McClean, Scotney, & Devlin, 2009). For instance, passive-infrared motion sensors are placed throughout the building in order to detect the location of occupants in key areas (Boers, Chodos, Gbyrzynski, et al. 2010). Alternatively it is used to offer a long-term care to seniors who demanded supportive healthcare services in their favorite environment. These systems are mainly designed to notice functional decline and call for an intervention when a deviation is detected (Rantz, Marek, Aud, et al., 2005). Contact switches are usually installed on the home appliances and doors to provide information on their interaction with the occupants. Low cost, easy installation, and low privacy concerns are the main advantages of using binary sensors (Ding, Cooper, Pasquina, & Pasquina, 2011). However, these sensors only provide information at an abstract level. Therefore, they cannot effectively infer the performed activities (Honga, Nugenta, Mulvenna, McClean, Scotney, & Devlin, 2009). Environmental binary sensors have also been used to track occupants and map their various behavioral patterns in order to detect atypical activities. Results showed that, the use of low-level ambient motion sensors is a promising solution to detect atypical behaviors on a day-to-day basis (Wong, Zhang, & Aghajan 2014).

3.2.2.2 Video Cameras

Video cameras have high-content sensors providing rich sources of information both for human observation and computer interpretation (Ding, Cooper, Pasquina, & Pasquina, 2011). However, their application incorporates some technical issues. These include storage requirements and data extraction along with social challenges associated with the use of these systems namely, privacy issues compared to simple binary sensors (Caine, Rogers, & Fisk, 2005; Demiris, Skubic, Rantz, et al. 2006). For instance, Microsoft's EasyLiving project based on context aware computing used tracking video to monitor residents (Krumm, Harris, Meyers, Brumitt, Hale, & Shafer, 2000; Brumitt, Meyers, Krumm, Kern, & Shafer. 2000). Images from the video feed were analyzed and processed through distributed computing. The system was able to identify people-shaped clusters of blobs in real time in order to enable tracking the occupants. Residents were recognized through an active badge system. Likewise, Tabar A, et al. (2006) used a network of three cameras in a room to complement a wearable accelerometer in order to detect falls (Taber, Keshavarz, & Aghajan, 2006). These cameras were triggered when a fall was detected based on the accelerometer signals. Real-time image processing was used to analyze the data and estimate the occupant's posture. This conserved the privacy of the occupants by minimizing transmissions when there was no need to transmit visual data. It also helped reducing the number of false alarms caused by sensitive accelerometer signals.

Mihailidis et al. (2004) developed a visionary-based system based on sensing, planning, and prompting. The system was capable of tracking the users' movements. Statistics-based and physics-based methods of segmenting skin colors in digital images were used to track face/hand movements in real time. They argued that, this system can be utilized in the design of a sensing agent for an intelligent environment assisting elderly people with dementia during daily routines (Mihailidis, Carmichael, & Boger, 2004). Likewise, Intille, et al. (2005) introduced PlaceLab, a live-in research laboratory to study the ubiquitous computing technologies in buildings (The PlaceLab was a real home where the routine activities could be monitored, recorded for later analysis and experimentally manipulated. In order to monitor the occupants' behaviors, infrared cameras, color cameras and microphones were installed. The application of PlaceLab can also be helpful in providing useful information about the health status of patients such as diabetes (Intille, Larson, Beaudin, Tapia, Kaushik, Nawyn, et al. 2005). An alternative study was undertaken to investigate the level of anxiety of occupants by observing the behavioral patterns of targeted residents. Their results were presented in terms of simple use of the kitchen scenarios. For example, the less he uses his cooker, the more anxious he is (West, Greehill, & Venkatesh, 2005). It is suggested that, this model can be used to recognize the occupants' activities (of similar length) captured by a video tracking system within a smart home (Riedel, Venkatesh, & Liu, 2005).

In summary, the use of video cameras in smart homes facilitates capturing behavioral patterns of the residents. A range of benefits can be gained ranging from health-caring policies to detecting security concerns. Using such systems, deviations from the residents' norms can be detected. These deviations are submitted to the nearest healthcare center with the help of other available intelligent technologies within the network. This system also provides significant promises for securing buildings against trespassing. Stone et al. (2015) evaluated a method for sending real-time fall alerts. The system contained an embedded hyperlink to an in-depth video clip of the suspected fall. Real-time alerts were sent via email to facility staff. The alerts contained an embedded hyperlink to a short depth video clip of the suspected fall. Recipients were able to click on the hyperlink in order to view the clip on any device supporting play back of MPEG-4 video such as smart phones. This was to immediately determine if the alert was for an actual fall or a false alarm. Removing the need to physically investigate false alarms significantly reduced the costs, both in terms of time and frustration associated with false alarms for staff members and residents (Stone, & Skubic, 2015).

3.2.2.3 Radio Frequency Identification (RFID)

RFID is defined as "a technology which creates communication via radio waves to exchange data between a reader and an electronic tag" (Ding, Cooper, Pasquina, & Pasquina, 2011). A RFID system consists of three basic components: the tag, the reader and the data processing application system (Finkenzeller, 2003). A tag contains unique identity information about the item to which it is affixed or embedded. The reader communicates with the tag to collect information and stores the received data. The data processing equipment, (ranging from a personal computer to a networked enterprise management information system), processes the collected data. In such systems, the RFID reader cross-examines the tags while the tags subsequently respond back with a unique identifier as well as the information stored in their memory. RFID tags are categorized to active and passive. Passive tags have no power source (often attached to an object for detecting user–object interaction) while active tags contain a battery and are capable of being carried by a person for personal identification (Ding, Cooper, Pasquina, & Pasquina, 2011). This intelligent system offers significant advantages including its ability to be installed out of sight as well as being able to track multiple users.

NTT DoCoMo, a multimedia laboratory in Japan, developed an intelligent model to recognize the occupants' behaviors through employing sensors and RFID-tagged objects (Isoda, Kurakake, & Nakano, 2004). This model was tested in an experimental building. The residents' daily activities were modeled as a sequence of states describing their varying contexts. The status of each user was represented in this study by their attributes. They expressed which objects were in the user's vicinity and how long the objects remained in that position. Modeling of the occupants' behaviors was performed through the raw data received from the RFID tags. The user's behavioral context at any given moment was obtained by matching the most recently detected states to previously defined task models. It was concluded that, their system was an effective way of acquiring the user's spatiotemporal context. Likewise, SmartPlug and SmartWave, were developed by Gator Tech Smart Home based on the RFID technology (Elzabadani, Helal, Abdulrazak, & Jansen 2005). In the SmartPlug system, every power outlet in the house was equipped with a RFID reader and the plugs of electrical devices such as lamps or radios were equipped with RFID tags. Whenever a device was plugged into an outlet, the RFID reader sent the respective data to the main computer. The main computer could directly identify each device and its location, as well as controlling the device. Provision of data concerning the residents' usage of electrical devices enabled the detection of deviations from daily routines. The SmartWave system was a pervasive microwave, designed for cooking activities. An RFID reader was installed under the countertop to determine which food packet needed to be scanned for obtaining the cooking instructions from a database. As a result, the microwave was programmed automatically based on the instructions (Russo, Sukojo, Helal, Davenport, & Mann, 2004). More recently Kim et al. (2013) proposed an indoor ubiquitous healthcare system. It used RFID technology to accurately locate and track the elderly. This system could provide real-time monitoring of elderly peoples' locations. The proposed system could analyze the elderly's locations in association with time slots and the length of time they stay in the same place, thus inferring information such as movement patterns, ranges, and frequencies. Hu et al. (2015) also investigated and proposed a scalable RFID-based architecture that could be deployed cost-effectively. The system supports delivery of accurate and timely healthcare to all patients.

3.2.2.4 Infrared Sensors (IR)

The working principle of IR sensor is based on detecting the radiations emitting from the objects with a temperature above the absolute zero. These sensors are titled passive since they do not need to produce/radiate energy to detect the target objects. IR sensors are used in smart homes as they can track objects. Researchers have used passive infrared sensors to develop automatic switches using lithium tantalite (LiTaO3) (Ismangil, Jenie, Irmansyah, & Irzaman, 2015). Automatic switches are electrical devices using sensor technology to detect movements or body temperature. These sensors can also be used for security purposes. Building security systems typically rely on an easy-to-install system of infrared motion sensors. These sensors are low-cost, easy to use and widely available commercially. However, reliability of these sensors is questionable since those installed outside the building are sensitive to insignificant objects e.g. pets, or even the wind (Soyer, 2009). Similarly, Budijono et al. (2014) designed a home security device through employing PIR (Passive Infrared) motion sensor as the primary sensor for motion detection. Other intelligent equipment were also utilized in this system to enhance the accuracy. These included cameras for capturing images, GSM modules for sending and receiving SMS, alarm buzzers and microcontroller AT Mega 328. This home security system monitored the surroundings through PIR sensors. Subsequently, the alarm was buzzed, notifying SMS was sent and trespassing images were immediately saved (Budijono, Andrianto, & Noor, 2014).

3.2.2.5 Other Sensors

Researchers have extensively investigated the application of creative technologies towards integrating various other sensors in smart homes (Intille, Larson, Beaudin, Tapia, Kaushik, Nawyn, et al. 2005; Rantz, Skubic, Miller, & Krampe, 2008; Chen, Kam, Zhang, Liu, & Shue, 2005; Gaddam, Mukhopadhyay, &

Gupta, 2010; Surie, Laguionie, & Pederson, 2008). For instance, installation of temperature, humidity, light and barometric pressure sensors has been recommended to capture the indoor climatic conditions for further potential adjustments (Intille, Larson, Beaudin, Tapia, Kaushik, Nawyn, et al. 2005).

Furthermore, Rantz, et al. (2008) suggested the utilization of a bed sensor. They used a pneumatic strip installed under the bed linens to detect the occupant's presence, respiration (normal/abnormal), pulse (low, normal, or high) and movements in the bed. Correspondingly, bed restlessness was automatically reported to remote caregivers in different levels. These reports included various data e.g. bradycardia (slow pulse rate of 1–30 beats per minute), essential to detect/predict critical medical conditions. This system enabled the users to manage their medical disorders and uplift their level of healthiness and independence. Their work supports the concept of aging in place allowing seniors to remain in their desired environment (Reeder, Meyer, Lazar, et al., 2013).

A number of studies have also considered the implementation of sensor networks for elderly-care purposes (Glascock & Kutzik, 2000; Haigh et al. 2006; Ransing, & Rajput, 2015; Tomita, & Nochajski, 2015; Suryadevara, & Mukhopadhyay, 2015). Application of motion sensors to infer daily activities has been commonly proposed. Heat, motion, vibration, and electric sensors have been utilized to record the presence/absence of selected behaviors and their time, date, duration and frequency of occurrence. As such approaches monitor strictly object-oriented behavioral indicators; the users are free from wearing special devices or performing required actions e.g. pressing buttons (Glascock & Kutzik, 2000). Similarly, placement of miniature omnidirectional microphones in bathrooms to detect and classify activities was tested. Primary application of these devices indicated 84% accuracy. Such systems can automatically generate customized personal hygiene behavioral reports for caregivers and geriatric clinicians. The system is efficient since in spaces such as bathrooms where the use of video sensors is not socially acceptable, sounds are an alternative source of information (Chen, Kam, Zhang, Liu, & Shue, 2005). In similar cases, intelligent wireless sensor networks have been developed in order to accommodate safe living for elderly people. Use of cognitive wireless sensors e.g. bed sensors, panic buttons and water flow sensors enabled detection of abnormality in the users' daily life patterns. The system was capable of generating early warning messages to care givers, in case of unforeseen abnormal condition occurring (Gaddam, Mukhopadhyay, & Gupta, 2010).

3.2.3 Infrastructure Mediated Systems (IMS)

Infrastructure Mediated System (IMS) is about the installation of sensors alongside the existing infrastructure resulting in a remarkable maintenance cost/complexity reduction (Patel, Reynolds, Abowd, & 2008). IMS uses the existing home infrastructure (e.g., electrical systems, or air conditioning systems) to mediate the transduction of events. Therefore, the necessity for further installations is avoided. This system offers various advantages e.g. an unobtrusive, low-cost, and practical method for activity classification in smart homes (Larson, Froehlich, Campbell, Haggerty, Atlas, Fogarty, et al. 2012). However, this system is unable to provide detailed data about the residents' activities (Demiris, 2009).

Patel, et al. (2008) instrumented an HVAC's air filter with five pressure sensors (each sensing in both directions) the magnitude of pressure changes across all sensors was used to identify unique variations in airflow. This captured human inter-room movements (such as a person walking through a doorway or the opening and closing of a door). The system enabled classification of unique transitions with up to 75–80% accuracy (Patel, Reynolds, Abowd, & 2008). Similar research developed a power line noise analyzer capable of being plugged into an ordinary wall outlet to detect a variety of electrical events throughout the building. The analyzer detects electrical noises in residential power lines created by the abrupt switching of electrical devices plus the noises from certain devices while in operation. Application of this system enabled the identification/classification of various electrical events with 85-90% accuracy (Patel, Roberston, Kientz, Reynolds, & Abowd, 2007). Similarly, HydoSense (a customized pressure sensor capable of being deployed at any accessible location within a building's existing water infrastructure e.g. an exterior hose bib) was utilized for activity sensing. Here, the continuous monitoring of pressure enabled estimation of building's water consumption with error rates comparable to utility-supplied water meters (Froehlich et al., 2009).

4.0 ENERGY MANAGEMENT IN SMART HOMES

This section aims to appraise energy management within smart homes, energy management in smart buildings is a crucial issue based on policy and demand. This issue is reviewed in two themes: by examining energy control methods in smart homes and outlining the opportunities that exist for real time energy management.

Observing the significant role of buildings in global energy consumption and annual GHG emissions various national/international level initiatives have been set out to enhance the sustainable performance of built environments (Lemmet, 2009; Robert, & Kummert, 2012). For instance, the EU Climate and Energy Objectives aims to reduce the GHG emissions by 20% by 2020 while simultaneously increasing the building energy efficiency by 20% (Missaoui, Joumaa, Ploix, & Bacha, 2014). Similarly, the US Federal Policy aims to decrease the energy demand in new buildings by 70% by 2020 (Knowles, 2008). Given these policy requirements and environmental needs home energy management systems are important measures to minimize building energy consumption. Energy management in smart building is a crucial issue (Veleva, Davcev, & Kacarska, 2011; Roy, Das Bhaumik, Bhattacharya, Basu, Cook, & Das, 2003; Han, & Lim, 2010; Mohsenian-Rad, Wong, Jatskevich, Schober, & Leon-Garcia, 2010; Zhou, Wu, Li, & Zhang, 2014; Hamed, B. 2012; Ehrenhard, Kijl, & Nieuwenhuis, 2014). It is highlighted that, "Energy Management System contains methods that coordinate the activities of energy consumers and energy providers in order to best fit energy production capabilities with consumer needs" (Missaoui, Joumaa, Ploix, & Bacha, 2014). The main objective of home energy management systems is to manage the load of appliances, reduce the building's electricity consumption and eventually maximize the users' level of satisfaction (Huang, Wang, & Wu, 2014). This concept has also been defined as "a system capable of exchange commands between households and energy providers to optimize the energy consumptions" (Molderink, Bakker, Bosman, Hurink, & Smit, 2010).

4.1 Energy Control in Smart Homes

Energy control management in smart homes is about attempting to increase the control over the household energy consumption. Embedded computer intelligence is used to optimize the power consumption of controllable appliances. This was done based on retail pricing schemes, knowledge about various home appliances and decision trees based on their consumption behavior. This platform provided an easy access to selected displays of switching status and consumption of all appliances. Remote overview of the information and power use control via smart phones and remote terminal computers was also enabled. This system could detect supply voltages out of the permitted limits and protect controllable appliances by switching off the supply (Veleva, Davcev, & Kacarska, 2011). Likewise, Roy et al. (2003) developed a predictive framework for location-aware resource optimization in smart homes capable of efficiently identifying locations/movements of occupants. This method supports pro-active resource management and on-demand operations of automated devices along with the users' future paths/locations therefore providing the desired level of comfort at a near-optimal cost. Alternatives to this include, network-based multi-sensing systems and hybrid algorithms (e.g. PSO-DE, Particle swarm optimization- Different evolution). These systems aim to automatically determine and control energy resources available to the end-users and identify the optimum operation costs (Huang, Wang, & Wu, 2014; Han, & Lim, 2010). Likewise, Cottone et al. (2013) proposed a model capable of recognizing users' daily life activities, through responding to the analysis of environmental sensory data to minimize the energy consumption. This model ensured peak demands would not exceed a given threshold thus rationalizing the household energy consumption. The proposed model was tested experimentally and the achieved results confirmed its effectiveness (Cottone, Gaglio, Re, & Ortolani, 2013).

4.2 Real-Time Energy Management in Smart Homes

The use of real-time approaches optimizes the efficiency of smart homes. Based on a two-way digital communication infrastructure system, researchers have used the game theory and formulated an energy consumption scheduling game. The players were the users and their strategies were the daily schedules of their household appliances and loads. The simulation results revealed that, the proposed system can decrease the peak-to-average ratio of the total energy demand, the total energy cost as well as users' individual daily electricity charge (Mohsenian-Rad, Wong, Jatskevich, Schober, & Leon-Garcia, 2010). To encourage households to participate in demand response services, researchers proposed a demand response (DR) mechanism (Zhou, Wu, Li, & Zhang, 2014). Consequently, real-time home management systems offer promising insights for future advancements of automation applications in smart homes (Hamed, B. 2012). Energy management systems in smart homes offer building energy savings through control and real-time management methods. The improved energy efficiency of smart homes significantly reduces the operating costs.

5.0 BENEFITS OF SMART HOMES

The implementation of smart homes brings a number of significant benefits. These benefits are categorized into health, security and environmental issues. With an aging population the presence of intelligent technologies in smart homes is highly promising for improving the occupants' quality of life. Smart homes can also provide substantially improved security, safety and comfort given the advances in technology. Environmental demands are significant and the application of smart devices equipped with creative technologies in smart homes can considerably mitigate the negative environmental impacts of buildings.

5.1 Health Benefits

The world population (in both developing and developed countries) is aging due to increased longevity and declining birth rates (Breslow, 2006; Ehrenhard, Kijl, & Nieuwenhuis, 2014). This urges the necessity to develop comprehensive health monitoring and management systems aiming to assist aging people to continue living on their own, independently (Institute of Medicine, 2012). It is therefore essential to develop new insights and creative methods predicting/preventing declines in community health status.

The design of smart homes should be inherently intertwined with the developments of effective, and technologically driven healthcare solutions to enhance the living standards. This should take cognizance of the elderly and disabled users suffering from chronic physical disorders (low mobility level) and cognitive illnesses (Alzheimers disease) (Hachiya, Sugiyama, & Ueda, 2012; Taati, Snoek, & Mihailidis, 2013). A growing interest in the design and development of intelligent technologies for healthcare-related issues has been observed (i.e. telemedicine or tele-monitoring for remote observations) (Ozkan, Davidson, Bicket, & Whitmarsh, 2013).

Jakkula, et al. (2007) proposed a predictive model for integration in smart homes. Their model identified the health trends over time and enabled the prediction of future trends which can contribute to providing preventive measures. This healthcare system targets to enable the elderly to maintain an independent lifestyle. Park, et al. (2009) proposed an automatic diagnostic method for detecting the metabolic syndrome via utilizing a collaborative community computing approach based on a well-being index. Whereas Kushwaha, et al. (2005) developed a health care system for monitoring the users' health conditions at home while promoting health awareness. They focused on the early symptoms of heart attack that would alert the patients about their medical conditions. The proposed system used Bayesian network model for inference and Microsoft Agent as human computer interface. Similarly, Fahad, et al. (2015) proposed the 'activity recognition' intelligent approach in smart homes with the capability of self-verification (ARSH-SV) in order to recognize the occupants' daily activities. The ultimate performance of ARSH-SV was evaluated based on nine real smart home datasets through comprehensive evaluation metrics. The final results indicated that, deploying ARSH-SV enhances activity recognition. It can achieve an average accuracy of 98.85% (6% higher compared to the existing approaches).

As part of the healthcare monitoring, patient activities, behavioral patterns and health status can now be automatically recognized and controlled (i.e. Monitoring the user's hygienic activities, eating, sleeping, and proper use of medicines and prescribed physical exercises) (Fahad, Khan, & Rajarajan, 2015). Several studies have reported the diversified healthcare-related services provided by smart homes (Fahad, Khan, & Rajarajan, 2015; Reeder, Meyer, Lazar, et al., 2013; Kelly, 2005; Tomita, Mann, Stanton, Tomita, & Sundar, 2007; Brownsell, Blackburn, & Hawley, 2008; Alwan, Kell, Turner, Dalal, Mack, & Felder, 2006; Glascock, & Kutzik, 2007; Mahoney, Mahoney, Liss, & Ease, 2009; Rantz, Skubic, & Miller, 2009; Kim, & Dave, 2010; Kaye, Maxwell, Mattek, et al., 2011; Van Hoof, Kort, Rutten, & Duijnstee, 2011; Jakkula, Cook, & Jain, 2007; Park, Jung, Park, Kim, & Cho, 2009; Kushwaha, & Kim, 2005). Table 3 outlines the key findings from a literature review presented the recent application of Health Smart Homes (HSH), and Home-based Consumer Health (HCH) technologies (Reeder, Meyer, Lazar, et al., 2013). The theoretical analysis concluded that, majority of these studies have predominantly included an activity-sensing component and passive infrared motion sensors.

In conclusion, the presence of intelligent technologies in smart homes is highly promising for improving the occupants' quality of life. Accordingly, healthcare services are considered a substantial benefit of smart homes. The embedded intelligent technologies should ensure independent living for the elderly with continuous medical monitoring and examination. In the near future, self-adjustability and learning capabilities of smart living environments will pave the way for more contributions to the healthcare benefits of smart homes.

Table 3. Health-based Smart Homes (HSH), and Home-based Consumer Health (HCH) technologies

Key Sources	Country	Study Description	Results
(Kelly, 2005)	Scotland	6-year community-level implementation of an integrated activity/environment monitoring system with medication reminders (historical controlled trial).	Mainstreamed a successful smart home system to anyone over 60 as a preventive measure. Increased quality of life for older adults, reduced hospital admissions, reduced length of stay in hospitals and reduced length of stay in nursing homes due to preventive measures. (1.4 per 1000 West Lothian older adults in hospital beds vs 2.74 per 1000 in Scotland overall, 30 days mean duration stay vs. 112 days in Scotland overall).
(Tomita, et al. 2007)	USA	2-year randomized controlled trial to evaluate the effectiveness of commercial smart home technology with sensing and automation capabilities to support independent aging in older adults.	Intervention group had a significant higher cognitive level after controlling for age and initial cognitive level. 80.4% of the intervention group lived at home versus 65.7% of control group at study end. 82.4% reported the computer very important/14.7% somewhat important at study end. All intervention group participants accepted a computer, sensor software, a lighting system, chimes for security and medication reminders; Types of problem were related to person, computer, 10× products and the home.
(Brownsell, et al. 2008)	UK	12-month non-randomized controlled trial to evaluate the effectiveness of a sensing system for activity and environmental monitoring.	Intervention group participants maintained times outside the home at 5 per week and increased time outside from 3.6 to 4 h while control reduced times outside from 5 to 4.4 and decreased from 2.6 to 2.4 h per week. Intervention group experienced a 1% increase in feeling safe during the day and a 5% increase at night while the control group experienced a 1% decrease during the day and 3% decrease at night. Intervention experienced 10% decrease in fear of crime while the control experienced a 6% decrease.
(Alwan, et al. 2006)	USA	4-month pilot study to evaluate the psychosocial impact of an activity monitoring system adapted to an independent retirement community.	Technology did not decrease participant QOL (older adults, family members) or increase informal caregiver strain. Mean number of hours of care rose from 5.16 to 8.10, suggesting that wellness reports prompted greater involvement by FMs in older adults' lives. 2 case studies indicate that lowered activity levels and increased restlessness could have prompted preventive measures prior to hospitalization.
(Rantz, et al. 2008)	USA	Using retrospective data analysis, demonstrated the ability to detect health status decline using a sensing system from an ongoing longitudinal study of 2+ years.	Changes in heart rate and restlessness in one case were indicators of decline in health status. Increase and decrease in restlessness during and following cardiac rehabilitation could have indicated increased/decreased pain in another case.
(Glascock, et al. 2007)	Canada	Longitudinal study of a sensing system for activity monitoring at 8 installations (1 site for 6 months).	3 cases regarding detected falls, decreases in eating and increases in lavatory use prompted participant contact and preventive measures resulting in positive results.
(Mahoney, et al. 2009)	USA	Pilot study implemented over 18 months (average 4 months/participant) to test a sensing system adapted to an independent retirement community setting and evaluate stakeholder perceptions.	Older adults and family members felt the system addressed their needs and was not intrusive. Unexpectedly, for older adults there was a categorical drop from strong agree to somewhat agree regarding feelings of security. Family members reported slight increase in concern but decrease in time need to check on relatives. Family members suggested the ability to see the reason for no activity alerts. 5 of 10 family members were willing to pay 60 USD/month. Water sensor alerts endorsed by staff.
(Rantz, et al. 2009)	USA	Using retrospective data analysis, demonstrated the ability to detect health status decline using a sensing system from an ongoing longitudinal study of 3+ years.	In one case, an increase in bed restlessness prior to a fall could have been used to prompt assessment for an older adult resident who was not feeling well. In another case, decreased activity and increased restlessness in a resident who experienced cognitive decline could have been used to raise levels of watchfulness.

continued on following page

Table 3. Continued

Key Sources	Country	Study Description	Results
(Skubic et al. 2009)	USA	Reported lessons learned from a 3+ year ongoing longitudinal study of a sensing system in a "living laboratory".	Typical patterns of activity for an individual were monitored for changes. Detection of increased pulse pressure was consistent with cerebral cardiovascular incident in one case. Decreases in activity were consistent with depression in another. Changes in restlessness and bed tachypnea (breathing rate > 30 bpm) were detected prior to a heart attack in another case. Changes in restlessness/ tachypnea were detected before a surgery and returned to normal afterwards.
(Kim, & Dave 2010)	South Korea	Evaluated participant perceptions of sensor technology installed for 10 years in 4 different apartment buildings for older adults.	Participants felt comforted by sensor technology but did not think it changed the patterns of their lives. Residents often overestimated the capabilities of the technology.
(Kaye, et al. 2011)	USA	Demonstrated feasibility of a large scale, longitudinal activity sensing project for older adults in their homes with average enrollment time of 33 months.	Times/day walked past in-home sensor: 22, Mean walking speed: 61.0 cm/s, Fast walking: 96.0 cm/s, Slow walking: 36.2 cm/s, Average times out of home: 2/day for a mean of 208 min, Average computer use time when used: 76 min/day, Average days of computer use: 43% of days. 83% reported physical health problems using the online form. Over half reported at least one fall and 35% at least one trip to the hospital/ER.
(van Hoof et al. 2011)	Netherlands	Investigated the use of ambient technologies by older adults enrolled for 8–23 months and the ability of technology to support aging in place.	Participants had a greater sense of security after technology installation. One participant developed a fear of the equipment and had it removed after a year. Two participants were dissatisfied with false alerts but kept the technology for the increased feeling of safety. Some participants felt the technology was too loud.

Source: Reeder et al., 2013.

5.2 Security Benefits

Smart homes provide improved security, safety and comfort. Integration of intelligent technologies into the living ambient of smart homes can deliver significant advantages for securing the building against trespassing and illegal intrusion. Using image sensor technology supplies rich sources of information about the living environment. Video surveillance systems are a practical solution for smart homes to address security requirements. In this regard, Zhang, et al. (2015) conducted a comprehensive review on the security in smart homes from 1994 to 2009.

Before 2000 few systems utilized cameras as their sensor sources, using traditional pressure sensors and infrared sensors. This was due to the limited computation power of computers and video analysis algorithms were not as mature and popular as today (Zhang, Shan, & Huang, 2015). Today, the use of video surveillance technology is an inherent part of smart living environments. The integration of video analysis systems in smart homes based on its linkage to other embedded sensors offers various advantages. These include fall recognition (Anderson, Luke, Keller, Skubic, Rantz, & Aud, 2009) and assistance with the completion of daily activities (Hoey, von Bertoldi, Poupart, & Mihailidis, 2007).

The security video technology enables simplified recognition of the occupants, their exact position within the environment and their behavioral patterns compared to other sensor technologies. Advanced video analyzing techniques (e.g. face recognition) enable assigning an identity to users. This provides a degree of personalized assistance (e.g. the personal home security system). Zhang, et al. (2015) proposed a new systematic video analysis architecture with the capability of producing rich sources of information about the home ambient. This system, called the ISEE Smart Home (ISH), can analyze various unfamiliar behaviors; provide real-time alarm generation and flexible video retrieval and video synopsis.

5.3 Environmental Benefits and Energy Efficiency

Observing the negative impacts of global warming, the building sector has been repeatedly criticized for consuming more than one-third of global energy consumption and producing approximately one-third of GHG emissions worldwide (Robert, & Kummert, 2012). There are several ways to decrease the environmental impacts of the building sector. These include: reducing fossil fuel dependency, increasing the use of renewable energy, reducing customer electricity consumption (monitoring and control), and converting older home appliances to smart, and energy-efficient versions (Al-Sumaiti, Ahmed, & Salama, 2014). In the context of smart homes, despite the initial predominant focus to create highly automated living environments, attention has recently been given to environmentally responsive features of embedded intelligent technologies. Application of smart devices equipped with creative technologies in smart homes can considerably mitigate the negative environmental impacts of buildings. The Advanced Metering Infrastructure (AMI) broadcasts real-time electricity data such as price messages to the smart meters located in living ambient of smart homes. Smart meters issue instructions to the integrated smart appliances and communicate with other devices to accomplish the power usage adjustment. This is for the purpose of energy management and improved power efficiency (Jin, & Kunz, 2011). AMI is an integrated system of smart meters, communications networks, and data management systems that enables two-way communication between utilities and users.

Another feature of smart home technology is the use of a smart home control panel. Several electronic appliances are automatically controlled, including lights, HVAC, TVs, computers, entertainment devices, and security systems. This is done through an integrated smart home control panel or a GSM (Global System for Mobile communication)/CDMA (Code division multiple access), Internet, and PSTN (public switched telephone network) networks (Li, 2012). Integration of emerging intelligent technologies and energy-oriented smart devices in living environments enhances the building energy management and mitigation of GHG emissions.

Different types of intelligent sensors in smart homes are the most advanced way to manage the building energy consumption. Lach et al. (2007) proposed an automatic monitoring system aiming to decrease the energy consumption of a typical home through WIFI technology with enabled smart switches. They added sensors to increase the automatic monitoring and control of the environment in accordance with the users' preference (Lach, Punchihewa, et al. 2007). Reinisch et al. (2011) also investigated the utilization of a multi-agent technique to reduce the energy consumption in a house.. The building operated according to an extensive knowledge-based system that stores all data required to realize the objectives of energy efficiency and user comfort. Its intelligence was within a multi-agent system that also caters for the system's openness to the outside world. They proposed several agents such as global goal agent, control agent, user agent, auxiliary data agent, and interface agent to operate the system. Different agents contain and provide intelligence regarding aspects such as user preferences, auxiliary data, and control parameters.

In conclusion, application of creative technologies in smart homes can significantly reduce the household energy consumption through smart regulation of energy usage. Smart appliances/devices can work homogenously within a network. They analyze the users' activities and issue relevant instructions to better manage the buildings energy consumption. The consequent energy saving is expected to mitigate the environmental emissions.

6.0 CHALLENGES OF SMART HOMES

6.1. Current Challenges of Smart Homes

In the context of intelligent environments, smart homes are often quoted as one of the key constituents of smarter living environments. In spite of their significant advantages in terms of environmental, social and health-care dimensions, their true potential is not yet fully explored. This is partially due to the existing technological challenges, financing barriers and obstacles to the proliferation of smart homes. The following sections discuss about the most critical challenges of smart homes and provide new insights about their future directions.

6.1.1 Integration of Smart Homes and Users' Life Styles

In essence, smart homes were primarily conceptualized and later developed to automatically address the daily requirements of the elderly and users with disabilities. Likewise, with the current global agendas for achieving sustainable urban future, smart homes have become more and more intertwined with the advanced sustainable technologies. More recently, other users have also shown interest to live in such highly automated homes. Nevertheless, there is an essential need for the smart homes to ensure a congruity between the design of living ambient, lifestyle of occupants, and the senses of embedded intelligent technologies. Smart homes must continuously adapt themselves to the rapid changes of technology and occupants' needs (Stringer, Fitzpatrick, & Harris, 2006; Li, Lee, Tsai, Xu, Son, Park, Moon, 2012). In addition to this the application of advanced technologies should not create a feeling of being out of control (Stringer, Fitzpatrick, & Harris, 2006). These smart technologies integrated into homes should be straightforwardly understandable enabling the users to easily utilize them without the need to gain particular knowledge (Li, Lee, Tsai, Xu, Son, Park, Moon, 2012). The intelligent technologies used in smart homes must be highly adaptable and evolvable to meet the changing needs, demands, and preferences of the occupants.

6.1.2 Interoperability

The living environment should be readily assimilated into the new devices which might be later applied in the smart home's network (Stringer, Fitzpatrick, & Harris, 2006). Intelligent appliances/devices used in smart homes have different operating systems, programming language, and hardware. These differences will cause potential issues for smart homes to perform a multiparty task. In the context of smart homes, interoperability can be defined as "the state of communicating different devices with each other into a same network context" (Ozkan, Davidson, Bicket, & Whitmarsh, 2013). Interoperability enables data and resources to be exchanged between different intelligent devices of smart home to execute an order. In order for a network in a smart home to be operating properly, all the integrated devices are required to be capable of communicating with each other. Nevertheless, achieving this can be highly complex as the integrated devices encompass different network media and communication protocols.

Interoperability in smart homes is concerned at basic connectivity, network, and syntactic levels (Perumal, Ramli, Leong, Mansor, & Samsudin, 2008). Basic connectivity interoperability provides common standards for data exchange and establishes a communication link. Network interoperability allows messages to be exchanged between systems across a variety of networks in smart home environments. It is defined as "an agreement of addressing the issues rising from information transfer between heterogeneous systems across multiple communication links" (Perumal et.al, 2008). Finally, syntactic interoperability refers to the ability of two or more components to work together through exchanging and interpreting data and messages. This level provides a mechanism to understand the data structure in messages exchanged between two entities in smart home environments.

6.1.3 Reliability

Concerning the reliability of smart homes, it is expressed that, "a smart home that its technical parts are functioning without flaw may still provide unreliable services, because the system is not intelligent enough to correctly understand and predict the needs of its users" (Ozkan, Davidson, Bicket, & Whitmarsh, 2013). In an integrated smart home, different appliances/devices are interconnected with variable tolerances for technical errors. This variation of tolerance raises serious concerns. For instance, boiler designers and home computer developers may have different assumptions regarding the appropriate level of tolerance for crashes. Combining these two products with dissimilar levels of tolerance within a network causes complications to the building. Likewise, even insignificant malfunctions in the home computer could potentially cause dangerous malfunctions in the boiler (Ozkan, Davidson, Bicket, & Whitmarsh, 2013). In this regard, certain services in smart homes (e.g. security, or fire alarm triggering) are more crucial to take into consideration for reliability purposes.

In order for the smart homes to reliably supply the intended services, the householder's desired outcomes must be accurately interpreted (Ozkan, Davidson, Bicket, & Whitmarsh, 2013). Thus, the degree to which the residents can trust the reliability of smart homes is a challenge for this widely developing context.

6.1.4 Privacy and Security

Smart homes need to collect extensive data about the occupants' lifestyles to be of optimum effectiveness. Occupants' movements, health status, energy consumption, purchases, even music preferences must be considered (Ozkan, Davidson, Bicket, & Whitmarsh, 2013). It is essential to ensure that all this private information collected by the smart home is adequately safeguarded. It is also critical to guarantee that control of the network's sensitive systems cannot be easily compromised. Therefore, the issue of safeguarding the users' private information and the smart home's sensitive systems is a major challenge for development and even promotion of this concept.

6.1.5 Other Challenges

Various other challenges concerned with smart homes have been identified. These include consumers' lack of awareness about the benefits of smart homes, costs and complexity of technology for most household users, lack of incentive for Internet providers, promoting networking technology, potential privacy issues and interface issues (Venkatesh, 2003). Ehrenhard, et al. (2014) suggested that the end users need to be convinced of the smart home values. Other major issues include unfamiliarity with the complex technology, fear of losing control and privacy, and maintenance costs (Ehrenhard, Kijl, & Nieuwenhuis, 2014).

Several real and potential challenges complicate the advancement process of using smart homes. The lack of common place awareness and understanding of the salient features of smart homes and their advantages is a major obstacle. Therefore, the role of governmental authorities to provide respective educational services is essential. It is advisable for governments to grant subsidies/loans for motivated applicants in order to promote widespread implementation of smart homes.

6.2 Consumer Perceptions on Smart Homes Adoption

The importance of users' demand response to the adoption of smart homes has been a focus point for several researchers. They identified a wide range of different barriers to the promotion of using smart homes. These included availability, financing and cost of demand response technologies, transaction costs involved in seeking out price and consumption information, relative share of savings compared to total expenditures and satisficing behavior in switching patterns. Difficult interfaces were identified as critical factors affecting the users' perception towards adoption of smart homes (Meyers, Williams, & Matthews, 2010). Since smart homes and related technologies are still in the early development/deployment stages (Ozkan, Davidson, Bicket, & Whitmarsh, 2013) the users are expected to perceive a technical gap between their expectations and the current solutions (Bonino, & Corno, 2011). Besides, common users mainly expect smart homes to simply provide an elevated level of comfort. This is already achievable through the application of existing commercial systems. Moreover, many users would prefer the comfort rather than the savings (Bartusch, Wallin, Odlare, Vassileva, & Wester, 2011). Finally, cost (including the cost of installation, operation and maintenance), comfort, and the state of being easy-to-use are also deemed to be additional significant factors affecting the users' perception. Therefore, the users' perception is highlighted as a key element towards future successfulness of smart homes.

7.0 SMART HOMES IN DIFFERENT CONTEXTS

Smart homes are residential units that are well integrated with intelligent devices such as sensors and actuators. These buildings aim to increase the occupants' control over the home's functionalities. This increase transforms homes from a solid and irresponsive shelter to a dynamic environment capable of interacting with its occupants. Smart home can simplify communications among the residents and the buildings' functionalities. These buildings can detect the occupants' activities and correspondingly adjust the level of energy consumption. They also offer continuous health monitoring and control. Alternatively, users can effectively supervise the building's functionalities through mediating sensors, actuators, etc. The following sections scrutinize the key features of smart homes in different contexts.

7.1 USA

In a relatively old yet innovative example, Mozer (1998) developed an adoptive house in Boulder, Colorado, originally a former three-room school house built in 1905 (Mozer, 1998). He used a neural network system called Adaptive Control of Home Environments (ACHE) to control temperature, heating and lighting without previous programming by the residents. ACHE aimed at monitoring the environment, observing the occupants' behavior (e.g., adjusting the thermostat, configuring lighting, etc) and attempting to infer patterns to predict the occupants' behavior. ACHE was designed to ensure the residences' needs (e.g. lighting, air temperature and ventilation) are maintained at their level of comfort. Occupants' manual adjustments of environmental set points was an indication that their needs have not been satisfied. This served as a training signal for ACHE. ACHE's ability to anticipate needs expected to significantly reduce manual control of the living environment. ACHE also focused on building energy savings, lights should be set to the minimum required intensity, and hot water should be maintained at the minimum needed temperature to satisfy the demand. Additionally only rooms that are likely to be occupied in the near future should be heated, when several heating options available (e.g., furnace, ceiling fans forcing hot air down, opening blinds to admit sunlight). The alternative with the least expected energy consumption should be selected.

Researchers at the University of Texas at Arlington focused on the creation of an intelligent and versatile home environment (the MavHome project) (Meyers, Williams, & Matthews, 2010). This project was aimed at creating a home acting as a rational agent. Perceiving the state of the home through sensors and acting in response to the environment maximizes the comfort while minimizing the operation costs. In order to achieve this objective, the agent must be able to sense and predict the occupants' mobility habits and their use of electrical appliances. Daily activities were operated in the MavHome following the subsequent order. At 6:45am, MavHome turns up the heat to warm the house to the user's preferred waking temperature. The alarm sounds at 7:00, after which the bedroom light and kitchen coffee maker turn on. The user steps into the bathroom and turns on the light. MavHome records this manual interaction, displays the morning news on the bathroom video screen and turns on the shower. Once the user finishes grooming, the bathroom light turns off while the kitchen light and display turn on. When the user leaves for work, MavHome makes sure that doors and windows are locked and starts the lawn sprinklers despite knowing the 30% predicted chance of rain. When the user arrives home, the hot tub is waiting for him. The so-called LeZi method (a technique of information theory), is employed in order to create a probabilistic model predicting the inhabitant's typical path segments, comfort management scheme, and appliance use. The Active LeZi (ALZ) algorithm calculates the probability of every possible action occurring in the currently observed sequence. It predicts the action with the highest probability (Helal, Mann, El-Zabadani, King, Kaddoura, Jansen, 2005). Technologies used in this system are categorized into four cooperating layers. The Decision layer selects actions for the agent to execute. The Information layer collects information and generates inferences useful for decision-making. The Communication layer routes information and requests between agents. The Physical layer contains the hardware including devices, transducers, and network equipment.

The University of Florida researchers developed the GatorTech Smart House. It aimed to provide a platform for experiencing and analyzing the application of intelligent technologies into a responsive house besides studying the responds of its users (Ghaffarianhoseini, et al., 2013). The main focus of this home, with an area of 2500 ft^2, was to help people with especial needs or the elderly live conveniently

(Ghaffarianhoseini, et al., 2013). The house also used a high-precision ultrasonic tracking system to detect the locations of its residents, evaluate their mobility habits and better control the environment.

Researchers at the Georgia Institute of Technology developed The Aware Home Research Initiative in three stories with an area of 5040 ft[2]. This project was a living laboratory for the design, development and evaluation of future domestic technologies (Aware Home Research Initiative). The building was capable of recognizing the users' needs and respond to them automatically. The smart floor could sense an individual's footsteps allowing the building to establish a model based on the user's habits and behavior. Different techniques were used to interpret the behavioral patterns of users namely, 'Markov models', 'simple feature-vector averaging', and 'neural networks'. The research aimed to enhance the quality of life of the elderly. Moreover, the building was equipped with a system of tracking and sensing technologies in order to assist the occupants in finding lost objects. Object tracking was performed based on the RFID technology. The users were able to interact with the system via LCD touch panels placed strategically throughout the house. The system also guided the users to their lost object using audio cues.

Researchers at the MIT Department of Architecture developed a multi-disciplinary project called, the house of the future. Their system encompasses three components, a set of state-change sensors utilized to gather information about using the objects, a context-aware experience sampling tool (ESM) employed by the subject to label its activities. As well as pattern recognition and classification algorithms for detecting the users' activities. Results indicated that, by extending the period of training and generating higher quality activity labels (e.g. using video observations, etc.), model accuracy and efficiency of the smart home will be improved (Chan, Esteve, Escriba, & Campo, 2008).

7.2 Asia

The smart home of 'Dr. Matsuoka' is an example of smart homes built in Japan. It was equipped with several sensors to detect unusual events potentially to be caused by disease or accidents (Matsuoka, 2004). Here, electrical devices were fitted with different sensors assigned to one or more activities e.g. getting up, going to bed, preparing meals, taking a shower, working in an office, etc. The smart home used a two-step method to translate raw sensor signals into behavioral data. Initially, the required data were obtained through the utilized sensors. At the second step, the data was analyzed and interpreted. Employment of diverse sensors at this stage enabled recognition of abnormalities leading to diseases. This smart home provided independent elderly people with a consistent health monitoring and controlling system. Similarly, Toyota Dream House Papi is another Japanese smart home equipped with 'ubiquitous computing systems and intelligent technologies' to facilitate an intelligent environment. This project aimed to assist the occupants with services and automation of functionalities as well as being responsive for energy savings and environmental concerns (Ghaffarianhoseini, et al., 2013).

University of Tokyo researchers developed a smart room encompassing data collection, data processing, and the integration of processed data components. The system was capable of gathering quantitative data about the users' daily activities, interpreting the achieved data, and learning from them (Noguchi, Mori, & Sato, 2002). The states of the floor, bed, table and switches were recorded by the sensing modules of the room. The combination of this data was defined as the room state. An algorithm named summarization was developed segmenting the accumulated sensor data at points where the outputs would change drastically. The segments were matched with and assigned to room states. The algorithm assisted in omitting the insignificant states which had only slightly changed. The system included switch sensors on a number of appliances in addition to the tables, chairs and beds. These sensors were sufficient to detect whether the user was standing or sleeping, to detect the position of their hands on the table and to detect the positions of objects on the table. The freezer, refrigerator, microwave, toaster, windows and chest of drawers were all equipped with switch sensors to detect whether their doors were open or closed.

7.3 Europe

The ComHOME project, a full- scale model constructed by a number of scenario-like set- ups, is a smart home developed in Sweden (Tollmar, & Junestrand, 1999). This instance was equipped with several sensors, voice controllers and voice- mediated communications. This case aimed to investigate home-based activates e.g. communication, distance, work and social activities as well as the impacts of employing these technologies on the users.

Likewise, a combination of different tele-care and hospital at home services such as a home emergency alarm, access to community health information, and ambulatory monitoring formed the CarerNet smart home in the UK. Diverse intelligent technologies namely, therapy units, a sensor set, a sensor bus, an intelligent monitoring system, and a control unit were implemented in this smart home (Williams, Doughty, Bradley, 1998). CarerNet was capable of collecting physiological data (ECG, photo plethysmograph, spirometry, temperature, galvanic skin response, colorimetry, and pulse). They were also able to determine the patient's lifestyle (through passive IR sensors, accelerometers, inductive badges, smart IR badges, and piezoelectric sensors), and 'environmental awareness (thermometer, microphone, IR smoke alarm). The system's distributed intelligence was based on the actions of different sensors such as smart sensors, smart therapy units, the body-hub, a Local Intelligence Unit, and the client's healthcare record.

Similarly, the British Telecom and Anchor Trust designed a smart home in UK to monitor the users' activities (Barnes, Edwards, Rose, Garner, 1998). This was done with the assistance of interior IR sensors, magnetic contacts on the entrance doors to recognize when the user enters and leaves their home, and another contact on the refrigerator door. Moreover, a temperature sensor was used to detect the ambient temperature. The smart home would trigger an alarm whenever sensing a deviation from the users' behavior. Based on this project, the Millennium Home, aiming to support the elderly in their own place of residence was developed. This offered a more sophisticated and sensitive approach towards monitoring activities and modeling behaviors in order to better control the alarms. The Millennium Home enabled users to cancel the false alarms through an easy and quick mechanism. Provision of the lifestyle monitoring system supported the independent-living needs of the users. This smart home utilized passive IR sensors to detect movements, pressure sensors under the chairs and beds and burglar alarm-style sensors on the windows and front doors to detect when they are opened. The system also included adjustable timers to remind the resident of medications. Temperature sensors were located to ensure the building is not getting too cold/warm for the residents' health. It also incorporated a computer-activated telephone, loudspeaker, TV screen and an interactive dialogue system between the users and their caregivers (Perry, Dowdall, Lines, Hone, 2004). Table 4 presents a holistic comparative overview of the selected smart homes in different contexts.

Regardless of the location of smart homes, these smart living environments can be classified based on their application areas, namely, security, eldercare, healthcare, childcare, energy efficiency and improved life quality. Smart homes can also be categorized based on their activity detection methods (e.g. audio based techniques, video based techniques, audio-visual techniques, sensor based techniques and mixture of audio, video and sensor based techniques) (De Silva, et al., 2012).

Table 4. Key intelligent characteristics of smart homes in different contexts

Intelligent Technologies Applied for Home-Based Usages	Intelligent Technologies Applied For Health-Based Usages	Intelligent Technologies Applied For Support-Based Usages
ComHOME **Location:** Sweden **Features:** Equipped with several sensors in order to investigate home-based activates as well as studying the impacts of employing these technologies on the users (Tollmar, & Junestrand, 1999).	*CarerNet Smart Home* **Location:** UK **Features:** Intended to provide telecare and hospital services at home through deploying various telecare services, namely a home emergency alarm, access to community health information, and ambulatory monitoring (Williams, et al., 1998). CarerNet is capable of determining the patient's lifestyle by collecting physiological data.	*Millennium Home* **Location:** UK **Features:** Intended to monitor the users' activities. This home aimed supporting elderly to stay in their own places without requiring consistence care (Perry, et al., 2004).
CASAS Smart Home **Location:** USA **Features:** Intended to enhance the mutual interaction between occupants and their living environment through deploying several sensors to perceive, and exploiting several actuators to respond to the environment. The goals of this project were laid upon maximizing the users' comfort and minimizing the maintaining cost (Ghaffarianhoseini, et al., 2013).	*Gloucester's Smart House.* **Location:** UK **Feature:** Intended to assist patients suffering from Dementia. This home is capable of continuously monitoring several items such as indoor environment, bathwater temperature (Orpwood, et al. 2001).	*Gator Tech Smart House* **Location:** USA **Features:** Intended to assist people with especial needs or the elderly to live conveniently. The house also used a high-precision ultrasonic tracking system to detect the locations of its residents, evaluate their mobility habits and better control the environment (Ghaffarianhoseini, et al., 2013).
Mozer House **Location:** USA **Features:** This home used a neural network system called Adaptive Control of Home Environments (ACHE) to ensure that the residences are maintained at their level of comfort (Mozer, 1998).	*TERVA* **Location:** Finland **Feature:** Capable of continually monitoring the physiological and psychological health status of occupants through employing vital sign measurements (e.g. arterial blood pressure, heart rate, body temperature) (Korhonen, et al. 1998).	*Elite CARE* **Location:** USA **Features:** It is inhabited by retirees, some of whom suffer from dementia or Alzheimer's disease. The main aim of this project was to prolong independence and help the staff identify health problems early (Elite-care)
MavHome **Location:** USA **Features:** Intended to enhance the house comfortability while minimizing the operation costs. This house aimed at predicting the habits of occupants' mobility and their use of electrical appliances (Meyers, et al., 2010).	*PROSAFE* **Location:** France **Features:** Developed as a means of continuously monitoring the mobility behavior of elderly. The goals of PROSAFE are twofold: to support autonomous living, and to sound an alarm in case of emergency (Chan, et al., 2005).	*Matilda Smart House* **Location:** USA **Features:** Developed to create smart spaces within a house which are responsive and supportive. The main focus of this project is on the automation of daily needs of users (Ghaffarianhoseini, et al., 2013).
Aware Home **Location:** USA **Features:** The building was capable of recognizing the users' needs and respond to them automatically (Aware Home Research Initiative). The concept was based on applying the ubiquitous computing systems to be linked to the entire homes' functionalities and activities. Application of technology for creating responsive environments has become a significant attribute.	*Smart home developed in New Zealand* **Location:** New Zealand **Features:** A smart house system was built capable of providing behavioral patterns by monitoring the user's habits, and making intelligent decisions based on these patterns (Diegel, 2005). This system allows to monitor the everyday health status of occupants, and creating a database accordingly. Later on, this database can be modified in which cause to increase the adoptability of system. Enhancement in user's medication and health care compliance rate has been shown resulting from the application of this system.	*ENABLE Home* **Location:** Norway, Finland, Ireland, Lithuania, and the U.K **Features:** Intended to support conveniently living for those who are suffering from mild to moderate dementia, demonstrating the impact of assistive technology on their quality of life (Adlam, et al. 2004).

8.0 LINKING ARTIFICIAL INTELLIGENCE, CREATIVITY, AND SMART CITIES

While smart cities are receiving much wider attention, there is still a lack of a universally acknowledged definition representing their true implications (Albino, et al., 2015). In addition, both in practice and academia, many related terms including intelligent, sustainable, resilient, digital, eco, low-carbon, etc.; have been interchangeably used to demonstrate the future of our so-called smart cities. It is clear that the meaning of a smart city is multi-faceted. As a result, many of the recent studies are in agreement that a smart city should be characterized by at least six interrelated indicators, namely, smart economy, smart mobility, smart environment, smart people, smart living and smart governance (Lazaroiu & Roscia, 2012).

Creativity has been proffered as a key driver of the smart city, with education, learning, and knowledge being at its core (Thuzar, 2011). Glaeser and Berry (2006) confirmed the most rapid urban growth rates occur in cities where a large part of the educated labor force is available. Successful knowledge based urban development requires clever, creative connected people (Dirks et al., 2010).

Smart homes therefore have the potential to play a key role in shaping the future smart cities. Creative technologies have always been a key driving force of forward-looking visions about the evolution of smart homes and smart cities. Nevertheless, there have been very few studies attempting to link the impacts of smart homes to the performance of smart cities.

In smart cities, information technology is used widely to help people in their daily lives. For instance, using smart grids (Siano, 2014), an optimal and efficient management of the energy production could be done at the scale of the city. Smart grids also allow the integration of renewable energy capacities to better handle the other sources and optimize the production (Potter, et al., 2009).

However, energy is not the only path that is explored nowadays for smart cities. Indeed, due to the rapid evolution of technologies, cities must be equipped with networks that are efficient and sufficient in size. Wi-Fi and data connection for smartphones are also essential requirements of the smart city. Using such networks enables a better comprehension about the inhabitants.

In the context of smart cities, IT/ICT can also improve tourism. Using the discussed data networks, artificial intelligence can be used to trace tourists' pathways and learn their behavior and provide tailored information to the tourist for their potential places of interest.

In contrast using the methodology known for the living labs, concepts are being developed to change the model of the Smart City into Human Smart City. This concept promotes human as the center of the project while ICT is only an enabler to develop users' creativity besides assisting them in daily living routines (The human Smart City Cookbook, 2014).

One recently tested project is MyNeighbourhood (Oliveira, 2014), this aims to reconnect people, interact with each other's and share new ideas on how can evolve their daily living so that it could be largely improved for all of them. Artificial intelligence (AI) here has an important place to link people that shares common things together and then emulation and creativity between them will allow the emergence of new ideas for everyday living. This can lead then to the idea of User Driven Open Innovation, the user being the citizen that will be able to have some power in their town. The most mature and co-conceived projects can be selected and then implemented in appropriately selected cities. This will require a new conception of Internet, with social and co-design capabilities, accessible by anyone in the city.

Finally, this idea of using the collective intelligence and gathering it with the power offered by the currently available ICT will give a new and hybrid system, used either for controlling energy efficiency, well-being (using technology for a smarter health), and also creativity emulation, with on one side the citizens and on the other the Artificial Intelligence helping them, creating a Smart Society. All this will be possible if there is holistic inclusion of technologies in our daily living (fully adapted and function AI). To facilitate this holistic inclusion of technologies would require the adaption of infrastructure and the decision making processes within a city.

9.0 FUTURE OF ARTIFICIAL INTELLIGENCE IN SMART ENVIRONMENTS

Researchers have constantly endeavored to apply knowledge-based methods in order to adapt the behavior of smart homes to its inhabitants and to determine the status of the users during long periods of time.

Artificial intelligence (AI) is mostly used to determine the activities of the inhabitants in smart homes. Such works have been well summarized by Cook et al. The detected activities can then be used in two ways. The first is to summarize the daily status of the users. This is to enable checking for apparitions of troubles known as being a part of some chronic/ageing related diseases (Noury, Berenguer, Teyssier, Bouzid, & Giordani, 2011). The aim is to identify indexes capable of being compared to the present clinical evaluations of the person and so to monitor, every day, the evolution of such an index to detect, as early as possible, the apparition of some critical signs. The second way is to adapt the response of building automation to the circumstances. It is achievable by altering the behavior of the building automation commands depending on the context (Vacher et al., 2011). AI is also used for energy consumption reduction in smart homes. It can be used to automatically change the heating habits (for a thermostat) depending on the prediction of occupancy status (Scott et al., 2011).

The future of AI in smart environments is expected at two levels. The first level is the building and its inhabitants. Better understanding the behavior of smart home occupants is essential. The application of more advanced learning techniques such as incremental techniques is essential, in order to adapt to first slight changes of the persons that are natural and also to changing conditions in long term measurements (seasoning). This improved comprehension will lead towards a more accurate and complete index computed in order to make them correspond to clinical evaluations. Moreover, better understanding of the behavior of the inhabitant will lead to an important change in these researches: scaling-up. Indeed, the current challenge is to develop a generic/adaptable model (e.g. during the first week of presence of the use) that will learn from the users. Models have to be adapted or are dependent of the person that is monitored. To ensure transferability this work has to be as generic as possible, capable of being installed, without extra-work, in every person's home, and to be linked to healthcare centers. The data analysis also has to be efficient, highlighting the important features that better describe the user, in order to be usable while providing the best view to the physician. Where the first level analysis monitors distress such as fall, the sensitivity and specificity have to be large enough to be usable. Such work, analyzing the behavior and habits of the person, can also be used to enhance the fitness of the automatized thermostats based on the users' expectation. This is beneficial in the improvement of users' well-being and the enhancement of building energy efficiency. Elimination of faulty sensor values is essential to improve the performance of smart homes. Systems that consider each sensor and actuator as an agent in a multi-agent system can have a better idea of the confidence on the data. Instead of the sensor, each room of the building can also be considered as an agent. It can then allow optimizing some actuator uses (e.g. heating) in a regulation system.

The second level of AI utilization is considering the smart home within a set of buildings e.g. in an urban context. This conceptualizes smart neighborhoods/cities. In this context, promising potentials exist through considering various smart buildings together in order to provide further services for the inhabitants. For instance, distribution of heat schemes linked among different smart buildings (the heat exchanges) will be recognized in addition to individual uses in stand-alone buildings. A second application would be some enhanced serious games, in which individuals would be compared to their neighbors for energy consumption/activities. It is increasingly significant when applied in larger communities resulting in substantial heat loss preventions. By promoting the competition among users to be better than the others in such serious games, energy is expected to be more effectively used in future smart environments.

Many countries have set up elderly villages in which the target individuals are well-secured and facilitated with access to their required services. In a second type of AI application, with the computation of a model for a user and the comparison of each user with these models (from data gathered in their own home), it would be possible to motivate each elderly user to be more active and more autonomous by comparing them and allowing them to be a part of a serious game at the scale of the village.

To conclude, the future of smart environments is expected to be formed based on integrating smart sensing and AI to obtain thorough and effective behavioral models of people in their environment. This is expected to enhance the well-being and sense of security.

10.0 CONCLUSION

With the emergence of information and communication technologies (ICT) and the development of advanced sensing systems, the concept of the smart home is receiving a growing attention worldwide. In past decades, smart homes were generally conceptualized as an innovative dream for future built environments. Nevertheless, this study demonstrated the rising interest in this field and confirmed the penetration of smart homes into urban areas, stressing that smart homes are gradually entering our lives.

This study provided a holistic overview about the current status, benefits and future direction of smart homes. It is revealed that, smart homes are predominantly influenced by the integration of ICT, creative technologies and intelligent systems such as sensors and actuators. With the aid of new technological initiatives, smart homes are capable of ensuring an independent lifestyle for all users. This is combined with a higher level of safety, security and comfort through continually monitoring and controlling the users' activities, behavioral patterns, health status of patients and automatically responding to the needs and preferences of the occupants. From the other side, smart homes promise to create adaptive, supportive and assistive living environments.

Traditionally, residential buildings are not flexible enough to correspond to the diversity of users' demands. They generally follow a singular pattern to meet the residents' demands. This inflexibility has resulted in an incongruity between the users' expectations, quality of living environment and the available integrated technologies. However, smart homes can revolutionize the traditional relationship between users and homes. They increase the level of users' participation in controlling the household activities and even, the energy consumption. Smart homes can be responsive and interactive towards the residents' needs. They deliver a consistent health caring, monitoring and control system. They provide a behavioral map and respond to any detected deviations from the developed pattern. Furthermore, smart environments recognize the level of users' activities in buildings and regulate the household energy consumption based on users' presence. Overall, smart homes should improve the static relationship, linkages, and communications between the occupants and the living environments. This results in ensuring a highly independent and convenient lifestyle.

Smart homes originated as a solution to offer highly automated living environments through deploying sophisticated technologies. However, future research is needed to examine the environmental performance of smart homes and their linkage to the smart cities. In fact, in recent years, researchers have initiated drawing more attention to the sustainable performance of smart homes. Through the integration of the energy management systems, renewable energy applications, intelligent active systems, and passive design initiatives, smart homes are expected to efficiently control the household energy consumption. Being integrated with sustainability principles, smart homes are a highly promising solution for the future of AEC industry due to their flexibility, adaptability and dynamic features. They result in a highly responsive, energy efficient and productive living environments as a fundamental step for achieving a sustainable urban future. It is expected that smart homes will become more intertwined with 'adaptability', 'self-adjustability', and 'self-learning capability' features allowing them to exceed their current position and to meet the ever-increasing demands of users.

Among the observed challenges, the high cost of the existing intelligent technologies and the lack of an operative financing mechanism are the key obstacles towards proliferating smart homes in urban areas. In this regard, governmental sectors and policy makers are highly recommended to develop new initiatives such as incentivized programs for the spread of smart homes into future urban areas. Likewise, the potential risks of the integration of untested creative technologies and lack of public awareness about the benefits of smart homes are the other key challenges.

Findings of this study encourage researchers to focus on further exploration and analytical evaluation of the social and environmental benefits of smart homes. This is to be done using cross-disciplinary collaborative approaches. This should include the perspectives of the whole team ranging from designers, architects and urban planners to civil, environmental, mechanical and computer engineers. Furthermore, future research is necessary to evaluate possible policies for encouraging the use of smart homes. Finally, further investigations towards ensuring the economic feasibility of proliferating smart homes as a part of the urban sustainability agenda should be encouraged.

REFERENCES

Adlam, T., Faulker, R., Orpwood, R., Jones, K., Macijauskiene, J., & Budraitiene, A. (2004). The installation and support of internationally distributed equipment for people with dementia. *IEEE Transactions on Information Technology in Biomedicine*, 8(3), 253–257. doi:10.1109/TITB.2004.834393 PMID:15484430

Al-Sumaiti, A. S., Ahmed, M. H., & Salama, M. M. A. (2014). Smart Home Activities: A Literature Review. *Electric Power Components and Systems*, 42(3-4), 294–305. doi:10.1080/15325008.2013.832439

Albino, V., Berardi, U., & Dangelico, R. M. (2015). Smart cities: Definitions, dimensions, performance, and initiatives. *Journal of Urban Technology*, 22(1), 3–21. doi:10.1080/10630732.2014.942092

Aldrich, F. K. (2003). *Smart homes: past, present and future. Inside the smart home.* Springer. doi:10.1007/1-85233-854-7_2

Aleksy, M., Korthaus, A., & Schader, M. (2005). *Implementing Distributed Systems with Java and CORBA*. Berlin: Springer.

Alonso, I. G., Fres, O. A., Fernández, A. A., Gómez del Torno, P., Maestre, J. M., De, P. A. M., & Fuente, G. (2012). Towards a new open communication standard between homes and service robots, the DH-Compliant case. *Robotics and Autonomous Systems, 60*(6), 889–900. doi:10.1016/j.robot.2012.01.006

Alwan, M., Kell, S., Turner, B., Dalal, S., Mack, D., & Felder, R. (2006). Psychosocial impact of passive health status monitoring on informal caregivers and older adults living in independent senior housing. In Information and Communication Technologies, CTTA'06. doi:10.1109/ICTTA.2006.1684477

Anderson, D., Luke, R. H., Keller, J. M., Skubic, M., Rantz, M., & Aud, M. (2009). Linguistic summarization of video for fall detection using voxel person and fuzzy logic. *Computer Vision and Image Understanding, 113*(1), 80–89. doi:10.1016/j.cviu.2008.07.006 PMID:20046216

Asada, H. H., Shaltis, P., Reisner, A., Rhee, S., & Hutchinson, R. C. (2003). Mobile monitoring with wearable photoplethysmographic biosensors. *IEEE Engineering in Medicine and Biology Magazine, 22*(3), 28–40. doi:10.1109/MEMB.2003.1213624 PMID:12845817

Aslan, M., Sengur, A., Xiao, Y., Wang, H., Ince, M. C., & Ma, X. (2015). Shape Feature Encoding via Fisher Vector for Efficient Fall Detection in Depth-Videos. *Applied Soft Computing, 37*, 1023–1028. doi:10.1016/j.asoc.2014.12.035

Aware Home Research Initiative. (n.d.). *About AHRI*. Georgia Tech. Available on: http://www.aware-home.gatech.edu/drupal/?q=content/about-ahri

Barnes, N. M., Edwards, N. H., Rose, D. A. D., & Garner, P. (1998). Lifestyle monitoring technology for supported independence. *Computing & Control Engineering Journal, 9*(4), 169–174. doi:10.1049/cce:19980404

Bartusch, C., Wallin, F., Odlare, M., Vassileva, I., & Wester, L. (2011). Introducing a demand-based electricity distribution tariff in the residential sector: Demand response and customer perception. *EnergPolicy, 39*, 5008–5025.

Berardi, U. (2013). Clarifying the new interpretations of the concept of sustainable building. *Sustainable Cities and Society, 8*, 72–78. doi:10.1016/j.scs.2013.01.008

Biswas, D., Cranny, A., Gupta, N., Maharatna, K., Achner, J., Klemke, J., & Ortmann, S. (2015). Recognizing upper limb movements with wrist worn inertial sensors using k-means clustering classification. *Human Movement Science, 40*, 59–76. doi:10.1016/j.humov.2014.11.013 PMID:25528632

Boers, N., Chodos, D., & Gbyrzynski, P. et al.. (2010). The smart condo project: services for independent living. In M. Ziefle & C. Röcker (Eds.), *E-Health, assistive technologies and applications for assisted living: challenges and solutions*. IGI Global.

Bonino, D., Corno, F. (2011). What would you ask to your home if it were intelligent? Exploring user expectations about next-generation homes. *Journal of Ambient Intelligence and Smart Environments, 3.*

Borja, R., De la Pinta, J. R., Álvarez, A., & Maestre, J. M. (2013). Integration of service robots in the smart home by means of UPnP: A surveillance robot case study. *Robotics and Autonomous Systems, 61*(2), 153–160. doi:10.1016/j.robot.2012.10.005

Bregman, D., & Korman, A. (2009). A universal implementation model for the smart home. *International Journal of Smart Home*, *3*(3), 15–30.

Breslow, L. (2006). Health measurement in the third era of health. *American Journal of Public Health*, *96*(1), 17–19. doi:10.2105/AJPH.2004.055970 PMID:16322463

Brownsell, S., Blackburn, S., & Hawley, M. S. (2008). An evaluation of second and third generation telecare services in older people's housing. *Journal of Telemedicine and Telecare*, *14*(1), 8–12. doi:10.1258/jtt.2007.070410 PMID:18318922

Brumitt, B., Meyers, B., Krumm, J., Kern, A., & Shafer, S. (2000). EasyLiving: Technologies for intelligent environments. *Lecture Notes in Computer Science*, *1927*, 12–29. doi:10.1007/3-540-39959-3_2

Buckman, A., Mayfield, M., & Beck, , S. (2014). What is a smart building? *Smart and Sustainable Built Environment*, *3*(2), 92–109. doi:10.1108/SASBE-01-2014-0003

Budijono, S., Andrianto, J., & Noor, M. A. N. (2014). Design and implementation of modular home security system with short messaging system. In EPJ Web of Conferences EDP Sciences. doi:10.1051/epjconf/20146800025

Buys, I., Barnett, K., Miller, E., & Bailey, C. (2005). Smart housing and social sustainability: Learning from the residents of Queensland's Research House. *Australian Journal of Emerging Technologies and Society*, *3*(1), 43–57.

Caine, K. E., Rogers, W. A., & Fisk, A. D. (2005). Privacy perceptions of an aware home with visual sensing devices. In *Proceedings of the Human Factors and Ergonomics Society Annual Meeting SAGE Publications*. doi:10.1177/154193120504902108

Cempel, W. A., & Mikulik, J. (2013). Intelligent building reengineering: Adjusting life and work environment to occupant's optimal routine processes. *Intelligent Buildings International*, *5*(1), 51–64.

Chan, M., Campo, E., & Est`eve, D. (2005). Assessment of activity of elderly people using a home monitoring system. *International Journal of Rehabilitation Research. Internationale Zeitschrift fur Rehabilitationsforschung. Revue Internationale de Recherches de Readaptation*, *28*(1), 69–76.

Chan, M., Campo, E., Estève, D., & Fourniols, J. Y. (2009). Smart Homes – Current Features and Future Perspectives. *Maturitas*, *64*(2), 90–97. doi:10.1016/j.maturitas.2009.07.014 PMID:19729255

Chan, M., Esteve, D., Escriba, C., & Campo, E. (2008). A Review of Smart Homes – Present State and Future Challenges. *Computer Methods and Programs in Biomedicine*, *91*(1), 55–81. doi:10.1016/j.cmpb.2008.02.001 PMID:18367286

Chan, M., Estève, D., Fourniols, J. Y., Escriba, C., & Campo, E. (2012). Smart wearable systems: Current status and future challenges. *Artificial Intelligence in Medicine*, *56*(3), 137–156. doi:10.1016/j.artmed.2012.09.003 PMID:23122689

Chen, J., Kam, A. H., Zhang, J., Liu, N., & Shue, L. (2005). Bathroom activity monitoring based on sound. In *Proceedings of the Pervasive* (LNCS), (vol. 3468, pp. 47 – 61). Berlin: Springer.

Choon, S.-W., Siwar, C., Pereira, J. J., Jemain, A. A., Hashim, H. S., & Hadi, A. S. (2011). A sustainable city index for Malaysia. *International Journal of Sustainable Development and World Ecology*, *18*(1), 28–35. doi:10.1080/13504509.2011.543012

Clements-Croome, D. (2013). *Intelligent Buildings: Design, Management and Operation*. ICE Publishing. Retrieved from https://books.google.co.nz/books?id=jwRUuAAACAAJ

Clements-Croome, D. J. (2011). Sustainable intelligent buildings for people: A review. *Intelligent Buildings International*, *3*(2), 67–86.

Cook, D. J., & Krishnan, N. C. (2015). *Activity Learning: Discovering, Recognizing, and Predicting Human Behavior from Sensor Data*. Wiley. Retrieved from https://books.google.co.nz/books?id=TMZ9BgAAQBAJ

Cottone, P., Gaglio, S., Re, G.L., & Ortolani, M. (2013). User activity recognition for energy saving in smart homes. *Sustainable Internet and ICT for Sustainability (SustainIT)*. IEEE.

Day, S. (2006). *Digital life, the future of humanity?* Available on: http://mms.ecs.soton.ac.uk/2007/papers/60.pdf

De Silva, L. C., Morikawa, C., & Petra, I. M. (2012). State of the art of smart homes. *Engineering Applications of Artificial Intelligence*, *25*(7), 1313–1321. doi:10.1016/j.engappai.2012.05.002

Demiris, G. (2009). *Privacy and social implications of distinct sensing approaches to implementing smart homes for older adults*. IEEE EMBS.

Demiris, G., & Hensel, B. (2009). Smart homes for patients at the end of life. *Journal of Housing for the Elderly*, *23*(1), 106–115. doi:10.1080/02763890802665049

Demiris, G., & Hensel, B. K. (2008). Technologies for an aging society: A systematic review of "smart home" applications. *Methods of Information in Medicine*, *47*(Suppl. 1), 33–40. PMID:18660873

Demiris, G., Skubic, M., & Rantz, M. et al.. (2006). Smart home sensors for the elderly: a model for participatory formative evaluation. In *Proceedings of the IEEE EMBS international special topic conference on information technology in biomedicine*. IEEE.

Deshmukh, S. D., & Shilaskar, S. N. (2015). Wearable sensors and patient monitoring system: A Review. In *Pervasive Computing (ICPC), 2015 International Conference on*. IEEE. doi:10.1109/PERVASIVE.2015.7086982

Dewsbury, G., Taylor, B., & Edge, M. (2001). The process of designing appropriate smart homes: including the user in the design. In *Proceedings of the 1st Equator IRC workshop on ubiquitous computing in domestic environments*. Nottingham, UK: University of Nottingham.

Diegel, O. (2005). Intelligent automated health systems for compliance monitoring. In *Proceedings of the IEEE Region 10 TENCON*. IEEE. doi:10.1109/TENCON.2005.301000

Ding, D., Cooper, R. A., Pasquina, P. F., & Pasquina, L. F. (2011). Sensor technology for smart homes. *Maturitas*, *69*(2), 131–136. doi:10.1016/j.maturitas.2011.03.016 PMID:21531517

Dingli, A., & Seychell, D. (2015). *Smart Homes*. The New Digital Natives. Springer Berlin Heidelberg.

Dirks, S., & Keeling, M. (2009). *A Vision of Smarter Cities: How Cities Can Lead the Way into a Prosperous and Sustainable Future.* Somers, NY: IBM Global Business Services.

Ehrenhard, M., Kijl, B., & Nieuwenhuis, L. (2014). Market adoption barriers of multi-stakeholder technology: Smart homes for the aging population. *Technological Forecasting and Social Change, 89,* 306–315. doi:10.1016/j.techfore.2014.08.002

Elite-care, smart home. (n.d.). Retrieved from http://www.elite-care.com

Elma, O., Selamogullari, U. S., Uzunoglu, M., & Ugur, E. (2013, October). Carbon emission savings with a renewable energy supplied smart home operation. In *Renewable Energy Research and Applications (ICRERA), 2013 International Conference on* (pp. 1129-1132). IEEE. doi:10.1109/ICRERA.2013.6749922

Elzabadani, H., Helal, A., Abdulrazak, B., & Jansen, E. (2005). Self-sensing spaces: smart plugs for smart environments. In *Proceedings of the third international conference on smart homes and health telematic.*

Fahad, L. G., Khan, A., & Rajarajan, M. (2015). Activity recognition in smart homes with self-verification of assignments. *Neurocomputing, 149,* 1286–1298. doi:10.1016/j.neucom.2014.08.069

File, T. (2013). *Computer and Internet Use in the United States.* Current Population Survey Reports.

Finkenzeller, K. (2003). *RFID handbook – fundamentals and applications in contactless smart cards and identification* (2nd ed.). Chichester, UK: JohnWiley.

Froehlich, J., Larson, E., Campbell, T., Haggerty, C., Fogarty, J., & Patel, S. N. (2009). Hydosense: infrastructure-mediated single-point sensing of whole-home water activity. In *Proceedings of the 11th international conference on Ubiquitous computing.*

Gaddam, A., Mukhopadhyay, S. C., & Gupta, G. S. (2010). Towards the development of a cognitive sensor network-based home for elder care. In *The 6th international conference on wireless and mobile communication.* doi:10.1109/ICWMC.2010.93

Gatzoulis, L., & Iakovidis, I. (2007). Wearable and portable eHealth systems. *IEEE Engineering in Medicine and Biology Magazine, 26*(5), 51–56. doi:10.1109/EMB.2007.901787 PMID:17941323

Gentry, T. (2009). Smart homes for people with neurological disability: State of the art. *NeuroRehabilitation, 25,* 209–217. PMID:19893189

Ghadi, Y. Y., Rasul, M. G., & Khan, M. M. K. (2014). Potential of Saving Energy Using Advanced Fuzzy Logic Controllers in Smart Buildings in Subtropical Climates in Australia. *Energy Procedia, 61,* 290–293. doi:10.1016/j.egypro.2014.11.1110

Ghaffarianhoseini, A. H., Berardi, U., AlWaer, H., Chang, S., Halawa, E., Ghaffarianhoseini, A., & Clements-Croome, D. (2015). What is an intelligent building? Analysis of recent interpretations from an international perspective. *Architectural Science Review,* 1-20.

Ghaffarianhoseini, A. H., Dahlan, N. D., Berardi, U., Ghaffarianhoseini, A., & Makaremi, N. (2013). The essence of future smart houses: From embedding ICT to adapting to sustainability principles. *Renewable & Sustainable Energy Reviews, 24,* 593–607. doi:10.1016/j.rser.2013.02.032

Glaeser, E. L., & Berry, C. R. (2006). *Why are Smart Places Getting Smarter? Taubman Centre Policy Brief 2006-2*. Cambridge, MA: Taubman Centre.

Glascock, A. P., & Kutzik, D. M. (2000). Behavioral Telemedicine: A new approach to continuous nonintrusive monitoring of activities of daily living. *Telemedicine Journal*, *6*(1), 33–44. doi:10.1089/107830200311833

Glascock, A. P., & Kutzik, D. M. (2007). An evidentiary study of the uses of automated behavioral monitoring. In *Proceedings of the 21st International Conference on Advanced Information Networking and Applications Workshops*. IEEE Computer Society. doi:10.1109/AINAW.2007.81

Hachiya, H., Sugiyama, M., & Ueda, N. (2012). Importance-weighted least-squares probabilistic classifier for covariate shift adaptation with application to human activity recognition. *Neurocomputing*, *80*(0), 93–101. doi:10.1016/j.neucom.2011.09.016

Haigh, K. Z., Kiff, L. M., & Ho, G. (2006). Independent Lifestyle Assistant: Lessons Learned. *Assistive Technology*, *18*(1), 87–106. doi:10.1080/10400435.2006.10131909 PMID:16796244

Hamed, B. (2012). Design & Implementation of Smart House Control Using LabVIEW. [IJSCE]. *International Journal of Soft Computing and Engineering*, *1*(6), 98–106.

Han, D. M., & Lim, J. H. (2010). *Smart home energy management system using IEEE 802.15.4 and zigbee. Consumer Electronics* (pp. 1403–1410). IEEE Transactions.

Hatler, M., Gurganious, D., & Chi, C. (2013). *Smart Building Wireless Sensor Networks A Market Dynamics Report*. ON World's Research.

Helal, S., Mann, W., El-Zabadani, H., King, J., Kaddoura, Y., & Jansen, E. (2005). The Gator Tech Smart House: A programmable pervasive space. *Computer*, *38*(3), 50–60. doi:10.1109/MC.2005.107

Hoey, J., von Bertoldi, A., Poupart, P., & Mihailidis, A. (2007). Assisting persons with dementia during handwashing using a partially observable markov decision process. In *Proceedings of the 5th international conference on computer vision systems*.

Hollands, R. G. (2008). Will the real smart city please stand up? Intelligent, progressive or entrepreneurial? *City*, *12*(3), 303–320. doi:10.1080/13604810802479126

Honga, X., Nugenta, C., Mulvenna, M., McClean, S., Scotney, B., & Devlin, S. (2009). Evidential fusion of sensor data for activity recognition in smart homes. *Pervasive and Mobile Computing*, *5*(3), 236–252. doi:10.1016/j.pmcj.2008.05.002

Hu, L., Ong, D. M., Zhu, X., Liu, Q., & Song, E. (2015). Enabling RFID technology for healthcare: Application, architecture, and challenges. Springer. *Telecommunication Systems*, *58*(3), 259–271. doi:10.1007/s11235-014-9871-x

Huang, Y., Wang, L., & Wu, Q. (2014). *A Hybrid PSO-DE Algorithm for Smart Home Energy Management* (pp. 292–300). Springer International Publishing Switzerland. doi:10.1007/978-3-319-11897-0_35

Hussain, S., Schaffner, S., Moseychuck, D. (2009). Applications of Wireless Sensor Networks and RFID in a Smart Home Environment. *Communication Networks and Services Research Conference CNSR '09. Seventh Annual.*

Institute of Medicine. (2012). *Living Well with Chronic Illness: A Call for Public Health Action.* Washington, DC: The National Academies Press.

Intille, S. S., Larson, K., Beaudin, S., Tapia, E. M., Kaushik, P., & Nawyn, J. et al.. (2005). *The Placelab: a live-in laboratory for pervasive computing research (video). Pervasive 2005.* Video Program.

Ismangil, A., Jenie, R. P., Irmansyah, , & Irzaman, . (2015). Development of lithium tantallite (LiTaO3) for automatic switch on LAPAN-IPB Satellite infrared sensor. *Procedia Environmental Sciences, 24,* 329–334. doi:10.1016/j.proenv.2015.03.043

Isoda, Y., Kurakake, S., & Nakano, H. (2004). Ubiquitous sensors based human behavior modeling and recognition using a spatio-temporal representation of user states. In *Proceedings of the 18th International Conference on Advanced Information Networking and Application (AINA'04).* doi:10.1109/AINA.2004.1283961

ITU. (2010). Applications of ITU-T G.9960. In ITU-T G.9961 Transceivers for Smart Grid Applications: Advanced Metering Infrastructure, Energy Management in the Home and Electric Vehicles (ITU-T, 06/2010). International Telecommunication Union Technical Paper.

Jakkula, V. R., Cook, D. J., & Jain, G. (2007). Prediction Models for a Smart Home Based Health Care System. *Advanced Information Networking and Applications Workshops, AINAW '07. 21st International Conference.* doi:10.1109/AINAW.2007.292

Jin, C., & Kunz, T. (2011). Smart Home Networking: Lessons from Combining Wireless and Powerline Networking. *Smart Grid and Renewable Energy, 2*(02), 136–151. doi:10.4236/sgre.2011.22016

Kaya, İ., & Kahraman, C. (2014). A comparison of fuzzy multicriteria decision making methods for intelligent building assessment. *Journal of Civil Engineering and Management, 20*(1), 59–69. doi:10.3846/13923730.2013.801906

Kaye, J. A., Maxwell, S. A., Mattek, N., Hayes, T. L., Dodge, H., Pavel, M., & Zitzelberger, T. A. et al. (2011). Intelligent systems for assessing aging changes: Home-based, unobtrusive, and continuous assessment of aging. *The Journals of Gerontology. Series B, Psychological Sciences and Social Sciences, 66*(Suppl. 1), i180–i190. doi:10.1093/geronb/gbq095 PMID:21743050

Kelly, D. (2005). Smart support at home: The integration of telecare technology with primary and community care systems. *Br. J. Healthc. Comput. Inform. Manage, 22*(3), 19–21.

Kim, S. C., Jeong, Y. S., & Park, S. O. (2013). RFID-based indoor location tracking to ensure the safety of the elderly in smart home environments. Springer. *Personal and Ubiquitous Computing, 17*(8), 1699–1707. doi:10.1007/s00779-012-0604-4

Kim, S. J., & Dave, B. (2010). Silver towns and smart technologies. In *Proceedings of the 22nd Conference of the Computer–Human Interaction Special Interest Group of Australia on Computer–Human Interaction.* ACM. doi:10.1145/1952222.1952256

Knowles, H. S. (2008). *Realizing residential building greenhouse gas emissions reductions: the case for a web-based geospatial building performance and social marketing tool.* The United States Environmental Protection Agency (EPA). Available from http://www.epa.gov/ttnchie1/conference/ei17/session5/knowles.pdf

Konstantas, D. (2007). An overview of wearable and implantable medical sensors. In IMIA year book of medical informatics. IMIA

Korhonen, I., Lappalainen, R., Tuomisto, T., Koobi, T., Pentikainen, V., Tuomisto, M., & Turjanmaa, V. (1998). TERVA: wellness monitoring system. In *Proceedings of the 20th Annual International Conference of IEEE Engineering in Medicine and Biology Society.* IEEE.

Krumm, J., Harris, S., Meyers, B., Brumitt, B., Hale, M., & Shafer, S. (2000). Multi-camera multi-person tracking for EasyLiving. In *Proceedings of 3rd IEEE International Workshop on Visual Surveillance.* IEEE. doi:10.1109/VS.2000.856852

Kushwaha, N., & Kim, M. (2005). Microsoft agent based health care alert system for smart home. *Enterprise networking and Computing in Healthcare Industry. HEALTHCOM. Proceedings of 7th International Workshop.* doi:10.1109/HEALTH.2005.1500453

Kwon, O., Lee, E., & Bahn, H. (2014). Sensor-aware elevator scheduling for smart building environments. *Building and Environment, 72,* 332–342. doi:10.1016/j.buildenv.2013.11.013

Lach, C., & Punchihewa, A. et al.. (2007). Smart home system operating remotely Via 802.11b/g wireless technology. *Proceedings of the Fourth International Conference Computational Intelligence and Robotics and Autonomous Systems (CIRAS2007).*

Larson, E., Froehlich, J., Campbell, T., Haggerty, C., Atlas, L., Fogarty, J., & Patel, S. N. (2012). Disaggregated water sensing from a single, pressure-based sensors: An extended analysis of HydroSense using staged experiments. *Pervasive and Mobile Computing, 8*(1), 82–102. doi:10.1016/j.pmcj.2010.08.008

Lazaroiu, G. C., & Roscia, M. (2012). Definition methodology for the smart cities model. *Energy, 47*(1), 326–332. doi:10.1016/j.energy.2012.09.028

Lemmet, S. (2009). Buildings and Climate Change: A Summary for Decision-Makers, UNEP's Sustainable Buildings & Climate Initiative (SBCI). Paris: Academic Press.

Lertlakkhanakul, J., Choi, J. W., & Kim, M. Y. (2008). Building data model and simulation platform for spatial interaction management in smart home. *Automation in Construction, 17*(8), 948–957. doi:10.1016/j.autcon.2008.03.004

Li, R. Y. M. (2012). A Content Analysis in Hong Kong Sustainable Smart Home Knowledge Sharing via World Wide Web. *Communications in Computer and Information Science, 350,* 265–269. doi:10.1007/978-3-642-35594-3_37

Li, W., Lee, Y. H., Tsai, W. T., Xu, J., Son, Y. S., Park, J. H., & Moon, K. D. (2012). Service-oriented smart home applications: Composition, code generation, deployment, and execution. *Service Oriented Computing and Applications, 6*(1), 65–79. doi:10.1007/s11761-011-0086-7

Lukowicz, P., Kirstein, T., & Tröster, G. (2004). Wearable systems for health care applications. *Methods of Information in Medicine, 43*, 232–238. PMID:15227552

Lymberis, A., & Dittmar, A. (2007). Advanced wearable health systems and applications, research and development efforts in the European Union. *IEEE Engineering in Medicine and Biology Magazine, 26*(3), 29–33. doi:10.1109/MEMB.2007.364926 PMID:17549917

Mahoney, D., Mahoney, E., Liss, E., & Ease, A. T. (2009). Automated technology for elder assessment, safety, and environmental monitoring. *Gerontechnology (Valkenswaard), 8*(1), 11–25. doi:10.4017/gt.2009.08.01.003.00

Manto, M., Topping, M., Soede, M., Sanchez-Lacuesta, J., Harwin, W., Pons, J., & Normie, L. et al. (2003). Dynamically responsive intervention for tremor suppression. *IEEE Engineering in Medicine and Biology Magazine, 22*(3), 120–132. doi:10.1109/MEMB.2003.1213635 PMID:12845828

Matsuoka, K. (2004). Aware home understanding life activities. In *Proceedings of the International Conference on ICOST'2004, Towards a Human-Friendly Assistive Environment*. IOS Press.

Matzeu, G., Florea, L., & Diamond, D. (2015). Advances in wearable chemical sensor design for monitoring biological fluids. *Sensors and Actuators. B, Chemical, 211*, 403–418. doi:10.1016/j.snb.2015.01.077

Meyers, R. J., Williams, E. D., & Matthews, H. S. (2010). Scoping the potential of monitoring and control technologies to reduce energy use in homes. *Energy and Building, 42*(5), 563–569. doi:10.1016/j.enbuild.2009.10.026

Mihailidis, A., Carmichael, B., & Boger, J. (2004). The use of computer vision in an intelligent environment to support aging-in-place, safety, and independence in the home. *IEEE Transactions on Information Technology in Biomedicine, 8*(3), 238–247. doi:10.1109/TITB.2004.834386 PMID:15484428

Missaoui, R., Joumaa, H., Ploix, S., & Bacha, S. (2014). Managing energy Smart Homes according to energy prices: Analysis of a Building Energy Management System. *Energy and Building, 71*, 155–167. doi:10.1016/j.enbuild.2013.12.018

Mohsenian-Rad, A. H., Wong, V. W. S., Jatskevich, J., Schober, R., & Leon-Garcia, A. (2010). Autonomous Demand-side Management Based on Game-theoretic Energy Consumption Scheduling for the Future Smart Grid. *IEEE Transactions on Smart Grid, 1*(3), 320–331. doi:10.1109/TSG.2010.2089069

Molderink, A., Bakker, V., Bosman, M. G. C., Hurink, J. L., & Smit, G. J. M. (2010). Management and Control of Domestic Smart Grid Technology. IEEE Transactions on Smart Grid, 1(2), 109 – 119.

Mozer, M. C. (1998). The neural network house: an environment that's adapts to its inhabitants. In *Proceedings of the AAAI Spring Symposium on Intelligent Environments*. AAAI Press.

Noguchi, H., Mori, T., & Sato, T. (2002). Construction of network system and the first step of summarization for human daily action in the sensing room. In *Proceedings of the IEEE Workshop on Knowledge Media Networking (KMN'02)*. IEEE. doi:10.1109/KMN.2002.1115157

Noury, N., Berenguer, M., Teyssier, H., Bouzid, M.-J., & Giordani, M. (2011). Building an index of activity of inhabitants from their activity on the residential electrical power line. *Information Technology in Biomedicine. IEEE Transactions on, 15*(5), 758–766.

Oliveira, A. (2014). MyNeihbourhood Vision. Presentation given at the "Human Smart Cities Conference - The future of cities today". Lisbon, Portugal.

Orpwood, R., Adlam, T., & Gibbs, C. (2001). User-centred Design of Support Devices for People with Dementia for Use in Smart House in Assistive Technology-added Value to the Quality of Life. IOS Press.

Ozkan, N. B., Amerighi, O., & Boteler, B. (2014). A comparison of consumer perceptions towards smart homes in the UK, Germany and Italy: Reflections for policy and future research. *Technology Analysis and Strategic Management*, *26*(10), 1176–1195. doi:10.1080/09537325.2014.975788

Ozkan, N. B., Davidson, R., Bicket, M., & Whitmarsh, L. (2013). Social barriers to the adoption of smart homes. *Energy Policy*, *63*, 363–374. doi:10.1016/j.enpol.2013.08.043

Park, J. W., Jung, Y. S., Park, H. J., Kim, S. D., & Cho, W. D. (2009). *WIS: A well-being index based health care system in smart home*. Pervasive Computing and Communications. PerCom 2009. IEEE International Conference. doi:10.1109/PERCOM.2009.4912804

Patel, S. N., Reynolds, M. S., & Abowd, G. D. (2008). *Detecting human movement by differential air pressure sensing in HVAC system ductwork: an exploration in infrastructure mediated sensing*. Pervasive.

Patel, S.N., Roberston, T., Kientz, J.A., Reynolds, M.S., Abowd, G.D. (2007). *At the flick of a switch: detecting and classifying unique electrical events on the residential power line*. Ubicomp.

Perry, M., Dowdall, A., Lines, L., & Hone, K. (2004). Multimodal and ubiquitous computing systems: Supporting independent-living older users. *IEEE Transactions on Information Technology in Biomedicine*, *8*(3), 258–270. doi:10.1109/TITB.2004.835533 PMID:15484431

Perumal, T., Ramli, A.R., Leong, C.H., Mansor, S., & Samsudin, K. (2008). Interoperability for Smart Home Environment Using Web Services. *International Journal of Smart Home, 2*(4).

Potter, C. W., Archambault, A., & Westrick, K. (2009, March). Building a smarter smart grid through better renewable energy information. In Power Systems Conference and Exposition, 2009. PSCE'09. IEEE/PES (pp. 1-5). IEEE. doi:10.1109/PSCE.2009.4840110

Ransing, R. S., & Rajput, M. (2015). Smart home for elderly care, based on Wireless Sensor Network. In *Nascent Technologies in the Engineering Field (ICNTE), 2015 International Conference*. IEEE. doi:10.1109/ICNTE.2015.7029932

Rantz, M., Skubic, M., Miller, S., & Krampe, J. (2008). Using technology to enhance aging in place. In S. Helal, S. Mitra, J. Wong, C. Chang, & M. Mokhtari (Eds.), *Smart homes and health telematics* (pp. 169–176). Berlin: Springer. doi:10.1007/978-3-540-69916-3_20

Rantz, M. J., Marek, K. D., Aud, M., Tyrer, H. W., Skubic, M., Demiris, G., & Hussam, A. (2005). A technology and nursing collaboration to help older adults age in place. *Nursing Outlook*, *53*(1), 40–45. doi:10.1016/j.outlook.2004.05.004 PMID:15761399

Rantz, M. J., Skubic, M., & Miller, S. J. (2009). Using sensor technology to augment traditional healthcare. In *Proceedings of the Annual International Conference of the IEEE of Engineering in Medicine and Biology Society 2009 (EMBC 2009)*. doi:10.1109/IEMBS.2009.5334587

Reeder, B., Meyer, E., Lazar, A., Chaudhuri, S., Thompson, H. J., & Demiris, G. (2013). Framing the evidence for health smart homes and home-based consumer health technologies as a public health intervention for independent aging: A systematic review. *International Journal of Medical Informatics*, *82*(7), 565–579. doi:10.1016/j.ijmedinf.2013.03.007 PMID:23639263

Reinisch, C., Kofler, M. J., Iglesias, F., & Kastner, W. (2011). Think home Energy Efficiency in Future Smart Homes. *EURASIP Journal on Embedded Systems*, 1–18.

Riedel, D. E., Venkatesh, S., & Liu, W. (2005). Spatial activity recognition in a smart home environment using a chemotactic model. In *Proceedings of the International Conference on Intelligent Sensors Networks and Information Processing*. doi:10.1109/ISSNIP.2005.1595596

Robert, A., & Kummert, M. (2012). Designing net-zero energy buildings for the future climate, not for the past. *Building and Environment*, *55*, 150–158. doi:10.1016/j.buildenv.2011.12.014

Rodden, T., & Benford, S. (2003). The evolution of buildings and implications for the design of ubiquitous domestic environments. In *Conference on human factors in computing systems, proceedings of the SIGCHI conference on human factors in computing systems*. New York: ACM Press. doi:10.1145/642611.642615

Roy, A., Das Bhaumik, S. K., Bhattacharya, A., Basu, K., Cook, D. J., & Das, S. K. (2003). Location Aware Resource Management in Smart Homes. *Proceedings of the First IEEE International Conference on Pervasive Computing and Communications*. IEEE. doi:10.1109/PERCOM.2003.1192773

Russo, J., Sukojo, A., Helal, A., Davenport, R., & Mann, W. C. (2004). SmartWave—intelligent meal preparation system to help older people live independently. In D. Zhang & M. Mokhtari (Eds.), *Toward a human-friendly assistive environment*. IOS Press.

Scott, F. (2007). *Teaching Homes to be Green: Smart Homes and the Environment*. London: Green Alliance.

Scott, J., Bernheim Brush, A., Krumm, J., Meyers, B., Hazas, M., Hodges, S., & Villar, N. (2011). PreHeat: controlling home heating using occupancy predictionACM. *Symposium conducted at the meeting of the Proceedings of the 13th international conference on Ubiquitous computing*. doi:10.1145/2030112.2030151

Siano, P. (2014). Demand response and smart grids—A survey. *Renewable & Sustainable Energy Reviews*, *30*, 461–478. doi:10.1016/j.rser.2013.10.022

Silva, R., Arakaki, J., Junqueira, F., Santos Filho, D., & Miyagi, P. (2012). Modeling of active holonic control systems for intelligent buildings. *Automation in Construction*, *25*, 20–33. doi:10.1016/j.autcon.2012.04.002

Sixsmith, A., & Johnson, N. (2004). A smart sensor to detect the falls of the elderly. *Pervasive Computing, IEEE*, *2*(2), 42–47. doi:10.1109/MPRV.2004.1316817

Skarmeta, A., & Moreno, M. V. (2014). Internet of Things. Lecture Notes in Computer Science, 8425, 48-53. doi:10.1007/978-3-319-06811-4_10

Skubic, M., Alexander, G., Popescu, M., Rantz, M., & Keller, J. (2009). A smart home application to eldercare: Current status and lessons learned. *Technology and Health Care*, *17*(3), 183–201. PMID:19641257

Soyer, E. B. (2009). *Pyroelectric Infrared (PIR) Sensor Based Event Detection*. Available from: http://www.thesis.bilkent.edu.tr/0003853.pdf

Stone, E. E., & Skubic, M. (2015). Testing Real-Time In-Home Fall Alerts with Embedded Depth Video Hyperlink. In *Smart Homes and Health Telematics* (pp. 41–48). Springer International Publishing. doi:10.1007/978-3-319-14424-5_5

Stringer, M., Fitzpatrick, G., & Harris, E. (2006). Lessons for the future: experiences with the installation and use of today's domestic sensors and technologies. In *Pervasive Computing: Proceedings of the 4th International Conference*. Springer- Verlag. doi:10.1007/11748625_24

Surie, D., Laguionie, O., & Pederson, T. (2008). Wireless sensor networking of everyday objects in a smart home environment. In *International conference intelligent sensors, sensor networks and information processing*. IEEE. doi:10.1109/ISSNIP.2008.4761985

Suryadevara, N. K., & Mukhopadhyay, S. C. (2015). Forecasting the Behaviour of an Elderly Person Using WSN Data. In *Smart Homes* (pp. 139–157). Springer International Publishing. doi:10.1007/978-3-319-13557-1_5

Taati, B., Snoek, J., & Mihailidis, A. (2013). Video analysis for identifying human operation difficulties and faucet usability assessment. *Neurocomputing, 100*(0), 163–169. doi:10.1016/j.neucom.2011.10.041

Taber, A., Keshavarz, A., & Aghajan, H. (2006). Smart home care network using sensor fusion and distributed vision-based reasoning. In *Proceedings of the VSSN '06 proceedings of the 4th ACM international workshop on Video surveillance and sensor networks*. ACM. doi:10.1145/1178782.1178804

Tanaka, K., Yoza, A., Ogimi, K., Yona, A., Senjyu, T., Funabashi, T., & Kim, C.-H. (2012). Optimal operation of DC smart house system by controllable loads based on smart grid topology. *Renewable Energy, 39*(1), 132–139. doi:10.1016/j.renene.2011.07.026

The human Smart City Cookbook, Planum. (2014). *The Journal of Urbanism, 28*(1). Retrieved from http://humansmartcities.eu/wpcontent/uploads/2014/06/The_Human_Smart_Cities_Cookbook_by_Planum_no.28_vol_I2014_low.pdf

Thuzar, M. (2011). *Urbanizationin South East Asia: Developing Smart Cities for the Future?*. Regional Outlook.

Tien, S. C., Feng, Y. Y., Chang, W. H., Lee, R. G., Huang, S. F., & Lee, T. Y. (2014). Smart textiles applied in emergency department patients with chest pain. In *Bioelectronics and Bioinformatics (ISBB), 2014 IEEE International Symposium on*. IEEE.

Tollmar, K., & Junestrand, S. (1999). Video Mediated Communication for Domestic Environments: Architectural and Technological Design. In N. Streiz, J. Siegel, V. Hartkopf, & S. Konomi (Eds.), *Cooperative Buildings: Integrating Information, organizations and Architecture, Proceedings of CoBuilding'99* (LNCS), (vol. 1670, pp. 176-89). Berlin: Springer.

Tomita, M. R., Mann, W. C., Stanton, K., Tomita, A. D., & Sundar, V. (2007). Use of currently available smart home technology by frail elders: Process and outcomes. *Top. Geriatr. Rehabil, 23*(1), 24–34. doi:10.1097/00013614-200701000-00005

Tomita, M. R., & Nochajski, S. M. (2015). Using Smart Home Technology and Health-Promoting Exercise. In *International Handbook of Occupational Therapy Interventions* (pp. 747–756). Springer International Publishing. doi:10.1007/978-3-319-08141-0_54

Tröster, G. (2004). The agenda of wearable healthcare. In R. Haux & C. Kulikowski (Eds.), *IMIA yearbook of medical informatics: ubiquitous health care systems* (pp. 125–138). Stuttgart, Germany: Schattauer.

Tuschl, R. H. (2013). Beyond the digital revolution: The structure between the governmental sphere and the civil society for hegemony in cyberspace. *Democracy in Crisis: The Dynamics of Civil Protest and Civil Resistance, 65.*

Vacher, M., Istrate, D., Portet, F., Joubert, T., Chevalier, T., Smidtas, S., & Chahuara, P. (2011). The sweet-home project: Audio technology in smart homes to improve well-being and reliance. *Symposium conducted at the meeting of the Engineering in Medicine and Biology Society, EMBC, 2011 Annual International Conference of the IEEE.* IEEE.

Van Hoof, J., Kort, H. S. M., Rutten, P. G. S., & Duijnstee, M. S. H. (2011). Ageing- in-place with the use of ambient intelligence technology: Perspectives of older users. *International Journal of Medical Informatics, 80*(5), 310–331. doi:10.1016/j.ijmedinf.2011.02.010 PMID:21439898

Veleva, S., Davcev, D., & Kacarska, M. (2011). *Wireless Smart Platform for Home Energy Management System.* The 2nd IEEE PES International Conference and Exhibition on Innovative Smart Grid Technologies (ISGT Europe), Manchester, UK. doi:10.1109/ISGTEurope.2011.6162798

Venkatesh, A. (2003). *Smart home concepts: current trends.* IT in the home series. Center for Research on Information Technology and Organizations. Available from http://escholarship.org/uc/item/6t16p6pf

Waterhouse, E. (2003). New horizons in ambulatory electroencephalography. *IEEE Engineering in Medicine and Biology Magazine, 22*(3), 74–80. doi:10.1109/MEMB.2003.1213629 PMID:12845822

West, G., Greehill, S., & Venkatesh, S. (2005). A probalistic approach to the anxious home for activity monitoring. In *Proceedings of the 29th Annual International Computer Software and Applications Conference (COMPSAC'05).* doi:10.1109/COMPSAC.2005.29

Williams, G., Doughty, K., & Bradley, D. A. (1998). A systems approach to achieving CarerNet—an integrated and intelligent telecare system. *IEEE Transactions on Information Technology in Biomedicine, 2*(1), 1–9. doi:10.1109/4233.678527 PMID:10719506

Wong, J., Li, H., & Wang, S. (2005). Intelligent building research: A review. *Automation in Construction, 14*(1), 143–159.

Wong, J. K. W., & Li, H. (2009). Development of intelligence analytic models for integrated building management systems (IBMS) in intelligent buildings. *Intelligent Buildings International, 1*(1), 5–22. doi:10.3763/inbi.2009.0011

Wong, K. B. Y., Zhang, T., & Aghajan, H. (2014). Extracting patterns of behavior from a network of binary sensors. *Journal of Ambient Intelligence and Humanized Computing,* 1-23.

Wood, A. (2015). The internet of things is revolutionising our lives, but standards are a must. *The Guardian.*

Zhang, J., Shan, Y., & Huang, K. (2015). ISEE Smart Home (ISH): Smart video analysis for home security. *Neurocomputing*, *149*, 752–766. doi:10.1016/j.neucom.2014.08.002

Zhou, S., Wu, Z., Li, J., & Zhang, X. P. (2014). Real-time Energy Control Approach for Smart Home Energy Management System. *Electric Power Components and Systems*, *42*(3–4), 315–326. doi:10.1080/15325008.2013.862322

Chapter 15
Exposing Core Competencies for Future Creative Technologists

Andy M. Connor
Auckland University of Technology, New Zealand

Maggie Buxton
Auckland University of Technology, New Zealand

Ricardo Sosa
Auckland University of Technology, New Zealand

Ann Marie Gribble
Auckland University of Technology, New Zealand

Sangeeta Karmokar
Auckland University of Technology, New Zealand

Anna G. Jackson
Auckland University of Technology, New Zealand

Stefan Marks
Auckland University of Technology, New Zealand

Jacques Foottit
Auckland University of Technology, New Zealand

ABSTRACT

This chapter suggests that in terms of preparing creative technologies graduates it is better to define what skill sets will be in the future rather than attempting to define either what creative technologies is now or what a current creative technologist should be capable of. The chapter is a collaborative attempt to explore the future definition of a creative technologist through a form of creative expression. The chapter utilizes a combination of self-reflective narrative and performative writing to develop position descriptions for jobs that may exist in the future, where each job is an extension of an author's life trajectory. A cluster analysis is undertaken to identify common themes that define the possible characteristics and attributes of future graduates that can be used to design the curricula for creative technologies programmes to meet the needs of the changing world.

INTRODUCTION

It seems a simple question to ask, "What is Creative Technologies?" However, simple questions often lead to complex answers and as yet there is no clear definition of creative technologies that is universally held. Different degree programmes exist under this banner, yet each maintains its own flavor of the field. Individuals tend to project their own experiences and requirements into definitions that suit them, for

DOI: 10.4018/978-1-5225-0016-2.ch015

example many occurrences of the job title creative technologist are found in creative agencies who are moving forward from their previous incarnations in advertising, but the use of creative technologies still maintains this heritage of advertising by emphasizing the importance of understanding brands and business. Such uncertainty and diversity is expressed by Avnet (2010) who states:

Back in the 90s, the first time "convergence" was brought up as an important idea, I was asked as a "new media expert" to write an article on its importance – and found just about as many definitions for the term as places I looked. When I was part of a panel of psychologists defining "media psychology," again, we found that just about everyone using the term defined it differently. Same with "engagement." These still remain relatively loosely described constructs, words or phrases that, to quote Carroll's Humpty Dumpty, "mean exactly what [we] choose it to mean – neither more nor less."

We're at a similar point with the term creative technology. What exactly IS a creative technologist? What makes her different from a programmer or a flash animator? What makes him different from a copywriter, brand manager, or strategist who can use Dreamweaver? What's the role of a creative technologist at an agency or in our industry? (Avnet, 2010)

The objective of this chapter is not to ask the question of what creative technologies is, but instead to ask the question of what a creative technologist might be in the future. The chapter brings together a varied collection of individuals with different experiences of creative technologies and utilizes a performative writing approach to develop a self-reflective narrative of a future creative technologist. These individual narratives are analyzed and common themes extracted that can be used to reframe current creative technologies degree programmes to ensure that they are preparing graduates for the future.

The remainder of the chapter is structured as follows. The next section provides a brief overview of the relevant literature related to creative technologies, graduate employability and methods of developing graduate outcomes. This is followed by an overview of the methodology used in this paper, which involves the specifying of job adverts for jobs that do not yet exist. The job adverts provide the basis for a reflective and reflexive analysis of common attributes and knowledge that are clustered into a number of high level groupings. The chapter concludes with a mapping of this cluster analysis to the current graduate profile of an established degree in Creative Technologies as a validation of the aims of the programme.

BACKGROUND

The following sections provide a brief overview of the related literature related to creative technologies, graduate employability and methods for producing graduate outcomes. It is argued that a perceived gap between graduate capabilities and the competencies required for employment in industry may be due to the use of too short a projected timescale when developing graduate outcomes for academic programmes.

Creative Technologies

This chapter does not aim to provide a single definition of creative technologies, however it is placed in the context of many existing definitions. Creative technology, or creative technologies, seems to be a relatively modern field however it can trace its origins back to the closing years of the Second World War (Connor, 2016). In many ways the field can be considered as a broad interdisciplinary domain that combines knowledge from a variety of traditional disciplines that include art, computer science, design, engineering and the humanities. In education, degrees of this ilk are typically presented to address needs for cross-disciplinary interaction and to develop lateral thinking skills across other more rigidly defined academic areas recognized as a valuable component in expanding technological horizons.

Avnet implicitly defines creative technologies whilst attempting to define a creative technologist as:

Here's my take on it. CTs understand the business of advertising, marketing, and branding, take a creative, strategic and people-centric view of how to connect people and brands, and understand the kinds of mediating technologies that can best be used to make those engaging experiences where the connection happens. They sketch with technology, just like a visual creative can sketch with a pencil. They're steeped in strategy, so the things they come up with make sense – it's not about technology just for the sake of technology. The experiences they design address real needs of people and brands. Creative technologists share a creative and inquisitive view of the world. They're on top of technology trends, aren't afraid of coding (just as a modern visual designer isn't afraid of Photoshop or Illustrator), and take both strategic and tactical approaches to creativity. They also understand that we're in a business, and we're solving business goals by addressing people's needs as a priority. (Avnet, 2010)

Such a definition is a pertinent starting point to consider the whole field, but in a world that is seeing the emergence of social enterprise over more traditional business models and a wide ranging set of global problems it raises the question as to whether business goals and brands are simply a projection of Avnet's own experience. This leads in to a range of questions such as what role do creative technologists play in the solution of global problems? What skills and knowledge are needed by creative technologists in order to undertake these roles? Ultimately, it is important to consider whether current creative technologies programmes are producing graduates that are capable of undertaking these roles.

An alternative definition of creative technologies is provided by Zagalo & Branco (2015) who suggest that creative technologies is "the basis for human expressivity: to sustain self-realization, to raise self-esteem, to increase community bonds, and to create a better society" (Zagalo & Branco, 2015, p. 3) and also that "creative technologies have as their main goal the task of facilitating creation by general people, to allow general people to self-discover the best of themselves that they can give back to the community" (Zagalo & Branco, 2015, p. 9).

The tension between this two definitions is clear, with Zagalo & Branco arguing that creative technologies is about self-expression whilst Avnet suggests that creative technologies is not only creative, but also strategic and business focused. The lack of rigid definition of the field is therefore a challenge in terms of understanding what is (and what is not) in scope of creative technologies. This challenge is further compounded by the rapid growth of new technologies and the changing nature of the field. This chapter therefore purposefully avoids attempt to work within a rigid definition of creative technologies, instead embracing the diversity of definition. The chapter sets out not to define what creative technologies might be, but instead what creative technologists should be able to do so as to inform the education of graduates prepared to be employed in this field in the future and to embrace the changing nature of their employment.

Graduate Employability

Perceptions of graduate employability is an on-going issue in academia, with many philosophical concerns around how to include employability in terms of curriculum design and delivery (Harvey, 2000). At a practical level, in many disciplines graduates themselves feel that they are ready for employment (Martin, Maytham, Case, & Fraser, 2005) whilst at the same time it is argued that there is a gap between graduate capabilities and the competencies required for employment in industry (Almi, Rahman, Purusothaman, & Sulaiman, 2011). This phenomenon is not limited to any particular discipline, with the readiness gap having been identified in a wide range of disciplines including healthcare (Edwards, 2011; Wolff, Pesut, & Regan, 2010), journalism (Cullen, Tanner, O'Donnell, & Green, 2014) and business (Raybould & Sheedy, 2005) to name but a few.

Both historically and more recently the nature of this gap has been investigated. For example, Candy and Crebert (1991) observe that:

One of the main criticisms that employers make of their new graduate employees is that they tend to emerge from university with their heads full of theories, principles, and information but are often ill-equipped to deal with aspects of the workplace such as problem solving, decision making, working in a team, or learning for themselves. (Candy & Crebert, 1991, p. 572)

Meanwhile, Jackson (2010) has undertaken an international meta-analysis of the nature of the gap for business graduates, though many of the competency gaps are applicable to other domains. Various studies have addressed issues related to closing the existing gap, for example Clapton (2013) discusses the role of academic staff in increasing readiness to be employed whereas other authors have considered different pedagogies for improving work readiness (Jollands, Jolly, & Molyneaux, 2012; Pegg, Waldock, Hendy-Isaac, & Lawton, 2012). However, there seems to be little recent work that investigates *why* there is such a gap between employers' expectations and graduate capabilities. One possible suggestion is that the time lines of preparing and updating current degree programmes is not fully considered during this process. As an example, a University may decide to develop a new programme and consult with industry as to the current needs. Given that it may take up to a year to develop the programme in order to meet these needs, then take another three years before the first graduates are entering the workforce, then there is a gap of four years from when the need was specified in which time technology and society have moved on.

There is therefore a pressing need to address the design or new programmes in such a way that the programmes are future proof, by incorporating and understanding the skills and knowledge that graduates are going to need in five, ten or twenty years time. There has been some work in this area, for example Gow and McDonald (2000) suggest that the attributes already identified across time and nations will not fully reflect the demands of future job markets and investigate new competences suggested in the literature as being essential for the future of work. There has been some attempts at accommodating future needs in current education for well defined disciplines, for example dentistry (Hunt & Bushong, 2010) and academia (Austin & McDaniels, 2006). However, for less well defined disciplines such as arts and creative industries, the main focus is on how to develop soft skills (Ball, 2002). In that regard, creative technologies as a field requires a unique mix of technical soft skills and the lack of definition of the field presents significant challenges in terms of what is needed to prepare graduates for the future.

Constructing Graduate Outcomes

The goal of this paper is to provide an understanding, not of what creative technologies is but instead what attributes and characteristics may be required to be a successful creative technologist in the future. This understanding can be used to develop a set of graduate outcomes that guide curriculum developments for creative technologies programmes.

As has already been mentioned, a typical curriculum design process will start with the definition of some form of graduate outcomes, normally phrased in terms of a graduate profile and some graduate attributes (Spronken-Smith et al., 2013). In recent years there has been a growing focus on the use of one or more personas that typify the graduate profile through creation of an archetype, an approach that has developed from introducing personas in to experience design (Adlin et al., 2006). Whilst such an approach is useful in helping tease out more subtle graduate attributes there is a need to consider how to project the persona into the future. Such an approach is utilized by Landis (2006) who considers the educational requirements for future librarians and suggests:

One challenge in thinking about core competencies and professional education programs at any point in time, but especially in the present, volatile technical world of the information and communication professions, is to figure out a creative way to avoid constraining future possibilities with too narrow a focus on the past and present. Surely the competencies we define today will play a role in steering (or not) creative new talent into our particular neighborhood of those information professions. (Landis, 2006, p. 41)

Landis goes on to describe in detail the persona of a future colleague using a self-reflective narrative. In the context of creative technologies, the only limitation of this approach is the relative narrow nature of collections librarianship and the fact that the development of a single persona by a single person is open to introducing bias. A more robust approach is to consider multiple personas developed by a wider range of individuals. Such an approach is utilized by Tu, Dong, Rau & Zhang (2010) who undertake a cluster analysis to find common elements.

Future Jobs

The method utilized in this paper draws on the work of both Landis (2006) and Tu, Dong, Rau & Zhang (2010), however also introduces aspects of performative writing (Pelias, 2005). Performative writing has been utilized methodologically as a means of highlighting the role of contemplation in teaching and learning (Blinne, 2014) and other forms of narrative have also been used in determining and communicating best teaching practice (Connor et al., 2014) and a wider research context (Hamilton, Smith, & Worthington, 2008). Whilst some authors argue that narrative based research needs to be approached cautiously (Atkinson & Delamont, 2006), in terms of the goals of this chapter the inclusion of narratives from multiple authors provides confidence that the outcomes are not overly influenced by a single voice.

Where the approach used in this chapter differs from other forms of performative writing or autoethnography is that pieces of writing are semi-fictional and project a narrative in to the future. Performative writing would typically feature a lived experience, recounting iconic moments that call forth the complexities of human life. Whilst the approach used in this paper does not recount the lived experience, it recounts the experience that could be. It also holds true to the aspect of performative writing that does not indiscriminately record experience. Instead, the approach is "a highly selective camera, aimed carefully to capture the most arresting angles" (Pelias, 2005, p. 418) .

The authors of this paper represent a wide range of individuals from different backgrounds and at different life stages, including undergraduate students in creative technologies, both Masters and PhD students and of course academic staff teaching on creative technologies programmes. Each author was tasked with self-reflecting on their life experiences and how they came to be involved in the creative technologies field and project their life trajectory in to a future in order to articulate a job that as yet does not exist. These "jobs as performances" are based on different narrative and interpretive practices that are all individually provide the writer a sense of grounding, or narrative coherence (Gubrium & Holstein, 1998). Each piece of writing is internally coherent, but it has been suggested that the use of narrative collage entails that performative writing "shows, rather than tells" (Denzin, 2001, p. 36). The approach acknowledges the suggestion by Pollock that performative writing should be evocative, reflexive, multi-voiced, cross-genres, and is always partial and incomplete (Pollock, 1998).

This process was carried out independently with no cross consultation between authors. Following the writing of the adverts the collected set of adverts were circulated for comment with a reflective component and an analytic component that will be reported in the discussion of this paper. The intention was to attempt to identify the core skills and attributes of creative technologists of the future in order to compare these to the current graduate outcomes of a creative technologies degree to identify whether the current programme is preparing graduates for the future. The following sections outline the "future jobs" that were the result of the performative writing exercise.

The adverts are presented in the same order as the authors list of the paper, however each author is also identified in the advert text for convenience. No constraints were placed on the authors in terms of whether the jobs were at a particular level (e.g. new graduate) or in any other form. The task presented to the authors was interpreted roughly equally in two ways, either the writing of a job advert or that of a job description. The latter have been edited in order to create a consistent set of adverts that make comparisons more easily, however the content of each modified advert has been cross-checked by the original author to confirm that the original intent has been maintained. The job adverts are as follows with the job title used as the section heading.

Naval Systems Repurposing Engineer

With the emergence of world peace, our world is facing new dilemmas and potential ecological disaster through inappropriate decommissioning of military assets. The large scale scuttling of Naval assets common in the Twentieth Century cannot be sustained due to the fragile state of our marine ecology and the diminishing fish stocks occurring as a result of poor fisheries practices.

We are currently seeking a Naval Systems Repurposing Engineer to join our Systems Engineering team at GAE Systems. The ideal candidate will have a minimum of a Bachelor of Creative Technologies (Masters of Creative Technologies preferred) with recent experience in a Systems Engineering role.

The successful candidate will report to the Director of Naval Systems Repurposing and will be responsible for identifying creative uses of subsystems extracted from both nuclear and fossil-fuel powered vessels. Currently our team has had great successes in repurposing flat panel radar systems as multiphase arrays for weather monitoring and aircraft carrier catapult launch systems in novel bushfire control mechanisms. However, the team requires an innovative thinking individual with the potential to see useful applications of a wider range of subsystems to work alongside the specialist engineers. The successful candidate will have the ability to interpret and understand technical documentation of naval systems, including requirements documents, CAD information, and both functional and simulation models. For legacy systems, the candidate will be expected to undertake practical investigations to reverse engineer subsystems in order to understand their behavior. The successful candidate will therefore have a sound knowledge of the interaction of mechanical, electrical and software components of complex systems. The candidate will be expected to demonstrate a "can-do" attitude and be prepared to learn new skills and gain new knowledge quickly as legacy systems are reverse engineered.

- **Minimum Qualification:** Creative Technologies degree and at least 5 years of experience in Systems Engineering.
- **Expertise and Knowledge:** Systems engineering methodologies, reverse engineering, fundamentals of mechanical, electrical and software engineering.
- **Candidate Attributes:** Lateral thinking, creative, methodical, self-motivated, good communicator, team player, quick learner.
- **Appointing Manager:** Andy M. Connor.

Senior Creativity Engineer

We are looking for a Senior Creativity Engineer to join our Strategic Design and Innovation team at H&P Healthcare.

You will be responsible for shaping a corporate culture based on creative, innovative and intrapreneurial teamwork. This will help consolidate a mind-set of collaborative and divergent reasoning across corporate departments aimed at developing next-generation products and services. You will plan, develop and deploy activities, tools, and ICT systems to support new design concepts in cross-disciplinary teams who will bring early ideas into market-ready products and subsequently research the entire product lifecycle including post-sale user experience. You will also lead staff training programmes on divergent reasoning, creative facilitation, and teamwork.

This generalist role includes:

- Lead field research initiatives with market, technology, and design specialists to reveal insights and identify new product and service opportunities
- Coordinate creative activities throughout the product lifecycle from needs assessment, strategic design, concept generation, product and service design, prototyping, testing and validation
- Develop corporate programmes that help consolidate an organizational culture centered around creativity, innovation, and intrapreneurship across areas and departments
- Plan, develop and deploy innovative tools, techniques and ICT systems that support creative initiatives and teamwork
- Initiate and oversee 'design stewardship' initiatives that bring early concepts into market and to learn from user-centered research analysis

You will have a Creative Technologies degree and more than 10 years of related experience in the design of innovative products and services. Experience including coordinating field research and evidence-based prototyping are required. Your design and technology background combined with managerial experience will be key to taking a leadership role in this position.

You will have a natural ability to bridge across disciplinary and cultural divides, and to build rapport to consolidate a culture of creative work with external partners as well as within the organization. You will possess strong scientific and academic writing skills and the ability to translate this information to suit diverse audiences. Your excellent communication skills will allow you to see the perspectives of different functions and to change your style to suit different environments. This is the perfect role to combine your strong interpersonal and technical skills with your passion for creativity and innovation.

We encourage original thinking and participatory leadership required to create better products, processes and practices. Show us your originality and apply now!

- **Minimum Qualification:** Creative Technologies degree and more than 10 years of related experience in the design of innovative products and services
- **Expertise and Knowledge:** Creative facilitation, product design and development, entrepreneurship, creative teamwork, innovation management
- **Candidate Attributes:** Leadership potential, inclusive, excellent communication skills
- **Appointing Manager:** Ricardo Sosa.

Human Experience and Entrepreneurial Guru

We are one of the leading technology service providers in human experience business development and our dream is to grow our business by transforming behavior through uplifting, meaningful human experiences through empathy. We believe experiences matter - they enhance lives and build stronger business.

We believe that a diverse thinking and the diversity of our team, creative thinkers and challenging work will make our business stronger and will generate new ventures. We are looking for professional people who are fearless, have empathy, understand human behavior, have a high level understanding of business competitiveness, experienced in providing support at management level, dedicated towards economic growth and will to take some risks.

So, if you like what you've read so far, and want to work for a company that values diversity and community outreach, professionalism and is industry-renowned for delivering growth in global competition.

You'll engage with community and industry to understand the needs and human experience, and using entrepreneurial skill develop a strategy for the growth or expansion of our business in both the short and long term. You will have skills to work under tight resources and deliver the expectations of community/users and clients. You will be responsible for learning the industries operation inside-out and developing a cutting edge concept that adds value to our business.

You will a strong passion for people and desire to uncover consumer behavior, to help our business to connect with customers in an impactful and desirable way. The successful candidate will build brilliant strategies across multiple verticals with their deep understanding of human experience. They will require strong passion to see big opportunities to thrive for economic success using meaningful and empathic approach.

You will serve as a key contact to receive community requests and investigate proposed and alternative solutions to maximize economic growth of the company. You will be key representative of our company in community to deliver human experience.

A successful applicant should have:

- A formal academic qualification (minimum Masters in Creative Technology, preferably Bachelor in Human Psychology)
- Professional experience in understanding human behavior and relevant experience in entrepreneurial area.
- 10+ years of experience in venture development and community enterprise in commercial environment
- 3+ years of experience focusing on community and social needs of humans in our society
- Experience developing strategically grounded, brilliant creative applied in digital and offline mediums.
- Well-versed portfolio of successful projects executed at national or international level.
- **Minimum Qualification:** Masters degree in Creative Technology with a background in Human Psychology
- **Expertise and Knowledge:** Human psychology, human experience, business acumen
- **Candidate Attributes:** Strategic, creative, entrepreneurial, risk taker
- **Appointing Manager:** Sangeeta Karmokar.

Human Swiss Army Knife

We are looking to appoint to a new role in our organization to work across multiple teams and provide customer facing solutions that need to incorporate a number of areas of different expertise. We consider this role a "Human Swiss Army Knife" that has a wide range of possible functions.

The successful candidate will have as a minimum a Bachelor of Creative Technologies degree.

Most of all, the successful applicant needs a "Can Do" attitude to see difficult projects as positive challenges and opportunities to learning on the job as well as to applying the acquired set of solid and established knowledge and practices.

An additional useful attribute is the ability to think out-of-the-box and an ability to approach problems using new, unusual, and/or unattempted methods. This in turn requires a certain level of courage and audaciousness.

With the nature of these challenges comes a certain requirement for adaptability and a willingness to learn – on the job as well as outside. Also helpful is an ongoing interest in keeping up with new developments and technologies.

Due to the multi-disciplinary nature of the projects, the successful candidate will need to be able to speak a variety of "languages" specific to the involved disciplines, and to be able to translate when dealing with two or more customers or suppliers of those different areas. This naturally requires strong communication and teamwork skills.

The successful candidate must be able to closely observe the problems that the customer struggles with and come up with one or more custom solutions. Those solutions must be as simple as possible, but have the potential to be extended beyond the original scope into full-blown installations or products.

The successful candidate must be able to think outside of any boxes seemingly defined by any software and hardware and must be able to make connections that are unusual, possibly counter-intuitive at first, but have the potential of yielding surprisingly efficient, elegant, and/or revolutionary results. However, this also requires an openness to failure and the skills to deconstruct and analyze those failures for a maximum learning effect.

Lastly, the successful candidate must develop a "vaguely specific" specialization, i.e., have a set of programming/crafting/design skills that is based on experience and best practice, but is also open for improvement and even a readiness for total abandonment in order to acquire a more suitable or modern set of skills.

- **Minimum Qualification:** Bachelor of Creative Technologies
- **Expertise and Knowledge:** Broad range of hardware and software knowledge
- **Candidate Attributes:** Courage, audaciousness, willingness to take calculated risks, lifelong learner, good communication and teamwork skills
- **Appointing Manager:** Stefan Marks.

Community Innovator

Communities today are faced with complex issues requiring sophisticated, cross-disciplinary solutions. In order to generated these solutions individuals need to use a number of different creative approaches which support social, economic, cultural and spiritual wellbeing.

Our community board is looking for someone who is technologically and socially adept with strong interpersonal communication skills. The person will have a solid network of connections and relationships within the community which crosses over cultural, political and disciplinary boundaries.

The individual will creatively use a number of different methodological and technological tools to address intractable problems facing our town: poverty, lack of educational achievement, division and exclusiveness. This may involve producing cross-disciplinary media-art projects, supporting technology-based advocacy, building cultural-digital literacy and facilitating cross-boundary project generation.

It is envisaged applicants will hold postgraduate qualifications in creative technologies, communications and/or social practice and have at least twenty-five year' experience working with a diverse range of groups including grass-roots community settings. A broad range of experience of different types of digital media is a requirement and preference is given to those who have experience using locative and augmented reality mobile applications.

- **Minimum Qualification:** A minimum of a Masters of Creative Technologies.
- **Expertise and Knowledge:** Systemic diagnosis and consulting skills, mobile learning, digital media, augmented reality, location aware systems, facilitation, leadership of interdisciplinary teams, production.
- **Candidate Attributes:** Ability to connect people, strong networker, culturally sensitive, leadership, exceptional organizational skills.
- **Appointing Manager:** Maggie Buxton.

Augmented Zoologist

Are you passionate about Animals and worry about the future possibility of land scarcity in zoos? Do you have innovative ideas for integrating a new zoological interactive immersive experience that takes up minimal space but have unlimited expansion. Do you enjoy seeing animals in their natural environments and being able to get up close and personal with lions, tigers and bears, oh my?

FutureZoo is a place for this real experience to happen. We are located in an old gutted cinema complex where each "cinema" is a difference Safari experience. We want to expand beyond the real and offer a wider range that includes more of a global menu. We as a company help in creating experiences that wouldn't occur otherwise, or anywhere else in the world. We present a highly visual experience and find through hiring creative technologists, the possibilities are endless.

The augmented zoologist we seek will work across the augmented team and will often travel on retreats to various locations across the globe to understand the real feeling of the places they create. The authenticity of production is key and is a crucial aspect to the company. The role will be working with the current eight Safaris, however this will be expanding soon as newer content is curated. Within the role, you will be the project manager of one Safari so that you know you contribution and involvement help towards a better experience. We believe in a collaborative environment and cross disciplinary input is key. You will ensure that FutureZoo is utilizing the best technology to strengthen its experience and ensure that disturbance in immersive connections are kept at a minimum. A Creative Technologies Qualification would be beneficial.

Key responsibilities:

- Project manage one Safari immersive environment programme;
- Develop new and innovative ways to bring animals to the public in an immersive environment;
- Work with your team members and managers on solutions for new technologies, bugs prevention and helping towards the preservation of existing environments around the world;
- Collaborate with curators and various external public exhibition developers such as Museum's and libraries to keep abreast with newly discovered and endangered/extinct species;
- Keep up to date with various emerging technologies and immersive environments being developed nationally and internationally.

The Future Zoo concept increases awareness globally of the need to preserve wildlife and is openly supported by the SPCA, PETA and WWF. We need a creative technologist to keep us moving forward and to help our guests feel even more immersed with the creatures. We want to create memorable experiences for all our guests. If you understand the need to preserve wildlife and are technologically minded, apply now for this excitingly wild opportunity.

- **Minimum Qualification:** Bachelor of Creative Technologies preferred
- **Expertise and Knowledge:** Project management, familiarity with a range of immersive technologies, understanding of conservation principles
- **Candidate Attributes:** Team player, good communication skills, lifelong learner
- **Appointing Manager:** Ann Marie Gribble.

Inter-Dimensional Transmediator

Limitless Entertainment is an innovator and industry leader in the field of inter-dimensional entertainment and educational experiences.

We are currently seeking an experienced transmediator to join our team as a creative technologies generalist. The successful candidate will be a strategic thinker with outstanding creative and communication skills and the ability to be equally effective as a supportive collaborator and as a leader. While transmediators are expected to have a wide range of general competencies, the successful candidate will be a highly specialised story architect and experience designer with a keen interest in the emerging field of inter-dimensional storytelling.

For the current role, the successful candidate must be an expert storyteller, able to construct multimodal narratives that facilitate a coherent and meaningful audience experience across multiple platforms and dimensions. This requires a strong literacy in a wide range of media (audio, visual, spatial, locative, performative, participatory, temporal and dimensional). The successful candidate will recruit and lead a team of experts to work collaboratively from concept to delivery, which requires sufficient technical competence to be able to communicate effectively with specialists such as programmers, quantum engineers, analysts and information architects. A familiarity with multiversal ethics and industry regulations is also a key requirement for this position.

Key responsibilities for this role will be ensuring that project objectives are aligned with audience expectations and behaviors, drawing on audience research, analytics, observation and user testing to ensure that content is delivered on the most appropriate platforms and employing well-tailored strategies for engagement and participation.

While they have a keen awareness of the latest developments in creative technologies, the successful candidate for this role will be able to tell the difference between novelty and innovation and will never compromise story or experience for the sake of a nifty gimmick.

- **Minimum Qualification:** Bachelor of Creative Technologies
- **Expertise and Knowledge:** Research and analysis approaches, storytelling ability, familiar with a range of analogue and digital media
- **Candidate Attributes:** Outstanding creative and communication skills, discerning, team player
- **Appointing Manager:** Anna Jackson

Computer Behaviorist

Asimov Robotics is at the forefront of human assistive robotic technologies. Our aim is to provide the best robotic assistive technologies for our clients. One of our key guiding principles is effective and intuitive interaction between our clients and their robotic assistive platforms. For this reason we are seeking a computer behaviorist to join our behavioral development team. As a computer behaviorist, you will play a key role in developing the behaviors and interaction our robot platforms have with our clients. Your responsibilities will include:

- Assessing the behavioral characteristics of our robot platforms.
- Designing behavioral algorithms to support intuitive and friendly interaction between our robot platforms and their owners.

- Working with our clients to ensure their robot platforms follow appropriate protocol and etiquette.
- Diagnose and treat robot platforms that exhibit behaviors outside of specification.

The successful applicant will have a Masters of Creative Technologies or equivalent qualification, with a focus on human-computer interaction. Experience in programming embedded systems is vital. Experience with developing mechanical systems is advantageous but not required. The ideal applicant will have excellent problem solving abilities and a passion for robotics. As this role involves working with clients, good communication skills are also essential. The ability to work with people from a diverse range of disciplines is also important.

If you see yourself working alongside a diverse, interdisciplinary team in this cutting edge industry then apply now.

- **Minimum Qualification:** Master of Creative Technologies degree
- **Expertise and Knowledge:** Knowledge of a range of hardware and software platforms, human computer interaction, rapid prototyping
- **Candidate Attributes:** Critical thinking, team player, good problem solver, good communication skills
- **Appointing Manager:** Jacques Foottit.

DISCUSSION

The job adverts presented in the previous section provide the basis for the discussion around definitions of what creative technologies might become. This discussion is structured around different approaches, namely a qualitative consideration of the adverts by the authors that is both reflective and reflexive, a clustering analysis to find common ground and finally a mapping back to current programmes in creative technologies.

Reflective and Reflexive Consideration

As has already been discussed, the job adverts were developed by the individual authors with no discussion around possible content. At the end of this process, the set of job adverts were circulated for consideration with a set of guiding questions, namely:

1. Describe your reaction to the adverts, either individually or as a set. Are you surprised by the adverts? Do they cover things that you would never see as creative technologies? Is there anything that you see that is missing that is creative technologies as we know it or how you think it should be?
2. Identify things that are common across at least two of the adverts.
3. Identify things that could be considered as differences that might stand out.
4. Identify anything that should be considered to be "core" for the future of creative technologies.

This reflective and reflexive consideration produced some interesting and useful responses. Some of these are detailed in Table 1.

Table 1. Comments from the reflective and reflexive consideration

Reaction to the Adverts
I enjoyed reading the article because it is unpredictable, an interesting mixture of weird and serious, and definitely points out that there is no "single" description of a Creative Technologist. [SM] Many of them sounded quite intangible and difficult to grasp in terms of what someone would be actually doing. This isn't necessarily a bad thing... reflective of the nature of a new breed of job that doesn't easily fit old categories which were siloed and prescribed. [MB] One thing that did surprise me is the extent to which interpersonal and communication skills were emphasised as key attributes for a creative technologist, so there is perhaps more emphasis on 'people skills' than on technical skills than I had expected. [AJ] Even though I coordinated the process, I didn't read any adverts until they were all received. I found the adverts to cover a broad spectrum of possible activity but all of them can be grounded into how we currently perceive creative technologies. [AMC]

Commonality
A focus on social value or need. [AJ] The common thread was the requirement for skills in multiple areas and particularly working with people from a range of disciplines. [JF] A combination of hard and soft skills (and skills which sit in between). [MB] Whilst not explicit in every advert, there seems to be a common need for people to be problem solvers. It was also interesting to see a focus on both hardware and software, though this seems to be more about familiarity rather than mastery. [AMC]

Differences
One thing that was interesting to note was that the jobs were so significantly different in some cases that the appropriate candidate for one job would be completely incompatible with another. [JF] There was a continuum of roles with one side seeming to be technology focused with a people component and on the other people roles with a technological component. [MB] I'm interested in how consistent the vision and language is. [AJ] The size of the projects. [SM] There are differences about whether roles needed leadership skills but this could be that some are seen as senior positions. I was surprised that there was not emphasis on project management. [AMC]

Core
I did appreciate the fact that all of the adverts touched on the multidisciplinary fact that is at the core of creative technologies. [AMC] The core of Creative Technologies is not in specific technical skills but rather is centered around interpersonal skills and the ability to understand and learn from people across a range of disciplines. [JF] Ability to collaborate across disciplinary boundaries, a removal of the distinction between hard and soft skills, removal of a hierarchy of experiences that are valued....a blending of science, art, social science, etc., and removal of strong disciplinary boundary distinctions. [MB] You can't define what I am as a creative technologist merely based on the project(s) that I am currently working on. And you also can't define which projects I will work on even with a specific creative technologies definition. [SM] Flexibility and adaptability (a tendency to be a generalist with a strong capacity to learn and adapt to fields that are constantly changing). [AJ] Outstanding social and interpersonal skills (the ability to collaborate and co-create and a deep understanding of human behavior). [AJ] The core seems to be very much about connecting people and working in teams. [AMC]

This qualitative analysis is very subjective, however consideration of the commentary does suggest that the technical skills and knowledge are less relevant than attitude and approach. The next section outlines the clustering analysis of key aspects extracted from the job adverts.

Cluster Analysis

Table 2 lists out all of the areas of expertise and candidate attributes extracted from the job adverts in the previous section. This list provides the basis of the clustering analysis used in this chapter.

Each of these entries can be clustered with other similar entries to provide an overall understanding of what might be expected of a future creative technologist. In this clustering approach when there is

Table 2. Candidate expertise, knowledge and attributes

Expertise/Knowledge	Attributes
• Systems engineering methodologies* • Reverse engineering* • Fundamentals of mechanical, electrical and software engineering • Creative facilitation • Product design and development • Entrepreneurship • Creative teamwork • Innovation management • Human psychology • Human experience • Business acumen* • Broad range of hardware and software knowledge • Systemic diagnosis and consulting skills • Mobile Learning • Digital media • Augmented reality • Location aware systems • Facilitation • Leadership of interdisciplinary teams • Production* • Project management • Familiarity with a range of immersive technologies • Understanding of conservation principles* • Research and analysis approaches • Storytelling ability* • Familiar with a range of analogue and digital media • Knowledge of a range of hardware and software platforms • Human computer interaction • Rapid prototyping*	• Lateral thinking • Creative • Methodical • Self-motivated • Good communicator • Team player • Leadership potential • Inclusive • Excellent communication skills • Quick learner • Strategic • Creative • Entrepreneurial • Risk taker • Courage • Audaciousness • Willingness to take calculated risks • Lifelong learner • good communication and teamwork skills • Ability to connect people • Strong networker • Culturally sensitive • Leadership • Exceptional organizational skills. • Team player • Good communication skills • Lifelong learner • Outstanding creative and communication skills • Discerning • Team player • Critical thinking • Team player • Good problem solver • Good communication skills

single entry which is not related to any other it is dropped from the analysis and considered an outlier. This items are marked with an asterisk in Table 1. The outcomes of the clustering is shown in Figure 1, where each cluster has been given a suitable label that describes the generic conceptual area.

This analysis has resulted in nine distinct clusters, three of which are related to knowledge and three of which are related to skills. The final three sit in the overlap between these areas. The creative technologist of the future is likely to need a broad coverage of all of these nine clusters with some depth in a number of them.

Interestingly there is a mismatch in places between the cluster analysis and the reflective/reflexive consideration. For example, the job adverts elicited a feeling that there was a common theme about social good that has not been picked up in the extraction of knowledge, expertise and attributes. This suggests that further analysis of the job adverts may be required to ensure that all relevant information has been extracted. This will be addressed in future work which will involve the addition of further authors/job adverts to this initial exploration of the idea.

Figure 1. Cluster analysis of expertise, knowledge, and attributes

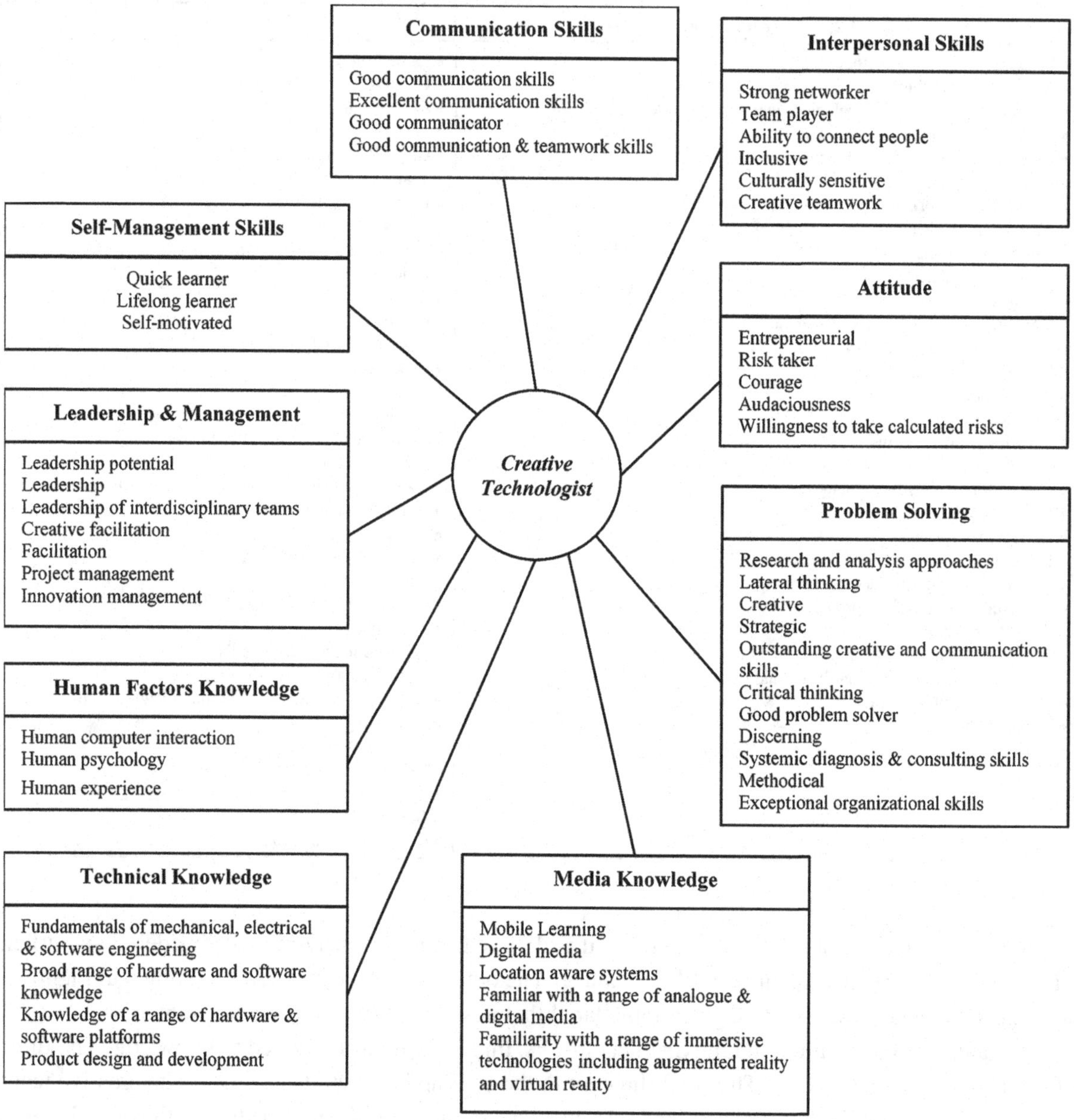

Communication Skills

Good communication skills
Excellent communication skills
Good communicator
Good communication & teamwork skills

Interpersonal Skills

Strong networker
Team player
Ability to connect people
Inclusive
Culturally sensitive
Creative teamwork

Self-Management Skills

Quick learner
Lifelong learner
Self-motivated

Attitude

Entrepreneurial
Risk taker
Courage
Audaciousness
Willingness to take calculated risks

Creative Technologist

Leadership & Management

Leadership potential
Leadership
Leadership of interdisciplinary teams
Creative facilitation
Facilitation
Project management
Innovation management

Problem Solving

Research and analysis approaches
Lateral thinking
Creative
Strategic
Outstanding creative and communication skills
Critical thinking
Good problem solver
Discerning
Systemic diagnosis & consulting skills
Methodical
Exceptional organizational skills

Human Factors Knowledge

Human computer interaction
Human psychology
Human experience

Technical Knowledge

Fundamentals of mechanical, electrical & software engineering
Broad range of hardware and software knowledge
Knowledge of a range of hardware & software platforms
Product design and development

Media Knowledge

Mobile Learning
Digital media
Location aware systems
Familiar with a range of analogue & digital media
Familiarity with a range of immersive technologies including augmented reality and virtual reality

Graduate Outcomes Mapping

The objective of this chapter is to identify common themes that can be used to reframe current creative technologies degree programmes to ensure that they are preparing graduates for the future. The final outcome of this chapter is therefore a mapping between the identified attributes and the current graduate outcome statements of an existing creative technologies programme to determine whether the programme is preparing "future proof graduates". The current graduate profile for the programme states:

Graduates from the Bachelor of Creative Technologies will present as ready for employment in emerging careers and professions in the creative industries. They will be flexible, innovative, curious and imaginative; experienced in problem-solving; technologically and creatively capable in their chosen domain, and; intellectually and commercially entrepreneurial in their approach.

Working in strongly team and studio-based environments, graduates will integrate discrete knowledge strands and will:

- *Work together in trans-disciplinary project teams;*
- *Embrace multiple creative and technological perspectives;*
- *Develop specialised knowledge and capabilities;*
- *Demonstrate skills of self, colleague and task management;*
- *Acquire an astute awareness of the technical and commercial contexts of the creative sector.*

More specifically, graduates of the Bachelor of Creative Technologies will integrate theory and practice. They will:

- *Work within and between a range of interlinking technological domains;*
- *Possess an awareness of new and emerging technologies;*
- *Scan, select and combine technologies suitable for specific projects;*
- *Measure project outcomes against the requirements of an original project briefing;*
- *Develop a range of visual, aural, verbal, non-verbal and multi-modal communication capabilities;*
- *Communicate with specialists and stakeholders from diverse disciplines and enterprise levels;*
- *Plan, organise and execute collaborative work;*
- *Generate ideas, concepts and artefacts encompassing creativity and innovation;*
- *Use analytical, synthetic and critical perspectives in the generative process;*
- *Produce elegant solutions to problems;*
- *Understand legal, ethical, and moral issues;*
- *Reflect on avenues for future development and improvement;*
- *Incorporate a concern for environmental sustainability;*
- *Base new learning and research on the cumulative knowledge gained during and after the course of study.*

At first glance it would appear that many of the attributes identified in the job adverts and cluster analysis are present in the current graduate profile. Indeed, in many cases the graduate profile extends the outcomes of the work described in this chapter with the inclusion of legal, ethical and moral issues as one example. In this regard the current programme is well set to prepare graduates to be the creative technologists of the future. However, the graduate profile would benefit from clarity of articulation and focusing on the key areas.

What is not clear from the graduate profile is to what extent each of the attributes are developed in the programme, nor is it clear from the current analysis to what extent they should be developed. There are unanswered questions as to whether it is achievable for graduates to be "technologically and creatively capable in their chosen domain" when typically this would require a degree programme in its own right. It is therefore useful to consider to what extent the delivery of the programme is achieving the graduate profile following on the validation of the graduate profile achieved in this chapter. Early work in this area (Sosa & Connor, 2015) investigates this by mapping both the graduate profile and the collected learning outcomes of core courses to Fink's Taxonomy of Significant Learning. Utilizing the learning outcomes provides a more fine grained analysis but the mapping into Fink's taxonomy provides an opportunity to directly compare the outcomes. Early comparisons suggest that there is a mismatch in what the learning outcomes produce in comparison to what the graduate profile promises.

CONCLUSION

This chapter has considered the future of creative technologies by considering what a creative technologist might be in the future. The approach used is based on performative writing and self-reflective narrative that has identified a range of potential knowledge, expertise and attributes for future creative technologists. This has enabled the examination of the graduate profile of a current creative technologies degree programme and validates the core embedded within the goals of the degree as being able to prepare future proof graduates. However, further work is required to ensure that the actual delivery of the programme meets the promises made in the graduate profile.

Whilst this chapter explores creative technologies as a field, it does so without adopting a single definition of what creative technologies actually is. The authors acknowledge the power of the undefined. In many regards, a tightly defined field would be less flexible and adaptive. In essence, creative technologies would become an interdisciplinary silo alongside the more traditional discipline based silos. Such sentiments are echoed by Avnet who argues that a "creative technologist shouldn't be a definition; it needs to be an attribute of what everyone does" (Avnet, 2012). The future of creative technologies needs to embrace both technology and creativity, to have individuals such as programmer whose function extends into a creative role and therefore expands what it means to be a developer, and a creative person who is more than usually technologically adept and uses that to expand what it means to be creative. Creative technologists of the future need more than a toolset; they need a mindset as well as a working knowledge of communication, culture and technology.

The role of creative technologies programmes should be to produce "T-shaped" thinkers that have both breadth and depth in terms of capabilities. However, each individual doesn't need to be the same shape of the letter T. The challenge for these programmes is to find structures and delivery mechanisms that promote self-actualization for creative technologies students to articulate their own future in a connected world.

REFERENCES

Adlin, T., Pruitt, J., Goodwin, K., Hynes, C., McGrane, K., Rosenstein, A., & Muller, M. J. (2006). *Putting personas to work*. Paper presented at the 2006 Conference on Human Factors in Computing Systems (CHI '06), Montreal, Canada.

Almi, N. E. A. M., Rahman, N. A., Purusothaman, D., & Sulaiman, S. (2011). *Software engineering education: The gap between industry's requirements and graduates' readiness.* Paper presented at the 2011 IEEE Symposium on Computers & Informatics, Kuala Lumpur, Malaysia. doi:10.1109/ISCI.2011.5958974

Atkinson, P., & Delamont, S. (2006). Rescuing narrative from qualitative research. *Narrative Inquiry*, *16*(1), 164–172. doi:10.1075/ni.16.1.21atk

Austin, A. E., & McDaniels, M. (2006). Preparing the professoriate of the future: Graduate student socialization for faculty roles. In J. C. Smart (Ed.), Higher Education: Handbook of Theory and Research (pp. 397–456). Dortrecht: Springer.

Avnet, M. (2010). *What the heck is a creative technologist?* Retrieved May 13, 2015, from https://markavnet.wordpress.com/2010/06/22/what-the-heck-is-a-creative-technologist/

Avnet, M. (2012, October 22). *Is this the end of the creative technologist?* Retrieved from https://markavnet.wordpress.com/2012/10/22/is-this-the-end-of-the-creative-technologist/

Ball, L. (2002). Preparing graduates in art and design to meet the challenges of working in the creative industries: A new model for work. *Art, Design & Communication in Higher Education*, *1*(1), 10–24. doi:10.1386/adch.1.1.10

Blinne, K. C. (2014). Awakening to lifelong learning: Contemplative pedagogy as compassionate engagement. *Radical Pedagogy*, *11*(2), 1524–6345.

Candy, P. C., & Crebert, R. G. (1991). Ivory tower to concrete jungle: The difficult transition from the academy to the workplace as learning environments. *The Journal of Higher Education*, *62*(5), 570–592. doi:10.2307/1982209

Clapton, G. (2013). Minding the gap: Assisting the transition from the academy to the profession. *Social Work Education*, *32*(3), 411–415. doi:10.1080/02615479.2012.657173

Connor, A. M. (2016). A historical review of creative technologies. In A. M. Connor & S. Marks (Eds.), *Creative Technologies for Multidisciplinary Applications*. Hershey, PA: IGI Global.

Connor, A. M., Berthelsen, C., Karmokar, S., Kenobi, B., Marks, S., & Walker, C. (2014). *An unexpected journey: experiences of learning through exploration and experimentation.* Paper presented at the 2014 DesignEd Asia Conference, Hong Kong.

Cullen, T., Tanner, S. J., O'Donnell, M., & Green, K. (2014). *Industry needs and tertiary journalism education: Views from news editors.* Paper presented at the 23rd Annual Teaching Learning Forum, Perth, Australia.

Denzin, N. K. (2001). The reflexive interview and a performative social science. *Qualitative Research*, *1*(1), 23–46. doi:10.1177/146879410100100102

Edwards, D. (2011). Paramedic preceptor: Work readiness in graduate paramedics. *The Clinical Teacher*, *8*(2), 79–82. doi:10.1111/j.1743-498X.2011.00435.x PMID:21585664

Gow, K., & McDonald, P. (2000). Attributes required of graduates for the future workplace. *Journal of Vocational Education and Training, 52*(3), 373–396.

Gubrium, J. F., & Holstein, J. A. (1998). Narrative practice and the coherence of personal stories. *The Sociological Quarterly, 39*(1), 163–187. doi:10.1111/j.1533-8525.1998.tb02354.x

Hamilton, M. L., Smith, L., & Worthington, K. (2008). Fitting the methodology with the research: An exploration of narrative, self-study and auto-ethnography. *Studying Teacher Education, 4*(1), 17–28. doi:10.1080/17425960801976321

Harvey, L. (2000). New realities: The relationship between higher education and employment. *Tertiary Education & Management, 6*(1), 3–17. doi:10.1080/13583883.2000.9967007

Hunt, R. J., & Bushong, M. (2010). ADEA CCI vision focuses on preparing graduates for discoveries of the future. *Journal of Dental Education, 74*(8), 819–823. PMID:20679450

Jackson, D. (2010). An international profile of industry-relevant competencies and skill gaps in modern graduates. *International Journal of Management Education, 8*(3), 29–58.

Jollands, M., Jolly, L., & Molyneaux, T. (2012). Project-based learning as a contributing factor to graduates' work readiness. *European Journal of Engineering Education, 37*(2), 143–154. doi:10.1080/0304 3797.2012.665848

Landis, W. E. (2006). Personas and archetypes: Envisioning the 21st century special collections professional. *RBM: A Journal of Rare Books. Manuscripts and Cultural Heritage, 7*(1), 40–48.

Martin, R., Maytham, B., Case, J., & Fraser, D. (2005). Engineering graduates' perceptions of how well they were prepared for work in industry. *European Journal of Engineering Education, 30*(2), 167–180. doi:10.1080/03043790500087571

Pegg, A., Waldock, J., Hendy-Isaac, S., & Lawton, R. (2012). *Pedagogy for employability*. York, UK: Higher Education Authority.

Pelias, R. J. (2005). Performative writing as scholarship: An apology, an argument, an anecdote. *Cultural Studies↔ Critical Methodologies, 5*(4), 415–424.

Pollock, D. (1998). Performing writing. In P. Phelan & J. Lane (Eds.), *The Ends of Performance* (pp. 73–103). New York: New York University Press.

Raybould, J., & Sheedy, V. (2005). Are graduates equipped with the right skills in the employability stakes? *Industrial and Commercial Training, 37*(5), 259–263. doi:10.1108/00197850510609694

Sosa, R., & Connor, A. M. (2015). *Orthodoxies in multidisciplinary design-oriented degree programmes*. Paper presented at the 2015 IASDR Conference: Interplay 2015, Brisbane, Australia.

Spronken-Smith, R., Bond, C., McLean, A., Frielick, S., Smith, N., Jenkins, M., & Marshall, S. (2013). *Toolkit to assist lecturers to engage with graduate outcomes*. Wellington: Ako Aotearoa.

Tu, N., Dong, X., Rau, P., & Zhang, T. (2010). *Using cluster analysis in persona development*. Paper presented at the 8th International Conference on Supply Chain Management and Information Systems, Hong Kong.

Wolff, A. C., Pesut, B., & Regan, S. (2010). New graduate nurse practice readiness: Perspectives on the context shaping our understanding and expectations. *Nurse Education Today*, *30*(2), 187–191. doi:10.1016/j.nedt.2009.07.011 PMID:19699561

Zagalo, N., & Branco, P. (2015). The creative revolution that is changing the world. In N. Zagalo & P. Branco (Eds.), *Creativity in the Digital Age* (pp. 3–15). Springer. doi:10.1007/978-1-4471-6681-8_1

Compilation of References

2013 *Sci-Tech Awards: Dr. Peter Hillman*. (2014). Retrieved from www.youtube.com/watch?v=7RZrLZCrh_c

2k Boston and 2k Australia. (2007). *Bioshock*. 2K Games.

Aarseth, E. (1997). *Cybertext: perspectives on ergodic literature*. Baltimore, MD: Johns Hopkins University Press.

Aarseth, E. J. (1997). *Cybertext: Perspectives on Ergodic Literature*. Baltimore, MD: Johns Hopkins University Press.

Ackernan, J., & Bargh, J. (2010). Two to tango: Automatic social coordination and the role of felt effort. In B. Bruya (Ed.), *Effortless Attention: A New Perspective in the Cognitiva Science of Attention and Action* (pp. 335–271). Cambridge, MA: MIT Press. doi:10.7551/mitpress/9780262013840.003.0015

Acosta-Marquez, C., & Bradley, D. A. (2005, June 28 - July 1). *The analysis, design and implementation of a model of an exoskeleton to support mobility*. Paper presented at the 9th International Conference on Rehabilitation Robotics, Chicago, IL. doi:10.1109/ICORR.2005.1501061

Adlam, T., Faulker, R., Orpwood, R., Jones, K., Macijauskiene, J., & Budraitiene, A. (2004). The installation and support of internationally distributed equipment for people with dementia. *IEEE Transactions on Information Technology in Biomedicine*, 8(3), 253–257. doi:10.1109/TITB.2004.834393 PMID:15484430

Adlin, T., Pruitt, J., Goodwin, K., Hynes, C., McGrane, K., Rosenstein, A., & Muller, M. J. (2006). *Putting personas to work*. Paper presented at the 2006 Conference on Human Factors in Computing Systems (CHI '06), Montreal, Canada.

Alberstat, P. (2004). *The Insider's Guide to Film Finance* (1st ed.). Oxford, UK: Focal Press.

Albino, V., Berardi, U., & Dangelico, R. M. (2015). Smart cities: Definitions, dimensions, performance, and initiatives. *Journal of Urban Technology*, 22(1), 3–21. doi:10.1080/10630732.2014.942092

Alderman, D. (2010, July 18). *Interview Bill Spitzak*. Retrieved from http://www.nukepedia.com/interviews/interview-bill-spitzak/

Aldrich, F. K. (2003). *Smart homes: past, present and future. Inside the smart home*. Springer. doi:10.1007/1-85233-854-7_2

Aleksy, M., Korthaus, A., & Schader, M. (2005). *Implementing Distributed Systems with Java and CORBA*. Berlin: Springer.

Alexander, O., Fyffe, G., Busch, J., Yu, X., Ichikari, R., Jones, A., Debevec, P., Jimenez, J., Danvoye, E., & Antionazzi, B., et al. (2013) Digital Ira: Creating a real-time photoreal digital actor. *ACM SIGGRAPH 2013 Posters 1*.

Alexander, O., Rogers, M., Lambeth, W., Chiang, M., & Debevec, P. (2009). *Creating a Media Production* (pp. 176–187). CVMP.

Almi, N. E. A. M., Rahman, N. A., Purusothaman, D., & Sulaiman, S. (2011). *Software engineering education: The gap between industry's requirements and graduates' readiness.* Paper presented at the 2011 IEEE Symposium on Computers & Informatics, Kuala Lumpur, Malaysia. doi:10.1109/ISCI.2011.5958974

Alonso, I. G., Fres, O. A., Fernández, A. A., Gómez del Torno, P., Maestre, J. M., De, P. A. M., & Fuente, G. (2012). Towards a new open communication standard between homes and service robots, the DHCompliant case. *Robotics and Autonomous Systems, 60*(6), 889–900. doi:10.1016/j.robot.2012.01.006

Al-Sumaiti, A. S., Ahmed, M. H., & Salama, M. M. A. (2014). Smart Home Activities: A Literature Review. *Electric Power Components and Systems, 42*(3-4), 294–305. doi:10.1080/15325008.2013.832439

Altmann, G., & Koch, W. A. (1998). *Systems: New Paradigms for the Human Sciences.* Berlin: W. de Gruyter. doi:10.1515/9783110801194

Alwan, M., Kell, S., Turner, B., Dalal, S., Mack, D., & Felder, R. (2006). Psychosocial impact of passive health status monitoring on informal caregivers and older adults living in independent senior housing. In Information and Communication Technologies, CTTA'06. doi:10.1109/ICTTA.2006.1684477

Anderson, C. (2008). *The end of theory, will the data deluge make the scientific method obsolete?* Retrieved July 20, 2014, from http://edge.org/3rd_culture/anderson08/anderson08_index.html

Anderson, E. F., McLoughlin, L., Liarokapis, F., Peters, C., Petridis, P., & Freitas, S. (2009). *Serious games in cultural heritage.* Paper presented at the 10th International Symposium on Virtual Reality, Archaeology and Cultural Heritag,e St. Julians, Malta.

Anderson, C. (2012). *Makers: The next industrial revolution.* New York, NY: Crown Business.

Anderson, D., Luke, R. H., Keller, J. M., Skubic, M., Rantz, M., & Aud, M. (2009). Linguistic summarization of video for fall detection using voxel person and fuzzy logic. *Computer Vision and Image Understanding, 113*(1), 80–89. doi:10.1016/j.cviu.2008.07.006 PMID:20046216

Ape and HAL Laboratory. (1995). *Earthbound/Mother 2.* Nintendo.

Apley, J. (1970). Clinical canutes. A philosophy of paediatrics. *Proceedings of the Royal Society of Medicine, 63*(5), 479. PMID:5453431

Appel, A. (1968). Some Techniques for Shading Machine Renderings of Solids. In *Proceedings of theSpring Joint Computer Conference* (pp. 37–45). New York, NY: ACM. doi:10.1145/1468075.1468082

Arbib, M. (2013). Five terms in search of synthesis. In M. Arbib (Ed.), *Language, Music, and the Brain: A Mysterious Relationship* (pp. 3–44). Cambridge, MA: MIT Press.

Ardizi, M., Martini, F., Alessandra Umilta, M., Sestito, M., Ravera, R., & Gallese, V. (2013). When early experiences build a wall to others' emotions: An electrophysiological and autonomic study. *PLoS ONE, 8*(4). PMID:23593374

Arellano, D., Spielmann, S., & Helzle, V. (2013). The Muses of Poetry - In search of the poetic experience. In: *Symposium on Artificial Intelligence and Poetry,* pp. 6–10

Arieti, S. (1980). New psychological approaches to creativity. In D. W. Fritz (Ed.), *Perspectives on creativity and the unconscious* (pp. 83–103). Oxford, OH: Miami University.

Aristotle. ([c335 BCE] 1952). 'Nicomachean Ethics' in Aristotle II (Founders' edn. Vol. 9). Chicago: W. Benton; Encyclopaedia Britannica Inc., University of Chicago.

Asada, H. H., Shaltis, P., Reisner, A., Rhee, S., & Hutchinson, R. C. (2003). Mobile monitoring with wearable photoplethysmographic biosensors. *IEEE Engineering in Medicine and Biology Magazine, 22*(3), 28–40. doi:10.1109/MEMB.2003.1213624 PMID:12845817

Aslan, M., Sengur, A., Xiao, Y., Wang, H., Ince, M. C., & Ma, X. (2015). Shape Feature Encoding via Fisher Vector for Efficient Fall Detection in Depth-Videos. *Applied Soft Computing, 37*, 1023–1028. doi:10.1016/j.asoc.2014.12.035

Astrid, M., Krämer, N. C., & Gratch, J. (2010). *How our personality shapes our interactions with virtual characters-implications for research and development.* Paper presented at the 10th International Conference on Intelligent Virtual Agents, Philadelphia, PA.

Atkinson, P. (2004). *Post-Industrial Manufacturing Systems: The impact of emerging technologies on design, craft and engineering processes.* Paper presented at Challenging Craft, Aberdeen, UK.

Atkinson, P. (2014). Orchestral manoeuvres in design. In B. van Abel, L. Evers, R. Klaassen, & P. Troxler (Eds.), *Open design now* (pp. 24–34). Amsterdam, Netherlands: BIS.

Atkinson, P., & Delamont, S. (2006). Rescuing narrative from qualitative research. *Narrative Inquiry, 16*(1), 164–172. doi:10.1075/ni.16.1.21atk

Austin, A. E., & McDaniels, M. (2006). Preparing the professoriate of the future: Graduate student socialization for faculty roles. In J. C. Smart (Ed.), Higher Education: Handbook of Theory and Research (pp. 397–456). Dortrecht: Springer.

Austin, J. (2010). The thalamic gateway: How the mediative training of attention evolves toward selfless transformations of consciousness. In B. Bruya (Ed.), *Effortless Attention: A New Perspective in the Cognitive Science of Attention and Action* (pp. 373–407). Cambridge, MA: MIT Press. doi:10.7551/mitpress/9780262013840.003.0016

Avnet, M. (2010). *What the heck is a creative technologist?* Retrieved from https://markavnet.wordpress.com/2010/06/22/what-the-heck-is-a-creative-technologist/

Avnet, M. (2010). *What the heck is a creative technologist?* Retrieved May 13, 2015, from https://markavnet.wordpress.com/2010/06/22/what-the-heck-is-a-creative-technologist/

Avnet, M. (2012, October 22). *Is this the end of the creative technologist?* Retrieved from https://markavnet.wordpress.com/2012/10/22/is-this-the-end-of-the-creative-technologist/

Aware Home Research Initiative. (n.d.). *About AHRI.* Georgia Tech. Available on: http://www.awarehome.gatech.edu/drupal/?q=content/about-ahri

Backe, H. J. (2012). Narrative rules? Story logic and the structures of games. *Joachim Literary and Linguistic Computing, 27*(3), 243–260. doi:10.1093/llc/fqs035

Baikadi, A., & Cardona-Rivera, R. E. (2012). Towards finding the fundamental unit of narrative: A Proposal for the Narreme.*Proceedings of the 2012 Workshop on Computational Models of Narrative (CMN2012).*

Baker, S. (2012). *Final Jeopardy: The Story of Watson, the Computer That Will Transform Our World.* New York: Mariner Books.

Bakkes, S., Tan, C. T., & Pisan, Y. (2012). Personalised gaming. *Journal of Creative Technologies,* (3).

Baldwin, J. R., Faulkner, S. L., Hecht, M. L., & Lindsley, S. L. (Eds.). (2006). *Redefining Culture: Perspectives Across the Disciplines.* Mahwah, NJ: Lawrence Erlbaum Associates.

Ball, R. (2008). *Oldest Animation Discovered in Iran. Animation Magazine.* Retrieved September 26, 2014, from http://www.animationmagazine.net/features/oldest-animation-discovered-in-iran/

Ball, L. (2002). Preparing graduates in art and design to meet the challenges of working in the creative industries: A new model for work. *Art, Design & Communication in Higher Education, 1*(1), 10–24. doi:10.1386/adch.1.1.10

Baltrusaitis, T., Robinson, P., & Morency, L. (2012). *3D constrained local model for rigid and non-rigid facial tracking.* Paper presented at the IEEE Conference on Computer Vision and Pattern Recognition, Providence, RI. doi:10.1109/CVPR.2012.6247980

Baraff, D. (2001). Physically based modeling: Rigid body simulation. *SIGGRAPH.* Retrieved from http://graphics.cs.cmu.edu/courses/15-869-F08/lec/14/notesg.pdf

Baranson, J. (1963). Economic and social considerations in adapting technologies for developing countries. *Technology and Culture, 4*(1), 22–29. doi:10.2307/3101333

Barceló, J. (2000). Visualizing what might be: an introduction to virtual reality techniques in archaeology. In Virtual Reality in Archaeology: Computer Applications and Quantitative Methods in Archaeology 1998 (pp. 9–35). ArcheoPress.

Barkow, J. H. (2006). *Missing the Revolution: Darwinism for Social Scientists.* Oxford, UK: Oxford University Press. doi:10.1093/acprof:oso/9780195130027.001.0001

Barnes, N. M., Edwards, N. H., Rose, D. A. D., & Garner, P. (1998). Lifestyle monitoring technology for supported independence. *Computing & Control Engineering Journal, 9*(4), 169–174. doi:10.1049/cce:19980404

Barthes, R., & Duisit, L. (1966). 1975). An Introduction to the Structural Analysis of Narrative. *New Literary History, 6*(2), 237–272. doi:10.2307/468419

Bartusch, C., Wallin, F., Odlare, M., Vassileva, I., & Wester, L. (2011). Introducing a demand-based electricity distribution tariff in the residential sector: Demand response and customer perception. *EnergPolicy, 39,* 5008–5025.

Bateman, C. (2006). Game Writing: Narrative Skills for. Charles River Media.

Baudrillard, J. (2001). *Impossible Exchange* (C. Turner, Trans.). London: Verso.

Bavelas, J., Gerwing, J., Allison, M., & Sutton, C. (2011). Dyadic evidence for grounding with abstract deictic gestures. In G. Starn & M. Ishino (Eds.), *Integrating Gestures: The Interdisciplinary Nature of Gesture* (pp. 49–60). Philadelphia, PA: John Benjamins Publishing Co.

Bayart, C., Bertezene, S., Vallat, D., & Martin, J. (2014). Serious games: Leverage for knowledge management. *The TQM Journal, 26*(3), 235–252. doi:10.1108/TQM-12-2013-0143

Bechdel, A. (2007). *Fun home: A family tragicomic.* Boston, MA: Houghton Mifflin Harcourt.

Beeman, M. J., & Bowden, E. M. (2000). The right hemisphere maintains solution-related activation for yet-to-be-solved problems. *Memory & Cognition, 28*(7), 1231–1241. doi:10.3758/BF03211823 PMID:11126944

Begley, S. (2015). The 30 most influential people on the internet. *Time Magazine.* Retrieved 8 May 2015 from http://time.com/3732203/the-30-most-influential-people-on-the-internet/

Benedict, E. (2014, January 8). *19 Scientific And Technical Achievements To Be Honored With Academy Awards®.* Retrieved May 12, 2015, from http://www.oscars.org/news/19-scientific-and-technical-achievements-be-honored-academy-awardsr

Benfey, O. T. (1958). August Kekulé and the birth of the structural theory of organic chemistry in 1858. *Journal of Chemical Education, 35*(1), 21–23. doi:10.1021/ed035p21

Benkler, Y. (2002). Freedom in the Commons: Towards a Political Economy of Information. *Duke Law Journal, 52,* 1245–1276.

Benyus, J. (2002). *Biomimicry: Innovation inspired by nature*. New York, NY: Harper Perennial.

Berardi, U. (2013). Clarifying the new interpretations of the concept of sustainable building. *Sustainable Cities and Society, 8*, 72–78. doi:10.1016/j.scs.2013.01.008

Berman, D. L., & Mase, H. (1983). The key to the productivity dilemma:"The performance manager. *Human Resource Management, 22*(3), 275–286. doi:10.1002/hrm.3930220308

Bickmore, T. W., Pfeifer, L. M., & Jack, B. W. (2009). Taking the time to care: empowering low health literacy hospital patients with virtual nurse agents. In *Proceedings of the SIGCHI Conference on Human Factors in Computing Systems* (pp. 1265-1274). ACM. doi:10.1145/1518701.1518891

Bills, J.-M. (2013, April 10). *I Have Seen The Future, And It Is... Slow*. Retrieved from http://www.vfxpdx.com/?p=815

Bisetti, S. (1979). *1941: the illustrated story*. New York, NY: Pocket Books.

Biswas, D., Cranny, A., Gupta, N., Maharatna, K., Achner, J., Klemke, J., & Ortmann, S. (2015). Recognizing upper limb movements with wrist worn inertial sensors using k-means clustering classification. *Human Movement Science, 40*, 59–76. doi:10.1016/j.humov.2014.11.013 PMID:25528632

Bjorklund, D., & Pellegrini, A. (2001). *The Origins of Human Nature: Evolutionary Developmental Psychology*. Washington, DC: American Psychological Association.

Blackmore, S. J. (2007). Memes, Minds and Imagination. In *'Imaginative Minds': Proceedings of the British Academy*. Retrieved from http://www.susanblackmore.co.uk/Chapters/ImaginativeMinds2007.htm

Blaikie, N. W. H. (2007). *Approaches to Social Enquiry* (2nd ed.). Cambridge, MA: Polity Press.

Blinne, K. C. (2014). Awakening to lifelong learning: Contemplative pedagogy as compassionate engagement. *Radical Pedagogy, 11*(2), 1524–6345.

Blomkamp, M., & Tatchell, T. (2015) *"Chappie"* [Film]. Columbia Pictures, Media Rights Capital, USA.

Bloore, P. (2013). *The Screenplay Business: Managing Creativity in the Film Industry*. London: Routledge.

Boden, M. A. (1991). *The creative mind: Myths and mechanisms*. New York, NY: Basic Books.

Boden, M. A. (2004). *The Creative Mind: Myths and Mechanisms* (2nd ed.). London: Routledge.

Boellstorff, T. (2006). A Ludicrous Discipline? Ethnography and Game Studies. *Games and Culture, 1*(1), 29–35. doi:10.1177/1555412005281620

Boers, N., Chodos, D., & Gbyrzynski, P. et al.. (2010). The smart condo project: services for independent living. In M. Ziefle & C. Röcker (Eds.), *E-Health, assistive technologies and applications for assisted living: challenges and solutions*. IGI Global.

Bogen, J. E., & Bogen, G. M. (1999). Split-brains: Interhemispheric exchange in creativity. In M. A. Runco & S. R. Pritzker (Eds.), *Encyclopedia of creativity* (Vol. 2, pp. 571–575). San Diego, CA: Academic Press.

Bogost, I. (2009). Videogames are a mess. *Keynote speech at DiGRA*. Retrieved August 20, 2015, from http://www.bogost.com/writing/videogames_are_a_mess.shtml

Bohm, D. (2005). *Wholeness and the Implicate Order*. London: Taylor and Francis. (Original work published 1980)

Bolter, J. D., & Grusin, R. (2000). *Remediation: Understanding New Media*. Cambridge, MA: MIT Press.

Bonafoux, P. (1985). *Portraits of the artist: the self-portrait in painting*. Rizzoli Intl Publishers.

Bonino, D., Corno, F. (2011). What would you ask to your home if it were intelligent? Exploring user expectations about next-generation homes. *Journal of Ambient Intelligence and Smart Environments, 3*.

Bordwell, D. (2011). *Common Sense + Film Theory = Common-Sense Film Theory?*. Retrieved from http://www.davidbordwell.net/essays/commonsense.php#_edn23

Bordwell, D. (2012). *The Viewer's Share: Models of Mind in Explaining Film.* Retrieved from http://www.davidbordwell.net/essays/viewersshare.php

Bordwell, D. (1997). *On the History of Film Style*. Cambridge, MA: Harvard University Press.

Bordwell, D. (2008). *Poetics of Cinema*. New York: Routledge.

Borja, R., De la Pinta, J. R., Álvarez, A., & Maestre, J. M. (2013). Integration of service robots in the smart home by means of UPnP: A surveillance robot case study. *Robotics and Autonomous Systems, 61*(2), 153–160. doi:10.1016/j.robot.2012.10.005

Bornmann, L., & Mutz, R. (2014). Growth rates of modern science: A bibliometric analysis based on the number of publications and cited references. *Journal of the Association for Information Science and Technology.* arXiv:1402.4578v3

Bornmann, L., & Marx, W. (2012). The Anna Karenina Principle: A Way of Thinking About Success in Science. *Journal of the American Society for Information Science and Technology, 63*(10), 2037–2051. doi:10.1002/asi.22661

Borshukov, G., Piponi, D., Larsen, O., Lewis, J., & Tempelaar-Lietz, C. (2005). Universal capture-image-based facial animation for The Matrix Reloaded, 16.

Bourdieu, P., & Johnson, R. E. (1993). *The Field of Cultural Production: Essays on Art and Literature*. New York: Columbia University Press.

Bowden, E. M., & Jung-Beeman, M. (2003). Aha! — Insight experience correlates with solution activation in the right hemisphere. *Psychonomic Bulletin & Review, 10*(3), 730–737. doi:10.3758/BF03196539 PMID:14620371

Bowden, E. M., & Jung-Beeman, M. (2007). Methods for investigating the neural components of insight. *Methods (San Diego, Calif.), 42*(1), 87–99. doi:10.1016/j.ymeth.2006.11.007 PMID:17434419

Bowker. (2013). *Self-Publishing In the United States, 2008-2013*. New Providence, NJ: Bowker (A ProQuest Affiliate).

Bowman, D. A., & Kruijff, E. Jr. (2004). *User Interfaces: Theory and Practice*. Boston, MA: Addison-Wesley Professional.

Boyd, B. (2009). *On The Origin Of Stories: Evolution, Cognition, and Fiction*. Cambridge, MA: Belknap Press of Harvard University Press.

Boyd, B. (2010). Art and Evolution: The Avant-Garde as Test Case – Spiegelman in The Narrative Corpse. In B. Boyd, J. Carroll, & J. Gottschall (Eds.), *Evolution, Literature and Film: A Reader*. New York: Columbia University Press.

Boyd, B., Carroll, J., & Gottschall, J. (2010). *Evolution, Literature and Film: A Reader*. New York: Columbia University Press.

Boyd, D., & Crawford, K. (2012). Critical Questions for Big Data. *Information Communication and Society, 15*(5), 662–679. doi:10.1080/1369118X.2012.678878

Braddock Clarke, S., & Harris, J. (2012). *Digital visions for fashion and textiles: Made in code*. London, UK: Thames & Hudson.

Braddock Clarke, S., & O'Mahony, M. (2008). *Techno textiles 2: Revolutionary fabrics for fashion and design* (2nd ed.). London, UK: Thames & Hudson.

Bradie, M., & Harms, W. (2012). Evolutionary Epistemology. *The Stanford Encyclopedia of Philosophy*. Retrieved from http://plato.stanford.edu/archives/win2012/entries/epistemology-evolutionary

Bradley, D., Heidrich, W., Popa, T., & Sheffer, A. (2010). High resolution passive facial performance capture.[TOG]. *ACM Transactions on Graphics*, *29*(4), 41. doi:10.1145/1778765.1778778

Braitmaier, M., & Kyriazis, D. (2011). *Virtual and Augmented Reality: Improved User Experience through a Service Oriented Infrastructure*. Paper presented at the Games and Virtual Worlds for Serious Applications (VS-GAMES), 2011 Third International Conference on.

Branigan, E. (1992). *Narrative Comprehension and Film*. London: Routledge.

Brauer, F., & Nohel, J. A. (1989). *The qualitative theory of ordinary differential equations: An introduction*. New York, NY: Dover.

Brave Heart Veterans. (n.d.). *BraveHeart: Welcome Back Veterans Southeast Initiative*. Retrieved August 28, 2014, from http://braveheartveterans.org/

Bredehoft, T. A. (2006). Comics architecture, multidimensionality, and time: Chris Ware's Jimmy Corrigan: the smartest kid on earth. *MFS Modern Fiction Studies*, *52*(4), 869–890. doi:10.1353/mfs.2007.0001

Bregman, D., & Korman, A. (2009). A universal implementation model for the smart home. *International Journal of Smart Home*, *3*(3), 15–30.

Bremer, H. W. (1998). *University technology transfer: evolution and revolution*. New York, NY: Council on Governmental Relations.

Breslow, L. (2006). Health measurement in the third era of health. *American Journal of Public Health*, *96*(1), 17–19. doi:10.2105/AJPH.2004.055970 PMID:16322463

Brittain, J. E. (1976). CP Steinmetz and EFW Alexanderson: Creative engineering in a corporate setting. *Proceedings of the IEEE*, *64*(9), 1413–1417. doi:10.1109/PROC.1976.10335

Broaders, S. C.-M., Cook, S. W., Mitchell, Z., & Goldin-Meadow, S. (2007). Making children gesture brings out implicit knowledge and leads to learning. *Journal of Experimental Psychology*, *136*(4), 539–550. doi:10.1037/0096-3445.136.4.539 PMID:17999569

Brockman, J. (2000). *The Greatest Inventions of the Past 2,000 Years*. New York: Simon & Schuster.

Brockman, J. (2010). *This Will Change Everything: Ideas That Will Shape the Future* (1st ed.). New York, NY: Harper Perennial.

Broin, D. O. (2011). *Using a Criteria-Based User Model for Facilitating Flow in Serious Games*. Paper presented at the Games and Virtual Worlds for Serious Applications (VS-GAMES), 2011 Third International Conference on.

Brown, J. S., & Adler, R. (2008). Minds on fire: Open education, the long tail and Learning 2.0. *EDUCAUSE Review*, (January/February), 17–32.

Brownsell, S., Blackburn, S., & Hawley, M. S. (2008). An evaluation of second and third generation telecare services in older people's housing. *Journal of Telemedicine and Telecare*, *14*(1), 8–12. doi:10.1258/jtt.2007.070410 PMID:18318922

Bruch, C. B. (1988). Metacreativity: Awareness of thoughts and feelings during creative experiences. *The Journal of Creative Behavior*, *22*(2), 112–122. doi:10.1002/j.2162-6057.1988.tb00672.x

Brumitt, B., Meyers, B., Krumm, J., Kern, A., & Shafer, S. (2000). EasyLiving: Technologies for intelligent environments. *Lecture Notes in Computer Science*, *1927*, 12–29. doi:10.1007/3-540-39959-3_2

Buchsbaum, S. J. (1986). Managing creativity–for fun and for profit. *International Journal of Technology Management*, *1*(1), 51–64.

Buckman, A., Mayfield, M., & Beck, , S. (2014). What is a smart building? *Smart and Sustainable Built Environment*, *3*(2), 92–109. doi:10.1108/SASBE-01-2014-0003

Budijono, S., Andrianto, J., & Noor, M. A. N. (2014). Design and implementation of modular home security system with short messaging system. In EPJ Web of Conferences EDP Sciences. doi:10.1051/epjconf/20146800025

Bulwer, J. (1649). *Pathomyotomia: Or a dissection of the significative muscles of the affections of the mind.* London: Humphrey Moseley.

Bunge, M. (1969). The Metaphysics, Epistemology and Methodology of Levels. In L. Whyte, A. Wilson, & D. Wilson (Eds.), *Hierarchical Structures.* New York: Elsevier.

Bunge, M. (1983). *Upshot.* Dordrecht: Springer. doi:10.1007/978-94-015-6921-7_6

Burke, B. (2014). *Gamify: How Gamification Motivates People to do Extraordinary Things.* Brookline, MA: Bibliomotion.

BusinessWire. (2015). *Research and Markets: Gamification Companies, Solutions, Market Outlook and Forecasts 2015 – 2020.* Retrieved March 3, 2015, from http://www.businesswire.com/news/home/20150224005574/en/Research-Markets-Gamification-Companies-Solutions-Market-Outlook#.VPduFIs5BwE

Buss, D. M. (2012). *Evolutionary Psychology: The New Science of the Mind* (4th ed.). Boston: Pearson Allyn & Bacon.

Buys, I., Barnett, K., Miller, E., & Bailey, C. (2005). Smart housing and social sustainability: Learning from the residents of Queensland's Research House. *Australian Journal of Emerging Technologies and Society*, *3*(1), 43–57.

Byrne, T. (2012). The evolving digital workplace. *KM World*, *21*(9), 12–14.

Cacchione, P. (2015). Interdisciplinary research teams. *Clinical Nursing Research*, *24*(2), 119–120. doi:10.1177/1054773815574790 PMID:25748854

Caillois, R. (1961). *Man, play, and games.* Champaign, IL: University of Illinois Press.

Caine, K. E., Rogers, W. A., & Fisk, A. D. (2005). Privacy perceptions of an aware home with visual sensing devices. In *Proceedings of the Human Factors and Ergonomics Society Annual Meeting SAGE Publications.* doi:10.1177/154193120504902108

Cameron, J., & Hurd, G. (1984) *"Terminator"* [Film]. Hemdale Film, Pacific Western, USA

Campbell, M. (2011). The audacious plan to make the world into a game. *New Scientist*, *209*(2794), 02–02.

Campbell, D. T. (1960). Blind Variation and Selective Retention in Creative Thought as in Other Knowledge Processes. *Psychological Review*, *67*(6), 380–400. doi:10.1037/h0040373 PMID:13690223

Campbell, D. T. (1974). Evolutionary Epistemology. In P. A. Schlipp (Ed.), *The Philosophy of Karl Popper* (Vol. 1, pp. 413–459). La Salle.

Campbell, J. (1949). *The Hero With A Thousand Faces.* New York: Pantheon Books.

Candy, L., & Edmonds, E. (2004). *Collaborative expertise for creative technology design.* Paper presented at the Design Thinking Research Symposium 6, Sydney, Australia. doi:10.1007/978-3-540-27795-8_7

Candy, L., & Edmonds, E. (2000). Creativity enhancement with emerging technologies. *Communications of the ACM*, *43*(8), 63–65. doi:10.1145/345124.345144

Candy, P. C., & Crebert, R. G. (1991). Ivory tower to concrete jungle: The difficult transition from the academy to the workplace as learning environments. *The Journal of Higher Education*, *62*(5), 570–592. doi:10.2307/1982209

Cantor, A., DeLauer, V., Martin, D., & Rogan, J. (2015). Training interdisciplinary "wicked problem" solvers: Applying lessons from HERO in community-based research experiences for undergraduates. *Journal of Geography in Higher Education*, 1–13. doi:10.1080/03098265.2015.1048508

Capra, F., & Luisi, P. L. (2014). *The Systems View of Life: A Unifying Vision*. Cambridge, UK: Cambridge University Press. doi:10.1017/CBO9780511895555

Carey, J. (1989). *Communication as Culture*. New York: Routledge.

Carroll, J. (1995). *Evolution and Literary Theory*. Columbia, MO: University of Missouri Press.

Carroll, J. (2008). Rejoinder to Responses - "An Evolutionary Paradigm for Literary Study," (target article to which scholars and scientists were invited to respond). *Style (DeKalb, IL)*, *42*(2 & 3), 103–135.

Carroll, J., McAdams, D. P., & Wilson, E. O. (Eds.). (in press). *Darwin's Bridge: Uniting the Sciences and Humanities*.

Carter, D. (1978). Industrial design - Is it engineering, art, or just a dirty word? *Journal of the Royal Society of Arts*, *126*(5265), 532–540.

Castells, M. (2002). The Internet galaxy: Reflections on the Internet, business and society. New York: Oxford. doi:10.1093/acprof:oso/9780199255771.001.0001

Castells, M. (2009). *The Global Network Society Communication Power* (pp. 24–37). New York: Oxford University Press.

Castronova, E., & Falk, M. (2009). Virtual Worlds: Petri Dishes, Rat Mazes, and Supercolliders. *Games and Culture*, *4*(4), 396–407. doi:10.1177/1555412009343574

Catmull, E. (1978). The problems of computer-assisted animation. *Computer Graphics*, *12*(3), 348–353. doi:10.1145/965139.807414

Cazden, C., Cope, B., Fairclough, N., Gee, J., Kalantzis, M., Kress, G., & Nakata, M et al.. (1996). A pedagogy of multiliteracies: Designing social futures. *Harvard Educational Review*, *66*(1), 60–92. doi:10.17763/haer.66.1.17370n67v22j160u

Cempel, W. A., & Mikulik, J. (2013).Intelligent building reengineering: Adjusting life and work environment to occupant's optimal routine processes. *Intelligent Buildings International*, *5*(1), 51–64.

Centre for Research on the Epidemiology of Disasters. (2015). Retrieved August 18, 2015, from http://www.cred.be/publications

Chaisson, E. (2001). *Cosmic Evolution: The Rise of Complexity in Nature*. Cambridge, MA: Harvard University Press.

Chang, F. (2002). Symbolically speaking: A connectionist model of sentence production, *Cognitive Science*. Cognitive Science Society. *Inc.*, *26*, 609–651.

Chan, L. K. Y., Kenderdine, S., & Shaw, J. (2013). Spatial user interface for experiencing Mogao caves. In *Proceedings of the 1st Symposium on Spatial User Interaction - SUI '13* (pp. 21–24). Los Angeles, CA: ACM. doi:10.1145/2491367.2491372

Chan, M., Campo, E., & Est`eve, D. (2005). Assessment of activity of elderly people using a home monitoring system. *International Journal of Rehabilitation Research. Internationale Zeitschrift für Rehabilitationsforschung. Revue Internationale de Recherches de Readaptation*, *28*(1), 69–76.

Chan, M., Campo, E., Estève, D., & Fourniols, J. Y. (2009). Smart Homes – Current Features and Future Perspectives. *Maturitas, 64*(2), 90–97. doi:10.1016/j.maturitas.2009.07.014 PMID:19729255

Chan, M., Esteve, D., Escriba, C., & Campo, E. (2008). A Review of Smart Homes – Present State and Future Challenges. *Computer Methods and Programs in Biomedicine, 91*(1), 55–81. doi:10.1016/j.cmpb.2008.02.001 PMID:18367286

Chan, M., Estève, D., Fourniols, J. Y., Escriba, C., & Campo, E. (2012). Smart wearable systems: Current status and future challenges. *Artificial Intelligence in Medicine, 56*(3), 137–156. doi:10.1016/j.artmed.2012.09.003 PMID:23122689

Chao, C., & Yim-Teo, T. (2004). *Corporate entrepreneurial behavior of latecomer technology firms.* Paper presented at the IEEE International Engineering Management Conference, Singapore. doi:10.1109/IEMC.2004.1407467

Chapin, A. (2011). The Future is a Videogame. *Canadian Business, 84*(4), 46–48.

Chen, J., Kam, A. H., Zhang, J., Liu, N., & Shue, L. (2005). Bathroom activity monitoring based on sound. In *Proceedings of the Pervasive* (LNCS), (vol. 3468, pp. 47 – 61). Berlin: Springer.

Chen, S.-Y. R. (2011). *Adolescents' linguistic practices in college-affiliated Bulletin Board Systems (BBSs) in Taiwan.* (Unpublished PhD dissertation). University of Lancaster.

Cheney, D. (1984). Category formation in vervet monkeys. In R. Harré & V. Reynolds (Eds.), *The Meaning of Primate Signals* (pp. 58–72). New York, NY: Cambridge University Press.

Cheredar, T. (2014). *Atlas raises $1.1M to power its Motion Genome Project, a motion database for wearables.* Retrieved May 5, 2015, from http://venturebeat.com/2014/10/08/atlas-raises-1-1m-to-power-its-motion-genome-project-a-motion-database-for-wearables/

Chick, G. (1999). *What's in a Meme? The Development of the Meme as a Unit of Culture.* Retrieved from http://www.personal.psu.edu/gec7/Memes.pdf

Chico, C. (2014, July-August). Machinima unplugged. *Computer Graphics World*, 24-28.

Chiu, C.-C., & Marsella, S. (2011). *A style controller for generating virtual human behaviors.* Paper presented at the 10th International Conference on Autonomous Agents and Multiagent Systems, Taipei, Taiwan.

Chomsky, N. (1957). *Syntactic Structures.* Berlin, Germany: Walter Gruyter GMBH.

Choon, S.-W., Siwar, C., Pereira, J. J., Jemain, A. A., Hashim, H. S., & Hadi, A. S. (2011). A sustainable city index for Malaysia. *International Journal of Sustainable Development and World Ecology, 18*(1), 28–35. doi:10.1080/13504509.2011.543012

Chops, (2014). *Cartoon Characters Come Alive For Children with Autism.* Retrieved August 22, 2014, from http://www.chops.com/blog/cartoon-characters-come-alive-for-children-with-autism/

Christensen, P. H., Fong, J., Laur, D. M., & Batali, D. (2006). Ray tracing for the movieCars. In *Interactive Ray Tracing 2006, IEEE Symposium on* (pp. 1–6). IEEE. Retrieved from http://ieeexplore.ieee.org/xpls/abs_all.jsp?arnumber=4061539

Christopher, M. (2011). *Logistics & supply chain management* (4th ed.). Harlow, UK: Prentice Hall.

Chung, P. J., Vanderbilt, D. L., Schrager, S. M., Nguyen, E., & Fowler, E. (2015). Active Videogaming for Individuals with Severe Movement Disorders: Results from a Community Study. *Games for Health Journal, 4*(3), 190–194. doi:10.1089/g4h.2014.0091 PMID:26182063

Cieply, M. (2009, November 9). A Movie's Budget Pops From the Screen. *The New York Times.* Retrieved from http://www.nytimes.com/2009/11/09/business/media/09avatar.html

Cirio, G., Marchal, M., Regia-Corte, T., & Lécuyer, A. (2009). The Magic Barrier Tape: A Novel Metaphor for Infinite Navigation in Virtual Worlds with a Restricted Walking Workspace. In *Proceedings of the 16th Symposium on Virtual Reality Software and Technology* (pp. 155–162). ACM. doi:10.1145/1643928.1643965

Clapton, G. (2013). Minding the gap: Assisting the transition from the academy to the profession. *Social Work Education*, *32*(3), 411–415. doi:10.1080/02615479.2012.657173

Clarke, D., & Duimering, P. R. (2006). How computer gamers experience the game situation: A behavioral study. *Computers in Entertainment*, *4*(3), 6. doi:10.1145/1146816.1146827

Clements-Croome, D. (2013). *Intelligent Buildings: Design, Management and Operation*. ICE Publishing. Retrieved from https://books.google.co.nz/books?id=jwRUuAAACAAJ

Clements-Croome, D. J. (2011). Sustainable intelligent buildings for people: A review. *Intelligent Buildings International*, *3*(2), 67–86.

Clemons, S. (1998). Computer Animation. A Creative Technology Tool. *Technology Teacher*, *58*(3), 8–12.

Cobb, S., Brooks, A. L., & Sharkey, P. M. (2013). Virtual Reality Technologies and the Creative Arts in the Areas of Disability, Therapy, Health, and Rehabilitation. In S. Kumar & E. R. Cohn (Eds.), *Telerehabilitation* (pp. 239–261). London: Springer. doi:10.1007/978-1-4471-4198-3_16

Cobley, P., & Schulz, P. (Eds.). (2013). *Theories and Models of Communication*. Boston: Walter de Gruyter. doi:10.1515/9783110240450

Cohen, D. (2006). Perception and responses to schemata in different cultures: Western and Arab music. In Music and Altered States: Consciousness, Transcendence, Therapy, and Addictions (pp. 60–73). London: Jessica Kingsley Publishers.

Cohen, J., Gehry, F., & Gehry, F. O. (2003). *Frank Gehry, architect*. New York, NY: Guggenheim Museum.

Coleman, S., & Dyer-Witheford, N. (2007). Playing on the digital commons: Collectivities, capital and contestation in videogame culture. *Media Culture & Society*, *29*(6), 934–953. doi:10.1177/0163443707081700

Colla, R., & Larson, G. (1978) "Battlestar Galactica" [Film]. Glen A. Larson Productions, Universal Television, USA.

Collins, A., Adams, M. J., & Pew, R. W. (1978). Effectiveness of an interactive map display in tutoring geography. *Journal of Educational Psychology*, *70*(1), 1–7. doi:10.1037/0022-0663.70.1.1

Collins, H. (2010). *Creative research: The theory and practice of research for the creative industries*. London, UK: AVA Publishing.

Connelly, B. (2013, April 5). *Weta Digital's Joe Letteri GIves Us A Cutting Edge Digital FX 101 - The Hobbit And Beyond*. Retrieved May 9, 2015, from http://www.bleedingcool.com/2013/04/05/wetas-joe-letteri-on-the-cutting-edge-of-cg-effects-the-hobbit-and-beyond/

Connor, A. M., Berthelsen, C., Karmokar, S., Kenobi, B., Marks, S., & Walker, C. (2014). *An unexpected journey: experiences of learning through exploration and experimentation*. Paper presented at the 2014 DesignEd Asia Conference, Hong Kong.

Connor, A. M. (2016). A historical review of creative technologies. In A. M. Connor & S. Marks (Eds.), *Creative Technologies for Multidisciplinary Applications*. Hershey, PA: IGI Global.

Connor, A. M., Karmokar, S., & Whittington, C. (2015). From STEM to STEAM: Strategies for Enhancing Engineering & Technology Education. *International Journal of Engineering Pedagogy*, *5*(2), 37–47. doi:10.3991/ijep.v5i2.4458

Connor, A. M., Marks, S., & Walker, C. (2015). Creating Creative Technologists: Playing With(in) Education. In N. Zagalo & P. Branco (Eds.), *Creativity in the Digital Age*. Berlin: Springer. doi:10.1007/978-1-4471-6681-8_3

Consalvo, M. (2007). *Cheating: Gaining advantage in videogames*. Cambridge, MA: MIT Press.

Consalvo, M. (2009). There is No Magic Circle. *Games and Culture*, *4*(4), 408–417. doi:10.1177/1555412009343575

Cook, D. J., & Krishnan, N. C. (2015). *Activity Learning: Discovering, Recognizing, and Predicting Human Behavior from Sensor Data*. Wiley. Retrieved from https://books.google.co.nz/books?id=TMZ9BgAAQBAJ

Cook, R. L., Carpenter, L., & Catmull, E. (1987). The Reyes Image Rendering Architecture. In *Proceedings of the 14th Annual Conference on Computer Graphics and Interactive Techniques* (pp. 95–102). New York, NY: ACM. http://doi.org/ doi:<ALIGNMENT.qj></ALIGNMENT>10.1145/37401.37414

Cooke, B., & Machann, C. (2012). Applied Evolutionary Criticism. *Style (DeKalb, IL)*, *46*(3/4), 277–296.

Cooke, B., & Turner, F. (1999). *Biopoetics: Evolutionary Explorations in the Arts*. Lexington, Ky.: ICUS.

Cooper, R. (2007). *Alter Ego: Avatars and their Creators*. London: Chris Boot Ltd.

Cope, B., & Kalantzis, M. (Eds.). (2000). Multiliteracies: Literacy learning and the design of social futures. Oxford, UK: Psychology Press.

Copeland, B., & Shagrir, O. (2013). Turing versus Gödel on computability and the mind. In J. Copeland, C. Posy, & O. Shagrir (Eds.), *Computability: Turing, Gödel, Church, and Beyond* (pp. 1–33). Cambridge, MA: MIT Press.

Corellianrogue. (2014). Everything Kinect 2 In "One" Place! (See What I Did There?). *123Kinect*. Retrieved September 22, 2015, from http://123kinect.com/everything-kinect-2-one-place/43136/

Cornblatt, M. (2011). Censorship as criticism. *Journal of Visual Culture*, *10*(1), 74–79. doi:10.1177/1470412910391565

Cottone, P., Gaglio, S., Re, G.L., & Ortolani, M. (2013). User activity recognition for energy saving in smart homes. *Sustainable Internet and ICT for Sustainability (SustainIT)*. IEEE.

Council, J. R., Bromley, K. A., Zabelina, D. L., & Waters, C. G. (2007). Hypnotic enhancement of creative drawing. *The International Journal of Clinical and Experimental Hypnosis*, *55*(4), 467–485. doi:10.1080/00207140701506623 PMID:17786662

CraftedPixels. (2012). *Why we need creative technologists*. Retrieved from http://craftedpixelz.co.uk/blog/why-we-need-creative-technologists/

Crogan, P. (2011). *Gameplay Mode: War, Simulation and Technoculture*. Minneapolis: U of Minnesota Press. doi:10.5749/minnesota/9780816653348.001.0001

Crogan, P., & Kennedy, H. (2009). Technologies Between Games and Culture. *Games and Culture*, *4*(2), 107–114. doi:10.1177/1555412008325482

Crookall, D. (2010). Serious Games, Debriefing, and Simulation/Gaming as a Discipline. *Simulation & Gaming*, *41*(6), 898–920. doi:10.1177/1046878110390784

Crump, J., & Sugarman, J. (2008). Ethical considerations for short-term experiences by trainees in global health. *Journal of the American Medical Association*, *300*(12), 1456–1458. doi:10.1001/jama.300.12.1456 PMID:18812538

Csikszentmihalyi, M. (1995). Creativity Across the Life-Span: A Systems View. Talent Development, 3, 9-18.

Csikszentmihalyi, M. (1999). Implications of a Systems Perspective for the Study of Creativity. In Handbook of Creativity. Cambridge, UK: Cambridge University Press.

Csikszentmihalyi, M., & Wolfe, R. (2000). New Conceptions and Research Approaches to Creativity: Implications for a Systems Perspective of Creativity in Education. In K. A. Heller, F. J. Mönks, R. Subotnik, & R. J. Sternberg (Eds.), International Handbook of Giftedness and Talent (2nd ed.). Amsterdam: Elsevier.

Csikszentmihalyi, M. (1988). Society, Culture, and Person: A Systems View of Creativity. In R. J. Sternberg (Ed.), *The Nature of Creativity* (pp. 325–339). New York: Cambridge University Press.

Csikszentmihalyi, M. (1996a, July-August). The Creative Personality. *Psychology Today*, 36–40.

Csikszentmihalyi, M. (1996b). *Creativity: Flow and the Psychology of Discovery and Invention* (1st ed.). New York: HarperCollins.

Csikszentmihalyi, M. (2006). A Systems Perspective on Creativity. In J. Henry (Ed.), *Creative Management and Development* (pp. 3–17). London: SAGE. doi:10.4135/9781446213704.n1

Csikszentmihalyi, M. (2014). The Systems Model of Creativity and Its Applications. In D. K. Simonton (Ed.), *The Wiley Handbook of Genius*. Chichester, UK: John Wiley & Sons Ltd. doi:10.1002/9781118367377.ch25

Csikszentmihalyi, M., & Massimini, F. (1985). On The Psychological Selection Of Bio-Cultural Information. *New Ideas in Psychology*, *3*(2), 115–138. doi:10.1016/0732-118X(85)90002-9

Csikszentmihalyi, M., & Nakamura, J. (2006). Creativity Through the Life Span from An Evolutionary Systems Perspective. In C. Hoare (Ed.), *Handbook of Adult Development and Learning* (pp. 243–254). New York: Oxford University Press.

Cudalbu, C., Anastasiu, B., Grecu, H., & Buzuloiu, V. (2006). Using stereo vision for real-time head-pose and gaze estimation. *University" Politehnica" Of Bucharest Scientific Bulletin, Series C. Electrical Engineering*, *68*(2), 15–26.

Cullen, T., Tanner, S. J., O'Donnell, M., & Green, K. (2014). *Industry needs and tertiary journalism education: Views from news editors*. Paper presented at the 23rd Annual Teaching Learning Forum, Perth, Australia.

Cullingford, G., Mawdesley, M., & Davies, P. (1979). Some experiences with computer based games in civil engineering teaching. *Computers & Education*, *3*(3), 159–164. doi:10.1016/0360-1315(79)90041-1

D'Altroy, T. (2003). *The Incas*. Oxford, UK: Blackwell Publishing.

Darwin, C. (1859). *On the Origin of Species by Means of Natural Selection, or The Preservation of Favoured Races in the Struggle For Life*. London: J. Murray.

Darwin, C. (1872). *The expression of the emotions in man and animals*. London: John Murray. doi:10.1037/10001-000

Davenport, R. (2010). More than a Game. *T+D, 64*(6), 26-29.

Davies, L., & Raziogova, E. (2013). Framing the contested history of digital culture. *Radical History Review*, (117), 5-31.

Dawkins, R. (1976). *The Selfish Gene*. Oxford, UK: Oxford University Press.

Dawkins, R. (1986). *The Blind Watchmaker* (1st American ed.). New York: Norton.

Day, S. (2006). *Digital life, the future of humanity?* Available on: http://mms.ecs.soton.ac.uk/2007/papers/60.pdf

de Eyto, A., Ryan, A., McMahon, M., Hassett, G., & Flynn, M. (2015). *Health Futures Lab-Transdisciplinary development of T shaped professionals through wicked problem challenges*. Paper presented at the 8th International Conference on Engineering Education for Sustainable Development, Vancouver, Canada.

de Leeuw, S., Kopczak, L., & Blansjaar, M. (2010). What really matters in locating shared humanitarian stockpiles: Evidence from the WASH Cluster. *IFIP Advances in Information and Communication Technology*, *336*, 166–172. doi:10.1007/978-3-642-15961-9_19

de Mönnink, M. I. (2014). *Inhabiting the border-A Cultural History of Privacy & Photography*. Academic Press.

De Silva, L. C., Morikawa, C., & Petra, I. M. (2012). State of the art of smart homes. *Engineering Applications of Artificial Intelligence*, *25*(7), 1313–1321. doi:10.1016/j.engappai.2012.05.002

De Vany, A. S., & Walls, W. D. (2004). Motion Picture Profit, the stable Paretian hypothesis, and the Curse of the Superstar. *Journal of Economic Dynamics & Control*, *28*(6), 1035–1057. doi:10.1016/S0165-1889(03)00065-4

Deacon, T. (1997). *The Symbolic Species: The Co-evolution of Language and the Brain*. New York, NY: WW Norton and Co.

Debevec, P. (2012). The light stages and their applications to photoreal digital actors. In SIGGRAPH Asia Technical Briefs, Singapore.

Deleuze, G., & Guattari, F. (1987). *A Thousand Plateaus: Capitalism and Schizophrenia*. Minneapolis, MN: University of Minnesota Press.

Delo, C. (2012). What is gamification, and how can I make it useful for my brand? *Advertising Age*, *83*(9), 58–58.

Demiris, G. (2009). *Privacy and social implications of distinct sensing approaches to implementing smart homes for older adults*. IEEE EMBS.

Demiris, G., & Hensel, B. (2009). Smart homes for patients at the end of life. *Journal of Housing for the Elderly*, *23*(1), 106–115. doi:10.1080/02763890802665049

Demiris, G., & Hensel, B. K. (2008). Technologies for an aging society: A systematic review of "smart home" applications. *Methods of Information in Medicine*, *47*(Suppl. 1), 33–40. PMID:18660873

Demiris, G., Skubic, M., & Rantz, M. et al.. (2006). Smart home sensors for the elderly: a model for participatory formative evaluation. In *Proceedings of the IEEE EMBS international special topic conference on information technology in biomedicine*. IEEE.

Dena, C. (2009). *Transmedia Practice: Theorising The Practice Of Expressing A Fictional World Across Distinct Media And Environments*. (PhD Thesis). University of Sydney. Retrieved from http://www.christydena.com/phd/

Dennett, D. C. (1984). Elbow Room: The Varieties of Free Will Worth Wanting. New York: Clarendon Press.

Dennett, D. (1984). Cognitive wheels: The frame problem of AI. In C. Hookaway (Ed.), *Minds, Machines, and Evolution* (pp. 129–151). Cambridge, MA: Cambridge University Press.

Dennett, D. (1991). *Consciousness Explained*. Toronto, Canada: Little, Brown and Co.

Dennett, D. C. (1995). *Darwin's Dangerous Idea: Evolution and the Meanings of Life*. New York: Simon & Schuster.

Dennett, D. C. (2003). *Freedom Evolves*. New York: Viking.

Denning, P. J. (2015). Emergent innovation. *Communications of the ACM*, *58*(6), 28–31. doi:10.1145/2753147

Denzin, N. K. (2001). The reflexive interview and a performative social science. *Qualitative Research*, *1*(1), 23–46. doi:10.1177/146879410100100102

Deshmukh, S. D., & Shilaskar, S. N. (2015). Wearable sensors and patient monitoring system: A Review. In *Pervasive Computing (ICPC), 2015 International Conference on.* IEEE. doi:10.1109/PERVASIVE.2015.7086982

Deterding, S. (2012). Gamification: designing for motivation. *Interactions, 19*(4), 14-17. doi: 10.1145/2212877.2212883

DeVault, D., Artstein, R., Benn, G., Dey, T., Fast, E., Gainer, A., & Morency, L. et al. (2014) SimSensei kiosk: a virtual human interviewer for healthcare decision support.*Proceedings of the 2014 international conference on Autonomous agents and multi-agent systems,Paris, France.* pp. 1061—1068.

Dewsbury, G., Taylor, B., & Edge, M. (2001). The process of designing appropriate smart homes: including the user in the design. In *Proceedings of the 1st Equator IRC workshop on ubiquitous computing in domestic environments.* Nottingham, UK: University of Nottingham.

Diamond, J. M. (1997). *Guns, Germs, and Steel: The Fates of Human Societies* (1st ed.). New York: W.W. Norton & Co.

Diegel, O. (2005). Intelligent automated health systems for compliance monitoring. In *Proceedings of the IEEE Region 10 TENCON.* IEEE. doi:10.1109/TENCON.2005.301000

Dietrich, A. (2003). Functional neuroanatomy of altered states of consciousness: The transient hypofrontality hypothesis. *Consciousness and Cognition, 12*(2), 231–256. doi:10.1016/S1053-8100(02)00046-6 PMID:12763007

Ding, D., Cooper, R. A., Pasquina, P. F., & Pasquina, L. F. (2011). Sensor technology for smart homes. *Maturitas, 69*(2), 131–136. doi:10.1016/j.maturitas.2011.03.016 PMID:21531517

Dingli, A. (2015). *The New Digital Natives: Cutting the Chord.* Springer. doi:10.1007/978-3-662-46590-5

Dingli, A., & Seychell, D. (2015). *Smart Homes.* The New Digital Natives. Springer Berlin Heidelberg.

Dirks, S., & Keeling, M. (2009). *A Vision of Smarter Cities: How Cities Can Lead the Way into a Prosperous and Sustainable Future.* Somers, NY: IBM Global Business Services.

Dorfman, E. (1969). *The Narreme in the Medieval Romance Epic: An Introduction to Narrative Structure.* Toronto: University of Toronto Press.

Dorfman, J., Shames, V. A., & Kihlstrom, J. F. (1996). Intuition, incubation, and insight: Implicit cognition in problem solving. In G. Underwood (Ed.), *Implicit cognition* (pp. 257–286). Oxford, UK: Oxford University Press.

Dovey, J., & Kennedy, H. W. (2006). *Game Cultures: Computer Games as New Media.* New York: Open University Press.

Dring, C. (2014). How PewDiePie fired Skate 3 back into the charts. *MCV Games.* Retrieved 8 May 2015 from http://www.mcvuk.com/news/read/how-pewdiepie-fired-skate-3-back-into-the-charts/0137447

Durgavich, J. (2009). Customs clearance issues related to the import of goods for public health programs. *US AID.* Retrieved March 21, 2015, from http://deliver.jsi.com/dlvr_content/resources/allpubs/policypapers/CustClearIssu.pdf

Dutton, D. (2009). *The Art Instinct: Beauty, Pleasure, and Human Evolution.* New York, NY: Bloomsbury Press.

Dutton, D. (2010). *The Art Instinct: Beauty, Pleasure and Human Evolution.* Oxford, UK: Oxford University Press.

DVorkin, L. (2011). Who's Doing It Right? How Machinima.com Got 70 Million Viewers on YouTube. *Forbes Business.* Retrieved 7 May 2015 from http://www.forbes.com/sites/lewisdvorkin/2011/05/25/whos-doing-it-right-how-machinima-com-got-70-million-viewers-on-youtube/

Dyer, D. (1991). *Cross-currents of Jungian thought: An annotated bibliography.* New York, NY: Shambhala.

Dyer-Witheford, N., & de Peuter, G. (2009). *Games of Empire: Capitalism and Video Games*. Minneapolis: University of Minnesota Press.

Ebert, R. (2000). *The ghost in the machinima*. Retrieved 7 May 2015 from http://web.archive.org/web/20000818183940/http://www.zdnet.com/yil/stories/features/0,9539,2572985,00.html

Edelman, G. (1992). Mind without biology. In *Bright Air, Brilliant Fire: On the Matter of the Mind* (pp. 211–252). New York, NY: Basic Books.

Edmonds, E. A., Weakley, A., Candy, L., Fell, M., Knott, R., & Pauletto, S. (2005). The studio as laboratory: Combining creative practice and digital technology research. *International Journal of Human-Computer Studies*, *63*(4), 452–481. doi:10.1016/j.ijhcs.2005.04.012

Edwards, D. (2011). Paramedic preceptor: Work readiness in graduate paramedics. *The Clinical Teacher*, *8*(2), 79–82. doi:10.1111/j.1743-498X.2011.00435.x PMID:21585664

Edwards-Groves, C. (2012). Interactive Creative Technologies: Changing learning practices and pedagogies in the writing classroom. *Australian Journal of Language and Literacy*, *35*(1), 99–113.

Egstad, J., Davis, M., & Lacewell, D. (2015). *Improved Deep Image Compositing Using Subpixel Masks*. Glendale, CA: Dreamworks Animation. doi:10.1145/2791261.2791266

Ehrenhard, M., Kijl, B., & Nieuwenhuis, L. (2014). Market adoption barriers of multi-stakeholder technology: Smart homes for the aging population. *Technological Forecasting and Social Change*, *89*, 306–315. doi:10.1016/j.techfore.2014.08.002

Ekman, P., & Friesen, E. (1978). *Facial action coding system: a technique for the measurement of facial movement*. Palo Alto.

Ekman, P., & Friesen, W. (1975). *Unmasking the face* (1st ed.). Englewood Cliffs, N.J.: Prentice-Hall.

Eliëns, A., & Ruttkay, Z. (2008). *Record, Replay & Reflect–a framework for understanding (serious) game play*. Paper presented at Euromedia 2009, Bruges, Belgium.

Elite-care, smart home. (n.d.). Retrieved from http://www.elite-care.com

Elizabeth, L. (2007). Walls, Doors, Condoms, and Duct Tape: Serious Games about National Security and Public Health. *Discourse (Berkeley, Calif.)*, *29*(1), 101–119.

Elma, O., Selamogullari, U. S., Uzunoglu, M., & Ugur, E. (2013, October). Carbon emission savings with a renewable energy supplied smart home operation. In *Renewable Energy Research and Applications (ICRERA), 2013 International Conference on* (pp. 1129-1132). IEEE. doi:10.1109/ICRERA.2013.6749922

El-Nasr, M. S., Zupko, J., & Miron, K. (2005). *Intelligent lighting for a better gaming experience*. Paper presented at CHI'05 Extended Abstracts on Human Factors in Computing Systems, Portland, OR, USA. doi:10.1145/1056808.1056852

Elzabadani, H., Helal, A., Abdulrazak, B., & Jansen, E. (2005). Self-sensing spaces: smart plugs for smart environments. In *Proceedings of the third international conference on smart homes and health telematic*.

England, D., Rupérez, M., Botto, C., Nimoy, J., & Poulter, S. (2007). *Creative technology and HCI*. Paper presented at the HCIed 2007, Aveiro, Portugal.

Erwin, S. I. (2000). Video games gaining clout as military training tools. *National Defense, November*, 62-63.

Eskelinen, M. (2001). The gaming situation. *Game Studies, 1*(1). Retrieved August 20, 2015, from http://www.gamestudies.org/0101/eskelinen/

Etcoff, N. (2000). *Survival of the Prettiest*. New York, NY: Anchor Books.

Eysenck, H. J. (1995). *Genius: The natural history of creativity*. Cambridge, UK: Cambridge University Press. doi:10.1017/CBO9780511752247

Ezzat, T., & Poggio, T. (2000). Visual speech synthesis by morphing visemes. *International Journal of Computer Vision*, *38*(1), 45–57. doi:10.1023/A:1008166717597

Fab Foundation. (n.d.). *FabLabs*. Retrieved August 24, 2015, from http://www.fabfoundation.org/fab-labs/

Faceshift. (2012). *Faceshift face animation software: we put marker-less motion capture at every desk*. Retrieved August 18, 2014, from http://www.faceshift.com/

Faceware Tech. (2014). *Faceware Tech, Facial Motion Capture & Animation*. Retrieved August 11, 2014, from http://facewaretech.com/

Fahad, L. G., Khan, A., & Rajarajan, M. (2015). Activity recognition in smart homes with self-verification of assignments. *Neurocomputing*, *149*, 1286–1298. doi:10.1016/j.neucom.2014.08.069

Failes, I. (2012, July 1). *Vampire Hunter: two killer sequences*. Retrieved from http://www.fxguide.com/featured/vampire-hunter-two-killer-sequences/

Failes, I. (2014). *Age of Extinction: ILM turns up its Transformers toolset*. Retrieved from http://www.fxguide.com/featured/age-of-extinction-ilm-turns-up-its-transformers-toolset/

Fauconnier, G., & Turner, M. (2002). *The Way We Think: Conceptual Blending and the Mind's Hidden Complexities*. New York: Basic Books.

Favreau, J., Theroux, J., & Lee, S. (2010) *"IronMan 2"* [Film]. Paramount Pictures, Marvel Entertainment, Marvel Studios, USA.

Fedkiw, R., Stam, J., & Jensen, H. W. (2001). Visual simulation of smoke. In Proceedings of the 28th annual conference on Computer graphics and interactive techniques (pp. 15–22). ACM. Retrieved from http://dl.acm.org/citation.cfm?id=383260

Feist, G. J. (1999). The influence of personality on artistic and scientific creativity. In R. J. Sternberg (Ed.), *Handbook of creativity* (pp. 273–296). Cambridge, UK: Cambridge University Press.

Fernandes, K. J., Raja, V., & Eyre, J. (2003, September). Cybersphere: The Fully Immersive Spherical Projection System. *Communications of the ACM*, *46*(9), 141–146. doi:10.1145/903893.903929

Ferrara, J. (2013). Games for Persuasion: Argumentation, Procedurality, and the Lie of Gamification. *Games and Culture*, *8*(4), 289–304. doi:10.1177/1555412013496891

Ferren, B. (1997). The future of museums: Asking the right questions. *Journal of Museum Education*, *22*(1), 3–7. doi:10.1080/10598650.1997.11510338

Feynman, R. P. (2005). Don't You Have Time To Think? London: Allen Lane (Penguin).

File, T. (2013). *Computer and Internet Use in the United States*. Current Population Survey Reports.

Film Research L.A. (2014). 2013 Feature Film Production Report. Los Angeles, CA: Author.

Finance, C., & Zwerman, S. (2009). The Visual Effects Producer: Understanding the Art and Business of VFX. Amsterdam: Focal Press.

Finkenzeller, K. (2003). *RFID handbook – fundamentals and applications in contactless smart cards and identification* (2nd ed.). Chichester, UK: JohnWiley.

Fischer, G., Jennings, P., Maher, M. L., Resnick, M., & Shneiderman, B. (2009). *Creativity challenges and opportunities in social computing.* Paper presented at CHI'09 Extended Abstracts on Human Factors in Computing Systems, Boston, MA. doi:10.1145/1520340.1520470

Fitch, T., & Friederici, A. (2012). Artificial grammar learning meets formal language learning: An overview. *Philosophical Transactions of the Royal Society, 367*(1598), 1933–1955. doi:10.1098/rstb.2012.0103 PMID:22688631

Fitch, T., Hauser, M., & Chomsky, N. (2005). The evolution of the language faculty: Clarifications and implications. *Cognition, 97,* 179–210. PMID:16112662

Flahiff, D. (2008). Aquaduct bike purifies water as you pedal. *Inhabitat.* Retrieved August 24, 2015, from http://inhabitat.com/aquaduct-bike-purifies-water-as-you-pedal/

Flusser, V. (1990). On Memory (Electronic or Otherwise). *Leonardo, 23*(4), 397. doi:10.2307/1575342

Foottit, J., Brown, D., Marks, S., & Connor, A. M. (2014). *An Intuitive Tangible Game Controller.* Paper presented at the 2014 Australasian Conference on Interactive Entertainment, Newcastle, Australia.

Forrester, J. W. (1980). Innovation and the economic long wave. *Planning Review, 8*(6), 6–15. doi:10.1108/eb053927

Fosk, K. (2011). Machinima is growing up. *Journal of Visual Culture, 10*(1), 25–30. doi:10.1177/1470412910391551

Foucault, M. (2010). *The Archaeology of Knowledge and the Discourse on Language* (R. Swyer, Trans.). New York: Vintage.

Foundry, T. (2012, October 4). *The Foundry & Weta Digital go DEEP.* Retrieved from http://www.thefoundry.co.uk/articles/2011/05/24/250/the-foundry-weta-digital-go-deep/

Frakes, J., Roddenberry, G., Berman, R., Braga, B., & Moore, R. D. (1996) *"Star Trek: First Contact"* [Film] Paramount Pictures, USA.

Frasca, G. (1999). Ludology meets narratology: similitude and differences between videogames and narrative. *Ludology.* Retrieved August 20, 2015, from www.ludology.org/articles/ludology.htm

Frasca, G. (2003a, November). Ludologists love stories, too: notes from a debate that never took place. In *DIGRA 2003 Conference Proceedings.* Academic Press.

Frasca, G. (2003b). Simulation vs. narrative: introduction to ludology. In M. J. P. Wolf & B. Perron (Eds.), *The video game theory reader* (pp. 221–235). New York, NY: Routledge.

Frasca, G. (2004). Videogames of the Oppressed. In P. Harrigan & N. Wardrip-Fruin (Eds.), *First person: New media as story, performance, and game* (pp. 85–94). Cambridge, MA: MIT Press.

French, J. E. (1952). Children's preferences for pictures of varied complexity of pictorial pattern. *The Elementary School Journal, 53*(2), 90–95. doi:10.1086/459405

Freud, S. (1948). *Leonardo da Vinci* (A. A. Brill, Trans.). London, UK: Routledge & Kegan Paul.

Freud, S. (1948a). The relation of the poet to day-dreaming. In *Collected papers of Sigmund Freud* (Vol. 4). London, UK: Hogarth Press.

Fritz, D. W. (Ed.). (1980). *Perspectives on creativity and the unconscious.* Oxford, OH: Miami University.

Froehlich, J., Larson, E., Campbell, T., Haggerty, C., Fogarty, J., & Patel, S. N. (2009). Hydosense: infrastructure-mediated single-point sensing of whole-home water activity. In *Proceedings of the 11th international conference on Ubiquitous computing*.

Fromm, E. (1978). Primary and secondary process in waking and in altered states of consciousness. *Journal of Altered States of Consciousness*, *4*, 115–128.

Fron, J. F. (2007). Playing dress-up: Costumes, roleplay and imagination. *Philosophy of Computer Games*.

Fuad-Luke, A. (2009). *Design activism*. London, UK: Earthscan.

Fuad-Luke, A. (2010). *Ecodesign: The sourcebook* (3rd ed.). San Francisco, CA: Chronicle.

Fuchs, M., Fizek, S., Ruffino, P., & Schrape, N. (Eds.). (2014). *Rethinking Gamification*. Luneberg Meson.

Fujita, T., & Karger, D. (1972). Managing R & D in Japan. *Management International Review*, *12*(1), 65–73.

Fulton, J., & McIntyre, P. (2013). Futures of Communication: Communication Studies ~ Creativity. *Review of Communication*, *13*(4), 269–289. doi:10.1080/15358593.2013.872805

Gabor, D. (1972). Re: Creativity Technology. *Security Dialogue*, *3*, 243.

Gadagkar, R. (1997). *Survival Strategies: Cooperation and Conflict in Animal Societies*. Cambridge, MA: Harvard University Press.

Gaddam, A., Mukhopadhyay, S. C., & Gupta, G. S. (2010). Towards the development of a cognitive sensor network-based home for elder care. In *The 6th international conference on wireless and mobile communication*. doi:10.1109/ICWMC.2010.93

Gallese, V., & Dio, D. I. C. (2012). Neuroaesthetics: The body in aesthetic experience. In Encyclopedia of Human Behavior (vol. 2, pp. 687–693). London: Academic Press.

Galloway, A. R. (2006). *Gaming: Essays on Algorithmic Culture*. Minneapolis, MN: University of Minnesota Press.

Gamez, D. (2014). Can we prove there are computational correlates of consciousness in the brain? *Journal of Cognitive Science*, *15*(2), 149–186. doi:10.17791/jcs.2014.15.2.149

Garber, L. (2013). Gestural technology: Moving interfaces in a new direction. *Computer*, *46*(10), 22–25. doi:10.1109/MC.2013.352

Gardner, H. (1993). Seven creators of the modern era. In J. Brockman (Ed.), *Creativity* (pp. 28–47). New York, NY: Simon & Schuster.

Garland, A. (2015) *"Ex Machina"* [Film]. Pinewood Studios, UK.

Gatzoulis, L., & Iakovidis, I. (2007). Wearable and portable eHealth systems. *IEEE Engineering in Medicine and Biology Magazine*, *26*(5), 51–56. doi:10.1109/EMB.2007.901787 PMID:17941323

Gaye, L., Tanaka, A., Richardson, R., & Jo, K. (2010). *Social inclusion through the digital economy: digital creative engagement and youth-led innovation*. Paper presented at the 9th International Conference on Interaction Design and Children, Barcelona, Spain. doi:10.1145/1810543.1810612

Gedo, J. E. (1997). Psychoanalytic theories of creativity. In M. A. Runco (Ed.), *The creativity research handbook* (Vol. 1, pp. 29–39). Cresskill, NJ: Hampton Press.

Gee, J. P. (2003). What video games have to teach us about learning and literacy. *Computers in Entertainment*, *1*(1), 20–20. doi:10.1145/950566.950595

Gee, J. P. (2003). *What videogames have to teach us about learning and literacy*. New York: Palgrave Macmillan.

Genette, G. (1997). *Paratexts: Thresholds of interpretation* (J. Lewin, Trans.). Cambridge, MA: Cambridge University Press. doi:10.1017/CBO9780511549373

Gentry, T. (2009). Smart homes for people with neurological disability: State of the art. *NeuroRehabilitation*, *25*, 209–217. PMID:19893189

Gerrig, R. J. (1993). *Experiencing Narrative Worlds*. New Haven, CT: Yale University Press.

Gershenfeld, N. (2007). *Fab: The coming revolution on your desktop–from personal computers to personal fabrication*. New York, NY: Basic Books.

Gershenson, C., & Heylighen, F. (2005). How Can We Think Complex? In K. A. Richardson (Ed.), Managing Organizational Complexity: Philosophy, Theory and Application (pp. 47-62). Greenwich, CT: IAP - Information Age Pub. Inc.

Ghadi, Y. Y., Rasul, M. G., & Khan, M. M. K. (2014). Potential of Saving Energy Using Advanced Fuzzy Logic Controllers in Smart Buildings in Subtropical Climates in Australia. *Energy Procedia*, *61*, 290–293. doi:10.1016/j.egypro.2014.11.1110

Ghaffarianhoseini, A. H., Berardi, U., AlWaer, H., Chang, S., Halawa, E., Ghaffarianhoseini, A., & Clements-Croome, D. (2015). What is an intelligent building? Analysis of recent interpretations from an international perspective. *Architectural Science Review*, 1-20.

Ghaffarianhoseini, A. H., Dahlan, N. D., Berardi, U., Ghaffarianhoseini, A., & Makaremi, N. (2013). The essence of future smart houses: From embedding ICT to adapting to sustainability principles. *Renewable & Sustainable Energy Reviews*, *24*, 593–607. doi:10.1016/j.rser.2013.02.032

Gibson, I., Rosen, D., & Stucker, B. (2014). *Additive manufacturing technologies: 3D printing, rapid prototyping and direct digital manufacturing* (2nd ed.). New York, NY: Springer.

Gibson, M. A., & Lawson, D. W. (Eds.). (2014). *Applied Evolutionary Anthropology*. New York: Springer. doi:10.1007/978-1-4939-0280-4

Giddens, A. (1984). *The Constitution of Society: Outline of the Theory of Structuration*. Cambridge, MA: Polity.

Giddings, S. (2007a). Dionysiac Machines: Videogames and the Triumph of the Simulacra. *Convergence (London)*, *13*(4), 417–431. doi:10.1177/1354856507082204

Giddings, S. (2007b). A 'Pataphysics Engine: Technology, Play, and Realities. *Games and Culture*, *2*(4), 392–404. doi:10.1177/1555412007309534

Gilbert, N. (2008). *Agent-Based Models*. London: SAGE.

Gilchrist, T. (2012, April 5). *"Avatar 2" Delayed Until at Least 2015, Says Jon Landau*. Retrieved May 19, 2015, from http://www.hollywoodreporter.com/heat-vision/avatar-2-delayed-at-2015-308743

Gildea, D. (2012). *Very clever: Google's Ingress masks Data-Collection in Gaming*. Retrieved June 15, 2013, from http://takefiveblog.org/2012/12/09/ingress-gathering-data-through-gaming/

Gill, R., & Pratt, A. (2008). Precarity and cultural work in the social factory? Immaterial labour, precariousness and cultural work. *Theory, Culture & Society*, *25*(7-8), 1–30. doi:10.1177/0263276408097794

Gisin, N. (2014). *Quantum Chance: Nonlocality, Teleportation and Other Quantum Marvels*. New York, NY: Springer.

Gitelman, L. (2008). *Always, Already New*. Cambridge, MA: MIT Press.

Glaeser, E. L., & Berry, C. R. (2006). *Why are Smart Places Getting Smarter? Taubman Centre Policy Brief 2006-2*. Cambridge, MA: Taubman Centre.

Glascock, A. P., & Kutzik, D. M. (2000). Behavioral Telemedicine: A new approach to continuous nonintrusive monitoring of activities of daily living. *Telemedicine Journal, 6*(1), 33–44. doi:10.1089/107830200311833

Glascock, A. P., & Kutzik, D. M. (2007). An evidentiary study of the uses of automated behavioral monitoring. In *Proceedings of the 21st International Conference on Advanced Information Networking and Applications Workshops*. IEEE Computer Society. doi:10.1109/AINAW.2007.81

Glaskin, M. (2013). *Strava users help sports science – unwittingly*. Retrieved May 1, 2015, 2015, from http://cycling-andscience.com/2013/11/20/strava-users-help-sports-science-unwittingly/

Gödel, K. (1962). On formally undecidable propositions of principia mathematica and related systems. In *On Formally Undecidable Propositions of Principia Mathematica and Related Systems*. New York, NY: Dover.

Gontier, N. (2012). Applied Evolutionary Epistemology: A new methodology to enhance interdisciplinary research between the life and human sciences. *Journal of Philosophy and Science, 4*, 7-49.

Gontier, N. (2014). Evolutionary Epistemology. *The Internet Encyclopedia of Philosophy* Retrieved 7th April, 2015, from http://www.iep.utm.edu/evo-epis/

Gordon, D. (1999). *Ants at Work*. New York, NY: Free Press.

Gordon, W. J. (1961). *Synectics: The development of creative capacity*. New York: Harper & Row.

Gottschall, J. (2008). *Literature, Science, and a New Humanities* (1st ed.). New York: Palgrave Macmillan. doi:10.1057/9780230615595

Gottschall, J. (2012). *The Storytelling Animal: How Stories Make Us Human*. Boston: Houghton Mifflin Harcourt.

Gow, K., & McDonald, P. (2000). Attributes required of graduates for the future workplace. *Journal of Vocational Education and Training, 52*(3), 373–396.

Grage, P., & Ross, S. (2014). *Inside VFX: An Insider's View Into The Visual Effects And Film Business* (1st ed.). CreateSpace Independent Publishing Platform.

Gray, J. (2010). *Show sold separately: promos, spoilers, and other media paratexts*. New York: New York University Press.

Greatorex, G. (2015). *3D printing and consumer product safety*. Retrieved July 18, 2015, from http://productsafetysolutions.com.au/3d-printing-call-for-action-on-product-safety/

Green, M. C., & Carpenter, J. M. A. (2011). Transporting Into Narrative Worlds. *The Future of Scientific Studies in Literature, 1*(1), 113–122.

Greenaway, P. (2010). *Peter Greenaway speaks at the 48Hour Film Project Machinima 2010*. Retrieved 6 February 2012, from http://vimeo.com/groups/8472/videos/15253336

Green, M. C., & Brock, T. C. (2000). The role of transportation in the persuasiveness of public narratives. *Journal of Personality and Social Psychology, 79*(5), 701–721. doi:10.1037/0022-3514.79.5.701 PMID:11079236

Green, M. C., & Brock, T. C. (2002). In the mind's eye: Imagery and transportation into narrative worlds. In M. C. Green, J. J. Strange, & T. C. Brock (Eds.), *Narrative Impact: Social and Cognitive Foundations* (pp. 315–341). Mahwah, NJ: Lawrence Erlbaum Associates.

Green, M. C., Chatham, C., & Sestir, M. A. (2012). Emotion and transportation into fact and fiction. *Scientific Study of Literature*, *2*(1), 37–59. doi:10.1075/ssol.2.1.03gre

Gregory, R. (1966). *Eye and Brain: The Psychology of Seeing*. Princeton, NJ: Princeton University Press.

Gregory, R., & Ramachandran, V. (1991). Perceptual filing in of artificially induced scotomas in human vision. *Nature*, *350*(6320), 699–702. doi:10.1038/350699a0 PMID:2023631

Greuter, S., & Roberts, D. J. (2015). Controlling viewpoint from markerless head tracking in an immersive ball game using a commodity depth-based camera. *Journal of Simulation*, *9*(1), 54–63. doi:10.1057/jos.2014.19

Greve, W. (2012). The importance of evolutionary theory in developmental psychology. *International Journal of Developmental Science*, *1-2*, 17–19.

Grimshaw, M. (2007, November 14—15). *The Resonating spaces of first-person shooter games*. Paper presented at the 5th International Conference on Game Design and Technology, Liverpool, UK.

Grimshaw, M. (2009). *The audio Uncanny Valley: Sound, fear and the horror game*. Paper presented at the Audio Mostly 2009 Conference, Glasgow, UK.

Grundberg, S., & Hansegard, J. (2014). YouTube's biggest draw plays games, earns $M a year. *The Wall Street Journal*. Retrieved 8 May 2015 from http://www.wsj.com/articles/youtube-star-plays-videogames-earns-4-million-a-year-1402939896

Grüter, C. (2011). Communication in social insects: Sophisticated problem solving by groups of tiny-brained animals. In R. Menzel & J. Fischer (Eds.), *Animal Thinking: Contemporary Issues in Comparative Cognition* (pp. 163–173). Cambridge, MA: MIT Press.

Gubrium, J. F., & Holstein, J. A. (1998). Narrative practice and the coherence of personal stories. *The Sociological Quarterly*, *39*(1), 163–187. doi:10.1111/j.1533-8525.1998.tb02354.x

Guinness World Records. (2011). Fastest-selling gaming peripheral. *Officially Amazing*. Retrieved from http://www.guinnessworldrecords.com/records-9000/fastest-selling-gaming-peripheral/

Habash, G. (2012). *Average Book Length: Guess How Many Words Are In A Novel*. Retrieved from http://www.huffingtonpost.com/2012/03/09/book-length_n_1334636.html

Hachiya, H., Sugiyama, M., & Ueda, N. (2012). Importance-weighted least-squares probabilistic classifier for covariate shift adaptation with application to human activity recognition. *Neurocomputing*, *80*(0), 93–101. doi:10.1016/j.neucom.2011.09.016

Hadamard, J. (1945). *An essay on the psychology of invention in the mathematical field*. Princeton, NJ: Princeton University Press.

Hahn, F., Jenson, S., & Tanev, S. (2014). Disruptive innovation versus disruptive technology: The disruptive potential of the value proposition of 3D printing technology start-ups. *Technology Innovation Management Review*, *4*(12), 27–36.

Haigh, K. Z., Kiff, L. M., & Ho, G. (2006). Independent Lifestyle Assistant: Lessons Learned. *Assistive Technology*, *18*(1), 87–106. doi:10.1080/10400435.2006.10131909 PMID:16796244

Halloran, J. D. (1998). Mass Communication Research: Asking The Right Questions. In A. Hansen (Ed.), *Mass Communication Research Methods* (pp. 9–34). New York: New York University Press. doi:10.1007/978-1-349-26485-8_2

Hamed, B. (2012). Design & Implementation of Smart House Control Using LabVIEW.[IJSCE]. *International Journal of Soft Computing and Engineering*, *1*(6), 98–106.

Hamilton, M. L., Smith, L., & Worthington, K. (2008). Fitting the methodology with the research: An exploration of narrative, self-study and auto-ethnography. *Studying Teacher Education, 4*(1), 17–28. doi:10.1080/17425960801976321

Hancock, H. (2015). *Has intellectual property law short changed machinima and gaming culture?* Retrieved 29 April 2015, from https://www.youtube.com/watch?v=0xHjcrIKYfM

Han, D. M., & Lim, J. H. (2010). *Smart home energy management system using IEEE 802.15.4 and zigbee. Consumer Electronics* (pp. 1403–1410). IEEE Transactions.

Hardt, M., & Negri, A. (2000). *Empire.* Cambridge, MA: Harvard University Press.

Harman, J. (2014). *The shark's paintbrush: Biomomicry and how nature is inspiring innovation.* Ashland, OR: White Cloud Press.

Harris, R. (1984). Must monkeys mean? In R. Harré & V. Reynolds (Eds.), *The Meaning of Primate Signals* (pp. 126–137). Cambridge, UK: Cambridge University Press.

Harteveld, C., Guimarães, R., Mayer, I. S., & Bidarra, R. (2010). Balancing Play, Meaning and Reality: The Design Philosophy of LEVEE PATROLLER. *Simulation & Gaming, 41*(3), 316–340. doi:10.1177/1046878108331237

Hartholt, A., Gratch, J., & Weiss, L. (2009, September 14-16). *At the virtual frontier: Introducing Gunslinger, a multi-character, mixed-reality, story-driven experience.* Paper presented at the 9th International Conference on Intelligent Virtual Agents, Amsterdam, The Netherlands. doi:10.1007/978-3-642-04380-2_62

Harvey, L. (2000). New realities: The relationship between higher education and employment. *Tertiary Education & Management, 6*(1), 3–17. doi:10.1080/13583883.2000.9967007

Harwood, T. (2010). *Participant observation in Machinima research.* Games Research Methods Seminar, Tampere, Finland.

Harwood, T. (2012b). Machinima as visual consumer culture. *7th Consumer Culture Theory Conference.* Oxford University.

Harwood, T. (2013). Machinima as a learning tool. *Digital Creativity.* Retrieved from http://www.tandfonline.com/eprint/uxKx4sNnsjMxt5N2YjuZ/full

Harwood, T. (2011). Towards a manifesto for Machinima. *Journal of Visual Culture, 10*(1), 6–12. doi:10.1177/1470412910391547

Harwood, T. (2012a). Emergence of Gamified Commerce: Turning Virtual to Real. *Journal of Electronic Commerce in Organizations, 10*(2), 16–39. doi:10.4018/jeco.2012040102

Harwood, T. (2013). Per un manifesto del machinima. In M. Bittanti & H. Lowood (Eds.), *MACHINIMA! Teorie. Pratiche. Dialoghi.* Ludologica, Edizioni Unicopli.

Harwood, T., & Garry, T. (2012). Book chapter: It's Mine: participation and ownership within virtual value co-creation environments. *Journal of Marketing Management., 26*(3), 290–301.

Harwood, T., & Garry, T. (2013). Co-Creation and Ambiguous Ownership within Virtual Communities: The Case of the Machinima Community. *Journal of Consumer Behaviour.*

Harwood, T., & Ward, J. (2013). The challenge of marketing research within 3D virtual worlds. *International Journal of Market Research, 55*(2). doi:10.2501/IJMR-2013-022

Hassenzahl, M., Diefenbach, S., & Göritz, A. (2010). Needs, affect, and interactive products – Facets of user experience. *Interacting with Computers, 22*(5), 353–362. doi:10.1016/j.intcom.2010.04.002

Hatfield, C. (2005). *Alternative comics: an emerging literature.* Jackson, MS: Univ. Press of Mississippi.

Hatler, M., Gurganious, D., & Chi, C. (2013). *Smart Building Wireless Sensor Networks A Market Dynamics Report.* ON World's Research.

Hauser, M. (1998). *The Evolution of Communication.* Cambridge, MA: MIT Press.

Havaldar, P. (2006). Performance Driven Facial Animation. *Proceedings of SIGGRAPH, 2006,* 23–42.

Hawken, P., Lovins, A., & Lovins, L. (2010). *Natural capitalism: The next industrial revolution.* London, UK: Earthscan.

Hawkins, T., Cohen, J., & Debevec, P. (2001, November 28-30). *A photometric approach to digitizing cultural artifacts.* Paper presented at the 2001 Conference on Virtual Reality, Archeology, and Cultural Heritage, Athens, Greece. doi:10.1145/584993.585053

Hawkins, J. (2005). *On Intelligence.* New York, NY: Owl Books.

Hay, J., & Couldry, N. (Eds.). (2011). Rethinking convergence/culture, special issue of Hayes, C.J. (2009). Changing the rules of the game: How video game publishers are embracing user-generated derivative works. *Harvard Journal of Law & Technology, 21*(2), 567–587.

Haykin, S. O. (2008). *Neural networks and learning machines* (3rd ed.). Upper Saddle River, NJ: Prentice-Hall.

Hayles, N. K. (1999). Simulating narratives: What virtual creatures can teach us. *Critical Inquiry, 26*(1), 1–26. doi:10.1086/448950

Hazelton, J. (2015, January 7). *Weta Digital: Maximum effect.* Retrieved May 5, 2015, from http://www.screendaily.com/awards/weta-digital-maximum-effect/5081538.article

Heberlein, A., & Adolphs, R. (2004). Impaired spontaneous anthropomorphizing despite intact perception and social knowledge. *Proceedings of the National Academy of Sciences of the United States of America, 101*(19), 7487–7491. doi:10.1073/pnas.0308220101 PMID:15123799

Heckenberg, D., Saam, J., Doncaster, C., & Cooper, C. (2010). Deep Compositing. Presented at the SIGGRAPH. Retrieved from http://www.johannessaam.com/deepImage.pdf

Heider, F., & Simmel, M.-A. (1944). An experimental study of human behavior. *The American Journal of Psychology, 2*(57), 243–259. doi:10.2307/1416950

Heisenberg, W. (1975). The meaning of beauty in the exact sciences. In W. Heisenberg (Ed.), *Across the frontiers* (P. Heath, Trans.). (pp. 166–183). New York, NY: Harper & Row.

Helal, S., Mann, W., El-Zabadani, H., King, J., Kaddoura, Y., & Jansen, E. (2005). The Gator Tech Smart House: A programmable pervasive space. *Computer, 38*(3), 50–60. doi:10.1109/MC.2005.107

Helmenstine, A. M. (2014). *How Many Atoms Are There in a Human Cell?* Retrieved from http://chemistry.about.com/od/biochemistry/f/How-Many-Atoms-Are-There-In-A-Human-Cell.htm

Helmholtz, H. L. (1896). *Vorträge und Reden* (5th ed.; Vol. 1–2). Braunschweig: Friedrich Vieweg und Sohn.

Herrero, J. (2005). A scientific point of view on perceptions. In *Mechanisms, Symbols, and Models Underlying Cognition* (pp. 416–426). Berlin, Germany: Springer Verlag. doi:10.1007/11499220_43

Hewett, T. T. (2005). Informing the design of computer-based environments to support creativity. *International Journal of Human-Computer Studies, 63*(4-5), 383–409. doi:10.1016/j.ijhcs.2005.04.004

Heylighen, F., & Chielens, K. (2009). Evolution of Culture, Memetics. In R. A. Meyers (Ed.), *Encyclopedia of Complexity and Systems Science* (pp. 3205–3220). Larkspur, CA: Springer. doi:10.1007/978-0-387-30440-3_189

Hill, R., Gratch, J., Johnson, W., Kyriakakis, C., LaBore, C., Lindheim, R., . . . Morie, J. (2001). *Toward the holodeck: integrating graphics, sound, character and story.* Paper presented at the Fifth International Conference on Autonomous Agents, Montreal, Canada. doi:10.1145/375735.376390

Hillman, P., Winquist, E., & Welford, M. (2010). *Compositing "Avatar".* Academic Press.

Himonides, E. (2009). Mapping a beautiful voice: Theoretical considerations. *Journal of Music, Technology, and Education, 2*(1), 25–54. doi:10.1386/jmte.2.1.25/1

Hines, T. (1991). The myth of right hemisphere creativity. *The Journal of Creative Behavior, 25*(3), 223–227. doi:10.1002/j.2162-6057.1991.tb01373.x

Hippo Water Roller Project. (n.d.). Retrieved August 24, 2015, from http://hipporoller.org/

Hoberman, P., Krum, D. M., Suma, E. A., & Bolas, M. (2012). *Immersive training games for smartphone-based head mounted displays.* Paper presented at the Virtual Reality Short Papers and Posters, Costa Mesa, CA. doi:10.1109/VR.2012.6180926

Hocking, C. (2009). Ludonarrative dissonance in Bioshock: The problem of what the game is about. In D. Davidson (Ed.), *Well Played 1.0* (pp. 255–259). Halifax, Canada: ETC Press.

Hodson, H. (2012). *Why Google's Ingress game is a data gold mine.* Retrieved June 15, 2013, from http://www.newscientist.com/article/mg21628936.200-why-googles-ingress-game-is-a-data-gold-mine.html#.UbzPl_aus9F

Hoey, J., von Bertoldi, A., Poupart, P., & Mihailidis, A. (2007). Assisting persons with dementia during handwashing using a partially observable markov decision process. In *Proceedings of the 5th international conference on computer vision systems.*

Holland Cotter. (2008). Buddha's Caves. *New York Times.* Retrieved May 18, 2015, from http://www.nytimes.com/2008/07/06/arts/design/06cott.html?pagewanted=1&_r=0

Hollander, R. (2011). *Deep Compositing in Rise of the Planet of the Apes.* Twentieth Century Fox Film Corporation. Retrieved from http://vimeo.com/37310443

Hollands, R. G. (2008). Will the real smart city please stand up? Intelligent, progressive or entrepreneurial? *City, 12*(3), 303–320. doi:10.1080/13604810802479126

Hollerbach, J. M., Christensen, R. R., Corp, S., & Jacobsen, S. C. (1999). Design Specifications for the Second Generation Sarcos Treadport Locomotion Interface. In *Haptics Symposium, Proc. ASME Dynamic Systems and Control Division* (pp. 1293–1298). Academic Press.

Honga, X., Nugenta, C., Mulvenna, M., McClean, S., Scotney, B., & Devlin, S. (2009). Evidential fusion of sensor data for activity recognition in smart homes. *Pervasive and Mobile Computing, 5*(3), 236–252. doi:10.1016/j.pmcj.2008.05.002

Hoskins, S. (2013). *3D Printing for Artists, Designers and Makers.* London: Bloomsbury.

Höysniemi, J. H. (2005). Children's intuitive gestures in vision-based action games. *Communications.*

Huang Ling, Y. (2011). *Designing Serious Games to Enhance Political Efficacy and Critical Thinking Disposition for College Students: The Case of Taiwan.* Paper presented at the Games and Virtual Worlds for Serious Applications (VS-GAMES), 2011 Third International Conference on.

Huang, L., Morency, L.-P., & Gratch, J. (2010). *Parasocial consensus sampling: combining multiple perspectives to learn virtual human behavior.* Paper presented at the 9th International Conference on Autonomous Agents and Multiagent Systems, Toronto, Canada.

Huang, Y., Wang, L., & Wu, Q. (2014). *A Hybrid PSO-DE Algorithm for Smart Home Energy Management* (pp. 292–300). Springer International Publishing Switzerland. doi:10.1007/978-3-319-11897-0_35

Huizinga, J. (1950). Homo Ludens: A Study of the Play-Element. In *Culture*. Boston: Beacon Press.

Huizinga, J. (1955). *Homo ludens: A study of the play element in culture* (R. Hull, Trans.). Boston, MA: Beacon.

Hu, L., Ong, D. M., Zhu, X., Liu, Q., & Song, E. (2015). Enabling RFID technology for healthcare: Application, architecture, and challenges. Springer. *Telecommunication Systems*, *58*(3), 259–271. doi:10.1007/s11235-014-9871-x

Hulsey, N. (2015). Houses in Motion: An Overview of Gamification in the Context of Mobile Interfaces. In A. De Souza e Silva & M. Sheller (Eds.), *Mobility and Locative Media: Mobile Communication in Hybrid Spaces*. New York: Routledge.

Hulsey, N., & Reeves, J. (2014). The Gift that Keeps on Giving: Google, Ingress, and the Gift of Surveillance. *Surveillance & Society*, *12*(3), 389–400.

Hundert, E. (1995). *Lessons from an Optical Illusion*. Cambridge, MA: Harvard University Press.

Hunt, M. (1993). *The Story of Psychology*. New York, NY: Doubleday.

Hunt, R. J., & Bushong, M. (2010). ADEA CCI vision focuses on preparing graduates for discoveries of the future. *Journal of Dental Education*, *74*(8), 819–823. PMID:20679450

Hussain, S., Schaffner, S., Moseychuck, D. (2009). Applications of Wireless Sensor Networks and RFID in a Smart Home Environment. *Communication Networks and Services Research Conference CNSR '09. Seventh Annual*.

Ibanez, G., & Legaretta, I. (2014) *"Automata"* [Film]. Green Moon, Nu Boyana Viburno, New Boyana Film Studios, Sofia, Bulgaria

IDE. (n.d.). *Treadle pumps*. Retrieved August 24, 2015, from http://www.ideorg.org/OurTechnologies/TreadlePump.aspx

IDEO. (2008). *Aquaduct concept vehicle*. Retrieved August 24, 2015, from http://www.ideo.com/work/aquaduct

Iglesias, K. (2001). *The 101 Habits of Highly Successful Screenwriters: Insider Secrets from Hollywood's Top Writers*. Avon, MA: Adams Media.

IMDb. (n.d.). *Waldo C. Graphic (Character)*. Retrieved September 5, 2014, from http://www.imdb.com/character/ch0116570/

Innovate or Die ! (2014). Retrieved August 24, 2015, from http://www.innovateordie.fi/#in-english

Institute of Medicine. (2012). *Living Well with Chronic Illness: A Call for Public Health Action*. Washington, DC: The National Academies Press.

Intille, S. S., Larson, K., Beaudin, S., Tapia, E. M., Kaushik, P., & Nawyn, J. et al.. (2005). *The Placelab: a live-in laboratory for pervasive computing research (video). Pervasive 2005*. Video Program.

Irrational Games & Looking Glass Studios. (1999). *System Shock 2*. Electronic Arts.

Ismangil, A., Jenie, R. P., Irmansyah, , & Irzaman, . (2015). Development of lithium tantallite (LiTaO3) for automatic switch on LAPAN-IPB Satellite infrared sensor. *Procedia Environmental Sciences*, *24*, 329–334. doi:10.1016/j.proenv.2015.03.043

Isoda, Y., Kurakake, S., & Nakano, H. (2004). Ubiquitous sensors based human behavior modeling and recognition using a spatio-temporal representation of user states. In *Proceedings of the 18th International Conference on Advanced Information Networking and Application (AINA'04)*. doi:10.1109/AINA.2004.1283961

Ito, M. (2011). Machinima in a fanvid ecology. *Journal of Visual Culture, 10*(1), 51–54. doi:10.1177/1470412910391557

Itti, L., Dhavale, N., & Pighin, F. (2004, August 3). *Realistic avatar eye and head animation using a neurobiological model of visual attention.* Paper presented at the Applications and Science of Neural Networks, Fuzzy Systems, and Evolutionary Computation VI, San Diego, CA. doi:10.1117/12.512618

ITU. (2010). Applications of ITU-T G.9960. In ITU-T G.9961 Transceivers for Smart Grid Applications: Advanced Metering Infrastructure, Energy Management in the Home and Electric Vehicles (ITU-T, 06/2010). International Telecommunication Union Technical Paper.

Itzhak, B., & Torrens, P. M. (2004a). *Modeling Urban Land-use with Cellular Automata. In Geosimulation: Automata-based modeling of urban phenomena* (pp. 90–152). Chichester, UK: Wiley.

Itzhak, B., & Torrens, P. M. (2004b). *System Theory, Geography and Urban Modeling. In Geosimulation: Automata-based modeling of urban phenomena* (pp. 47–90). Chichester, UK: Wiley.

Iverson, J., Patel, A., & Ohgushi, K. (2008). Perception of rhythmic grouping depends on auditory experience. Acoustical Society of America, 2263–2271.

Iwata, H., Yano, H., Fukushima, H., & Noma, H. (2005). CirculaFloor. *IEEE Computer Graphics and Applications, 25*(1), 64–67. doi:10.1109/MCG.2005.5 PMID:15691174

Iwata, H., Yano, H., & Tomiyoshi, M. (2007). String Walker. In *ACM SIGGRAPH 2007 Emerging Technologies* (pp. 5–9). New York, NY: ACM; doi:10.1145/1278280.1278301

Jackson, D. (2010). An international profile of industry-relevant competencies and skill gaps in modern graduates. *International Journal of Management Education, 8*(3), 29–58.

Jacobs, D. (2008). Multimodal constructions of self: autobiographical comics and the case of Joe Matt's Peepshow. *Biography, 31*(1).

Jacobs, D. (2013). *Graphic Encounters: Comics and the Sponsorship of Multimodal Literacy.* New York, NY: Bloomsbury Publishing USA.

Jacobson, J., & Lewis, M. (2005). Game engine virtual reality with CaveUT. *Computer, 38*(4), 79–82. doi:10.1109/MC.2005.126

Jakkula, V. R., Cook, D. J., & Jain, G. (2007). Prediction Models for a Smart Home Based Health Care System. *Advanced Information Networking and Applications Workshops, AINAW '07.21st International Conference.* doi:10.1109/AINAW.2007.292

James, C. (2013) *"The Machine"* [Film]. Red & Black Films, UK

Jenkins, H. (2011). Transmedia 202: Further Reflections. *Journal of Memetics.*

Jenkins, H. (2015). *Minecraft and the future of transmedia learning.* Retrieved 5 May 2015 from http://henryjenkins.org/2015/04/minecraft-and-the-future-of-transmedia-learning.html

Jenkins, H. (1992). *Textual poachers: television fans and participatory culture.* New York: Routledge.

Jenkins, H. (2006). *Fans, bloggers and gamers: Exploring participatory culture.* New York: New York University Press.

Jenkins, H. (2007). The future of fandom. In J. Gray, C. Sandvoss, & C. L. Harrington (Eds.), *Fandom: Identities and Communities in a Mediated World.* New York: New York University Press.

Jenkins, H. (2008). *Convergence Culture: Where Old and New Media Collide.* New York: NYU Press.

Jenkins, H. (2014). Rethinking 'rethinking convergence/culture'. *Cultural Studies, 28*(2), 267–297. doi:10.1080/09502 386.2013.801579

Jenkins, H., Ford, S., & Green, J. (2013). *Spreadable Media: Creating Value and Meaning in a Networked Culture*. New York: New York University Press.

Jensen, H. W., Marschner, S. R., Levoy, M., & Hanrahan, P. (2001). A practical model for subsurface light transport. In Proceedings of the 28th annual conference on Computer graphics and interactive techniques (pp. 511–518). ACM. Retrieved from http://dl.acm.org/citation.cfm?id=383319 doi:10.1145/383259.383319

Jin, C., & Kunz, T. (2011). Smart Home Networking: Lessons from Combining Wireless and Powerline Networking. *Smart Grid and Renewable Energy, 2*(02), 136–151. doi:10.4236/sgre.2011.22016

Jittlov, M. (1997). *Puffin Commotion 1.0.5 - Photoshop for Video*. NewMedia.

Johnson, D., & Wiles, J. (2003). Effective affective user interface design in games. *Ergonomics, 46*(13-14), 1332-1345.

Johnson, S. D. (1991). Productivity, the workforce, and technology education. *Journal of Technology Education, 2*(2).

Johnson, W. L., & Rickel, J. (1997). Steve: An animated pedagogical agent for procedural training in virtual environments. *ACM SIGART Bulletin, 8*(1-4), 16–21. doi:10.1145/272874.272877

Jollands, M., Jolly, L., & Molyneaux, T. (2012). Project-based learning as a contributing factor to graduates' work readiness. *European Journal of Engineering Education, 37*(2), 143–154. doi:10.1080/03043797.2012.665848

Jones, P., & Wilks-Heeg, S. (2004). Capitalising culture: Liverpool 2008. *Local Economy, 19*(4), 341–360. doi:10.1080/0269094042000286846

Jones, R. (2011). Does machinima really democratize? *Journal of Visual Culture, 10*(1), 59–65. doi:10.1177/1470412910391559

Jonze, S. (2013) *"Her"* [Film]. Annapurna Pictures, USA.

Jørgensen, K. (2012). Between the Game System and the Fictional World: A Study of Computer Game Interfaces. *Games and Culture, 7*(2), 142–163. doi:10.1177/1555412012440315

Jung, C. G. (CW). The collected works of C. G. Jung. H. Read, M. Fordham, & G. Adler (Eds.). London: Routledge & Kegan Paul, 1953–78; New York: Pantheon, 1953–60, and Bollingen Foundation, 1961–67; Princeton, NJ: Princeton University Press, 1967–78.

Jung, C. G. (1934). *Modern man in search of a soul* (W. S. Dell & C. F. Baynes, Trans.). New York, NY: Harcourt Brace.

Jung, R. E., Mead, B. S., Carrasco, J., & Flores, R. A. (2013). The structure of creative cognition in the human brain. *Frontiers in Human Neuroscience, 7*, 330. doi:10.3389/fnhum.2013.00330 PMID:23847503

Juul, J. (2010). The game, the player, the world: Looking for a heart of gameness. *PLURAIS-Revista Multidisciplinar da UNEB, 1*(2).

Juul, J. (2011). *Half-real: Video games between real rules and fictional worlds*. Cambridge, MA: MIT Press.

Kafka, P. (2012). Google gets deeper into the content business, by putting money into Machinima. *All Things D*. Retrieved 7 May 2015 from http://allthingsd.com/20120507/google-gets-deeper-into-the-content-business-by-putting-money-into-machinima/

Kahneman, D. (2011). *Thinking, Fast and Slow* (1st ed.). New York: Farrar, Straus and Giroux.

Kain, E. (2013, December). Another reason why YouTube's video game copyright crackdown doesn't make sense. *Forbes, 12*. Retrieved from http://www.forbes.com/sites/erikkain/2013/12/12/another-reason-why-youtubes-video-game-copyright-crackdown-doesnt-make-sense/

Kainz, F., & Bogart, R. (2012, August 5). *Technical Introduction to OpenEXR*. Industrial, Light & Magic. Retrieved from https://github.com/openexr/openexr/blob/master/OpenEXR/doc/TechnicalIntroduction_2.0.pdf

Kalleberg, A. L. (1982). Work: Postwar trends and future prospects. *Business Horizons, 25*(4), 78–84. doi:10.1016/0007-6813(82)90030-1

Kandalaft, M., Didehbani, N., Krawczyk, D., Allen, T., & Chapman, S. (2013). Virtual reality social cognition training for young adults with high-functioning autism. *Journal of Autism and Developmental Disorders, 43*(1), 34–44. doi:10.1007/s10803-012-1544-6 PMID:22570145

Kang, N., Brinkman, W., van Riemsdijk, M., & Neerincx, M. (2011) Internet-delivered multipatient virtual reality exposure therapy system for the treatment of anxiety disorders," In Canadian Human-Computer Communications Society. pp. 233–236.

Kannenberg, E. P. (2002). *Form, function, fiction: Text and image in the comics narratives of Winsor McCay, Art Spiegelman, and Chris Ware. (Unpublished Doctoral Dissertation)*. University of Connecticut.

Kaplan, S. (2012). Leading disruptive innovation. *Ivy Business Journal*. Retrieved July 22 2015 from http://iveybusinessjournal.com/publication/leading-disruptive-innovation/

Kaufman, J. C., & Beghetto, R. A. (2009). Beyond big and little: The Four C Model of Creativity. *Review of General Psychology, 13*(1), 1–12. doi:10.1037/a0013688

Kaufman, J. C., & Beghetto, R. A. (2013). Do people recognize the four Cs? Examining layperson conceptions of creativity. *Psychology of Aesthetics, Creativity, and the Arts, 7*(3), 229–236. doi:10.1037/a0033295

Kaya, İ., & Kahraman, C. (2014). A comparison of fuzzy multicriteria decision making methods for intelligent building assessment. *Journal of Civil Engineering and Management, 20*(1), 59–69. doi:10.3846/13923730.2013.801906

Kaye, J. A., Maxwell, S. A., Mattek, N., Hayes, T. L., Dodge, H., Pavel, M., & Zitzelberger, T. A. et al. (2011). Intelligent systems for assessing aging changes: Home-based, unobtrusive, and continuous assessment of aging. *The Journals of Gerontology. Series B, Psychological Sciences and Social Sciences, 66*(Suppl. 1), i180–i190. doi:10.1093/geronb/gbq095 PMID:21743050

Kekulé, A. (1890). Benzolfest: Rede. *Berichte der Deutschen Chemischen Gesellschaft, 23*(1), 1302–1311.

Kelland, M., Morris, D., & Lloyd, D. (2005). *Machinima: Making Movies in 3D Virtual Environments*. Cambridge: The Ilex Press.

Kelly, D. (2005). Smart support at home: The integration of telecare technology with primary and community care systems. *Br. J. Healthc. Comput. Inform. Manage, 22*(3), 19–21.

Kelly, M. J. (1950). The Bell Telephone Laboratories-an example of an institute of creative technology. *Proceedings of the Royal Society of London. Series A, Mathematical and Physical Sciences, 203*(1074), 287–301. doi:10.1098/rspa.1950.0140

Kelly, M. J. (1955). Training programs of industry for graduate engineers. *Electrical Engineering, 74*(10), 866–869. doi:10.1109/EE.1955.6439586

Kelly, M. J. (1957). The Nation's Research and Development-Their Deficiencies and Means for Correction. *Proceedings of the American Philosophical Society, 101*(4), 386–391.

Kelly, M. J. (1959). Development of the Nation's scientific and technical potential. *Electrical Engineering*, 78(4), 315–318. doi:10.1109/EE.1959.6446332

Kemp, S. (2012). 'Vertigo' Tops 'Citizen Kane' in Poll of Greatest Films of All Time. *The Hollywood Reporter*. Retrieved from http://www.hollywoodreporter.com/news/vertigo-citizen-kane-greatest-film-of-all-time-357266

Kenderdine, S., Chan, L. K. Y., & Shaw, J. (2014). Pure Land: Futures for Embodied Museography. *Journal on Computing and Cultural Heritage*, 7(2), 1–15. doi:10.1145/2614567

Kenderdine, S., & Shaw, J. (2009). New media in situ: The re-socialisation of public space. *International Journal of Arts and Technology*, 2(4), 258–276. doi:10.1504/IJART.2009.029235

Keogh, B. (2014). Across worlds and bodies: Criticism in the age of video games. *Journal of Games Criticism*, 1(1), 1–26.

Kerrigan, S., & Velikovsky, J. T. (2015). Examining Documentary Transmedia Narratives Through 'The Living History of Fort Scratchley' Project. *Convergence*. doi: 10.1177/1354856514567053

Keys, P., & Hall, A. D. (1985). A step beyond OR. *The Journal of the Operational Research Society*, 36(9), 864–867. doi:10.2307/2582175

Kim, B. (2012). Harnessing the power of game dynamics. *College & Research Libraries News*, 73(8), 465–469.

Kim, S. C., Jeong, Y. S., & Park, S. O. (2013). RFID-based indoor location tracking to ensure the safety of the elderly in smart home environments. Springer. *Personal and Ubiquitous Computing*, 17(8), 1699–1707. doi:10.1007/s00779-012-0604-4

Kim, S. J., & Dave, B. (2010). Silver towns and smart technologies. In *Proceedings of the 22nd Conference of the Computer–Human Interaction Special Interest Group of Australia on Computer–Human Interaction*. ACM. doi:10.1145/1952222.1952256

King, R., Weiss, B., Buyyala, P., & Sehgal, M. (2008). Bridging the Gap Between Education and Professional Production. In *ACM SIGGRAPH ASIA 2008 Educators Programme* (pp. 13:1–13:3). New York, NY: ACM. doi:10.1145/1507713.1507728

Kipling, R. (1937/1952). Working tools. In B. Ghiselin (Ed.), *The creative process: A symposium* (pp. 157–159). Berkeley, CA: University of California Press.

Kittler, F. (1986). *Grammaphone, Film, Typewriter*. Stanford, CA: Stanford University Press.

Kittler, F. (2010). *Optical Media*. Cambridge, MA: Polity Press.

Klabbers, J. H. G. (2009). Terminological Ambiguity: Game and Simulation. *Simulation & Gaming*, 40(4), 446–463. doi:10.1177/1046878108325500

Klepek, P. (2015). Who invented let's play videos? *Kotaku*. Retrieved 8 May 2015 from http://kotaku.com/who-invented-lets-play-videos-1702390484

Knowles, H. S. (2008). *Realizing residential building greenhouse gas emissions reductions: the case for a web-based geospatial building performance and social marketing tool*. The United States Environmental Protection Agency (EPA). Available from http://www.epa.gov/ttnchie1/conference/ei17/session5/knowles.pdf

Koch, C., & Tononi, G. (2011). A test for consciousness. *Scientific American*, 4(6), 44–47. doi:10.1038/scientificamerican0611-44 PMID:21608402

Koelsch, S. (2011). Toward a neural basis of musical perception: A review and updated model. *Frontiers in Psychology*, 2(110).

Koestler, A. ([1978] 1979). Janus: A Summing Up (1st Vintage Books ed.). London: Pan Books.

Koestler, A. (1964). *The Act of Creation*. London: Hutchinson.

Koestler, A. (1967). The Ghost. In *The Machine*. London: Hutchinson.

Koestler, A. (1978). *Janus: A Summing Up*. London: Hutchinson.

Kolb, J. (2013). *The Hidden Side of Ingress*. Retrieved June 15, 2013, from http://www.applieddatalabs.com/content/hidden-side-ingress

Konstantas, D. (2007). An overview of wearable and implantable medical sensors. In IMIA year book of medical informatics. IMIA

Korhonen, I., Lappalainen, R., Tuomisto, T., Koobi, T., Pentikainen, V., Tuomisto, M., & Turjanmaa, V. (1998). TERVA: wellness monitoring system. In *Proceedings of the 20th Annual International Conference of IEEE Engineering in Medicine and Biology Society*. IEEE.

Korris, J., & Macedonia, M. (2002). The end of celluloid: Digital cinema emerges. *Computer, 35*(4), 96–98. doi:10.1109/MC.2002.993781

Kovács, G., & Spens, K. (2007). Humanitarian logistics in disaster relief operations. *International Journal of Physical Distribution & Logistics Management, 36*(2), 99–114.

Kozbelt, A., Beghetto, R. A., & Runco, M. A. (2010). Theories of Creativity. In J. C. Kaufman & R. J. Sternberg (Eds.), *The Cambridge handbook of Creativity* (pp. 20–47). Cambridge, UK: Cambridge University Press. doi:10.1017/CBO9780511763205.004

Kress, G. (2000). Multimodality. In Multiliteracies: Literacy learning and the design of social futures. Oxford, UK: Psychology Press.

Kress, G. (2003). *Literacy in the new media age*. London: Routledge. doi:10.4324/9780203164754

Kress, G. (2010). *Multimodality: A social semiotic approach to contemporary communication*. London: Routledge.

Kress, G., & Leeuwen, T. (2001). *Muiltimodal discourse: the modes and media of contemporary communications*. London: Arnold.

Kringiel, D. (2011). Machinima and modding: pedagogic means for enhancing computer game literacy. In The Machinima Reader (pp. 241-256). Massachusetts Institute of Technology.

Kris, E. (1952). *Psychoanalytic explorations in art*. New York, NY: International Universities Press.

Kris, E. (1953). Psychoanalysis and the study of creative imagination. *Bulletin of the New York Academy of Medicine, 29*, 334–351. PMID:13032689

Kroeber, A. L., & Kluckhohn, C. (1952). *Culture: A Critical Review of Concepts and Definitions*. Cambridge, MA: The Museum.

Krumm, J., Harris, S., Meyers, B., Brumitt, B., Hale, M., & Shafer, S. (2000). Multi-camera multi-person tracking for EasyLiving. In *Proceedings of 3rd IEEE International Workshop on Visual Surveillance*. IEEE. doi:10.1109/VS.2000.856852

Kuhn, T. (1970). *The structure of scientific revolutions* (2nd ed.). Chicago, IL: University of Chicago Press.

Kumar, J. M., & Herger, M. (2013). *Gamification at Work: Designing Engaging Business Software*. New York: The Interactions Design Foundation.

Kumar, V. (2012). *101 design methods: A structured approach for driving innovation in your organization.* Wiley.

Kushwaha, N., & Kim, M. (2005). Microsoft agent based health care alert system for smart home. *Enterprise networking and Computing in Healthcare Industry. HEALTHCOM.Proceedings of 7th International Workshop.* doi:10.1109/HEALTH.2005.1500453

Kwon, O., Lee, E., & Bahn, H. (2014). Sensor-aware elevator scheduling for smart building environments. *Building and Environment, 72,* 332–342. doi:10.1016/j.buildenv.2013.11.013

L'Hermitte, C., Tatham, P. H., & Bowles, M. (2013). Classifying logistics-relevant disasters: Conceptual model and empirical illustration. *Journal of Humanitarian Logistics and Supply Chain Management, 4*(2), 155–178. doi:10.1108/JHLSCM-07-2013-0025

Lach, C., & Punchihewa, A. et al.. (2007). Smart home system operating remotely Via 802.11b/g wireless technology. *Proceedings of the Fourth International Conference Computational Intelligence and Robotics and Autonomous Systems (CIRAS2007).*

Lakoff, G., & Johnson, M. (1980). *Metaphors We Live By.* Chicago, IL: The University of Chicago Press.

Lakoff, G., & Núñez, R. (2000). *Where Mathematics Comes from: How the Embodied Mind Brings Mathematics into Being.* New York, NY: Perseus Books.

Lamer, B. (2015). Caves of Faith. *National Geographic Magazine.* Retrieved May 18, 2015, from http://ngm.nationalgeographic.com/print/2010/06/dunhuangcaves/

Landis, W. E. (2006). Personas and archetypes: Envisioning the 21st century special collections professional. *RBM: A Journal of Rare Books. Manuscripts and Cultural Heritage, 7*(1), 40–48.

Landow, G. P. (2006). *Hypertext 3.0: Critical theory and new media in an era of globalization.* Baltimore, MD: Johns Hopkins University Press.

Lange, B., Koenig, S., McConnell, E., Chang, C., Juang, R., Suma, E., . . . Rizzo, A. (2012). *Interactive game-based rehabilitation using the Microsoft Kinect.* Paper presented at the Virtual Reality Short Papers and Posters, Costa Mesa, CA. doi:10.1109/VR.2012.6180935

Lange, B., Rizzo, A., Chang, C.-Y., Suma, E. A., & Bolas, M. (2011). *Markerless full body tracking: Depth-sensing technology within virtual environments.* Paper presented at the Interservice/Industry Training, Simulation, and Education Conference (I/ITSEC), Orlando, FL.

Lange, B., Flynn, S. M., & Rizzo, A. (2009). Game-based telerehabilitation. *European Journal of Physical and Rehabilitation Medicine, 45*(1), 143–151. PMID:19282807

Lankshear, C., & Knobel, M. (2010). *New literacies: Everyday practices and social learning* (3rd ed.). Maidenhead, UK: Open University Press.

Larson, G., & Moore, R. (2004) "Battlestar Galactica" [Television Programme]. British Sky Broadcasting (BSkyB), David Eick Productions, NBC Universal Television, USA.

Larson, E., Froehlich, J., Campbell, T., Haggerty, C., Atlas, L., Fogarty, J., & Patel, S. N. (2012). Disaggregated water sensing from a single, pressure-based sensors: An extended analysis of HydroSense using staged experiments. *Pervasive and Mobile Computing, 8*(1), 82–102. doi:10.1016/j.pmcj.2010.08.008

Laszlo, E. (1972). *Introduction to Systems Philosophy: Toward a New Paradigm of Contemporary Thought.* New York: Gordon and Breach.

Latonero, M., & Sinnreich, A. (2014). The hidden demography of new media ethics. *Information Communication and Society*, *17*(5), 572–593. doi:10.1080/1369118X.2013.808364

Lawrence-Lightfoot, S. (1997). *The art and science of portraiture*. San Francisco: Jossey-Bass.

Lazaroiu, G. C., & Roscia, M. (2012). Definition methodology for the smart cities model. *Energy*, *47*(1), 326–332. doi:10.1016/j.energy.2012.09.028

Lazzarato, M. (1996). Immaterial Labour. In Radical Thought in Italy: A Potential Politics (pp. 133–47). Minneapolis, MN: University of Minnesota Press.

Leap Motion, I. (2015). *Leap Motion Controller*. Retrieved September 22, 2015, from https://www.leapmotion.com/

LeDoux, J. (1998). *The Emotional Brain*. New York, NY: Touchstone.

LeDoux, J. (2002). *The Synaptic Self: How Our Brains Become Who We Are*. New York, NY: Penguin Books.

Lee, S. H. (2005). A gesture-based American Sign Language game for deaf children. *CHI'05 Extended Abstracts on Human Factors in Computing Systems*. ACM.

Lemmet, S. (2009). Buildings and Climate Change: A Summary for Decision-Makers, UNEP's Sustainable Buildings & Climate Initiative (SBCI). Paris: Academic Press.

Lerdahl, F. (1992). Cognitive constraints on compositional systems. *Contemporary Music Review*, *6*(2), 97–121. doi:10.1080/07494469200640161

Lertlakkhanakul, J., Choi, J. W., & Kim, M. Y. (2008). Building data model and simulation platform for spatial interaction management in smart home. *Automation in Construction*, *17*(8), 948–957. doi:10.1016/j.autcon.2008.03.004

Lessig, L. (2001). *The Future of Ideas: The Fate of the Commons in a Connected World*. New York: Random House.

Lessig, L. (2008). *Remix: Making art and commerce thrive in the hybrid economy*. London: Penguin. doi:10.5040/9781849662505

Levison, L. (2013). *Filmmakers and Financing: Business Plans for Independents* (7th ed.). New York: Focal Press.

Levy, P. (1997). The Art and Architecture of Cyberspace: The Aesthetics of Collective Intelligence (R. Bononno, Trans.). In Collective Intelligence: Mankind's Emerging World in Cyberspace (pp. 117-130). Cambridge: Perseus Books.

Lewis, J. (2013). *Ingress - Crowdsourcing Solutions to NP-Hard Problems?* Retrieved June 15, 2013, from http://de-complecting.org/blog/2013/01/22/ingress-crowdsourcing-solutions-to-np-hard-problems/

Lewis, J. P., & Pighin, F. (2006). Performance-driven Facial Animation Introduction. *Proceedings of SIGGRAPH, 2006*, 5–9.

Lewis, K. (2003). Measuring transactive memory systems in the field: Scale development and validation. *The Journal of Applied Psychology*, *88*(4), 587–604. doi:10.1037/0021-9010.88.4.587 PMID:12940401

Leys, P. (2015). *The Killer Apps of 3D printing*. Paper presented at Inside 3D Printing, New York, NY.

Lifestraw. (2014). Retrieved August 24, 2015, from http://www.buylifestraw.com/en/

Lin, H. W. (2014). Selfie Quality Assessment Based on Angle. *IPPR Conference on Computer Vision, Graphics, and Image Processing*. Academic Press.

Lindheim, R., & Swartout, W. (2001). Forging a new simulation technology at the ICT. *Computer*, *34*(1), 72–79. doi:10.1109/2.895120

Lin, Y., Duan, X., Zhao, C., & Xu, L. (2013). *Systems Science: Methodological Approaches*. Boca Raton, FL: CRC Press.

Lionhead Games. (2005). *Fable: The Lost Chapters*. Microsoft Game Studios.

Lipson, H., & Kurman, M. (2013). *Fabricated: The new world of 3D printing*. Wiley.

Li, R. Y. M. (2012). A Content Analysis in Hong Kong Sustainable Smart Home Knowledge Sharing via World Wide Web. *Communications in Computer and Information Science*, *350*, 265–269. doi:10.1007/978-3-642-35594-3_37

Livingstone, I., & Hope, A. (2011). Next Gen. *Nesta*. Retrieved from http://www.nesta.org.uk/publications/next-gen

Li, W., Lee, Y. H., Tsai, W. T., Xu, J., Son, Y. S., Park, J. H., & Moon, K. D. (2012). Service-oriented smart home applications: Composition, code generation, deployment, and execution. *Service Oriented Computing and Applications*, *6*(1), 65–79. doi:10.1007/s11761-011-0086-7

Lokovic, T., & Veach, E. (2000). Deep Shadow Maps. Presented at the SIGGRAPH. Los Angeles, CA: Addison-Wesley. Retrieved from http://graphics.stanford.edu/papers/deepshadows/

Long, W. A., & Ohtani, N. (1988). Entrepreneurship education and adding value to new ventures. *Journal of Marketing Education*, *10*(1), 11–20.

Lovelock, J. (1995). *Gaia: A New Look At Life On Earth*. Oxford, UK: Oxford University Press.

Lowood, H. (2005). Real time performance: Machinima and game studies. *The International Digital Media & Arts Association Journal*, *2*(1), 10–17.

Lowood, H. (2011). Perfect capture: Three takes on replay, machinima and the history of virtual worlds. *Journal of Visual Culture*, *10*(1), 113–124. doi:10.1177/1470412910391578

Lowood, H., & Nitsche, M. (2011). *The machinima reader*. London: MIT Press. doi:10.7551/mitpress/9780262015332.001.0001

Loy, J. (2014). ELearning and eMaking: 3D printing blurring the digital and the physical. *Education Sciences*, *4*(1), 108–121. doi:10.3390/educsci4010108

Loy, J., & Canning, S. (2013). *Reconnecting through digital making*. *IDEN*. Sydney, Australia: Industrial Design Educators Network.

Loy, J., & Welch, D. (2013). A brave new creativity. *Art. Design and Communication in Higher Education*, *12*(1), 91–102. doi:10.1386/adch.12.1.91_1

Lubart, T. (2005). How can computers be partners in the creative process: Classification and commentary on the special issue. *International Journal of Human-Computer Studies*, *63*(4-5), 365–369. doi:10.1016/j.ijhcs.2005.04.002

Lu, D., & Pan, Y. (2010). *Digital Preservation for Heritages*. Berlin, Germany: Springer-Verlag; doi:10.1007/978-3-642-04862-3

Lukowicz, P., Kirstein, T., & Tröster, G. (2004). Wearable systems for health care applications. *Methods of Information in Medicine*, *43*, 232–238. PMID:15227552

Lunenfeld, P. (2000). *The digital dialectic: New essays on new media*. Cambridge, MA: MIT Press.

Lusty, S. Jr. (1969). Educational technology. *Peabody Journal of Education*, *47*(1), 53–56. doi:10.1080/01619566909537677

Lutz, E. (1920). *Animated Cartoons: How They Are Made, Their Origin and Development*. Bedford, MA: Applewood Books, Charles Schribner.

Lymberis, A., & Dittmar, A. (2007). Advanced wearable health systems and applications, research and development efforts in the European Union. *IEEE Engineering in Medicine and Biology Magazine, 26*(3), 29–33. doi:10.1109/MEMB.2007.364926 PMID:17549917

MacCallum-Stewart, E., & Parsler, J. (2007). Illusory agency in Vampire: a Masquerade-Bloodlines. *Dichtung-Digital, 37.* Retrieved August 20, 2015, from http://www.dichtung-digital.org/2007/Stewart%26Parsler/maccallumstewart_parsler.htm

Macdonald, I. W. (2004). *The Presentation of the Screen Idea in Narrative Film-making.* (PhD Dissertation). Leeds Metropolitan University, Leeds, UK.

Macdonald, I. W. (2013). *Screenwriting Poetics and the Screen Idea.* New York: Palgrave Macmillan. doi:10.1057/9780230392298

MacDorman, K., Green, R., Ho, C., & Koch, C. (2009). Too real for comfort? Uncanny responses to computer generated faces. *Computers in Human Behavior, 25*(3), 695–710. doi:10.1016/j.chb.2008.12.026 PMID:25506126

Macedonia, M. (2002). Games soldiers play. *IEEE Spectrum, 39*(3), 32–37. doi:10.1109/6.988702

Mackey, M. (2002). *Literacies across media: Playing the text.* London: Routledge. doi:10.4324/9780203218976

MacLennan, B. J. (2015). Living Science. *Progress in Biophysics & Molecular Biology, 119*(3), 410–419. doi:10.1016/j.pbiomolbio.2015.08.009

MacLennan, B. J. (2006). Evolutionary Jungian psychology. *Psychological Perspectives, 49*(1), 9–28. doi:10.1080/00332920600732968

MacLennan, B. J. (2010). The U-machine: A model of generalized computation. *International Journal of Unconventional Computing, 6,* 265–283.

MacLennan, B. J. (2014). Neoplatonism in science: Past and future. In R. Berchman & J. Finamore (Eds.), *Metaphysical patterns in Platonism: Ancient, medieval, renaissance, and modern* (pp. 199–214). Somerset, UK: Prometheus.

Mahoney, D., Mahoney, E., Liss, E., & Ease, A. T. (2009). Automated technology for elder assessment, safety, and environmental monitoring. *Gerontechnology (Valkenswaard), 8*(1), 11–25. doi:10.4017/gt.2009.08.01.003.00

Makela, T. (2005). Multimedia software as culture: Towards critical interaction design. *IEEE MultiMedia, 12*(1), 14–15. doi:10.1109/MMUL.2005.8

Makepeace, J. (1995). *Makepeace: The spirit of adventure in craft and design.* London, UK: Conran Octopus.

Malaby, T. M. (2007). Beyond Play: A New Approach to Games. *Games and Culture, 2*(2), 95–113. doi:10.1177/1555412007299434

Malloy, T. (2012). Bankroll: A New Approach to Financing Feature Films (2nd ed.). Studio City, CA: Michael Wiese Productions.

Manresa, C. P. (2005). Hand tracking and gesture recognition for human-computer interaction. *ELCVIA. Electronic Letters on Computer Vision and Image Analysis.*

Manto, M., Topping, M., Soede, M., Sanchez-Lacuesta, J., Harwin, W., Pons, J., & Normie, L. et al. (2003). Dynamically responsive intervention for tremor suppression. *IEEE Engineering in Medicine and Biology Magazine, 22*(3), 120–132. doi:10.1109/MEMB.2003.1213635 PMID:12845828

Mao, W., & Gratch, J. (2004, July 19 - 23). *A utility-based approach to intention recognition.* Paper presented at the AAMAS 2004 Workshop on Agent Tracking: Modeling Other Agents from Observations, New York, NY.

Marino, P. (2004). *3D Game-Based Filmmaking: The Art of Machinima*. Scottsdale, Arizona: Paraglyph Press.

Marks, S., Estevez, J. E., & Connor, A. M. (2014). *Towards the Holodeck: fully immersive virtual reality visualisation of scientific and engineering data*. Paper presented at the 29th International Conference on Image and Vision Computing New Zealand, Hamilton, New Zealand. doi:10.1145/2683405.2683424

Marsh, T. (2011). Serious games continuum: Between games for purpose and experiential environments for purpose. *Entertainment Computing*, *2*(2), 61–68. doi:10.1016/j.entcom.2010.12.004

Martindale, C. (1989). Personality, situation, and creativity. In J. A. Glover, R. R. Ronning, & C. R. Reynolds (Eds.), *Handbook of creativity* (pp. 211–228). New York, NY: Plenum. doi:10.1007/978-1-4757-5356-1_13

Martindale, C. (1999). Biological bases of creativity. In R. J. Sternberg (Ed.), *Handbook of creativity* (pp. 137–152). Cambridge, UK: Cambridge University Press.

Martin, R., Maytham, B., Case, J., & Fraser, D. (2005). Engineering graduates' perceptions of how well they were prepared for work in industry. *European Journal of Engineering Education*, *30*(2), 167–180. doi:10.1080/03043790500087571

Marvin, C. (1988). *When Old Technologies Were New: Thinking about Electric Communication in the Late Nineteenth Century*. Oxford, UK: Oxford University Press.

Marwick, A. E., & Boyd, D. (2011). I tweet honestly, I tweet passionately: Twitter users, context collapse, and the imagined audience. *New Media & Society*, *13*(1), 114–133. doi:10.1177/1461444810365313

Mason, T. R. (1976). New directions for modeling? *New Directions for Institutional Research*, *1976*(9), 105–111. doi:10.1002/ir.37019760909

Matsuoka, K. (2004). Aware home understanding life activities. In *Proceedings of the International Conference on ICOST'2004, Towards a Human-Friendly Assistive Environment*. IOS Press.

Matt, J. (1992). *Peepshow*. Quebec, Canada: Drawn and Quarterly.

Matzeu, G., Florea, L., & Diamond, D. (2015). Advances in wearable chemical sensor design for monitoring biological fluids. *Sensors and Actuators. B, Chemical*, *211*, 403–418. doi:10.1016/j.snb.2015.01.077

Mauss, M. (2000). *The Gift: The Form and Reason for Exchange in Archaic Societies*. New York: W.W. Norton & Co.

Mayr, E. (2002). What Evolution Is. London: Phoenix.

May, R. M. (1976). Simple mathematical models with very complicated dynamics. *Nature*, *261*(5560), 459–467. doi:10.1038/261459a0 PMID:934280

McCloud, S. (1993). *Understanding comics: The invisible art*. Northampton, MA: Paradox Press.

McDonald, S., & Howell, J. (2012). Watching, creating and achieving: Creative technologies as a conduit for learning in the early years. *British Journal of Educational Technology*, *43*(4), 641–651. doi:10.1111/j.1467-8535.2011.01231.x

McIntyre, P. (2012). *Creativity and Cultural Production: Issues for Media Practice*. Basingstoke, UK: Palgrave Macmillan.

McNamara, A. (2011). Can we measure memes? *Frontiers in Evolutionary Neuroscience*, *3*(1). doi:10.3389/fnevo.2011.00001 PMID:21720531

McQuaid, M. (2005). *Extreme textiles*. Princeton, NJ: Princeton Architectural Press.

Mead, G. H. (1934). *Mind, Self, and Society* (C. W. Morris, Ed.). Chicago: U of Chicago Press.

Medina, E., Fruland, R., & Weghorst, S. (2008). Virtusphere: Walking in a Human Size VR "Hamster Ball". In *Proceedings of the Human Factors and Ergonomics Society Annual Meeting* (Vol. 52, pp. 2102–2106). Los Angeles, CA: Sage. doi:10.1177/154193120805202704

Medley, S. (2010). Discerning pictures: How we look at and understand images in comics. *Studies in Comics*, *1*(1), 53–70. doi:10.1386/stic.1.1.53/1

Mednick, S. A. (1962). The associative basis of the creative process. *Psychological Review*, *69*(3), 220–232. doi:10.1037/h0048850 PMID:14472013

Mendel, J. M. (1999). Establishing academic programs in integrated media systems. *IEEE Signal Processing Magazine*, *16*(1), 67–76. doi:10.1109/79.743869

Mendelsohn, G. A. (1976). Associative and attentional processes in creative performance. *Journal of Personality*, *44*(2), 341–369. doi:10.1111/j.1467-6494.1976.tb00127.x

Merchant, G. (2001). Teenagers in cyberspace: An investigation of language use and language change in internet chatrooms. *Journal of Research in Reading*, *24*(3), 293–306. doi:10.1111/1467-9817.00150

Merchant, G. (2013). The Trashmaster: Literacy and new media. *Language and Education*, *27*(2), 144–160. doi:10.1080/09500782.2012.760586

Merickel, M. L. (1992). *A Study of the Relationship between Virtual Reality (Perceived Realism) and the Ability of Children To Create, Manipulate and Utilize Mental Images for Spatially Related Problem Solving*. Paper presented at the Annual Convention of the National School Boards Association, Orlando, FL.

Merickel, M. L. (1990). The creative technologies project: Will training in 2D/3D graphics enhance kids' Cognitive skills? *T.H.E. Journal*, *18*(5), 55.

Metz, C. (1991). Film Language: A Semiotics of the Cinema (University of Chicago Press ed.). Chicago: University of Chicago Press.

Meyers, R. J., Williams, E. D., & Matthews, H. S. (2010). Scoping the potential of monitoring and control technologies to reduce energy use in homes. *Energy and Building*, *42*(5), 563–569. doi:10.1016/j.enbuild.2009.10.026

Microsoft. (2014). *Microsoft Kinect for Windows*. Retrieved September 22, 2015, from http://www.microsoft.com/en-us/kinectforwindows/

Mihailidis, A., Carmichael, B., & Boger, J. (2004). The use of computer vision in an intelligent environment to support aging-in-place, safety, and independence in the home. *IEEE Transactions on Information Technology in Biomedicine*, *8*(3), 238–247. doi:10.1109/TITB.2004.834386 PMID:15484428

Miller, T. (2012). The Shameful Trinity: Game Studies, Empire, and the Cognitariat. In G. A. Voorhees, J. Call, & K. Whitlock (Eds.), Guns, Grenades, and Grunts: First-Person Shooter Games (pp. 2033-2368). New York: Continuum.

Miller, F., Janson, K., Varley, L., Costanza, J., & Kane, B. (2002). *Batman: The dark knight returns*. New York, NY: Random House.

Miller, J. G. (1968). Living Systems: Basic Concepts. In W. Gray, F. J. Duhl, & N. D. Rizzo (Eds.), *General Systems Theory and Psychiatry*. Boston: Litte, Brown & Co.

Miller, J. G. (1978). *Living Systems*. New York: McGraw-Hill.

Milone, J. (1994). Multimedia authors, one and all. *Technology and Learning*, *5*(2), 25–31.

Milton, A., & Rodgers, P. (2013). *Research methods for product design*. London, UK: Laurence King.

Missaoui, R., Joumaa, H., Ploix, S., & Bacha, S. (2014). Managing energy Smart Homes according to energy prices: Analysis of a Building Energy Management System. *Energy and Building, 71*, 155–167. doi:10.1016/j.enbuild.2013.12.018

Mixamo. (2014). *Mixamo: Production-quality 3d character animation in seconds*. Retrieved 18 August 2014, from https://www.mixamo.com/faceplus

Mobus, G. E., & Kalton, M. C. (2014). *Principles of Systems Science*. New York: Springer.

Mohsenian-Rad, A. H., Wong, V. W. S., Jatskevich, J., Schober, R., & Leon-Garcia, A. (2010). Autonomous Demand-side Management Based on Game-theoretic Energy Consumption Scheduling for the Future Smart Grid. *IEEE Transactions on Smart Grid, 1*(3), 320–331. doi:10.1109/TSG.2010.2089069

Molderink, A., Bakker, V., Bosman, M. G. C., Hurink, J. L., & Smit, G. J. M. (2010). Management and Control of Domestic Smart Grid Technology. IEEE Transactions on Smart Grid, 1(2), 109 – 119.

Montgomery, J. (2007, March 10). *D2 Software's Nuke Acquired by The Foundry*. Retrieved from http://www.fxguide.com/featured/d2_softwares_nuke_acquired_by_the_foundry/

Moore, A., Gibbons, D., & Higgins, J. (1987). *Watchmen*. New York, NY: Random House.

Morbini, F., DeVault, D., Georgila, K., Artstein, R., Traum, D., & Morency, L. (2014). A Demonstration of Dialogue Processing in SimSensei Kiosk. In *15th Annual Meeting of the Special Interest Group on Discourse and Dialogue*, 2014, p. 254. doi:10.3115/v1/W14-4334

Moreno-Ger, P., Torrente, J., Hsieh, Y. G., & Lester, W. T. (2012). Usability Testing for Serious Games: Making Informed Design Decisions with User Data. *Advances in Human-Computer Interaction, 2012*, 1–13. doi:10.1155/2012/369637

Moretti, F. (2000). The Slaughterhouse of Literature. *MLQ: Modern Language Quarterly, 61*(1), 207–227. doi:10.1215/00267929-61-1-207

Moretti, F. (2007). *Graphs, Maps, Trees: Abstract Models for Literary History*. London: Verso.

Mori, M. (1970). Bukimi no tani[the uncanny valley]. *Energy*, (7): 33–35.

Morini, M. (2015). Multimodal Thought Presentation in Chris Ware's Building Stories. *Multimodal Communication, 4*(1), 31–41.

Mostow, J., Ferris, M., & Brancato, J. (2009) *"Surrogates"* [Film]. Touchstone Pictures, Mandeville Films, Top Shelf Productions, Wintergreen Productions, USA.

Mozer, M. C. (1998). The neural network house: an environment that's adapts to its inhabitants. In *Proceedings of the AAAI Spring Symposium on Intelligent Environments*. AAAI Press.

Muller, L. A. (1967). The role of industry in the introduction of educational change. *New York State Education, LV, 3*, 4–7.

Murray, J. H. (2005). The last word on ludology v narratology in game studies. In *DiGRA 2005 Conference: Changing views of worlds in play*. Retrieved August 20, 2015, from http://inventingthemedium.com/2013/06/28/the-last-word-on-ludology-v-narratology-2005/

Murray, J. H. (1997). *Hamlet on the holodeck: The future of narrative in cyberspace*. New York, NY: Simon and Schuster.

Myers, D. (1999). Simulation, Gaming, and the Simulative. *Simulation & Gaming, 30*(4), 482–489. doi:10.1177/104687819903000406

Myers, D. (2006). Signs, Symbols, Games, and Play. *Games and Culture*, *1*(1), 47–51. doi:10.1177/1555412005281778

Nadis, F. (2005). *Wonder Shows: Performing Science, Magic and Religion in America*. New Brunswick, NJ: Rutgers University Press.

Naef, M., Staadt, O., & Gross, M. (2002). *Spatialized audio rendering for immersive virtual environments*. Paper presented at the ACM Symposium on Virtual Reality Software and Technology, Shatin, Hong Kong. doi:10.1145/585740.585752

Nakamichi, T. (2011). *Pattern magic 2*. London, UK: Laurence King.

Nemytskii, V. V., & Stepanov, V. V. (1989). *Qualitative theory of differential equations*. New York, NY: Dover.

NeoNurture. (n.d.). In *Design that matters*. Retrieved August 24, 2015, from http://www.designthatmatters.org/neonurture/

Nericcio, W. A. (1995). Artif [r] acture: Virulent pictures, graphic narrative and the ideology of the visual. *Mosaic (Winnipeg)*, *28*(4), 79–109.

Neumann, E. (1971). *Art and the creative unconscious* (R. Manheim, Trans.). New York, NY: Princeton University Press.

Ng, J. (Ed.). (2013). *Understanding machinima*. Bloomsbury.

Nickerson, R. S. (1999). Enhancing creativity. In R. J. Sternberg (Ed.), *Handbook of creativity* (pp. 392–430). Cambridge, UK: Cambridge University Press.

Nielsen, J. (1995). Usability inspection methods. *Conference companion on Human factors in computing systems*. Academic Press.

Nikias, C. (1999). Integraded Media Systems. *IEEE Signal Processing Magazine*, *16*(1), 32–32. doi:10.1109/MSP.1999.743865

Nissan, N., & Schocken, S. (2005). *The Elements of Computing Systems: Building a Modern Computer from First Principles*. Cambridge, MA: MIT Press.

Nitsche, M. (2011). Machinima as media. In The Machinima Reader (pp. 113-126). Massachusetts Institute of Technology.

Nitsche, M. (2006). Film live: an excursion into machinima. In B. Bushoff (Ed.), *Developing interactive content: Sagas_Sagasnet_Reader* (pp. 210–243). Munich, Germany: High Text.

Nitsche, M. (2009). *Video Game Spaces. Image, Play, and Structure in 3D Worlds*. Cambridge, MA: MIT Press.

Noguchi, H., Mori, T., & Sato, T. (2002). Construction of network system and the first step of summarization for human daily action in the sensing room. In *Proceedings of the IEEE Workshop on Knowledge Media Networking (KMN'02)*. IEEE. doi:10.1109/KMN.2002.1115157

Noppe, L. D. (1999). Unconscious. In M. A. Runco & S. R. Pritzker (Eds.), *Encyclopedia of creativity* (Vol. 2, pp. 673–679). San Diego: Academic Press.

Norman, D. A. (2002). *The design of everyday things*. Basic Books.

Noury, N., Berenguer, M., Teyssier, H., Bouzid, M.-J., & Giordani, M. (2011). Building an index of activity of inhabitants from their activity on the residential electrical power line. *Information Technology in Biomedicine. IEEE Transactions on*, *15*(5), 758–766.

Nussbaum, B. (2010). Is humanitarian design the new imperialism? *Fastcompany*. Retrieved April 27, 2015, from http://www.fastcodesign.com/1661859/is-humanitarian-design-the-new-imperialism

Oculus, V. R. (2014). *Oculus Rift*. Retrieved September 22, 2015, from http://www.oculusvr.com/

Okada, N. (1993). Entrepreneurship in the new technological regime. In A. E. Andersson, D. F. Batten, K. Kobayashi, & K. Yoshikawa (Eds.), *The Cosmo-Creative Society* (pp. 121–135). Berlin: Springer. doi:10.1007/978-3-642-78460-6_9

Okun, J. A., & Zwerman, S. (Eds.). (2010). *The VES Handbook of Visual Effects: Industry Standard VFX Practices and Procedures* (1st ed.). Burlington, MA: Focal Press.

Oliveira, A. (2014). MyNeihbourhood Vision. Presentation given at the "Human Smart Cities Conference - The future of cities today". Lisbon, Portugal.

Olson, J. L., Krum, D. M., Suma, E. A., & Bolas, M. (2011). *A design for a smartphone-based head mounted display.* Paper presented at the 2011 IEEE Virtual Reality Conference, Singapore. doi:10.1109/VR.2011.5759484

One Laptop per Child. (n.d.). Retrieved August 24, 2015, from http://one.laptop.org/

Orpwood, R., Adlam, T., & Gibbs, C. (2001). User-centred Design of Support Devices for People with Dementia for Use in Smart House in Assistive Technology-added Value to the Quality of Life. IOS Press.

Osberg, K. M. (1993). Virtual reality and education: A look at both sides of the sword. Seattle, WA: Human Interface Technology Laboratory Technical Report.

Osborn, K. (2009, 15 March). "Army Robots: Will Humans Still Be in Control?". *Time magazine.*

Oxfam. (2013). *Oxfam GB Catalogue.* Retrieved January 25, 2014, from http://www.oxfam.org.uk/equipment/catalogue/introduction

Oxfam. (2015). *WASH project.* Retrieved August 24, 2015, from http://policy-practice.oxfam.org.uk/our-work/water-health-education/wash

Ozkan, N. B., Amerighi, O., & Boteler, B. (2014). A comparison of consumer perceptions towards smart homes in the UK, Germany and Italy: Reflections for policy and future research. *Technology Analysis and Strategic Management, 26*(10), 1176–1195. doi:10.1080/09537325.2014.975788

Ozkan, N. B., Davidson, R., Bicket, M., & Whitmarsh, L. (2013). Social barriers to the adoption of smart homes. *Energy Policy, 63*, 363–374. doi:10.1016/j.enpol.2013.08.043

Paharia, R. (2014). Can You Architect Virality? Absolutely. Here's How. *Gamification Blog.*

Paharia, R. (2013). *Loyalty 3.0: How to Revolutionize Customer and Employee Engagement with Big Data and Gamification.* New York: McGraw-Hill.

Pantaleoni, J., Fascione, L., Hill, M., & Aila, T. (2010). PantaRay: Fast Ray-traced Occlusion Caching of Massive Scenes. In ACM SIGGRAPH 2010 Papers (pp. 37:1–37:10). New York, NY: ACM. doi:<ALIGNMENT.qj></ALIGNMENT>10.1145/1833349.1778774

Papanek, V. (1971). *Design for the real world.* London, UK: Thames & Hudson.

Parikka, J. (2012). *What is Media Archaeology.* London: Polity Press.

Park, J. W., Jung, Y. S., Park, H. J., Kim, S. D., & Cho, W. D. (2009). *WIS: A well-being index based health care system in smart home.* Pervasive Computing and Communications. PerCom 2009. IEEE International Conference. doi:10.1109/PERCOM.2009.4912804

Parke, F. (1972). Computer Generated Animation of Faces. In *Proceedings of the ACM annual conference-Volume 1* (pp. 451-457). ACM. doi:10.1145/800193.569955

Parnes, S. J. (1967). *Creative behavior guidebook.* New York: Scribner.

Parsons, T., & Rizzo, A. (2008). Affective outcomes of virtual reality exposure therapy for anxiety and specific phobias: A meta-analysis. *Journal of Behavior Therapy and Experimental Psychiatry, 39*(3), 250–261. doi:10.1016/j.jbtep.2007.07.007 PMID:17720136

Patel, S.N., Roberston, T., Kientz, J.A., Reynolds, M.S., Abowd, G.D. (2007). *At the flick of a switch: detecting and classifying unique electrical events on the residential power line.* Ubicomp.

Patel, S. N., Reynolds, M. S., & Abowd, G. D. (2008). *Detecting human movement by differential air pressure sensing in HVAC system ductwork: an exploration in infrastructure mediated sensing.* Pervasive.

Pauli, W. (1955). The influence of archetypal ideas on the scientific theories of Kepler. In C. G. Jung & W. Pauli (Eds.), *The interpretation of nature and psyche* (pp. 147–240). New York, NY: Pantheon Books.

Pauli, W. (2001). *Atom and archetype: The Pauli/Jung letters, 1928–1958* (C. A. Meier, Ed.). Princeton, NJ: Princeton University Press.

Pausch, R., Burnette, T., Brockway, D., & Weiblen, M. E. (1995). Navigation and locomotion in virtual worlds via flight into hand-held miniatures. In *Proceedings of the 22nd annual conference on Computer graphics and interactive techniques - SIGGRAPH '95* (pp. 399–400). New York: ACM Press. doi:10.1145/218380.218495

Payne, M. T. (2011). Everything I need to know about filmmaking I learned from playing video games: the educational promise of machinima. In *The Machinima Reader* (pp. 241–256). Massachusetts Institute of Technology. doi:10.7551/mitpress/9780262015332.003.0015

Pearce, C. (2006). Productive Play: Game Culture From the Bottom Up. *Games and Culture, 1*(1), 17–24. doi:10.1177/1555412005281418

Pearl, J. (1984). *Heuristics.* New York: Addison-Wesley.

Peer, W. v., Hakemulder, J., & Zyngier, S. (2012). *Scientific Methods for the Humanities.* Amsterdam: John Benjamins Pub. Co. doi:10.1075/lal.13

Pegg, A., Waldock, J., Hendy-Isaac, S., & Lawton, R. (2012). *Pedagogy for employability.* York, UK: Higher Education Authority.

Pelechano, N., Allbeck, J. M., & Badler, N. I. (2007). Controlling individual agents in high-density crowd simulation. In Proceedings of the 2007 ACM SIGGRAPH/Eurographics symposium on Computer animation (pp. 99–108). Eurographics Association. Retrieved from http://dl.acm.org/citation.cfm?id=1272705

Pelias, R. J. (2005). Performative writing as scholarship: An apology, an argument, an anecdote. *Cultural Studies↔ Critical Methodologies, 5*(4), 415–424.

Peppler, K. A., & Kafai, Y. B. (2007). From SuperGoo to Scratch: Exploring creative digital media production in informal learning. *Learning, Media and Technology, 32*(2), 149–166. doi:10.1080/17439880701343337

Perry, M., Dowdall, A., Lines, L., & Hone, K. (2004). Multimodal and ubiquitous computing systems: Supporting independent-living older users. *IEEE Transactions on Information Technology in Biomedicine, 8*(3), 258–270. doi:10.1109/TITB.2004.835533 PMID:15484431

Perumal, T., Ramli, A.R., Leong, C.H., Mansor, S., & Samsudin, K. (2008). Interoperability for Smart Home Environment Using Web Services. *International Journal of Smart Home, 2*(4).

Pessoa, L., & Adolphs, R. (2010). Emotion processing and the amygdala: From 'low road' to 'many roads' of evaluating biological significance. *Nature Reviews. Neuroscience, 11*(11), 773–783. doi:10.1038/nrn2920 PMID:20959860

Petridis, P., Dunwell, I., Arnab, S., Scarle, S., Qureshi, A., de Freitas, S., et al. (2011). *Building Social Commmunities around Alternate Reality Games*. Paper presented at the Games and Virtual Worlds for Serious Applications (VS-GAMES), 2011 Third International Conference on.

PGA. (2010). Producers Guild Of America Code Of Credits - New Media. *Producers Guild of America Code of Credits*. Retrieved from http://www.producersguild.org/?page=coc_nm#transmedia

Piaget, J. (1962). *Play, dreams and imitation in childhood*. New York: Norton.

Piaget, J. (1962). *Play, Dreams, and Imitation in Childhood*. New York: W.W. Norton and Co.

Piaget, J. (1971). *Genetic Epistemology*. New York, NY: WW Norton.

Pias, C. (2011). On the Epistemology of Computer Simulation. *Zeitschrift für Medien- und Kulturforschung, 1*(11).

Pierce, J. R. (1975). Mervin Joe Kelly. *Biographical Memoirs, 46*, 191–219.

Pigliucci, M., & Müller, G. (2010). *Evolution: The Extended Synthesis*. Cambridge, MA: MIT Press. doi:10.7551/mitpress/9780262513678.001.0001

Pilloton, E. (2009). *Design revolution*. New York, NY: Metropolis Books.

Pink, D. (2009). *The puzzle of motivation*. Retrieved from http://www.ted.com/talks/dan_pink_on_motivation?language=en

Pinker, S. (1997). *How the Mind Works*. New York, NY: WW Norton.

Pinker, S. (1997). *How The Mind Works*. New York: Norton.

Pisoni, D. B. (1997). Perception of synthetic speech. In J. P. H. V. Santen, R. W. Sproat, J. P. Olive, & J. Hirschberg (Eds.), *Progress in Speech Synthesis* (pp. 541–560). New York: Springer Verlag. doi:10.1007/978-1-4612-1894-4_43

Pitchfork. (n.d.). Mother 2/Earthbound. *Socks Make People Sexy*. Retrieved August 20, 2015, from http://www.socksmakepeoplesexy.net/index.php?a=earthbound

Poincaré, H. (1908/1952). Mathematical creation. In B. Ghiselin (Ed.), *The creative process: A symposium* (pp. 33–42). Berkeley, CA: University of California Press.

Poincaré, H. (1929). *The foundations of science: Science and hypothesis, the value of science, science and method* (G. B. Halstead, Trans.). New York, NY: The Science Press.

Pollock, D. (1998). Performing writing. In P. Phelan & J. Lane (Eds.), *The Ends of Performance* (pp. 73–103). New York: New York University Press.

Polson, D., Cook, A.-M., Brackin, A., & Velikovsky, J. T. (Eds.). (2014). *Transmedia Practice: A Collective Approach*. London: ID-Press.

Popper, B. (2013). Field of streams: how Twitch made video games a spectator sport. *The Verge*. Retrieved 7 May 2015 from http://www.theverge.com/2013/9/30/4719766/twitch-raises-20-million-esports-market-booming

Popper, K. R. ([1972] 1979). Objective Knowledge: An Evolutionary Approach (Rev. ed.). Oxford, UK: Oxford University Press.

Popper, K. R. (1963). *Conjectures and Refutations: The Growth of Scientific Knowledge. (Essays and Lectures.)*. London: Routledge & Kegan Paul.

Popper, K. R. (1978a). Natural Selection and the Emergence of Mind. *Dialectica, 32*(3-4), 339–355. doi:10.1111/j.1746-8361.1978.tb01321.x

Popper, K. R. (1978b). *Three Worlds*. Salt Lake City, UT: University of Utah.

Popper, K. R. (1999). *All Life is Problem Solving*. London: Routledge.

Postill, J. (2010). Introduction: Theorising media and practice. In B. Bräuchler & J. Postill (Eds.), *Theorising Media and Practice*. Oxford. doi:10.7551/mitpress/9780262014816.003.0001

Potter, C. W., Archambault, A., & Westrick, K. (2009, March). Building a smarter smart grid through better renewable energy information. In Power Systems Conference and Exposition, 2009. PSCE'09. IEEE/PES (pp. 1-5). IEEE. doi:10.1109/PSCE.2009.4840110

Powell, W. (2014). *September. Time for a checkup: Health and Social Care. Future Tech Feature/ Interviewer McCallion, J* (p. 41). PC Pro Magazine.

Powell, W., Garner, T., Tonks, D., & Lee, T. (2014). Evidence Based Facial Design of an Interactive Virtual Advocate. *Proceedings 10th Intl Conf. Disability, Virtual Reality & Associated Technologies*, pp. 355-358.

Prahalad, C. K., & Ramaswamy, V. (2004). Creating Unique Value with Customers. *Strategy and Leadership, 32*(3), 4–9. doi:10.1108/10878570410699249

Prinstein, M. J. (2008). *Understanding peer influence in children and adolescents*. Guilford Press.

Proffitt, R., Lange, B., Chen, C., & Winstein, C. (2015). A comparison of older adults' subjective experiences with virtual and real environments during dynamic balance activities. *Journal of Aging and Physical Activity, 23*(1), 24–33. doi:10.1123/JAPA.2013-0126 PMID:24334299

Propp, V. (1958). *Morphology of the Folk Tale*. Bloomington, IN: Indiana University Press.

Proyas, A., & Goldsman, A. (2004) *"I Robot"* [Film]. Twentieth Century Fox Film Corporation, Mediastream Vierte Film GmbH & Co. Vermarktungs KG, Davis Entertainment.

Pullin, G. (2011). *Design meets disability*. Cambridge, MA: MIT Press.

Qian, M. (2015). Metal powder for additive manufacturing. *JOM, 67*(3), 536–537. doi:10.1007/s11837-015-1321-z

Qiao, S., & Eglin, R. (2011). Accurate behaviour and believability of computer generated images of human head, In *Proceedings of the 10th International Conference on Virtual Reality Continuum and Its Applications in Industry*. pp. 545-548. doi:10.1145/2087756.2087860

Radnitzky, G., Bartley, W. W., & Popper, K. R. (1987). *Evolutionary Epistemology, Rationality, and the Sociology of Knowledge*. Open Court.

Ramello, G. B. (2005). Property rights, firm boundaries, and the republic of science—A note on Ashish Arora and Robert Merges. *Industrial and Corporate Change, 14*(6), 1195–1204. doi:10.1093/icc/dth085

Randall, W., Hill, J., Han, C., & Lent, M. V. (2002). *Perceptually driven cognitive mapping of urban environments*. Paper presented at the First International Joint Conference on Autonomous Agents and Multiagent Systems, Bologna, Italy.

Ransing, R. S., & Rajput, M. (2015). Smart home for elderly care, based on Wireless Sensor Network. In *Nascent Technologies in the Engineering Field (ICNTE), 2015 International Conference*. IEEE. doi:10.1109/ICNTE.2015.7029932

Rantz, M. J., Marek, K. D., Aud, M., Tyrer, H. W., Skubic, M., Demiris, G., & Hussam, A. (2005). A technology and nursing collaboration to help older adults age in place. *Nursing Outlook*, *53*(1), 40–45. doi:10.1016/j.outlook.2004.05.004 PMID:15761399

Rantz, M. J., Skubic, M., & Miller, S. J. (2009). Using sensor technology to augment traditional healthcare. In *Proceedings of the Annual International Conference of the IEEE of Engineering in Medicine and Biology Society 2009 (EMBC 2009)*. doi:10.1109/IEMBS.2009.5334587

Rantz, M., Skubic, M., Miller, S., & Krampe, J. (2008). Using technology to enhance aging in place. In S. Helal, S. Mitra, J. Wong, C. Chang, & M. Mokhtari (Eds.), *Smart homes and health telematics* (pp. 169–176). Berlin: Springer. doi:10.1007/978-3-540-69916-3_20

Rao, K., & Skouge, J. (2015). Using multimedia technologies to support culturally and linguistically diverse learners and young children with disabilities. In K. L. Heider & M. Renck Jalongo (Eds.), *Young Children and Families in the Information Age* (pp. 101–115). Dordrecht: Springer. doi:10.1007/978-94-017-9184-7_6

Raybould, J., & Sheedy, V. (2005). Are graduates equipped with the right skills in the employability stakes? *Industrial and Commercial Training*, *37*(5), 259–263. doi:10.1108/00197850510609694

Razzaque, S., Kohn, Z., & Whitton, M. (2001). Redirected Walking (short paper presentation). In *Proceedings of EUROGRAPHICS 2001*. Manchester, UK: The European Association for Computer Graphics.

Reeder, B., Meyer, E., Lazar, A., Chaudhuri, S., Thompson, H. J., & Demiris, G. (2013). Framing the evidence for health smart homes and home-based consumer health technologies as a public health intervention for independent aging: A systematic review. *International Journal of Medical Informatics*, *82*(7), 565–579. doi:10.1016/j.ijmedinf.2013.03.007 PMID:23639263

Reichhenbach, H. (1938). *Experience and prediction*. Chicago, IL: University of Chicago Press.

Reinisch, C., Kofler, M. J., Iglesias, F., & Kastner, W. (2011). Think home Energy Efficiency in Future Smart Homes. *EURASIP Journal on Embedded Systems*, 1–18.

Remo, C. (2010). Analysis: System Shock 2 – structure and spoilers. *Gamasutra*. Retrieved August 20, 2015, from http://www.gamasutra.com/view/news/27684/Analysis_System_Shock_2__Structure_And_ Spoilers.php

Resnick, M. (2006). Computer as paint brush: Technology, play, and the creative society. In D. Singer, R. Golikoff, & K. Hirsh-Pasek (Eds.), *Play= learning: How play motivates and enhances children's cognitive and social-emotional growth* (pp. 192–208). Oxford, UK: Oxford University Press. doi:10.1093/acprof:oso/9780195304381.003.0010

Rhyne, T.-M. (2002). Computer games and scientific visualization. *Communications of the ACM*, *45*(7), 40–44. doi:10.1145/514236.514261

Richards, C. E. (2012). Complementarities in Physics and Psychology. In L. J. Miller (Ed.), *The Oxford Handbook of Psychology and Spirituality*. Oxford, UK: Oxford University Press. doi:10.1093/oxfordhb/9780199729920.013.0005

Rickel, J., Marsella, S., Gratch, J., Hill, R., Traum, D., & Swartout, W. (2002). Toward a new generation of virtual humans for interactive experiences. *IEEE Intelligent Systems*, *17*(July/August), 32–38. doi:10.1109/MIS.2002.1024750

Riedel, D. E., Venkatesh, S., & Liu, W. (2005). Spatial activity recognition in a smart home environment using a chemotactic model. In *Proceedings of the International Conference on Intelligent Sensors Networks and Information Processing*. doi:10.1109/ISSNIP.2005.1595596

Rigney, R. (2013). Want to sell your game? Don't tick off YouTubers. *Wired*. Retrieved 8 May 2015 from http://www.wired.com/2013/10/stanley-parable-sales/

RITA. (2014) *RITA: Responsive Interactive Advocate.* Retrieved April 22, 2015, from http://rita.me.uk/

Rizzo, A. A., Requejo, P., Winstein, C. J., Lange, B., Ragusa, G., Merians, A., . . . Aisen, M. (2011). *Virtual reality applications for addressing the needs of those aging with disability.* Paper presented at Medicine Meets Virtual Reality 2011, Newport Beach, CA.

Rizzo, A., Pair, J., McNerney, P., Eastlund, E., Manson, B., Gratch, J., . . . Roy, M. (2004). *An immersive virtual reality therapy application for Iraq war veterans with PTSD: from training to toy to treatment.* Paper presented at the 24th Annual Army Science Conference, Orlando, FL.

Rizzo, A., Cukor, J., Gerardi, M., Alley, S., Reist, C., Roy, M., & Difede, J. et al. (2015). Virtual reality exposure for ptsd due to military combat and terrorist attacks. *Journal of Contemporary Psychotherapy*, 1–10. doi:10.1007/s10879-015-9306-3

Rizzo, A., Sagae, K., Forbell, E., Kim, J., Lange, B., & Buckwalter, J. et al.. (2011). SimCoach: An intelligent virtual human system for providing healthcare information and support. *Studies in Health Technology and Informatics*, (163): 503–509. PMID:21335847

Robert, A., & Kummert, M. (2012). Designing net-zero energy buildings for the future climate, not for the past. *Building and Environment*, *55*, 150–158. doi:10.1016/j.buildenv.2011.12.014

Robertson, B. (1988). 'Mike, the Talking Head'. *Computer graphics world*, 11(7) pp. 15-17.

Robertson, B. (1992). 'Moving pictures'. *Computer Graphics World*, *15*, 38–38.

Rodden, T., & Benford, S. (2003). The evolution of buildings and implications for the design of ubiquitous domestic environments. In *Conference on human factors in computing systems, proceedings of the SIGCHI conference on human factors in computing systems.* New York: ACM Press. doi:10.1145/642611.642615

Rosegrant, J. (1980). Adaptive regression of two types. *Journal of Personality Assessment*, *6*(6), 592–599. doi:10.1207/s15327752jpa4406_4 PMID:16366913

Rosegrant, J. (1987). A reconceptualization of adaptive regression. *Psychoanalytic Psychology*, *4*(2), 115–130. doi:10.1037/h0079128

Roth, S. (2015). Serious Gamification: On the Redesign of a Popular Paradox. *Games and Culture.* doi:10.1177/1555412015581478

Rouse, J. (2006). Practice Theory. In S. Turner & M. Risjord (Eds.), *Philosophy of Anthropology and Sociology: A Volume in the Handbook of the Philosophy of Science Series* (pp. 639–681). Amsterdam: Elsevier B.V.

Roussou, M. (2002). Virtual heritage: from the research lab to the broad public. In F. Niccolucci (Ed.), *Virtual Archaeology:Proceedings of the VAST 2000 Euroconference* (pp. 93–101). Arezzo, Italy: Archaeopress Oxford.

Roussou, M. (2007). The Components of Engagement in Virtual Heritage Environments. In Y. Kalay, T. Kvan, & J. Affleck (Eds.), *New Heritage, New Media and Cultural Heritage* (pp. 225–241). London, UK: Routledge - Taylor and Francis Group; doi:10.4324/9780203937884

Roy, J. (2012). *Much Like GOOG-411, Google's New Augmented Reality Game Ingress Is a Genius Ploy to Get You To Collect Data.* Retrieved June 15, 2013, from http://betabeat.com/2012/11/much-like-goog-411-googles-new-augmented-reality-game-ingress-is-a-genius-ploy-to-get-you-to-collect-data/

Roy, A., Das Bhaumik, S. K., Bhattacharya, A., Basu, K., Cook, D. J., & Das, S. K. (2003). Location Aware Resource Management in Smart Homes.*Proceedings of the First IEEE International Conference on Pervasive Computing and Communications*. IEEE. doi:10.1109/PERCOM.2003.1192773

Ruffino, P. (2014). From engagement to life, or: how to do things with gamification? In M. Fuchs, S. Fizek, P. Ruffino, & N. Schrape (Eds.), *Rethinking Gamification* (pp. 47–70). Lüneburg, Germany: Meson Press.

Rummelhart, D., & McClelland, J. (1986). *Parallel Distributed Processing: Explorations in the Microstructure of Cognition*. Cambridge, MA: MIT Press.

Runco, M. A., & Jaeger, G. J. (2012). The Standard Definition of Creativity. *Creativity Research Journal, 24*(1), 92–96. doi:10.1080/10400419.2012.650092

Russell, A., Ito, M., Richmond, T., & Tuters, M. (2008). Culture: Media convergence and networked participation. In K. Varnelis (Ed.), *Networked publics*. Cambridge, MA: MIT Press. doi:10.7551/mitpress/9780262220859.003.0003

Russo, J., Sukojo, A., Helal, A., Davenport, R., & Mann, W. C. (2004). SmartWave—intelligent meal preparation system to help older people live independently. In D. Zhang & M. Mokhtari (Eds.), *Toward a human-friendly assistive environment*. IOS Press.

Ryan, C. (2004). *Digital eco-sense: Sustainability and ICT – a new terrain for innovation*. Carlton, Australia: lab.3000 – innovation in digital design.

Ryan, M. L. (2001). *Narrative as virtual reality: Immersion and interactivity in literature and electronic media*. Baltimore, MD: Johns Hopkins University Press.

Sacco, J. (2003). *Palestine*. New York, NY: Random House.

Sadowski, P. (1999). *Systems Theory as an Approach to the Study of Literature: Origins and Functions of Literature*. Lewiston, NY: E. Mellen Press.

Salovaara, A., Helfenstein, S., & Oulasvirta, A. (2011). Everyday appropriations of information technology: A study of creative uses of digital cameras. *Journal of the American Society for Information Science and Technology, 62*(12), 2347–2363. doi:10.1002/asi.21643

Sarah Kenderdine. (2012a). Pure Land Augmented Reality Edition. *Alive Lab, City University of Hong Kong*. Retrieved May 18, 2015, from http://alive.scm.cityu.edu.hk/projects/alive/pure-land-ii-2012/

Sarah Kenderdine. (2012b). Pure Land: Inside the Mogao Grottoes at Dunhuang. *Alive Lab, City University of Hong Kong*. Retrieved May 18, 2015, from http://alive.scm.cityu.edu.hk/projects/alive/pure-land-inside-the-mogao-grottoes-at-dunhuang-2012/

Sarah Kenderdine. (2013). "Pure Land": Inhabiting the Mogao Caves at Dunhuang. *Curator: The Museum Journal, 56*(2), 199–218. doi:10.1111/cura.12020

Saren, M., Harwood, T., Ward, J., & Venkatesh, A. (Eds.). (2013). Special Issue: Virtual worlds research in marketing. Journal of Marketing Management.

Sasaki, M. (2003). Kanazawa: A creative and sustainable city. *Policy Sciences, 10*(2), 17–30.

Satrapi, M. (2007). *The Complete Persepolis*. New York, NY: Pantheon Books.

Sawyer, R. K. (2012). Explaining Creativity: The Science of Human Innovation (2nd ed.). New York: Oxford University Press.

Sawyer, R. K. (2006). *Explaining creativity: The science of human innovation*. Oxford, UK: Oxford University Press.

Saygin, A. P., Cicekli, I., & Akman, V. (2000). Turing Test: 50 Years Later. *Minds and Machines*, *10*(4), 463–518. doi:10.1023/A:1011288000451

Scott, J., Bernheim Brush, A., Krumm, J., Meyers, B., Hazas, M., Hodges, S., & Villar, N. (2011). PreHeat: controlling home heating using occupancy predictionACM. *Symposium conducted at the meeting of the Proceedings of the 13th international conference on Ubiquitous computing*. doi:10.1145/2030112.2030151

Scott, F. (2007). *Teaching Homes to be Green: Smart Homes and the Environment*. London: Green Alliance.

Scott, L. M. (1994). Images in advertising: The need for a theory of visual rhetoric. *The Journal of Consumer Research*, *21*(2), 252–273. doi:10.1086/209396

Searle, J. (1980). Minds, brains, and programs. *Behavioral and Brain Sciences*, *3*(03), 417–424. doi:10.1017/S0140525X00005756

Seixas, M. C. (2015). *The Leap Motion Movement for 2D Pointing Tasks: Characterisation and Comparison to Other Devices*. Academic Press.

Senft, T. M. (2015). Selfies Introduction~ What Does the Selfie Say? Investigating a Global Phenomenon. *International Journal of Communication*.

Senztech. (2012). *Virtual Reality let Users Walk in Rotating Sphere*. Retrieved September 22, 2015, from http://www.senztech.cc/shownews.aspx?newid=28

Seymour, M. (2012, July 5). *Alvy Ray Smith: RGBA, the birth of compositing & the founding of Pixar*. Retrieved from http://www.fxguide.com/featured/alvy-ray-smith-rgba-the-birth-of-compositing-the-founding-of-pixar/

Seymour, M. (2013, April 25). *The science of Spherical Harmonics at Weta Digital*. Retrieved from http://www.fxguide.com/featured/the-science-of-spherical-harmonics-at-weta-digital/

Sfard, A. (2008). *Thinking as Communicating: Human Development, the Growth of Discourse, and Mathemetizing*. New York, NY: Cambridge University Press. doi:10.1017/CBO9780511499944

Shaker, L. (2006). Google we trust: Information integrity in the digital age. Academic Press.

Shanahan, M., & Baars, B. (2005). Applying the global workspace theory to the frame problem. *Cognition*, *98*(2), 157–176. doi:10.1016/j.cognition.2004.11.007 PMID:16307957

Shapeways. (n.d.). Retrieved August 24, 2015, from http://www.shapeways.com/

Shapiro, A., Pighin, F., & Faloutsos, P. (2003). *Hybrid control for interactive character animation*. Paper presented at the 11th Pacific Conference on Computer Graphics and Applications, Canmore, Canada.

Shavinina, L. V., & Ponomarev, E. A. (2003). Developing innovative ideas through high intellectual and creative educational multimedia technologies. In L. V. Shavinina (Ed.), *The international handbook on innovation* (pp. 401–418). Amsterdam: Elsevier. doi:10.1016/B978-008044198-6/50028-0

Shepard, R. (1999). Cognitive psychology and music. In P. Cook (Ed.), *Music, Cognition and Computerized Sound* (pp. 21–35). Cambridge, MA: MIT Press.

Shettleworth, S. (1998). *Cognition. Evolution, and Behavior*. New York, NY: Oxford University Press.

Siano, P. (2014). Demand response and smart grids—A survey. *Renewable & Sustainable Energy Reviews*, *30*, 461–478. doi:10.1016/j.rser.2013.10.022

Sifakis, E., Selle, A., Robinson-Mosher, A., & Fedkiw, R. (2006) Simulating speech with a physics-based facial muscle model. In *Proceedings of the 2006 ACM SIGGRAPH/Eurographics symposium on Computer animation, Vienna, Austria.* pp. 261-270.

SIGGRAPH. (2014). Retrieved May 17, 2015, from http://www.siggraph.org/learn/open-access-s2014-conference-proceedings

Silva, R., Arakaki, J., Junqueira, F., Santos Filho, D., & Miyagi, P. (2012). Modeling of active holonic control systems for intelligent buildings. *Automation in Construction, 25,* 20–33. doi:10.1016/j.autcon.2012.04.002

Silverman, R. E. (1968). Two kinds of technology. *Educational Technology, VIII*(1), 3.

SimGraphics. (n.d.). *SimGraphics VActor.* Retrieved August 11, 2014, from http://www.simg.com/

Simon, H. A. (1991). *Models of My Life.* New York: Basic Books.

Simon, H. A. (1996). *The Sciences of the Artificial* (3rd ed.). Cambridge, MA: MIT Press.

Simons, J. (2007). Narrative, games, and theory. *Game studies, 7*(1), 1-21. Retrieved August 20, 2015, from http://gamestudies.org/0701/articles/simons

Simonton, D. K. (1999). *Origins of genius: Darwinian perspectives on creativity.* New York, NY: Oxford.

Simonton, D. K. (2007). Is Bad Art The Opposite Of Good Art? Positive Versus Negative Cinematic Assessments of 877 Feature Films. *Empirical Studies of the Arts, 25*(2), 143–161. doi:10.2190/2447-30T2-6088-7752

Simonton, D. K. (2011). *Great Flicks: Scientific Studies of Cinematic Creativity and Aesthetics.* New York: Oxford University Press. doi:10.1093/acprof:oso/9780199752034.001.0001

Simonton, D. K. (2012a). Creative Thought as Blind Variation and Selective Retention: Why Creativity is Inversely Related to Sightedness. *Journal of Theoretical and Philosophical Psychology, 33*(4), 253–266. doi:10.1037/a0030705

Simonton, D. K. (2012b). Fields, Domains, and Individuals (Chapter). In M. D. Mumford (Ed.), *Handbook of Organizational Creativity* (pp. 67–86). Oxford, UK: Elsevier Science. doi:10.1016/B978-0-12-374714-3.00004-5

Simpson, E. (1963). *You and Research.* Washington, DC: American Vocational Association, Inc.

Sinnreich, A., Latonero, M., & Gluck, M. (2009). Ethics reconfigured: How today's media consumers evaluate the role of creative reappropriation. *Information Communication and Society, 12*(8), 1242–1260. doi:10.1080/13691180902890117

Sirois, S., & Karmiloff-Smith, A. (2009). Ontogenetic development matters. In L. Tommasi, M. Peterson, & L. Nadel (Eds.), *Cognitive Biology: Evolutionary and Developmental Perspectives on Mind, Brain, and Behavior* (pp. 322–334). Cambridge, MA: MIT Press. doi:10.7551/mitpress/9780262012935.003.0293

Sivers, D. (2010). *Leadership Lessons from Dancing Guy.* Retrieved from https://sivers.org/ff

Sixsmith, A., & Johnson, N. (2004). A smart sensor to detect the falls of the elderly. *Pervasive Computing, IEEE, 2*(2), 42–47. doi:10.1109/MPRV.2004.1316817

Skarmeta, A., & Moreno, M. V. (2014). Internet of Things. Lecture Notes in Computer Science, 8425, 48-53. doi:10.1007/978-3-319-06811-4_10

Skinner, L. (1996). The media lab at the university of the West of England, Bristol. *Local Economy, 11*(2), 181–184. doi:10.1080/02690949608726326

Skinner, R. (1994). Creative technology projects in science: The CREST-Creativity in Science and Technology-model. *Australian Science Teachers Journal, 40*(4), 26.

Skubic, M., Alexander, G., Popescu, M., Rantz, M., & Keller, J. (2009). A smart home application to eldercare: Current status and lessons learned. *Technology and Health Care, 17*(3), 183–201. PMID:19641257

Slater, M., Pertaub, D., & Steed, A. (1999). Public speaking in virtual reality: Facing an audience of avatars. *Computer Graphics and Applications, IEEE, 19*(2), 6–9. doi:10.1109/38.749116

Slingerland, E. G., & Collard, M. (2012). *Creating Consilience: Integrating the Sciences and the Humanities.* New York: Oxford University Press.

Sliwinski, A. (2012). Machinima.com cuts staff by 10%, EIC calls it 'growing pains'. *Engadget.* Retrieved 7 May 2015 from http://www.engadget.com/2012/12/14/machinima-layoffs/

Sloan, P.-P. (2008). Stupid spherical harmonics (sh) tricks. Presented at the GDC. Austin, TX: Microsoft Corporation. Retrieved from http://ppsloan.org/publications/StupidSH36.pdf

Sloan, P.-P., Kautz, J., & Snyder, J. (2002). Precomputed Radiance Transfer for Real-time Rendering in Dynamic, Low-frequency Lighting Environments. In *Proceedings of the 29th Annual Conference on Computer Graphics and Interactive Techniques* (pp. 527–536). New York, NY: ACM. doi:10.1145/566570.566612

Smith, A. R. (1982). Special Effects for Star Trek II: The Genesis Demo, Instant Evolution with Computer Graphics. *American Cinematographer, 63*(10), 1038–1039, 1048–1050.

Smith, S. M., & Dodds, R. A. (1999). Incubation. In M. A. Runco & S. R. Pritzker (Eds.), *Encyclopedia of creativity* (Vol. 2, pp. 39–44). San Diego, CA: Academic Press.

Smithsonian, Cooper-Hewitt National Design Museum. (n.d.). *Design with the other 90%.* Retrieved August 24, 2015, from http://www.designother90.org/

Snow, C. P. (1959). *The Two Cultures and the Scientific Revolution.* Cambridge University Press.

Solo, R. A. (1961). Creative technology and economic growth. *International Development Review, 3*(1).

Sosa, R., & Connor, A. M. (2015). *Orthodoxies in multidisciplinary design-oriented degree programmes.* Paper presented at the 2015 IASDR Conference: Interplay 2015, Brisbane, Australia.

Soyer, E. B. (2009). *Pyroelectric Infrared (PIR) Sensor Based Event Detection.* Available from: http://www.thesis.bilkent.edu.tr/0003853.pdf

Soyinka, W. (1978). Technology and the artist. *Science & Public Policy, 5*(1), 65–66.

Spangler, T. (2014a). Warner Bros is buying a stake in struggling YouTube net Machinima. Here's why. *Variety.* Retrieved 7 May 2015 from http://variety.com/2014/digital/news/warner-bros-is-buying-a-stake-in-struggling-youtube-net-machinima-heres-why-1201127883/

Spangler, T. (2014b). Machinima hires cable exec Chad Gutstein as CEO. *Variety.* Retrieved 7 May 2015 from http://variety.com/2014/digital/exec-shuffle-people-news/machinima-hires-cable-exec-chad-gutstein-as-ceo-1201150400/

Spiegelmock, M. (2013). *Leap Motion Development Essentials.* Packt Publishing Ltd.

Spielberg, S., & Aldiss, B. (2001) *"A.I."* [Film]. Warner Bros., DreamWorks SKG, Amblin Entertainment, USA.

Spronken-Smith, R., Bond, C., McLean, A., Frielick, S., Smith, N., Jenkins, M., & Marshall, S. (2013). *Toolkit to assist lecturers to engage with graduate outcomes.* Wellington: Ako Aotearoa.

StandardGamer. (2014). A new genre of games is emerging: Pewdiepie bait. *IGN*. Retrieved 8 May 2015 from http://uk.ign.com/blogs/standardgamer/2014/10/19/a-new-genre-of-games-is-emerging-pewdiepie-bait

Stapleton, C., Hughes, C., & Moshell, J. M. (2002). *Mixed reality and the interactive imagination*. Paper presented at the First Swedish-American Workshop on Modeling and Simulation, Orlando, FL.

Staten, J., & Boren, B. (2001). *Halo* [video game]. Microsoft Game Studios, Gearbox Software, Bungie Software, Westlake Interactive.

Stecker, R. (2000). Is it reasonable to attempt to define art? In N. Carroll (Ed.), *Theories of Art Today* (pp. 45–64). Madison, WI: University of Wisconsin Press.

Steel, E., & Dembosky, A. (2013). *Health apps run into privacy snags*. Retrieved September 20, 2014, from http://www.ft.com/intl/cms/s/0/b709cf4a-12dd-11e3-a05e-00144feabdc0.html#axzz3JHHno8bz

Steinkuehler, C. (2006). The Mangle of Play. *Games and Culture*, *1*(3), 199–213. doi:10.1177/1555412006290440

Stein, M. I. (1967). Creativity and culture. In R. L. Mooney & T. A. Razik (Eds.), *Explorations in creativity*. New York, NY: Harper.

Stein, M. I. (1974). Stimulating creativity: *Individual procedures (vol. 1)*. New York, NY: Academic Press.

Stelarc, S. (2013). Aliveness & affect: Alternate art & anatomies. In P. Baler (Ed.), *The next thing: Art in the twenty-first century* (pp. 133–150). Fairleigh Dickinson University Press.

Stern, E. (2011). Massively multiplayer machinima mikusuto. *Journal of Visual Culture*, *10*(1), 42–50. doi:10.1177/1470412910391556

Stevens, A. (1993). *The two million-year-old self*. College Station, TX: Texas A&M University Press.

Stevens, A. (1998). *Ariadne's clue: A guide to the symbols of humankind*. Princeton, NJ: Princeton University Press.

Stevens, A. (2003). *Archetype revisited: An updated natural history of the self*. Toronto, Canada: Inner City Books.

Stohr, K., & Sinclair, C. (2012). *Design like you give a damn: Building change from the ground up*. New York, NY: Harry N. Abrams.

Stoltz, R. B. (1945). The fortieth annual meeting of the american dairy science association. *Journal of Dairy Science*, *28*(8), 625–649. doi:10.3168/jds.S0022-0302(45)95216-7

Stone, G. P. (1990). Appearance and the self: A slightly revised version. In *Life as theater: A dramaturgical sourcebook*. Academic Press.

Stone, E. E., & Skubic, M. (2015). Testing Real-Time In-Home Fall Alerts with Embedded Depth Video Hyperlink. In *Smart Homes and Health Telematics* (pp. 41–48). Springer International Publishing. doi:10.1007/978-3-319-14424-5_5

Stringer, M., Fitzpatrick, G., & Harris, E. (2006). Lessons for the future: experiences with the installation and use of today's domestic sensors and technologies. In *Pervasive Computing:Proceedings of the 4th International Conference*. Springer- Verlag. doi:10.1007/11748625_24

Stuart, T. (2013). Rage against the machinima. *Houston Press*. Retrieved 7 May 2015 from http://www.houstonpress.com/arts/rage-against-the-machinima-6596834

Stumpfel, J., Tchou, C., Jones, A., Hawkins, T., Wenger, A., & Debevec, P. (2004). *Direct HDR capture of the sun and sky*. Paper presented at the 3rd International Conference on Computer Graphics, Virtual Reality, Visualisation and Interaction in Africa, Cape Town, South Africa.

Stumpfel, J., Tchou, C., Yun, N., Martinez, P., Hawkins, T., Jones, A., . . . Debevec, P. E. (2003). *Digital Reunification of the Parthenon and its Sculptures.* Paper presented at the 4th International Symposium on Virtual Reality, Archaeology and Intelligent Cultural Heritage, Brighton, UK.

Suma, E. a., Bruder, G., Steinicke, F., Krum, D. M., & Bolas, M. (2012). A taxonomy for deploying redirection techniques in immersive virtual environments. In Proceedings - IEEE Virtual Reality (pp. 43–46). IEEE. doi:10.1109/VR.2012.6180877

Suma, E. A., Lipps, Z., Finkelstein, S., Krum, D. M., & Bolas, M. (2012). Impossible spaces: Maximizing natural walking in virtual environments with self-overlapping architecture. *Visualization and Computer Graphics. IEEE Transactions on*, *18*(4), 555–564.

Suranyi-Unger, T. (1963). The role of knowledge in invention and economic development. *American Journal of Economics and Sociology*, *22*(4), 463–472. doi:10.1111/j.1536-7150.1963.tb00910.x

Surie, D., Laguionie, O., & Pederson, T. (2008). Wireless sensor networking of everyday objects in a smart home environment. In *International conference intelligent sensors, sensor networks and information processing*. IEEE. doi:10.1109/ISSNIP.2008.4761985

Suryadevara, N. K., & Mukhopadhyay, S. C. (2015). Forecasting the Behaviour of an Elderly Person Using WSN Data. In *Smart Homes* (pp. 139–157). Springer International Publishing. doi:10.1007/978-3-319-13557-1_5

Sutton, J. (2013). *Air painting with Corel Painter Freestyle and the leap motion controller: a revolutionary new way to paint!*. ACM. doi:10.1145/2503673.2503694

Swan, C. (2012). Gamification: A new way to shape behavior. *Communication World*, *29*(3), 13–14.

Swartout, W., Traum, D., Artstein, R., Noren, D., Debevec, P., Bronnenkant, K., & White, K. et al. (2010). Ada and Grace: Toward Realistic and Engaging Virtual Museum Guides. In J. Allbeck, N. Badler, T. Bickmore, C. Pelachaud, & A. Safonova (Eds.), *Intelligent Virtual Agents (IVA)* (pp. 286–300). Heidelberg: Springer. doi:10.1007/978-3-642-15892-6_30

Swartout, W., & van Lent, M. (2003). Making a game of system design. *Communications of the ACM*, *46*(7), 32–39. doi:10.1145/792704.792727

Taati, B., Snoek, J., & Mihailidis, A. (2013). Video analysis for identifying human operation difficulties and faucet usability assessment. *Neurocomputing*, *100*(0), 163–169. doi:10.1016/j.neucom.2011.10.041

Taber, A., Keshavarz, A., & Aghajan, H. (2006). Smart home care network using sensor fusion and distributed vision-based reasoning. In *Proceedings of the VSSN '06 proceedings of the 4th ACM international workshop on Video surveillance and sensor networks*. ACM. doi:10.1145/1178782.1178804

Tanaka, K. (1993). Neural mechanisms of object recognition. *Science*, *262*(5134), 685–688. doi:10.1126/science.8235589 PMID:8235589

Tanaka, K., Yoza, A., Ogimi, K., Yona, A., Senjyu, T., Funabashi, T., & Kim, C.-H. (2012). Optimal operation of DC smart house system by controllable loads based on smart grid topology. *Renewable Energy*, *39*(1), 132–139. doi:10.1016/j.renene.2011.07.026

Tan, B., & Rahaman, H. (2009). Virtual Heritage : Reality and Criticism. In T. Tidafi & T. Dorta (Eds.), *CAAD Futures 2009: Joining languages, cultures and visions* (pp. 143–156). Montreal, Canada: Les Presses de l'Université de Montréal.

Tang, H.-K., & Yeo, K.-T. (1994). The new audacious technopreneurs. *Journal of Enterprising Culture*, *2*(3), 857–870. doi:10.1142/S021849589400029X

Taormina, A. (2014). Microsoft paying YouTubers for secret, only-positive Xbox One advertising. *Game Rant*. Retrieved 7 May 2015 from http://gamerant.com/microsoft-machinima-youtube-xbox-one-advertising/

Tapscott, D., & Williams, A. D. (2006). *Wikinomics: How Mass Collaboration Changes Everything*. New York: Portfolio.

Tatham, P., & Hughes, K. (2011). Humanitarian logistic metrics: Where we are, and how we might improve. In M. Christopher & P. H. Tatham (Eds.), *Humanitarian logistics: Meeting the challenge of preparing for and responding to disasters* (pp. 65–84). London, UK: Kogan Page.

Tatham, P., Loy, J., & Peretti, U. (2015). Three dimensional printing – a key tool for the humanitarian logistician? *Journal of Humanitarian Logistics and Supply Chain Management*, 5(2), 188–208. doi:10.1108/JHLSCM-01-2014-0006

Tatham, P., & Pettit, S. (2010). Transforming humanitarian logistics: The journey to supply network management. *International Journal of Physical Distribution & Logistics Management*, 40(8/9), 609–622. doi:10.1108/09600031011079283

Tatum, J. (2004). The challenge of responsible design. *Design Issues*, 20(3), 66–80. doi:10.1162/0747936041423307

Taylor, A., Kalogridis, L., Lussier, P., Cameron, J., & Hurd, G. (2015) *"Terminator Genisys"* [Film]. Paramount Pictures, Skydance Productions, USA.

Taylor, N. T. (2008). Periscopic Play: Re-positioning 'The Field' in MMO Research. *Loading...* 1(3).

Taylor, R. (1996). *Encyclopedia of Animation Techniques*. London: Quarto Publishing Ltd.

Taylor, T. L. (2006). Does WoW Change Everything?: How a PvP Server, Multinational Player Base, and Surveillance Mod Scene Caused Me Pause. *Games and Culture*, 1(4), 318–337. doi:10.1177/1555412006292615

Taylor, T. L. (2006). *Play Between Worlds: Exploring online game culture*. Cambridge, MA: MIT Press.

Taylor, T. L. (2009). The Assemblage of Play. *Games and Culture*, 4(4), 331–339. doi:10.1177/1555412009343576

Techland. (2013). *Call of Juarez: Gunslinger*. Ubisoft.

Terzopoulos, D., & Waters, K. (1990). Physically-based facial modelling, analysis, and animation. *The Journal of Visualization and Computer Animation*, 1(2), 73–80. doi:10.1002/vis.4340010208

The human Smart City Cookbook, Planum. (2014). *The Journal of Urbanism*, 28(1). Retrieved from http://humansmart-cities.eu/wpcontent/uploads/2014/06/The_Human_Smart_Cities_Cookbook_by_Planum_no.28_vol_I2014_low.pdf

The Museum of Modern Art. (2004) *Walt Disney, Steamboat Willie (1928)*. Retrieved September 26, 2014, from http://www.moma.org/collection/object.php?object_id=89284

Thierstein, A., & Gabi, S. (2004). When creativity meets metropolitan governance. *disP-The Planning Review*, 40(158), 34-40.

Thilmany, J. (2010). Rapid prototyping gains new roles in humanitarian causes. *Mechanical Engineering (New York, N.Y.)*, (January): 46–49.

Thomas, M. (2015). *Language learning with machinima*. EU funded CAMELOT project (2013-2015). Retrieved 30 April 2015 from http://camelotproject.eu/

Thomas, A., & Mizushima, M. (2005). Logistics training: Necessity or luxury? *Forced Migration Review*, 22, 60–61.

Thomassen, A., & Rive, P. (2010). How to enable knowledge exchange in Second Life in design education? *Learning, Media and Technology*, 35(2), 155–169. doi:10.1080/17439884.2010.494427

Thuzar, M. (2011). *Urbanizationin South East Asia: Developing Smart Cities for the Future?*. Regional Outlook.

Thwaites, H. (2013). Visual Heritage in the Digital Age. In E. Ch'ng, V. Gaffney, & H. Chapman (Eds.), *Springer Series on Cultural Computing* (pp. 327–348). London, UK: Springer; doi:10.1007/978-1-4471-5535-5

Tien, S. C., Feng, Y. Y., Chang, W. H., Lee, R. G., Huang, S. F., & Lee, T. Y. (2014). Smart textiles applied in emergency department patients with chest pain. In *Bioelectronics and Bioinformatics (ISBB), 2014 IEEE International Symposium on*. IEEE.

Tinbergen, N. (1963). On the aims and methods of ethology. *Zeitschrift für Tierpsychologie, 4*(20), 410–433.

Tinwell, A., & Grimshaw, M. (2009) 'Survival horror games - an uncanny modality', paper presented at the Thinking After Dark Conference, Montreal, Canada, 23-25 April.

Tinwell, A., Grimshaw, M., Nabi, D. A., & Williams, A. (2011). Facial expression of emotion and perception of the Uncanny Valley in virtual characters. *Computers in Human Behavior, 27*(2), 741–749. doi:10.1016/j.chb.2010.10.018

Tobler, W. (1970). A computer movie simulating urban growth in the Detroit region. *Economic Geography, 46*(2), 234–240. doi:10.2307/143141

Toffler, A. (1980). *The Third Wave*. New York: Bantam Books.

Tolentino, G. P., Battaglini, C., Pereira, A. C. V., de Oliveria, R. J., & de Paula, M. G. M. (2011). *Usability of Serious Games for Health*. Paper presented at the Games and Virtual Worlds for Serious Applications (VS-GAMES), 2011 Third International Conference on.

Tollmar, K., & Junestrand, S. (1999). Video Mediated Communication for Domestic Environments: Architectural and Technological Design. In N. Streiz, J. Siegel, V. Hartkopf, & S. Konomi (Eds.), *Cooperative Buildings: Integrating Information, organizations and Architecture, Proceedings of CoBuilding'99* (LNCS), (vol. 1670, pp. 176-89). Berlin: Springer.

Tomita, M. R., Mann, W. C., Stanton, K., Tomita, A. D., & Sundar, V. (2007). Use of currently available smart home technology by frail elders: Process and outcomes. *Top. Geriatr. Rehabil, 23*(1), 24–34. doi:10.1097/00013614-200701000-00005

Tomita, M. R., & Nochajski, S. M. (2015). Using Smart Home Technology and Health-Promoting Exercise. In *International Handbook of Occupational Therapy Interventions* (pp. 747–756). Springer International Publishing. doi:10.1007/978-3-319-08141-0_54

Tooby, J., & Cosmides, L. (1992). The psychological foundations of culture. In The Adapted Mind: Evolutionary Psychology and the Generation of Culture (pp. 19–136). New York, NY: Oxford Press.

Tooby, J., & Cosmides, L. (2005). Conceptual Foundations of Evolutionary Pyschology. In D. Buss (Ed.), The Handbook of Evolutionary Psychology. Hoboken, NJ: John Wiley & Sons.

Troika Games. (2004). *Vampire: The Masquerade – Bloodlines*. Activision.

Tröster, G. (2004). The agenda of wearable healthcare. In R. Haux & C. Kulikowski (Eds.), *IMIA yearbook of medical informatics: ubiquitous health care systems* (pp. 125–138). Stuttgart, Germany: Schattauer.

Trovato, K. I. (2001). *Simulated environment using procedural animation in a simulated city*. Google Patents. Retrieved from https://www.google.com/patents/US6183364

Truby, J. (2007). *The Anatomy of Story: 22 Steps to Becoming a Master Storyteller* (1st ed.). New York: Faber and Faber.

Tu, N., Dong, X., Rau, P., & Zhang, T. (2010). *Using cluster analysis in persona development*. Paper presented at the 8th International Conference on Supply Chain Management and Information Systems, Hong Kong.

Tulloch, R. (2010). A man chooses, a slave obeys: Agency, interactivity and freedom in video gaming. *Journal of Gaming & Virtual Worlds*, *2*(1), 27–38. doi:10.1386/jgvw.2.1.27_1

Turing, A. (1936). *On computable numbers, with an application to the entscheidungsproblem. In The Essential Turing* (pp. 58–90). New York, NY: Oxford, University Press.

Turing, A. (2004). *The Essential Turing* (J. B. Copeland, Ed.). Oxford, UK: Oxford U Press.

Turing, A. M. (1950). Computing machinery and intelligence. *Mind*, *59*(236), 433–460. doi:10.1093/mind/LIX.236.433

Turing, A., Post, E., & Davies, D. W. (2004). On Computer Numbers: Corrections and Critiques. In J. B. Copeland (Ed.), *The Essential Turing* (pp. 91–124). Oxford, UK: Oxford U. Press.

Tuschl, R. H. (2013). Beyond the digital revolution: The structure between the governmental sphere and the civil society for hegemony in cyberspace. *Democracy in Crisis: The Dynamics of Civil Protest and Civil Resistance, 65*.

Twomey Fosnot, C. (Ed.), *Constructivism: Theory, Perspectives, and Practice*. New York, NY: Teachers College, Columbia University.

Twomey Fosnot, C., & Perry, R. (2005). Constructivism: A psychological theory of learning. In C. Twomey Fosnot (Ed.), *Constructivism: Theory, Perspectives, and Practice* (pp. 8–38). New York, NY: Teachers College, Columbia University.

University of Cambridge. (2013). *Face of the future rears its head*. Retrieved August 1, 2014, from http://www.cam.ac.uk/research/news/face-of-the-future-rears-its-head

USC ICT. (2010). *Talking with Ada and Grace. YouTube*. Retrieved August 28, 2014, from https://www.youtube.com/watch?v=K6kcv3zwoo8

USC ICT. (2013). *SimSensei & MultiSense: Virtual Human and Multimodal Perception for Healthcare Support. YouTube*. Retrieved 2 September, 2014, from https://www.youtube.com/watch?v=ejczMs6b1Q4

Usoh, M., Arthur, K., Whitton, M. C., Bastos, R., Steed, A., Slater, M., & Brooks, F. P. (1999). Walking > walking-in-place > flying, in virtual environments. In *Proceedings of the 26th annual conference on Computer graphics and interactive techniques - SIGGRAPH '99* (pp. 359–364). New York, NY: ACM Press/Addison-Wesley Publishing Co. doi:10.1145/311535.311589

Vacher, M., Istrate, D., Portet, F., Joubert, T., Chevalier, T., Smidtas, S., & Chahuara, P. (2011). The sweet-home project: Audio technology in smart homes to improve well-being and reliance. *Symposium conducted at the meeting of the Engineering in Medicine and Biology Society, EMBC, 2011 Annual International Conference of the IEEE*. IEEE.

Van Hoof, J., Kort, H. S. M., Rutten, P. G. S., & Duijnstee, M. S. H. (2011). Ageing- in-place with the use of ambient intelligence technology: Perspectives of older users. *International Journal of Medical Informatics*, *80*(5), 310–331. doi:10.1016/j.ijmedinf.2011.02.010 PMID:21439898

Van Laer, T., De Ruyter, K., Visconti, L. M., & Wetzels, M. (2014). The Extended Transportation-Imagery Model: A Meta-Analysis of the Antecedents and Consequences of Consumers' Narrative Transportation. *The Journal of Consumer Research*, *40*(5), 797–817. doi:10.1086/673383

Van Peer, W. (1997). Two Laws of Literary Canon: Growth and Predictability in Canon Formation. *Mosaic: A Journal for the Interdisciplinary Study of Literature*, *30*(2), 113-132.

Van Peer, W. (1996). Canon Formation: Ideology or Aesthetic Quality? *The British Journal of Aesthetics*, *36*(2), 97–108. doi:10.1093/bjaesthetics/36.2.97

Van Peer, W., Hakemulder, J., & Zyngier, S. (2007). *Muses and Measures: Empirical Research Methods for the Humanities*. Newcastle, UK: Cambridge Scholars.

Varzi, A. (2015). Mereology. *The Stanford Encyclopedia of Philosophy (Spring 2015 Edition)*. Retrieved from http://plato.stanford.edu/archives/spr2015/entries/mereology/

Veen, M., Fenema, P., & Jongejan, P. (2012). Towards a Framework for Unraveling the Hidden Curriculum in Military Training Simulators. In S. Wannemacker, S. Vandercruysse, & G. Clarebout (Eds.), *Serious Games: The Challenge* (Vol. 280, pp. 65–73). Springer Berlin Heidelberg. doi:10.1007/978-3-642-33814-4_10

Veleva, S., Davcev, D., & Kacarska, M. (2011). *Wireless Smart Platform for Home Energy Management System*. The 2nd IEEE PES International Conference and Exhibition on Innovative Smart Grid Technologies (ISGT Europe), Manchester, UK. doi:10.1109/ISGTEurope.2011.6162798

Velikovsky, J. T. (2013a). Brave New Storyworlds: An Introduction to Creating Transmedia Narratives. *Screen Education, 68*.

Velikovsky, J. T. (2013b). *The Holon/Parton Structure of the Meme, the Unit of Culture*. Retrieved from http://storyality.wordpress.com/2013/12/12/storyality-100-the-holonic-structure-of-the-meme-the-unit-of-culture/

Velikovsky, J. T. (2014a). *Flow Theory, Evolution & Creativity: or, 'Fun & Games'*. Paper presented at the Interactive Entertainment 2014 (IE2014), Newcastle, Australia.

Velikovsky, J. T. (2014b). The Hero's Journey: It's Not What You Think. *The StoryAlity screenwriting research weblog*. Retrieved 9th February, 2015, from http://storyality.wordpress.com/2013/08/23/storyality-73-the-heros-journey-its-not-what-you-think/

Velikovsky, J. T. (2014c). A Hierarchy of Memes. *Practical Memetics*. Retrieved from http://www.practicalmemetics.com/index.php/memetics-101/202-mem-101-holons.html?showall=1&limitstart=

Velikovsky, J. T. (2014d). Review of the book 'The Screenplay Business: Managing Creativity and Script Development in the Film Industry', by Peter Bloore, 2013. *Journal of Screenwriting, 5*(2), 283–285. doi:10.1386/josc.5.2.283_5

Venkatasawmy, R. (2013). *The Digitization of Cinematic Visual Effects: Hollywood's Coming of Age*. Rowman & Littlefield.

Venkatesh, A. (2003). *Smart home concepts: current trends*. IT in the home series. Center for Research on Information Technology and Organizations. Available from http://escholarship.org/uc/item/6t16p6pf

Vikram, S. L. (2013). *Handwriting and Gestures in the Air, Recognizing on the Fly*. CHI.

Virtuix. (2014). *Virtuix Omni*. Retrieved September 22, 2015, from http://www.virtuix.com/

Vogler, C. (1992). *The Writer's Journey: Mythic Structures for Storytellers and Screenwriters*. Studio City, CA: M. Wiese Productions.

von Bertalanffy, L. (1950). An Outline of General System Theory. *The British Journal for the Philosophy of Science, 1*(2), 134–165. doi:10.1093/bjps/I.2.134

von Franz, M.-L. (1974). *Number and time: Reflections leading toward a unification of depth psychology and physics* (A. Dykes, Trans.). Evanston, IL: Northwestern University Press.

Vygotsky, L. (1978). *Mind in Society: the Development of Higher Psychological Processes*. Cambridge, MA: Harvard University Press.

Vygotsky, L. E. (2012). *Thought and language*. MIT Press.

Wageman, R., Gardner, H., & Mortensen, M. (2012). The changing ecology of teams: New directions for teams' research. *Journal of Organizational Management, 3*(33), 301–315.

Wallach, H. (2010). High-resolution photography at the Dunhuang grottoes: Northwestern University's role in the Mellon International Dunhuang Archive. In N. Agnew (Ed.), *Conservation of ancient sites on the Silk Road: Proceedings of the Second International Conference on the Conservation of Grotto Sites, Mogao Grottoes, Dunhuang, People's Republic of China* (pp. 259–261). Los Angeles, CA: The Getty Conservation Institute.

Wallas, G. (1926). *The art of thought.* New York, NY: Harcourt.

Wallin, D. L. (1990). Televised interactive education: Creative technology for alternative learning. *Community Junior College Research Quarterly of Research and Practice, 14*(3), 259–266. doi:10.1080/0361697900140309

Walters, G. (1989). 'The Story of Waldo C. Graphic'. 3D Character Animation by Computer. In *Proceedings of ACM SIGGRAPH,1989.* Boston. pp. 65-79.

Wang, X. (2012). Future Dunhuang. *NODEM 2012 Hong Kong: Future Culture. Hong Kong.* Hong Kong, China: NODEM 2012. Retrieved September 22, 2015, from http://repo.nodem.org/?objectId=23

Wan, V., Anderson, R., Blokland, A., Braunschweiler, N., Chen, L., Kolluru, B., & Yanagisawa, K. et al. (2013). *Photorealistic expressive text to talking head synthesis* (pp. 2667–2669). INTERSPEECH.

Ward, T. (2014). *Confessions of a Strava cycling addict.* Retrieved September 8, 2014, from http://www.theguardian.com/environment/bike-blog/2014/jan/14/confessions-of-a-strava-cycling-addict-app

Ward, L. (1913). *The Outlines of Sociology.* Norwood, MA: Macmillan. (Original work published 1898)

Ward, T. B., & Kolomyts, Y. (2010). Cognition and creativity. In J. C. Kaufman & R. J. Sternberg (Eds.), *The Cambridge handbook of creativity* (pp. 93–112). New York, NY: Cambridge University Press. doi:10.1017/CBO9780511763205.008

Ware, C. (2001). *Jimmy Corrigan: The smartest kid on earth.* New York, NY: Random House.

Ware, C. (2012). *Building Stories.* New York, NY: Pantheon Books.

Warfield, J. N. (2006). *An Introduction to Systems Science.* Hackensack, NJ: World Scientific.

Warren, T. (2014) *The story of Cortana, Microsoft's Siri killer.* Retrieved April 2, 2014, from http://www.theverge.com/2014/4/2/5570866/cortana-windows-phone-8-1-digital-assistant

Waterhouse, E. (2003). New horizons in ambulatory electroencephalography. *IEEE Engineering in Medicine and Biology Magazine, 22*(3), 74–80. doi:10.1109/MEMB.2003.1213629 PMID:12845822

Wearing, S., & McGehee, N. (2013). Volunteer tourism – a review. *Tourism Management, 38*, 120–130. doi:10.1016/j.tourman.2013.03.002

Webster, R., & Sudweeks, F. (2006). Enabling effective collaborative learning in networked virtual environments. *Current Developments in Technology-Assisted Education, 2*, 1437-1441.

Webster, S. (2003). *Thinking About Biology.* Cambridge, UK: Cambridge University Press. doi:10.1017/CBO9780511754975

Wegbreit, E., Suzuki, S., Grabowecky, M., Kounios, J., & Beeman, M. (2014). Visual attention modulates insight versus analytic solving of verbal problems. *Journal of Problem Solving, 4*(2), 94–115. PMID:24459538

Weichert, F. B., Bachmann, D., Rudak, B., & Fisseler, D. (2013). Analysis of the accuracy and robustness of the leap motion controller. *Sensors (Basel, Switzerland), 13*(5), 6380–6393. doi:10.3390/s130506380 PMID:23673678

Weiden+Kennedy. (2011). *Why we are not hiring creative technologists*. Retrieved from http://blog.wk.com/2011/10/21/why-we-are-not-hiring-creative-technologists/

Weinschenck, S. (2011). *100 things every designer needs to know about people*. San Francisco, CA: New Riders.

Weisberg, R. W. (2006). *Creativity: Understanding Innovation in Problem Solving, Science, Invention, and the Arts*. Hoboken, NJ: John Wiley & Sons.

Weise, T., Bouaziz, S., Li, H., & Pauly, M. (2011). Real-time performance-based facial animation.[TOG]. *ACM Transactions on Graphics*, *30*(4), 77. doi:10.1145/2010324.1964972

Welling, D., Ryan, J., Burris, D., & Rich, N. (2010). Seven sins in humanitarian medicine. *World Journal of Surgery*, *34*(3), 466–470. doi:10.1007/s00268-009-0373-z PMID:20063094

Wellman, B. (2002). Little boxes, glocalization, and networked individualism. In Digital cities II: Computational and sociological approaches (pp. 10–25). Berlin: Springer. doi:10.1007/3-540-45636-8_2

Wendt, B. (2014). *The allure of the selfie: Instagram and the new self-portrait*. Academic Press.

Weng, Y.-J., Weng, Y.-C., Wong, Y.-C., Yang, S.-Y., & Liu, H.-K. (2009). *Fabrication of optical waveguide devices using electromagnetic assisted nanoimprinting*. Paper presented at the 2009 International Conference on Signal Processing Systems, Singapore. doi:10.1109/ICSPS.2009.179

Wertheimer, M. (1982). Productive thinking (M. Wertheimer, Ed.). Chicago, IL: University of Chicago Press.

West, G. B., & Brown, J. H. (2005). The origin of allometric scaling laws in biology from genomes to ecosystems: Towards a quantitative unifying theory of biological structure and organization. *The Journal of Experimental Biology*, *208*(9), 1575–1592. doi:10.1242/jeb.01589 PMID:15855389

West, G., Greehill, S., & Venkatesh, S. (2005). A probalistic approach to the anxious home for activity monitoring. In *Proceedings of the 29th Annual International Computer Software and Applications Conference (COMPSAC'05)*. doi:10.1109/COMPSAC.2005.29

Whewell, W. (1840). *The Philosophy of the Inductive Sciences, Founded Upon Their History*. London: J.W. Parker.

White, D. S., Gunasekaran, A., & Roy, M. H. (2014). Performance measures and metrics for the creative economy. *Benchmarking: An International Journal*, *21*(1), 46–61. doi:10.1108/BIJ-03-2012-0017

Whiting, C. S. (1958). *Creative thinking*. New York, NY: Reinhold.

Whitson, J. R. (2013). Gaming the Quantified Self. *Surveillance & Society*, *11*(1/2), 163–176.

Wiener, N. (1948). Cybernetics: Or Control and Communication in the Animal and the Machine. New York: J. Wiley.

Wiener, J., Shettleworth, S., Bingman, V., Cheng, K., Healy, S., Jacobs, L., & Newcombe, N. et al. (2011). Animal navigation: A synthesis. In R. Menzel & J. Fischer (Eds.), *Animal Thinking: Contemporary Issues in Comparative Cognition* (pp. 51–76). Cambridge, MA: MIT Press.

Wild, C. (1965). Creativity and adaptive regression. *Journal of Personality and Social Psychology*, *2*(2), 161–169. doi:10.1037/h0022404 PMID:14316976

Willett, R., Robinson, M., & Marsh, J. (Eds.). (2008). *Play, creativity and digital cultures*. London: Routledge.

Williams, G., Doughty, K., & Bradley, D. A. (1998). A systems approach to achieving CarerNet—an integrated and intelligent telecare system. *IEEE Transactions on Information Technology in Biomedicine*, *2*(1), 1–9. doi:10.1109/4233.678527 PMID:10719506

Williams, L. (1990). Performance-driven facial animation.[). ACM]. *Computer Graphics*, *24*(4), 235–242. doi:10.1145/97880.97906

Wilson, E. O. ([1998] 1999). Consilience: The Unity of Knowledge (1st Vintage Books ed.). New York: Knopf.

Wilson, E. O. (1998). Consilience: The Unity of Knowledge (1st ed.). New York: Knopf.

Winnicott, D. (1971). *Playing and Reality*. New York, NY: Routeledge Classics.

Winter, J. (2013). *Selfie-loathing*. Slate.

WizDish. (2008). *ROVR*. Retrieved September 21, 2015, from http://www.wizdish.com/

Wolff, E. (2008, August 13). *RenderMan@20: Ed Catmull and Dana Batali Reflect On Pixar's Killer App*. Retrieved May 10, 2015, from http://www.awn.com/vfxworld/renderman20-ed-catmull-and-dana-batali-reflect-pixars-killer-app

Wolff, A. C., Pesut, B., & Regan, S. (2010). New graduate nurse practice readiness: Perspectives on the context shaping our understanding and expectations. *Nurse Education Today*, *30*(2), 187–191. doi:10.1016/j.nedt.2009.07.011 PMID:19699561

Wolf, M. J. P. (2006). Game Studies and Beyond. *Games and Culture*, *1*(1), 116–118. doi:10.1177/1555412005281787

Wolfram, S. (2002). *A new kind of science*. Champaign, IL: Wolfram Media.

Wong, K. B. Y., Zhang, T., & Aghajan, H. (2014). Extracting patterns of behavior from a network of binary sensors. *Journal of Ambient Intelligence and Humanized Computing*, 1-23.

Wong, J. K. W., & Li, H. (2009). Development of intelligence analytic models for integrated building management systems (IBMS) in intelligent buildings. *Intelligent Buildings International*, *1*(1), 5–22. doi:10.3763/inbi.2009.0011

Wong, J., Li, H., & Wang, S. (2005). Intelligent building research: A review. *Automation in Construction*, *14*(1), 143–159.

Wood, A. (2015). The internet of things is revolutionising our lives, but standards are a must. *The Guardian*.

Wooff, T. (1979). The south wales association for design education: Schools exhibition. *Studies in Design Education Craft & Technology*, *11*(2), 105–107.

Wright, J. (2012). Borrowed intelligence: Observing and implementing the culture of the art world. In *Création et Transmission en Anthropologie Visuelle* (pp. 399–422). AFA.

Wright, J. (2013a). Can you tell me how to get, how to get to e-learning: Development and complexity. *Journal of e-Learning and Knowledge Society. Complexity*, *9*(3), 41–53.

Wright, J. (2013b). Discovering the non-self: The construction of language, trance, and space, *Leonardo Electronic Almanac, Publications: Not Here and Not There. Leonardo and MIT Press*, *19*(2), 146–167.

Wright, J. (2014a). Why just teach art: The development of the hippocampus. *Bioscience and Engineering: An International Journal*, *1*(1), 1–10.

Wright, J. (2014b). Why we might augment reality: Art's role in the development of cognition. In V. Geroimenko (Ed.), *Augmented Reality Art: From an Emerging Technology to a Novel Creative Medium* (pp. 201–214). New York, NY: Springer. doi:10.1007/978-3-319-06203-7_12

Wright, J. (2015). Calculation in art: The inconspicuous heuristics of computation, *Rupkatha Journal on Interdisciplinary Studies in Humanities. SI: Digital Humanties*, *7*(1), 120–130.

Wu, X., Downes, M. S., Goktekin, T., & Tendick, F. (2001). Adaptive nonlinear finite elements for deformable body simulation using dynamic progressive meshes. In *Computer Graphics Forum* (Vol. 20, pp. 349–358). Wiley Online Library. doi:10.1111/1467-8659.00527

Zagalo, N., & Branco, P. (2015). The creative revolution that is changing the world. In N. Zagalo & P. Branco (Eds.), *Creativity in the Digital Age* (pp. 3–15). London: Springer. doi:10.1007/978-1-4471-6681-8_1

Zeiler, W. (2014). The difference in communication between architects and engineers and the effectiveness within integral design. In E. Bohemia et al. (Eds.), *Proceedings of the EPDE 2014 16th International Conference on Engineering and Product Design Education* (pp. 238-243). Bristol, UK: Design Society.

Zhang, J., Shan, Y., & Huang, K. (2015). ISEE Smart Home (ISH): Smart video analysis for home security. *Neurocomputing, 149*, 752–766. doi:10.1016/j.neucom.2014.08.002

Zhao, J., Hahn, U., & Osherson, D. (2014). Perception and identification of random events. *Journal of Experimental Psychology, 40*(4), 1358–1371.

Zhou, S., Wu, Z., Li, J., & Zhang, X. P. (2014). Real-time Energy Control Approach for Smart Home Energy Management System. *Electric Power Components and Systems, 42*(3–4), 315–326. doi:10.1080/15325008.2013.862322

Zicherman, G., & Cunningham, C. (2011). *Gamification by design: implementing game mechanics in web and mobile apps*. New York: O'Reilly Media.

Zicherman, G., & Linder, J. (2010). *Game-based marketing: inspire customer loyalty through rewards, challenges and contests*. Wiley.

Zimmer, C. (2011). 100 Trillion Connections: New Efforts Probe and Map the Brain's Detailed Architecture. *Scientific American*. Retrieved from http://www.scientificamerican.com/article/100-trillion-connections/

Zuckerman, E. (2012). Attention, activism and advocacy in the digital age. *Connected Learning*. Retrieved 30 April 2015 from http://connectedlearning.tv/ethan-zuckerman-attention-activism-and-advocacy-digital-age

About the Contributors

Andy M. Connor is a Senior Lecturer at Colab, the "collaboratory" at Auckland University of Technology in New Zealand. His undergraduate training is in mechanical engineering and he holds a PhD in mechatronics. He has worked at the Engineering Design Centres at both the University of Bath and the University of Cambridge in the UK. Following a number of years of commercial experience as a software engineer and a systems engineering consultant, Andy migrated to New Zealand and took up a number of roles in software engineering and computer science at Auckland University of Technology prior to joining Colab in 2012. Andy has a broad range of research interests that include automated design, computational creativity, education, evolutionary computation, machine learning and software engineering.

Stefan Marks is a Senior Lecturer at Colab, the "collaboratory" at Auckland University of Technology in New Zealand. He has several years of industry experience as a hardware and software developer, a diploma in microinformatics, a master's degree in human-computer interaction, and a PhD from the University of Auckland for his research on virtual reality medical teamwork simulation. His research interests include virtual and interactive environments, 3D data visualization, human-computer interaction, simulation of physical processes, serious games, robotics and electronics, and computer science education. In his spare time, he enjoys photography, preferably while exploring beautiful New Zealand's outdoors.

* * *

Vince Briffa is a multimedia artist and researcher. He produces gallery and site-specific artwork, objects and installations which integrate drawing, painting, text, photography, sculpture and the moving image. He is also a curator of contemporary art exhibitions, writes for various local and international publications and organizes discussions, exhibitions and art residencies. Having studied drawing and painting as well as digital media, he investigates the integration of digital media and traditional artistic practices to establish a vehicle that seamlessly communicates the artistic concept. Apart from notions that draw from contemporary artistic and aesthetic concerns, his trans-mediatic work often integrates approaches and concerns from the areas of sociology, advertising, film studies, literature and philosophy. Over the past thirty five years, Briffa's work has been exhibited in some of the world's most prestigious museums and galleries. He has also been chosen to represent Malta in many international exhibitions, including the Venice Biennale (1999) amongst others, and his work forms part of many local and international private and public collections. As an academic, he is the head of the Department of Digital Arts, an Associate of the Electronic and Digital Arts Unit (EDAU) of the University of Central Lancashire, and a visiting academic at Contemporary Art Practice, Leeds University. He is also external examiner for the Bradford Bradford Film School in the UK.

Maggie Buxton is a transdisciplinary community practitioner, creative producer, tertiary educator and writer. She specialises in connecting people to places and opening minds to other realities and ways of knowing. She has worked internationally in a diverse range of settings from grass-roots communities to large corporates and political institutions. She has just completed a PhD on her creative work with technology in her own community.

Samuel Canning is originally from the United Kingdom, where he trained as a hand French Polisher with one of the UK's oldest furniture manufacturers. On moving to Australia, Sam studied Industrial Design as a means of accessing state of the art technology to enhance his Furniture Making. Since this time Sam has worked as an Industrial Designer and is now a lecturer into the Industrial Design and 3D Design courses at the Gold Coast Campus of Griffith University in Queensland, Australia.

Natalie Corbett received her BSc in Computer Animation with first class honours from the University of Portsmouth in 2013. Following this she has been working as a research assistant on the Innovate UK funded RITA (Responsive InTeractive Advocate) project, with a particular focus on research in Virtual Humans, and in facial animation techniques.

Alexiei Dingli is an Associate Professor of Artificial Intelligence within the Faculty of ICT at the University of Malta. He was also a founder member of the ACM student chapter in Malta, the Web Science Research group, the International Game Developers Association (IGDA) Malta and of the Gaming group at the same University. He also heads the Gaming in Education group and represents the University of Malta on the BeSmartOnline initiative. He pursued his Ph.D. on the future of the Internet at the University of Sheffield in the UK under the supervision of Professor Yorick Wilks. His work was rated World Class by a panel of international experts whose chair was Professor James Handler (one of the creators of the Semantic Web) and was used as a core component of the application that won the first Semantic Web challenge (2003). His research in Mobile Technology and Smart Cities (2011) was also awarded a first prize by the European Space Agency and an e-Excellence Gold Seal at the prestigious CeBit Conference in Germany. He has published several posters, papers, book chapters and books in the area. He also pursued an MBA with the Grenoble Business School in France specialising on Technology Management.

Daniel J. Dunne is currently a PhD Candidate at the Swinburne University of Technology. His work focuses mainly upon the combination of both narrative and gameplay elements to create a sense of story and place. Previously Daniel has presented and written on the intersection of narrative within paratext, multimodality, Brechtian alienation theory and ergodic literature.

Anthony Fleury received an Engineer (Computer Science) and a M.Sc. (Signal Processing) degree in 2005 in Grenoble and a PhD degree in Signal Processing from the University Joseph Fourier of Grenoble in 2008 for his work on Health Smart Homes and activity recognition. He joined then the LMAM team at Swiss Federal Institute of Technology and is now, since sept. 2009, Assistant Professor at Ecole des Mines de Douai. His research interests include the modelling of human behaviours and activities, machine learning and pattern recognition with applications to biomedical engineering and smart environments.

Jacques Foottit received his Bachelor of Creative Technologies in 2014 and is currently working towards his Masters of Creative Technologies. His current research is investigating the application of haptic feedback and motion capture glove systems in sensory rehabilitation.

Ali Ghaffarianhoseini is an academician (Auckland University of Technology, Auckland, New Zealand) and a professional architect (NZIA Academic Member) holds PhD and MSc degrees in Architectural Studies and a BSc in Architecture Engineering. He has achieved well-recognized international innovation awards in addition to publication of various international level patent, journal articles, books, conference papers, etc. He has been an active member of scientific/technical committees for international academic conferences in Australia, Canada, China, Croatia, Czech Republic, Egypt, Finland, France, Germany, Greece, Hong Kong, Iran, Italy, Japan, Kuwait, New Zealand, Portugal, Romania, Singapore, Slovenia, South Korea, Switzerland, Sri Lanka, Thailand, Turkey, United Arab Emirates (UAE), United Kingdom (UK) and the United States of America (USA).

Amirhosein Ghaffarianhoseini is a senior lecturer in the field of building science, energy efficient design, urban greening and environmental modelling at University of Malaya (UM), Malaysia. He is holding Ph.D in Architectural Studies, MArch and BArch. He has secured several national and international funding for interdisciplinary research projects related to the environmental optimization of built environments. In addition to his academic work, he has practiced as architect, urban designer and project manager. He currently serves as editorial board member, scientific/technical committee member and reviewer for various international journals and conferences.

Mahdiar Ghaffarianhoseini sincerely believes that architecture is not only the art of designing innovative aesthetic forms or reproduction of contemporary idol shapes, but architecture means designing suitable and purposeful platforms for humans' life, emotions, feelings, moments and inspirations to get shaped." He is studying for a PhD in Environmental Design at the University of Calgary and has numerous awards and honours including; Royal Architectural Institute of Canada Honour Roll Certificate (2013), Top Admission Entrance Scholarship Award, University of Toronto, John H Daniels (2012), University of Calgary's Admission Entrance Scholarship Murray W. Waterman Architectural Scholarship and Award (2011) Many scientific, academic and design publications including the most recent article "Paskan Tower-City", previously published in Globe and Mail paper, in Evolo skyscrapers book 2014 Participated and recognized for many competitions, such as Evolo Skyscrapers 2013, "The Flexchair" Battery Park bench design and "The Ambient Exchange" Helsinki Central Library Competition. He has several years of experience in computational design, digital architecture, digital fabrication and conceptual design, his areas of interest and specialty are Parametric and Generative Design, Agility, flexibility and responsiveness in architecture and his area of research is Alive Architecture; Designing buildings as live forms based on architecture of change and the concept of biomimicry.

Stefan Greuter is the Foundation Director of the Centre for Game Design Research (CGDR) in the School of Media and Communication at RMIT University. He holds a Doctorate of Philosophy in Visual Communication and his postgraduate studies were supported by two prestigious scholarships from the German Academic Exchange program (DAAD) and the Australian International Postgraduate Research

Scholarship (IPRS). Stefan Greuter's research is interested in solving existing problems using innovative game design experiences that bring together research from multiple disciplines including Business, Construction, Occupational Health and Safety, Art, Design and Information Technology. Stefan has a track record of working with experts from other fields and specialises in solutions involving the latest game technology. He has over ten years of teaching experience and is teaching Experimental Game Design in the Bachelor of Design (Games) program. He supervises several PhD candidates whose work seeks to solve existing problems through the use of gaming technology.

Ann Marie Gribble is a graduate from the Bachelor of Creative Technologies. Through a variety of projects undertaken within this course at Auckland University of Technology as well as hands on experience externally, she is well trained in Transmedia Storytelling, Digital Fabrication and Creative Interactivity for Marketing and eBusiness.

Tracy Harwood is Senior Research Fellow at the Institute of Creative Technologies and also manages the facility's Usability Lab. Her research focuses on consumer behaviour/usability, technology/usability in emerging contexts (marketing, retail), virtual/online commerce, e-communities/tribes, marketing, machinima/digital arts and e-commerce interface.

Ry Healy is a Griffith University graduate, who completed his Master's Degree in Digital Design majoring in Fabrication (3D Printing). Starting out with a hands on approach as an apprentice carpenter, through to the final viva of his academic pursuit, he has learnt a great deal of discipline and found his strength in practicality.

Nathan Hulsey completed his doctoral studies at the Communication, Rhetoric and Digital Media program at North Carolina State University. He is active in the fields of Game Studies and Media Studies and has been previously published in Surveillance and Society. His current research concerns a genealogy of gamification.

Anna Jackson is a creative producer and lecturer at Colab working in the areas of transmedia production and documentary innovation. Anna's professional experience spans a range of creative industries including theatre, film, documentary, and transmedia production. She is the co-director of Transmedia NZ, one of the executive producers of online documentary initiative "Loading Docs", a blogger for "The Big Idea" and an ambassador for arts crowdfunding platform "Boosted". In 2014 she completed a joint PhD at The University of Melbourne and the University of Auckland, "Innovation and Change in New Zealand's documentary production ecology (2010-2013).

Sangeeta Karmokar has worked in the education industry across business and design disciplines. This provided her opportunity to bring all her past teaching experience and education in business, design and information technology together. Her research study covered user centred design in interface design process, bringing innovation using design methods for developing business strategies, developing design methodologies for innovation, designing new digital business models. Her experience includes teaching across various disciplines such as communication Design, Business Design, Creative Technology and entrepreneurship.

Sarah Kenderdine researches at the forefront of interactive and immersive experiences for museums and galleries. In widely exhibited installation works, she has amalgamated cultural heritage with new media art practice, especially in the realms of interactive cinema, augmented reality and embodied narrative. She is considered a pioneer in the field digital heritage / humanities and is a regular keynote speaker at related forums internationally. Sarah concurrently holds the position of Professor and Deputy Director of the National Institute for Experimental Arts (NIEA), University of New South Wales | Art & Design (2013–) where she directs the Lab for Innovation in Galleries, Libraries, Archives and Museums (iGLAM) and an Associate Director, iCinema Research Centre. She continues a life-long position as head of Special Projects for Museum Victoria, Australia (2003–) and is Director of Research at the Applied Laboratory for Interactive Visualization and Embodiment (ALiVE), City University of Hong Kong. Prof. Kenderdine has conceived and created interactive installations on UNESCO world heritage sites including Angkor, Cambodia; The Monuments at Hampi, India; Olympia, Greece and at numerous sites throughout Turkey. Between 2012-2015 she directed Pure Land: Inside the Mogao Grottoes at Dunhuang, Pure Land Augmented Reality Edition, Pure Land Henqin and Pure Land UnWired in collaboration with the Dunhaung Academy. In 2012, ECloud WWI for Europeana. She conceived and curated Kaladham | PLACE-Hampi as a permanent museum located at Vijayanagar, Karnataka, inaugurated in November 2012, and co-directed two new installations based on 'Pacifying of the South China Sea Pirates' scroll which recently premiered at Maritime Museum, Hong Kong (2013). In 2104, she completed Museum Victoria's data browser for 100,000 objects, in a 360-degree 3D interactive installation in the galleries. Formerly, Kenderdine was Creative Director of Special Projects at the Powerhouse Museum, Sydney (1998-2003). She is a maritime archaeologist, former curator at the Western Australian Maritime Museum (1994-1997) and has written a number of authoritative books on shipwrecks. In 1994-1995, she designed and built one of the world's earliest museum websites (for the Maritime Museum) and subsequently award-winning cultural networks/websites for: Australian Museums Online (AMOL), the ten South East Asian Nations (ASEAN) and, Intel Corporation's Olympic Games Olympia projects, Sydney 2000.

Jan Kruse is a Lecturer in Visual Effects in the Digital Design Department at Auckland University of Technology. He started his career in Video and Audio Editing, spent more than 15 years in the Visual Effects Industry, and worked as a Supervisor, Producer and Compositor in various companies across New Zealand, Canada and Europe. His portfolio includes work on high profile projects such as Lord of the Rings, King Kong, X-Men and Rise of the Planet of the Apes. He recently left his position at Weta Digital in Wellington, New Zealand, to pursue an academic career. An interest in Industrial and Hobby Robotics led him to explore a few projects outside of his area of expertise, including the introduction of the first autonomous UAV (Quadrotor) in New Zealand in 2007, and several other electronics and automation ventures.

Jennifer Loy is Program Leader of Industrial Design at Griffith University and Deputy Director of the Griffith Centre for Creative Arts Research. Loy has a PhD in Industrial Design and a background in manufacturing. Her research and teaching focus on design for process, with a particular interest in digital fabrication, sustainable design and creative practice.

Bruce J. MacLennan has a BS in mathematics (with honours, 1972) from Florida State University, and an MS (1974) and PhD (1975) in computer science from Purdue University. He was a Senior Software Engineer with Intel Corp. (1975–9), after which he joined the Computer Science faculty of the Naval Postgraduate School (Monterey, CA) as Assistant Professor (1979–83), Associate Professor (1983–7), and Acting Chair (1984–5). Since 1987, he has been an Associate Professor in the Dept. of Electrical Engineering and Computer Science of the University of Tennessee, Knoxville. Since the mid-1980s, his research has focused on new approaches to artificial intelligence based on neuroscience and informed by phenomenological philosophy, embodied cognitive science, and psychology. His research focus is basic science: What can AI reveal about natural intelligence and the relation of mind and matter? Prof. MacLennan has more than 80 refereed journal articles and book chapters and has published two books. He has made more than 70 invited or refereed presentations. MacLennan was also founding Editor-in-Chief of the International Journal of Nanotechnology and Molecular Computation.

Nicola Naismith is a Senior Lecturer in the School of Engineering at Auckland University of Technology.

Hossein Omrany received his Bachelor of Architecture Engineering from Islamic Azad University of Shiraz – Iran in 2010. He followed with his mater studies in Universiti Teknologi Malaysia (UTM) - Malaysia in the field of Construction Management, and graduated in 2014.

Vaughan Powell has a degree in Biology, a Master's degree in Archaeology, and a PhD in Creative Technologies. His primary research interest is in the interface between humans and computers, and the way in which the design of interactive technology and virtual reality systems mediates the behaviour and perception of the users. He is a regular speaker at conferences and workshops, and also teaches interaction design. He also has a particular interest in research ethics, and is chair of the Creative and Cultural Industries faculty ethics committee at the University of Portsmouth.

Wendy Powell has degrees in Computer Science and in Chiropractic, and was awarded a PhD in Creative Technologies from the University of Portsmouth in 2012. She is currently a Reader in Virtual Reality, with a particular interest in the use of advanced interactive technologies for health and well-being. She has been the recipient of a number of research grants, and has led the development of a human-like avatar to support elderly people. She lectures and publishes in the area of human interaction with virtual reality, and is a regular speaker on the use of creative technology for healthcare and rehabilitation.

Dylan Seychell is lecturer and the Head of the Department of Computer Information Systems at the St. Martin's Institute of Higher Education, a University of London Affiliate Centre. He is also a visiting lecturer at the University of Malta in the Faculty of Media and Knowledge Sciences. He teaches topics in Mobile Technology and Interaction Design of various levels. Mr Seychell is a co-author of various international peer-reviewed publications and a book chapter. After graduating with honours in IT from the University of Malta, he completed a Master of Science degree in the field of Intelligent Computer Systems in Mobile Technology and is currently reading for a PhD in Computer and Communication

Engineering. Mr Seychell is a co-creator of the award winning project "DINOS for Smart Cities". With this idea, Mr Seychell won two prestigious international awards; European Satellite Navigation Competition 2010 – First Place in Media and CeBIT 2011 Gold Seal of e-Excellence. He also worked in various software houses and with large scale telecommunication companies.

Jeffrey Shaw has been a leading figure in new media art since its emergence from the performance, expanded cinema and installation paradigms of the 1960s to its present day technology-informed and virtualized forms. In a prolific career of widely exhibited and critically acclaimed work he has pioneered the creative use of digital media technologies in the fields of virtual and augmented reality, immersive visualization environments, navigable cinematic systems and interactive narrative. Professor Shaw was co-founder of the Eventstructure Research Group in Amsterdam (1969-1979), and founding director of the ZKM Institute for Visual Media Karlsruhe (1991-2002). At the ZKM he conceived and ran a seminal artistic research program that included the ArtIntAct series of digital publications, the Multi-Mediale series of international media art exhibitions, over one hundred artist-in-residence projects, and the invention of new creative platforms such as the EVE Extended Virtual Environment (1993) PLACE (1995) and the Panoramic Navigator (1997). In 1995 Shaw was appointed Professor of Media Art at the State University of Design, Media and Arts (HfG), Karlsruhe, Germany. Professor Shaw's landmark art works include The Legible City (1989), The Virtual Museum (1991), The Golden Calf (1994), Place-A Users Manual (1995), conFiguring the CAVE (1997) and the Web of Life (2002). He co-curated the seminal FUTURE CINEMA exhibition at the ZKM Karlsruhe, the catalogue of which was published by MIT Press. Shaw's career is further distinguished by his collaborations with fellow artists including Peter Gabriel, David Pledger, Agnes Hegedues, The Wooster Group, William Forsyth, Harry de Wit, Theo Botschuijer, Dennis Del Favero, Peter Weibel, Bernd Lintermann, Dirk Goeneveld, Leslie Stuck, Paul Doornbusch, Jean Michel Bruyere, Saburo Teshigawara, Ulf Langheinrich and Sarah Kenderdine. Shaw has been the recipient of numerous awards including Ars Electronica, Linz, Austria, L'Immagine Elettronica, Ferrara, Italy, the Oribe Prize, Gifu, Japan and an IDEA Gold Medal in 2009. In 2003 Professor Shaw was awarded the prestigious Australian Research Council Federation Fellowship and returned to Australia to co-found and direct the UNSW iCinema Centre for Interactive Cinema Research in Sydney from 2003-2009. At iCinema he led a theoretical, aesthetic and technological research program in immersive interactive post-narrative systems, which produced pioneering artistic and research works such as Place-Hampi and T_Visionarium, the latter shown at the Biennale of Seville in 2008. In September 2009 Shaw joined City University in Hong Kong as Chair Professor of Media Art and Dean of the School of Creative Media (SCM). Professor Shaw has a position at UNSW as co-director of the iCinema Centre for the purposes of academic and research co-operation with CityU. He established a SCM research facility at the Hong Kong Science Park in 2010.

Ricardo Sosa is a researcher and lecturer at Colab. He combines a creative background as an industrial designer with a passion for the systematic study of computational systems.

Peter Tatham retired as a Commodore (1*) after 35 years as logistician in the (UK) Royal Navy and moved into academia in 2004. He joined the faculty of Griffith University's Business School in July 2010 where he teaches and researches in humanitarian supply chain management. He is the Asian and Australasian Editor of the Journal of Humanitarian Logistics and Supply Chain Management, and a member of the Editorial Board of the International Journal of Physical Distribution and Logistics Management.

Cassie Tapper is a Griffith University graduate who has been working as a Research Assistant. She completed her Bachelor in Digital Design majoring in 3D Design. Tapper's work is focused on design responsibility and creating positive change, both socially and environmentally.

John Tookey is the head of the Department of Built Environment Engineering at Auckland University of Technology, having previously worked at the University of Auckland, Glasgow Caledonian University (UK) and Bradford University (UK). He has published widely across a range of discipline areas including supply chain management, logistics, procurement and latterly sustainability.

J. T. Velikovsky is a Story / Screenplay / Movie / Transmedia / Culture Researcher & Evolutionary Systems Theorist, see: http://aftrs.academia.edu/JTVelikovsky and also a produced feature film screenwriter and million-selling transmedia writer-director-producer. He has been a professional story analyst for major movie studios, film funding organizations, and for the national writer's guild. He is also a member of the Digital Humanities Research Group. For more see: http://on-writing.blogspot.com/.

Judson Wright makes Behavioural Art, programming computers in order to study cognition. His software experiments/artwork, papers, music and performances have been featured extensively around the world since 1996 (circus tents in Europe, the Smithsonian International Art Gallery, the Brooklyn Museum of Art with the Brooklyn Philharmonic, the 809 International Art District in China, the Journal of Science and Technology of the Arts, ...). He graduated from Brown University and has an MA from the Interactive Telecommunications Program at New York University.

Index

Printed in the United States
By Bookmasters